THE
WORLD CUP
A COMPLETE RECORD

1930
1990

THE WORLD CUP
COMPLETE RECORD

1930
1990

IAN MORRISON

Breedon Books Sport

First published in Great Britain by
The Breedon Books Publishing Company Limited
44 Friar Gate, Derby DE1 1DA.

© Ian Morrison 1990

ISBN 0 907969 62 3

Printed by Butler and Tanner Limited, Frome, Somerset.
Jacket printed by Arkle Print Ltd, Northampton.

Contents

The most controversial goal ever scored in the World Cup. Geoff Hurst's shot bounces down off the crossbar in the 1966 Final between England and West Germany at Wembley. A quarter of a century later there is still debate about whether the ball crossed the line. Slow-motion film and countless photographs have failed to settle the argument, but the fact remains that the goal was allowed and England went on to win the trophy for the only time.

Previous page: The opening ceremony of the 1990 World Cup in the Stadio Giuseppe Meazza, better known as Milan's San Siro Stadium.

Following page: The first World Cup Final. Action from the game between Uruguay and Argentina in the Centenary Stadium, Montevideo, in 1930.

Many of the photographs in this book
have been supplied by PETER
ROBINSON (FIFA's official
photographer) and STEVE HALE.
Other sources include Action Images
and Colorsport of London, Empics of
Nottingham and there has also been
much help from Serge Van Hoof of
Belgium, Janusz Kukulski of Poland,
Dan Cristea of Romania, Ján Podolský
of Czechoslovakia and Tony Quinn,
Fudge Browne and Willow Walmsley of
the United States.

Author's Notes & Acknowledgements

COMPILING *The World Cup: A Complete Record* has been a long and arduous task. At the same time, it has been one of the most interesting and enjoyable of all the books I have written because it is a subject in which I have been interested ever since that day in 1956 when I was given Maurice Golesworthy's *The Encyclopedia of Association Football* as a Christmas present. I now feel honoured to have been involved in the compilation of one of the most definitive books ever published on this vast topic.

Whilst soccer in general is a well-documented sport, I found that, even with a topic as popular as the World Cup, there have been discrepancies between various sources over the years. I believe that, after lengthy research, the information in this book is as accurate as anything ever attempted but, of course, there are pitfalls. I know that people may pull me up and say, for instance, that the name 'Banichevski' should end with a 'y' and not an 'i', but there are many grey areas over the spelling of foreign names, particularly with Eastern Bloc countries where names are spelt using either the Roman or Cyrillic alphabet. Without deciding on the merits of each system, I have simply endeavoured to find a level of consistency.

Romania, in particular, posed problems with the names of players in the 1930 tournament because some were Hungarian immigrants, who used their Hungarian names whilst other sources quoted their 'new' Romanian names. An example is the outside-right who most sources, particularly English ones, list as 'Covaci'. Apparently he was a Hungarian immigrant called Kovacs and that is what the Romanian FA call him in their records. I beg not to differ.

Brazilian names were also a problem and, again for consistency's sake, I have used the following guideline: Where a player is known by a nickname — 'Pelé', for instance — I have used that nickname in both match reports and record sections. However, where a player does not have a nickname, but is referred to by a single name, I have used his widely-acknowledged name. A good example is Gilmar Do Santos Neves. In match reports he is known simply as 'Gilmar' but in the record and statistical section I have called him by his full name.

There are other areas where people will say: 'He's got it wrong'. For example, many British sources give Ademir of Brazil as being the top scorer in the 1950 series with seven goals. I give his total as nine, as do many Continental sources. The Brazilian FA have confirmed to me that Ademir scored two goals in their 6-1 win over Spain. British sources generally ignore this fact, hence the difference of two goals.

Attendances are the one major area where there has been poor documentation and the years before 1950 are a minefield of potential error. The figures I have quoted for the first three tournaments are those supplied to me by FIFA, who pointed out that they were aware of probable inaccuracies. A few early matches do not have attendance figures at all, as FIFA have no record of them and my own exhaustive search of newspapers from many countries has failed to yield further information. To preserve the credibility of this book, I have chosen to indicate where attendances are not known — and probably never will be — rather than hazard wild guesses.

In every entry in this book I have delved into such matters and arrived at what I feel is the correct answer. I accepted nothing on face value when presented with team line-ups etc, and when I made my ultimate decision, I did so in the firm belief that it was correct.

To have eventually arrived at my conclusions would not have been possible without the enormous help from various Football Associations around the world and the following should be singled out for their extra special assistance: Guido Tognoni and Andreas Herren (FIFA), Omar Paolillo (Uruguayan FA), Michael Listkiewicz (Polish FA), Ester Kristensson (Swedish FA), Edgar Obertüfer (Swiss FA), David L.Raterman (US Soccer Federation), Cristian Bivolaru (Romanian FA) and Americo Faria (Brazilian FA). In addition, I would like to express my sincerest thanks to Ron Templeton for helping me verify facts and allowing me to delve into the extensive records which he has collated over the years. Thanks also to Chris Rhys for his help with European line-ups. Finally, a special thanks to the man who invented the fax machine, without whom my job would have been even more difficult.

Ian Morrison
Cheshire
July 1990

The Beginning of the Dream

C.A.W.Hirschman, the Dutch banker who mooted the idea of a world governing body for soccer.

ORGANIZED soccer can trace its birthdate to 26 October 1863, when the English Football Association was founded at the Freemason's Tavern, London. There followed competitions in the form of the FA Cup, the world's oldest soccer tournament, the formation of the Football League and, eventually, dozens of other cups and leagues across Britain.

By 1880, there were Football Associations in all the four 'home' countries — England, Scotland, Ireland and Wales — but the real growth of soccer was still to come, when the game was taken across the English Channel and into Europe.

British expatriots took soccer with them wherever they went and the first FA outside the British Isles was the Boldspil Union of Denmark, which was inaugurated in 1889. As clubs sprang up, their make-up was largely of English immigrants at first. Then they became mixed and then totally dependent on home-grown talent.

By the early part of the 20th century, organized football was being played across Europe and the idea of a 'world' governing body was mooted by a Dutch banker, C.A.W.Hirschman, and a Frenchman, Robert Guérin. They had the foresight to see the need of such a body, even though football was still in its infancy.

On 21 May 1904, in Paris, delegates from Belgium, Denmark, France, Holland, Spain, Sweden and Switzerland founded the *Federation Internationale de Football Association,* better known as FIFA. One notable absentee at the inaugural meeting was a representative from the English Football Association, to whom the founder members had turned for guidance. They refused because the English felt that there was no need for a world body to run soccer.

The English FA was regarded as the 'father' of the game and, before FIFA was formed, had been approached by Hirschman to take control of the International Board. The FA, displaying a great show of single-mindedness, refused.

Frenchman Robert Guérin. He also had the foresight to see the need for an organization like FIFA.

Hirschman tried everything he could to get the FA to join FIFA, but his efforts were in vain. He had approached the FA as early as 1902 and asked if they would be interested in sponsoring an international tournament which, if it had won their seal of approval, would probably have borne the label of the World Cup.

In June 1902, the secretary of the FA, Frederick Wall, replied to Hirschman's request, saying the matter would be considered and discussed at their next meeting — two months later. This decision alone showed how aloof the FA was at that time and how it displayed an obvious lack of regard for the game outside the confines of its own boundaries.

Wall's next letter to Hirschman was in April 1903, when he advised that the matter would be brought up at their next meeting, in June 1903, a year after Hirschman's first approach.

It was at this point that the Frenchman, Guérin, also approached the English FA and suggested the founding of a federation for European nations. Predictably, the FA replied saying 'they could not see the advantages' of such a body.

Guérin and Hirschman could see that they were getting nowhere and set about forming the new international body without help from the 'father' association. In 1904 the fruits of their efforts were realized when FIFA came into being at their inaugural meeting in Paris.

D.B.Woolfall of Lancashire was elected president of FIFA in succession to Guérin.

However, after a couple of years of 'waiting and seeing' the FA eventually acknowledged the need for FIFA, in view of the development of soccer on the Continent. In 1906 they were represented at a FIFA meeting for the first time. Daniel Burley Woolfall of Lancashire was elected FIFA president in succession to Guérin.

The formation of FIFA brought about the opportunity to organize a competition for member nations. Had the English FA shown more interest in the new international body when initially approached by Hirschman in 1902, there could well have been a World Cup competition then, instead of which the game had to wait over a quarter of a century for its eventual birth.

The competition which Hirschman proposed to the FA is believed to have been the idea of a Dutchman, Count van der Straten Ponthoy. Had the tournament got off the ground then, who knows, footballers the world over could have ended up playing for the 'van der Straten Ponthoy Cup' instead of the Jules Rimet Trophy.

However, the outbreak of war in 1914 interrupted FIFA's plans and in 1918 the world body lost one of its instigators when Robert Guérin died. That was only one of the many problems which FIFA faced in the immediate post-war years.

The British nations and their allies refused to play against nations with whom they had lately been at war. This in itself posed a problem for FIFA. The Scandinavian countries, however, wanted the right to play against any country they chose. The FA decided to boycott matches against, not only 'enemy' nations, but also against countries who played the Germans etc. Consequently, the English FA withdrew from FIFA.

Jules Rimet, the FIFA president who gave his name to the World Cup.

L. Muhlinghaus of Belgium, who was general secretary of FIFA for the first two years of the organization's existence, from 1904 to 1906.

I. Shricker of Switzerland was the third general secretary of FIFA, taking over in 1932, in time to prepare for the second World Cup tournament. Shricker looked after FIFA's interests through the difficult war years. C.A.W.Hirschman had acted as secretary from 1906 to 1928.

Uruguay's 'professional' team which was the first South American side to win the Olympic soccer title in Paris in 1924. Back row (left to right): Scarone, Romano, Cea, Mazzali, Andrade, Petrone, Vidal. Front row (players only): Urdinaràn, Tomasini, Ghierra.

The problems lasted two years until the intervention of Austrian, Hugo Meisl. In 1923 England met Sweden, who had previously been black-listed for playing Hungary and Austria. Normality was restored and FIFA continued its task of controlling the international game.

By now FIFA had a new president. Jules Rimet, a 48-year-old Frenchman, who took up office on 1 March 1921 in succession to the late Daniel Burley Woolfall. Rimet was born at Theuley, Haute-Saote, in 1873 and founded the Red Star club in France. He was recognized as a fine adminstrator and served on many bodies before becoming FIFA president, a post he was to hold for 33 years. It was Rimet who did much to get the British Associations back into FIFA and they rejoined *en bloc* in 1924.

Whilst Europe had been at conflict, soccer had been making progress in far off corners of the globe, notably in North and South America. The game had been played in the United States since the latter part of the 19th century. In 1884, an American Football Association came into being, at a time when the game was played mostly by British immigrants. It was not until 1905 that soccer started to attract widespread interest.

On 5 April 1913, the United States Football Association was born and soon became affiliated to FIFA. Three years later, on 9 July 1916, the *Federacion Sudamericana de Football* was instituted and that same year, Uruguay became the first winners of the South American championship which featured three other nations, Argentina, Brazil and Chile.

Uruguay, Argentina and Brazil were regarded as the 'Big Three' of South American football, but gradually other nations joined the championship, although Paraguay was the only other country to pose anything like a threat to the three giants.

The only true international footballing feast was the Olympic tournament which was held every four years, but that was for amateurs only. However, more and more nations had adopted professionalism and 'shamateurism' was creeping into the amateur game. This was apparent at the Paris Olympics in 1924, when the very 'professional' Uruguay team became the first South American nation to win the title.

FIFA and the International Olympic Committee were at loggerheads over who should control the Olympic soccer tournament. FIFA announced that they were the highest footballing

authority and so should run a tournament claiming to be the biggest soccer event in the world. But, irrespective of the right to control the event, the problem of amateurism was the main source of aggravation between the two bodies. Because of 'shamateurism', Britain did not send a team to Paris.

In 1921, the Belgian FA announced that they were to allow 'broken time' payment to amateurs who lost wages because of time taken off work to play football. Soon afterwards, France, Italy, Norway and Switzerland followed suit.

In December 1923, having experienced such problems in their early days, the English FA asked FIFA for a definition of an amateur player. FIFA did not have one and said that they left it to the consciences of the individual countries. The FA asked FIFA to accept their definition of an amateur. FIFA refused and Britain withdrew its team from the 1928 Olympics, a decision which was supported by Denmark, who also withdrew.

Britain also refused to go to the Amsterdam Olympics when 'shamateurism' was even more prevalent. Furthermore, at a meeting at Sheffield on 17 February 1928, they announced that they were withdrawing from FIFA, yet again. This time the British were to operate outside the world body for nearly 20 years and missed the first three celebrations of the World Cup.

The Olympic soccer tournament still took place in Amsterdam, even without British involvement, but there must be some considerable doubt as to whether they could have mastered the skill of the South American nations.

Uruguay went to Paris four years earlier and captured the title. In 1928 it was the turn of the Dutch fans to be treated to their skills and they retained the title after beating their South American neighbours, Argentina, 2-1 in a replay.

The Uruguayan side which retained the Olympic title in 1928, beating Argentina 2-1 in the Final in Amsterdam after a replay. Back row (left to right): Andrade, Nasazzi, Arispe, Mazzali, Gestido, Fernàdez. Front row: Urdinaràn, Gastro, Petrone, Cea, Campolo and the team masseur.

South American soccer was firmly established as one of the hotbeds of the international game, not that the British would hear anything of it. Uruguay had been the first winners of the South American championship and were now double Olympic champions. There was little doubting their place at the top of world soccer. But how different might it have been in Amsterdam, had 'shamateurism' been stamped out as the English FA wanted.

While all the talk of 'broken time' payments was taking place in Amsterdam, it was also during the Olympics that FIFA made an important decision. They accepted the resolution of Henri Delaunay, secretary of the French FA since 1919 until his death in 1956, that a World Cup competition be organized immediately.

The acceptance of his proposal came two years after he had announced to the footballing authorities: 'International football can no longer be held within the confines of the Olympics and many countries where professionalism is now recognized and organized cannot any longer be represented there by their best players.' His resolution was passed by 25 votes to five.

FIFA duly announced its plans to run its own competition, open to all affiliated countries. They did not immediately give a name to the competition, but the world's Press were quick to give it their own title. 'World Cup', 'World Soccer Championship' and 'La Coupe de Monde' were favourite descriptions. Another was the 'Jules Rimet Trophy'. Eventually that was how the World Cup officially became known, thus honouring the man who had done so much for FIFA in drumming up support amongst member nations.

By 1930, FIFA had 41 members, a figure which had steadily increased from the initial complement of seven in 1904, to 24 in 1914, and 31 in 1923.

Hugo Meisl of the Austrian FA had mooted the idea of a European Cup in 1926, but this was put aside because of FIFA's intention to run the 1928 Olympics under the guise of a world championship. FIFA eventually set up a special commission under the chairmanship of G.Bonnet of the Swiss FA to look into the possibility of running a 'World Cup' — a term FIFA used when they established the committee, although they did not choose that name when eventually announcing plans for the competition in 1930.

By May 1929, FIFA still had not finalized plans for the first championship, although they had announced it would take place in 1930. The host nation had not been selected and as the talks dragged on, it was apparent that finance was to be the biggest problem in running such a tournament, particularly if it was to be a true world championship.

Rodolfe Seeldrayers, the FIFA vice-president, proposed that the country given the honour of staging the first tournament should make funds available for (in the following order of priority) transport and accommodation expenses for referees, FIFA members and the teams. This was clearly going to be an expensive proposition for any national FA to undertake, but there were some willing takers.

Holland, Hungary, Italy, Spain, Sweden and Uruguay had all put their names forward, but Holland and Sweden soon withdrew and lent their support to Italy's claim. Argentina supported Uruguay's claim, as did the other South American nations. Hungary withdrew their application and then so did Spain and Italy. The latter's decision was strange because they were certainly one of the countries who could have withstood the financial burden. Perhaps they opted out because of the uncertainty of it all.

So it was left to Uruguay, the only remaining nominee. At last the dream was about to be realized, the date was set and the host country selected. It was a case of 'Uruguay, here we come'.

Shortly after the fourth World Cup tournament, K.Gassman, also from Switzerland, succeeded Shricker as general secretary of FIFA. He remained in office until 1960, by which time the World Cup had grown into a truly global competition.

Rodolfe Seeldrayers, the FIFA vice-president who proposed that the World Cup host country should fund players' and officials' expenses.

MEN WHO MADE THE HEADLINES - 1930

Guillermo Stàbile
(Argentina)

A PROLIFIC goalscorer, Guillermo Stàbile was top scorer in the 1930 World Cup competition with eight goals. And in Argentina's 6-3 win over Mexico, he created World Cup history by becoming the first man to score a hat-trick — and he came into the side only because skipper Ferreira was not available. Born in 1905, Stàbile was playing for Huracán at the time of the inaugural World Cup but, like so many top South Americans in the 1930s, he found the lure of the lire too great and joined the Italian club, Genoa. He was soon proclaimed a local hero after scoring a hat-trick on his debut against the League leaders, Bologna. Like his present-day counterpart and fellow Argentinian, Diego Maradona, Stàbile later moved to Napoli before finishing his career in the French League with Red Star Paris. He was also capped by France and once scored four goals against Austria.

Héctor Scarone
(Uruguay)

HÉCTOR Scarone was one of the finest inside-forwards to play for Uruguay. He was born in 1898 and was a key member of their 1924 and 1928 Olympic gold medal winning teams. He completed a hat-trick of medals in the inaugural World Cup in Montevideo, one of four players to appear in all three winning teams. A hard worker and tough competitor, Scarone was in the classic Uruguayan mould of the era and was adept at playing an individual role as well as being an important team member. He began his career at the age of 14 with the Third Division Montevideo club, Sportsman. The following year he was signed by Nacional. Known as El Magico (The Magician), he made his international debut in 1919. Scarone was tempted to Spain in 1926 and signed for Barcelona, but his stay in Europe lasted only six months. However, he returned to Europe after the war and coached Real Madrid. In 1953, he returned to Nacional as a player, despite being 55, and later coached their team. He won a total of 64 international caps. Héctor Scarone died in 1968.

José Leandro Andrade
(Uruguay)

JOSÉ Andrade was the classy wing-half in the Uruguayan team which enjoyed such success in the 1920s and 1930s. He was born in 1901 and started his career with the Montevideo club, Bella Vista, before being snapped up by Nacional. By the time Uruguay won the 1924 Olympic title, Andrade was an established international and was the first of the world's outstanding coloured footballers. Having played a major role in Nacional's capture of three successive Uruguayan championships between 1922 and 1924, he earned the respect of the Europeans when he toured Europe with Nacional in 1925. Andrade figured in Uruguay's 1928 Olympic winning team as well as their South American Championship-winning sides of 1923, 1924 and 1926. He quit international football after the 1928 Olympic triumph but was recalled for the inaugural World Cup, where his tremendous skills contributed to many of the goals scored by the Uruguayan forwards. Andrade ended his career with Peñarol in 1933, at the age of 32, and died in 1957. However, the name of Andrade was not lost with his retirement. His nephew, Victor Rodríguez Andrade, was a member of the second Uruguayan team to win the World Cup, in 1950.

At Last, the First World Cup
Uruguay 1930

FIFA president Jules Rimet presents the first World Cup trophy to Dr Paul Jude, president of the Uruguayan Football Association after his country's success in 1930.

Lucien Laurent, scorer of the first-ever World Cup finals goal, when he put France on the way to a 4-1 win over Mexico. It was his only World Cup goal.

King Carol of Romania selected his country's squad for the first World Cup.

THIRTEEN countries made the trip to Montevideo for the first championship which took place between 13-30 July 1930. The prize for the eventual winners was a 32cm (12½in) high trophy made of solid gold and weighing 12lb. Designed by the French sculptor, Abel Lafleur, its sporting value was priceless and there were 13 captains all eager to get their hands on the trophy.

Because of the travelling involved, the number of European entrants totalled only four. The journey across the Atlantic in 1930 was not the easy task it is today. There were no scheduled air routes, so the journey had to be made by boat and that took anything up to a month.

The European representation was not the best the Continent could muster. Romania, for example, were not supposed to be sending a team to Uruguay until their young King, Carol, intervened and pleaded with employers to give three months leave to employees selected for the Romanian squad. They agreed and the King then set about picking the team himself.

Because of the strong French influence in getting the competition off the ground in the first place, France was compelled to send a team to Uruguay. Alas, they knew that they were not good enough to combat the might of the Uruguayans or Argentinians. The other two European nations, Belgium and Yugoslavia, were not the best in Europe in 1930 and many wondered why they had bothered to make the long trip.

The Uruguayan FA was somewhat perturbed by the lack of interest shown by the other European nations, particularly Italy, Hungary, Holland, Sweden and Spain who, at one time, had all put in a bid to host the event. The remainder of the entrants came from America — eight from the South and a representative team from the United States.

It was appropriate, for several reasons, that Uruguay should be chosen to host the first tournament. They were the holders of the Olympic title, good enough credentials in its own right. Furthermore, in July 1930 the country was celebrating the centenary of its independence. It was certainly going to be carnival time in Montevideo during the two weeks of the World Cup.

The Uruguayans had guaranteed the expenses of all teams and officials and also agreed to build a new 100,000 capacity stadium for the big occasion. But heavy rain in Montevideo in the months leading up to the tournament meant the new stadium was not completed for the start of the tournament on 13 July. However, working nearly 24 hours a day and under floodlights, it was completed in time for Uruguay's opening match against Peru five days later.

The opening matches, however, were played at the Pocitos and Central Park stadiums in Montevideo, the homes of Peñarol and Nacional respectively.

1930 Tournament

Group One

Luís Monti, whose quickly-taken free-kick led to Argentina's winning goal against France.

FRANCE 4   MEXICO 1 (Half-time 3-0)

Pocitos, Montevideo, 13 July
Attendance: 1,000

AT last the dream of Henri Delaunay and Jules Rimet got underway and it was quite appropriate that France should have the honour of appearing in the first-ever World Cup game.

The French desperately wanted to do well in the first competition and not disappoint Delaunay and Rimet, both of whom had worked so hard to launch the tournament.

Their opening match was played on the eve of Bastille Day and the Uruguayan supporters in the crowd strongly favoured the French, confirming the bond between the two nations.

Despite losing goalkeeper Alex Thépot, who was kicked on the jaw after only ten minutes, France managed to overcome the unimaginative Mexicans by a margin of three goals.

Repeated first-half attacks saw France take the lead after 19 minutes when a shot from Lucien Laurent was too powerful for goalkeeper Oscar Bonfiglio. Thus, the honour of scoring the World Cup's first goal fell to the inside-left.

Continued raids on the Mexican goal produced two more goals, from Marcel Langiller and André Maschinot, before the half-time whistle was blown by referee Lombardi.

The Aztecs were shaken into action in the second half and reduced the arrears through inside-right Juan Carreño, who beat the stand-in 'keeper Augustin Chantrel. But France sealed an easy victory with their fourth goal three minutes from time, when Maschinot netted his second.

Skippering the French team that day was Alex Villaplane, the footballer who was to meet an unpleasant death. In 1944, after the liberation of France, he was executed by firing squad for collaborating with the Germans.

Mexican defenders Manuel and Felipe Rosas made history as the first brothers to play in the World Cup.

France: Thépot; Mattler, Capelle, Villaplane, Pinel, Chantrel, Libérati, Delfour, Maschinot, Laurent, Langiller.
Scorers: Laurent, Langiller, Maschinot 2
Mexico: Bonfiglio; R.Guitiérrez, M.Rosas, F.Rosas, Sanchez, Amezcúa, Pérez, Carreño, Mejia, Ruíz, López.
Scorer: Carreño
Referee: Domingo Lombardi (Uruguay)

ARGENTINA 1   FRANCE 0 (Half-time 0-0)

Central Park, Montevideo, 15 July
Attendance: 3,000

ARGENTINA made the trip to Montevideo as one of the favourites to become the first holders of the World Cup. They certainly had the right credentials, being runners-up to Uruguay in the 1928 Olympic Final in Amsterdam. On home soil in 1929, they retained the South American championship.

France, however, stood in their way. The Europeans had not made the long trip just to enjoy Bastille Day celebrations. They also wanted to celebrate a World Cup triumph and, after their opening performance, there was no eliminating them from the list of potential champions.

Central Park Stadium was nearly full for the Argentinians' first appearance. Alex Thépot was back in goal for France after missing 80 minutes of the opening match against Mexico. Despite his return, Argentina were the favourites, but the neutrals in the large crowd were behind the French because of the political tension between Uruguay and their South American neighbours at the time.

Argentina possessed a powerful team, a blend of old masters and new youngsters, who were to serve their country for many years. Amongst the old guard were goalkeeper Angel Bossio, full-backs José Della Torre and Ramón Muttis, 'hard man' Luís Monti, Natàlio Perinetti, Roberto Cierro and 'The Maestro' — captain 'Nolo' Ferreira. The new brigade consisted of wing-half Arico Suàrez, the Evaristo brothers and Francisco Varallo.

Argentina attacked from the start and had every intention of breaking through the French defence early on, but a magnificent display by Thépot kept the strong Argentinian attack at bay. Despite having Laurent as a passenger from the tenth minute, when he was hurt following a tackle from Luís Monti. France managed to keep the scoreline goalless for 81 minutes.

French goalkeeper Alex Thépot gathers an Argentinian cross during the Group One match in Central Park, Montevideo.

WORLD CUP FACT

In the first competition only three players played their club football in a country different from the one they represented, and all three were Yugoslavian – Stefanović, Beck (both Sete, France) and Seculić (Montpellier, France). Remarkably, a look at the 1990 squads for Italy showed that over 100 players were playing their league football abroad.

Etiénne Mattler (France).

By then, the thousands of Argentinian supporters were getting restless, but their frustration ended nine minutes from time, when Argentina were awarded a free-kick just outside the penalty area. Monti took the kick quickly, while the French were still organizing their wall. Centre-half Marcel Pinel, who had played magnificently all afternoon, left Thépot unsighted and the ball sped past him and into the net.

Brazilian referee Almeida Rego blew for time as French winger Marcel Langiller was breaking through the Argentine defence. It was then realized he had blown six minutes early. The French protested as the Argentinian fans rushed on to the pitch to congratulate their heroes. Rego then realized his mistake and tried to reorganize the teams, whilst mounted policemen cleared the pitch. The Argentine inside-left Cierro apparently fainted at the prospect of carrying on.

Unfortunately for the French, they could not compose themselves, but the traditional firework celebrations did not follow the Argentinian win. Their fans were relieved to get over the first hurdle of a championship that they already thought would be theirs. But how difficult the French had made it for them.

Argentina: Bossio; Della Torre, Muttis, Suàrez, Monti, J.Evaristo, Perinetti, Varallo, Ferreira, Cierro, M.Evaristo
Scorer: Monti
France: Thépot; Mattler, Capelle, Villaplane, Pinel, Chantrel, Libérati, Delfour, Maschinot, Laurent, Langiller.
Referee: Almeida Rego (Brazil)

CHILE 3   MEXICO 0 (Half-time 1-0)

Central Park, Montevideo, 16 July
Attendance: 500

ANOTHER lacklustre performance by Mexico saw them go out of the tournament after

Manuel Ferreira of Argentina, who played in four of his country's five games in the 1930 tournament.

Argentina's Stàbile scored a hat-trick against Mexico and finished as leading scorer in the first World Cup tournament.

two matches. The Chileans had the support of their own fans, who made the 'short' journey from the other side of the Andes, and also from the Uruguayans, who had never hidden their friendship with their South American neighbours.

Despite dominating play, Chile could not build on their fourth-minute goal from inside-right Guillermo Subiabre. However, second-half goals from Subiabre in the 50th minute and Vidal 14 minutes later, made the match safe as Chile started their campaign with a 3-0 win. They left the field to a standing ovation from the crowd.

Chile: Cortés; Morales, Poirier, A.Torres, Saavedra, Elgueta, Ojeda, Subiabre, Villalobos, Vidal, Schneeberger.
Scorers: Vidal, Subiabre 2
Mexico: Sota; R.Guitiérrez, M.Rosas, F.Rosas, Sanchez, Amezcúa, Pérez, Carreño, Ruíz, Gayòn, López.
Referee: Henri Chrisophe (Belgium)

CHILE 1   FRANCE 0 (Half-time 0-0)

Centenary Stadium, Montevideo, 19 July
Attendance: 2,000

AFTER opening with an easy win over Mexico and then giving their all against Argentina, the French failed miserably in their final group match against Chile and thus ended their dreams of winning the trophy.

The only goal of the game was scored by Chilean idol Subiabre, who headed home his third goal of the tournament in the 64th minute. He was the 1930s equivalent of today's 'midfield dynamo' and was a brilliant link between Chile's defence and attack. France's hero, once again, was their goalkeeper Alex Thépot, but even he could not prevent another 1-0 defeat and an exit from the competition.

Chile: Cortés; Chaparro, Morales, A.Torres, Saavedra, C.Torres, Ojeda, Subiabre, Villalobos, Vidal, Schneeberger.
Scorer: Subiabre
France: Thépot; Mattler, Capelle, Chantrel, Delmer, Villaplane, Libérati, Delfour, Pinel, Veinante, Langiller.
Referee: Anibal Tejeda (Uruguay)

ARGENTINA 6   MEXICO 3 (Half-time 3-0)

Centenary Stadium, Montevideo, 19 July
Attendance: 5,000

PLAYING immediately after the Chile-France game in the Estadio Centenario, Argentina knew that they had to win to remain in contention with Chile at the top of the group. They were without skipper Ferreira, who had to return to his country to sit a vital university examination, upon which his graduation depended. He was replaced as captain by Adolfo Zumelzù.

The Argentinians' performance was ragged to say the least. Their defence was vulnerable and allowed the insignificant Mexican attack to score three goals. Goalkeeper Angelo Bossio, nicknamed 'The Elastic Wonder' after his performances in the 1928 Olympics was no longer 'elastic'.

Nevertheless, the Argentina forwards Varallo, Stàbile, Demerìa, Spadaro and newcomer Peucelle, were in much better form and hammered six goals past the Mexicans.

Argentina were three up after 17 minutes thanks to two goals from centre-forward Stàbile and one from the new captain Zumelzù. Seven minutes before the interval Manuel Rosas pulled one back when he converted the World Cup's first-ever penalty. Varallo scored two goals within the first ten minutes of the restart to send Argentina into a 5-1 lead. But then came a lapse in defence.

Felipe Rosas emulated his brother and scored Mexico's second goal in the 65th minute and ten minutes later the arrears were reduced further as López made it 5-3. However, ten minutes from time Stàbile made the game safe when he became the first player to score a hat-trick in the World Cup Finals.

But the big question asked was: How could a team with no star players, and having suffered heavy defeats by France and Chile, score three goals against the fortress-like defence of the Argentinians? Perhaps the light blues did not justify their tag as outstanding favourites.

Argentina returned to their headquarters, in the quiet and serene setting next to the Santa Lucia river, to rethink plans for their showdown with Chile, the match which would decide which nation progressed to the semi-final.

Argentina: Bossio; Della Torre, Paternoster, Cividini, Zumelzù, Orlandini, Peucelle, Varallo, Stàbile, Demerìa, Spadaro.
Scorers: Stàbile 3, Varallo 2, Zumelzù
Mexico: Bonfiglio; R.Guitiérrez, F.Guitiérrez, M.Rosas, Sánchez, Rodríguez, F.Rosas, López, Gayòn, Carreño, Olivares.
Scorers: M.Rosas (pen), F.Rosas, López
Referee: Ulrico Saucedo (Bolivia)

Montevideo's Centenary Stadium.

Group One – Final Table

	P	W	D	L	F	A	Pts
Argentina	3	3	0	0	10	4	6
Chile	3	2	0	1	5	3	4
France	3	1	0	2	4	3	2
Mexico	3	0	0	3	4	13	0

ARGENTINA 3   CHILE 1 (Half-time 2-1)

Centenary Stadium, Montevideo, 22 July
Attendance: 1,000

THE final Group One match between these two South American countries had been eagerly awaited. The winners would progress to a semi-final clash with the United States.

Until their unimpressive win over Mexico, few would have bet against Argentina progressing to the next stage, but after that performance it left the outcome of the group more in the balance.

Ferreira was back from his exams and returned to the Argentine attack. But it was their defence which needed sorting out and only Orlandini remained in the half-back line. Monti returned to centre-half, while Juan Evaristo was brought in at right-half for his first game of the tournament. The only changes made by Chile from their win over France were to replace the two wingers, Tomás Ojeda and captain Carlos Schneeberger, with Guillermo Arellano and Juan Aguilera.

Argentina had slightly more of the play, which was a fair reflection of the difference between the two teams. The combination of Ferreira and Mario Evaristo proved to be a decisive one which the Chilean defence could not control. The new goalscoring sensation, Stàbile, scored in the 12th and 14th minutes before Subiabre, Chile's own goalscoring star, reduced the arrears two minutes later. Shortly before half-time a free-for-all broke out following a foul by Argentine centre-half Monti. Police had to come on to the pitch to separate the brawling players.

Fortunately, the second-half was free from such incident as the Chilean forwards made life tough for the Argentinian defence. Bossio was called upon to make some good saves, but Mario Evaristo made the game safe when he scored his second and Argentina's third goal in the 51st minute. He took the blue and whites into a semi-final clash against the surprise nation of the tournament, the United States.

Fernando Paternoster of Argentina.

Argentina: Bossio; Della Torre, Paternoster, J.Evaristo, Monti, Orlandini, Peucelle, Varallo, Stàbile, Ferreira, M.Evaristo.
Scorers: Stàbile 2, M.Evaristo
Chile: Cortés; Chaparro, Morales, A.Torres, Saavedra, C.Torres, Arellano, Subiabre, Villalobos, Vidal, Aguilera.
Scorer: Subiabre
Referee: Jean Langenus (Belgium)

Group Two

YUGOSLAVIA 2   BRAZIL 1 (Half-time 2-0)

Central Park, Montevideo, 14 July
Attendance: 5,000

IT was Yugoslavia, one of the four European entrants, who gained the advantage over Brazil, one of the fancied South American sides and the seeded side in Group Two.

Their victory, and that of France the day before, indicated that the European nations had not undertaken the long trip just to make up the numbers. Skippered by their Olympic

Milorad Arseniević (Yugoslavia).

Yugoslavia (right) and Brazil (below) pictured before the start of their Group One match. The Slavs topped the group with Brazil as runners-up, but in future years it was the Brazilians who became a major force in the World Cup.

Dr Milutin Ivković (Yugoslavia).

star Milutin Ivkovic, they were in Uruguay to try and take the trophy back to its European 'birthplace'.

Alexsandar Tirnanić and Ivan Beck, a professional in France at the time, gave Yugoslavia a 2-0 first-half lead with goals in the 21st and 31st minutes. A second-half goal by captain Preguinho in the 62nd minute reduced the arrears to 2-1. But that was the final scoreline and Brazil's hopes of becoming the first World Champions were severely dented.

Yugoslavia: Yavović; Ivković, Milhailović, Arsenievíc, Stefanović, Djokić, Tirnanić, Marianović, Beck, Vujadinović, Seculić.
Scorers: Tirnanić, Beck
Brazil: Joel; Brilhante, Italia, Hernògenes, Fausto, Fernando, Poly, Nilo, Araken, Preguinho, Teofilo.
Scorer: Preguinho
Referee: Anibal Tejeda (Uruguay)

YUGOSLAVIA 4   BOLIVIA 0 (Half-time 0-0)

Central Park, Montevideo, 17 July
Attendance: 800

THIS was the first of two 'back-to-back' matches played at the Central Park that day and the crowd saw Yugoslavia clinch their place in the semi-finals with an emphatic second-half display which left the Bolivians bewildered.

The Europeans made one change from their opening win over Brazil when they brought in Dragutin Naidanović on the left wing for Branislav Seculić. After a goalless first half the game sprang to life on the hour when beck opened the scoring. Marianović made it 2-0 five minutes later and in the 67th minute Beck scored a second to make it 3-0. The

Blagoje Marianović of Yugoslavia scored the second goal against Bolivia.

rout was completed five minutes from time through inside-left Vujadinović and Yugoslavia had finished top of Group Two.

Yugoslavia: Yavović; Ivković, Milhailović, Arsenievič, Stefanović, Djokić, Tirnanić, Marianović, Beck, Vujadinović, Naidanović.
Scorers: Beck 2, Marianović, Vujadinović
Bolivia: Bermúdez; Durandal, Civarría, Argote, Lara, Valderama, Gómez, Bustamente, Mendez, Alborta, Fernández.
Referee: Francisco Mateucci (Uruguay)

BRAZIL 4   BOLIVIA 0 (Half-time 1-0)
Centenary Stadium, Montevideo, 20 July
Attendance: 1,200

WITH Yugoslavia guaranteed to head Group Two, all that was left to play for in this match in the new Estadio Centenario was the 'wooden spoon'. Brazil, one of the pre-tournament favourites, saved themselves that embarrassment by inflicting another big defeat on the Bolivians.
    Brazil made wholesale changes, notably to their forward line where only skipper Preguinho remained from the Yugoslavia match. It paid dividends as new left winger Moderato netted twice, after 37 and 73 minutes. Preguinho also scored twice, after 57 and 83 minutes.

Brazil: Veloso; Italia, Zé Luis, Hernògenes, Fausto, Fernando, Benedito, Russinho, Leite, Preguinho, Moderato.
Scorers: Moderato 2, Preguinho 2
Bolivia: Bermúdez; Durandal, Civarría, Sáinz, Lara, Valderama, Ortiz, Bustamante, Mendez, Alborta, Fernández.
Referee: Thomas Balway (France)

Group Three

ROMANIA 3   PERU 1 (Half-time 1-0)
Pocitos, Montevideo, 14 July
Attendance: 300

WITH this game played on Bastille Day, a public holiday in Uruguay, the people of Montevideo were out celebrating and obviously had better things to do than go to the Pocitos Stadium to watch a World Cup match between two of the less-fancied teams.
    The Romanian team only made the trip following the intervention of their king and he took responsibility for picking the team. He did not do too bad a job because the Europeans enjoyed an opening win.
    The clash between the two sides was, to say the least, 'heated'. Romania's right-back, Adalbert Steiner, suffered a broken leg following a tackle and Peru's captain, Mario De Las Casas, had the unwanted distinction of becoming the first man to be sent off in the World Cup, when he received his marching orders from the Chilean referee, Alberto Warken, for increasingly violent play. The standard of refereeing again came in for criticism.
    As for the football, Romania were superior in all departments, Desu scoring in the very first minute. Souza equalized after 63 minutes but 13 minutes from time Stanciu put Romania back in front and five minutes from the end Kovacs made it 3-1.
    Romania won 3-1 and thus emulated France and Yugoslavia, their European counterparts, by winning their opening match.

Romania: Lapuseanu; Steiner, Bürger, Rafinski, Vogl, Eisembeisser, Kovacs, Desu, Wetzer, Stanciu, Barbu.
Scorers: Desu, Stanciu, Kovacs
Peru: Valdivieso; De Las Casas, Soria, Galindo, García, Valle, Flores, Villanueva, Denegri, Neira, Souza.
Scorer: Souza
Referee: Alberto Warken (Chile)

URUGUAY 1   PERU 0 (Half-time 0-0)
Centenary Stadium, Montevideo, 18 July
Attendance: 70,000

THE big day eventually arrived for the Uruguayan fans when the home team started its campaign. Their opening match had been delayed until 18 July, the 100th anniversary of the nation's independence. It was truly a great day for Uruguay.
    The tournament was five days old when the hosts played their first match in the newly-constructed Estadio Centenario (Centenary Stadium). However, it was only just ready on time. At the start of the tournament, its completion was well behind schedule, but days and nights of labour saw it ready for use shortly before the start of Uruguay's opening match.
    Scheduled for a 100,000 capacity, because there was still work to be finished, it was reduced

Group Two – Final Table

	P	W	D	L	F	A	Pts
Yugoslavia	2	2	0	0	6	1	4
Brazil	2	1	0	1	5	2	2
Bolivia	2	0	0	2	0	8	0

Djordje Vujadinović of Yugoslavia, completed the scoring against the Bolivians.

Branislav Seculić, who was left out of the Yugoslavian team to meet Bolivia.

Uruguayan skipper, José Nasazzi.

Uruguay's Pedro Cea *(top)* and Héctor Castro *(bottom)*.

to 80,000 for the inaugural match. Scaffolding was still in evidence, but the near-capacity crowd was seated and ready for the big occasion.

Peru had been disappointing in their opening match against Romania. Their defence was weak and their attack virtually non-existent. Their performance gave rise to optimism amongst the Uruguayan fans that an easy first match was expected. But how wrong they were.

As the Uruguayan Press reported: 'The devil was hidden; he had stayed in the Inca's dressing-room against Romania without ever appearing on the pitch'.

But he emerged against Uruguay in the shape of the coloured right winger Lavalle, just one of several changes made by Peru. Lavalle was to menace the Uruguay defence and at times the partisan crowd were forced to stop their chanting of 'U-R-U-G-U-A-Y' and hold their breath. From the onset he proved too much for left-half Alvaro Gestido and left-back Tejera.

The first half was goalless and the Uruguay fans were grateful for that scoreline. However, the packed house went wild, some 15 minutes into the second half, when 'Manco' Castro picked up a pass from Pedro Petrone to score the only goal of the game.

For the last half-hour, however, the Uruguay supporters were less than happy with their team's performance and were worried every time Lavalle got the ball.

Uruguay held on for a 1-0 win, but it was an uncomfortable debut for the host nation. Changes were needed for the Romanian game if a place in the semi-finals was going to be won.

Uruguay: Ballesteros; Nasazzi, Tejera, Andrade, Fernàndez, Gestido, Urdinaràn, Castro, Petrone, Cea, Iriarte.
Scorer: Castro
Peru: Pardón; De Las Casas, Maquilón, Denegri, Galindo, Astengo, Lavalle, Flores, Villanueva, Neira, Souza.
Referee: Jean Langenus (Belgium)

URUGUAY 4   ROMANIA 0 (Half-time 4-0)

Centenary Stadium, Montevideo, 22 July
Attendance: 80,000

URUGUAY did not have a team manager at the time of the 1930 World Cup. Instead, the players preferred to talk about tactics and strategies amongst themselves. It had worked in the past and helped produced a winning formula. Now it was time for some real talking amongst the players.

They decided that Domingo Tejera could have problems if the Romanian winger, in the classic European style, turned out to be another Lavelle. So, he was replaced by Ernesto Mascheroni, who was to become a vital part of the defence. Up front Pablo Dorado, Héctor Scarone and Peregrino Anselmo all found a place in the team.

The short-passing game of the revamped forward line soon reaped dividends and Dorado opened the scoring after seven minutes. Scarone added a second 17 minutes later and in the 30th minute, Anselmo made it 3-0. With only 35 minutes gone, Pedro Cea made it 4-0. The euphoria in the Centenary Stadium made up for the previous match.

The home team did not add to the scoreline, nor did the 'visitors'. In the second half, Uruguay chose to preserve themselves for the more difficult semi-final clash with Yugoslavia in a week's time.

Their display in the first half against Romania was one of the finest of the tournament and those privileged to be at the Centenary Stadium talked about it long after the final ball of the 1930 World Cup competition was kicked.

Uruguay: Ballesteros; Nasazzi, Mascheroni, Andrade, Fernàndez, Gestido, Dorado, Scarone, Anselmo, Cea, Iriarte.
Scorers: Dorado, Scarone, Anselmo, Cea
Romania: Lapuseanu; Bürger, Czako, Robe, Vogl, Eisembeisser, Kovacs, Desu, Wetzer, Rafinski, Barbu.
Referee: Almeida Rego (Brazil)

The Romanian team which lost to Uruguay. Back row (left to right): Kovacs, Desu, Wetzer, Rafinski, Barbu, trainer. Front row: Robe, Vogl, Eisembeisser, Lapuseanu, Czako, Bürger.

Group Three – Final Table

	P	W	D	L	F	A	Pts
Uruguay	2	2	0	0	5	0	4
Romania	2	1	0	1	3	5	2
Peru	2	0	0	2	1	4	0

Group Four

UNITED STATES 3   BELGIUM 0 (Half-time 2-0)

Central Park, Montevideo, 13 July
Attendance: 10,000

ON the same day that France and Mexico got the World Cup underway, the surprise team of the tournament, the United States, opened their account in the Central Park Stadium against one of the four European nations.

Two years earlier, the United States had been hammered 11-2 by Argentina during the Olympic competition in Amsterdam. Curiously, though, they were one of the seeded teams for the first World Cup, but this decision was justified by the fact that many British professionals, mostly from Scotland, had emigrated to the United States since the Olympics and were now members of the American national side.

Included in the US squad were Alec Wood, James Gallacher, Andrew Auld, James Brown, Bart McGhee and George Moorhouse. Some of them, however, appeared to have seen better days and appeared rather 'large' to say the least. The French were quick to nickname them the 'Shot-putters'.

Despite their size, they were still too good for the Belgians, who were not one of the strongest European soccer nations at the time. A large crowd came to Central Park out of curiosity to see the American team.

The North Americans played a system of three men up front and the remainder in defence. It worked as the front runners showed extreme skill and did enough to help the Americans to a 3-0 win, thanks to two goals from Scottish left winger McGhee and one from Fall River FC centre-forward, Bert Patenaude. It was the first win at major international level for the States and they had more in store for their fans before the end of World Cup '30.

Héctor Scarone (Uruguay).

The Belgian team which lost 3-0 to the United States. Back row (left to right): Hellemans, Pierre Braine, Torten Goetinck (manager), Badjou, Nouwens, Hoydonckx, De Clercq. Front row: Versijp, Voorhoof, Adams, Moeschal, Diddens.

United States: Douglas; Wood, Moorhouse, Gallacher, Tracey, Brown, Gonsalvez, Florie, Patenaude, Auld, McGhee.
Scorers: McGhee 2, Patenaude
Belgium: Badjou; Nouwens, Hoydonckx, Braine, Hellemans, De Clercq, Diddens, Moeschal, Adams, Voorhoof, Versijp.
Referee: Jose Macias (Argentina)

UNITED STATES 3   PARAGUAY 0 (Half-time 2-0)

Central Park, Montevideo, 17 July
Attendance: 800

HAVING played a typically British game in the first match against Belgium, the Americans changed their tactics and adopted the short-passing game against Paraguay. And their change of tactics surprised the South American team.

Paraguay went to Montevideo full of confidence. They had beaten Uruguay, one of the pre-tournament favourites, 3-0 in the previous year's South America Cup. The Uruguay team was made up of many of their 1928 Olympic winning team that day. It was certainly a worthy performance by the Paraguayans.

But, despite their confidence, the South Americans were brought down to earth by centre-forward Patenaude, who added two goals to the one he scored in the opening match. He scored his first goal after ten minutes and five minutes later the scoreline was increased to 2-0 with the help of an own-goal from Gonzáles, the first in the World Cup. American skipper Thomas Florie also claimed the goal although the record books show it as a Gonzáles own-goal.

Paraguay were 'sent packing' when a second Patenaude goal sealed their fate in the 50th

Bernard Voorhoof, a great Belgian star of the 1930s, although the Belgians were not one of Europe's strongest soccer nations at that time.

Group Four – Final Table

	P	W	D	L	F	A	Pts
USA	2	2	0	0	6	0	4
Paraguay	2	1	0	1	1	3	2
Belgium	2	0	0	2	0	4	0

minute. The United States team, on the other hand, had emerged from 'no hopers' to reach the semi-finals and had become one of the favourites to win the trophy.

United States: Douglas; Wood, Moorhouse, Gallacher, Tracey, Auld, Brown, Gonsalvez, Patenaude, Florie, McGhee.
Scorers: Patenaude 2, Gonzales (og)
Paraguay; Denis; Olmedo, Miracca, Etcheverri, Díaz, Aguirre, Nessi, Domínguez, Gonzáles, Benítez Cáceres, Peña.
Referee: Jose Macias (Argentina)

PARAGUAY 1   BELGIUM 0 (Half-time 1-0)
Centenary Stadium, Montevideo, 20 July
Attendance: 900

THE final match in Group Four was of academic value only. The United States had seen to that with their two emphatic wins over Paraguay and Belgium. All that was left to play for was the right to prop up the table and that unwanted distinction went to the Europeans, who fell to a single first-half goal.

There was little to choose between the two sides and the winner was scored by Paraguay's captain and outside-left, Peña, five minutes before the interval.

It was Paraguay's first win over a European opponent, but that was little compensation for a side which had gone to Uruguay with so much optimism but were now out of the tournament.

Paraguay: P.Benítez; Olmedo, Flores, S.Benítez, Díaz, Garcete, Nessi, Romero, Gonzáles, Benítez Cárceres, Peña.
Scorer: Pena
Belgium: Badjou; De Deken, Hoydonckx, Braine, Hellemans, Moeschal, Versijp, Delbeke, Adams, Nouwens, Diddens.
Referee: Ricardo Vallarino (Uruguay)

Santos Iriarte of Uruguay.

Semi-finals

ARGENTINA 6   UNITED STATES 1 (Half-time 1-0)
Centenary Stadium, Montevideo, 26 July
Attendance: 80,000

AFTER two impressive Group wins, the United States team was, perhaps surprisingly, installed as the favourites to become the first world champions. But the Argentinians were pleased with their own performance against Chile and would, in no way, consider defeat at the hands of their opponents.

The American team, managed by Jack Coll of Brooklyn Wanderers, had surprised the Uruguayan fans with their varying skills, tough defending, and surprising pace. The home fans were grateful that the Americans were playing Argentina in the semi-final and not their own team. Before the semi-final the American's manager declared that the Argentinians didn't worry him and that he was concerned only about the Final.

The Argentinians, on the other hand, had a team of class players, who had gained invaluable experience on the international scene. They were more of a 'team' than the Americans, who were somewhat extravagent and individual.

Argentina, however, were without the services of inside-right Varallo, known as 'El Canonito' — the Little Cannon. But in 'Conejo' (the Rabbit) Scopelli, they had an adequate replacement.

Despite being members of a team filled with star names, the likes of Monti and Stàbile were not renowned for the most gentlemanly of conduct and the American dream of reaching the Final lay in tatters after only a few brief minutes of the semi-final in front of a near full-house.

Centre-half Raphael Tracy (Bel Millers) had his leg broken after only ten minutes play. And by the end of the first half, goalkeeper Jim Douglas (New York Nationals) was a near-cripple. Left-half Andy Auld (Providence FC) was suffering from a severe mouth injury following a kick in the face. The rough tactics of the Argentinians had reduced the US side to a team of 'walking wounded'.

By half-time, the North Americans had done remarkably well to hold Argentina to one goal, scored by Monti after 20 minutes when 'keeper Douglas misjudged the ball. But in the second half it was a different story and they could not control the barrage of attacks which the Argentinians threw at them.

Scopelli and his Estudiantes teammate, 'Nolo' Ferreira, did most of the damage and created repeated opportunities for Stàbile and Carlos Peucelle, who each scored twice, three of the goals coming in a hectic seven-minute spell. Scopelli also got on the score-sheet and Brown scored a consolation goal for the United States two minutes from time.

The American officials were unimpressed with the refereeing of Belgian Jean Langenus. After he blew for a foul against one of their players, the US trainer ran on to the field and threw his medical equipment at the official.

José Andrade of Uruguay.

The United States team had played some good football in reaching the semi-finals, but their performance was hardly noticed in the States where the staple diet of ice-hockey, baseball and 'grid-iron' football still attracted most of the column inches of the sports pages.

On their way home, the Americans stopped off to play a friendly against Brazil and were narrowly beaten 4-3, with Patenaude scoring twice. The result showed that the Americans were one of the top soccer nations at the time — or did it merely show that Brazil had not emerged as the force they were to become 25 years later?

For a brief moment, Argentina could rightly claim to be the leading South American soccer nation. They had reached the first World Cup Final. Would South American dominancy be confirmed the next day when Uruguay took on Yugoslavia in the other semi-final?

Argentina: Botasso; Della Torre, Paternoster, J.Evaristo, Monti, Orlandini, Peucelle, Scopelli, Stàbile, Ferreira, M.Evaristo.
Scorers: Monti, Scopelli, Stàbile 2, Peucelle 2
United States: Douglas; Wood, Moorhouse, Gallacher, Tracey, Auld, Brown, Gonsalvez, Patenaude, Florie, McGhee.
Scorer: Brown
Referee: Jean Langenus (Belguim)

URUGUAY 6   YUGOSLAVIA 1 (Half-time 3-1)

Centenary Stadium, Montevideo, 27 July
Attendance: 93,000

A FULL house greeted the home team on to the pitch at the new Centenary Stadium. They knew their side was only one match away from a meeting with their South American neighbours, Argentina, and the chance to become the first holders of the World Cup. But in their way stood Yugoslavia, the strongest of the four European countries.

In only the fourth minute of this semi-final, Yugoslavia's Seculić put his side ahead, but it was not long before Cea and Anselmo had turned the panic amongst the fervent fans into delight with goals after 18 and 20 minutes.

The Yugoslavs had more of the play and were unlucky to concede the first goal, which had more than a hint of offside about it. They were equally unlucky to have a goal disallowed when trailing 2-1. And when Uruguay scored their third goal through Anselmo after 31 minutes the ball appeared to go out of play before being netted. The European side trailed 3-1 but had every right to feel their luck was deserting them. The half-time interval did nothing to help lift their spirits and they came back for the second half with their heads down.

After the break, Uruguay completed the rout with three more goals, the first from Iriarte on the hour before Cea completed his hat-trick with goals in the 67th and 72nd minutes. Remarkably, the second semi-final ended up with the same scoreline as the first, 6-1.

The hosts had confirmed South American football as the best in the world — at least that part of the world which was embraced by FIFA — and set up a meeting with the Argentinians in a repeat of the 1928 Olympic Final, which Uruguay won. The hosts had been the first South American champions in 1917. They were also the reigning Olympic champions. Could they now become the first World Champions as well? They were only one match away from finding out the answer to that question.

Uruguay: Ballesteros; Nasazzi, Mascheroni, Andrade, Fernàndez, Gestido, Dorado, Scarone, Anselmo, Cea, Iriarte.
Scorers: Cea 3, Anselmo 2, Iriarte
Yugoslavia: Yavović; Ivković, Milhailović, Arsenievič, Stefanović, Djokić, Tirnanić, Marianović, Beck, Vujadinović, Seculić.
Scorer: Seculić
Referee: Almeida Rego (Brazil)

Final

URUGUAY 4   ARGENTINA 2 (Half-time 1-2)

Centenary Stadium, Montevideo, 30 July
Attendance: 93,000

SOCCER history was made at the Estadio Centenario on Wednesday, 30 July 1930, when the host nation, Uruguay, and South American neighbours, Argentina, met in the Final of the first World Cup.

Thousands of Argentine supporters crossed the River Plate by the boatload, ready to cheer on their heroes. But the majority of the 93,000 crowd inside the new stadium were very much on the side of the home team.

Uruguay left out Anselmo and replaced him with the one-armed Castro at centre-forward. The traditional pre-match team selection by the players decided that stamina rather the artistry would be better on the day and that is why 'Manco' Castro returned to the team for his second game of the championship.

Aleksandar Tirnanić (Yugoslavia).

WORLD CUP FACT

Pedro Cea of Uruguay was the first person to score a goal in both the Olympic and World Cup Finals. He scored in the 1924 Olympic Final in Paris and in the inaugural World Cup Final six years later.

Uruguayan goalkeeper Enrique Ballesteros.

José Nasazzi (Uruguay) and Manuel Ferreria (Argentina) exchange pennants before the 1930 World Cup Final, watched by Belgian referee Jean Langenus.

José Nasazzi and Manuel Ferreira captained the two sides, just as they had in Amsterdam two years earlier, and the match was refereed by the experienced Belgian, Jean Langenus.

The opening minutes saw the two teams 'discovering' each other, but after 12 minutes the home side took the lead when Pablo Dorado shot through the legs of Botasso. Eight minutes later, the scores were level when outside-right Carlos Peucelle picked up a pass from Francisco Varallo and beat goalkeeper Enrique Ballesteros with a powerful shot.

Argentina took the lead in the 37th minute after Stàbile scored, but it was to be one of the game's most controversial incidents. When he collected the ball, Stàbile looked offside — the Uruguay captain, Nasazzi, later agreed with that -— but despite appeals to the referee, Langenus would not change his mind and the goal stood.

The incident unsettled the Uruguayans and it was perhaps fortunate that the half-time whistle soon blew and gave them the opportunity to cool down in the dressing-room.

The 12th minute of each half turned out to be significant. Just as Dorado had scored for Uruguay after 12 minutes of the first half, so Pedro Cea did the same after the same period in the second half. Uruguay had now settled down after the disputed first-half goal and the scores were level again, at 2-2.

For the first time in the match, the hosts were getting on top and the noise from their fans was deafening. However, the Argentinian wingers, Peucelle and Mario Evaristo, together with centre-forward Stàbile, were still proving to be dangerous and were always capable of a quick breakaway. The crowd were well aware they could spoil the celebrations in an instant.

Above: Andrade watches his goalkeeper Enrique Ballesteros in a goalmouth tussle with an Argentinian forward.

Left, above: The opening goal of the first World Cup Final. Right winger Pablo Dorado shoots past Juan Botasso.

Left, below: Stàbile's controversial goal that gave Argentina a 2-1 lead in the 37th minute.

Pedro Cea's 57th-minute goal brought Uruguay back into the match.

STATISTICS

Goalscorers:
8 — Guillermo Stàbile (Argentina).
5 — Pedro Cea (Uruguay).
4 — Guillermo Subiabre (Chile).
3 — Carlos Peucelle (Argentina), Bert Patenaude (United States), Ivan Beck (Yugoslavia), Peregrino Anselmo (Uruguay), Preguinho (Brazil).
2 — Luís Monti, Francisco Varallo (both Argentina), Bert McGhee (United States), Moderato Wisintainer (Brazil), André Maschinot (France), Héctor Castro, Pablo Dorado, Santos Iriarte (all Uruguay).
1 — Adolfo Zumelzù, Mario Evaristo, Alejandro Scopelli (all Argentina), James Brown (United States), Blagoje Marianović, Djordje Vujadinović, Alexsandar Tirnanić, Branislav Seculić (all Yugoslavia), Lucien Laurent, Marcel Langiller (both France), Carlos Vidal (Chile), Juan Carreño, Felipe Rosas, Manuel Rosas, Hilário López (all Mexico), Constantin Stanciu, Nikolai Kovacs, Andalbert Desu (all Romania), Luís Vargas Peña (Paraguay), Luis Ferreira Souza (Peru), Héctor Scarone (Uruguay).

Own-goal
Ramón Gonzáles (Paraguay v United States).

Hat-tricks
Guillermo Stàbile (Argentina v Mexico), Pedro Cea (Uruguay) v Yugoslavia).

Fastest goal
1 minute — Adalbert Desu (Romania v Peru).

Most goals (team)
18 Argentina

Teams failing to score
Belgium and Bolivia

Total goals scored: 70
Average per game: 3.88

Penalties
Scored: Manuel Rosas (Mexico v Argentina) *Referee: Ulrico Saucedo (Bolivia).*

Most appearances
5 — José Della Torre (Argentina)

Sendings-off
Mario De Las Casas (Peru v Romania) *Referee; Alberto Warken (Chile)*

Number of players used by Finalists
15 — Uruguay
20 — Argentina

Uruguay eased any concern in the 68th minute, when 'El Canario' — Santos Iriarte — scored a cracking goal from more than 25 yards. He received a pass from Ernesto Mascheroni and was being covered by Argentine defender Juan Evaristo. The wing-half just did not believe that Iriarte would try a shot from such a distance and 'dropped his guard'. To everyone's amazement, the winger's shot flew into the net for one of the best goals of the tournament.

Uruguay were back in front, but their lead was slender. They were looking for a vital fourth goal, but it was Argentina who came close to scoring next, when a shot from Stàbile, the centre-forward who later managed Argentina, hit the bar.

Then came that crucial fourth goal for the hosts. It was scored in the last minute by Castro, who headed home a Dorado cross. The man who lost part of his left arm in a childhood accident suddenly became a national hero. He had scored Uruguay's only goal of their opening match against Peru but was then dropped. His return was certainly a timely one as he completed a notable 'double' of scoring the host country's first and last goals of the inaugural tournament.

The final whistle went and Uruguay were world champions. There were tears of joy in the stadium and dancing in the streets of Montevideo, well into the next day which was declared a national holiday. The Argentina fans, who had arrived in Montevideo chanting 'Victory or death', returned home subdued. They made their anger in defeat known by throwing bricks through the windows of the Uruguayan Embassy in Buenos Aires — times do not change all that much.

Uruguay could not have been given a better birthday present than the honour to stage the first World Cup. The icing on the cake was the winning of the prize. It has been said that other nations have their history and that Uruguay has its football. On 30 July 1930, she certainly had her football and that day will never be forgotten.

Argentina's World Cup line-up. Back row (left to right): Jaun Evaristo, Paternoster, Monti, Bossio, Della Torre, Suàrez, Peucelle. Front row: Varallo, Stàbile, Ferreira, Marioe Evaristo.

Left, above: **Uruguay retake the lead as Santos Iriarte's tremendous 25-yard shot beats Botasso and nestles in the net.**

Héctor Castro (left) is hugged by Héctor Scarone after scoring the crucial last goal in the 1930 World Cup Final. Castro had also scored Uruguay's first-ever goal in the competition.

Uruguay: Enrique Ballesteros; José Nasazzi, Ernesto Mascheroni, José Leandro Andrade, Lorenzo Fernàndez, Alvaro Gestido, Pablo Dorado, Héctor Scarone, Héctor Castro, Pedro Cea, Santos Iriarte.
Scorers: Dorado, Cea, Iriarte, Castro
Argentina: Juan Botasso; José Della Torre, Fernando Paternoster, Juan Evaristo, Luís Monti, Pedro Arico Suàrez, Carlos Peucelle, Francisco Varallo, Guillermo Stàbile, Manuel Ferreira, Mario Evaristo.
Scorers: Peucelle, Stabile
Referee: Jean Langenus (Belgium)

Left, below: **Castro seals it for Uruguay in the last minute.**

Argentina's goalkeeper, Juan Botasso, dives bravely at the feet of Uruguay's Héctor Castro.

Uruguay, the first World Cup winners. Back row (left to right): Andrade, Gestido, Nasazzi, Ballesteros, Mascheroni, Fernàndez. Front row: Dorado, Scarone, Castro, Cea, Iriarte.

MEN WHO MADE THE HEADLINES - 1934

Giuseppe Meazza
(Italy)

MILAN-born 'Peppino' Meazza was Italy's most prolific goalscorer in the 1930s and his 33 goals in 53 appearances for the national side was a record until beaten by Luigi Riva. Meazza began as a centre-forward with Internazionale in 1927, at the age of 17. The following season he scored 33 goals and in 1929-30 was the Italian League's top scorer, a feat he repeated twice more. In all he scored 355 goals at senior level. He scored twice on his international debut, against Switzerland in February 1930, and was a virtual ever-present until 1939. Vittorio Pozzo moved Meazza to inside-forward and it paid dividends, culminating in Meazza playing a crucial role in Italy's first World Cup success. He was captain when they retained the title four years later, but shortly afterwards he suffered an injury which put him out of action for most of 1938-9. He moved to AC Milan at the end of 1939 but played only occasionally until 1942. He guested for Juventus and Varese during the war before moving to Atalanta for one season in 1945 and then became manager at Inter, occasionally turning out for them. Giuseppe Meazza died in 1979, aged 69. In 440 games in the Italian First Division he scored 269 goals.

Matthias Sindelar
(Austria)

A STAR of the 'Wunderteam', Matthias Sindelar was a tall, elegant centre-forward and, although known as *Der Paperiener (Man of Paper)* because of his frail appearance, he displayed tremendous skill. Born in Vienna in 1903, he joined FK Austria as a 20-year-old, following a brief spell with Hertha Vienna and Amateure. He succeeded Kalman Konrad at centre-forward and modelled his style on the great Hungarian. Outstanding on the ground, if not quite so effective in the air, Sindelar scored many goals during Austria's great spell between 1931 and 1934, having made his debut against Czechoslovakia in 1926. In the 8-2 defeat of Hungary in Vienna, he scored three and had a hand in the other five. With FK Austria he won three Cup-winners' and two Championship medals and scored a last-minute winner in the 1933 Mitropa Cup Final against Ambrosia-Inter of Italy. Sindelar appeared in three of Austria's four World Cup matches in 1934, scoring against France. Altogether, he netted 17 goals in 44 internationals. In 1939, Sindelar, a Jew, was betrayed by a Nazi member of the 'Wunderteam' and gassed himself. It was a tragic end for one of the finest centre-forwards of the pre-war era.

Frantisek Plánička
(Czechoslovakia)

IN 1934, Frantisek Plánička and Giampiero Combi of Italy made history as the first, and so far only, goalkeepers to skipper World Cup Finalists in the same game. Combi went on to lift the trophy and it is ironic that, after such a wonderful tournament in which his acrobatics saved his side on several occasions, Plánička should be best remembered for Orsi's dipping shot which beat him to level the scores with only ten minutes to go. Born in 1904, Plánička was one of Europe's finest pre-war goalkeepers and his 74 caps was a Czech record until overhauled by Ladislav Novák in 1966. In 1938, Plánička was again playing an heroic role as his country reached the quarter-finals. He thwarted Brazil's Leónidas time after time and, after what was later dubbed 'The Battle of Bordeaux', it was revealed that Plánička played for part of the game with a broken arm. Without him, the Czechs lost the replay. He was also an inspirational captain of his club side, Slavia Prague, who dominated Czech soccer in the 1920s and '30s. Plánička played for SK Bubanec before progressing via Slavia's youth teams and made more than 700 senior appearances before his retirement in 1939. Thirty years later he was still turning out in veterans' soccer.

Europe's Turn to Play Host
Italy 1934

A T A FIFA Congress on 8 October 1932, after eight lengthy conferences, Italy was chosen as the venue for the second World Cup. At the time Italy was under the Fascist rule of Benito Mussolini, *Il Duce*, who had taken power in 1922. The awarding of the World Cup to his country was seen by the dictator as a great propaganda platform and he ensured that Italy would provide a footballing spectacle that would be the envy of the world.

Since the first World Cup tournament in Uruguay, the number of countries affiliated to FIFA had passed the 50 mark. And 32 of them entered the second competition. However, because many European nations had snubbed the Uruguayans in 1930, they and some other South American countries refused to travel to Italy. Uruguay, therefore, remain the only reigning champions not to defend their title.

The 1930 runners-up, Argentina, did send a squad to Italy but it was a very weak outfit. They had already lost some of their top players, including one of their 1930 heroes, Luis Monti, to the Italian League. With the World Cup being staged on Italian soil, they felt that the competition would serve as a 'shop window' for their star players and, consequently, Argentina's finest were not allowed to make the trip.

The British associations were still at loggerheads with FIFA and the four Home Countries did not enter. The Republic of Ireland — then known as the Irish Free State — did enter but were eliminated by Belgium on goal-difference in the qualifying competition.

Because of the increased number of entrants it was necessary to reduce the 32 applicants to 16 for the Finals, although 17 teams were represented in Italy.

The United States were late entrants and FIFA decided they should meet Mexico, the winners of qualifying pool one. The match was played in Milan only three days before the start of the competition proper. The United States won 4-2 and Mexico had made the long trip to play only one game. When the final 16 teams were established, 12 were from Europe. The only exceptions were Egypt, the United States and South America's only two entrants, Brazil and Argentina.

Mexico, however, were not the only nation to make the long haul for just 90 minutes' football. For the first time the final stages of the World Cup were organized on a straight knock-out basis, which meant that half the competing nations had to make the trip for a single game only. However, unlike 1930 when the organizers overlooked a third-place match, one was arranged in 1934, between the losing semi-finalists. This match has since been a common feature of World Cup competitions.

Fearful that the draw could pair leading nations and thus have an effect on the financial viability of the tournament, eight teams were seeded to prevent them meeting in the first round. They were Italy, Czechoslovakia, Brazil, Hungary, Austria, Argentina, Holland and Germany.

Unlike the first tournament, when all the matches were played in one city, Montevideo, the 1934 competition was spread around Italy with Rome as the headquarters. On 27 May 1934, Italy had the honour of getting the competition underway. Mussolini's propaganda machine was rolling. The only possible hiccup to his plans was an Italian defeat. But that was unthinkable. The hosts were out to win, at almost any cost. . .

Italy's Meazza looks on as Greece's goalkeeper Grammaticopulos gathers the ball during the qualifying match between the two countries in Milan in March 1934. This was the first World Cup game for either side. Italy won 4-0 and went through, the return game in Greece not being played.

1934 Qualifying Competition

BECAUSE it was necessary to reduce the 32 entrants to a manageable 16 for the final stages in Italy, FIFA decided to organize a qualifying competition for the first time. There were 12 groups and one country from each group, with the exceptions of Groups 8, 10, 11 and 12 (two countries from each of them) qualified for Italy.

Even the host nation had to qualify, although the Italians faced little difficulty in overcoming Greece. The United States did not put in their entry until after the qualifying groups had been drawn up. It was then decided that they should meet the winner of the triangular Group 1 which comprised Cuba, Haiti and Mexico. The 'play-off', however, was to be staged in Italy and the USA and Mexico each faced an 8,000-mile round trip, knowing that one of them would be eliminated after only one game. That unwanted distinction eventually fell to the Mexicans.

The Republic of Ireland — then known as the Irish Free State — was the only British Isles representative. They were placed in Group 11, with Holland and Belgium, and were eliminated on the slenderest of goal-averages — having 0.66 to Belgium's 0.74. However, in their famous 4-4 draw with the Belgians in Dublin, centre-forward Paddy Moore made World Cup history by becoming the first man to score four goals in a game.

Controversy raged in the Switzerland-Romania match at Berne. The game ended 2-2 but, on appeal, the match was awarded to Switzerland because the Romanians fielded an ineligible player, Baratki. At one time it was thought that the Romanians, who had qualified as runners-up and were therefore eligible for the World Cup Finals in Italy, were going to be ejected from the competition. However, after another appeal they were allowed to make the journey.

Results

Group One

Round One
28 Jan 1934 *Port au Prince* Haiti .... 1 Cuba 3
1 Feb 1934 *Port au Prince* Haiti .... 0 Cuba 6
4 Feb 1934 *Port au Prince* Haiti .... 1 Cuba 1
Round Two
4 Mar 1934 *Mexico City* Mexico .... 3 Cuba 2
11 Mar 1934 *Mexico City* Mexico .... 5 Cuba 0
18 Mar 1934 *Mexico City* Mexico .... 4 Cuba 1
Group Final
24 May 1934 *Rome* United States .... 4 Mexico 2
United States qualified

Group Two
Brazil qualified (Peru withdrew)

Group Three
Argentina qualified (Chile withdrew)

Group Four
16 Mar 1934 *Cairo* Egypt .... 7 Palestine 1
6 Apr 1934 *Tel Aviv* Palestine .... 1 Egypt 4
Egypt qualified (Turkey withdrew)

Group Five
11 Jun 1933 *Stockholm* Sweden .... 6 Estonia 2
29 Jun 1933 *Kaunas* Lithuania .... 0 Sweden 2
Estonia v Lithuania not played.
Sweden qualified

Group Six
11 Mar 1934 *Madrid* Spain .... 9 Portugal 0
18 Mar 1934 *Lisbon* Portugal .... 1 Spain 2
Spain qualified

Group Seven
25 Mar 1934 *Milan* Italy .... 4 Greece 0
Greece v Italy not played.
Italy qualified

Group Eight
25 Mar 1934 *Sofia* Bulgaria .... 1 Hungary 4
25 Apr 1934 *Vienna* Austria .... 6 Bulgaria 1
28 Apr 1934 *Budapest* Hungary .... 4 Bulgaria 1
Bulgaria v Austria, Austria v Hungary and Hungary v Austria not played.

	P	W	D	L	F	A	Pts	
Hungary	2	2	0	0	8	2	4	**Hungary and**
Austria	1	1	0	0	6	1	2	**Austria qualified**
Bulgaria	3	0	0	3	3	14	0	

Group Nine
15 Oct 1933 *Warsaw* Poland .... 1 Czechoslovakia .. 2
15 Apr 1934 *Prague* Czechoslovakia .. 2 Poland 0
Czechoslovakia qualified

Group Ten
24 Sep 1933 *Belgrade* Yugoslavia .... 2 Switzerland 2
29 Oct 1933 *Berne* *Switzerland ...... 2 Romania 0
29 Apr 1934 *Bucharest* Romania .... 2 Yugoslavia 1
*This game ended 2-2 but after an appeal against Romania fielding an ineligible player, FIFA awarded the match to Switzerland, 2-0.

	P	W	D	L	F	A	Pts	
Switzerland	2	1	1	0	4	2	3	**Switzerland and**
Romania	2	1	0	1	2	3	2	**Romania qualified**
Yugoslavia	2	0	1	1	3	4	1	

Group Eleven
25 Feb 1934 *Dublin* Irish Free State .. 4 Belgium 4
8 Apr 1934 *Amsterdam* Holland .... 5 Irish Free State 2
29 Apr 1934 *Brussels* Belgium .... 2 Holland 4

	P	W	D	L	F	A	Pts	
Holland	2	2	0	0	9	4	4	**Holland and**
Belgium	2	0	1	1	6	8	1	**Belgium (on goal-**
Irish Free State	2	0	1	1	6	9	1	**average) qualified**

Group Twelve
11 Mar 1934 *Luxembourg* Luxembourg ..... 1 Germany 9
15 Apr 1934 *Luxembourg* Luxembourg ..... 1 France 6
France v Germany not played.

	P	W	D	L	F	A	Pts	
Germany	1	1	0	0	9	1	2	**France and**
France	1	1	0	0	6	1	2	**Germany qualified**
Luxembourg	2	0	0	2	2	15	0	

1934 Tournament

Round One

ITALY 7   UNITED STATES 1 (Half-time 3-0)
PNF Stadium, Rome, 27 May
Attendance: 30,000

ITALY, the pre-tournament favourites, included three Argentinians from the Italian League in their squad — Luis Monti, centre-half in the team beaten in the 1930 Final, Raimundo Orsi, a brilliant winger who collected a silver medal at the 1928 Olympics but missed the 1930 World Cup, and Enrique Guaita, who did not play in the opening match against the USA.

The Italian team was assembled by Vittorio Pozzo, one of the game's great coaches, who, as a student in England, watched the great Manchester United team of 1908. He silenced his critics by pointing out that the Argentinians had Italian fathers and could be called up to serve in the Italian forces. "If they can die for Italy, they can play football for Italy," he said.

Six weeks before the start of the tournament the Italians had been taken away to a near-monastic life at a mountainside retreat near Lake Maggiore. The Americans, meanwhile, had entered the competition at the last minute and only three players — full-back George Moorhouse, centre-half Bill Gonsalvez and skipper Thomas Florie — remained from their team that reached the 1930 semi-finals.

The Americans hung on for 18 minutes before the floodgates opened. Angelo Schiavio, who won a bronze medal at the 1928 Olympics, opened the scoring. Two minutes later, Orsi made it 2-0 and Schiavio scored a third after 29 minutes. In the 57th minute, Aldo 'Buff' Donelli, an Italian immigrant who stayed on after the World Cup to play for Naples, pulled back a goal for the USA but Giovanni Ferrari made it 4-1 after 63 minutes, Schiavio completed his hat-trick a minute later and in the 69th minute Orsi scored his second to make it 6-1. Right on the final whistle, Giuseppe Meazza, one of the most gifted Italian forwards of all-time, scored Italy's seventh.

Mussolini went away happy. His team had cleared the first hurdle with ease and with a new World Cup record score.

Italy: Combi; Rosetta, Allemandi, Pizziolo, Monti, Bertolini, Guarisi, Meazza, Schiavio, Ferrari, Orsi.
Scorers: Schiavio 3, Orsi 2, Meazza, Ferrari
United States: Hjulian; Czerkiewicz, Moorhouse, Pietras, Gonsalvez, Florie, Ryan, Nilsen, Donelli, Dick, Maclean.
Scorer: Donelli
Referee: Rene Mercet (Switzerland)

Raimundo Orsi, one of three Argentinians playing in the Italian League and selected by Italy. Orsi scored twice as his adopted nation beat the United States.

The United States squad pictured before the start of the tournament.

CZECHOSLOVAKIA 2   ROMANIA 1 (Half-time 0-1)
Littorio Stadium, Trieste, 27 May
Attendance: Not recorded

ROMANIA included only two survivors from their 1930 squad, inside-forward Nikolai Kovacs and full-back Emmerich Vogl. Czechoslovakia were one of the seeds but were lucky to overcome the plucky Romanians.

Left winger Dobai put the outsiders ahead after ten minutes and they held on to their lead until the 49th minute, when the Czech left winger, Antonin Puč, levelled the scores.

Czechoslovakia's winner came in the 69th minute when centre-forward Sobotka won the ball from a dropped-ball and was lucky to get a pass to the talented inside-left Oldrich Nejedlý, who scored the vital goal.

The Czechs had been saved from an embarrassing defeat by their goalkeeper and captain,

Stefan Dobai of Romania.

Outside-left Dobai gives outsiders
Romania a tenth-minute lead
against Czechoslovakia in Trieste.

Frantisek Plánička, who brought off some acrobatic saves and kept his team in the game. In the end they were fortunate, and grateful, to squeeze through 2-1. They certainly did nothing to justify their seeding.

Czechoslovakia: Plánička; Ženíšek, Čtyřoký, Košťálek, Čambal, Krčil, Junek, Silný, Sobotka, Nejedlý, Puč.
Scorers: Puč, Nejedlý
Romania: Zombori; Vogl, Albu, Deheleanu, Kotormani, Moravez, Bindea, Kovacs, Sepi, Bodola, Dobai.
Scorer: Dobai
Referee: Jean Langenus (Belgium)

GERMANY 5   BELGIUM 2 (Half-time 1-2)
Giovanni Berta Stadium, Florence, 27 May
Attendance: 8,000
ANOTHER team who did not do their seeding justice was Germany. They played the 'third-back' game but were uninspiring. Only their captain, the blond-haired Fritz Szepan, gave anything like an honest performance. He was certainly the most versatile player on the field and it was fortunate for the Germans that their opposition was weak and could not capitalize on a 2-1 half-time lead.

Germany opened the scoring through Stanislaus Kobierski in the 26th minute but two goals by Belgium's inside-right Voorhoof, in the 31st and 43rd minutes, gave them a surprise lead at the interval. Siffling levelled the scores before the German centre-forward, Edmund Conen, scored a hat-trick. His first goal came in the 67th minute, the second three minutes later and his hat-trick was completed ten minutes from time.

The scoreline looked impressive at 5-2 but it was not a reflection of the way Germany played, more a reflection on how bad was the opposition.

Germany: Kress; Haringer, Schwartz, Janes, Szepan, Zielinksi, Lehner, Hohmann, Conen, Siffling, Kobierski.
Scorers; Conen 3, Kobierski, Siffling
Belgium: Van de Weyer; Smellinckx, Joacim, Peeraer, Welkenhuyzen, Klaessens, Devries, Voorhoof, Capelle, Grimmonprez, Heremans.
Scorer: Voorhoof 2
Referee: Francesco Mattea (Italy)

AUSTRIA 3   FRANCE 2 (a.e.t.) (Half-time 1-1; 90 mins 1-1)
Mussolini Stadium, Turin, 27 May
Attendance: Not recorded
AUSTRIA were second favourites behind Italy and, like the hosts, they were guided by one of the game's leading coaches of the time, Hugo Meisl. His right-hand man was Lancashire-born Jimmy Hogan and it was Hogan who introduced the Austrians to the effective Scottish-style of keeping the ball on the ground.

Nicknamed the *Wunderteam*, the Austrians had run England close in a friendly in 1932, going down 4-3 at Stamford Bridge. However, when they arrived in Italy, Meisl announced that his team was tired and he doubted if they could win the trophy, despite having such world-class players as left-back Karl Sesta, roving centre-half Josef Smistik and the brilliant ball-playing centre-forward Matthias Sindelar.

Skipper Franz Szepan, the only
German to give an honest
performance against Belgium.

Fortune, though, smiled on Austria in their opening game. French centre-forward, Jean Nicolas, suffered a bad head injury early in the game, although that did not prevent him from opening the scoring in the 19th minute.

Sindelar made it 1-1 in the last minute of the first half and that is the way it stayed throughout an entertaining second half. Even before the start of extra-time it had been the most entertaining match of the tournament but the World Cup's first-ever period of extra-time held even more in store, including three goals.

The game turned sour for the French after only four minutes when Anton Schall put the Austrians in front with a goal that was blatantly offside. Two minutes later, still fuming over the decison, the French allowed Josef Bican to make it 3-1. They pulled a goal back six minutes from time, when centre-half Georges Verriest converted a penalty, but it was too late. Schall refused to comment on his controversial goal, but years later he admitted in a newspaper article that he felt he was offside.

Austria: Platzer; Cisar, Sesta, Wagner, Smistik, Urbanek, Zischek, Bican, Sindelar, Schall, Viertl.
Scorers: Sindelar, Schall, Bican
France: Thépot; Mairesse, Mattler, Delfour, Verriest, Llense, Keller, Alcazar, Nicolas, Rio, Aston.
Scorers: Nicolas, Verriest (pen)
Referee: John Van Moorsel (Holland)

Austria's team that beat France 3-2. From left to right: Sesta, Viertl, Urbanek, Bican, Wagner, Sindelar, Cisar, Zischek, Smistik, Schall, Platzer.

The Spanish team that beat Brazil 3-1. Back row (left to right, players only): Marculeta, Quincoces, Zamora, Muguerza, Ciriaco, Lecue, Iraragorri. Front row: Langara, Cilauren, Lafuente, Gorostiza.

SPAIN 3   BRAZIL 1 (Half-time 2-0)

Luigi Ferraris Stadium, Genoa, 27 May
Attendance: Not recorded

SPAIN should probably have been seeded for the 1934 World Cup, but were not. Brazil were seeded and probably should not have been, despite having a squad of highly talented players. And when the draw brought the two teams together in the first round, this point was underlined.

Brazil's only survivor from the inaugural competition four years earlier was José Luis Oliveira, who had preferred to be known as *Ze Luis* in 1930.

Brazil's Leónidas pulled back a goal for his side against Spain.

Jacinto Francisco Fernandez de Quincoces of Spain.

José Iraragorri put Spain in front from the penalty-spot in the 18th minute and nine minutes later the Spaniards increased their lead through centre-forward Isidro Langara.

Spain were content to sit on that two-goal cushion and save themselves for the next round, but their complacency nearly backfired when Leónidas pulled one back for the Brazilians in the 56th minute. However, Spain made sure of their passage into round two when Langara scored his second goal in the 77th minute.

The Brazilians had made the long journey for nothing because their hugely gifted side had failed to play well as a team.

Valdemar de Brito of Brazil made history during this game by becoming the first man in World Cup history to miss a penalty. However, later in life he was forgiven because he was the man who discovered and coached the legendary Pelé.

Spain: Zamora; Ciriaco, Quincoces, Cilauren, Muguerza, Lafuente, Iraragorri, Langara, Lecue, Marculeta, Gorostiza.
Scorers: Iraragorri (pen), Langara 2
Brazil: Pedrosa; Silvio, Luz, Tinoco, Martin Silveira, Canalli, Oliviera, de Brito, Leónidas, Armadinho, Bartesko.
Scorer: Leónidas
Referee: Alfred Birlem (Germany)

SWITZERLAND 3   HOLLAND 2 (Half-time 2-1)
San Siro Stadium, Milan, 27 May
Attendance: Not recorded

HOLLAND qualified for the final stages after comfortable wins over Belgium and the Irish Free State in the qualifying round and were rightly made one of the seeded teams. It was a shock, then, when they got it so wrong in their first-round match against Switzerland.

The Dutch fell behind to a Leopold Kielholz goal in the 14th minute and were battling for the rest of the game. Smit made it 1-1 in the 22nd minute but two minutes before half-time, Kielholz struck a demoralizing blow when he scored his second goal.

Switzerland put themselves into an even stronger position after 64 minutes when Andre Abegglen III made it 3-1. Holland offered little resistance and a late goal by Leen Vente was scant consolation. Holland took a squad of 22 players to Italy in the hope of doing well but they needed only 11 of them.

Switzerland: Sechehaye; Minelli, Weiler, Guinchard, Jaccard, Hufschmid, von Känel, Passello, Kielholz, Abeggien III, Bossi.
Scorers: Kielholz 2, Abeggien III
Holland: Van der Meulen; Weber, van Run, Pellikaan, Anderiesen, van Heel, Wels, Vente, Bakhuijs, Smit, van Nellen.
Scorers: Smit, Vente
Referee: Ivan Eklind (Sweden)

Sweden's Rydberg punches clear from De Vincenzi of Argentina in Bologna.

SWEDEN 3   ARGENTINA 2 (Half-time 1-1)
Littoriale Stadium, Bologna, 27 May
Attendance: Not recorded

FOLLOWING Brazil's sad exit, it was now the turn of the other South American entrant to bid farewell to World Cup 1934. The first World Cup had belonged to the South Americans. The second tournament was becoming a wholly European affair.

Brazil had only one survivor from the 1930 tournament but the Argentinians, runners-up last time around, could not boast any. Their star players were kept at home, the Argentine FA fearing that they would be 'poached' by the top Italian clubs.

Whilst Sweden could not match the technique of the South Americans, they made up for it with an all-round team display. Despite falling behind to a tremendous 25-yard shot from full-back Belis in the third minute, the Scandinavians were not rattled and five minutes later they equalized through centre-forward Sven Jonasson.

Argentina took the lead again two minutes after the interval, when Alberto Galateo scored, and their lead was longer lived this time. It was 20 minutes before Sweden pulled level again, once more through Jonasson. Then, 11 minutes from the end, the Swedes polished off a satisfactory performance when outside-left Knut Kroon gave them the lead for the first time. They held on and South American interest in the competition evaporated.

Sweden: Rydberg; Axelsson, S.Andersson, Carlsson, Rosen, E.Andersson, Dunker, Gustafsson, Jonasson, Keller, Kroon.
Scorers: Jonasson 2, Kroon
Argentina: Freschi; Pedevilla, Belis, Nehin, Sosa-Urbieta, Lopez, Rua, Wilde, De Vincenzi, Galateo, Irañeta.
Scorers: Belis, Galateo
Referee: M.Braun (Austria)

HUNGARY 4   EGYPT 2 (Half-time 2-1)
Ascarelli Stadium, Naples, 27 May
Attendance: Not recorded

EGYPT went into the World Cup record books as Africa's first competing nation. And, despite losing at the first attempt, they were certainly not disgraced by going down to Hungary, one of Europe's leading teams.

The Hungarians were still smarting from a shock 3-0 defeat inflicted upon them by the Egyptians in the 1924 Olympics in Paris, in one of the greatest upsets in Olympic soccer history. And in Amsterdam four years later, Egypt reached the semi-final of the Olympic tournament. The Egyptians had also embarrassed Hungary by holding them to a goalless draw in a friendly international in Cairo in 1932. Their presence in Italy was not taken lightly, certainly not by the Hungarians, even though the Magyars were one of the fancied 'outsiders'.

Egypt fell behind to a Teleki goal in the 12th minute. However, Hungary did not score again until the half-hour mark, when inside-left Géza Toldi netted. Egypt responded with a goal from Abdel Rahman Fawzi eight minutes later and at half-time the score was 2-1 in Hungary's favour.

The second half belonged to the skilful, ball-playing Hungarians. Goals from Toldi and Vincze, after 52 and 59 minutes respectively, made it 4-1 and thus ended Egypt's brave effort. Fawzi scored his second goal in the 67th minute but the Hungarians played out the rest of the game at their own pace.

Hungary: A.Szabó; Futo, Sternberg, Palotas, Szücs, Lázár, Markos, Vincze, Teleki, Toldi, G.Szabó.
Scorers: Teleki, Toldi 2, Vincze
Egypt: Kamel Taha; El Said, Hamidu, El Far, Rafaat, Ragab, Latif, Fawzi, Mokhtar, Kamel Mansour, Hassan.
Scorer: Fawzi 2
Referee: Rinaldo Barlassini (Italy)

Eberhard Bakhuijs of Holland.

Round Two

GERMANY 2   SWEDEN 1 (Half-time 0-0)
San Siro Stadium, Milan, 31 May
Attendance: 3,000

GERMANY went to Italy as one of the more fancied teams but were disappointing in the way they disposed of Belgium in the first round. Now, against the Swedish amateurs, they showed little imagination in scraping home with a narrow win.

The game was played in heavy rain and Sweden had the opportunity to take an early lead, but Kroon missed an easy chance. The game remained goalless for an hour before two goals in three minutes, both from inside-right Karl Hohmann, put Germany in a commanding position. Sweden were reduced to ten men when left-half Ernest Andersson went off injured. However, they still managed to pull a goal back seven minutes from time, when right winger Gosta Dunker found the net.

Germany: Kress; Haringer, Busch, Gramlich, Szepan, Zielinski, Lehner, Hohmann, Conen, Siffling, Kobierski.
Scorer: Hohmann 2
Sweden: Rydberg; Axelsson, S.Andersson, Carlsson, Rosen, E.Andersson, Dunker, Jonasson, Gustafsson, Keller, Kroon.
Scorer: Dunker
Referee: Rinaldo Barlassini (Italy)

Joop Smit, equalized for Holland with a 22nd-minute goal against Switzerland but his side still lost.

Austria's Matthias Sindelar.

Johann Horvath gives Austria a
fifth-minute lead against Hungary.

AUSTRIA 2   HUNGARY 1 (Half-time 1-0)

Littoriale Stadium, Bologna, 31 May
Attendance: Not recorded

THE second round drew together Austria and Hungary, two teams who played similar styles of football. The Hogan influence on the Austrian *Wunderteam* had crept into the Hungarian style of play and a large crowd at Bologna eagerly anticipated this clash.

Hugo Meisl drafted the diminutive Johann Horvath into the side and he proved to be the greatest menace to the Hungarian defence. In the fifth minute, Horvath was on the end of a classy Austrian move to open the scoring.

Hungary were playing under par and their usually effective centre-forward, György Sárosi was off form. The Austrians took advantage of their opponents' lapses and in the 53rd minute, classy winger Karl Zischek cut in from the right to unleash a shot and put Austria 2-0 ahead.

The Magyars pulled a goal back when Sárosi converted a penalty in the 67th minute, but they could not equalize and to complete Hungary's misery outside-right Imre Markos was sent off.

The game had promised so much because both sides had very skilful players. Alas, it turned into a running battle which Meisl described as 'a brawl, not a football match'.

Austria: Platzer; Cisar, Sesta, Wagner, Smistik, Urbanek, Zischek, Bican, Sindelar, Horvath, Viertl.
Scorers: Horvath, Zischek
Hungary: A.Szabó; Vágó, Sternberg, Palotas, Szücs, Szalay, Markos, Avar, Sárosi, Toldi, Kemény.
Scorer: Sárosi (pen)
Referee: Francesco Mattea (Italy)

ITALY 1   SPAIN 1 (a.e.t.) (Half-time 0-1; 90 mins 1-1)

Giovanni Berta Stadium, Florence, 31 May
Attendance: 35,000

ITALY'S skipper, Virginio Rosetta, was injured in the opening game against the United States and missed the clash with Spain. The captaincy went to experienced goalkeeper Giampiero Combi, who was playing in his 44th international, but it was the Spanish 'keeper, Ricardo Zamora, who stole the limelight.

Zamora had a habit of raising his game against the Italians and in the past had often appeared to take them on single-handed. This time was no different.

The Italians knew how Zamora could frustrate them and he was subjected to some rough treatment early in the game. However, poor refereeing from Louis Baert of Belgium allowed many fouls on the goalkeeper to go unpunished.

It was Spain who took the lead in the 31st minute, when a miskick from Regueiro wrong-footed Combi. However, a minute after the start of the second half, the Italian fans went wild when Giovanni Ferrari equalized. The goal was surrounded with controversy because Schiavio apparently impeded Zamora but it stood, despite the Spanish protests.

At the end of 120 minutes' play, both sides counted the cost of a bruising affair — the Italian wing-half Pizziolo had broken his leg during the game — and sweeping changes had to be made for the replay the next day.

Italy: Combi; Monzeglio, Allemandi, Pizziolo, Monti, Castellazzi, Guaita, Meazza, Schiavio, Ferrari, Orsi.
Scorer: Ferrari

Spain's right-back, Ciriaco.

Spain: Zamora; Ciriaco, Quincoces, Cillauren, Muguerza, Fede, Lafuente, Iraragorri, Langara, Regueiro, Gorostiza.
Scorer: Regueiro
Referee: Louis Baert (Belgium)

Replay
ITALY 1   SPAIN 0 <small>(Half-time 1-0)</small>
Giovanni Berta Stadium, Florence, 1 June
Attendance: 43,000

SPAIN were forced to make seven changes because of their massive injury list. Amongst their casualties was goalkeeper Zamora, who had done so well to hold the Italians at bay the previous day.

Italy had to make four changes — Pizziolo and his fellow wing-half Castellazzi, together with strikers Schiavio and Ferrari (their scorer in the first game) were all ruled out — but the most significant change of all was that of the referee.

Belgian Louis Baert was replaced by Rene Mercet of Switzerland but, alas, his handling of the game was no better and he was subsequently suspended by the Swiss FA. Mercet was obviously affected by the fierce partisanship of the home crowd and he became wrapped up in the Italian 'win-at-all-costs' approach to the world title.

Both sides were subdued and the replay offered little excitement for the army of Italian fans, who packed the Giovanni Berta Stadium for the second time in 24 hours.

Zamora's stand-in, Nogues, was as defiant as his mentor and fought hard to keep the Italians at bay after Meazza headed the only goal of the game in the 12th minute. Spain's reserves did well to contain the Italians to one goal, particularly as outside-left Bosch was a passenger after being injured in the fifth minute. And Spain were very unlucky to have two goals disallowed for offside. Both were disputed decisions and one was a blatant error by the referee.

Italy: Combi; Monzeglio, Allemandi, Ferraris IV, Monti, Bertolini, Guaita, Meazza, Borel, De Maria, Orsi.
Scorer: Meazza
Spain: Nogues; Zabalo, Quincoces, Cillauren, Muguerza, Lecue, Vantolra, Regueiro, Campanal, Chacho, Bosch.
Referee: Rene Mercet (Switzerland)

CZECHOSLOVAKIA 3   SWITZERLAND 2 <small>(Half-time 1-1)</small>
Mussolini Stadium, Turin, 31 May
Attendance: Not recorded

THE best game of the second round was undoubtedly this clash in Turin. Both sides took it in turn to lead and the outcome was in doubt until the very last minute.

Considering they were one of the outsiders at the start of the tournament, the Swiss gave a very commendable performance against the more fancied Czechs and took the lead in the 18th minute, when Leopold Kielholz scored a breakaway goal. Svoboda equalized six minutes later, however, and three minutes into the second half, the Czechs led for the first time when Sobotka netted.

The match was all-square again after 71 minutes when Abegglen got to the ball at full stretch to put it past Plánička. But the end to Switzerland's brave effort came seven minutes from time when the fine inside-left, Oldrich Nejedlý, scored Czechoslovakia's winning goal.

Czechoslovakia: Plánička; Ženíšek, Čtyřoký, Koštálek, Čambal, Krčil, Junek, Svoboda, Sobotka, Nejedlý, Puč.
Scorers: Svoboda, Sobotka, Nejedlý
Switzerland: Sechehaye; Minelli, Weiler, Guinchard, Jaccard, Hufschmid, von Känel, Jaeggi IV, Kielholz, Abegglen III, Jaeck.
Scorers: Kielholz, Abegglen III
Referee: Alois Beranek (Germany)

Ricardo Zamora, the great Spanish goalkeeper who missed the replay against Italy through injury.

Swiss goalkeeper Sechehaye gathers the ball from Czechoslovakia's Svoboda in the Mussolini Stadium, Turin.

Semi-finals

ITALY 1   AUSTRIA 0 (Half-time 1-0)

San Siro Stadium, Milan, 3 June
Attendance: 60,000

Italy's Meazza tends to his injured
comrade, Schiavio, who has just
collided with Platzer, the Austrian
goalkeeper who is also lying on the
line.

LESS than four months before this match, Austria had beaten Italy 4-2 in Turin. Now the Italians were seeking revenge in a match which many people had hoped would be reserved for the World Cup Final. Austria were regarded as the unofficial champions of Europe, whilst Italy, under the guidance of Vittorio Pozzo, were rapidly catching them up. This clash would resolve who were the new 'champions of Europe', irrespective of the Final outcome.

The game was played in a downpour and the sticky pitch was a disadvantage to the ball-playing Austrians. Italy's three Argentinians — Monti, Orsi and Guaita — were outstanding and Monti completely shut out Austria's star centre-forward, Matthias Sindelar. His ineffectiveness proved to be Austria's downfall.

The game was settled by a 19th-minute goal scored by outside-right Enrique Guaita. Austria's goalkeeper, Peter Platzer, had enjoyed a memorable tournament but when Schiavio shot, he punched the ball instead of holding it and Guaita rammed the ball home.

Austria were missing the injured Horvath and did not have their first shot at goal until the 42nd minute. But in the second half they did most of the attacking without finding

the net. Italy had their own star 'keeper, Combi, to thank as he brought off a succession of fine saves. In the last minute Austria had a great chance to level the scores when inside-right Zischek broke away, but he shot wide of an open goal.

Mussolini, who was in the crowd, was delighted that his team had reached the World Cup Final, for it substantially helped his propaganda campaign. For Austria, it marked the end of an era which had seen them so dominant on mainland Europe.

Italy: Combi; Monzeglio, Allemandi, Ferraris IV, Monti, Bertolini, Guaita, Meazza, Schiavio, Ferrari, Orsi.
Scorer: Guaita
Austria: Platzer; Cisar, Sesta, Wagner, Smistik, Urbanek, Zischek, Bican, Sindelar, Schall, Viertl.
Referee: Ivan Eklind (Sweden)

CZECHOSLOVAKIA 3   GERMANY 1 (Half-time 1-0)
PNF Stadium, Rome, 3 June
Attendance: 10,000

IF anyone had been asked to pick a winner out of these teams at the start of the tournament, they would probably have chosen Germany. Now it was a different matter. Germany had played poorly in their first two matches, whilst Czechoslovakia, although given a scare by the Swiss in the second round, were the more attractive team.

Only 10,000 fans turned up to watch the game in Rome's National Stadium. The Italians were more interested in what was happening in Milan, where the host nation were playing Austria.

The fury of the Czech attacks caught the Germans unawares from the start and in the 21st minute, Oldrich Nejedlý put Czechoslovakia in front with his third goal of the tournament.

Germany, who were missing Hohmann, levelled the scores after 50 minutes when Noack latched on to a corner. His lob sailed over the head of the normally reliable Plánička in the Czech goal. The Germans nearly took the lead a few minutes later, but the Czech 'keeper smothered a powerful drive from Lehner. However, on the hour Nejedlý restored the Czechs' lead when he scored after following up a Puč free-kick which rebounded off the crossbar.

By now the Czechs had stepped up a gear and dominated all areas of play. They were on their way to a comfortable win and sealed the victory with a third goal nine minutes from time when Nejedlý completed his hat-trick following a corner. Czechoslovakia were thus the surprise Finalists, and booked to meet the host country.

Czechoslovakia; Plánička; Čtyřoký, Bürgr, Košťálek, Čambal, Krčil, Junek, Svoboda, Sobotka, Nejedlý, Puč.
Scorers: Nejedlý 3
German: Kress; Busch, Haringer, Zielinski, Szepan, Bender, Lehner, Siffling, Conen, Noack, Kobierski.
Scorer: Noack
Referee: Rinaldo Barlassini (Italy)

Italy's Felice Placido Borel II, one of four changes for the second-round replay against Spain. He was omitted for the semi-final and so the Spanish game turned out to be his only appearance in the World Cup finals.

Third place play-off
GERMANY 3   AUSTRIA 2 (Half-time 3-1)
Asarelli Stadium, Naples, 7 June.
Attendance: 7,000

HUGO Meisl's *Wunderteam* were showing signs of tiredness when they got bogged down in the Milan mud during their semi-final with Italy. Their performance in this third place play-off match with Germany confirmed that they were ready to make their way home.

As a contest, the game was over by the interval, at which point the Germans had built up a 3-1 lead. They had taken the lead after only 30 seconds when Ernest Lehner scored the fastest goal of the tournament.

Conen made it 2-0 in the 29th minute, but within a minute Austria had pulled one back through Horvath, who was fit again after being sorely missed in Milan. Lehner scored his second goal three minutes before half-time to complete the first-half goal spree and, had the Germans played this well against Czechoslovakia, they would surely have been in the Final instead of having to fight it out for third place.

The game produced only one more goal, scored in the 55th minute by Austrian left-back Sesta. When the team returned home, the Austrian people blamed the team's poor showing on Meisl and he promptly offered his resignation, although the Austrian FA refused to accept it.

Germany: Jakob; Janes, Busch, Zielinski, Münzenberg, Bender, Lehner, Siffling, Conen, Szepan, Heidemann.
Scorers: Lehner 2, Conen.
Austria: Platzer; Cisar, Sesta, Wagner, Smistik, Urbanek, Zischek, Braun, Bican, Horvath, Viertl.
Scorers: Horvath, Sesta.
Referee: Albino Carraro (Italy)

Edmund Conen gave Germany a 2-0 lead in the 29th minute.

Above: Frantisek Plánička, captain of Czechoslovakia. *Right:* Italy take the field at the PNF Stadium for the 1934 World Cup Final.

Final

ITALY 2   CZECHOSLOVAKIA 1 (a.e.t.) (Half-time 0-0; 90 mins 1-1)

PNF Stadium, Rome, 10 June
Attendance: 55,000

THE political use of the World Cup was working wonders for Mussolini and with one match remaining, victory for Italy would put the seal on a memorable tournament for the dictator. But Czechoslovakia had played stylish football in the Austrian mould to reach the Final and now looked quite capable of providing an upset.

Both sides were captained by their goalkeepers — Italy by Giampiero Combi, playing his 47th and last international, Czechoslovakia by the equally experienced Frantisek Plánička.

The Czechs opened with determination and pushed the ball around to better effect than in any of their previous matches. Their attacking centre-half, Čambal, and Italy's stopper,

The Czechoslovakian squad line up before the kick-off. From left to right: Kalocsay, Boucek, Kopecky, Junek, Puč, Plánička, Bürgr, Sobotka, Nejedlý, Čambal, Silný, Svoboda, Koštálek, Ženíšek, Čtyřoký, Vodicka, Krčil.

Monti, had some fierce battles in the Italian half of the field but Italy showed more flair when attacking.

Despite both sides' positive approach, however, it was 70 minutes before a goal was scored. Then, the Czech left winger, Antonin Puč, who had just returned to the field after an attack of cramp, took a corner and, when the ball came back to him, he fired home a powerful shot from an acute angle to crown a great individual performance.

Czechoslovakia should have put the issue beyond doubt but Sobotka missed a great chance and then a Svoboda shot hit a post. The Czechs would have reason to rue those misses, for, as the game went into the last ten minutes, the Italians scored a remarkable equalizer.

Orsi gathered a pass from his fellow Argentinian, Guaita. He ran through the Czech defence

Above: Giampiero Combi, skippered Italy in what was his 47th and last international appearance. *Left (top and bottom):* Action from the Final. In the lower picture, Meazza tries a shot with Plánička looking on, but the ball went over the bar.

WORLD CUP FACT

When Czechoslovakia reached the 1934 Final, their team consisted of 11 players from only two clubs – Sparta and Slavia. No other World Cup Final team has contained such a small club representation.

Above: Schiavio tries an overhead shot at the Czech goal but on this occasion his spectacular effort failed. Meazza is the Italian to Schiavio's left. Orsi is the Italian player on the right.

Opposite page (top): Ecstatic Italian players and officials immediately after the final whistle. *(bottom)*: The Italian Press gather round.

and dummied a shot with his left foot, instead shooting with the outside of his right boot to send a curling, dipping ball over the hands of Plánička. The 'keeper seemed to have it covered but the ball eluded him. It was probably a fluke, but Orsi insisted he could do it any time he liked. The next day, in front of a barrage of reporters and photographers, he tried the shot 20 times — and failed to hit the target every time.

The teams had been evenly matched in a furious 90 minutes. Now it was down to stamina. Italy were the fitter of the two sides but were handicapped by an injury to Meazza. Nevertheless, his injury was turned into Italy's advantage in the 95th minute.

The Czechs were not bothering to mark him and when he got the ball on the wing, he crossed to Guaita, who fed the tired Schiavio. The centre-forward rounded a defender and beat Plánička with a shot which crept in just under the crossbar. Vittorio Pozzo's team were the World Champions.

Skipper Combi received the trophy from *Il Duce* and the hosts had achieved their goal. The players were lavished with gifts from Mussolini and for centre-half Luís Monti, who added a winners' medal to the runners-up award he had gained in Uruguay, there was the added distinction of becoming the first man to win successive World Cup medals with different nations.

However, the 1934 World Cup left a bitter taste outside Italy. There was little doubt that Italy won because they were the host nation and local fanaticism had intimidated referees. FIFA also had doubts about Mussolini's use of the tournament for his own political ends. Nevertheless, the second World Cup tournament was a resounding financial success and established the competition as a major world sporting event.

The victorious Italian team. Back row (left to right): Combi, Monti, Ferraris IV, Allemandi, Guaita, Ferrari. Front row: Schiavio, Meazza, Monzeglio, Bertolini, Orsi.

Italy: Giampiero Combi; Eraldo Monzeglio, Luigi Allemandi, Attilo Ferraris IV, Luís Monti, Luigi Bertolini, Enrique Guaita, Giuseppe Meazza, Angelo Schiavio, Giovanni Ferrari, Raimundo Orsi.
Scorers: Orsi, Schiavio

Czechoslovakia: Frantisek Plánička; Ladislav Žéníšek, Josef Čtyřoký, Josef Koštálek, Stefan Čambal, Rudolf Krčil, Frantisek Junek, Frantisek Svoboda, Jiří Sobotka, Oldrich Nejedlý, Antonin Puč.
Scorer: Puč
Referee: Ivan Eklind (Sweden)

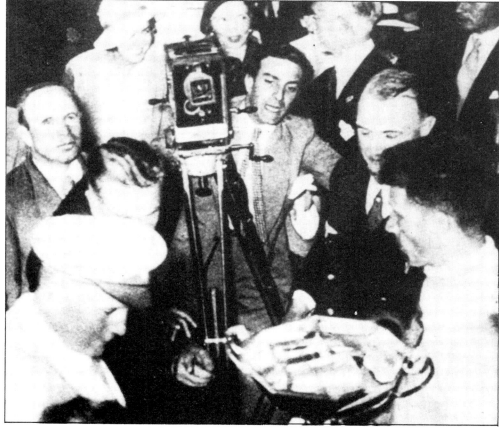

MEN WHO MADE THE HEADLINES - 1938

Silvio Piola
(Italy)

IN a World Cup dominated by fine centre-forwards, one of the best was Silvio Piola, who scored four goals, including two in Italy's win over Hungary in the Final. Piola was born at Robbio Lomellina in 1913 and began as a 16-year-old with Pro Vercelli. Five years later he won his first cap, scoring both goals in a 2-0 win over Austria in Vienna in March 1935. The previous year he had joined Lazio of Rome and spent eight years with them before further success with Torino, Juventus and Novara. In 1951 he passed Giuseppe Meazza's Italian League record with his 336th goal. Piola appeared in an Italian League record of 566 matches and was top scorer in 1937 and 1943. He retired in 1954, after 25 years' senior football. There followed a spell as manager of Lazio and of the national Under-23 squad. He won the last of his 34 caps against England in 1952, at the age of 38, but could not add to his total of 30 goals for Italy. One of those, against England in Milan in 1939, came after Piola had handled the ball past Vic Woodley for the sort of effort which was labelled a 'Hand of God' goal when Maradona tried the same thing in 1986.

Györgi Sárosi
(Hungary)

GYÖRGI Sárosi and Gyula Zsengellér were one of the most lethal strike forces in the 1938 World Cup as they helped Hungary to their first Final. Sárosi, the Hungarian skipper, scored in the Final but could not prevent Italy winning 4-2. Born in September 1912, he became one of the most talented and versatile of Hungarian footballers. After a successful career with Ferencváros, where he was one of their most popular players of all time, he was 'poached' by Italian club, Juventus, after his great display in the 1938 World Cup. And after ending his playing days, the man equally at home in the heart of defence or attack, spent some time in the USA before taking up coaching jobs at Bologna, Roma and Juventus. In 1952, he guided the latter club to the Italian Championship, seven points clear of AC Milan. His international career lasted from 1931 to 1943 and he won 62 caps and scored 42 goals, including all five in the 5-3 win over Austria in 1936 and seven against Czechoslovakia in 1937. Sárosi was an excellent all-round sportsman and gained honours as a swimmer, fencer and tennis player. He also obtained a post-graduate degree in law.

Leónidas
(Brazil)

LEÓNIDAS da Silva was top scorer in the 1938 World Cup with eight goals, including a four-goal haul in the remarkable 6-5 win over Poland. Leónidas was the first man to score four goals in a World Cup match — five minutes ahead of Poland's Ernst Willimowski — and for the semi-final against Italy, manager Ademar Pimenta rested him. It was an overconfident move and the Italians won 2-1. Despite his size, Leónidas, capped 23 times, was one of the most outstanding pre-war centre-forwards and famed for his bicycle-kick. Born in 1913, he was known as the 'Black Diamond' or the 'Rubber Man'. He began his career with local Río teams before joining Peñarol of Uruguay in 1933, a year after scoring two goals on his international debut against Uruguay. He returned to Brazil after a year and helped Vasco da Gama to the Rio championship. After appearing in the 1934 World Cup, he was a key member of the Botafogo team which won the 1935 Río title. The following year he signed for Flamengo, where he stayed until 1942. He then spent eight years at São Paulo before retiring in 1950. He returned to São Paulo as manager in 1953, before becoming a radio reporter and later the proprietor of a furniture store in São Paulo.

Last Competition for 12 Years
France 1938

Stanley Rous was secretary of the FA when they were still outside FIFA and great players like Raich Carter, Tommy Lawton and Eddie Hapgood were thus denied the unique experience of playing in the World Cup. Ironically, Rous eventually became president of FIFA.

*I*N 1934, Mussolini had used the World Cup Finals in Italy to full advantage as a propaganda platform. Two years later, Adolf Hitler tried to do the same with the Berlin Olympics. Now, with Europe teetering towards the brink of war, FIFA had to be diplomatic over its choice of venue for the 1938 World Cup.

Argentina had applied to stage the competition and, believing the venue would alternate between South America and Europe, they were confident of playing host to the world's leading soccer tournament. But FIFA were mindful of the problems with the first competition in Uruguay, not to mention the travelling difficulties.

FIFA membership was up to 57 nations in 1938 and most of those were from Europe. It therefore made sense to give the third World Cup to a European country and that honour fell to France. FIFA's choice was probably out of loyalty to Jules Rimet, the man who played a big part in getting the tournament started in the first place. The International Olympic Committee had made a similar choice in 1900, when Paris staged the Games as a testimony to Baron Pierre de Coubertin, the founder of the modern Olympics.

With the venue decided for the third World Cup, 36 nations entered. The British sides were still absent, Spain entered but then withdrew because the country was engaged in a civil war. Argentina, the reigning South American champions, snubbed the competition because they had not been allocated the tournament. At first they decided not to enter, then submitted a late entry which FIFA accepted — and then withdrew.

Uruguay were absent for the second successive tournament. It was understandable why they had snubbed the Italians in 1934, for Italy had done the same to them four years earlier. But why they should refuse to travel to France was a mystery. The French, after all, had made the trip to Uruguay in 1930. The Uruguayans were in the throes of adopting professionalism and probably knew they would be no match for the more powerful European nations. Brazil, therefore, were the only South American representatives in France.

To add further confusion, Austria came through the qualifying competition but their nation was then swallowed up by Germany after the *Anschluss*. Consequently, Austria had to withdraw. However, the Germans, who were not one of the strongest soccer nations at the time, recruited four top Austrian players and found themselves one of the seeded teams.

The qualifying competition helped reduce the final number of teams to 16 — but only 15 went to France. With the vacancy left by Austria's demise, the 16th place was offered to England but they again turned their backs on the championship designed to find the best team in the world. England had already beaten the World Champions, Italy, in what became known as the 'Battle of Highbury' in 1934, when England, battered and bruised, won 3-2.

An English presence in the World Cup would certainly have added to its credibility but, despite the pleas of FIFA secretary Dr Ivo Schricker to FA secretary Stanley Rous, England ignored the tournament. The 1938 World Cup was far from a true representation of the world's finest nations.

Like the previous tournament, the teams played a straight knock-out competition and the following nations were seeded: Germany, France, Brazil, Czechoslovakia, Cuba, Hungary, Italy and, initially, Austria, whose opponents in the first round, Sweden, eventually received a bye.

The tournament got under way at the Parc des Princes on 4 June when Germany played Switzerland. Hitler's team was held to a draw in the first of many surprises to be thrown up by the third World Cup.

Front page of the Italian newspaper *La Gazzetta dello Sport*, proclaiming Italy's victory in the 1938 World Cup Final.

1938 Qualifying Competition

FOR the first time, the holders were exempt from the qualifying tournament, as were the host nation. Clearly the organizers had realized what a financial disaster the 1934 tournament would have been without Italy. The same applied in 1938, for had France not taken part, then FIFA's investment of some two million francs would have looked extremely sick.

A total of 34 teams had to 'pre-qualify'. Argentina, Colombia, Costa Rica, Dutch Guinea, El Salvador, Mexico, Spain and the United States all withdrew before being allocated fixtures whilst Egypt and Japan both withdrew after being drawn in the same group as Romania and Dutch East Indies respectively.

After coming through matches against Palestine, Greece met the strong Hungarians and were beaten 11-1. It was the first time that a nation had reached double-figures in a World Cup game and it stood as the highest score until West Germany beat Cyprus 12-0 in the 1970 qualifying competition.

Results

Group One

16 Jun 1937	*Stockholm*	Sweden 4	Finland 0
20 Jun 1937	*Stockholm*	Sweden 7	Estonia 2
29 Jun 1937	*Helsinki*	Finland...........0	Germany 2
19 Aug 1937	*Turku*	Finland...........0	Estonia 1
29 Aug 1937	*Konigsberg*	Germany 4	Estonia 1
21 Nov 1937	*Hamburg*	Germany 5	Sweden 0

Final Table

	P	W	D	L	F	A	Pts	
Germany	3	3	0	0	11	1	6	**Germany and**
Sweden	3	2	0	1	11	7	4	**Sweden qualified**
Estonia	3	1	0	2	4	11	2	
Finland	3	0	0	3	0	7	0	

Group Two

Norway played the Republic of Ireland and Poland played Yugoslavia. Aggregate winners of each match qualified.

10 Oct 1937	*Oslo*	Norway 3	Rep of Ireland ...2
10 Oct 1937	*Warsaw*	Poland............4	Yugoslavia 0
7 Nov 1937	*Dublin*	Rep of Ireland ...3	Norway...........3
3 Apr 1938	*Belgrade*	Yugoslavia 1	Poland............0

Norway and Poland qualified

Group Three

Romania qualified (Egypt withdrew)

Group Four

1 May 1938	*Milan*	Switzerland 2	Portugal..........1

Switzerland qualified

Group Five

Round One

22 Jan 1938	*Tel Aviv*	Palestine 1	Greece 3
20 Feb 1938	*Athens*	Greece 1	Palestine 0

Round Two

25 Mar 1938	*Budapest*	Hungary 11	Greece 1

Hungary qualified

Group Six

7 Nov 1937	*Sofia*	Bulgaria 1	Czechoslovakia..1
24 Apr 1938	*Prague*	Czechoslovakia ..6	Bulgaria 0

Czechoslovakia qualified

Group Seven

Round One

29 Jul 1937	*Riga*	Latvia.............4	Lithuania 2
3 Sep 1937	*Kaunas*	Lithuania 1	Latvia.............5

Round Two

5 Oct 1937	*Vienna*	Austria............2	Latvia.............1

Austria qualified

Group Eight

28 Nov 1937	*Rotterdam*	Holland 4	Luxembourg.....0
13 Mar 1938	*Luxembourg*	Luxembourg.....2	Belgium 3
3 Apr 1938	*Antwerp*	Belgium 1	Holland 1

Final Table

	P	W	D	L	F	A	Pts	
Holland	2	1	1	0	5	1	3	**Holland and**
Belgium	2	1	1	0	4	3	3	**Belgium qualified**
Luxembourg	2	0	0	2	2	7	0	

Group Nine

Cuba and Brazil qualified (No other teams entered group)

Group Ten

Dutch East Indies qualified (Japan withdrew)

The Bulgarian team that drew 1-1 with Czechoslovakia in Sofia. Back row (left to right): Angelov, unknown, Maznikov, Bolakciev, Lozanov, Stefanov, Jordanov, trainer. Front row: Gabrovski, Dermonski, Kalocev, Petrov, Nikolov, Pacendziev.

THE LAST COMPETITION FOR TWELVE YEARS — FRANCE 1938

1938 Tournament

Round One

Switzerland's centre-forward Alfred Bickel.

GERMANY 1   SWITZERLAND 1 (a.e.t.) (Half-time 1-1; 90 mins 1-1)

Parc des Princes, Paris, 4 June
Attendance: 30,000

THE Germans suffered a severe set-back to their plans in the opening game of the tournament. First, the Swiss stood defiant and refused to give the Nazi salute during the German national anthem. Then, when the action started, the Germans were outplayed by the Swiss and were lucky to hold on for a draw after extra-time.

Andre Abegglen III, one of the stars in the Swiss team in Italy four years earlier and now playing in France with FC Sochaux, was injured early in the game after a tackle by Kitzinger and had to leave the field.

Shortly after his return, Germany opened the scoring in the 29th minute when Josef Gauchel converted a cross from the Austrian Hans Pesser. Two minutes before the interval, Abegglen levelled the scores when he headed home a cross from Walaschek which was misjudged by Schmaus, another Austrian-born player.

There were no goals in the second half and, as the game went into extra-time, Hans Pesser of Germany was sent off for kicking the Swiss captain, Severino Minelli.

Despite their numerical advantage, the Swiss could not snatch the game and a replay was scheduled for five days later.

Germany: Raftl; Janes, Schmaus, Kupfer, Mock, Kitzinger, Lehner, Gellesch, Gauchel, Hahnemann, Pesser.
Scorer: Gauchel
Switzerland: Huber; Minelli, Lehmann, Springer, Vernati, Lörtscher, Amadò, Walaschek, Bickel, Abegglen III, Aebi.
Scorer: Abegglen III
Referee: Jean Langenus (Belgium)

Fritz Szepan, recalled by Germany for the replay.

Replay
SWITZERLAND 4   GERMANY 2 (Half-time 1-2)

Parc des Princes, Paris, 9 June
Attendance: 22,000

MIDWAY through the first half, Germany were two up and cruising to what looked like an easy win. But the Swiss proved that their performance five days earlier was no fluke and showed tremendous resilience to come back and record a major upset.

Switzerland played for most of the game with ten men after Aebi was injured. He returned in the second half but was a virtual passenger and being a man short simply added more to the magnitude of Switzerland's performance.

An eighth-minute goal by Hahnemann and a own-goal by Swiss left-half Lörtscher, 14 minutes later, gave Germany a 2-0 lead before Walaschek pulled back a goal for the Swiss in the 41st minute.

Alfred Bickel made it 2-2 in the 64th minute and then Abegglen scored twice in three minutes (75 and 78) to seal a remarkable performance. Sepp Herberger's so called 'Greater Germany' team had been humiliated.

Switzerland: Huber; Minelli, Lehmann, Springer, Vernati, Lörtscher, Amadò, Abegglen III, Bickel, Walaschek, Aebi.
Scorers: Abegglen III 2, Walaschek, Bickel
Germany: Raftl; Janes, Streitle, Kupfer, Goldbrunner, Skoumal, Lehner, Stroh, Hahnemann, Szepan, Neumer.
Scorers: Hahnemann, Lörtscher (og)
Referee: Ivan Eklind (Sweden)

Severino Minelli, the Swiss skipper.

Germany give the Nazi salute before their first game against the Swiss, who keep their arms firmly by their sides.

Joop Smit, a star in domestic Dutch football, who was nevertheless unable to help his side make any impression against the Czechs.

CUBA 3   ROMANIA 3 (a.e.t.) (Half-time 1-1; 90 mins 2-2)

Chapou Stadium, Toulouse, 5 June
Attendance: 6,000

CUBA were making their first — and to date only — World Cup appearance. The Romanians, however, were one of the pioneers back in 1930 and half their team had World Cup experience. Bürger, Rafinski and Kovacs had all played in the first tournament.

The Europeans were favourites to reach the second round with ease but, like Germany, they were to suffer a tremendous shock. Bindea opened the scoring in the 35th minute before Socorro equalized right on half-time. The Romanians retook the lead through Baratki in the 59th minute and their tactical superiority was beginning to show. But ten minutes later the Cubans had drawn level again when Maquina made it 2-2.

There were no further goals and the game went into extra-time and two minutes before the end of the first half Cuba took the lead for the first time when Socorro scored his second goal. But right on the whistle to indicate the first half of the extra period, Dobai made it 3-3. That is how it stayed and the Toulouse crowd looked forward to the replay four days later.

Cuba: Carvajeles; Barquín, Chorens, Arías, Rodriguez, Berges, Maquina, Fernández, Socorro, Tunas, Sosa.
Scorers: Socorro 2, Maquina
Romania: Pavlovici; Bürger, Cossini, Chiroiu, Rasinaru, Rafinski, Bindea, Kovacs, Baratki, Bodola, Dobai.
Scorers: Bindea, Baratki, Dobai
Referee: Giovanni Scarpi (Italy)

Replay
CUBA 2   ROMANIA 1 (Half-time 0-1)

Chapou Stadium, Toulouse, 9 June
Attendance: 5,000

CUBA sprang a surprise by dropping their star goalkeeper Benito Carvajeles, one of the heroes of the first game. In his place came the equally brilliant Juan Ayra, who gave an outstanding performance. Indeed, credit for the Cuban victory went largely to his acrobatics between the posts.

Dobai opened the scoring for the new-look Romanian team in the ninth minute and they held on to that lead for nearly an hour until Socorro equalized. Ten minutes from time the Romanians were sent embarrassingly out of the tournament when Carlos Maquina netted the winner. The goal looked offside and, indeed, the linesman flagged but was overruled by referee Birlem.

The 1938 World Cup was to be noted for its shock results and Cuba's performance was as sensational as any. And it must be remembered that they qualified for the final stages only because Mexico withdrew from their qualifying pool.

Cuba: Ayra; Barquín, Chorens, Arías, Rodriguez, Berges, Maquina, Fernández, Socorro, Tunas, Sosa.
Scorers: Socorro, Maquina
Romania: Sadowski; Bürger, Felecan, Barbulescu, Rasinaru, Rafinski, Bogden, Moldoveanu, Baratki, Prassler, Dobai.
Scorer: Dobai
Referee: Alfred Birlem (Germany)

CZECHOSLOVAKIA 3   HOLLAND 0 (a.e.t.) (Half-time 0-0; 90 mins 0-0)

Stade de la Cavée Verte, Le Havre, 5 June
Attendance: Not recorded

HOLLAND came close to bringing off yet another shock when they held Czechoslovakia, runners-up in Italy in 1934, for 90 minutes before succumbing to the footballing skills of their Eastern European opponents.

Holland were playing without their top scorer, Bakhuijs, and also had inside-right Fritz Van Der Veen injured in the second half. In the end it proved too great a handicap for the courageous Dutch. Czechoslovakia, on the other hand, fielded an experienced side and four members of their 1934 World Cup Final team of four years earlier lined up at Le Havre. Their skipper and centre-half, Jaroslav Boucek, played League soccer in France at the time, so the local fans knew plenty about him.

It was not until six minutes into extra-time that the first goal was scored, by Koštálek. Two goals in the second period sealed Holland's fate. The first was from the experienced Nejedlý. In the very last minute, inside-left Zeman added a third to ease the tension for the few Czech fans who had made the trip.

Czechoslovakia: Plánička; Bürgr, Daučik, Koštálek, Boucek, Kopecky, Říha, Simunek, Zeman, Nejedlý, Puč.
Scorers: Koštálek, Nejedlý, Zeman
Holland: Van Male; Weber, Caldenhove, Paawe, Anderiesen, Van Heel, Wels, Van Der Veen, Smit, Vente, De Harder.
Referee: Lucien Leclercq (France)

Raymond Braine, whose World Cup was restricted to only one game after Belgium lost to France.

FRANCE 3   BELGIUM 1 (Half-time 2-1)

Stade Colombes, Paris, 5 June
Attendance: Not recorded

IT was appropriate that France should open their campaign against their traditional rivals, Belgium. The teams had been playing each other since 1904, in one of the oldest international fixtures outside the United Kingdom.

France's captain, Etiénne Mattler, and inside-left Edmond Delfour were appearing in their third successive World Cup, as was the Belgian inside-forward Bernard Voorhoof.

The French were greeted by the large Parisian crowd, who were still settling down when Emile Veinante put their side ahead in the first minute. Eleven minutes later, Jean Nicolas, France's skipper in 1934, made it 2-0.

The celebrations were temporarily dampened seven minutes before the interval, when Isemborghs pulled one back for Belgium, but Nicolas netted his second after 69 minutes and the match was safe for the hosts.

France: Di Lorto; Cazenave, Mattler, Bastien, Jordan, Diagne, Aston, Heisserer, Nicolas, Delfour, Veinante.
Scorers: Nicolas 2, Veinante
Belgium: Badjou; Paverick, Seys, Van Alphen, Stijnen, De Winter, Van de Wouwer, Voorhoof, Isemborghs, Braine, Buyle.
Scorer: Isemborghs
Referee: Hans Wuthrich (Switzerland)

HUNGARY 6   DUTCH EAST INDIES 0 (Half-time 4-0)

Stade Vélodrome Municipal, Reims, 5 June
Attendance: Not recorded

IN a first round of shocks and surprises, only two matches did not go to extra-time. Had the Hungarians been taken to an extra period by the Dutch East Indies, making their one

Italy's Silvio Piola was shut out for much of the game against Norway but broke free of Nils Eriksen to restore the Italians' lead in extra-time.

Ernst Willimowski, whose four goals were still not enough to beat Brazil.

Brazil's Leónidas, seen here in action against the Poles, also netted four and helped his side to victory in a remarkable game.

and only World Cup appearance, it would certainly have been one of the biggest shocks in World Cup history.

Leading up to the tournament, Hungary had been scoring a lot of goals in friendlies, including eight against Czechoslovakia when György Sárosi, a qualified doctor, put seven past the Czech's top-class goalkeeper, Plánička. And in their qualifier against Greece, the Hungarians netted a World Cup record of 11 goals.

In their opening match against the Dutch East Indies, the Magyars were far too good for their opponents and by half-time were 4-0 ahead. The prospect of extra-time was the last thing being talked about at the interval — the topic of conversation was about the number of goals the Europeans might eventually score.

The scoring spree had started in the 18th minute when Kohut scored. Toldi made it 2-0 five minutes later and in the 28th minute, Sárosi, who had reverted to centre-forward after a spell at centre-half, made it 3-0. Zsengeller netted twice, seven minutes before half-time and again seven minutes after the break. The scoring was completed in the 77th minute when Sárosi shot home his second and Hungary's sixth.

For the Dutch East Indies it was a long journey for only one game — but what tales those 11 players had to tell their grandchildren in years to come.

Hungary: Háda; Koranyi, Bíró, Lázár, Turai, Balogh, Sas, Zsengeller, Sárosi, Toldi, Kohut.
Scorers: Zsengeller 2, Sárosi 2, Toldi, Kohut
Dutch East Indies: Mo Heng; Hu Kom, Samuels, Nawir, Meng, Anwar, Hong Dijen, Soedarmadji, Sommers, Pattiwael, Taihuttu.
Referee: M.Conrie (France)

ITALY 2   NORWAY 1 (a.e.t.) (Half-time 1-0; 90 mins 1-1)

Stade Velódrome, Marseilles, 5 June
Attendance: Not recorded

ITALY arrived in France as the defending World Champions and with a team that Vittorio Pozzo declared was more skilful than the one which had won the World Cup on home soil in 1934.

Italy had upset Hitler's Germany by winning the Olympic title at Berlin in 1936 and some members of that team had been drafted into Pozzo's World Cup side, notably the full-backs Alfredo Foni and Pietro Rava.

Into the national team had also come the latest Italian goalscoring sensation, Silvio Piola, who would carry on playing international soccer until 1952. Rugged centre-half Monti, the Argentinian, had been replaced by another South American, Andreolo of Uruguay. The only two survivors from Italy's 1934 winning team were Giuseppe Meazza and Giovanni Ferrari.

Despite a host of old and new talent, the Italians were given a fright by the amateurs from Norway, who had shown what they were capable of at the Berlin Olympics when they ousted Germany and were narrowly beaten by the eventual champions, Italy, in the semi-final before winning the bronze medal. Six of Norway's Olympic team were in the side for the battle against the top Italian professionals.

Italy got off to a fortunate start when they scored after less than two minutes, when Norway's goalkeeper, Johansen, failed to hold a shot from Ferrari. The same player followed up to score from the rebound. The Norwegians immediately counter-attacked. They hit the woodwork three times and had a goal disallowed for offside as their blond centre-forward, Brynildsen, caused the Italian defence all sorts of problems.

However, it was not until the 83rd minute that they were rewarded for their endeavour with a late equalizer from Brustad. The game went into extra-time and the Italians were considerably relieved when Piola, who had been shut out of the game by centre-half Eriksen for most of the match, restored their lead after four minutes of the extra period. The goal was similar to Italy's first as Piola was on hand to follow up a rebound after the Norwegian goalkeeper again failed to hold a shot, this time from Pasinati.

Italy: Olivieri; Monzeglio, Rava, Serantoni, Andreolo, Locatelli, Pasinati, Meazza, Piola, Ferrari, Ferraris II.
Scorers: Ferrari, Piola
Norway: Johansen; Johannesen, Holmsen, Henriksen, Eriksen, Holmberg, Frantzen, Kvammen, Brynildsen, Isaksen, Brustad.
Scorer: Brustad
Referee: Alois Beranek (Germany)

BRAZIL 6   POLAND 5 (a.e.t.) (Half-time 3-1; 90 mins 4-4)

Stade de la Meinau, Strasbourg, 5 June
Attendance: Not recorded

THE most remarkable match of the 1938 competition — and probably in World Cup history — was this game which saw Brazil and Poland share 11 goals. Furthermore, two players, Leónidas (Brazil) and Willimowski (Poland) each scored four goals.

Brazil fielded four players who were making their international debuts, whilst the entire Polish team was new to the World Cup Finals.

The first half belonged to Brazil and to the diminutive black inside-forward Leónidas, who scored two goals. The second period, though, belonged to Poland and Ernst Willimowski, who, in contrast to Leónidas, was tall and blond.

The goal glut started after 18 minutes when Leónidas opened the scoring. Four minutes later, Willimowski equalized. After 25 minutes Leónidas put Brazil back in front and a minute before the interval, the same player completed his hat-trick. The Brazilians were playing the exciting football for which they have become known over the years.

But the second half saw Poland attack them with their own brand of football. Piontek pulled a goal back in the 50th minute and, just on the hour, Willimowski scored his second to level the scores at 3-3.

Peracio put Brazil back in front after 72 minutes and with just two minutes of normal time remaining, Willimowski completed his hat-trick to make it 4-4.

It was perhaps inevitable that the first goal of the extra period would be scored by either Leónidas or Willimowski and it was the Brazilian who netted after three minutes. Brazil's lead was extended to 6-4 after 12 minutes of extra-time, when Romeo scored. Not to be outdone, Willimowski also scored his fourth, but it came too late to prevent Brazil winning a remarkable match which was played in a wonderful spirit. The Poles sent their opponents a congratulatory telegram after the match and wished them the best of luck for the rest of the competition.

Brazil: Batatais; Domingos, Machado, Zezé Procopio, Martim Silveira, Alfonsinho, Lopez, Romeo, Leónidas, Peracio, Hercules.
Scorers: Leónidas 4, Peracio, Romeo
Poland: Madejski; Szczepaniak, Galecki, Gora, Nyc, Dytko, Piec I, Piontek, Szerfke, Willimowski, Wodarz.
Scorers: Willimowski 4, Piontek
Referee: Ivan Eklind (Sweden)

Berjum Peracio of Brazil heads his side back in front after 72 minutes. Teammate Leónidas watches the ball on its way past Edward Madejski in the Polish goal.

Round Two

ITALY 3 FRANCE 1 (Half-time 1-1)

Stade Colombes, Paris, 12 June
Attendance: 58,000

THE match of the round saw the hosts and holders pitched together, so it was hardly surprising that the Stade Colombes was full to its capacity with the largest crowd of the championship.

Seven months earlier, France had held the reigning champions to a goalless draw in Paris and their fans were now hoping for a win over Italy, particularly after their uninspiring performance against the Norwegian amateurs in the first round.

Italy played in Fascist black shirts and took the lead after ten minutes, thanks to a fortunate goal when the French goalkeeper, Di Lorto, misjudged a cross from left winger Gino Colaussi and the ball crept into the net. The French equalized a minute later, when Heisserer finished off a clever move involving the wingers, Aston and Veinante.

The sides were well matched and in the second half France played a more attacking game.

Etiénne Mattler of France.

Jean Nicolas of France.

But this proved to be their downfall as Italy's new goalscoring sensation, Piola, was given too much freedom and netted twice to finish off the French challenge.

With the French defence exposed in the 52nd minute, he scored his first and, 20 minutes later, headed home a cross from Biavati to make it 3-1. Piola had been subdued in the first half after being shut out by centre-half Gusti Jordan, but when he was given the freedom that all centre-forwards enjoy, he gave a great second-half performance.

Italy: Olivieri; Foni, Rava, Serantoni, Andreolo, Locatelli, Biavati, Meazza, Piola, Ferrari, Colaussi.
Scorers: Piola 2, Colaussi
France: Di Lorto; Cazenave, Mattler, Bastien, Jordan, Diagne, Aston, Heisserer, Nicolas, Delfour, Veinante.
Scorer: Heisserer
Referee: Louis Baert (Belgium)

SWEDEN 8   CUBA 0 (Half-time 4-0)

Stade du Fort Carré, Antibes, 12 June
Attendance: Not recorded

AFTER their shock win over Romania, the Cubans were brought down to earth by Sweden, who were playing their first game after receiving a first-round bye, following Austria's withdrawal.

While the Swedes were fresh and raring to go, the Cubans looked tired after their two gruelling games against Romania and it soon showed when they fell behind to a Harry Andersson goal in the 15th minute.

Sweden were, however, held to that one goal in the first half hour but then the floodgates opened and it was one-way traffic for the rest of the game. Jonasson made it 2-0 after 32 minutes and by half-time, outside-right Gustav Wetterström had added two more to make it 4-0. The clever winger completed his hat-trick seven minutes into the second period and, two minutes later, skipper Tore Keller scored to make it six. Fourteen years earlier, Keller had won a bronze medal at the Olympic Games and was now confident of picking up a World Cup-winners' medal.

Nyberg scored Sweden's seventh on the hour and in the last minute, Wetterström struck again to become the third man of the tournament to score four goals in a game. It was certainly an unhappy recall for Cuban goalkeeper Benito Carvajeles.

Sweden: Abrahamsson; Eriksson, Källgren, Almgren, Jacobsson, Svanström, Wetterström, Keller, H.Andersson, Jonasson, Nyberg.
Scorers: Wetterström 4, Nyberg, H.Andersson, Jonasson, Keller
Cuba: Carvajeles; Barquín, Chorens, Arías, Rodriguez, Berges, Ferrer, Fernández, Socorro, Tunas, Alonzo.
Referee: M.Kirst (Czechoslovakia)

HUNGARY 2   SWITZERLAND 0 (Half-time 1-0)

Stade Victor Boucquey, Lille, 12 June
Attendance: Not recorded

FROM the moment it was announced that their captain and star defender, Severino Minelli, and winger Aebi, would not be fit, the Swiss knew that their task against Hungary, one of the more fancied nations, was going to be an uphill one.

The Hungarian team selector, Dr Diest, announced that if his team lost to the Swiss, then he would walk all the way back to Budapest. Fortunately, the good doctor's feet were spared, thanks to their classy inside-forward Gyula Zsengeller, who scored his side's first in the 42nd minute and ensured their victory by adding a second after 68 minutes.

Switzerland enjoyed their moment of glory in beating the Germans in the previous round, but the two matches took their toll and the result of this second-round match was never in doubt.

Hungary: Szabó; Koranyi, Bíró, Szalay, Turai, Lázár, Sas, Vincze, Sárosi, Zsengeller, Kohut.
Scorer: Zsengeller 2
Switzerland: Huber; Stelzer, Lehmann, Springer, Vernati, Lörtscher, Amadò, Walaschek, Bickel, Abegglen III, Grassi.
Referee: Rinaldo Barlassina (Italy)

György Sárosi of Hungary.

BRAZIL 1   CZECHOSLOVAKIA 1 (a.e.t.) (Half-time 1-0; 90 mins 1-1)

Parc de Lescure, Bordeaux, 12 June
Attendance: 25,000

THIS game was chosen as a showpiece for the opening of Bordeaux's new stadium. Brazil, after their impressive win over Poland in the first round, and Czechoslovakia, runners-up in 1934, were two of the favourites to lift the World Cup. But what a disgraceful display of football the sides gave as their battle turned into a bloody, ugly affair.

Three players received their marching orders and two Czech players suffered broken limbs. It was, by far, the most savage game of football in World Cup history.

The aggravation started very early when Brazil's wing-half, Zezé Procopio, kicked the Czech inside-forward, Nejedlý. The Brazilian was sent off by referee Paul Van Hertzka of Hungary, who had the job of trying to restore order more than once.

After half an hour, Leónidas scored his fifth goal of the tournament to put Brazil in front. But a minute before half-time, trouble flared up again when Říha and Machado began fighting and both were sent off.

After 64 minutes, the top Brazilian defender, Domingos, handled the ball in the penalty area and Nejedlý made no mistake with the spot-kick. Domingos was the father of Ademir, a star of the next World Cup in 1950.

Despite the handicap of losing Nejedlý with a broken leg and with 'keeper Plánička playing part of the game with a broken arm, the Czechs held on to force a replay after extra-time. Both teams ended the match with only nine players on the field.

Brazil: Walter; Domingos, Machado, Zezé Procopio, Martim Silveira, Alfonsinho, Lopez, Romeo, Leónidas, Peracio, Hercules.
Scorer: Leónidas
Czechoslovakia: Plánička; Bürgr, Daučik, Koštálek, Bouček, Kopecky, Říha, Simunek, Ludl, Nejedlý, Puč.
Scorer: Nejedlý (pen)
Referee: Paul Van Hertzka (Hungary)

Brazil made nine changes for their replay against Czechoslovakia, only goalkeeper Walter and Leónidas keeping their places. This line-up was involved in the 11-goal thriller against Poland in the first round. From left to right: Unknown, Ademar Pimenta (coach), Leónidas, Zezé Procopio, Machados, Hercules, Peracio, Lopez, Alfonsinho, Romeo, Domingos, Batatais, Martim Silveira.

Replay
BRAZIL 2   CZECHOSLOVAKIA 1 (Half-time 0-1)

Parc de Lescure, Bordeaux, 14 June
Attendance: Not recorded

AFTER such a fierce first game, the Bordeaux fans and officials did not know what the replay would have in store but, to everyone's amazement and delight, it was a mild game which was decided on football alone.

Czechoslovakia were at a big disadvantage, being without Nejedlý and Plánička, and their

Frantisek Plánička, missed the replay against Brazil through injury.

Karel Burket, the Czech
goalkeeper, gets down to a
Brazilian shot during the replay in
Bordeaux.

forward line was completely revamped as they were forced to introduce six new faces to the team. However, they were given a glimmer of hope when the Brazilians made an astonishing nine changes. Only goalkeeper Walter and scoring sensation Leónidas remained. Thus, only seven of the 22 men who played in the first game turned out for the replay.

Kopecky put Czechoslovakia in the lead in the 30th minute and they held that until 11 minutes into the second half, when Leónidas equalized. The Czechs were unlucky not to get back in front when a shot from Kopecky was stopped by goalkeeper Walter. There were many around the ground who felt that Walter had retrieved the ball after it had crossed the line. Referee Capdeville of France thought otherwise and the goal was disallowed. In the very next breakaway, Roberto crowned his international debut by volleying the winner for Brazil.

A battle-torn Czech side made a sad exit, while South America's only representatives marched on to the semi-finals. It was the last replayed game in the World Cup finals.

Brazil: Walter; Jaú, Narìz, Brito, Brandao, Argemiro, Roberto, Luizinho, Leónidas, Tim, Patesko.
Scorers: Leónidas, Roberto
Czechoslovakia: Burket; Bürgr, Daučik, Koštálek, Bouček, Ludl, Horák, Senecky, Kreutz, Kopecky, Rulc.
Scorer: Kopecky
Referee: Georges Capdeville (France)

Semi-finals

ITALY 2   BRAZIL 1 (Half-time 0-0)
Stade Velódrome, Marseilles, 16 June
Attendance: 35,000

BRAZIL and Italy were now joint favourites to win the 1938 World Cup, but fate pitched them together in the semi-final. For the Marseilles fans there was now the prospect of an intriguing battle between two of the game's outstanding goalscorers — Brazil's 'Black Diamond', Leónidas, and Italy's Silvio Piola.

Alas, the duel was never staged because Brazil's coach, Ademar Pimenta, left out Leónidas, the man who had scored six goals in the first two rounds. It was one of the strangest decisions in World Cup history, although Pimenta defended it by announcing that he was saving Leónidas for the Final!

Both sides played good football and the Brazilian defence did not give any room to Piola, who was subdued for a large part of the game. It was outside-left Colaussi who scored the first goal, in the 55th minute. Five minutes later, Brazil's right-back, Domingos, spoilt what had been a magnificent performance by conceding a penalty after bringing down Piola, who made his tumble look more dramatic than necessary. Referee Wuthrich had no hesitation

Italy's Silvio Piola, one of pre-war
soccer's greatest goalscorers.

Piola (far left) is foiled by Brazilian goalkeeper Walter in the semi-final.

Attackers Ferrari (left) and Piola (third from left) watch as Brazil clear an Italian attack.

in pointing to the spot and skipper Meazza converted the kick to make it 2-0 and set Italy on their way to a second successive final. Brazil pulled a goal back three minutes from time, through Romeo, but it was too late for the South Americans.

Italy: Olivieri; Foni, Rava, Serantoni, Andreolo, Locatelli, Biavati, Meazza, Piola, Ferrari, Colaussi.
Scorers: Colaussi, Meazza (pen)
Brazil: Walter; Domingos, Machado, Zezé Procopio, Martim Silveira, Alfonsinho, Lopez, Luizinho, Peracio, Romeo, Patesko.
Scorer: Romeo
Referee: Hans Wuthrich (Switzerland)

HUNGARY 5 SWEDEN 1 (Half-time 3-1)

Parc des Princes, Paris, 16 June
Attendance: 17,000

AFTER their 8-0 win over Cuba, Sweden were looking forward to their semi-final clash with Hungary, particularly as the game was being played on the 80th birthday of their monarch, King Gustav V. They knew it would not be an easy match but were still confident. However, they were taught the harsh realities of soccer and were on the wrong end of a drubbing by the classy Magyars.

Remarkably, Sweden struck in the first minute, when they broke from the kick-off and winger Arne Nyberg scored with his first kick of the match. The goal was timed at 35 seconds, which made it the second fastest World Cup goal at the time.

Hungary's scoring sensation, Zsengeller, equalized in the 18th minute with a goal that seemed to be helped into the net by full-back Ivar Eriksson. Titkos (26 minutes) and Zsengeller (38 minutes) saw Hungary go in at half-time with a comfortable 3-1 lead. Dr Sárosi made it 4-1 in the 61st minute and Zsengeller completed a comprehensive victory with his third goal 13 minutes from time. In the second half, the Swedes were under so much pressure that a blackbird took up near-permanent residency in the Hungarian half of the field without being unduly interrupted.

Hungary had swept into the Final and their goalscoring exploits must have had worried the Italians. The Magyars had netted 13 goals in only three matches.

Hungary: Szabó; Koranyi, Bíró, Szalay, Turai, Lázár, Sas, Zsengeller, Sárosi, Toldi, Titkos.
Scorers: Zsengeller 3, Titkos, Sárosi
Sweden: Abrahamsson; Eriksson, Källgren, Almgren, Jacobsson, Svanström, Wetterström, Keller, H.Andersson, Jonasson, Nyberg.
Scorer: Nyberg
Referee: Lucien Leclercq (France)

Third place play-off
BRAZIL 4 SWEDEN 2 (Half-time 1-2)

Parc de Lescure, Bordeaux, 19 June
Attendance: Not recorded

BRAZIL recalled Leónidas into their attack, installed him as captain for the day and he repaid them with two goals which overcame a surprise Swedish lead. Leónidas was not, however, the only star of the game and, despite trailing by a goal at half-time, the Brazilians were superior to the Swedish amateurs in every department.

As they had done in the semi-final against Hungary, Sweden opened the scoring when Jonasson netted in the 18th minute. Nyberg, the man who had scored that sensational 35th-second goal against the Magyars, made it 2-0 in the 38th minute but two minutes before the break, Romeo pulled one back for Brazil.

The South Americans exploded into action in the second half and Leónidas scored in the 63rd and 73rd minutes to take his tally to eight and make him the tournament's top scorer. Peracio added a fourth, ten minutes from time and, despite the Swedes' early two-goal lead, the final scoreline was a true reflection of the difference between the teams.

Brazil: Batatais; Domingos, Machado, Zezé Procopio, Brandao, Alfonsinho, Roberto, Romeo, Leónidas, Peracio, Patesko.
Scorers: Leónidas 2, Romeo, Peracio
Sweden: Abrahamsson; Eriksson, Nilsson, Almgren, Linderholm, Svanström, Perssen, H.Andersson, Jonasson, A.Andersson, Nyberg.
Scorers: Jonasson, Nyberg
Referee: Jean Langenus (Belgium)

Giuseppe Meazza (above) and Giovanni Ferrari (below), two of Italy's great World Cup stars.

Final

ITALY 4 HUNGARY 2 (Half-time 3-1)

Stade Colombes, Paris, 19 June
Attendance: 55,000

THE Colombes Stadium was not quite filled to capacity for the third World Cup Final. After France's exit, interest in the tournament dwindled and this was reflected in the attendances for the later matches.

However, the crowd was eager to see whether the Hungarians, with their flowing style of football, could halt Vittorio Pozzo's Italian side which boasted the outstanding centre-forward, Silvio Piola.

Twenty-five-year-old Piola was a man of rare talent. He was a centre-forward who could not only score goals with his feet and head, but also had magnificent distribution skills. He could easily have fitted into the midfield of the Italian team, but it was his goalscoring skills that were vital to Italy's cause.

When the Italians journeyed to the stadium, the streets were so crowded that their motor-coach could not get near the ground. Manager Pozzo immediately told the driver to turn

Giuseppe Meazza collects the World Cup trophy after Italy's victory in a Final which was not the classic encounter many had expected.

French referee Georges Capdeville watches Meazza (left) of Italy and Sárosi (right) of Hungary greet each other before the 1938 World Cup Final at the Stade Colombes in Paris.

Alfredi Foni, a spectacular Italian defender.

around and take the team back to the hotel. He did not want his players sitting around on a bus before such a crucial game. It was another psychological ploy by the master tactician.

The Italians reached the ground at the second attempt and then wasted no time in taking the lead. Colaussi finished off a great move down the left when he volleyed into the corner of the net to beat the diving Szabó.

It took Hungary only two minutes to level the scores, when Titkos hit a powerful shot into the roof of the net from an acute angle. Titkos later became secretary to the Hungarian FA and was eventually the national team coach.

Piola, who had been the 'Player of the Tournament', got his name on the score-sheet in the 16th minute when he finished off an intricate four-pass move in the Hungarian penalty area. Italy went in at half-time with a 3-1 lead after Colaussi scored his second goal in the 35th minute.

Italy played a solid defensive game in the second half, but came unstuck in the 70th minute when Hungary's captain, Sárosi, brought them back into the game with a goal which made it 3-2. However, eight minutes from time, Piola, perhaps appropriately, scored the last goal

of the tournament when his powerful left-foot shot from 12 yards gave the Hungarian goalkeeper no chance.

The game was not a classic encounter, but one which saw occasional flashes of brilliance from some exciting players. Vittorio Pozzo said that his new team was better than the one which won the World Cup in 1934. And in Meazza he had one of the game's most inspirational captains. For Meazza and Ferrari it was a second successive winners' medal. The trio of Foni, Rava and Locatelli added a World Cup-winners' medal to their Olympic gold won in 1936.

For Pozzo to mould two different World Cup-winning teams was a remarkable achievement and earned him a place in the game's history. Sadly, the 1938 success was to be his last triumph. Shortly afterwards Europe was at war and the World Cup, along with all other major sporting events, came to an end while the nations fought for superiority on the battlefields instead.

Piola thumps the ball high into Szabó's net for Italy's fourth goal and the last of the 1938 World Cup tournament.

Below: The victorious Italian team. Back row (left to right, players only): Biavati, Piola, Ferrari, Colaussi. Front row: Locatelli, Meazza, Foni, Olivieri, Rava, Serantoni. Andreolo is lying in front of Foni. Coach Vittorio Pozzo is holding aloft the trophy.

Opposite page (top): Italian goalkeeper Aldo Olivieri and his defenders clearing a Hungarian attack.

Opposite page (bottom): Hungary's skipper Sárosi brings his side back into the game with their second goal.

Italy: Aldo Olivieri; Alfredo Foni, Pietro Rava, Pietro Serantoni, Michele Andreolo, Ugo Locatelli, Amedeo Biavati, Giuseppe Meazza, Silvio Piola, Giovanni Ferrari, Gino Colaussi.
Scorers: Colaussi 2, Piola 2
Hungary: Antal Szabó; Gyula Polgar, Sándor Bíró, Antal Szalay, György Szücs, Gyula Lázár, Ferenc Sas, Jenö Vincze, György Sárosi, Gyula Zsengeller, Pál Titkos.
Scorers: Titkos, Sárosi
Referee: Georges Capdeville (France)

Own-goals
Ernst Lörtscher (Switzerland v Germany)

Hat-tricks
Leónidas da Silva (4 goals, Brazil v Poland). Gustav Wetterström (4 goals, Sweden v Cuba). Ernst Willimowski (4 goals, Poland v Brazil). Gyula Zsengeller (Hungary v Sweden).

Fastest goal
35 seconds — Arne Nyberg (Sweden v Hungary)

Most goals (team)
15 — Hungary

Teams failing to score
Dutch East Indies, Holland

Total goals scored: 84
Average per game: 4.67

Penalties
Scored: Oldrich Nejedlý (Czechoslovakia v Brazil, 1st game) *Referee: Paul Van Hertzka (Hungary).* Giuseppe Meazza (Italy v Brazil) *Referee: Hans Wuthrich (Switzerland).*

Most appearances
4 — Alfonsinho, Antonio da Guia Domingos, Leónidas da Silva, Arthur Machado, Berjum Peracio, Romeo Pellicciari, Zezé Procopio (all Brazil), Michele Andreolo, Giovanni Ferrari, Ugo Locatelli, Giuseppe Meazza, Aldo Olivieri, Silvio Piola, Pietro Rava, Pietro Serantoni (all Italy), Sándor Bíró, Gyula Lázár, György Sárosi, Ferenc Sas, Gyula Zsengeller (all Hungary).

Sendings-off
Hans Pesser (Germany v Switzerland, 1st game) *Referee: Jean Langenus (Belgium).* Zezé Procopio (Brazil v Czechoslovakia, 1st game) *Referee: Paul Van Hertzka (Hungary).* Arthur Machado (Brazil v Czechoslovakia 1st game) *Referee: Paul Van Hertzka.* Jan Říha (Czechoslovakia v Brazil, 1st game) *Referee: Paul Van Hertzka (Hungary).*

Most players used
21 — Brazil

Number of players used by Finalists
14 — Italy
17 — Hungary

MEN WHO MADE THE HEADLINES - 1950

Juan Schiaffino
(Uruguay)

NOT a particularly big player, Juan Alberto Schiaffino defied those who thought he would fail against some of the toughest defenders in international soccer and became one of the best inside-forwards of the 1950s. Born in Montevideo in 1925, Schiaffino broke into the Peñarol youth team as a 17-year-old and a year later was a first-teamer. At 19, he was a member of Uruguay's South American Championship squad. In the 1950 World Cup he was the second-highest scorer with six goals, including an equalizer against Brazil in the Final which set Uruguay on the road to victory. Four years later, an injury to Schiaffino in the semi-final against Hungary saw the South Americans defeated. AC Milan paid a world record £72,000 for Schiaffino shortly after the 1954 World Cup. Six months later he played his first game for Italy and then helped his club to three Championships and to the 1958 European Cup Final. When he was 35, he moved to AS Roma and spent two seasons with them before retiring in 1962. In 1976, after nearly 15 years away from the game, Schiaffino took charge of Peñarol and had a brief spell as the Uruguayan national team manager. He played for Uruguay 45 times and Italy on four occasions.

Ademir
(Brazil)

ADEMIR Marques de Meneses was one of the finest centre-forwards produced by Brazil. With Jair and Zizinho either side of him, the Brazilian attack in the 1950 World Cup was one of the most lethal in the history of the tournament. Ademir was responsible for nine of Brazil's impressive total of 22 goals and four of those came in the 7-1 win over Sweden during the final group matches. He was the complete all-rounder and had great dribbling skills, magnificent balance and a lethal shot with either foot. Born at Recife in 1924, he was the son of Domingos da Guia, a Brazilian international defender in the 1930s. Ademir began his career with Esporte Recife at the age of 19. He joined the Rio club, Vasco da Gama, in 1944 and the following year collected a Championship medal. He moved to Fluminense in 1946 and another Championship medal followed, but a year later he was back at Vasco da Gama and between 1947 and 1952 he won another four Championship medals. He retired in 1956, having scored 32 goals in 37 international appearances and 303 goals in 461 appearances for Vasco da Gama. He went into broadcasting after hanging up his boots.

Lennart Skoglund
(Sweden)

LENNART 'Nacka' Skoglund was a star of two Swedish World Cup sides, as a young inside-left in 1950 and then as a mature left winger on home soil in 1958. Born at Stockholm in 1929, blond-haired Skoglund was spotted as a 19-year-old playing for Third Division Hammerby by the top Swedish club, AIK Stockholm. A little over a year later, Skoglund was making an impact in the World Cup, where he formed a great partnership with Karl-Erik Palmer as Sweden finished third. Before Sweden's next World Cup appearance, 'Nacka' joined Inter-Milan, where his fine ball-control, excellent left foot and fine distribution made him a favourite with the fans. By now he had been turned into a dashing winger and played a vital role in Milan's two Championship wins, in 1953 and 1954. Sweden failed to qualify for the 1954 World Cup finals because they would not recall exiles like Skoglund, but when the Swedes played host to the 1958 tournament, they had a change of heart and Skoglund appeared in all six of Sweden's matches as they finished runners-up. He continued playing in Italy for a while before returning to his native Sweden and a second spell with AIK Stockholm.

War Clouds are Lifted
Brazil 1950

O N THE opening day of the 1938 World Cup in Paris, FIFA met to discuss the venue for the 1942 tournament. Brazil and Germany had both staked claims to host the next World Cup but, in view of the political situation in Europe, the matter was adjourned until the next congress, scheduled to be held in Luxembourg in 1940. In the meantime a third nation, Argentina, made a bid to stage the tournament. By the date arranged for the Luxembourg conference, German troops were moving through the Low Countries and, inevitably, the meeting was cancelled.

During the war, Dr Ivo Schricker kept the FIFA offices open in Zurich and the gold World Cup trophy was deposited in a bank in Rome, although some reports state that Jules Rimet slept with the trophy under his bed.

By the time the next congress did take place, in Luxembourg on 1 July 1946, Brazil was the only candidate and they were allocated the fourth World Cup tournament, which was originally planned for 1949. At the same meeting, Switzerland applied to stage the 1954 tournament and the congress agreed to their request.

The decision to stage the fourth tournament in South America stemmed from the fact that a large part of Europe was still in turmoil after the war. The choice of Brazil was to be a good one. They were the reigning South American champions and interest in football was reaching remarkable levels of fanaticism in that vast country. FIFA was confident Brazil would stage a spectacular carnival of football.

At their 1946 congress, FIFA also announced that, from 1950, the World Cup trophy would in future be known as the Jules Rimet Cup, although it was subsequently referred to as the Jules Rimet Trophy. This was to mark Rimet's 25th anniversary as FIFA president.

The British associations rejoined FIFA in 1946 and a representative match between Great Britain and the Rest of Europe was staged at Hampden Park in 1947. Britain won 6-1 in front of a staggering attendance of 135,000. With their share of the gate receipts, FIFA were financially sound for the first time in their history. They did need British soccer after all.

In 1950 there were 73 FIFA members, but, because of the aftermath of war, only 31 entered the fourth World Cup. In the UK, the 1949-50 Home International Championship was used as a qualifying pool, with the top two being eligible to make the trip to Río. However, notable absentees from the list of entrants included Czechoslovakia and Hungary, runners-up in the last two competitions.

The qualifying competition turned into something of a farce with teams qualifying then withdrawing — and teams already eliminated being offered places. India withdrew because FIFA would not let them play in bare feet!

However, once the tournament moved to Brazil for the final stages, the local fans showed tremendous enthusiasm and the competition turned out to be the most successful so far. The newly-constructed Maracana Stadium was full for the 1950 World Cup Final and the 200,000 crowd is still a world record attendance for a football match.

The authorities had panicked just before the start of the tournament, when scaffolding still adorned the Maracana. Like Uruguay in 1930, the show-piece stadium was not complete for the start of the World Cup. It had, though, staged its first match, despite being incomplete. On 10 June 1950, junior representative sides from Río and São Paulo met. The honour of scoring the first goal in the world's largest soccer stadium went to Didi, who later gained World Cup-winners' medals with Brazil in 1958 and 1962.

The success of the fourth World Cup was due largely to the brilliant footballing flair of the Brazilians and the enthusiasm of their fans. But the late withdrawals and the totally unacceptable system of playing all matches on a pool basis could well have turned the tournament into a disaster, had it been staged in any other country.

Thirteen teams eventually took part in the final stages and were divided into four pools. One would have thought the pools would have contained either three or four teams, but two groups contained four teams, one comprised three teams and Uruguay were fortunate enough to be in a pool of only two teams.

The four group winners then went through to a final pool and all teams played each other once. As it happened, the final match of the pool, between Brazil and Uruguay, was, in everything but name, the World Cup Final. This absurd system has never been attempted again, although one could see FIFA's reasoning behind the idea. They did not want nations making the long trip to Brazil to play only one game, as some did when the tournament was last played in South America 20 years earlier.

To make matters worse, the pool matches were not played at a single venue. This meant a great deal of travelling for most of the teams.

Brazil were the favourites to win the Jules Rimet Cup but the one team they feared was England. Yet both fell. The hosts played some of the finest football ever seen at international level but could not lay their hands on the trophy their fans so passionately wanted. For England, meanwhile, gracing football's finest stage for the first time, disaster lay ahead.

1950 Qualifying Competition

THIRTY-ONE teams, plus holders Italy and hosts Brazil, entered the fourth World Cup — and what a farce the qualifying competition turned out to be. Indonesia and the Philippines both withdrew before the draw for the qualifying competition was held in January 1949. Argentina then withdrew because of their differences with the Brazilian FA, which meant that the two other teams from their qualifying group, Bolivia and Chile, automatically qualified for the Finals.

Ecuador and Peru withdrew from Group 8, which meant that Uruguay and Paraguay also qualified without playing. And in Group 10, Burma withdrew to give India automatic entry to the final stages. Then India subsequently withdrew after FIFA announced that their barefooted players would have to wear boots in the Finals.

Scotland also upset the organizers. The British Home International Championship of 1949-50 had been designated a World Cup qualifying group with the top two teams eligible to make the trip to Brazil. England and Scotland were thus guaranteed places before they met at Hampden Park in April 1950, but after a Roy Bentley goal gave England a 1-0 win, the Scots announced that they would not compete in the World Cup as runners-up and promptly added to the list of withdrawals.

Austria, who missed the 1938 tournament, were missing again in 1950. They should have played the winners of the Turkey-Syria group but withdrew on the grounds that their young team was too inexperienced. Yet, on the eve of the 1950 World Cup Final, the Austrians held Italy to a draw. Belgium withdrew without playing in the qualifying competition, whilst Turkey qualified but later withdrew.

FIFA were desperate to fill the places created by the withdrawal of Scotland and Turkey. They invited France and Portugal — both of whom had been eliminated — to fill their places. The Portuguese declined but France accepted and went into the same pool as Uruguay and Bolivia.

The four pools should then have looked like this (first-named teams were the 'seeds'):

Pool 1 Brazil, Mexico, Switzerland, Yugoslavia.
Pool 2 England, Chile, Spain, United States.
Pool 3 Italy, India, Paraguay, Sweden.
Pool 4 Uruguay, Bolivia, France.

However, India subsequently pulled out of Pool 3 and France withdrew from Pool 4 when they saw how much travelling was involved. It was too late for FIFA to make another draw and so the tournament got underway with four unbalanced groups.

Results

Group One

1 Oct 1949 *Belfast*	N. Ireland ....2 Scotland 8
15 Oct 1949 *Cardiff*	Wales ....1 England 4
9 Nov 1949 *Glasgow*	Scotland ....2 Wales 0
16 Nov 1949 *Manchester*	England ....9 N. Ireland 2
8 Mar 1950 *Wrexham*	Wales ....0 N. Ireland 0
15 Apr 1950 *Glasgow*	Scotland ....0 England 1

	P	W	D	L	F	A	Pts	
England	3	3	0	0	14	3	6	**England and**
Scotland	3	2	0	1	10	3	4	**Scotland qualified**
Wales	3	0	1	2	1	6	1	**(Scotland subse-**
N. Ireland	3	0	1	2	4	17	1	**quently withdrew)**

Group Two
20 Nov 1949 *Ankara*   Turkey............7 Syria 0
Turkey qualified (Turkey should have met Austria in the next match but the Austrians withdrew. Turkey also subsequently withdrew)

Group Three
First Round
21 Aug 1949 *Belgrade*   Yugoslavia ....6 Israel 0
18 Sep 1949 *Tel Aviv*   Israel ....2 Yugoslavia 5
Second Round
9 Oct 1949 *Belgrade*   Yugoslavia ....1 France 1
30 Oct 1949 *Paris*   France ....1 Yugoslavia 1
Play-off
11 Dec 1949 *Florence*   Yugoslavia ....3 France 2
Yugoslavia qualified

Group Four
26 Jun 1949 *Zurich*   Switzerland ......5 Luxembourg.....2
18 Sep 1949 *Luxembourg* Luxembourg.....2 Switzerland 3
Switzerland qualified. (They should have met Belgium in the next match but the Belgians withdrew)

Group Five

2 Jun 1949 *Stockholm*	Sweden ....3 Rep of Ireland ...1
8 Sep 1949 *Dublin*	Rep of Ireland ...3 Finland...........0
9 Oct 1949 *Helsinki*	Finland...........1 Rep of Ireland ...1
13 Nov 1949 *Dublin*	Rep of Ireland ...1 Sweden 3

The Sweden-Finland fixtures were not played

	P	W	D	L	F	A	Pts	
Sweden	2	2	0	0	6	2	4	**Sweden qualified**
Rep of Ireland	4	1	1	2	6	7	3	
Finland	2	0	1	1	1	4	1	

Group Six
2 Apr 1950 *Madrid*   Spain ....5 Portugal..........1
9 Apr 1950 *Lisbon*   Portugal..........2 Spain 2
Spain qualified

Group Seven
Bolivia and Chile qualified (Argentina withdrew)

Group Eight
Uruguay and Paraguay qualified (Ecuador and Peru withdrew)

Group Nine

4 Sep 1949 *Mexico City*	Mexico............6 United States 0
11 Sep 1949 *Mexico City*	Mexico............2 Cuba 0
14 Sep 1949 *Mexico City*	United States ....1 Cuba 1
18 Sep 1949 *Mexico City*	United States ....2 Mexico............6
21 Sep 1949 *Mexico City*	Cuba ....2 United States 5
25 Sep 1949 *Mexico City*	Cuba ....0 Mexico............3

	P	W	D	L	F	A	Pts	
Mexico	4	4	0	0	17	2	8	**Mexico**
United States	4	1	1	2	8	15	3	**and United States**
Cuba	4	0	1	3	3	11	1	**qualified**

Group Ten
India qualified (Burma withdrew. India also withdrew later)

1950 Tournament

Pool One

BRAZIL 4   MEXICO 0 (Half-time 1-0)

Maracana Stadium, Río de Janeiro, 24 June
Attendance: 81,649

THE splendid Maracana Stadium was not finished by the time Brazil lined up against Mexico for the opening game. But this did not stop the Brazilians laying on a pageant which included a 21-gun salute, firework display and the release of 5,000 pigeons. The carnival atmosphere that would be a big part of this championship had begun.

The crowd revelled in the atmosphere but had to wait 30 minutes before their heroes opened the scoring. The honour of scoring the first goal of the tournament fell to Ademir, one of the finest footballers of the day and one of the best attacking players ever to have pulled on the famous yellow jersey of Brazil.

For more than an hour, the Mexicans did well to contain their more illustrious opponents, who were the reigning South American champions, but after 66 minutes Jair added a second goal before Baltazar and Ademir completed the scoring with two goals in the last 20 minutes. It was not exactly the best of starts for Mexico's goalkeeper, Antonio Carbajal, who was to go on to make World Cup history by playing in five consecutive tournaments.

The favourites had overcome the first hurdle which has often proved a difficult obstacle to other fancied teams over the years. Now the Brazilian fans were expecting nothing less than ultimate victory.

Brazil: Barbosa; Augusto, Juvenal, Eli, Danilo, Bigode, Maneca, Ademir, Baltazar, Jair, Friaça.
Scorers: Ademir 2, Jair, Baltazar
Mexico: Carbajal; Zetter, Montemajor, Ruíz, Ochoa, Roca, Septien, Ortíz, Casarin, Pérez, Velásquez.
Referee: George Reader (England)

YUGOSLAVIA 3   SWITZERLAND 0 (Half-time 2-0)

Sete de Setembro Stadium, Belo Horizonte, 25 June
Attendance: 7,336

YUGOSLAVIA impressed in their opening match and showed the Brazilians they would be tough opponents in Pool One. Runners-up to Sweden at the 1948 Olympics, their side was well-balanced and contained two outstanding inside-forwards, Stjepan Bobek and Bernard Vukas. The team was well martialled by skipper and wing-half, Zlatko Ciakowski.

Carbajal of Mexico.

Bernard Vukas of Yugoslavia.

Mitić (left) of Yugoslavia and Alfred Bickel (Switzerland) lead out their respective teams. Two weeks before their World Cup encounter, the sides met in Berne, where Yugoslavia won 4-0.

Jacques Fatton of Switzerland.

The game was a stroll for the Eastern Europeans as the Swiss failed to reproduce the form that earned them much praise in the 1938 tournament in France. They had one survivor from that tournament, new skipper Alfred Bickel.

Yugoslavia's superiority told with two goals in six minutes from Kosta Tomasević in the first half. Outside-right Ognjanov sealed the victory with a third goal eight minutes from time.

Yugoslavia: Mrkusić; Horvat, Stanković, Ciakowski, Jovanović, Djajić, Ognjanov, Mitić, Tomasević, Bobek, Vukas.
Scorers: Tomasević 2, Ognjanov
Switzerland: Stuber; Neury, Bocquet, Lusenti, Eggimann, Guinche, Bickel, Antenen, Tamini, Bader, Fatton.
Referee: Giovanni Galeati (Italy)

The Yugoslavian team which beat Switzerland. Back row (left to right): Stanković, Mitić, Ognjanov, Jovanović, Bobek, Horvat, Mrkusić. Front row: Tomasević, Vukas, Djajić, Ciakowski.

BRAZIL 2   SWITZERLAND 2 (Half-time 2-1)
Pacaembu Stadium, São Paulo, 28 June
Attendance: 42,032

BRAZIL changed their team for their first match at the Pacaembu Stadium and selected several local São Paulo players to keep the home fans happy. But the decision by coach Flavio Costa nearly backfired as the Swiss produced the first shock of the tournament.

Switzerland fell behind to an Alfredo goal after only two minutes. The Europeans did well to come back after such a magnificent start by the hosts and got their just reward in the 16th minute, when outside-left Jacques Fatton equalized. Brazil regained the lead just before the interval when Baltazar scored.

Brazil seemed to be nervously holding on for a 2-1 win when Fatton levelled the scores two minutes from time in a rare second-half Swiss attack. Brazil's goals were rather fortunate affairs and many felt that Switzerland could have won, despite having much less of the play.

Costa, the coach, was attacked by a large section of the crowd as he left the ground. The Brazilian fans were not prepared to accept anything other than outright success and the pressure was now on Costa and his team to do well in their final match against Yugoslavia.

Brazil: Barbosa; Augusto, Juvenal, Bauer, Ruy, Noronha, Alfredo, Maneca, Baltazar, Ademir, Friaça.
Scorers: Alfredo, Baltazar
Switzerland: Stuber; Neury, Bocquet, Lusenti, Eggimann, Quinche, Tamini, Bickel, Friedländer, Bader, Fatton.
Scorer: Fatton 2
Referee: Ramon Azon Roma (Spain)

YUGOSLAVIA 4   MEXICO 1 (Half-time 2-0)
Beira-Río Stadium, Pôrto Alegre, 29 June
Attendance: 11,078

BRAZIL'S demise against Switzerland gave Yugoslavia the chance to head the group and another fine display of flowing football saw them easily beat Mexico, who conceded four goals for the second successive game.

The Yugoslavs brought in Zeliko Ciakowski, brother of their skipper, at outside-left in place of Vukas and the newcomer turned out to be the man of the match with two fine goals.

Bobek opened the scoring after 19 minutes and replacement winger, Ciakowski, made it 2-0 three minutes later. He scored his second after 62 minutes and Tomasević made it 4-0

Srdjan Mrkusić of Yugoslavia under pressure from Ademir of Brazil.

nine minutes from time. Mexico scored a late consolation goal from the penalty-spot in the 88th minute, through Casarin.

This Yugoslavian win meant the outcome of Pool One would be decided by their match against Brazil.

Yugoslavia: Mrkusić; Horvat, Stanković, Zlatko Ciakowski, Jovanović, Djajić, Mihailović, Mitić, Tomasević, Bobek, Zeliko Ciakowski.
Scorers: Zeliko Ciakowski 2, Bobek, Tomasević
Mexico: Carbajal; Gutiérrez, Ruíz, Gómez, Ochoa, Ortíz, Flores, Naranjo, Casarin, Pérez, Velásquez.
Scorer: Casarin (pen)
Referee: Reg Leafe (England)

BRAZIL 2   YUGOSLAVIA 0 (Half-time 1-0)

Maracana Stadium, Río de Janeiro, 1 July
Attendance: 142,409

BRAZIL had a score to settle with Yugoslavia because the Europeans had ousted them from the inaugural World Cup in 1930. However, after only three minutes of this crucial game, Brazil's legendary striker Ademir put the hosts in front. But for more than an hour, until Zizinho scored the second, the Brazilian fans had their hearts in their mouths. A draw was no good for Brazil, they had to win, and only when that second goal went in could they breathe a sigh of relief.

Yugoslavia were forced to start the game with ten men because Rajko Mitić, their star inside-right, failed to see a beam above his head as he was leaving the dressing-room. He ran into it and was badly cut and shaken. He had to be taken back to the dressing-room and did not join the game until after Ademir had opened the scoring. Heavily bandaged and obviously suffering the effects of the injury, he played little part in the game.

The Brazilian trio of Ademir, Zizinho and Jair were to become one of the great strike forces of the tournament and scored 13 goals between them. And wing-half José Carlos Bauer, the man who made both goals, was the equivalent of the modern-day midfield general and was an inspirational member of the team.

For Zizinho, the winning goal was an outstanding solo effort and was a memorable way to celebrate his World Cup debut. The Brazilian fans had a new hero.

Brazil: Barbosa; Augusto, Juvenal, Bauer, Danilo, Bigode, Maneca, Zizinho, Ademir, Jair, Chico.
Scorers: Ademir, Zizinho
Yugoslavia: Mrkusić; Horvat, Brokela, Zlatko Ciakowski, Jovanović, Djajić, Vukas, Mitić, Tomasević, Bobek, Zelico Ciakowski.
Referee: Mervyn Griffiths (Wales)

SWITZERLAND 2   MEXICO 1 (Half-time 2-0)

Beira-Río Stadium, Pôrto Alegre, 2 July
Attendance: 3,580

ALL that was left for Switzerland and Mexico to play for at Pôrto Alegre was the 'wooden spoon', which went to Mexico.

Both sides made changes and gave World Cup debuts to some of their players. Switzerland led 2-0 at half-time, through goals from René Bader after 12 minutes and Antenen right on the stroke of half-time. For Mexico there was a late consolation when Casarin scored two minutes from time.

Switzerland: Hug; Neury, Bocquet, Lusenti, Eggimann, Quinche, Tamini, Antenen, Friedländer, Bader, Fatton.
Scorers: Bader, Antenen
Mexico: Carbajal; Gutiérrez, Gómez, Ortíz, Ochoa, Roca, Flores, Guevara, Casarin, Borbolla, Velásquez.
Scorer: Casarin
Referee: Ivan Eklind (Sweden)

Pool Two

ENGLAND 2   CHILE 0 (Half-time 1-0)

Maracana Stadium, Río de Janeiro, 25 June
Attendance: 29,703

THE thin Río air did not suit the England players but they still managed to come through their first-ever World Cup match with a win.

In the Chile team was that country's only full-time professional, George Robledo, who played his soccer in the English First Division with Newcastle United. In contrast, England

Pool One – Final Table

	P	W	D	L	F	A	Pts
Brazil	3	2	1	0	8	2	5
Yugoslavia	3	2	0	1	7	3	4
Switzerland	3	1	1	1	4	6	3
Mexico	3	0	0	3	2	10	0

Jean Tamini of Switzerland.

José Carlos Bauer of Brazil.

England's line-up against Chile. Back row (left to right): John Aston, Wilf Mannion, Alf Ramsey, Laurie Hughes, Billy Wright, Bert Williams. Front row: Jimmy Mullen, Roy Bentley, Jimmy Dickinson, Stan Mortensen, Tom Finney.

Billy Wright leads out England in the Maracana Stadium to meet Chile. He is followed by Bert Williams.

fielded some of the best-known players in the world against their part-time opponents. However, they made a simple task look difficult.

At the interval, England led by a single goal, scored by Stan Mortensen, and sealed their victory seven minutes into the second half when Wilf Mannion finished off a close-passing move involving the mercurial Tom Finney.

England went to Brazil as second favourites behind the hosts, but this unimpressive performance did not justify their odds. Their next match was even less impressive.

England: Williams; Ramsey, Aston, Wright, Hughes, Dickinson, Finney, Mortensen, Bentley, Mannion, Mullen.
Scorers: Mortensen, Mannion
Chile: Livingstone; Farias, Roldan, Alvarez, Busquet, Carvalho, Mayanes, Cremaschi, Robledo, Muñoz, Diaz.
Referee: Karel Van Der Meer (Holland)

SPAIN 3   UNITED STATES 1 (Half-time 0-1)

Brito Stadium, Curitiba, 25 June
Attendance: 9,511

THE United States, who were to pull off the biggest shock in World Cup history in their next match, nearly brought off a surprise in their opening match against Spain before three late goals saved the Spaniards' blushes.

Inside-right John Souza put the Americans in the lead in the 18th minute and for the next 62 minutes their defence, marshalled by full-back Maca, was magnificent as they thwarted countless Spanish attacks.

With ten minutes remaining, the Americans were hanging on to their slender lead but then their defence crumbled. Basora levelled the scores in the 80th minute and with the American players now demoralized, Basora netted again two minutes later. In the 85th minute, Zarra completed a miserable five-minute spell for the United States.

The Americans, of course, did not know it at the time, but victory would probably have qualified the team for the final pool. Considering most of their players were part-timers, their performance was a remarkable one — but even that paled into insignificance compared to their next match.

Spain: Eizaguirre; Alonzo, Antuñez, J.Gonzalvo, M.Gonzalvo, Puchades, Basora, Hernández, Zarra, Igoa, Gaínza.
Scorers: Basora 2, Zarra
United States: Borghi; Keough, Maca, McIlvenny, Colombo, Bahr, Craddock, J.Souza, Gaetjens, Pariani, Valentini.
Scorer: J.Souza
Referee: Mario Viana (Brazil)

SPAIN 2   CHILE 0 (Half-time 2-0)

Maracana Stadium, Río de Janeiro, 29 June
Attendance: 19,790

AFTER their fright against the USA, the Spaniards made three team changes and encountered very few problems in their second match against Chile.

Estanislao Basora of Spain, who scored twice against the USA.

Two first-half goals, from Basora and Zarra, their goalscorers in the first match, were enough to see them register their second win and go to the top of the pool. Basora's goal came after 19 minutes, whilst Zarra's contribution came in the 35th minute.

Spain: Ramallets; Alonzo, Parra, J.Gonzalvo, M.Gonzalvo, Puchades, Basora, Igoa, Zarra, Panizo, Gaínza.
Scorers: Basora, Zarra
Chile: Livingstone; Farias, Roldan, Alvarez, Busquet, Carvalho, Prieto, Cremaschi, Robledo, Muñoz, Diaz.
Referee: Alberto Gama Malcher (Brazil)

Bert Williams of England.

The United States team that scored a sensational victory over England. Back row (left to right): Chubby Lyons (team manager), Joe Maca, Charlie Colombo, Frank Borghi, Harry Keogh, Walter Baer, Bill Jeffrey (coach). Front row: Frank Wallace, Ed McIlvenny, Gino Pariani, Joe Gaetjens, John Souza, Ed Souza.

The England side humiliated by the USA. Back row (left to right): Alf Ramsey, John Aston, Roy Bentley, Laurie Hughes, Billy Wright, Bert Williams. Front row: Jimmy Mullen, Tom Finney, Stan Mortensen, Wilf Mannion, Jimmy Dickinson.

UNITED STATES 1   ENGLAND 0 (Half-time 1-0)

Mineiro Stadium, Belo Horizonte, 29 June
Attendance: 10,151

ENGLAND travelled 300 miles north to Belo Horizonte for their second game, against the United States. They could not have failed to notice what a scare their opponents had given Spain in their opening match. Yet, still England approached the game with the wrong attitude. Of course, on paper, a team containing players like Bert Williams, Billy Wright, Jimmy Dickinson, Tom Finney, Stan Mortensen, and Wilf Mannion should not have experienced any problems against a team of part-timers. But the United States enjoyed the greatest day in its soccer history.

England full-back Alf Ramsey was in the side humiliated by the USA. But 16 years later, Ramsey managed the side which won the World Cup.

England skipper Billy Wright (left) and the USA's Ed McIlvenny at the toss-up.

Bert Williams can only stare in disbelief as 'Larry' Gaetjens' effort enters the net.

American inside-forward John Souza.

The American skipper was Eddie McIlvenny, one of only three non-US born players in the team. He had played for Wrexham before being given a free transfer in 1949 and later went on to play for Manchester United. Full-back Joe Maca was born in Belgium and the only other non-American was the Haitian, Joseph 'Larry' Gaetjens. The American team was moulded together by Scotsman Bill Jeffrey of Penn State and one of the most successful soccer coaches in US college history.

England did plenty of attacking and had enough chances to win by a big score — but they could not find the net, due largely to the acrobatics of Frank Borghi in the US goal and the glove-wearing centre-half, Charles Colombo. The Americans, on the other hand, did score and that one goal was enough to provide the biggest upset in World Cup history.

Gaetjens met a cross from Walter Bahr and glanced it past goalkeeper Williams. The unthinkable had happened. America had withstood 37 minutes of English pressure, broken away and scored what turned out to be the match-winner.

England continued to raid the American goal constantly in the second half and it must be said that a Jimmy Mullen header from a free-kick appeared to cross the line, although the referee thought different.

For America it was their finest hour. For England it was their most humiliating. What of Larry Gaetjens? He went to France to finish his playing career with Racing Club de Paris and then Alès. During troubled times in Haiti in 1970, the hero of the 1950 World Cup mysteriously disappeared.

United States: Borghi; Keough, Maca, McIlvenny, Colombo, Bahr, Wallace, Pariani, Gaetjens, J.Souza, E.Souza.
Scorer: Gaetjens
England: Williams; Ramsey, Aston, Wright, Hughes, Dickinson, Finney, Mortensen, Bentley, Mannion, Mullen.
Referee: Generoso Dattilo (Italy)

An American hero – 'Larry' Gaetjens is carried off the field after his historic goal earned the USA victory.

SPAIN 1   ENGLAND 0 (Half-time 0-0)

Maracana Stadium, Río de Janeiro, 2 July
Attendance: 74,462

IT was back to the Maracana for England's final pool game against Spain. The best they could hope for was a play-off match but first they had to beat Spain — and a team that could not beat the United States was always going to have problems.

England made four changes. They brought Stan Matthews in for his first World Cup game. Matthews had not been fully fit before leaving for Brazil, but coach Walter Winterbottom had to include him after the miserable performance against the USA. Also coming into the team after injury was Newcastle United centre-forward Jackie Milburn, whilst Bill Eckersley (Blackburn) and Eddie Baily (Spurs) both won their first caps.

England gave a dazzling performance in a goalless first half and should have taken a 12th-minute lead. What appeared to be a perfectly good goal by Jackie Milburn was disallowed because of a dubious offside decision by the referee. The Italian official was harsh on England and throughout the match persistently let the Spaniards get away with some bruising tackling.

Nevertheless, Zarra headed Spain into the lead in the 49th minute and immediately the Spaniards put up the shutters and packed their own half of the field with players. At the end of the match, the Brazilian fans booed them off the field.

Tom Finney, another great England star whose talents could not prevent a sensational World Cup result.

Spanish goalkeeper Antonio Ramallets in action against England at the Maracana Stadium.

Pool Two – Final Table

	P	W	D	L	F	A	Pts
Spain	3	3	0	0	6	1	6
England	3	1	0	2	2	2	2
Chile	3	1	0	2	5	6	2
United States	3	1	0	2	4	8	2

England went unceremoniously out of the tournament. They had arrived as one of the favourites, but were dumped out after three unimpressive performances.

Spain: Ramallets; Alonzo, Parra, J.Gonzalvo, M.Gonzalvo, Puchades, Basora, Igoa, Zarra, Panizo, Gaínza.
Scorer: Zarra
England: Williams; Ramsey, Eckersley, Wright, Hughes, Dickinson, Matthews, Mortensen, Milburn, Baily, Finney.
Referee: Giovanni Galeati (Italy)

Three Chilean stars (left to right): Atílio Cremaschi, George Robledo and Manuel Muñoz.

CHILE 5   UNITED STATES 2 (Half-time 2-0)

Ilha do Retiro Stadium, Recife, 2 July
Attendance: 8,501

WHAT a strange pool this turned out to be. England lost to the United States and Spain. The Americans surprised both England and Spain. And then Chile, who were outplayed by the two fancied teams, beat the USA in the last game.

As it turned out, the result had no bearing on the eventual outcome of the pool, but had England beaten Spain, then the Americans could have forced a play-off situation. The harsh reality, however, was that Chile won handsomely.

Chile's 'Englishman', George Robledo, started the scoring in the 20th minute and Cremaschi made it 2-0 after half an hour. Within four minutes of the start of the second half, though, Pariani and Ed Souza (from the penalty-spot) had levelled the scores.

It was turning out to be the best match of the group. Chile regained the lead through Cremaschi in the 54th minute and five minutes later they had re-established a two-goal advantage when Andrés Prieto scored.

The Americans could not come back a second time and the scoring glut ended one minute from the end when Cremaschi completed his hat-trick to make it 5-2.

Chile: Livingstone; Machuca, Alvarez, Busquet, Farias, Rojas, Riera, Cremaschi, Robledo, Prieto, Ibañez.
Scorers: Cremaschi 3, Robledo, Prieto
United States: Borghi; Keough, Maca, McIlvenny, Colombo, Bahr, Wallace, Pariani, Gaetjens, J.Souza, E.Souza.
Scorers: Pariani, E.Souza (pen)
Referee: Mario Gardelli (Brazil)

Pool Three

Italian centre-half Carlo Parola.

SWEDEN 3   ITALY 2 (Half-time 2-1)

Pacaembu Stadium, São Paulo, 25 June
Attendance: 56,502

ITALY arrived in Brazil, not only as the reigning champions but also undefeated in the World Cup. When they beat Hungary in the 1938 Final, it was their ninth game in two tournaments and they had still to taste defeat.

However, gone was coach Vittorio Pozzo, who had been replaced in 1949. The rebuilding

The Italian team that met Sweden.

Riccardo Carapellese gives Italy the lead as Karl Svensson is stranded, but the Swedes went on to win 3-2 in the first major upset of the 1950 tournament.

had started after the war but suffered a tragic blow when 17 members of the Torino team, eight of them internationals, were killed when their plane crashed into the Superga Basilica on a hillside near Turin in May 1949. This was a tremendous set-back to Italy's new mentor, Lajos Czeizler, who had to muster up a team experienced enough to compete in Brazil.

Because of the Superga disaster, the Italians travelled by boat to Río and the long journey did not give them enough time on dry land before their opening match against Sweden, the reigning Olympic champions. The result provided the first shock of this remarkable tournament as the Swedes won 3-2 and thus inflicted the first-ever World Cup defeat on Italy. Sweden were coached by an Englishman, George Raynor, and their win was more satisfying because they had lost several of their Olympic-winning team — Gunnar Nordahl, Gunnar Gren, and Nils Liedholm — to AC Milan. The team Raynor took to Brazil was comprised entirely of amateurs.

Italy were confident of reaching the final pool and when their new skipper, Carapellese, opened the scoring in the seventh minute, that confidence grew visibly. However, Hans Jeppson and Sune Andersson gave the Swedes a 2-1 lead at the interval. Jeppson stunned the Italians with a second goal after 68 minutes. Muccinelli pulled one back seven minutes later, but they could not snatch the equalizer and the Swedes had pulled off a sensational result.

Whilst the victory was a memorable occasion for the Swedes, it resulted in eight members of the team being snapped up by professional Italian clubs after the World Cup and Sweden once more paid the price of success.

Giampiero Boniperti of Italy.

Sweden: Svensson; Samuelsson, E.Nilsson, Andersson, Nordahl, Gärd, Sundqvist, Palmer, Jeppson, Skoglund, S.Nilsson.
Scorers: Jeppson 2, Andersson
Italy: Sentimenti IV; Giovannini, Furiassi, Annovazzi, Parola, Magli, Muccinelli, Boniperti, Cappello, Campatelli, Carapellese.
Scorers: Carapellese, Muccinelli
Referee: M.Lutz (Switzerland)

SWEDEN 2 PARAGUAY 2 (Half-time 2-1)

Brito Stadium, Curitiba, 29 June
Attendance: 7,903

SWEDEN needed only to draw to guarantee a place in the next phase of the competition and they seemed to be coasting at 2-0, but then threw away their lead. They held on, though, and gained the point that took them into the final pool.

The Swedes burst into life in the 23rd minute when Sundqvist put them ahead. Two minutes later, Palmer made it 2-0 and a comfortable victory looked likely. But ten minutes before half-time, Atilo López scored for Paraguay. Their second goal, from López Fretes, came ten minutes from the end. Any earlier and Sweden could well have thrown away their chance.

Sweden: Svensson; Samuelsson, E.Nilsson, Andersson, Nordahl, Gärd, Jönsson, Palmer, Jeppson, Skoglund, Sundqvist.
Scorers: Sundqvist, Palmer
Paraguay: Vargas; González, Céspedes, Gavilan, Lequízamon, Cantero, Avalos, López, Saguir, López Fretes, Unzaín.
Scorers: López, López Fretes
Referee: Bobby Mitchell (Scotland)

Two members of Sweden's Olympic gold medal-winning team of 1948. Gunnar Nordahl (left) was missed by Sweden in the 1950 World Cup but his brother Knut Nordahl (right) proved to be one of their stars.

Pool Three – Final Table

	P	W	D	L	F	A	Pts
Sweden	2	1	1	0	5	4	3
Italy	2	1	0	1	4	3	2
Paraguay	2	0	1	1	2	4	1

ITALY 2 PARAGUAY 0 (Half-time 1-0)

Pacaembu, São Paulo, 2 July
Attendance: 25,811

ITALY'S exit from the 1950 World Cup was already assured. Paraguay, on the other hand, could force a play-off with Sweden if they beat the Italians. But, despite coming up against probably the weakest side ever fielded by Italy in the history of the World Cup, Paraguay were no match for their European opponents, who ran out 2-0 winners.

Italy made seven changes for the match but Carapellese put them ahead after 12 minutes and Pandolfini made it 2-0 in the 62nd minute. But the victory was scant compensation for the Italians, who had nothing to look forward to except a long boat journey home.

Italy: Moro; Blason, Furiassi, Fattori, Remondini, Mari, Muccinelli, Pandolfini, Amadei, Cappello, Carapellese.
Scorers: Carapellese, Pandolfini
Paraguay: Vargas; González, Céspedes, Gavilan, Lequízamon, Cantero, Avalos, López, Saguir, López Fretes, Unzaín.
Referee: Arthur Ellis (England)

Riccardo Carapellese gives Italy a seventh-minute lead against Paraguay.

Pool Four

URUGUAY 8 BOLIVIA 0 (Half-time 4-0)

Mineiro Stadium, Belo Horizonte, 2 July
Attendance: 5,284

FORTUNE certainly smiled on Uruguay during the fourth World Cup. Competing for the first time since winning the inaugural competition on home soil in 1930, they did not have to play a game before arriving in Brazil, thanks to the withdrawal of Peru and Ecuador from their qualifying pool. And when the pools were drawn for the final stages, France

Uruguayan centre-half Matías Gonzáles clears his lines in a rare Bolivian attack.

withdrew, which meant Uruguay had just one match to play, against the weak and inexperienced Bolivians.

The result was a one-sided win for the light blues, who ran in four goals in the first half and repeated the performance in the second. Indeed, some reports suggest that if they had not eased off, then the final scoreline would have been well into double figures.

Schiaffino, with a hat-trick, and Vidal scored the first-half goals. The second period saw Schiaffino add another, whilst Míguez scored twice and Ghiggia completed the scoring seven minutes from time. Bolivia, incidentally, have not qualified for the final stages of the World Cup since this defeat.

Uruguay's 8-0 win equalled the record for the final stages of the World Cup set by Sweden when they beat Cuba by the same score in 1938. Uruguay's outstanding inside-left, Juan Schiaffino of Peñarol, and later AC Milan, became the fourth man in World Cup history to score four goals in one game.

Uruguay: Máspoli; M.Gonzáles, Tejera, J-C.Gonzáles, Varela, Andrade, Ghiggia, Pérez, Míguez, Schiaffino, Vidal.
Scorers: Schiaffino 4, Míguez 2, Vidal, Ghiggia
Bolivia: B.Gutiérrez; Achá, Bustamente, Greco, Valencia, Ferrel, Algarañaz, Ugarte, Caparelli, E.Gutiérrez, Maldonado.
Referee: George Reader (England)

Pool Four – Final Table

	P	W	D	L	F	A	Pts
Uruguay	1	1	0	0	8	0	2
Bolivia	1	0	0	1	0	8	0

> **WORLD CUP FACT**
>
> **Alfred Bickel (Switzerland) and Erik Nilsson (Sweden) are the only men to have played in the final stages both before and after World War Two. They both appeared in 1938 and 1950.**

Final Pool

BRAZIL 7   SWEDEN 1 (Half-time 3-0)
Maracana Stadium, Río de Janeiro, 3 July
Attendance: 138,886

BY the time Brazil ran out for the first game of the final pool, they were bubbling with confidence. Like Italy in 1934 and 1938, Brazil were improving all the time. Their forward line, particularly the mercurial Ademir, was unstoppable and, despite the fact that they had ousted Italy, very few people gave Sweden any chance of preventing another barrage of Brazilian attacks. They were correct.

Brazil destroyed the amateurs with a display of fast non-stop football and by half-time had three goals on the score-board — from Ademir (17 and 36 minutes) and Chico (39 minutes).

The second half told the same story and by the 64th minute, Ademir had added two more goals, before Andersson pulled one back from the penalty-spot for the demoralized Swedes. Maneca and Chico added two further goals in the last five minutes to seal a comprehensive victory. Uruguay, playing out a draw at São Paulo, must have been quaking when they heard the result from Río.

Brazil: Barbosa; Augusto, Juvenal, Bauer, Danilo, Bigode, Maneca, Zizinho, Ademir, Jair, Chico.
Scorers: Ademir 4, Chico 2, Maneca
Sweden: Svensson; Samuelsson, E.Nilsson, Andersson, Nordahl, Gärd, Sundqvist, Palmer, Jeppson, Skoglund, S.Nilsson.
Scorer: Andersson (pen)
Referee: Arthur Ellis (England)

English referee Arthur Ellis officiated in the 1950 World Cup. Ellis later became a household name in Britain when he refereed BBC television's *It's A Knockout*.

From left to right: Augusto, Barbosa and Juvenal of Brazil.

Omar Míguez of Uruguay.

Alcides Ghiggia of Uruguay.

SPAIN 2   URUGUAY 2 *(Half-time 2-1)*

Pacaembu Stadium, São Paulo, 9 July
Attendance: 44,802

WHILST Brazil were in rampant form against Sweden, Uruguay, the only nation regarded as a serious challenger to Brazil, were being surprisingly held by Spain at São Paulo in a game marred by some fierce and ugly tackling.

Despite taking the lead through outside-right Ghiggia after half an hour, Uruguay found themselves trailing ten minutes later when Basora scored two quick goals for Spain.

Uruguay did not have the freedom they were given by Bolivia and the solid defence of the Spaniards kept Uruguay at bay until the 73rd minute when their captain, Obdulio Varela, pushed forward from his wing-half role to hammer home the equalizer.

Whilst Brazil were outstanding at Río, Uruguay were disappointing in São Paulo and the odds on Brazil winning the Jules Rimet Cup for the first time shortened even further.

Spain: Ramallets; Alonzo, Parra, J.Gonzalvo, M.Gonzalvo, Puchades, Basora, Igoa, Zarra, Molowny, Gaínza.
Scorer: Basora 2
Uruguay: Máspoli; M.Gonzáles, Tejera, J-C.Gonzáles, Varela, Andrade, Ghiggia, Pérez, Míguez, Schiaffino, Vidal.
Scorers: Ghiggia, Varela
Referee: George Reader (England)

BRAZIL 6   SPAIN 1 *(Half-time 3-0)*

Maracana Stadium, Río de Janeiro, 13 July
Attendance: 152,772

BRAZIL returned to the Maracana Stadium four days after their resounding win over Sweden, and again they treated the large crowd to a magnificent display of attacking football. This time Spain were on the receiving end of the wonderful skills of the Brazilians which produced another big scoreline.

Because of his reputation, and the fact that he had already scored seven goals, the Spaniards marked Ademir with two men but he still managed to increase his tally by two.

After half an hour, Brazil were three up with Ademir, Jair, and Chico getting the goals. Chico scored a second after 55 minutes and then Ademir scored his ninth goal of the tournament to make it 5-0. Brazil certainly did not need any help from the Spanish defence to score goals — but they got it.

Zizinho made it 6-0 in the 67th minute and with 20 minutes remaining they eased off and saved themselves for their last match. During this period, Spain pulled back a consolation goal through Igoa.

With 13 goals in the last two games, how could anyone bet against Brazil winning the 1950 World Cup?

Brazil: Barbosa; Augusto, Juvenal, Bauer, Danilo, Bigode, Friaça, Zizinho, Ademir, Jair, Chico.
Scorers: Ademir 2, Chico 2, Zizinho, Jair
Spain: Ramallets; Alonzo, Parra, J.Gonzalvo, M.Gonzalvo, Puchades, Basora, Igoa, Zarra, Panizo, Gaínza.
Scorer: Igoa
Referee: Reg Leafe (England)

Nacka Skogland of Sweden.

URUGUAY 3   SWEDEN 2 (Half-time 1-2)

Pacaembu Stadium, São Paulo, 13 July
Attendance 7,987

AFTER their disappointing performance against Spain, Uruguay made two changes to their defence for their second match. In came a new goalkeeper, Anibal Paz, and at wing-half Juan-Carlos González was replaced by Schubert Gambetta.

Despite the changes, Uruguay still struggled to beat a Swedish side that was truly destroyed by Brazil. For 71 minutes they trailed the Swedish amateurs.

Palmer put Sweden in front after only five minutes before Ghiggia equalized in the 39th minute. However, their joy was short-lived because, a minute later, Sundqvist put Sweden back in front. The Swedes held on to their lead until the 77th minute, when Míguez struck with the first of two quick goals, the winner coming five minutes from time.

Uruguay held on to their narrow win and were now the only team capable of topping Brazil and the final match of the pool turned out to be the equivalent of the World Cup Final.

Uruguay: Paz; M.Gonzáles, Tejera, Gambetta, Varela, Andrade, Ghiggia, Pérez, Míguez, Schiaffino, Vidal.
Scorers: Míguez 2, Ghiggia
Sweden: Svensson; Samuelsson, E.Nilsson, Andersson, Johansson, Gärd, Jönsson, Palmer, Mellberg, Skoglund, Sundqvist.
Scorers: Palmer, Sundqvist
Referee: Giovanni Galeati (Italy)

SWEDEN 3   SPAIN 1 (Half-time 2-0)

Pacaembu Stadium, São Paulo, 16 July
Attendance: 11,227

AFTER their disappointing opening game against Brazil, Sweden had shown their true capabilities against Uruguay, despite narrowly losing. They wound up their programme with this fine win over Spain to clinch third place.

Sundqvist and Mellberg gave Sweden a first-half lead and ten minutes from time, Palmer confirmed himself as one of Europe's top strikers when he made it 3-0. Spain pulled one back two minutes later through Zarra, but it was all academic. The small crowd were not interested, all that captured their imagination was the outcome of the Brazil-Uruguay match at the Maracana.

Sune Andersson, Knut Nordahl and Erik Nilsson added their World Cup bronze medals to the Olympic gold they won at Wembley two years earlier. Stellan Nilsson also completed the same 'double' although he did not play in this match.

Sweden: Svensson; Samuelsson, E.Nilsson, Andersson, Johansson, Gärd, Jönsson, Mellberg, Rydell, Palmer, Sundqvist.
Scorers: Sundqvist, Mellberg, Palmer
Spain: Eizaguirre; Asensi, Parra, Alonzo, Silva, Puchades, Basora, Hernández, Zarra, Panizo, Juncosa.
Scorer: Zarra
Referee: Karel Van Der Meer (Holland)

Ademir of Brazil.

URUGUAY 2   BRAZIL 1 (Half-time 0-0)

Maracana Stadium, Río de Janeiro, 16 July
Attendance: 199,854

A WORLD record crowd greeted the teams and, despite efforts to restrict the capacity to 150,000, the official attendance was just short of 200,000, although the actual paying attendance

The magnificent Maracana Stadium in Río de Janeiro, where a world-record attendance of some 200,000 greeted the teams.

was 172,772. There were very few in the overcrowded stadium who expected anything but a Brazilian success. Even the many Uruguayan fans present must have given their team little chance.

Brazil came to what was effectively the World Cup Final having scored 13 goals in their two final pool matches. Uruguay had scored a mere five against the same opposition and had struggled on both occasions. Brazil were 1/10 on favourites to win and stood to collect mammoth bonuses of around £10,000 if they lifted the trophy.

The Brazilian players, officials and fans were confident. But perhaps over-confidence crept in, just as it had done with the England team embarrassingly beaten by the United States.

Needing only a draw to win the trophy, Brazil could not resist the temptation to attack. Their forwards had been majestic throughout the tournament and they thought they would rely upon attack as their best form of defence in the final game. But the Uruguayans defended solidly and kept Ademir and company at bay.

After a goalless first half, Ademir slipped the ball to Friaça, who put the hosts in front two minutes into the second half. Then came a tactical error. Coach Flavio Costa gave instructions for Jair to drop back into defence. The instructions never reached him. But, if Brazil had a captain other than one in name only, he would have insisted that Jair, or another forward, aided the defence. Being one goal in front and only needing a draw, Brazil were in a strong position — but they continued to attack. Uruguay's 34-year-old captain, Obdulio Varela, was an inspiration to his team and kept driving them forward.

Right winger Ghiggia was a dangerman and the Brazilian left-half, Bigode, gave him too much room in the second half. After one such lapse, the winger gathered a pass from his skipper Varela, beat his man and crossed for Schiaffino to head home the equalizer after 66 minutes.

Top: Five Brazilian stars (top to bottom): Alfredo, Noronha, Baltazar, Rui and Bauer. *Below:* Zizinho, another Brazilian soccer hero.

Opposite page: Friaça puts Brazil ahead two minutes into the second half.

Despite allowing Uruguay to level the scores, Brazil still attacked but their efforts failed to produce any more goals. By now, Uruguay were attacking more and more and wing-half Victor Andrade, whose uncle José was in the 1930 winning team, set up many attacking moves.

With 11 minutes remaining, Ghiggia got round Bigode once more and this time, when the defence was expecting another centre, he ran for the goal and slotted the ball in between the near post and goalkeeper Barbosa.

Little more than ten minutes later, English referee George Reader blew the final whistle. The improbable and 'impossible' had happened. Brazil had lost and Uruguay joined Italy as two-times winners of the World Cup.

The Brazilian fans openly wept in the Maracana and in the streets of Río. Despite their anguish, the Brazilian fans inside the giant stadium nevertheless found time to warmly applaude the victors as they paraded the trophy.

It brought an end to a three-week Brazilian carnival. The final result may not have been what the home fans wanted, but it signalled the rebirth of the World Cup after a 12-year absence.

Opposite page (top): Schiaffino's equalizer enters the net as Friaça, scorer of the first goal, watches helplessly. *Opposite page (bottom):* Ghiggia (hidden by the post) turns away after scoring the winner with Barbosa lying out of his goal.

Jair of Brazil.

Uruguay's Máspoli dives to save as Gonzáles covers. The other players are Brazil's Ademir (centre) and Gambetta of Uruguay.

Máspoli is under pressure from Brazil but it does not matter, for English referee George Reader (far right) signals the end of the game.

Final Pool – Final Table

	P	W	D	L	F	A	Pts
Uruguay	3	2	1	0	7	5	5
Brazil	3	2	0	1	14	4	4
Sweden	3	1	0	2	6	11	2
Spain	3	0	1	2	4	11	1

Uruguay: Roque Gaston Máspoli; Matías Gonzáles, Eusébio Tejera, Schubert Gambetta, Obdulio Jacinto Varela, Victor Rodríguez Andrade, Alcides Edgardo Ghiggia, Julio Pérez, Omar Oscar Míguez, Juan Alberto Schiaffino, Rubén Morán.
Scorers: Schiaffino, Ghiggia
Brazil: Moacir Barbosa; Augusto de Costa, Amanso Juvenal, José Carlos Bauer, Danilo Alvim, João Ferreira Bigode, Albino Cardosa Friaça, Tomas Soares da Silva 'Zizinho', Ademir Marques de Menezes, Jair Rosa Pinto, Francisco Arambura 'Chico'.
Scorer: Friaça
Referee: George Reader (England)

Top: The stunned Brazilian crowd at the end of the 1950 World Cup Final. *Below:* Uruguay skipper Obdulio Varela collects the trophy.

Opposite page (top): The victorious Uruguayan team. Back row (left to right, players only): Varela, Tejera, Gambetta, Gonzáles, Máspoli, Andrade. Front row: Ghiggia, Pérez, Míguez, Schiaffino, Morán. *Opposite page (bottom):* Brazil back row (left to right): Barbosa, Augusto, Juvenal, Bauer, Danilo, Bigode. Front row: Johnson (masseur), Friaça, Zizinho, Ademir, Jair, Chico, Americo (masseur).

STATISTICS

Goalscorers:
9 — Ademir Marques de Menezes (Brazil).
5 — Juan Schiaffino (Uruguay), Estanislao Basora (Spain).
4 — Chico (Brazil), Telmo Zarra (Spain), Omar Míguez, Alcides Ghiggia (both Uruguay).
3 — Costa Tomasević (Yugoslavia), Karl-Erik Palmer, Stig Sundqvist (both Sweden), Atilio Cremaschi (Chile).
2 — Baltazar, Jair Rosa Pinto, Zizinho (all Brazil), Zeliko Ciakowski (Yugoslavia), Hans Jepsson, Sune Andersson (both Sweden), Riccardo Carapellese (Italy), Jacques Fatton (Switzerland), Horacio Casarin (Mexico).
1 — Alfredo, Maneca, Albino Friaça (all Brazil), Tihomir Ognjanov, Stjepan Bobek (both Yugoslavia), Bror Mellberg (Sweden), Ermes Muccinelli, Egisto Pandolfini (both Italy), Ernesto José Vidal, Obdulio Jacinto Varela (both Uruguay), John Souza, Joseph Gaetjens, Gino Pariani, Ed Souza (all United States), Atilio López, Cesar López Fretes (both Paraguay), George Robledo, Andres Prieto (both Chile), Rene Bader, Charles Antenen (both Switzerland), Stan Mortensen, Wilf Mannion (both England), Silvestre Igoa (Spain).

Own-goals:
None

Hat-tricks
Ademir Marques de Menezes (4 goals, Brazil v Sweden). Juan Schiaffino (4 goals, Uruguay v Bolivia). Atilio Cremaschi (Chile v United States).

Fastest goal
2 minutes — Alfredo Ramos dos Santos (Brazil v Switzerland)

Most goals (team)
22 — Brazil

Teams failing to score
Bolivia

Total goals scored: 88
Average per game: 4.00

Penalties
Scored: Horacio Casarin (Mexico v Yugoslavia) *Referee: Reg Leafe (England)*, Ed Souza (United States v Chile) *Referee: Mario Gardelli (Brazil)*, Sune Andersson (Sweden v Brazil) *Referee: Arthur Ellis (England)*.

Most appearances
6 — Ademir Marques de Menezes, Augusto Da Costa, Moacir Barbosa, Amanso Juvenal (all Brazil), Gabriel Aristiaguirre Alonso, Estanislao Basora, Antonio Puchades, Telmo Zarraonandia Zarra (all Spain).

Sendings-off
None

Most players used
18 — Italy and Spain

Number of players used by Finalists
17 — Brazil
14 — Uruguay

MEN WHO MADE THE HEADLINES - 1954

Fritz Walter
(West Germany)

FRITZ Walter's international career was shortened by Germany's absence from the scene from 1942 to 1950, but he returned to captain them to World Cup triumph in 1954. Born at Kaiserlautern in October 1920, it was with his home-town team that Walter, a wartime paratrooper, spent his 20-year first-class career, winning Championship medals in 1951 and 1953. He made his international debut against Romania in 1940, scoring a hat-trick in a 9-2 win and altogether won 61 caps, scored 31 goals and was an outstanding skipper. A skilful inside-left with a powerful shot, Walter was partnered in the German forward line by his brother, Ottmar. When they collected World Cup-winners' medals it was the first such family double. Fritz made the first goal in the Final against Hungary and also set up Rahn's winner. Manager Sepp Herberger brought him out of semi-retirement for the 1958 World Cup finals, after 16 months out of the national team, and he played in five of Germany's six matches. Badly injured in the semi-final against Sweden, he missed the third-place match against France. After retiring he turned down lucrative coaching offers and went into business.

Sandor Kocsis
(Hungary)

TOP scorer in the 1954 World Cup with 11 goals, Sandor Kocsis, was a superb header of the ball and known as 'The Man With the Golden Head'. In 68 internationals he scored 75 goals, including a record seven hat-tricks. Born in Budapest in September 1929, he began with KTC before moving to Ferencváros and at 19 helped them win the 1949 Hungarian title. After Ferencváros were amalgamated into the new Honvéd team, he established a great partnership with Ferenc Puskás at both club and international level. Kocsis made his international debut in 1949 and in the early 1950s was the Hungarian League's top scorer three times. A key member of the Hungarian side that remained unbeaten from the start of the decade, he was in the team that beat England 6-3 at Wembley in 1953. He scored two extra-time goals in the World Cup 1954 semi-final against Uruguay but could not add to his 1952 Olympic gold medal. In 1956, Honvéd were playing in Spain during the Hungarian uprising and Kocsis, Puskás and others decided not to return home. Kocsis became player-coach of Young Boys Berne, then joined Barcelona in 1957 and scored in their defeat by Benfica in the 1961 European Cup Final. He retired in 1966, at the age of 37, and died in 1980.

Ernst Ocwirk
(Austria)

ERNST Ocwirk was the backbone of the great Austrian team of the 1950s, an attacking wing-half with outstanding ball-control who was famed for his accurate passing. His captaincy skills were twice recognized at the highest level when he skippered Rest of Europe sides against the FA in 1953 and against the Irish FA in 1955. Born in Vienna on 10 March 1926, Ocwirk began with Stadlau before moving to Florisdorfer during the war. He made his international debut in 1947, the year he was transferred to FK Austria. He was a member of the Austrian team in the 1948 Olympics and altogether won 62 caps. Ocwirk was at his inspirational best in the 1954 World Cup, guiding Austria to their best-ever finish of third place. After nine years at FK, he signed for Sampdoria and stayed in Italy for five years before a 12-month spell back at FK Austria. Then it was back to Sampdoria as mananger in 1962. He returned to manage FK in 1965 and during five years with his old club, guided them to two League Championships and a Cup Final success. He later managed Cologne and Admira of Vienna.

Back to Europe
Switzerland 1954

SWITZERLAND was the obvious choice of venue for the fifth World Cup. FIFA's headquarters were in Zurich and 1954 marked the 50th anniversary of its formation. The Swiss had been granted the tournament at FIFA's first post-war Congress in 1946 and they had spent eight years building new stadiums for the great occasion.

They did not quite live up to their promise and were not really up to the organizational requirements of such a tournament. Nevertheless, the competition proved to be a financial success, despite the fact that most stadiums had small capacities. Germany — now playing as West Germany — enjoyed a great run to the Final and this contributed towards the overall success of the competition.

The tournament received limited television coverage for the first time and the Swiss showed a piece of marketing know-how by having special commemorative coins minted.

FIFA had a new president, Rodolphe Seeldrayers of Belgium, and once more the governing body found it necessary to change the format, reverting to a pool and knock-out system. But this time the 16 qualifying nations were divided into four groups, with two teams in each group seeded. However, the two seeds did not play each other. They met only the non-seeded teams. At the end of the pool matches, the four winners played off on a knock-out basis to find one finalist while the four runners-up did the same. It became apparent, therefore, that the top two in one pool stood every chance of meeting each other in the World Cup Final. And that is what happened.

The seedings took on an unexpected and farcical air when Spain were eliminated in the preliminary competition by Turkey. The seedings had been announced before the 16 finalists were known. Spain had been seeded, whereas West Germany had not. When the pools for Switzerland were decided, Germany and Turkey were in the same group. But, because they had beaten Spain in the qualifiers, Turkey became the second seeds after Hungary.

The four pools were made up as follows:

Pool One: Brazil, France, Mexico, Yugoslavia.
Pool Two: Hungary, Turkey, South Korea, West Germany.
Pool Three: Austria, Czechoslovakia, Scotland, Uruguay.
Pool Four: Belgium, England, Italy, Switzerland.
(The first two named were the seeded teams).

Absurdly, it was necessary to play extra-time if the scores were level at the end of 90 minutes of the pool matches. Goal-difference separated the first and second teams in each pool but, if the second and third teams were level on points, there had to be a play-off match.

Brazil, who had been involved in the World Cup's most violent match against Czechoslovakia in 1938, were involved in yet another disgraceful match. This time it was against Hungary in what was dubbed 'The Battle of Berne'. English referee Arthur Ellis had to send off three players. There were further ugly scenes when the Brazilian referee, Mario Viani, was chased off the field by irate Italian players after they had lost to Switzerland. The fifth World Cup certainly produced some unsavoury moments.

On the positive side, goals were plentiful. There were 140 in 26 matches. Hungary scored a staggering 27 from five games, including 17 in their two group matches. Germany were only two behind, although they played one more game. For sheer excitement, the Austria-Switzerland match provided a World Cup record 12 goals. Austria beat the hosts by the remarkable scoreline of 7-5.

Hungary had established themselves as firm favourites but, as we saw in 1950, favourites do not always win the World Cup, and this tournament was no exception. West Germany ran out winners — the first time an unseeded team had lifted the trophy since seeding was introduced.

Forty-one teams originally entered. The European nations were back in the competition after the many withdrawals in 1950 and Uruguay were competing on European soil for the first time. But it was Hungary who went to Switzerland as the hottest-ever favourites to win the World Cup.

Jules Rimet addressing the crowd at the Wankdorf Stadium in Berne, scene of the 1954 World Cup Final.

1954 Qualifying Competition

FORTY-ONE nations had entered by the closing date of 31 January 1953. However, before the draw for the qualifying matches was made, Vietnam, Peru and India had all withdrawn. Poland and China later withdrew and Poland's absence meant that hot favourites Hungary progressed to the final stages without qualifying, as did hosts Switzerland and the defending world champions, Uruguay, who were competing in Europe for the first time.

In Britain, the Home International Championship was to serve as a qualifying group, as it had in 1950. It was the only one of the 13 groups where two teams, rather than one, qualified for the Finals. England won the group and Scotland were runners-up. However, unlike their decision in 1950, the Scots decided to make the trip, although they did so on a shoe-string budget, taking only 13 players, including two goalkeepers. Their results reflected this decision.

The biggest World Cup shock since England's defeat by the United States was in Group 6. Spain had already been seeded for the Finals, but were eliminated by the totally unfancied Turks. After each country had won one game, the play-off in Rome resulted in a 2-2 draw and Spain went out after lots were drawn.

Sweden, who had established themselves in the previous two World Cups, had their team plans shattered by the Italian clubs who poached the Swedes' best players. Sweden thus failed to qualify for the final stages in 1954.

The 57 qualifying matches produced 209 goals and France hammered 20 of those in four matches against the Republic of Ireland and Luxembourg, whilst Mexico scored 19 times. The biggest win of the qualifying competition was Austria's 9-1 hammering of Portugal. By contrast, Group 10 produced only seven goals from its six matches, Greece's 2-0 win over Israel being the highest individual score of the group. That, of course, was no indication of what was to come in Switzerland in the summer of 1954.

Results

Group One

24 Jun 1953 *Oslo*	Norway...........2 Saar................3
19 Aug 1953 *Oslo*	Norway...........1 West Germany...1
11 Oct 1953 *Stuttgart*	West Germany...3 Saar................0
8 Nov 1953 *Saarbrücken*	Saar................0 Norway...........0
22 Nov 1953 *Hamburg*	West Germany...5 Norway...........1
28 Mar 1954 *Saarbrücken*	Saar................1 West Germany...3

Final Table

	P	W	D	L	F	A	Pts	
W.Germany	4	3	1	0	12	3	7	**West Germany**
Saar	4	1	1	2	4	8	3	**qualified**
Norway	4	0	2	2	4	9	2	

Group Two

25 May 1953 *Helsinki*	Finland..........2 Belgium..........4
28 May 1953 *Stockholm*	Sweden...........2 Belgium..........3
5 Aug 1953 *Helsinki*	Finland..........3 Sweden...........3
16 Aug 1953 *Stockholm*	Sweden...........4 Finland..........0
23 Sep 1953 *Brussels*	Belgium..........2 Finland..........2
8 Oct 1953 *Brussels*	Belgium..........2 Sweden...........0

Final Table

	P	W	D	L	F	A	Pts	
Belgium	4	3	1	0	11	6	7	**Belgium qualified**
Sweden	4	1	1	2	9	8	3	
Finland	4	0	2	2	7	13	2	

Group Three

3 Oct 1953 *Belfast*	N. Ireland........1 Scotland..........3
10 Oct 1953 *Cardiff*	Wales.............1 England..........4
4 Nov 1953 *Glasgow*	Scotland.........3 Wales.............3
11 Nov 1953 *Liverpool*	England..........3 N. Ireland.......1
31 Mar 1954 *Wrexham*	Wales.............1 N. Ireland.......2
3 Apr 1954 *Glasgow*	Scotland.........2 England..........4

Final Table

	P	W	D	L	F	A	Pts	
England	3	3	0	0	11	4	6	**England and**
Scotland	3	1	1	1	8	8	3	**Scotland qualified**
N. Ireland	3	1	0	2	4	7	2	
Wales	3	0	1	2	5	9	1	

Group Four

20 Sep 1953 *Luxembourg*	Luxembourg.....1 France...........6
4 Oct 1953 *Dublin*	Rep of Ireland...3 France...........5
28 Oct 1953 *Dublin*	Rep of Ireland...4 Luxembourg.....0
25 Nov 1953 *Paris*	France...........1 Rep of Ireland...0
17 Dec 1953 *Paris*	France...........8 Luxembourg.....0
7 Mar 1954 *Luxembourg*	Luxembourg.....0 Rep of Ireland...1

Final Table

	P	W	D	L	F	A	Pts	
France	4	4	0	0	20	4	8	**France qualified**
Rep of Ireland	4	2	0	2	8	6	4	
Luxembourg	4	0	0	4	1	19	0	

Group Five

| 27 Sep 1953 *Vienna* | Austria...........9 Portugal..........1 |
| 29 Nov 1953 *Lisbon* | Portugal..........0 Austria...........0 |

Austria qualified

Group Six

| 6 Jan 1954 *Madrid* | Spain.............4 Turkey...........1 |
| 14 Mar 1954 *Istanbul* | Turkey...........1 Spain.............0 |

Play-off

| 17 Mar 1954 *Rome* | Turkey...........2 Spain.............2 |

Turkey qualified after drawing lots

Group Seven

Hungary qualified (Poland withdrew)

Group Eight

14 Jun 1953 *Prague*	Czechoslovakia..2 Romania.........0
28 Jun 1953 *Bucharest*	Romania.........3 Bulgaria..........1
6 Sep 1953 *Sofia*	Bulgaria..........1 Czechoslovakia..2
11 Oct 1953 *Sofia*	Bulgaria..........1 Romania.........2
25 Oct 1953 *Bucharest*	Romania.........0 Czechoslovakia..1
8 Nov 1953 *Prague*	Czechoslovakia..0 Bulgaria..........0

Final Table

	P	W	D	L	F	A	Pts	
Czechoslovakia	4	3	1	0	5	1	7	**Czechoslovakia**
Romania	4	2	0	2	5	5	4	**qualified**
Bulgaria	4	0	1	3	3	7	1	

Group Nine

| 13 Nov 1953 *Cairo* | Egypt ....1 Italy ....2 |
| 24 Jan 1954 *Milan* | Italy ....5 Egypt ....1 |

Italy qualified

Group Ten

9 May 1953 *Belgrade*	Yugoslavia ....1 Greece 0
1 Nov 1953 *Athens*	Greece ....1 Israel..............0
8 Nov 1953 *Skopje*	Yugoslavia ....1 Israel..............0
8 Mar 1954 *Tel Aviv*	Israel..............0 Greece 2
21 Mar 1954 *Tel Aviv*	Israel..............0 Yugoslavia 1
28 Mar 1954 *Athens*	Greece ....0 Yugoslavia 1

	P	W	D	L	F	A	Pts	
Yugoslavia	4	4	0	0	4	0	8	**Yugoslavia**
Greece	4	2	0	2	3	2	4	**qualified**
Israel	4	0	0	4	0	5	0	

Group Eleven

19 Jul 1953 *Mexico City*	Mexico............8 Haiti 0
27 Dec 1953 *Port au Prince*	Haiti ....0 Mexico............4
10 Jan 1954 *Mexico City*	United States ....0 Mexico............4
14 Jan 1954 *Mexico City*	Mexico............3 United States 1
3 Apr 1954 *Port au Prince*	Haiti ....2 United States 3
4 Apr 1954 *Port au Prince*	United States ....3 Haiti 0

	P	W	D	L	F	A	Pts	
Mexico	4	4	0	0	19	1	8	**Mexico qualified**
United States	4	2	0	2	7	9	4	
Haiti	4	0	0	4	2	18	0	

Group Twelve

14 Feb 1954 *Asunción*	Paraguay ....4 Chile..............0
21 Feb 1954 *Santiago*	Chile..............1 Paraguay 3
28 Feb 1954 *Santiago*	Chile..............0 Brazil 2
7 Mar 1954 *Asunción*	Paraguay ....0 Brazil 1
14 Mar 1954 *Río de Janeiro*	Brazil ....1 Chile..............0
21 Mar 1954 *Río de Janeiro*	Brazil ....4 Paraguay 1

	P	W	D	L	F	A	Pts	
Brazil	4	4	0	0	8	1	8	**Brazil qualified**
Paraguay	4	2	0	2	8	6	4	
Chile	4	0	0	4	1	10	0	

Group Thirteen

| 7 May 1954 *Tōkyō* | Japan ....1 South Korea .....5 |
| 14 Mar 1954 *Tōkyō* | South Korea .....2 Japan ....2 |

South Korea qualified (China withdrew)

The Home International Championship served as the United Kingdom's qualifying group. *Left:* England's Nat Lofthouse gets a shot past Welsh defender Ray Daniel at Ninian Park, Cardiff.

Below: Northern Ireland's goalkeeper Billy Smyth fails to get to a shot from Harold Hassell (not in picture) and the ball rolls under his body to give England a first-minute lead at Goodison Park. The England player following up is Albert Quixall.

1954 Tournament

Pool One

Vladimir Beara of Yugoslavia, who trained as a ballet dancer before turning to soccer.

YUGOSLAVIA 1   FRANCE 0 (Half-time 1-0)
La Pontaise Stadium, Lausanne, 16 June
Attendance: 16,000

THE opening day of the tournament saw the first shock as France, one of the seeded teams, lost to Yugoslavia by a 15th-minute goal from their brilliant young outside-right, Milutinović. Ironically, Milutinović was later to become one of the stars of the Racing Club de Paris team.

Yugoslavia fielded ten of their side which won the silver medal at the Helsinki Olympics two years earlier and were an extremely underrated team. Their forward line, containing 1950 World Cup stalwarts Bobek, Mitić and Vukas, was one of the most feared in the tournament.

France, on the other hand, paraded some talented World Cup debutants like Raymond Kopa, Robert Jonquet and Jean Vincent, who were all to become household names in later years. But even they could not break through the Yugoslav defence, admirably marshalled by their captain Zlatko Ciakowski, who skippered the side in Brazil four years earlier.

Yugoslavia: Beara; Stanković, Crnković, Ciakowski, Horvat, Boskov, Milutinović, Mitić, Vukas, Bobek, Zebec.
Scorer: Milutinović
France: Remetter; Gianessi, Kaelbel, Penverne, Jonquet, Marcel, Kopa, Glovacki, Strappe, Dereuddre, Vincent.
Referee: Mervyn Griffiths (Wales)

BRAZIL 5   MEXICO 0 (Half-time 4-0)
Les Charmilles, Geneva, 16 June
Attendance: 12,500

BRAZIL certainly did justice to their seeding in the opening 45 minutes against Mexico, when they ran in four goals. The second half could have seen an avalanche but the Brazilians eased off, almost taking pity on their Central American opponents.

The Brazilian team had been subject to a rebuilding programme since the Finals four years earlier. The outstanding inside-forward trio of Zizinho, Ademir, and Jair had gone and only Francisco Rodrigues, Baltazar and Bauer remained from the 1950 squad. However, they had produced two outstanding full-backs in Djalma and Nilton Santos and the forward line contained a new sensation, Julinho. The new team boss was Zezé Moreira, who had replaced Flavio Costa.

Their first match in Switzerland was a one-sided affair. Baltazar opened the scoring in the 23rd minute and before half-time Didí and Pinga (2) had added to the scoreline. Julinho netted a fifth goal in the 60th minute.

Brazil: Castilho; D.Santos, N.Santos, Brandaozinho, Pinheiro, Bauer, Julinho, Didí, Baltazar, Pinga, Rodrigues.
Scorers: Pinga 2, Baltazar, Didí, Julinho
Mexico: Mota; López, Gomez, Cardenas, Romo, Avalos, Torres, Naranjo, Lamadrid, Balcazar, Arellano.
Referee: Raymon Wyssling (Switzerland)

Raymond Kopa of France, who was making his debut in the World Cup finals.

BRAZIL 1   YUGOSLAVIA 1 (a.e.t.) (Half-time 0-0; 90 mins 1-1)
La Pontaise Stadium, Lausanne, 19 June
Attendance: 21,000

THIS was by far the most entertaining match of the group, between two extremely talented teams, and the scoreline was a fair reflection of a very even match.

The first half was goalless but Branko Zebec, moved from the left wing to the centre-forward role, put the Europeans in front three minutes after the interval. Didí, Brazil's clever inside-forward, equalized with 20 minutes to go and the scores remained level at the end of 90 minutes, despite Brazil twice hitting the woodwork and Yugoslavia creating their fair share of chances.

The rules of the competition demanded a further 30 minutes but defences dominated proceedings and no further goals resulted in an extra-time period played at a casual pace because, if the game ended 1-1, then both sides were assured of getting through to the next phase.

Despite being held to a draw Brazil, who started as one of the favourites, were still regarded as potential champions, even taking into account Hungary's short odds. The new-look Brazilian team with its overlapping full-backs, and with Didí dominant up front, looked impressive.

Brazil's Brandaozinho (number 4) in an aerial battle with Vukas of Yugoslavia. Looking on (nearest to camera) are Nilton Santos, Boskov and Pinheiro.

Beara blocks a shot from Brazil's Pinga.

Brazil: Castilho; D.Santos, N.Santos, Brandaozinho, Pinheiro, Bauer, Julinho, Didí, Baltazar, Pinga, Rodriguez.
Scorer: Didí
Yugoslavia: Beara; Stanković, Crnković, Ciakowski, Horvat, Boskov, Milutinović, Mitić, Zebec, Vukas, Dvornić.
Scorer: Zebec
Referee: Edward Faultless (Scotland)

FRANCE 3   MEXICO 2 (Half-time 1-0)

Les Charmilles, Geneva, 19 June
Attendance: 19,000

THE remaining match in Pool One was academic. All that remained to be established were

Pool One – Final Table

	P	W	D	L	F	A	Pts
Brazil	2	1	1	0	6	1	3
Yugoslavia	2	1	1	0	2	1	3
France	2	1	0	1	3	3	2
Mexico	2	0	0	2	2	8	0

the occupants of fourth place in the group and that distinction fell to the Mexicans, after France clinched victory with a last-gasp disputed penalty.

Vincent scored the only goal of the first half and four minutes into the second period Cardenas put through his own goal to give France a 2-0 lead. They seemed to be coasting to an easy win until captain Naranjo pulled one back for the Mexicans in the 54th minute. Balcazar equalized with five minutes to go, but their joy was short-lived because Kopa converted the penalty two minutes from time.

For both sides it was an exit from the fifth World Cup. It was Mexico's third appearance in the Finals and they still had not won a match.

France: Remetter; Gianessi, Marche, Marcel, Kaelbel, Mahjoub, Kopa, Dereuddre, Strappe, Ben Tifour, Vincent.
Scorers: Vincent, Cardenas (og), Kopa (pen)
Mexico: Carbajal; López, Romo, Cardenas, Avalos, Martínez, Torres, Naranjo, Lamadrid, Balcazar, Arellano.
Scorers: Naranjo, Balcazar
Referee: Manuel Asensi (Spain)

Mexico's goalkeeper Carbajal fails to stop France taking the lead through Jean Vincent.

Hungary's spectacular goalkeeper, Gyula Grosics.

Pool Two

HUNGARY 9   SOUTH KOREA 0 (Half-time 4-0)

Sportzplatz Hardturm, Zurich, 17 June
Attendance: 13,000

THE hot favourites gave their rivals plenty to think about after scoring nine goals in their opening match against the World Cup debutants, South Korea.

While the Koreans played with a great deal of enthusiasm, their skill was no match for the Magyars, who were skippered by one of the all-time greats of international soccer, Ferenc Puskás, better known as 'The Galloping Major'.

The Hungarians went to Switzerland with the enviable record of not losing an international since May 1950. They won the 1952 Olympic title and in November 1953 became the first Continental side to beat England on home soil when they won 6-3 at Wembley. After that memorable day, the names of Puskás, Hidegkuti, Grosics, Bozsik, Kocsis and Czibor became household names, unlike those of their first opponents in Switzerland, who gave us such wonderfully named players as Jae-sung Park, Young-kweng Chu and Nam-sick Chung.

Shortly before the start of the World Cup, Hungary gave England the chance of revenge in Budapest but there was even greater embarrassment for the English — Hungary won 7-1. Little wonder they were such odds-on favourites to win the Jules Rimet Cup.

The unfortunate Koreans were the first to feel the might of the Magyars and in the first half, Puskás, full-back Lantos and Kocsis (2) had put the favourites into a commanding position. Kocsis completed his hat-trick in the 50th minute. Ten minutes later, Czibor made it 6-0 before the Hungarians eased off. However, three more goals in the final 15 minutes, from Palotas (2) and a last-minute goal from Puskás, completed the rout as Hungary established a new record score in the final stages of the World Cup.

Hungary: Grosics; Buzánszky, Lantos, Bozsik, Lóránt, Szojka, Budai, Kocsis, Palotas, Puskás, Czibor.
Scorers: Kocsis 3, Puskás 2, Palotas 2, Czibor, Lantos
South Korea: Duk-yung Hong; Kyu-jong Park, Chang-gi Kang, Ji-sung Min, Jae-sung Park, Young-kweng Chu, Nam-sick Chung, Il-kap Park, Nak-woon Sung, Sang-gwoon Woo, Jung-mih Choi.
Referee: Raymond Vincenti (France)

WEST GERMANY 4   TURKEY 1 (Half-time 1-1)
Wankdorf Stadium, Berne, 17 June
Attendance: 28,000

GERMANY were back in the World Cup after failing to appear in 1950, because they were not members of FIFA at the time. But now their nation was divided and only West Germany competed. They were not one of the fancied teams, but what shocks they had in store as their clever coach, Sepp Herberger, guided them to the Final.

Turkey, not Germany, were the other seeds in this group but one would not have thought so, considering the way the Germans romped to an easy victory, despite being held at half-time.

The Turks took a lead as early as the second minute, through Suat, but 12 minutes later Hans Schäfer made it 1-1. The second half was a one-sided affair with the Germans playing at only half pace. Klodt made it 2-1 in the 52nd minute before one of the Walter brothers, Ottmar, added a third on the hour. Morlock completed the scoring nine minutes from time and Germany headed the group along with the favourites, Hungary. But the next game saw Herberger at his tactical best.

West Germany: Turek; Laband, Kohlmeyer, Eckel, Posipal, Mai, Klodt, Morlock, O.Walter, F.Walter, Schäfer.
Scorers: Schäfer, Klodt, Morlock, O.Walter
Turkey: Turgay; Ridvan, Basri, Mustafa, Çetin, Rober, Erol, Suat, Feridun, Burhan, Lefter.
Scorer: Suat
Referee: Jose Da Costa (Portugal)

Sandor Kocsis' hat-trick against South Korea saw him well on the way to 11 goals in the tournament.

Fritz Walter floats a free-kick over the Turkish wall, most of whom have their backs to the ball.

HUNGARY 8   WEST GERMANY 3 (Half-time 3-1)
St Jakob Stadium, Basle, 20 June
Attendance: 56,000

THIS was one of only three games of the 1954 World Cup to attract an attendance of over 50,000. The Basle fans wanted to see if the Magyars could produce another feast of goals. They were not disappointed as the Hungarians took their tally to 17 from two pool matches. But how Sepp Herberger lulled them into a false sense of security.

Having assessed the format of the competition, Herberger knew that if Germany lost to Hungary, they would engage in a play-off with either Turkey or Korea for the remaining place in the next phase. And, as runners-up, they would avoid a clash with the strong Brazilians and set up a quarter-final meeting with the weaker Yugoslavs instead. Herberger was confident of beating either Turkey or Korea with a full side and he engaged in one of the World Cup's great gambles.

He completely revamped his team for the match against Hungary, even recalling Helmut Rahn to international duty, although the player was on tour with his club in Uruguay at the time.

Only four Germans remained from the win over Turkey — full-back Kohlmeyer, wing-

József Bozsik of Hungary.

The Hungarian side that beat West Germany 8-3. From left to right: Puskás, Grosics, Lóránt, Hidegkuti, Bozsik, Lantos, Buzánszky, Zakariás, Toth, Czibor and Kocsis.

half Posipal, inside-forward Horst Eckel and captain Fritz Walter. Hungary made a couple of changes, but fielded a near-full strength side.

More than 30,000 Germans made the journey to Basle and were very disappointed when the German line-up was announced. The match was played amidst long periods of whistling from those fans, who showed their disgust at Herberger's decision. And for several days after the match he was a very unpopular man. But in the end they forgave him.

Hungary were as rampant as they were against the Koreans and opened the scoring through Kocsis in the third minute. Puskás added a second 15 minutes later and after 20 minutes, Kocsis scored his second to make it 3-0. Pfaff pulled one back for the Germans, but Hungary went into a 3-1 lead at the interval.

Hidegkuti, who missed the first game, scored twice within four minutes of the restart. Kocsis complete his second hat-trick of the tournament after 67 minutes and became the first person to score two hat-tricks in one World Cup. József Tóth made it 7-1 with 17 minutes to go, before Rahn scored a second German goal after 77 minutes. However, less than a minute later Kocsis netted his fourth goal of the game, before the 11 goals scoring spree ended nine minutes from the end when Herrmann made it 8-3.

Ottmar Walter (left), who did not play against the Hungarians, and Werner Liebrich. Walter returned for the play-off game against Turkey.

Ferenc Puskás is surrounded by German defenders as they try to contain the onslaught which produced eight goals for the Magyars.

Sepp Herberger was undeterred by the result, provided his team won the play-off match, which was to be against Turkey. Hungary swept the Germans aside and Herberger knew that, if the two sides should meet in the Final, then Hungary would certainly go into the match full of confidence. But next time, Herberger would field a very different team. His ploy in fielding a weakened team had served its purpose.

Hungary, however, were unlucky to lose their skipper Puskás, following a tackle from Liebrich, and the 'Galloping Major' was to miss his country's next two matches. Many felt the tackle eventually cost Hungary the title and won it for Germany.

Hungary: Grosics; Buzánszky, Lantos, Bozsik, Lóránt, Zakariás, J.Tóth, Kocsis, Hidegkuti, Puskás, Czibor.
Scorers: Kocsis 4, Hidegkuti 2, Puskás, J.Tóth
West Germany: Kwiatkowski; Bauer, Kohlmeyer, Posipal, Liebrich, Mebus, Rahn, Eckel, F.Walter, Pfaff, Herrmann.
Scorers: Pfaff, Rahn, Herrmann
Referee: Bill Ling (England)

TURKEY 7 SOUTH KOREA 0 (Half-time 4-0)
Les Charmilles, Geneva, 20 June
Attendance: 4,000

A crowd of only 4,000, the lowest of the tournament, turned out to watch two of the least fancied teams in the competition. For the Koreans it was a sad farewell as they conceded another seven goals on top of the nine the Hungarians put past them in their opening match.

Suat after ten minutes, Lefter (24 minutes), and Suat again (30 minutes) saw the Turks race into a 3-0 lead within half an hour. Inside-left Sargun Burhan scored the first of his three goals eight minutes before half-time and by the 70th minute he had completed his hat-trick as Turkey scored their sixth goal. Erol made it 7-0 after 76 minutes.

The South Koreans bid farewell to their first World Cup, whilst Turkey had to play-off against the Germans for the right to progress to the next stage.

Turkey: Turgay; Ridvan, Basri, Mustafa, Çetin, Rober, Erol, Suat, Necmi, Burhan, Lefter.
Scorers: Burhan 3, Suat 2, Lefter, Erol
South Korea: Duk-yung Hong; Kyu-jong Park, Gi-choo Lee, Chang-gi Kang, C-H Han, Ji-sung Kim, Soo-nam Lee, Jung-mih Choi, John-kap Lee, Sang-gwoon Woo, Nak-woon Sung.
Referee: Esteban Marino (Uruguay)

Play-off
WEST GERMANY 7 TURKEY 2 (Half-time 3-1)
Sportzplatz Hardturm, Zurich, 23 June
Attendance: 17,000

HERBERGER brought his established stars back for the play-off game and they duly beat the Turks with the ease that he had predicted when he fielded his below-par team against Hungary.

Ottmar Walter and Schäfer put the Germans two up after only 12 minutes and, despite a goal from Mustafa, the Turks were never a match for their much more organized opponents. Morlock scored a third goal after half an hour and the same player made it 4-1 right on the hour. Fritz Walter joined in the goalscoring two minutes later and then two goals in two minutes, from Morlock, completing his hat-trick, and Schäfer, made it 7-1. Lefter scored a consolation goal for Turkey in the 82 minute.

The gamble taken by Herberger against Hungary had paid off handsomely and Germany progressed to the quarter-finals and a meeting with Yugoslavia. Herberger was confident that a place in the semi-finals beckoned them.

West Germany: Turek; Laband, Bauer, Eckel, Posipal, Mai, Klodt, Morlock, O.Walter, F.Walter, Schäfer.
Scorers: Morlock 3, Schäfer 2, O.Walter, F.Walter
Turkey: Sükrü; Ridvan, Basri, Naci, Çetin, Rober, Erol, Mustafa, Necmi, Coskun, Lefter.
Scorers: Mustafa, Lefter
Referee: Raymond Vincent (France)

Pool Three

AUSTRIA 1 SCOTLAND 0 (Half-time 1-0)
Sportzplatz Hardturm, Zurich, 16 June
Attendance: 25,000

AFTER 24 years, Scotland eventually made their World Cup debut. Their first opponents were Austria, who were one of the top teams before the war but were no longer the world force they used to be. However, they were still good enough to be one of the seeded teams.

The Scotland squad was considerably depleted due to the fact that Rangers would not

Pool Two – Final Table

	P	W	D	L	F	A	Pts
Hungary	2	2	0	0	17	3	4
Turkey	2	1	0	1	8	4	2
W.Germany	2	1	0	1	7	9	2
South Korea	2	0	0	2	0	16	0

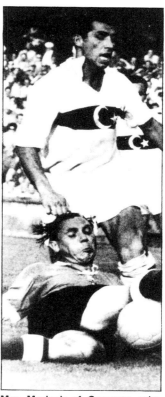

Max Morlock of Germany, who scored a hat-trick in the play-off, is grounded after a tackle by a Turkish defender.

Zoltan Czibor of Hungary.

Scotland's John McKenzie and Austria's Hanappi in action in Zurich.

release players, including captain George Young, for international duty. Scotland also missed the delicate skills of Lawrie Reilly who was absent through injury.

Despite these set-backs, the Scots fared well in the opening game but fell behind to a 33rd-minute goal from Erich Probst. Scotland made several raids on the Austrian goal but could not get past goalkeeper Schmied, who certainly had more to do than Martin in the Scottish goal. It took a magnificent late save to deny centre-forward Mochan and maintain Austria's narrow lead.

Austria: Schmied; Hanappi, Barschandt, Ocwirk, Happel, Koller, R.Körner, Schleger, Dienst, Probst, A.Körner.
Scorer: Probst
Scotland: Martin; Cunningham, Aird, Docherty, Davidson, Cowie, McKenzie, Fernie, Mochan, Brown, Ormond.
Referee: Laurent Franken (Belgium)

URUGUAY 2   CZECHOSLOVAKIA 0 (Half-time 0-0)

Wankdorf Stadium, Berne, 16 June
Attendance: 20,500

URUGUAY went into their ninth match in three World Cup tournaments with the record of never having lost. They were, of course, the holders and maintained their unbeaten record by winning 2-0 over a Czech side that offered less resistance than anticipated.

The South Americans were captained by Obdulio Varela, who led the side to their 1950 triumph. He was now in his 39th year and became the oldest man to appear in the final stages of the competition. Goalkeeper Máspoli, Andrade, Míguez and their lethal scorer, Schiaffino, all remained from the successful 1950 team as the Uruguayans played their first World Cup match on European soil. At the heart of their defence was José Santamaria, who was to earn fame in the great Real Madrid side in the 1950s.

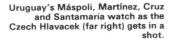

Uruguay's Máspoli, Martínez, Cruz and Santamaria watch as the Czech Hlavacek (far right) gets in a shot.

Uruguayan line-up that beat Czechoslovakia. From left to right (players only): Abbadíe, Andrade, Santamaria, Cruz, Míguez, Ambrois, Borges, Schiaffino, Martínez, Verela, Máspoli. All but skipper Verela and goalkeeper Máspoli are wearing tracksuit tops over their sky-blue shirts.

Opposite page: Uruguayan skipper Obdulio Varela (left) and Czech captain Ladislav Novak, pictured with a FIFA official before the start of their Pool Three game.

Ernst Ocwirk of Austria.

Czechoslovakia's team that lost 5-0 to Austria. Left to right: Krauss, Hlavacek, Hertl, Hemele, Kacany, Safranek, Pazicky, Trnka, Pluskal, Stacho and Novak.

Scotland's Tommy Docherty struggled to contain Uruguay's Schiaffino and the South American wingers ran Scotland ragged.

Oscar Míguez of Uruguay is foiled by Scottish goalkeeper Fred Martin, but the South Americans still managed seven goals.

Czechoslovakia did well to hold Uruguay for 70 minutes but then Míguez scored. Schiaffino added a second eight minutes from time and Uruguay had taken the first steps towards retaining the title.

Uruguay: Máspoli; Santamaria, Martínez, Andrade, Varela, Cruz, Abbadíe, Ambrois, Míguez, Schiaffino, Borges.
Scorers: Míguez, Schiaffino
Czechoslovakia: Reiman; Safranek, Novak, Trnka, Hledik, Hertl, Hlavacek, Hemele, Kacany, Pazicky, Kraus.
Referee: Arthur Ellis (England)

AUSTRIA 5   CZECHOSLOVAKIA 0 (Half-time 4-0)

Sportzplatz Hardturm, Zurich, 19 June
Attendance: 21,000

AFTER a quiet performance against Scotland, Austria showed against Czechoslovakia why they were one of the seeded teams and gave a polished performance with full-back Hanappi and captain Ernst Ocwirk supporting their forwards brilliantly.

Four first-half goals saw off the Czechs. Within the first four minutes Austria had netted twice, through Stojaspal and Probst, and the latter notched further goals in the 21st and 24th minutes to complete his hat-trick.

The only goal of the second half came from Stojaspal, his second of the game.

Austria: Schmied; Hanappi, Barschandt, Ocwirk, Happel, Koller, R.Körner, Wagner, Stojaspal, Probst, A.Körner.
Scorers: Probst 3, Stojaspal 2
Czechoslovakia: Stacho; Safranek, Novak, Trnka, Pluskal, Hertl, Hlavacek, Hemele, Kacany, Pazicky, Kraus.
Referee: Vasa Stefanović (Yugoslavia)

URUGUAY 7   SCOTLAND 0 (Half-time 2-0)

St Jakob Stadium, Basle, 19 June
Attendance: 34,000

SCOTLAND'S plight became even worse, even before they took to the field against the defending champions, when manager Andy Beattie quit. Disillusioned, he announced his decision after the Austria match. The morale of the Scottish players was low and it showed as their defence crumbled under the weight of the Uruguayan attacks. Their own attack, meanwhile, did little to dent the powerful Uruguay defence.

The game was played in scorching heat, which suited the South Americans, and within half an hour they had beaten 'keeper Martin twice with goals from Borges and Míguez.

The second half was a constant barrage of attacks and even talented wing-half Tommy Docherty was powerless against Schiaffino, the best inside-forward he reckoned he ever played against at international level.

Within 12 minutes of the start of the second half Borges, with two more goals, and Abbadíe had made it 5-0. The two wingers were far too strong for the Scottish defenders. In the closing minutes, Míguez and Abbadíe both netted their second goals to end Scotland's misery and put them out of their first World Cup.

Uruguay: Máspoli; Santamaria, Martínez, Andrade, Varela, Cruz, Abbadíe, Ambrois, Míguez, Schiaffino, Borges.
Scorers: Borges 3, Míguez 2, Abbadíe 2
Scotland: Martin; Cunningham, Aird, Docherty, Davidson, Cowie, McKenzie, Fernie, Mochan, Brown, Ormond.
Referee: Vincenzo Orlandini (Italy)

Pool Three – Final Table

	P	W	D	L	F	A	Pts
Uruguay	2	2	0	0	9	0	4
Austria	2	2	0	0	6	0	4
Czechoslovakia	2	0	0	2	0	7	0
Scotland	2	0	0	2	0	8	0

Schiaffino and Varela of Uruguay.

Above: **Scotland's John Aird (number 3) is beaten in the air by Uruguay's Luis Cruz.** *Left:* **Martin's outstretched leg fails to stop Carlos Borges scoring one of his hat-trick goals.**

Pool Four

ENGLAND 4   BELGIUM 4 (a.e.t.) (Half-time 2-1; 90 mins 3-3)

St Jakob Stadium, Basle, 17 June
Attendance: 14,000

ENGLAND threw away a glorious chance in their opening game of their second World Cup campaign when they let slip a 3-1 lead to allow Belgium to come back and force extra-time.

The England players must still have had their recent 7-1 hammering by the Hungarians

England's Sid Owen and Jimmy Dickinson (number 6) in a midfield battle with Léopold Anoul (10) and Henri Coppens of Belgium.

Ivor Broadis (not in picture) scores for England with Léopold Gerneay on the ground. Tommy Taylor is the England player on the left, Nat Lofthouse is falling nearer the goal.

on their minds and their defence was very shaky, as the scoreline suggests. Goalkeeper Gil Merrick, still smarting from conceding those seven Magyar goals, was far from his usual confident self. Fortunately for England, outside-right Stanley Matthews was in brilliant form.

Léopold Anoul put Belgium ahead after five minutes, but their lead was wiped out 20 minutes later when Ivor Broadis scored. Ten minutes before half-time, Nat Lofthouse put England in front and their lead was extended after 63 minutes when Broadis scored his second goal. With 20 minutes to go, England seemed to be heading for a comfortable win, but then Anoul scored his second in the 71st minute and 12 minutes from time Coppens made it 3-3.

Extra-time was needed, but it failed to separate the teams. England's fourth came from Lofthouse in the first minute of the extra period, when he finished off a fine move involving Broadis and Tommy Taylor. Despite England's dominance, Belgium drew level again when Jimmy Dickinson headed Dries' free-kick into his own net and thus ended what was an unhappy opening game for England.

England: Merrick; Staniforth, Byrne, Wright, Owen, Dickinson, Matthews, Broadis, Lofthouse, Taylor, Finney.
Scorers: Broadis 2, Lofthouse 2
Belgium: Gerneay; Dries, Van Brandt, Huysmans, Carré, Mees, Mermans, Houf, Coppens, Anoul, P.Van Den Bosch.
Scorers: Anoul 2, Coppens, Dickinson (og)
Referee: Emil Schmetzer (West Germany)

SWITZERLAND 2   ITALY 1 (Half-time 1-1)

La Pontaise Stadium, Lausanne, 17 June
Attendance: 40,500

THE hosts' debut was marred by some ugly tackling from both sides in a match which Brazilian referee Viana lost control of.

The Swiss were not innocent for their part and employed similar tactics to their Italian counterparts. Nobody gave the Swiss much chance of beating the former world champions — and, had they not retaliated, they probably would have been soundly beaten.

The Swiss surprisingly took the lead after 17 minutes when Ballaman beat Ghezzi. Boniperti equalized shortly before the half-time whistle, but the game was no longer the spectacle

Belgium's Marcel Dries robs Tom Finney as the England winger tries to get in a centre.

Swiss goalkeeper Eugene Parlier and his defenders hang on to preserve their slender lead over the Italians.

for which the large Lausanne crowd had hoped. Large periods of the game got out of hand and the referee seemed powerless to do anything about it.

The second half was much the same as the first and 12 minutes from the end, Josef Hügi, the Swiss centre-forward who had been switched to the wing after being injured, popped up to score the winning goal and put the unseeded hosts surprisingly at the top of Pool Four.

The Italian outside-left, Lorenzi, had been constantly querying the referee's decisions and when he had a goal ruled out because of an offside decision it caused further aggravation between the referee and the man nicknamed 'Poison'. Lorenzi was lucky to stay on the field. At the end of the match the referee was chased off the pitch by the Italian players.

Switzerland: Parlier; Neury, Kernen, Flückiger, Bocquet, Casali, Ballaman, Vonlanthen, Hügi, Meier, Fatton.
Scorers: Ballaman, Hügi
Italy: Ghezzi; Vincenzi, Giacomazzi, Neri, Tognon, Nesti, Muccinelli, Boniperti, Galli, Pandolfini, Lorenzi.
Scorer: Boniperti
Referee: Mario Viana (Brazil)

Giampiero Boniperti of Italy.

Ron Staniforth of England.

Parlier in action again, this time challenged by England's Tommy Taylor.

Taylor (number 10) and Dennis Wilshaw (15) are thwarted by Parlier once more.

This time Taylor finds Parlier and Neury in his way.

Wilshaw rounds off England's win with a 69th-minute goal to ensure progress to the quarter-finals.

ENGLAND 2   SWITZERLAND 0 (Half-time 1-0)

Wankdorf Stadium, Berne, 20 June
Attendance: 43,500

IN a dull game, England brought the Swiss harshly down to earth after their unexpected win over Italy.

England had to make changes. Centre-half Syd Owen was injured and so too was Stanley Matthews, the star of the game against Belgium until he pulled a muscle which ruled him out of England's second game. Captain Billy Wright was moved from right-half to centre-half and this was to be the position he played for the remainder of his international career.

Gil Merrick was retained in goal and this time he kept a clean sheet as England ran out 2-0 winners. The Swiss held England at bay until two minutes before the interval when Jimmy Mullen opened the scoring. His Wolves teammate, Dennis Wilshaw, rounded off the win with a second goal after 69 minutes.

England completed their programme in the knowledge that they had topped their group. Switzerland were still in the tournament and lived to fight another day.

England: Merrick; Staniforth, Byrne, McGarry, Wright, Dickinson, Finney, Broadis, Wilshaw, Taylor, Mullen.
Scorers: Mullen, Wilshaw
Switzerland: Parlier; Neury, Kernen, Eggimann, Bocquet, Bigler, Antenen, Vonlanthen, Meier, Ballaman, Fatton.
Referee: Istvan Zsolt (Hungary)

ITALY 4   BELGIUM 1 (Half-time 1-0)

Comunale di Cornaredo, Lugano, 20 June
Attendance: 24,000

THE only match at Lugano's Comunale Stadium did not reproduce any of the ugly football seen in Italy's opening match. In fact the crowd were treated to some skilful soccer from the Italian forwards who, once they had found the net, became a rampant force.

It took them 40 minutes to get their first goal when Pandolfini scored but, within 13 minutes of the start of the second half, they were 4-0 in front, thanks to goals from Galli, Frignani and Lorenzi. Anoul, the man who scored twice against England, netted again for Belgium, but all his 81st-minute goal did was to make the scoreline look a bit more respectable.

Italy had at last shown they could play good football but, before they advanced any further, they had to meet Switzerland again in a play-off.

Italy: Ghezzi; Magnini, Giacomazzi, Neri, Tognon, Nesti, Frignani, Cappello, Galli, Pandolfini, Lorenzi.
Scorers: Pandolfini, Galli, Frignani, Lorenzi
Belgium: Gerneay; Dries, Van Brandt, Huysmans, Carré, Mees, Mermans, H.Van Den Bosch, Coppens, Anoul, P.Van Den Bosch.
Scorer: Anoul
Referee: Erich Steiner (Austria)

Play-off
SWITZERLAND 4 ITALY 1 (Half-time 1-0)
St Jakob Stadium, Basle, 23 June
Attendance: 29,000

THE host nation beat Italy for the second time in less than a week in a match that was not as ill-tempered as the first.

Switzerland's win was certainly memorable, but it also served to indicate that Italy were only a shadow of their former selves and were no longer amongst the élite of world soccer.

The choice of players by Italy's Hungarian-born coach, Lajos Czeizler, for this important play-off match was peculiar to say the least. Several key men were omitted altogether, whilst others were played out of position.

Mervyn Griffiths was designated as the new match official and the experienced Welsh referee certainly kept both sets of players in check.

Josef Hügi, the man who scored the winner in the first match, but had to miss the England game because of injuries sustained at Lausanne, put Switzerland ahead after 14 minutes. They maintained this lead until half-time. Three minutes after the start of the second half, Ballaman put them further ahead and midway through the second period, Nesti pulled one back for the Italians. But two goals in the last five minutes, from Hügi again, and little winger Fatton, sent Switzerland into the next round at the expense of one of the fancied teams.

Switzerland: Parlier; Neury, Kernen, Eggimann, Bocquet, Casali, Antenen, Vonlanthen, Hügi, Ballaman, Fatton.
Scorers: Hügi 2, Ballaman, Fatton
Italy: Viola; Magnini, Giacomazzi, Mari, Tognon, Nesti, Muccinelli, Pandolfini, Lorenzi, Segato, Frignani.
Scorer: Nesti
Referee: Mervyn Griffiths (Wales)

Quarter-finals

AUSTRIA 7 SWITZERLAND 5 (Half-time 5-4)
La Pontaise Stadium, Lausanne, 26 June
Attendance: 31,000

IT was a shame that the sun-baked Lausanne ground was not filled to capacity for this remarkable match, which produced a World Cup record of 12 goals — nine of them in the first half.

The host nation had done well to reach this stage of the competition and when they scored three goals in the first 23 minutes, the Swiss fans must have been booking tickets for the semi-final. But Austria made a remarkable comeback with five goals in a ten-minute spell.

The glut of goals got under way in the 16th minute when Ballaman scored for Switzerland. A minute later, Hügi found the net for his fourth goal of the tournament and in the 23rd minute he made it 3-0. But three goals in three minutes, from Wagner, Alfred Körner and Wagner again, made it 3-3. The Austrian skipper and midfield general, Ocwirk, gave his side the lead after 32 minutes and two minutes later, Körner scored his second to put Austria 5-3 in front. Ten minutes earlier they had trailed 3-0.

The first-half scoring was still not complete. Ballaman scored his second goal of the game to reduce the deficit to just one goal at the interval.

Wagner completed his hat-trick after 52 minutes to make it 6-4 but again Switzerland pulled one back, when Hügi also completed a hat-trick six minutes later. However, Switzerland could not find the resources to draw level and Probst completed the scoring in the 76th minute.

All 12 goals came within the space of 60 minutes, the first nine within 23 minutes. Scoring

	P	W	D	L	F	A	Pts
England	2	1	1	0	6	4	3
Italy	2	1	0	1	5	3	2
Switzerland	2	1	0	1	2	3	2
Belgium	2	0	1	1	5	8	1

Benito Lorenzi of Italy.

England skipper Billy Wright.

Austria's team that beat Uruguay in the third-place play-off. Back row (left to right, players only): Probst, R.Körner, Dienst, Koller, Hanappi. Front row: Ocwirk, Schmied, Kollmann, Barschandt, Wagner and Stojaspal.

Austria's Ocwirk (left) and Hanappi (nearest ball) in action during the 12-goal thriller against Switzerland.

England centre-forward Nat Lofthouse gets up high to head the ball as Uruguayan goalkeeper Máspoli is beaten. The other England player is Dennis Wilshaw.

like that had never been seen in the World Cup before, or since, and it beat the scoring-rate in the 11-goal extravaganza of the Brazil-Poland match in 1938.

Austria were inspired by their two wingers, Alfred and Robert Körner, while Ocwirk gave a classic display. Switzerland's most outstanding player was inside-right Vonlanthen who, despite not getting on the score-sheet, played a prominent part in most of his team's goals.

Austria: Schmied; Hanappi, Barschandt, Ocwirk, Happel, Koller, R.Körner, Wagner, Stojaspal, Probst, A.Körner.
Scorers: Wagner 3, A.Körner 2, Ocwirk, Probst
Switzerland: Parlier; Neury, Kernen, Eggimann, Bocquet, Casali, Antenen, Vonlanthen, Hügi, Ballaman, Fatton.
Scorers: Hügi 3, Ballaman 2
Referee: Edward Faultless (Scotland)

URUGUAY 4   ENGLAND 2 (Half-time 2-1)

St Jakob Stadium, Basle, 26 June
Attendance: 50,000

ENGLAND and Uruguay provided an entertaining game of football for the Basle fans, who had the added bonus of having the score from Lausanne relayed to them. Uruguay maintained

England's Tom Finney is just beaten to the ball by Máspoli, the Uruguayan goalkeeper.

Borges opens the scoring for Uruguay after only five minutes, squeezing the ball past England's Bill McGarry and goalkeeper Gil Merrick.

their unbeaten World Cup record, although England could probably have beaten them had it not been for some erratic goalkeeping from Gil Merrick, whose performance came in for a lot of criticism.

The two centre-halves and respective captains, Wright and Varela, were outstanding at the heart of their own defences. England had Matthews and Lofthouse back in attack and Matthews once again had a good game. It was his pass that sent Wilshaw away to set up England's equalizer from Lofthouse in the 16th minute, after Borges had put Uruguay in front after just five minutes.

The Uruguayan skipper, Varela, caught Merrick unawares just before half-time and a shot from outside the box beat the England 'keeper. Varela left the field shortly afterwards after pulling a muscle, but returned in the second half with his leg heavily bandaged.

The teams were finely balanced after 45 minutes but Uruguay were carrying three passengers in Varela, Andrade and Abbadíe, who had all received injuries. Lofthouse might have equalized from the kick-off at the start of the second half, but seconds later Schiaffino latched on to a dubious free-kick from Varela. Merrick was slow in getting down to the shot and Uruguay increased their lead.

The scoreline was hardly a true reflection of the play and Tom Finney added respectability in the 67th minute, when he scrambled a second goal for England. Stanley Matthews nearly levelled the score, but his shot hit the post. A series of errors by the England forwards followed and they cost them dearly.

The killer blow came 12 minutes from the end when Ambrois added a fourth goal for Uruguay and England's hopes were dashed, despite giving one of their best international performances for two years.

Uruguay: Máspoli; Martínez, Santamaria, Andrade, Varela, Cruz, Abbadíe, Ambrois, Míguez, Schiaffino, Borges.
Scorers: Borges, Varela, Schiaffino, Ambrois
England: Merrick; Staniforth, Byrne, McGarry, Wright, Dickinson, Matthews, Broadis, Lofthouse, Wilshaw, Finney.
Scorers: Lofthouse, Finney
Referee: Erich Steiner (Austria)

Nat Lofthouse, equalized in the 16th minute.

Opposite page (top): The ball seems to have been cleared towards the Brazilian right flank. Players include goalkeeper Castillo and the Hungarian forward Czibor. Number-six for Brazil is Bauer. *Opposite page (bottom):* Castillo dives bravely at the feet of Czibor.

Right: Captains Bauer of Brazil (left) and Bozsik (right) of Hungary, together with English referee Arthur Ellis, who, despite being an experienced official, was unable to prevent some ugly scenes.

Didí and Lantos tussle.

Didí of Brazil.

HUNGARY 4   BRAZIL 2 (Half-time 2-1)

Wankdorf Stadium, Berne, 27 June
Attendance: 40,000

THE quarter-final match between two great footballing nations should have produced a classic game of football. Instead, it produced disgraceful scenes as three players were sent off in a match since dubbed the 'The Battle of Berne'.

The experienced English referee, Arthur Ellis, was the man in charge but, despite his many years in the game, he was unable to prevent some of the ugliest scenes witnessed on a football field.

Both sides were over keen to do well at the expense of discipline, which the two teams lacked. Hungary were without their captain, Puskás, who was injured in their previous match against West Germany.

The game was played in wet conditions, which suited the Europeans. Hungary's centre-half, Lóránt, committed the first bad foul in the opening minutes and was booked by Ellis. The defender laughed at the referee's decision and was lucky not to be sent off.

The Brazilians could not compose themselves in the bad conditions and fell behind to a Hidegkuti goal in the fourth minute. Kocsis headed home a Hidegkuti centre three minutes later and Hungary were *en route* to the semi-finals.

It was only after going two goals in arrears that Brazil played the sort of football seen in 1950. In the 18th minute, Djalma Santos converted a penalty after Indio had been bustled

Hidegkuti opens the scoring in the seventh minute.

Fighting breaks out and policemen appear as Bozsik and Nilton Santos are sent off.

Castillo, almost in tears after conceding a fourth goal.

Brandaozinho (4) and Czibor (8) in an aerial battle.

over by Buzánszky in the penalty area. Brazil were, at this stage, on top and both teams were tackling aggressively.

An injury to Mihaly Tóth in the first half made him a virtual passenger on the wing in the second period. Brazil now had a numerical advantage but could not capitalize. Some very dangerous tackles were committed by both sides and the game was ready to explode — which it did when Ellis awarded a penalty to Hungary after both sides thought that the offence was against the Hungarian Kocsis.

The Brazilians were furious at the decision but Lantos eventually converted the spot-kick. Thereafter, the tackling became even more ferocious. Humberto was lucky to stay on the field after a bad foul and Czibor should also have been removed. Brazil pulled another goal back 20 minutes into the second half through Julinho, but five minutes later the game erupted once more and a fight broke out which resulted in Hungary's captain, and Member of Parliament, Bozsik, together with Nilton Santos, receiving marching orders.

Four minutes from time, Humberto was also sent off, for violently kicking Lóránt, and in the last minute Kocsis headed home a Czibor cross to put the result beyond doubt. By now the pitch resembled a boxing ring. The final whistle sounded, but the fighting continued and the players still threw punches on their way back to the dressing-rooms. Referee Ellis was escorted to his changing-room by armed guards.

Hungary were lucky to hold out for the win. The favourites were through to the semi-final but their contribution to the 'Battle of Berne' did little to enhance their popularity.

Hungary: Grosics; Buzánszky, Lantos, Bozsic, Lóránt, Zakariás, M.Tóth, Kocsis, Hidegkuti, Czibor, J.Tóth.
Scorers: Kocsis 2, Hidegkuti, Lantos (pen)
Brazil: Castilho; D.Santos, N.Santos, Brandaozinho, Pinheiro, Bauer, Julinho, Didí, Indio, Humberto, Maurinho.
Scorers: D.Santos (pen), Julinho
Referee: Arthur Ellis (England)

WEST GERMANY 2   YUGOSLAVIA 0 (Half-time 1-0)

Les Charmilles, Geneva, 27 June
Attendance: 17,000

AFTER Sepp Herberger's gamble in the pool matches, he had to beat Yugoslavia to thwart any possible embarrassment.

Despite taking the lead in the ninth minute, when Yugoslav centre-half Horvat put through his own goal after a defensive mix up, Yugoslavia had most of the play and it appeared to be only a matter of time before they equalized. Kohlmeyer saved the Germans by clearing off the goal-line no fewer than three times.

The German defence was solid and well organized and they managed to withstand any pressure Bobek, Mitić and Vukas could throw at them. Their resilience was rewarded five minutes from time when winger Helmut Rahn broke away to seal Germany's win and thus save Herberger from that acute embarrassment.

Many underestimated the German victory. Whilst it was, to a large extent, against the run of the play, they were a well-organized outfit and their performance deserved more credit than was given at the time. Yugoslavia were one of the fancied teams before the start of the tournament. West Germany certainly were not.

West Germany: Turek; Laband, Kohlmeyer, Eckel, Liebrich, Mai, Rahn, Morlock, O.Walter, F.Walter, Schäfer.
Scorers: Horvat (og), Rahn
Yugoslavia: Beara; Stanković, Crnković, Ciakowski, Horvat, Boskov, Milutinović, Mitić, Vukas, Bobek, Zebec.
Referee: Istvan Zsolt (Hungary)

From left to right: West Germany's Kohlmeyer, Mai and Morlock.

Eckel (left) and Rahn of West Germany.

Beara watches the ball sail wide of the Yugoslavian goal.

**Kocsis, netted twice against
Uruguay.**

Semi-finals

HUNGARY 4   URUGUAY 2 (a.e.t.) (Half-time 1-0; 90 mins 2-2)

La Pontaise Stadium, Lausanne, 30 June
Attendance: 37,000

AFTER their disgraceful performance against Brazil in the quarter-final, Hungary dished up a dazzling display of football in this semi-final clash with Uruguay which resulted in the South Americans suffering World Cup defeat for the first time since the tournament began in 1930.

Although, as it transpired, there was no trouble, the Swiss authorities took no chances and arranged for the pitch to be surrounded by troops.

Hungary were still missing the injured Puskás, but Uruguay were without the services of three key players — captain Varela, Míguez and Abbadíe.

The match was played in torrential rain and Hungary struck first in the 13th minute when they broke the Uruguayan rearguard and Czibor volleyed home a Kocsis header after a defensive error. A minute into the second half it was 2-0. This time it was the head of Hidegkuti which sent the ball into the net.

Hungary seemed to be coasting into the Final but, 15 minutes from the end, Schiaffino sent Juan Eduardo Hohberg through to beat Hungarian 'keeper Grosics. Four minutes from time Uruguay levelled the scores with a similar goal when Hohberg netted from a Schiaffino

pass. However, the centre-forward nearly made a mess of it. He lost the ball after taking the pass, but was fortunate enough to regain control. Hungary's tactics of playing for time had failed and the game went into an extra period.

The first 15 minutes produced no further goals, although Hohberg nearly scored with another breakaway when his shot hit the post. Uruguay were to then receive a set-back when Schiaffino was injured and they were, effectively, down to ten men.

With nine minutes remaining, Kocsis headed Hungary back into the lead while Andrade, who had been the inspiration of the Uruguayan midfield, was receiving treatment for cramp. There were a lot of tired legs on the park as night began to fall. Four minutes from the end, Kocsis made sure of the victory with another header. It was his 11th goal of the tournament — a new World Cup record.

After what had happened in Berne, Hungary's latest quest for World Cup glory was a treat for the large Lausanne crowd. The contrasting styles of the two teams made it an interesting and exciting encounter. It was the best match of the 1954 tournament and one of the finest ever seen in the World Cup.

Hungary: Grosics; Buzánszky, Lantos, Bozsik, Lóránt, Zakariás, Budai, Kocsis, Palotas, Hidegkuti, Czibor.
Scorers: Kocsis 2, Czibor, Hidegkuti
Uruguay: Máspoli; Santamaria, Martínez, Andrade, Carballo, Cruz, Souto, Ambrois, Schiaffino, Hohberg, Borges.
Scorer: Hohberg 2
Referee: Mervyn Griffiths (Wales)

Carballo and Máspoli of Uruguay are stranded as Hidegkuti heads Hungary into a 2-0 lead.

Fritz Walter, scorer of two penalties as Austria were trounced by the Germans.

WEST GERMANY 6   AUSTRIA 1 (Half-time 1-0)

St Jakob Stadium, Basle, 30 June
Attendance: 58,000

SURPRISINGLY, this game between two of Switzerland's adjacent neighbours attracted the biggest crowd of the tournament so far, with a large proportion of the attendance made up of Austrian and West German fans.

Both were confident of victory, although the Austrian supporters must have felt uneasy at the way their defence conceded five goals in the quarter-final match. As a consequence, Austria recalled out-of-form goalkeeper Walter Zeman for his first match of the tournament — but it was to prove an unhappy return for him.

Morlock added to Schäfer's first-half goal after 47 minutes before Probst, in the 51st minute, pulled one back for Austria. After that it was one German attack after another — and each seemed to yield a goal.

A Fritz Walter penalty in the 54th minute made it 3-1 and after an hour, he centred for his brother, Ottmar, to score with a back-header. Fritz converted a second penalty in the 65th minute and right on time Ottmar scored with another header to make it 6-1.

Before the match the Hungarians admitted they feared the Austrians more than any other team left in the competition. Now they would have to have a rethink because Germany's win was no fluke. They had reached the World Cup Final and were real contenders for the title.

West Germany: Turek; Posipal, Kohlmeyer, Eckel, Liebrich, Mai, Rahn, Morlock, O.Walter, F.Walter, Schäfer.
Scorers: F.Walter 2 (2 pens), O.Walter 2, Schäfer, Morlock
Austria: Zeman; Hanappi, Schleger, Ocwirk, Happel, Koller, R.Körner, Wagner, Stojaspal, Probst, A Körner.
Scorer: Probst
Referee: Vincenzo Orlandini (Italy)

Third place play-off
AUSTRIA 3   URUGUAY 1 (Half-time 1-1)

Sportzplatz Hardturm, Zurich, 3 July
Attendance: 31,000

BASED on their semi-final performance, Uruguay were clear favourites to occupy third place. But, just as Austria had been upset by Germany in their semi-final clash, it was now their turn to upset the odds and inflict a second World Cup defeat on the South Americans in the World Cup's 100th match.

Stojaspal, the best forward on the field, put Austria ahead from the penalty-spot in the 16th minute but they held the lead for only five minutes before that galloping forward, Hohberg, equalized. Uruguay, however, were playing like a demoralized team after their defeat by Hungary and a first-half injury to Schiaffino did not help.

Luís Cruz, an ever-present at the heart of the Uruguayan defence, put through his own goal after 59 minutes and Austria made sure of third place when their skipper Ocwirk, one of the stars of the tournament, completed the scoring 11 minutes from time with a goal from 25 yards.

Opposite page: Uruguay's Máspoli denies Dienst but the Austrians still finished in third place. Martínez is the player on the floor.

Below: Stojaspal (right) celebrates Ocwirk's third goal for Austria in the third place match.

Austria: Schmied; Hanappi, Barschandt, Ocwirk, Kollmann, Koller, R.Körner, Wagner, Dienst, Stojaspal, Probst.
Scorers: Stojaspal (pen), Cruz (og), Ocwirk
Uruguay: Máspoli; Santamaria, Martínez, Andrade, Carballo, Cruz, Abbadíe, Hohberg, Méndez, Schiaffino, Borges.
Scorer: Hohberg
Referee: Raymon Wyssling (Switzerland)

STATISTICS

Goalscorers:
11 — Sandor Kocsis (Hungary).
6 — Maximilian Morlock (West Germany), Josef Hügi (Switzerland).
5 — Erich Probst (Austria).
4 — Ferenc Puskás, Nandor Hidegkuti (both Hungary), Hans Schäfer, Ottmar Walter, Helmut Rahn (all West Germany), Carlos Borges (Uruguay), Ernst Stojaspal (Austria), Robert Ballaman (Switzerland).
3 — Mamat Suat, Sargun Burhan (both Turkey), Zoltan Czibor (Hungary), Fritz Walter (West Germany), Oscar Míguez, Juan Eduardo Hohberg (both Uruguay), Theodor Wagner (Austria), Leopold Anoul (Belgium), Nat Lofthouse (England).
2 — Kucucandoniadis Lefter (Turkey), Pinga, Julinho, Didí (all Brazil), Peter Palotas, Mihaly Lantos (both Hungary), Juan Alberto Schiaffino, Julio César Abbadie (both Uruguay), Alfred Körner, Ernst Ocwirk (both Austria), Ivor Broadis (England).
1 — Milos Milutinović, Branko Zebec (both Yugoslavia), Jean Vincent, Raymond Kopa (both France), José Naranjo, Tomás Balcazar (both Mexico), Keksin Erol, Ertan Mustafa (both Turkey), Baltazar, Djalma Santos (both Brazil), József Tóth (Hungary), Bernhard Klodt, Alfred Pfaff, Richard Herrmann (all West Germany), Obdulio Jacinto Varela, Javier Ambrois (both Uruguay), Henri Coppens (Belgium), Jacques Fatton (Switzerland), Jimmy Mullen, Dennis Wilshaw, Tom Finney (all England), Gianpiero Boniperti, Egisto Pandolfini, Carlo Galli, Amleto Frignani, Benito Lorenzi, Fulvio Nesti (all Italy).

Own-goals
Raúl Cardenas (Mexico v France). Jimmy Dickinson (England v Belgium). Ivan Horvat (Yugoslavia v West Germany). Luís Cruz (Uruguay v Austria).

Hat-tricks
Sandor Kocsis (Hungary v South Korea). Sandor Kocsis (4 goals, Hungary v West Germany, 1st game). Sargun Burhan (Turkey v South Korea). Josef Hügi (Switzerland v Austria). Theodor Wagner (Austria v Switzerland). Maximilian Morlock (West Germany v Turkey, 2nd game). Erich Probst (Austria v Czechoslovakia). Carlos Borges (Uruguay v Scotland).

Fastest goal
2 minutes — Mamat Suat (Turkey v West Germany, 1st game).

Most goals (team)
27 — Hungary

Teams failing to score
Czechoslovakia, Scotland, South Korea

Total goals scored: 140
Average per game: 5.38

Berne's Wankdorf Stadium, venue for the 1954 World Cup Final.

Final

WEST GERMANY 3   HUNGARY 2 (Half-time 2-2)

Wankdorf Stadium, Berne, 4 July
Attendance: 60,000

A PACKED Wankdorf Stadium saw West Germany and Hungary do battle in one of the finest Finals the World Cup had seen.

In appalling weather, the wet conditions were not ideal for football but both sides displayed great skills in a game that was a repeat of their Pool Two match, which Hungary won 8-3. Then, of course, West German coach Sepp Herberger shrewdly fielded a weakened team. Now, two weeks later, it was a different story.

Hungary went to Switzerland expecting to win the Jules Rimet Trophy. West Germany were not even one of the seeds, although Herberger had great confidence in his side.

The Magyars were, perhaps over-confident, and lulled into a false sense of security by that big scoreline in their pool game. Not that one would have thought it by the way they started.

Puskás insisted on playing, even though he was not fully fit, and the 'Galloping Major' put his side in front after only six minutes when he followed up a Kocsis shot that rebounded to him. Two minutes later, Czibor scored after a back-pass by the German left-back, Werner Kohlmeyer, was not gathered by 'keeper Turek. The Wankdorf Stadium was certainly not a happy hunting ground for Czibor. He was to eventually end up on the losing side, and seven years later in the same stadium, playing for Barcelona in the European Cup Final, he was again on the losing side after scoring.

Hungary led 2-0 after only eight minutes and there could not have been anybody prepared to back a West German victory at this stage. But what a turnaround the large crowd were to witness.

After ten minutes, Morlock reduced the arrears when he latched on to a great pass from left winger Schäfer which split the Hungarian defence. A mistake by the Hungarian 'keeper, Gyula Grosics, in the 18th minute allowed Rahn to equalize from a corner. The winger had been recalled for international duty for the first game with Hungary and had turned out to be one of the stars of the German team.

Hungary came close to restoring their lead in the second half. Hidegkuti hit the post, Kocsis hit the bar, Kohlmeyer kicked off the line and Turek brought off a series of amazing saves.

Six minutes from the end, with the prospect of extra-time looming, Rahn picked up a half-hearted clearance from Lantos. The German winger raced to the edge of the penalty area and hit the ball, which skidded low past the diving 'keeper.

With two minutes remaining, Puskás raced on to a Tóth pass and put the ball past the German 'keeper. But the Welsh linesman, Mervyn Griffiths, had his flag raised for an offside decision against Puskás. It was certainly a close call and one that was talked about for a long time after the final whistle was blown.

Top: Puskás puts Hungary ahead after following up a rebound in the sixth minute. *Middle:* Two minutes later, Czibor gets the second after a defensive error by Werner (3). *Bottom:* Rahn equalizes following a corner in the 18th minute, after Morlock had reduced the arrears for the Germans in the tenth.

Penalties
Scored: Raymond Kopa (France v Mexico) *Referee: Manuel Asensi (Spain).* Djalma Santos (Brazil v Hungary) *Referee: Arthur Ellis (England).* Mihaly Lantos (Hungary v Brazil) *Referee: Arthur Ellis (England).* Fritz Walter 2 (West Germany v Austria) *Referee: Vincenzo Orlandini (Italy).* Ernst Stojaspal (Austria v Uruguay) *Referee: Mervyn Griffiths (Wales).*

Most appearances
6 — Horst Eckel, Fritz Walter (both West Germany).

Sendings-off
József Bozsik (Hungary v Brazil) *Referee: Arthur Ellis (England).* Nilton Santos (Brazil v Hungary) *Referee: Arthur Ellis (England).* Humberto Barbosa Tozzi (Brazil v Hungary) *Referee: Arthur Ellis (England).*

Most players used
18 — West Germany

Number of players used by Finalists
18 — West Germany
15 — Hungary

Turek brought off a magnificent save from a powerful Czibor shot in the dying seconds and Hungary were thwarted for the final time.

Referee Ling blew for full time and Hungary, one of the hottest ever favourites to win the World Cup, suffered their first defeat in 30 internationals, stretching back to May 1950.

West Germany became the first unseeded team to win the World Cup and coach Sepp Herberger received much individual praise for the way he had tactically guided his team to their ultimate honour. Two weeks earlier, of course, he had come in for a lot of criticism for fielding a weakened side against the Hungarians.

West Germany: Anton Turek; Josef Posipal, Werner Kohlmeyer, Horst Eckel, Werner Liebrich, Karl Mai, Helmut Rahn, Maximilian Morlock, Ottmar Walter, Fritz Walter, Hans Schäfer.
Scorers: Rahn 2, Morlock
Hungary: Gyula Grosics; Jenö Buzánszky, Mihaly Lantos, József Bozsik, Gyula Lóránt, József Zakariás, Zoltan Czibor, Sandor Kocsis, Nandor Hidegkuti, Ferenc Puskás, József Tóth.
Scorers: Puskás, Czibor
Referee: Bill Ling (England)

Opposite page (top): **Morlock opens the scoring for Germany.** *Opposite page (bottom):* **Hungary line up before the kick-off. Skipper Ferenc Puskás is on the extreme left of the line.**

Hungary's 'Galloping Major', Ferenc Puskás.

Rahn (20) hits the winning goal past Grosics and Hungary's World Cup dreams are shattered.

Top: Puskás beats Turek and the ball lands in the net, but Hungary's celebrations are premature for the goal is disallowed.

Middle: Kocsis watches as Posipal (right) receives the ball from Mai.

Bottom: Puskás, although not fully fit, still managed to cause problems for the Germans. Here, he gets in another shot.

Mihaly Lantos of Hungary.

József Zakariás of Hungary.

Opposite page (top left): Kocsis tries a shot as Liebrich challenges. *Opposite page (top right):* Grosics tips the ball away from Rahn. *Opposite page (middle left):* Czibor in action. *Opposite page (middle right):* Grosics gathers the ball. *Opposite page (bottom left):* Turek is beaten but the ball went wide of the post. *Opposite page (bottom right):* Rahn, Germany's two-goal hero, gets in another challenge on the Hungarian 'keeper.

West Germany before the Final. From left to right: F.Walter, Turek, Eckel, Rahn, O.Walter, Liebrich, Posipal, Schäfer, Kohlmeyer, Mai, Morlock.

Puskás, the lone Hungarian amidst the celebrating Germans.

Jules Rimet presents the World Cup to Fritz Walter.

Walter and Puskás exchange pennants before the start.

Fritz Walter, the victorious captain, with the trophy.

MEN WHO MADE THE HEADLINES - 1958

Nils Liedholm
(Sweden)

NILS Liedholm, with Gunnar Gren and Gunnar Nordahl, all members of Sweden's 1948 Olympic gold medal-winning team, left Swedish soccer for Italy in the early 1950s. Liedholm was born at Walermarkvic in October 1922 and made his name with IFK Norrköping, who won the Swedish League five times between 1943 and 1948. Then Norrköping's manager, Lajos Czeizler, took charge of AC Milan and soon afterwards the trio were members of the AC attack which became one of the best in Europe. In 1951, Milan won their first Italian League title for 44 years. Liedholm moved from inside-forward to wing-half, then to sweeper where his tall frame and aerial skills were very much part of Milan's success. He won two more Italian League Championship medals and a European Cup runners-up medal in 1957. When Sweden played host to the World Cup, the exiles were recalled after being overlooked four years earlier and Liedholm, now reverted to midfield, helped his country to the World Cup Final. The following year he won his fourth Italian League Championship medal and retired in 1961 at the age of 33. He later enjoyed a successful managerial career with Fiorentina, Milan and Roma. Liedholm won 23 Swedish caps.

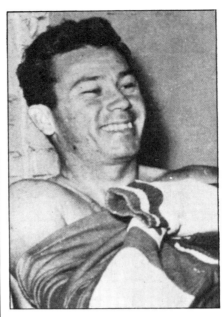

Juste Fontaine
(France)

JUSTE Fontaine's record 13 World Cup goals in 1958 included four in the third place play-off against West Germany, as France achieved their best-ever finish in the tournament. Fontaine, who was born at Marrakesh in Morocco in 1933, began his career with Nice and won League and Cup winners' medals before making his international debut against Hungary in October 1956. He was in and out of the national team and won a place in Sweden only after an injury to René Biliard. But he combined with Raymond Kopa to provide one of the tournament's most lethal strike forces and he scored in every game. Fontaine, who scored 27 goals in 20 internationals, moved to Rheims shortly after his World Cup exploits and appeared for them the 1959 European Cup Final, when they lost to Raymond Kopa's Real Madrid. His career was cut short at the age of 27, when he broke a leg for a second time. He became president of the French Footballers' Union and had a brief spell in charge of the national team and Paris Saint-Germain. Fontaine's 13 goals remained an overall World Cup record until surpassed by Gerd Müller in 1974, although no man has bettered his tally in one series.

Pelé
(Brazil)

PELÉ does not belong only to the 1958 World Cup, for he can claim a place as one of the stars of 1970, but it was in Sweden that he first made an impact with skills that belied his 17 years. Born Edson Arantes do Nascimento at Três Corações on 23 October 1940, he went on to become arguably the greatest footballer of all time. He made his senior debut for Santos in 1956, a month before his 16th birthday and ten months later played for Brazil against Argentina. Pelé missed the first two games of the 1958 World Cup before making his debut against Russia. His first World Cup goal came in the 1-0 quarter-final win over Wales and he scored a hat-trick in the semi-final and two more in the Final. Scoring goals was Pelé's trademark, but he was also a clever, quick-thinking player who could create goals for others. He scored 97 goals in 111 appearances for Brazil and various sources suggest he netted 1,281 in 1,363 senior games overall. He played his final game for Santos in 1974 but was persuaded out of retirement the following year, when he joined NASL club, New York Cosmos in a $4 million deal. He played his last game for Cosmos in 1977, in front of 75,646 fans.

Arrival of those Great Brazilians
Sweden 1958

THE sixth World Cup tournament will be remembered for the arrival of those wonderful Brazilians, and in particular a 17-year-old who was later to become one of the legends of the game. His name was, of course, Pelé. For the first time the World Cup received international television coverage and the world could revel in the mastery of Pelé, Garrincha, Vavá, Zagalo *et al*, as for the first time since 1938, the favourites went on to win the trophy.

A record number of 53 nations entered, although only 46 played in the qualifying competition. For the first time, all four United Kingdom teams qualified and this must have annoyed those countries who had previously complained to FIFA that using the Home International Championship as a qualifying pool gave an unfair advantage to the four Home countries, because two nations were previously eligible to qualify from the pool. To placate their critics, FIFA split the four UK countries into different groups — and four qualified, although Wales had more than a small piece of good fortune in qualifying for the final stages.

The England team which made the trip to Sweden had been decimated following the Munich air tragedy a few months earlier. They sorely missed the Manchester United trio of Roger Byrne, Tommy Taylor and Duncan Edwards. It would have been interesting to see how England, with these three outstanding players in their side, would have fared against the talented Brazilians.

Hungary, the heroes of 1954, were no longer the force they were four years earlier, due mostly to the invasion of their country by the Soviet Union in 1956. Leading players, Puskás, Czibor and Kocsis, all defected after the invasion. The Soviets, on the other hand, entered and reached the final stages for the first time in their history and were installed as one of the favourites.

Argentina appeared for the first time since 1934 and were managed by Guillermo Stábile, one of their stars of the inaugural World Cup. However, there were two very notable absentees from the 1958 finals — Uruguay and Italy, both dual winners of the trophy. They were both suprisingly eliminated at the qualifying stage. Another fancied team not to make the trip to Sweden was Spain. Since the last World Cup, European soccer had seen the launch of the Fairs Cup and European Championship Cup. Spain had been dominant, with Barcelona and Real Madrid winning both tournaments. Their national side was one of the fancied teams for the 1958 World Cup, had they qualified.

The clear favourites were Brazil, who brought with them an innovative 4-2-4 system. It would not be long before the rest of the soccer world employed the same formation. Brazil played an attacking game and their skills were exhilarating to say the least and their performance in the semi-final against France was one of the finest in World Cup history.

In the Final, Brazil met the host nation Sweden, who were coached by an Englishman, George Raynor. He had predicted before the start of the tournament that his team would reach the Final. Few took him seriously, but he knew that once the Swedish FA had a change of heart and adopted professionalism, he could recall such outstanding players as Nils Liedholm, Gunnar Gren, Kurt Hamrin, Bengt Gustavsson and Nacka Skoglund from their duties in the Italian League. They added their immense skills to the Swedish national side and it was soon apparent they would be a team to be reckoned with — as Raynor had suggested.

The format for the 1958 World Cup was changed yet again. The 16 Finalists were split into four pools. However, unlike 1954, all four teams in each pool played each other once with the top two qualifying for the next phase, a knock-out competition. If teams tied for second and third place, then the outcome was decided by a play-off. Thankfully, extra-time was not played in pool matches this time.

The teams were not seeded as in 1954, but each of the four groups contained one team from Western Europe, one from Eastern Europe, one from the United Kingdom and one from Latin America. England found themselves in Pool Four with Brazil and Russia in what was the toughest group of them all.

Pelé, aged 17, pictured just before the start of his first match in a World Cup finals, the stage he was to grace for years to come.

1958 Qualifying Competition

FOR the first — and so far only — time the four home countries, England, Scotland, Wales and Northern Ireland, all qualified for the final stages of the World Cup. And what an eventful series of qualifying matches it turned out to be.

England eventually won their group by two points from the Republic of Ireland, but they came within 60 seconds of a possible exit, trailing 1-0 with a minute to go in Dublin when John Atyeo snatched a last-gasp equalizer. Had the Irish won, then they would have forced a play-off match.

England's last qualifying match was in May 1957, when the Manchester United trio of Roger Byrne, Tommy Taylor and Duncan Edwards were all major figures. Alas, the dreadful air disaster at Munich on 6 February 1958 meant that England went to Sweden four months later with the backbone of their team destroyed.

Northern Ireland scored a memorable success by eliminating Italy, one of the favourites to win the World Cup. But had the Italians not been so petty, they would have qualified instead. The Irish had to win the match between the two countries in Belfast to qualify. However, dense fog resulted in the appointed FIFA referee, Istvan Zsolt of Hungary, being stranded at London Airport. The Italians would not accept another official and refused to play the qualifier. The match still went ahead but was dubbed a 'friendly' — although it hardly lived up to that billing. The Italians indulged in some ferocious tackling and the match later became known as 'The Battle of Belfast'.

The game ended 2-2 and, had it been the qualifier, Italy would have been on their way to Sweden. When the match was replayed the following month, with Zsolt in charge, Northern Ireland won a tame affair 2-1 and Italy failed to qualify for the World Cup Finals for the first time.

Scotland qualified from their group at the expense of the Spaniards, who threw away their chances in the very first match against Switzerland. The 120,000 crowd was stunned as the unfancied Swiss held the home team to a 2-2 draw. It was Switzerland's only point in the group. Scotland beat Switzerland twice and Spain once to qualify. For Spain it

was a bitter disappointment. With players like Di Stefano, Suarez, Ghento and Kubala in the team, they were favourites to win the group and to figure prominently in Sweden.

Wales were by far the luckiest of the four home countries — they qualified for the final stages after being eliminated. The Welsh finished second to Czechoslovakia in Group Four but their good fortune came after Israel won the Asia-Africa qualifying competition, only after their opponents, Turkey, Indonesia, Egypt and Sudan all withdrew. For the first time, FIFA ruled that no country, other than the holders and hosts, could reach the final stages without playing a match.

Consequently, the runners-up from all the other groups were invited to take part in a draw to see who would face Israel in a two-match play-off. Wales were the lucky nation and had no problems in winning both matches 2-0 and thus qualifiying via the 'back door'.

The Welsh team boss was Jimmy Murphy, Matt Busby's assistant at Manchester United. Murphy should have been with Busby and the United team for the European Cup-tie against Red Star Belgrade, which preceded the Munich air disaster. However, on the day of the crash, Wales were playing their second match against Israel at Cardiff and Murphy was with the Welsh squad instead.

The Soviet Union, who entered for the first time, qualified, but only after beating Poland in a play-off. And the once-mighty Magyars of Hungary only just scraped through after losing to the Norwegian amateurs in their first match. France qualified, thanks to a 6-3 home win over one of their 'bogey' teams, Belgium. But spare a thought for Iceland in this group — they conceded 26 goals in four matches.

The champions elect, Brazil, were also lucky to survive the qualifiers after being held to a 1-1 draw by Peru in Lima. They won the return by a solitary goal. Uruguay, however, were not so fortunate. They were eliminated after failing to beat a weak Colombian side and then getting thrashed 5-0 by Paraguay.

For the United States there was no chance of a repeat of their 1950 exploits. They finished bottom of their CONCACAF group, conceding 21 goals in the process.

Results

EUROPE

Group One

3 Oct 1956 *Dublin*	Rep of Ireland ...2 Denmark 1
5 Dec 1956 *Wolverh'ton*	England ....5 Denmark 2
8 May 1957 *London*	England ....5 Rep of Ireland ...1
15 May 1957 *Copenhagen*	Denmark ....1 England 4
19 May 1957 *Dublin*	Rep of Ireland ...1 England 1
2 Oct 1957 *Copenhagen*	Denmark ....0 Rep of Ireland ...2

	P	W	D	L	F	A	Pts	
England	4	3	1	0	15	5	7	**England qualified**
Rep of Ireland	4	2	1	1	6	7	5	
Denmark	4	0	0	4	4	13	0	

Group Two

11 Nov 1956 *Paris*	France ....6 Belgium 3
2 Jun 1957 *Nantes*	France ....8 Iceland............0
5 Jun 1957 *Brussels*	Belgium ....8 Iceland............3
1 Sep 1957 *Reykjavik*	Iceland............1 France 5
4 Sep 1957 *Reykjavik*	Iceland............2 Belgium 5
27 Oct 1957 *Brussels*	Belgium ....0 France 0

	P	W	D	L	F	A	Pts	
France	4	3	1	0	19	4	7	**France**
Belgium	4	2	1	1	16	11	5	**qualified**
Iceland	4	0	0	4	6	26	0	

Group Three

22 May 1957 *Oslo*	Norway...........1 Bulgaria..........2
12 Jun 1957 *Oslo*	Norway...........2 Hungary 1
23 Jun 1957 *Budapest*	Hungary ....4 Bulgaria..........1
15 Sep 1957 *Sofia*	Bulgaria ....1 Hungary 2
3 Nov 1957 *Sofia*	Bulgaria ....7 Norway...........0
10 Nov 1957 *Budapest*	Hungary ....5 Norway...........0

	P	W	D	L	F	A	Pts	
Hungary	4	3	0	1	12	4	6	**Hungary qualified**
Bulgaria	4	2	0	2	11	7	4	
Norway	4	1	0	3	3	15	2	

Group Four

1 May 1957 *Cardiff*	Wales ....1 Czechoslovakia ..0
19 May 1957 *Leipzig*	East Germany ...2 Wales 1
26 May 1957 *Prague*	Czechoslovakia ..2 Wales 0
16 Jun 1957 *Brno*	Czechoslovakia ..3 East Germany ...1
25 Sep 1957 *Cardiff*	Wales ....4 East Germany ...1
27 Oct 1957 *Leipzig*	East Germany ...1 Czechoslovakia ..4

	P	W	D	L	F	A	Pts	
Czechoslovakia	4	3	0	1	9	3	6	**Czechoslovakia**
Wales	4	2	0	2	6	5	4	**qualified**
East Germany	4	1	0	3	5	12	2	

(Wales also qualified after meeting Israel, winners of the Asia-African group)

The Welsh team before their qualifying game in Prague. From left to right: John Charles, Harris, Kelsey, Palmer, Thomas, Medwin, Jones, Vernon, Hopkins, Mel Charles, Daniel.

Group Five

30 Sep	1956	*Vienna*	Austria............7 Luxembourg.....0
30 Mar	1957	*Rotterdam*	Holland ....4 Luxembourg.....1
26 May	1957	*Vienna*	Austria............3 Holland 2
11 Sep	1957	*Rotterdam*	Luxembourg.....2 Holland 5
25 Sep	1957	*Amsterdam*	Holland ....1 Austria............1
29 Sep	1957	*Luxembourg*	Luxembourg.....0 Austria............3

	P	W	D	L	F	A	Pts	
Austria	4	3	1	0	14	3	7	**Austria qualified**
Holland	4	2	1	1	12	7	5	
Luxembourg	4	0	0	4	3	19	0	

Group Six

23 Jun	1957	*Moscow*	Soviet Union ....3 Poland............0
5 Jun	1957	*Helsinki*	Finland..........1 Poland............3
27 Jul	1957	*Moscow*	Soviet Union ....2 Finland...........1
15 Aug	1957	*Helsinki*	Finland..........0 Soviet Union ...10
20 Oct	1957	*Chorzów*	Poland............2 Soviet Union 1
3 Nov	1957	*Warsaw*	Poland............4 Finland...........0

	P	W	D	L	F	A	Pts
Soviet Union	4	3	0	1	16	3	6
Poland	4	3	0	1	9	5	6
Finland	4	0	0	4	2	19	0

Play-off

24 Nov 1957 *Leipzig*	Soviet Union ....2 Poland............0

Soviet Union qualified

Group Seven

5 May	1957	*Athens*	Greece ....0 Yugoslavia 0
16 May	1957	*Athens*	Greece ....1 Romania 2
29 Sep	1957	*Bucharest*	Romania ....1 Yugoslavia 1
3 Nov	1957	*Bucharest*	Romania ....3 Greece 0
10 Nov	1957	*Belgrade*	Yugoslavia ....4 Greece 1
17 Nov	1957	*Belgrade*	Yugoslavia ....2 Romania 0

	P	W	D	L	F	A	Pts	
Yugoslavia	4	2	2	0	7	2	6	**Yugoslavia**
Romania	4	2	1	1	6	4	5	**qualified**
Greece	4	0	1	3	2	9	1	

Group Eight

16 Jan	1957	*Lisbon*	Portugal..........1 N. Ireland 1
24 Apr	1957	*Rome*	Italy...............1 N. Ireland 0
1 May	1957	*Belfast*	N. Ireland ....3 Portugal..........0
26 May	1957	*Lisbon*	Portugal..........3 Italy...............0
22 Dec	1957	*Milan*	Italy...............3 Portugal..........0
15 Jan	1958	*Belfast*	N. Ireland ....2 Italy...............1

	P	W	D	L	F	A	Pts	
N. Ireland	4	2	1	1	6	3	5	**Northern Ireland**
Italy	4	2	0	2	5	5	4	**qualified**
Portugal	4	1	1	2	4	7	3	

Group Nine

10 Mar	1957	*Madrid*	Spain ....2 Switzerland 2
8 May	1957	*Glasgow*	Scotland ....4 Spain 2
19 May	1957	*Basle*	Switzerland ......1 Scotland 2
26 May	1957	*Madrid*	Spain ....4 Scotland 1
6 Nov	1957	*Glasgow*	Scotland ....3 Switzerland 2
24 Nov	1957	*Lausanne*	Switzerland ......1 Spain 4

	P	W	D	L	F	A	Pts	
Scotland	4	3	0	1	10	9	6	**Scotland qualified**
Spain	4	2	1	1	12	8	5	
Switzerland	4	0	1	3	6	11	1	

Switzerland's team which started well with a 2-2 draw in Madrid's Bernabéu Stadium. Alas, that proved to be their only point of the qualifying competition. Back row (left to right): Kernen, Meier, Frosio, Morf, Hügi II. Front row: Antenen, Schneiter, Parlier, Koch, Ballaman, Riva IV.

SOUTH AMERICA

Group One

| 14 Apr 1957 *Lima* | Peru | 1 Brazil | 1 |
| 21 Apr 1957 *Río de Janeiro* | Brazil | 1 Peru | 0 |

Brazil qualified

Group Two

22 Sep 1957 *Santiago*	Chile	2 Bolivia	1
29 Sep 1957 *La Paz*	Bolivia	3 Chile	0
6 Oct 1957 *La Paz*	Bolivia	2 Argentina	0
13 Oct 1957 *Santiago*	Chile	0 Argentina	2
20 Oct 1957 *Buenos Aires*	Argentina	4 Chile	0
27 Oct 1957 *Buenos Aires*	Argentina	4 Bolivia	0

	P	W	D	L	F	A	Pts	
Argentina	4	3	0	1	10	2	6	**Argentina qualified**
Bolivia	4	2	0	2	6	6	4	
Chile	4	1	0	3	2	10	2	

Group Three

16 Jun 1957 *Bogotá*	Colombia	1 Uruguay	1
20 Jun 1957 *Bogotá*	Colombia	2 Paraguay	3
30 Jun 1957 *Montevideo*	Uruguay	1 Colombia	0
7 Jun 1957 *Asunción*	Paraguay	3 Colombia	0
14 Jul 1957 *Asunción*	Paraguay	5 Uruguay	0
28 Jul 1957 *Montevideo*	Uruguay	2 Paraguay	0

	P	W	D	L	F	A	Pts	
Paraguay	4	3	0	1	11	4	6	**Paraguay qualified**
Uruguay	4	2	1	1	4	6	5	
Colombia	4	0	1	3	3	8	1	

CONCACAF
(Central & North America)

Group One

10 Feb 1957 *Guatemala*	Guatemala	2 Costa Rica	6
17 Feb 1957 *San José*	Costa Rica	3 Guatemala	1
3 Mar 1957 *San José*	Costa Rica	4 Curaçao	0
10 Mar 1957 *Guatemala*	Guatemala	1 Curaçao	3
1 Aug 1957 *Willemstad*	Curaçao	1 Costa Rica	2

Curaçao v Guatemala not played due to attack on the Guatemalan president, as a result of which the team was refused permission to leave the country.

	P	W	D	L	F	A	Pts	
Costa Rica	4	4	0	0	15	4	8	**Costa Rica**
Curacao	3	1	0	2	4	7	2	**qualified for**
Guatemala	3	0	0	3	4	12	0	**CONCACAF Final**

Group Two

7 Apr 1957 *Mexico City*	Mexico	6 United States	0
28 Apr 1957 *Los Angeles*	United States	2 Mexico	7
22 Jun 1957 *Toronto*	Canada	5 United States	1
30 Jun 1975 *Mexico City*	Canada	0 Mexico	3
4 Jul 1957 *Mexico City*	Mexico	2 Canada	0
6 Jul 1957 *St Louis*	United States	2 Canada	3

	P	W	D	L	F	A	Pts	
Mexico	4	4	0	0	18	2	8	**Mexico qualified**
Canada	4	2	0	2	8	8	4	**for CONCACAF**
United States	4	0	0	4	5	21	0	**Final**

Final

| 20 Oct 1957 *Mexico City* | Mexico | 2 Costa Rica | 0 |
| 27 Oct 1957 *San José* | Costa Rica | 1 Mexico | 1 |

Mexico qualified

ASIA-AFRICA

Group One

Formosa-China withdrew

| 12 May 1957 *Djakarta* | Indonesia | 2 China | 0 |
| 2 Jun 1957 *Peking* | China | 4 Indonesia | 3 |

Play-off

| 23 Jun 1957 *Rangoon* | Indonesia | 0 China | 0 |

Indonesia qualified for second phase on goal-average

Group Two

Israel qualified for next phase following Turkey's withdrawal

Group Three

Egypt qualified for next phase after Cyprus withdrew

Group Four

| 8 May 1957 *Khartoum* | Sudan | 1 Syria | 0 |
| 24 May 1957 *Damascus* | Syria | 1 Sudan | 1 |

Sudan qualified for next phase

Second Phase

Indonesia and Egypt withdrew. Sudan and Israel qualified for final phase

Final Phase

Sudan withdrew, making Israel the Asia-African winners. However, FIFA ruled that no team could qualify for the Finals without playing a match and a special play-off tie with Wales was arranged.

Special Play-off

| 15 Jan 1958 *Tel Aviv* | Israel | 0 Wales | 2 |
| 5 Feb 1958 *Cardiff* | Wales | 2 Israel | 0 |

Wales qualified

The Chinese (right) and Indonesian teams parade their national flags as they take the field for a qualifying group match.

1958 Tournament

Pool One

NORTHERN IRELAND 1   CZECHOSLOVAKIA 0 (Half-time 1-0)

Örjans vall, Halmstad, 8 June
Attendance: 10,647

NORTHERN Ireland celebrated their World Cup debut with a 1-0 win over the powerful Czechs, thanks to a first-half goal from Wilbur Cush. It was a fairy-tale start for the Irish, whose captain, Danny Blanchflower, summed up the tactics of his team in true Irish style when he said: "Our tactics are to equalize before the other team scores!"

The Czechs threw everything at Northern Ireland, but magnificent goalkeeping from Harry Gregg and expert leadership from Blanchflower saw the proud Irish hold out for a great win.

The only goal was scored after 20 minutes, when the 5ft 5in tall inside-right Cush rose to meet a centre from Jimmy McIlroy and headed the ball past goalkeeper Dolejsi.

It was a magnificent World Cup baptism for the Irish, but they may never have appeared in the competition, had the Irish FA not backed down on their rule which forbade players to turn out on a Sunday. Several matches in Sweden were scheduled for the Sabbath.

Northern Ireland: Gregg; Keith, McMichael, Blanchflower, Cunningham, Peacock, Bingham, Cush, Dougan, McIlroy, McParland.
Scorer: Cush
Czechoslovakia: Dolejsi; Mraz, Novák, Pluskal, Cadek, Masopust, Hovorka, Dvorak, Borovicka, Hartl, Kraus.
Referee: Eric Seipelt (Austria)

Northern Ireland's Peter McParland, a star of the tournament.

WEST GERMANY 3   ARGENTINA 1 (Half-time 2-1)

Malmö Stadium, 8 June
Attendance: 31,156

WEST Germany fielded four of their 1954 winning team — Fritz Walter, Hans Schäfer, Horst Eckel and Helmut Rahn — and it was Rahn who destroyed the Argentinians with two goals. His international career seemed to be over in the four years between the two World Cups but here he was, continuing where he had left off in Switzerland. Making his World Cup debut for the Germans was Uwe Seller, who was to become one of the legendary figures of the competition, appearing in a record 21 matches.

Argentina had won the 1957 South American championship with a powerful young team and were one of the favourites for the sixth World Cup. But many of their top players had moved to Italy and the Argentinian FA refused to recall them for World Cup duties. Consequently, they were not the force many expected, as West Germany found out in their opening match, although there was a scare in the opening minutes when Corbatta put the Argentinians in front.

The Germans, again managed by Sepp Herberger, soon composed themselves and Rahn netted after 32 minutes to level the scores. Three minutes before the break, Seeler crowned his World Cup debut with Germany's second goal. The scoring was completed a minute from time when Rahn made it 3-1.

West Germany: Herkenrath; Stollenwerk, Juskowiak, Eckel, Erhardt, Szymaniak, Rahn, Walter, Seeler, Schmidt, Schäfer.
Scorers: Rahn 2, Seeler
Argentina: Carrizo; Lombardo, Vairo, Rossi, Dellacha, Varacka, Corbatta, Prado, Menendez, Rojas, Cruz.
Scorer: Corbatta
Referee: Reg Leafe (England)

ARGENTINA 3   NORTHERN IRELAND 1 (Half-time 1-1)

Örjans vall, Halmstad, 11 June
Attendance: 14,174

POOL One was thrown wide open when Argentina beat Northern Ireland — but how close the Irish came to bringing off yet another surprise.

Winger Peter McParland opened the scoring after only three minutes, but the Argentinians remained unusually calm and seven minutes before half-time they equalized when Corbatta scored from the penalty-spot after Dick Keith handled in the area.

Instead of attacking, Danny Blanchflower's team went on the defensive, perhaps thinking the wet conditions would be to their advantage. But they were not and the South Americans gave a fine display of attacking football which resulted in Menendez putting them in the lead ten minutes into the second half. On the hour, Avio wrapped it up with a third goal. The Irishmens' luck had eventually run out on them.

Helmut Rahn, whose goals helped destroy Argentina.

Gustav Mraz of Czechoslovakia.

The young Argentinians were bolstered by the experience of Angel Labruna, who was recalled to the side. He was to give the Irish a lesson in the delicate skills of the game.

Argentina: Carrizo; Lombardo, Vairo, Rossi, Dellacha, Varacka, Corbatta, Avio, Menendez, Labruna, Boggio.
Scorers: Corbatta (pen), Menendez, Avio
Northern Ireland: Gregg; Keith, McMichael, Blanchflower, Cunningham, Peacock, Bingham, Cush, Coyle, McIlroy, McParland.
Scorer: McParland
Referee: Sten Ahlner (Sweden)

CZECHOSLOVAKIA 2   WEST GERMANY 2 (Half-time 2-0)

Olympia Stadium, Halsingborg, 11 June
Attendance: 25,000

WEST Germany showed, for the second successive game, that they were a team to be taken seriously when, once more, they came from behind. This time they pulled back a two-goal deficit to force a draw with the Czechs, who showed their true form for the first time.

Inside-right Milan Dvorak put the East Europeans ahead from the penalty-spot midway through the first half and two minutes before the break, Zikan added a second goal.

A disputed goal by Schäfer, who bundled the Czech 'keeper over the line, brought West Germany back into the game after 60 minutes and ten minutes later, that man Rahn was there again to score his third goal of the tournament and put the Germans on top of a very close pool.

The Germans were expected to beat Czechoslovakia easily after the form of both teams in their opening pool matches. But wholesale changes to the Czech attack turned them into a different team and in the end the holders were fortunate to hold on for a draw.

Czechoslovakia: Dolejsi; Mraz, Novák, Pluskal, Popluhár, Masopust, Hovorka, Dvorak, Molnar, Feureisl, Zikan.
Scorers: Dvorak (pen), Zikan
West Germany: Herkenrath; Stollenwerk, Juskowiak, Schnellinger, Erhardt, Szymaniak, Rahn, Walter, Seeler, Schäfer, Klodt.
Scorers: Schäfer, Rahn
Referee: Arthur Ellis (England)

Uwe Seeler, equalized against the Irish.

NORTHERN IRELAND 2   WEST GERMANY 2 (Half-time 1-1)

Malmö Stadium, 15 June
Attendance: 21,990

TO make sure of qualifying for the next stage, Northern Ireland had to beat West Germany. And with ten minutes to go it looked as though they had achieved their goal. But then Uwe Seeler struck to score an equalizer.

Germany had proved themselves to be the strongest team in a very tight group and were expected to win. But how well the Irish team, managed by Peter Doherty, performed. Winger Peter McParland established himself as one of the stars of the 1958 competition.

The tall outside-left scored first in the 17th minute but the Irish joy was was short-lived because Germany's own goalscoring sensation, Helmut Rahn, equalized three minutes later.

McParland restored the Irish lead after 58 minutes and they looked as though they were going to hold out for a memorable win until Seeler scored the equalizer ten minutes from time.

This was unquestionably the best match of the pool with Rahn outstanding for the Germans, notably in the first half, and Gregg outstanding in the Northern Ireland goal.

The draw ensured West Germany qualified and Northern Ireland had to face Czechoslovakia in a play-off.

Northern Ireland: Gregg; Keith, McMichael, Blanchflower, Cunningham, Peacock, Bingham, Cush, Casey, McIlroy, McParland.
Scorer: McParland 2
West Germany: Herkenrath; Stollenwerk, Juskowiak, Eckel, Erhardt, Szymaniak, Rahn, Walter, Seeler, Schäfer, Klodt.
Scorers: Rahn, Seeler
Referee: Joaquim Campos (Portugal)

CZECHOSLOVAKIA 6   ARGENTINA 1 (Half-time 3-0)

Olympia Stadium, Halsingborg, 15 June
Attendance: 16,418

THIS was a game that both sides needed to win if they hoped to progress to the quarter-

Top: The Czech team that hammered Argentina. From left to right (players only): Novák, Dolejsi, Popluhár, Mraz, Hovorka, Dvorak, Borovicka, Feureisl, Zikan, Molnar, Masopust.
Bottom: Milan Dvorak is congratulated by his teammates after giving them an eighth-minute lead against the Argentinians.

Zdenek Zikan makes it 2-0 after 17 minutes and Argentina are on their way out of the World Cup.

Jan Popluhár of Czechoslovakia.

Right: The Northern Ireland team that beat Czechoslovakia to reach the quarter-final stage. From left to right: Blanchflower, Cunningham, Uprichard, Cush, McIlroy, Bingham, Scott, Peacock, McParland, Keith, McMichael.

Josef Masopust of Czechoslovakia.

final stage. But three first-half goals by Czechoslovakia ensured they would be engaged in a play-off with Northern Ireland.

The young Argentinian side were hopelessly outclassed by a Czech side who had improved with every game. Dvorak scored after only eight minutes and two more first-half goals from Zikan, in the 17th and 40th minutes, put Czechoslovakia into a commanding 3-0 lead.

After 65 minutes, Corbatta pulled one back with his second penalty of the tournament, but Feureisl maintained the Czechs' three-goal advantage four minutes later. And two goals from Hovorka in the final eight minutes saw them register their biggest-ever World Cup score.

Had Argentina won, they would have stayed in the tournament. However, the Czechoslovakian victory meant a play-off between them and Northern Ireland. Argentina made the long journey home and on their arrival in Buenos Aires were pelted with stones and rubbish by their fans, who were disgusted with their showing against the Czechs.

Czechoslovakia: Dolejsi; Mraz, Novák, Dvorak, Popluhár, Masopust, Hovorka, Borovicka, Molnar, Feureisl, Zikan.
Scorers: Zikan 2, Hovorka 2, Dvorak, Feureisl
Argentina: Carrizo; Lombardo, Vairo, Rossi, Dellacha, Varacka, Corbatta, Avio, Menendez, Labruna, Cruz.
Scorer: Corbatta (pen)
Referee: Arthur Ellis (England)

Play-off
NORTHERN IRELAND 2 CZECHOSLOVAKIA 1 (a.e.t.) (Half-time 1-1; 90 mins 1-1)
Malmö Stadium, 17 June
Attendance: 6,196

DESPITE beating the Czechs in the opening game, Northern Ireland were given no chance in the return match and their opponents were 1/4 on favourites. Those odds looked about right when Zikan gave Czechoslovakia the lead in the 19th minute, after a disastrous defensive error involving a defender and goalkeeper Norman Uprichard, who was playing in place of the injured Harry Gregg.

But the Czechs did not allow for the pluck of the Irish and a minute before half-time, McParland scored his fourth goal in three games. He eventually put the ball in the net after Wilbur Cush had three attempts at scoring. The second half brought no further goals and the game went into extra-time.

Ten minutes from the end, McParland scored his fifth goal of the tournament when he latched on to a Blanchflower free-kick and hammered the ball into the roof of the net.

Czechoslovakia ended the match with ten men after French referee Maurice Guigue sent off wing-half Titus Bubernik. Ireland finished the game with a few casualties. Peacock, who was a virtual passenger, and Uprichard who played on gallantly after receiving an injury. All 11 men played with great will and determination. And the 'no-hopers' of Northern Ireland were in the World Cup quarter-finals.

Northern Ireland: Uprichard; Keith, McMichael, Blanchflower, Cunningham, Peacock, Bingham, Cush, Scott, McIlroy, McParland.
Scorer: McParland 2
Czechoslovakia: Dolejsi; Mraz, Novák, Bubernik, Popluhár, Masopust, Dvorak, Borovicka, Feureisl, Molnar, Zikan.
Scorer: Zikan
Referee: Maurice Guigue (France)

Pool Two

SCOTLAND 1   YUGOSLAVIA 1 (Half-time 0-1)

Arosvallen, Västerås, 8 June
Attendance: 9,591

SCOTLAND were seeking their first-ever World Cup win, in their second tournament. The Yugoslavs, meanwhile, were seeking to rediscover the glory which made them a feared nation in the early days of the competition. At the end of 90 minutes both sides settled for a draw.

Scotland were thrown out of their stride after only six minutes when Petaković put the Yugoslavs ahead, whilst the Scots were still settling down. That was the only goal of the first half and shortly after the interval, the Scottish goal was protected only by the woodwork after a Petaković shot hit the upright.

From nearly going two down, Scotland quickly broke away and the honour of scoring their first-ever goal in the final stages of the World Cup fell to inside-right Jim Murray.

Scotland were driven on by a determined will and were the fitter of the two sides. Their 35-year-old wing-half, Eddie Turnbull, was an inspiration to the younger members of the team.

It was Scotland's first-ever point in the World Cup — and also their last until 1974, when they beat Zaïre.

Scotland: Younger; Caldow, Hewie, Turnbull, Evans, Cowie, Leggat, Murray, Mudie, Collins, Imlach.
Scorer: Murray

Pool One – Final Table

	P	W	D	L	F	A	Pts
W.Germany	3	1	2	0	7	5	4
Czechoslovakia	3	1	1	1	8	4	3
N. Ireland	3	1	1	1	4	5	3
Argentina	3	1	0	2	5	10	2

Danny Blanchflower, Northern Ireland's inspirational captain.

Scotland's Doug Cowie (12) throws up his arms in dismay as Yugoslavia take a sixth-minute lead. Veselinović (13) is the Yugoslavian inside-right.

Jean Vincent of France.

Yugoslavia: Beara; Sijaković, Crnković, Krstić, Zebec, Boškov, Petaković, Veselinović, Milutinović, Šekularac, Rajkov.
Scorer: Petaković
Referee: Paul Wyssling (Switzerland)

FRANCE 7   PARAGUAY 3 (Half-time 2-2)

Idrottsparken, Norrköping, 8 June
Attendance: 16,518

AFTER eliminating Uruguay in the qualifying competition, Paraguay must have been confident of faring well in Sweden. But how disillusioned they were, as France brought them down to earth with a dazzling display of attacking football, notably from Juste Fontaine, who was to end the tournament as its top scorer.

The Moroccan-born Fontaine had made his international debut two years earlier, but was still unsure of a regular place as he went to Sweden. But what an impact he was to have on the tournament.

It was Paraguay who took the lead when Amarilla scored after 20 minutes, but then Fontaine struck with two goals in the 24th and 30th minutes. In the closing minute of the half, Amarilla scored his second goal of the match when he converted a penalty.

After 50 minutes, the South Americans took the lead for the second time when Romero found the net. But thereafter the French forwards commanded the game.

Piantoni scored two minutes after Romero's goal and in the 61st minute, Wisnieski put France back in front. Fontaine completed his hat-trick in the 67th minute and a minute later, that other outstanding French striker, Raymond Kopa, made it 6-3. Kopa was the 1958 European Footballer of the Year and was a star of the great Real Madrid side at the time. Jean Vincent, who was manager of the Cameroon side which reached the final stages in 1982, added the seventh goal with six minutes remaining.

It was a resounding start for the French team which contained seven members of the Rheims side and was managed by their former World Cup centre-forward, Paul Nicolas. France turned out to be one of the outstanding teams of an outstanding tournament.

France: Remetter; Kaelbel, Lerond, Penverne, Jonquet, Marcel, Wisnieski, Fontaine, Kopa, Piantoni, Vincent.
Scorers: Fontaine 3, Piantoni, Wisnieski, Kopa, Vincent
Paraguay: Mageregger; Arevalo, Miranda, Achucaro, Lezcano, Villalba, Aguero, Parodi, Romero, Re, Amarilla.
Scorers: Amarilla 2 (1 pen), Romero
Referee: Juan Gardeazabal Garay (Spain)

PARAGUAY 3   SCOTLAND 2 (Half-time 2-1)

Idrottsparken, Norrköping, 11 June
Attendance: 11,665

HARDLY surprisingly, after conceding seven goals against France, Paraguay made alterations to their defence, including bringing in a new goalkeeper, Samuel Aguilar.

Bobby Collins (left) and Willie Fernie in action for Scotland against Paraguay.

The South Americans learnt a lot from their defeat by France and played with more resolution. Scotland, however, appeared to be tired, with the exception of Bobby Evans, who was outstanding in their defence.

Scotland found themselves trailing after only four minutes, when Aguero scored. Jackie Mudie equalized 20 minutes later but right on half-time, Re scored a crucial goal for Paraguay.

As the second half unfolded, the South Americans were the fitter and stronger of the two teams, although Scotland had been handicapped following an injury to Mudie. Parodi added a third for Paraguay in the 71st minute and, even though Bobby Collins pulled one back a minute later, Paraguay were strong enough to hold on for their win.

Paraguay: Aguilar; Arevalo, Echague, Achucaro, Lezcano, Villalba, Aguero, Parodi, Romero, Re, Amarilla.
Scorers: Aguero, Re, Parodi
Scotland: Younger; Parker, Caldow, Turnbull, Evans, Cowie, Leggat, Collins, Mudie, Robertson, Fernie.
Scorers: Mudie, Collins
Referee: Vincenzo Orlandini (Italy)

Juste Fontaine hit a hat-trick against Paraguay and two goals against Yugoslavia. He finished the tournament with a record total of 13.

YUGOSLAVIA 3 FRANCE 2 (Half-time 1-1)
Arosvallen, Västerås, 11 June
Attendance: 12,217

JUSTE Fontaine added two more goals to his tally in France's second match, but once more his defence conceded three goals and this time Fontaine was on the losing side.

In a very tough game, French optimism from the first game was missing and they allowed the Yugoslavs to dominate for large periods. It was Fontaine, however, who opened the scoring as early as the fourth minute, but Petaković levelled the scores after a quarter of an hour.

After 61 minutes, Veselinović put the Eastern Europeans 2-1 in front before Fontaine snatched an equalizer five minutes from time. However, instead of settling for the draw, the Yugoslavs pushed forward and Veselinović scored a last-minute winner following a breakaway. The win put Yugoslavia on top of the group.

Yugoslavia: Beara; Tomić, Crnković, Krstić, Zebec, Boškov, Petaković, Veselinović, Milutinović, Šekularac, Rajkov.
Scorers: Veselinović 2, Petaković
France: Remetter; Kaelbel, March, Penverne, Jonquet, Lerond, Wisnieski, Fontaine, Kopa, Piantoni, Vincent.
Scorers: Fontaine 2
Referee: Mervyn Griffiths (Wales)

Raymond Kopa of France.

FRANCE 2 SCOTLAND 1 (Half-time 2-0)
Eyravallen, Örebro, 15 June
Attendance: 13,554

FRANCE had to beat Scotland to qualify for the quarter-finals, whilst the Scots had to win to stand an outside chance of qualifying. France went into the match as clear favourites but, after their impressive start against Paraguay, had done little to encourage their fans against Yugoslavia. However, they tightened up their game and took no chances, which had cost them goals in both games so far. Kopa opened the scoring midway through the first half and as the first period came to a close, Fontaine made it 2-0 with his sixth goal in three games.

Sammy Baird gave the Scots some hope when he pulled one back from a throw-in in the 58th minute, but there was no more scoring and France qualified for the quarter-final.

Whilst the defeat appeared to be a narrow one for Scotland, it was only thanks to the heroics of debutant goalkeeper Bill Brown that France were held to two goals.

For Scotland it was a sad exit. They were the only one of the four Home countries not to be involved in a play-off.

France: Abbès; Kaelbel, Lerond, Penverne, Jonquet, Marcel, Wisnieski, Fontaine, Kopa, Piantoni, Vincent.
Scorers: Kopa, Fontaine
Scotland: Brown; Caldow, Hewie, Turnbull, Evans, Mackay, Collins, Murray, Mudie, Baird, Imlach.
Scorer: Baird
Referee: Juan Brozzi (Argentina)

PARAGUAY 3 YUGOSLAVIA 3 (Half-time 1-2)
Tunavallen, Eskilstuna, 15 June
Attendance: 13,103

THIS pool certainly produced a variety of strange results and Paraguay, who suffered that heavy defeat by France in the opening game, were not too far away from qualifying for the quarter-final. For the first time they produced the form which had taken them to a 7-0 aggregate win over Uruguay in the qualifying competition.

Claude Abbès, who replaced Francois Remetter in the French goal for the vital game against Scotland.

Pool Two – Final Table

	P	W	D	L	F	A	Pts
France	3	2	0	1	11	7	4
Yugoslavia	3	1	2	0	7	6	4
Paraguay	3	1	1	1	9	12	3
Scotland	3	0	1	2	4	6	1

They held Yugoslavia to a 3-3 draw in their last game after coming from behind on three occasions and poor goalkeeping by Beara nearly cost the Yugoslavs a place in the last eight.

Ognjanović gave the Yugoslavs a 12th-minute lead which Parodi equalized eight minutes later. Veselinović restored the Yugoslav lead in the 28th minute before Aguero drew Paraguay level once more, in the 52nd minute. Seventeen minutes from time, Rajkov made it 3-2 before Romero equalized again with a goal ten minutes from the end. Alas for Paraguay, the draw was not good enough to give them a second chance in a play-off match.

Paraguay: Aguilar; Arevalo, Echague, Villalba, Lezcano, Achucaro, Aguero, Parodi, Romero, Re, Amarilla.
Scorers: Parodi, Aguero, Romero
Yugoslavia: Beara; Tomić, Crnković, Krstić, Zebec, Boškov, Petaković, Veselinović, Ognjanović, Šekularac, Rajkov.
Scorers: Ognjanović, Veselinović, Rajkov
Referee: Martin Macko (Czechoslovakia)

Gunnar Gren of Sweden.

Pool Three

SWEDEN 3   MEXICO 0 (Half-time 1-0)
Råsunda Stadium, Solna, 8 June
Attendance: 34,107

AT 2pm on 8 June, the host nation got the sixth World Cup underway and there could not have been a better start for the home fans or for Sweden's Yorkshire-born trainer, George Raynor. Victory over Mexico set them on the way to an appearance in the World Cup Final, which Raynor had predicted for them before the start of the tournament.

The Scandinavians were once more one of the world's leading soccer nations. Their Italian exports Nils Liedholm (AC Milan), Kurt Hamrin (Padova), Arne Selmonsson (Lazio), 'Nacka' Skoglund (Inter Milan), and Bengt Gustavsson (Atalanta) were in the national side after Sweden's acceptance of professionalism and their presence was certainly felt by the other teams.

The opening match was played in a tremendous spirit and this championship went on to rightly earn a reputation for being the 'friendly World Cup'.

Sweden had little difficulty in disposing of Mexico, for whom Antonio Carbajal was appearing in his third successive tournament — and he still had to appear on a winning side.

Simonsson, with a goal in each half, and a Liedholm penalty in the second half were enough to see Sweden gain a comfortable 3-0 win.

The match was refereed by Nikolai Latychev, the first Soviet referee in the final stages of the World Cup. His appearance coincided with that of his country, who were also making their debut.

Sweden: Svensson; Bergmark, Axbom, Liedholm, Gustavsson, Parling, Hamrin, Mellberg, Simonsson, Gren, Skoglund.
Scorers: Simonsson 2, Liedholm (pen)
Mexico: Carbajal; Del Muro, Villegas, Portugal, Romo, Flores, Hernández, Reyes, Calderon, Gutiérrez, Sesma.
Referee: Nikolai Latychev (USSR)

Agne Simonsson of Sweden.

The Swedish players are presented to their king, Gustav.

Sweden's team which beat Mexico. Back row (left to right): Liedholm, Simonsson, Parling, Skoglund, Gren, Gustavsson. Front row: Bergmark, Svensson, Axbom, Hamrin, Mellberg.

HUNGARY 1   WALES 1 (Half-time 1-1)

Jernvallen, Sandviken, 8 June
Attendance: 15,343

THE Hungarian uprising of 1956 had taken its toll on the Magyars' national soccer team. Only goalkeeper Grosics, defender Bozsik and forward Hidegkuti remained from the team which fought out the 1954 Final and Hidegkuti was now 38 years old. But in Sándor and Tichy, they had two exciting forwards and were expected to gain an easy victory over the Welsh, who were lucky to be in the final stages at all. But what a shock the once-mighty Magyars got.

Wales turned out to be the surprise team of the tournament as John Charles, his brother Mel, Dave Bowen, Ivor Allchurch and so on gave opposing teams plenty to think about. John Charles arrived in Sweden only the day before the opening match, after the Italian FA gave last-minute permission for him to be released from domestic duties with Juventus.

Bozsik swept the favourites into a fifth-minute lead when he took a pass from Hidegkuti and put the ball past Kelsey in the Welsh goal after a great solo effort.

The 15,000 crowd now expected an avalanche of goals from the Hungarians. But, despite being superior, they could not find the net again and the game's only other goal was scored by John Charles in the 27th minute. He had been a marked man from the first whistle, but rose to head home a Cliff Jones cross to earn the Welsh a momentous draw against one of the former giants of world soccer.

Hungary: Grosics; Mátrai, Sárosi, Bozsik, Sipos, Berendi, Sándor, Hidegkuti, Tichy, Bundzsák, Fenyvesi.
Scorer: Bozsik
Wales: Kelsey; Williams, Hopkins, Sullivan, M.Charles, Bowen, Webster, Medwin, J.Charles, Allchurch, Jones.
Scorer: J.Charles
Referee: Jose Maria Codesal (Uruguay)

MEXICO 1   WALES 1 (Half-time 0-1)

Råsunda Stadium, Solna, 11 June
Attendance: 15,150

MEXICO made several changes for their second match, including moving left winger Gutiérrez to left-back. The South Americans were very popular with the Stockholm crowd, who were trying to lift them, but it was Wales who scored first when Allchurch volleyed home a Medwin pass after half an hour.

Despite the support of the home fans, and countless raids on Jack Kelsey's goal, the Mexicans could not score until the very last minute, when Belmonte headed the equalizer, much to the delight of most of the 15,000 fans.

Wales were disappointed at failing to win, particularly after holding Hungary to a draw. And with one game remaining, against group favourites Sweden, Welsh hopes of qualifying for the next phase were diminishing.

Sweden's goalkeeper Karl Svensson.

Welsh goalkeeper Jack Kelsey and teammate Mel Charles.

Mexico: Carbajal; Del Muro, Gutiérrez, Cardenas, Romo, Flores, Belmonte, Reyes, Blanco, González, Sesma.
Scorer: Belmonte
Wales: Kelsey; Williams, Hopkins, Baker, M.Charles, Bowen, Webster, Medwin, J.Charles, Allchurch, Jones.
Scorer: Allchurch
Referee: Leo Lemesić (Yugoslavia)

SWEDEN 2   HUNGARY 1 (Half-time 1-0)

Råsunda Stadium, Solna, 12 June
Attendance: 38,850

THE day after Wales' poor showing against Mexico, the hosts did the Welsh a big favour by beating Hungary.

Hungary dropped Hidegkuti and moved Bozsik, to a deep-lying centre-forward role. But this move did little to improve the Hungarian firepower and they gave a very unimpressive performance. Sweden were equally off-form and perhaps a little fortunate to win.

When Hamrin scored after 34 minutes there appeared to be a suspicion of offside, but Scottish referee Mowat ruled in Hamrin's favour and Sweden led at the interval.

It was only the powerful shooting of Tichy which gave the Hungarians any hope of breaking through and in the 55th minute he beat the Swedish goalkeeper with an effort which hit the underside of the bar. Many thought the ball rebounded over the line, but referee Mowat was adamant that it had not. Less than a minute later, Hamrin scored his second goal when his lob was deflected past Grosics.

Sweden's lead was ill-deserved but, even though Tichy eventually scored for Hungary in the 77th minute, it was too late to salvage anything and Sweden hung on for a narrow win.

Sweden: Svensson; Bergmark, Axbom, Liedholm, Gustavsson, Parling, Hamrin, Mellberg, Simonsson, Gren, Skoglund.
Scorer: Hamrin 2
Hungary: Grosics; Mátrai, Sárosi, Szojka, Sipos, Berendi, Sándor, Tichy, Bozsik, Bundzsák, Fenyvesi.
Scorer: Tichy
Referee: Jack Mowat (Scotland)

The Hungarian line-up which lost to Sweden. Left to right: Bozsik (partly hidden), Grosics, Tichy, Mátrai, Sipos, Szojka, Bundzsák, Sárosi, Sándor, Fenyvesi, Berendi.

SWEDEN 0   WALES 0 (Half-time 0-0)

Råsunda Stadium, Solna, 15 June
Attendance: 29,800

AS Sweden were assured of qualifying for the quarter-finals, they rested some of their established stars and fielded five reserves. The Welshmen knew that a draw would guarantee them a play-off game and they played for the point. Their plans could have come unstuck, however, had it not been for a magnificent display by goalkeeper Jack Kelsey. Wales held out for the World Cup's second goalless draw, in what can only be described as a drab match.

Sweden: Svensson; Bergmark, Axbom, Börjesson, Gustavsson, Parling, Berndtsson, Selmonsson, Källgren, Löfgren, Skoglund.
Wales: Kelsey; Williams, Hopkins, Sullivan, M.Charles, Bowen, Vernon, Hewitt, J.Charles, Allchurch, Jones.
Referee: Lucien Van Nuffel (Belgium)

HUNGARY 4   MEXICO 0 (Half-time 1-0)

Jernvallen, Sandviken, 15 June
Attendance: 13,310

BOTH teams started this, their final match, with one point and needed to win to progress further. A draw would have eliminated both sides and put Wales through, although neither side knew that until half-time, by which time Hungary led 1-0, thanks to a goal from their new scoring sensation, Lajos Tichy.

The Sweden-Wales match had kicked-off earlier and as the players took their half-time break, they learned of the score from Stockholm. The news gave Hungary the greater motivation and they attacked from the restart. Within a minute, Tichy had scored his second goal.

Hungary were now cruising and Sándor made it 3-0 in the 54th minute. González put through his own goal 30 minutes from time to seal a miserable afternoon for the Mexicans.

Victory put Hungary into a play-off with Wales, but for Mexico it was their 11th World Cup match in four tournaments without a win.

Hungary: Ilku; Mátrai, Sárosi, Szojka, Sipos, Kotász, Budai, Bencsics, Hidegkuti, Tichy, Sándor.
Scorers: Tichy 2, Sándor, González (og)
Mexico: Carbajal; Del Muro, Gutiérrez, Cardenas, Sepúlveda, Flores, Belmonte, Reyes, Blanco, González, Sesma.
Referee: A.Eriksson (Finland)

Pool Three – Final Table

	P	W	D	L	F	A	Pts
Sweden	3	2	1	0	5	1	5
Hungary	3	1	1	1	6	3	3
Wales	3	0	3	0	2	2	3
Mexico	3	0	1	2	1	8	1

Nacka Skoglund of Sweden.

Welsh centre-forward John Charles gets back to try to block a centre from Hungary's Lászlo Budai.

Play-off
WALES 2   HUNGARY 1 (Half-time 0-1)

Råsunda Stadium, Solna, 17 June
Attendance: 2,832

SINCE their opening match, when they did well to hold Hungary, Wales' performance had deteriorated and they were given little chance against the Magyars, who had reached their top form for the first time against Mexico. The Swedish fans did not give much for Wales' chances and stayed away in their thousands.

Wales fell behind to a tremendous Tichy goal, his fourth in three games, after 33 minutes. Ivor Allchurch levelled the scores ten minutes into the second half, when his 35-yard volley beat Grosics. Then, with 14 minutes left, Terry Medwin latched on to a short kick from Grosics to one of his defenders and scored the winner in cheeky fashion, much to the embarrassment of the established Hungarian goalkeeper, who had a nightmare of a match.

It was a remarkable victory and Wales, the team originally eliminated from the qualifying competition, were in the quarter-finals.

The game was refereed by the Soviet official, Nikolai Latychev, who, after ignoring many of the Hungarian foul tactics, was eventually forced to dismiss Sipos for a vicious tackle on Hewitt. John Charles was the victim of many of the violent tackles dished out by the Magyars in one of the roughest games of the tournament.

Wales: Kelsey; Williams, Hopkins, Sullivan, M.Charles, Bowen, Medwin, Hewitt, J.Charles, Allchurch, Jones.
Scorers: Allchurch, Medwin
Hungary: Grosics; Mátrai, Sárosi, Bozsik, Sipos, Kotász, Budai, Bencsics, Tichy, Bundzsák, Fenyvesi.
Scorer: Tichy
Referee: Nikolai Latychev (USSR)

Mel Hopkins, Tottenham Hotspur's Welsh international full-back.

Pool Four

Lev Yashin of the USSR, one of the world's greatest post-war goalkeepers.

BRAZIL 3   AUSTRIA 0 (Half-time 1-0)

Rimnersvallen, Uddevalla, 8 June
Attendance: 21,000

SINCE the war, Brazil had emerged as one of the most exciting footballing nations. After failing to win the World Cup on their home soil in 1950, their disappointment was acute. Four years later, in Switzerland, they had expected to fare better — and failed again. But now they had a new and exciting team. Some faces remained, like Nilton and Djalmar Santos and Didí. But new stars like Garrincha, Vavá, Zagalo and the 17-year-old wonderboy, Pelé, constituted the 'new' Brazil, who brought their innovative 4-2-4 line-up to Sweden.

Pelé did not appear in the opening match because he was suffering from an injury, but Brazil still had no problem in disposing of Austria at Uddevalla. The Europeans paid the penalty for not calling up the talented Ernst Ocwirk. He was playing League soccer in Italy at the time and they could have done with the experienced defender against the rampant Brazilian forwards.

Goals from Mazzola, seven minutes before half-time, Nilton Santos after 49 minutes and Mazzola again, with a magnificent goal in the last minute, ensured Brazil started their sixth World Cup campaign with a win.

Brazil: Gilmar; De Sordi, N.Santos, Dino, Bellini, Orlando, Joel, Didí, Mazola, Dida, Zagalo.
Scorers: Mazola 2, N.Santos
Austria: Szanwald; Halla, Swoboda, Hanappi, Happel, Koller, Horak, Senekowitsch, Buzek, Körner, Schleger.
Referee: Maurice Guigue (France)

ENGLAND 2   SOVIET UNION 2 (Half-time 0-1)

Nya Ullevi Stadium, Gothenburg, 8 June
Attendance: 49,348

The Brazilian squad photographed outside their Swedish hotel.

WHEN the draw for the sixth World Cup was made, England knew that their pool was by far the toughest. Brazil were clearly the favourites, but in recent years the Russians had

emerged as one of Europe's top soccer nations. To make matters worse for England, the Munich air disaster had torn the heart from their team.

It was, therefore, perhaps strange that they should leave behind such talented players as Stanley Matthews and Nat Lofthouse, when their experience could have been invaluable in such a situation.

England had met the Russians in a friendly in Moscow, only three weeks before the start of the World Cup, and returned with a commendable 1-1 draw. They were feeling confident about this World Cup opener, particularly after it was announced that the Russian skipper, Igor Netto, was unfit.

However, England suffered a set-back after only 13 minutes. The Russian centre-forward, Nikita Simonian, put his side in front after goalkeeper McDonald could not hold a shot from Alexander Ivanov. The Soviets held on to that lead up to half-time and ten minutes into the second half, Ivanov made it 2-0.

Ten minutes later, England centre-forward Derek Kevan headed past Lev Yashin from a Billy Wright free-kick taken five yards inside his own half. It was not a spectacular goal, but at least the unfashionable centre-forward had opened England's account.

As the game went into the last five minutes, Johnny Haynes was brought down around the edge of the penalty area. It looked as though it might have been outside the area, but experienced Hungarian referee, Istvan Zsolt, had no hesitation in pointing to the spot. This decision made up for the possible penalty which England claimed when Tom Finney was brought down early in the half.

Finney stepped up and scored with what was virtually his last kick in World Cup football. He had salvaged a draw for one of the tournament's favourites, but if England were going to progress any further, then they would have to perform more convincingly than they did in this opening match.

England: McDonald; Howe, Banks, Clamp, Wright, Slater, Douglas, Robson, Kevan, Haynes, Finney.
Scorers: Kevan, Finney (pen)
Soviet Union: Yashin; Kesarev, Kuznetsov, Voinov, Krijevski, Tsarev, A.Ivanov, V.Ivanov, Simonian, Salnikov, Ilyin.
Scorers: Simonian, A.Ivanov
Referee: Istvan Zsolt (Hungary)

Nikita Simonian, gave Russia the lead against England after 13 minutes.

Tom Finney's penalty draws England level after being 2-0 down against the Russians.

Pelé did not play against England in what turned out to be the first-ever goalless draw in a World Cup finals.

Brazil's Nilton Santos keeps Derek Kevan and Alan A'Court (partly hidden) at bay as Gilmar falls on the ball during the game against England in Gothenburg.

SOVIET UNION 2   AUSTRIA 0 (Half-time 1-0)

Ryavallen, Borås, 11 June
Attendance: 21,239

THE Soviets, still without Netto, were simply too good for Austria who, once again, failed to score a World Cup goal. The nation which had occupied third place in the 1954 tournament were only a shadow of their former selves and allowed the World Cup newcomers to dominate them. Seven changes from the opening match did nothing but weaken the Austrian line-up. The Soviet Union team was unchanged.

One goal in each half, by Ilyin after 15 minutes and Valentin Ivanov in the 62nd minute, gave the Soviets their comfortable win.

Soviet Union: Yashin; Kesarev, Kuznetsov, Voinov, Krijevski, Tsarev, A.Ivanov, V.Ivanov, Simonian, Salnikov, Ilyin.
Scorers: Ilyin, V.Ivanov
Austria: Schmied; E.Kozlicek, Swoboda, Hanappi, Stotz, Koller, Horak, P.Kozlicek, Buzek, Körner, Senekowitsch.
Referee: Carl Jorgensen (Denmark)

BRAZIL 0   ENGLAND 0 (Half-time 0-0)

Nya Ullevi Stadium, Gothenburg, 11 June
Attendance: 40,895

THE fans flocked in their thousands to see England again, just as they had done in their opening match, and although the crowd had to witness the first-ever goalless draw in a World Cup Finals, they were treated to a most exciting game.

Both teams made one change. Brazil brought in Vavá at inside-left for Dida, whilst England were forced to leave out the badly injured Tom Finney, who was replaced by Alan A'Court on the left wing.

In contrast to their first performance against the Soviets, England played much better. At coach Bill Nicholson's instigation the defence was switched around, although the same players were used — and the changes worked.

The game was one of contrasting styles. Brazil had more of the play in the first half but the England defence kept their forwards at bay whilst goalkeeper Colin McDonald was outstanding and brought off some near-miraculous saves.

Brazil opted for a defensive game in the second half and England nearly scored a last-gasp winner. They were also unlucky not to have been awarded a penalty after Bellini brought down Derek Kevan in the first half. This was the only game Brazil failed to win on their way to lifting the trophy.

Brazil: Gilmar; De Sordi, N.Santos, Dino, Bellini, Orlando, Joel, Didí, Mazola, Vavá, Zagalo.
England: McDonald; Howe, Banks, Clamp, Wright, Slater, Douglas, Robson, Kevan, Haynes, A'Court.
Referee: Albert Dusch (West Germany)

AUSTRIA 2   ENGLAND 2 (Half-time 1-0)

Ryavallen, Borås, 15 June
Attendance: 16,800

ENGLAND knew that they had to beat Austria to be sure of qualifying for the quarter-finals. A draw might have been good enough, but that all depended on the result of the Brazil-Soviet Union game in Gothenburg.

England applied a lot of early pressure, but their ambitions were shattered when Koller scored from 30 yards to put Austria in front after 16 minutes.

Haynes equalized after 60 minutes, following an error by Austrian goalkeeper Szanwald, and then England continued to attack and were looking for the winner when another long-range effort beat McDonald. This time it was Körner who put the Austrians back in front in the 70th minute. Eight minutes later, Kevan became the England saviour once again when he levelled the scores. And that is how it stayed, despite late England pressure.

Before they left the pitch the England players knew the result from Gothenburg. It meant a second meeting with the Soviets in a play-off.

Austria: Szanwald; Kollmann, Swoboda, Hanappi, Happel, Koller, E.Kozlicek, P.Kozlicek, Buzek, Körner, Senekowitsch.
Scorers: Koller, Körner
England: McDonald; Howe, Banks, Clamp, Wright, Slater, Douglas, Robson, Kevan, Haynes, A'Court.
Scorers: Haynes, Kevan
Referee: A.Asmussen (Denmark)

BRAZIL 2   SOVIET UNION 0 (Half-time 1-0)

Nya Ullevi Stadium, Gothenburg, 15 June
Attendance: 50,928

NEARLY 51,000 fans — the highest attendance of the first phase matches — packed into the Nya Ullevi Stadium to watch these attractive teams. It was the Brazilians, giving Zito, Garrincha and Pelé their first games in the 1958 World Cup, who were most impressive and they secured their place in the last eight.

Pool Four – Final Table

	P	W	D	L	F	A	Pts
Brazil	3	2	1	0	5	0	5
England	3	0	3	0	4	4	3
Soviet Union	3	1	1	1	4	4	3
Austria	3	0	1	2	2	7	1

Garrincha, 'The Little Bird', was selected against Hungary after his teammates pleaded for his inclusion.

Nilton Santos performs an acrobatic clearance against the Soviet Union.

Valentin Ivanov of the USSR.

Garrincha, the man born with a deformed leg, was selected only after the Brazilian players pleaded with team manager Vicente Feola to include him. They were right and 'The Little Bird' ran rings around the Russian defence.

The Russian captain, Netto, was also making his first appearance and was given the role of marking Didí. But Didí was outstanding as the dynamo of the Brazilian team which had, for the first time in the tournament, showed their true form.

Both Brazilian goals were scored by Vavá, in the third and 77th minutes, and victory saw Brazil win the pool with only one dropped point. Their performance against the Soviet Union certainly served as a warning of what they had in store for the rest of the tournament.

Brazil: Gilmar; De Sordi, N.Santos, Zito, Bellini, Orlando, Garrincha, Didí, Vavá, Pelé, Zagalo.
Scorers: Vavá 2
Soviet Union: Yashin; Kesarev, Kuznetsov, Voinov, Krijevski, Tsarev, A.Ivanov, V.Ivanov, Simonian, Netto, Ilyin.
Referee: Maurice Guigue (France)

Play-off
SOVIET UNION 1   ENGLAND 0 (Half-time 0-0)
Nya Ullevi Stadium, Gothenburg, 17 June
Attendance: 23,182

ENGLAND changed their right-wing combination by giving first caps to Peter Brabrook and Peter Broadbent. Many felt the young Bobby Charlton should have been given his chance, but his day was yet to come.

The newcomers did well and both created plenty of chances, although Brabrook missed an easy opportunity to score and two other efforts hit the woodwork. England seemed to be well on top, but when Ilyin gathered a poor throw out from Colin McDonald in the 63rd minute, the winger's shot hit the post and rolled over the line.

The Russians held on to that lead and celebrated their World Cup debut by reaching the quarter-finals. England packed their bags and went home — but how different it might have been had Roger Byrne, Tommy Taylor and Duncan Edwards been in the side.

Ironically, it was the first time that the four Home countries had qualified for the final stages and the two more fancied teams, England and Scotland, were both eliminated. The United Kingdom flag was now being flown by Wales and Northern Ireland.

Soviet Union: Yashin; Kesarev, Kuznetsov, Voinov, Krijevski, Tsarev, Apoukhtin, V.Ivanov, Simonian, Falin, Ilyin.
Scorer: Ilyin
England: McDonald; Howe, Banks, Clayton, Wright, Slater, Brabrook, Broadbent, Kevan, Haynes, A'Court.
Referee: Albert Dusch (West Germany)

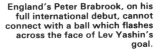

England's Peter Brabrook, on his full international debut, cannot connect with a ball which flashes across the face of Lev Yashin's goal.

Quarter-finals

WEST GERMANY 1   YUGOSLAVIA 0 (Half-time 1-0)

Malmö Stadium, 19 June
Attendance: 20,000

IN a dour defensive battle, the holders scraped through, thanks to a 12th-minute goal from Helmut Rahn. However, just as in Switzerland four years earlier, when the two sides met, the Yugoslavs were the better team but could not find that vital goal.

Neither side was giving anything away and their performances gave the 20,000 crowd little to cheer. For Rahn, it was to be his penultimate World Cup goal. He was one of the heroes of the German side which lifted the trophy four years earlier, but fell out of favour in the intervening years. Herberger recalled him for the 1958 tournament and the choice paid off as Rahn, once again, became one of the German stars as they marched into the semi-final.

West Germany: Herkenrath; Stollenwerk, Juskowiak, Eckel, Erhardt, Szymaniak, Rahn, Walter, Seeler, Schmidt, Schäfer.
Scorer: Rahn
Yugoslavia: Krivokuca; Sijaković, Crnković, Krstić, Zebec, Boškov, Petaković, Ognjanović, Milutinović, Veselinović, Rajkov.
Referee: Paul Wyssling (Switzerland)

Horst Szymaniak, the powerhouse of the West German side.

Fritz Walter of West Germany fires at the Yugoslavian goal as two defenders close in.

Helmut Rahn, star of West Germany's earlier World Cup triumph, puts his side into the semi-finals with a 12th-minute goal.

Nils Liedholm of Sweden.

France line up before their quarter-
final game against Northern
Ireland. From left to right: Jonquet,
Abbés, Kopa, Piantoni, Fontaine,
Wisnieski, Penverne, Vincent,
Marcel, Lerond, Kaelbel.

Didí of Brazil.

SWEDEN 2   SOVIET UNION 0 (Half-time 0-0)

Råsunda Stadium, Solna, 19 June
Attendance: 31,900

THE Russians, like Wales and Northern Ireland, had to face their quarter-final match less than 48 hours after their play-off game. The short rest period took its toll and the Swedes ran out deserved winners, helping to maintain George Raynor's prediction that the hosts would reach the Final.

The Russians curtailed the efforts of the Swedish forwards in the first half but in the 49th minute, outside-left Skoglund set up the first goal for his fellow winger, Hamrin. Despite being the best side, the Swedes could not find the net again, until two minutes from time when Simonsson sealed the victory with a powerful shot that beat Russian goalkeeper Yashin. That brought to an end the Soviets' hopes of progressing further. Nevertheless, they fared well on their World Cup debut.

Sweden: Svensson; Bergmark, Axbom, Börjesson, Gustavsson, Parling, Hamrin, Gren, Simonsson, Liedholm, Skoglund.
Scorers: Hamrin, Simonsson
Soviet Union: Yashin; Kesarev, Kuznetsov, Voinov, Krijevski, Tsarev, A.Ivanov, V.Ivanov, Simonian, Salnikov, Ilyin.
Referee: Reg Leafe (England)

FRANCE 4   NORTHERN IRELAND 0 (Half-time 1-0)

Idrottsparken, Norrköping, 19 June
Attendance: 11,800

THE handicap of playing two games in three days, as well as an eight-hour coach journey to Norrköping, took its toll on the Irish players. But, even without those obvious handicaps, they probably would still have been unable to stop the dynamic Juste Fontaine, who added two more goals to his already impressive tally.

Ireland were tired after their hard game against Czechoslovakia and were also nursing several injuries. Norman Uprichard was so badly hurt that Harry Gregg was forced to return to the Irish goal, despite still suffering from a leg injury received in the game against West Germany. Inside-right Tom Casey played with four stitches in his shin.

Considering all the facts, the Irish did remarkably well to hold the powerful French forwards until two minutes before half-time, when right winger Maryan Wisnieski scored the goal which France had threatened for most of the half.

In the second half, it was one French attack after another, with Raymond Kopa outstanding. Inevitably, a flood of goals followed. Fontaine scored twice, in the 55th and 63rd minutes, and 20 minutes from time, Piantoni wrapped it up with the fourth goal. Northern Ireland, meanwhile, hardly had a shot.

France: Abbès; Kaelbel, Lerond, Penverne, Jonquet, Marcel, Wisnieski, Fontaine, Kopa, Piantoni, Vincent.
Scorers: Fontaine 2, Wisnieski, Piantoni
Northern Ireland: Gregg; Keith, McMichael, Blanchflower, Cunningham, Cush, Bingham, Casey, Scott, McIlroy, McParland.
Referee: Juan Gardeazabal Garay (Spain)

BRAZIL 1   WALES 0 (Half-time 0-0)

Nya Ullevi Stadium, Gothenburg, 19 June
Attendance: 25,923

AS the quarter-final scores were flashed around the other grounds, the one shock was from Gothenburg where the gallant Welsh were holding the powerful Brazilians to a goalless first half.

Who could ever have imagined that Wales, without the injured John Charles, could have

Wales line up for their group game against Sweden in Solna. Players only (left to right): Bowen, John Charles, Kelsey, Jones, Hewitt, Allchurch, Hopkins, Williams, Vernon, Sullivan, Mel Charles. By the time the Welsh had fought their way through to the quarter-finals, they were without the services of the injured John Charles.

Vicente Feola, manager of Brazil.

Pelé gets in a challenge on Kelsey, but the ball flies harmlessly past the Welsh post.

checked the likes of Garrincha, Pelé, Didí and Zagalo? For more than 70 minutes the Welsh held their more illustrious opponents, thanks to a well-disciplined defence. However, in the 73rd minute they allowed 17-year-old Pelé to score his first-ever World Cup goal, which he later described as 'the most important goal of my career'.

It came after the Welsh full-backs hesitated and Pelé found a gap through the defence. When he struck the ball from the edge of the six-yard box it was not hit fully and it scraped past the advancing Jack Kelsey after being deflected off the Welsh right-back, Stuart Williams.

Wales kept on fighting to the final whistle, but could not get an equalizer. They went out of the tournament in a blaze of glory after coming in as complete no-hopers. In view of the next two performances the Brazilians were to give, the Welsh effort cannot be described any less accurately than 'brilliant'.

Brazil: Gilmar; De Sordi, N.Santos, Zito, Bellini, Orlando, Garrincha, Didí, Mazola, Pelé, Zagalo.
Scorer: Pelé
Wales: Kelsey; Williams, Hopkins, Sullivan, M.Charles, Bowen, Medwin, Hewitt, Webster, Allchurch, Jones.
Referee: Erich Seipelt (Austria)

Pelé in the back of the net after scoring Brazil's winner against Wales.

Above: Pelé's shot beats Jack Kelsey and Wales' brave World Cup fight is over. *Right:* Garrincha's shot goes wide as Kelsey covers.

Uwe Seeler tries to break through the Swedish defence in the semi-final.

Semi-finals

SWEDEN 3   WEST GERMANY 1 (Half-time 1-1)

Nya Ullevi Stadium, Gothenburg, 24 June
Attendance: 49,471

FOR the first time since the tournament started, the home fans got behind their team. The attendances up to the semi-final stage had been disappointing and the Swiss had taken little notice of what George Raynor had to say before the start of the tournament. But now they were in the semi-finals and beginning to believe in their team. Indeed, the scenes of patriotism in Gothenburg had never been seen on a Swedish football ground before.

Much against the run of the play, Hans Schäfer gave the Germans the lead midway through the first half with a brilliant volley from an Uwe Seeler cross. 'Nacka' Skoglund scored from an acute angle ten minutes later, after Liedholm had blatantly handled the ball without being penalized.

On paper Germany had a stronger team, whilst the Swedes, although skilful, were an ageing side and many expected them to tire in the second half.

Germany, however, were reduced to ten men in the 58th minute when referee Zsolt sent off full-back Juskowiak for retaliating after being fouled by Hamrin. The decision angered the Germans and for several minutes there were angry scenes as the German players surrounded the referee. Despite his pleas, Juskowiak had to make his way to the dressing-room.

The incident unsettled the Germans, who also had the misfortune of losing their captain, Fritz Walter, for ten minutes while he received treatment to an injury after a bad foul by Parling. Despite their set-backs and handicaps, West Germany held out until nine minutes from time, when Gunnar Gren put the Swedes in front for the first time. The home fans went wild and when Hamrin dribbled through the German defence to make it 3-1, two minutes from time, one would have thought Sweden had just won the World Cup.

West Germany's reign as holders of the Jules Rimet Trophy came to a sad and controversial end.

West Germany's Juskowiak (centre) is sent off after retaliating against Hamrin.

Sweden: Svensson; Bergmark, Axbom, Börjesson, Gustavsson, Parling, Hamrin, Gren, Simonsson, Liedholm, Skoglund.
Scorers: Skoglund, Gren, Hamrin
West Germany: Herkenrath; Stollenwerk, Juskowiak, Eckel, Erhardt, Szymaniak, Rahn, Walter, Seeler, Schäfer, Cieslarczyk.
Scorer: Schäfer
Referee: Istvan Zsolt (Hungary)

BRAZIL 5   FRANCE 2 (Half-time 2-1)

Råsunda Stadium, Solna, 24 June
Attendance: 27,100

WHAT a match this promised to be. The skills of Raymond Kopa and the goalscoring brilliance of Juste Fontaine for France against the dazzling Brazilian forwards. Indeed, it

Juste Fontaine gives France hope as he makes the score 1-1 against Brazil. It is the first goal conceded by the Brazilians in the tournament.

This time Gilmar just manages to foil Fontaine as France's top-scoring striker races in.

Brazil's Gilmar, a fine goalkeeper in a great team.

was a match to savour and turned out to be the best game of what was a great World Cup tournament.

Vavá gave the Brazilians the lead in the first minute when he gathered the ball on his chest, let it drop and then volleyed it past the French 'keeper, Claude Abbès. Less than eight minutes later, France had drawn level when Fontaine, perhaps predictably, scored after he finished off a move involving himself and Kopa. It was the first goal conceded by Brazil in the 1958 tournament.

The game was played at a furious pace as both sides gave displays of flowing attractive football. Sadly for France, their centre-half Jonquet received a bad injury and spent the remainder of the game as a limping passenger in the forward line. It was perhaps surprising that the game went so long before the next goal, which came in the 39th minute and was scored by Didí.

But the second half belonged to one man, Pelé. He scored a hat-trick in just over 20 minutes. The first was a simple goal after the 'keeper made a mistake and the ball dropped at the Brazilian's feet. The second was a well-taken half-chance from the edge of the six-yard box. But the third was sheer Pelé brilliance — a volley from the edge of the penalty area.

For the first 45 minutes it was a close affair. Thirty minutes later Brazil led 5-1. And it could well have been 7-1, had Welsh referee, Mervyn Griffiths, not disallowed two first-half efforts, one after a linesman had signalled a goal.

Piantoni added a second goal for France seven minutes from the end, but this semi-final belonged to Pelé as Brazil burst into life and played the brand of football that the world was to see many times over the next ten years or so.

Brazil: Gilmar; De Sordi, N.Santos, Zito, Bellini, Orlando, Garrincha, Didí, Vavá, Pelé, Zagalo.
Scorers: Pelé 3, Vavá, Didí
France: Abbés; Kaelbel, Lerond, Penverne, Jonquet, Marcel, Wisnieski, Fontaine, Kopa, Piantoni, Vincent.
Scorers: Fontaine, Piantoni
Referee: Mervyn Griffiths (Wales)

Pelé, the revelation of the 1958 World Cup, scored a hat-trick against France. Here he watches as goalkeeper Abbés dives towards the ball.

Roger Piantoni of France.

Two World Cup 'greats' – Didí (left) of Brazil and Raymond Kopa (France) after the semi-final.

Vavá volleys home to give Brazil a first-minute lead.

Right: The French defence is in disarray as West Germany celebrate another goal in the high-scoring third place match.

Hans Schäfer (West Germany) and Sven Axbom (Sweden) during the semi-final game in Gothenburg.

Scoring hero Juste Fontaine is chaired off after scoring four goals against the Germans to establish a new World Cup record.

Defender Georg Stollenwerk (left) of West Germany gets in a challenge during the third-place match.

Third place play-off
FRANCE 6   WEST GERMANY 3 (Half-time 3-1)

Nya Ullevi Stadium, Gothenburg, 28 June
Attendance: 32,482

JUSTE Fontaine joined a select band of players when he scored four goals in the third place play-off match against West Germany. It was the only four-goal haul of the 1958 tournament and his final tally of 13 goals remains an all-time record! Quite an achievement for a man who went to Sweden as a reserve.

The Germans fielded a much reorganized side and the large crowd was treated to a nine-goal extravaganza. Fontaine opened his account in the 14th minute but three minutes later, Cieslarczyk equalized. Kopa made it 2-1 to France from the penalty-spot after 26 minutes and ten minutes later, Fontaine completed the first-half scoring.

Yvon Douis, playing in his first match of the tournament, made it 4-1 shortly after the start of the second half. Rahn scored his sixth goal of the tournament in the 51st minute to make it 4-2. Fontaine increased the French lead again, when he completed his hat-trick 12 minutes from time. Schäfer made it 5-3, six minutes from the end and, with less than 20 seconds remaining, Juste Fontaine scored his fourth goal.

France took third place and this remained their best-ever performance in the World Cup until it was equalled in 1986.

France: Abbés; Kaelbel, Lerond, Penverne, Lafont, Marcel, Wisnieski, Douis, Kopa, Fontaine, Vincent.
Scorers: Fontaine (4), Kopa (pen) Douis
West Germany: Kwiatkowski; Stollenwerk, Erhardt, Schnellinger, Wewers, Szymaniak, Rahn, Sturm, Kelbassa, Schäfer, Cieslarczyk.
Scorers: Cieslarczyk, Rahn, Schäfer
Referee: Juan Brozzi (Argentina)

Final

BRAZIL 5   SWEDEN 2 (Half-time 2-1)

Råsunda Stadium, Solna, 29 June
Attendance: 49,737

AS the tournament progressed, the Brazilians got better and better. And they still had more brilliance in store for the 50,000 crowd in the Råsunda Stadium and the millions more watching on television.

The match was played on a slippery surface after 24 hours of rain. Brazil brought in Djalma Santos for his first game of the tournament, after his recovery from injury. He, Nilton Santos and Didí, were Brazil's only survivors from the 1954 World Cup.

After four minutes, a magnificently worked goal by Sweden's 'Italian Connection' resulted in Liedholm scoring. This was the first time Brazil had been a goal behind and there were many who thought that, should this ever happen, then the ball-playing South Americans might crumble. But the goal only spurred the Brazilians on to greater things.

The Swedish joy was short-lived and five minutes later, Garrincha beat his marker to cross the ball around the back of the Swedish defence for Vavá to level the scores.

After half an hour, Brazil scored an almost identical goal. Garrincha went down the flank, crossed at the back of the defence — and there was Vavá again.

The second half once more belonged to Pelé, just as it did in the semi-final. Ten minutes after the restart he scored a great goal when he trapped the ball with his chest, rounded his man, and volleyed the ball into the net.

Indecision in the Swedish defence after a Zagalo corner allowed the winger to follow up his own cross and ram home the fourth goal after 68 minutes. Ten minutes from time,

Gilmar collects a high ball in the Final.

Djalma Santos, who came in for the Final.

Garrincha takes on Swedish defender Gustavsson.

Garrincha is presented to King Gustav of Sweden before the start of the 1958 World Cup Final. Pelé and Djalma Santos are next in line.

Above: Garrincha centres for Vavá (20) to pounce. *Right (top):* Vavá completes his job and Brazil are level.

Right (bottom): Sweden score their second goal through Simonsson.

Aerial battle in the Final between Djalmar Santos and Bergmark. The other Brazilian player is Bellini.

Sweden scored a second goal when Simonsson was at the end of a brilliant passing move in which Gunnar Gren was prominent.

The match was well beyond Sweden's grasp, as it had been since Pelé hit the third goal, and with almost the last attack of the match, Pelé scored his second goal. He started the move with a cheeky back-heel to Zagalo and then collected the winger's cross to head home Brazil's fifth.

Brazil showed, even on the slippery, wet surface more suited to the European style of play, that they were superior.

Top: Pelé's great volley, ten minutes after the restart. *Middle:* Vavá (20) scores his second goal. *Bottom:* Zagalo (7) makes it 4-0, following up from his own corner which was not cleared.

STATISTICS

Goalscorers:

13 — Juste Fontaine (France).

6 — Pelé (Brazil), Helmut Rahn (West Germany).

5 — Peter McParland (Northern Ireland), Vavá (Brazil).

4 — Agne Simonsson, Kurt Hamrin (both Sweden), Zdenek Zikan (Czechoslovakia), Lájós Tichy (Hungary).

3 — Hans Schäfer (West Germany), Todor Veselinović (Yugoslavia), Orestes Omar Corbatta (Argentina), Roger Piantoni, Raymond Kopa (both France).

2 — Uwe Seeler (West Germany), Aleksandar Petaković (Yugoslavia), Maryan Wisnieski (France), Nils Liedholm (Sweden), Ivor Allchurch (Wales), Mazola (Brazil), Derek Kevan (England), Anatoli Ilyin (Soviet Union), Milan Dvorak, Vaclav Hovorka (both Czechoslovakia), Florencio Amarilla, Jorgelino Romero, Juan Bautista Aguero, José Parodi (all Paraguay).

1 — Wilber Cush (Northern Ireland), Hans Cieslarczyk (West Germany), Radivoje Ognjanović, Zdravko Rajkov (both Yugoslavia), Jean Vincent, Yvon Douis (both France), Lennart Skoglund, Gunnar Gren (both Sweden), John Charles, Terry Medwin (both Wales), Nilton Santos, Didí, Zagalo (all Brazil), Tom Finney, Johnny Haynes (both England), Nikita Simonian, Alexander Ivanov, Valentin Ivanov (all Soviet Union), Karl Koller, Alfred Körner (both Austria), Norberto Menendez, Ludovico Avio (both Argentina), Jiri Feureisl (Czechoslovakia), Sammy Baird, Bobby Collins, Jackie Mudie, Jimmy Murray (all Scotland), Cayetano Re (Paraguay), József Bozsik, Karoly Sándor (both Hungary), Jaime Belmonte (Mexico).

Own-goals
Juan Gómez González (Mexico v Hungary).

Hat-tricks
Juste Fontaine (France v Paraguay). Pelé (Brazil v France). Juste Fontaine (4 goals, France v West Germany).

Fastest goal
90 seconds — Vavá (Brazil v France)

Most goals (team)
23 — France

Teams failing to score
None

Total goals scored:	126
Average per game:	3.60

At the end, Pelé was in tears. He had certainly enjoyed an outstanding competition and he remained the youngest World Cup player until the arrival of Northern Ireland's Norman Whiteside in 1982.

The 1958 World Cup was the best and friendliest so far. As if to symbolize the spirit of the tournament, the Brazilians did a lap of honour, carrying a huge Swedish flag.

World Cup 1958 was also, perhaps, the most conclusive. Brazil arrived as favourites and, after six attempts at winning the coveted trophy, eventually carried it back home as the first team to win the Cup in a different continent from their own.

Brazil: Gilmar do Santos Neves; Djalmar Santos, Nilton Santos, Zito, Hideraldo Luiz Bellini, Orlando Peçanha de Canalho, Garrincha, Didí, Vavá, Pelé, Mario Zagalo.
Scorers: Vavá 2, Pelé 2, Zagalo
Sweden: Karl Svensson, Orvar Bergmark, Sven Axbom, Rejno Börjesson, Bengt Gustavsson, Sigvard Parling, Kurt Hamrin, Gunnar Gren, Agne Simonsson, Nils Liedholm, Lennart Skoglund.
Scorers: Liedholm, Simonsson
Referee: Maurice Guigue (France)

Above: Pelé challenges Svensson. *Right (top):* Brazil on their lap of honour. *Right (bottom):* The victorious Brazilian line-up. Back row (left to right): V.Feola (chief coach), D.Santos, Zito, Bellini, N.Santos, Orlando, Gilmar. Front row: Garrincha, Didí, Pelé, Vavá, Zagalo, trainer. *Opposite page:* Pelé (10) in tears, surrounded by teammates at the climax of his remarkable debut in the World Cup.

Penalties
Scored: Florencio Amarilla (Paraguay v France) *Referee: Juan Gardeazabal Garay (Spain).* Nils Liedholm (Sweden v Mexico) *Referee: Nikolai Latychev (Soviet Union).* Tom Finney (England v Soviet Union) *Referee: Istvan Zsolt (Hungary).* Orestes Omar Corbatta (Argentina v Northern Ireland) *Referee: Sten Ahlner (Sweden).* Milan Dvorak (Czechoslovakia v West Germany) *Referee: Arthur Ellis (England).* Orestes Omar Corbatta (Argentina v Czechoslovakia) *Referee: Arthur Ellis (England).* Raymond Kopa (France v West Germany) *Referee: Juan Brozzi (Argentina).*

Most appearances
6 — Hideraldo Luíz Bellini, Didí, Gilmar do Santos Neves, Nilton Santos, Orlando, Zagalo (all Brazil), Juste Fontaine, Raymond Kaelbel, Raymond Kopa, André Lerond, Armand Penverne, Jean Vincent, Maryan Wisnieski (all France), Herbert Erhardt, Helmut Rahn, Hans Schäfer, George Stollenwerk, Horst Szymaniak (all West Germany), Sven Axbom, Orvar Bergmark, Bengt Gustavsson, Sigvard Parling, Lennart Skoglund, Karl Svensson (all Sweden).

Sendings-off
Titus Bubernik (Czechoslovakia v Northern Ireland) *Referee: Maurice Guigue (France).* Ferenc Sipos (Hungary v Wales, play-off). *Referee: Nikolai Latychev (Soviet Union)* Erich Juskowiak (West Germany v Sweden) *Referee: Istvan Zsolt.(Hungary).*

Most players used
18 — West Germany

Number of players used by Finalists
16 — Brazil
16 — Sweden

MEN WHO MADE THE HEADLINES - 1962

Florian Albert
(Hungary)

FLORIAN Albert was the next Hungarian 'superstar' after Puskás, Kocsis and Hidegkuti and, whilst he is remembered for his outstanding 1966 World Cup when, practically single-handed, he helped beat the Brazilians at Goodison Park, it was in 1962 that his skills were first paraded on the world stage. The son of a farmer, he was born on the Yugoslavian border in 1940 but the family moved to Budapest when he was a teenager and he spent his senior career with Ferencváros. He made his international debut, aged 17, in 1958 and appeared in the 1960 Rome Olympics. Albert replaced Hidegkuti as Hungary's centre-forward and from 1960 he was always at or near the top of the Hungarian League scorers' list. In the 1962 World Cup, he scored the winner against England and then hit a hat-trick in the 6-1 win over Bulgaria. He had superb close control, good balance, tremendous speed and a lethal right foot. In 1965 he helped Ferencváros become the first Hungarian side to win a European trophy when they beat Juventus 1-0 in the Fairs Cup Final and he was the 1967 European Footballer of the Year. He scored 31 goals in 75 internationals before retiring in 1974 to become a journalist.

Josef Masopust
(Czechoslovakia)

ONE of the stars of the Czechoslovakian side which reached their second World Cup Final in 1962 was attacking left-half, Josef Masopust. The son of a miner, he was born at Most, in Northern Bohemia, in February 1931 and joined the Teplice club in 1948. Masopust started as an inside-left before moving into what would now be termed midfield. He became a member of the Czech Army team, Dukla Prague, in 1951, although they were known as UDA at the time. Masopust eventually rose to the rank of major and teamed up with Pluskal to form a great partnership which also prospered in the Czech national team, along with Jan Popluhár. The trio formed one of the best half-back lines in Europe and played a key role in Czechoslovakia's rise to the top of world soccer in the early 1960s. Masopust scored only one goal in the 1962 finals, but it was a well-taken strike which opened the scoring in the Final. Brazil won the game but Masopust's great skills were rewarded with the European Footballer of the Year trophy in 1962. He won 87 caps and appeared in two World Cup finals, in 1958 and 1962, before winding up his career with a brief spell in the Belgian League.

Garrincha
(Brazil)

MANOEL dos Santos Francisco — Garrincha — was born a cripple and the operation that enabled him to walk left him with a distorted left leg, yet he went on to gain two World Cup winners' medals. Born at Pau Grande in 1933, he joined Botafogo in 1953 and made his international debut in the 1957 South American Championship but was left out of the first two games of the 1958 World Cup. Teammates begged manager Feola to include him and he created Brazil's first two goals in the Final. 'The Little Bird', who perfected the 'banana' shot, was called up when the injured Pelé quit the 1962 tournament and he helped Brazil to another Final, despite being sent off in the semifinal. He had a cartilage operation in 1963 and was involved in a scandal when he left his wife and eight children to marry a local singer. He was also in dispute with the income tax authorities and with Botafogo over pay. After defeat by Hungary in the 1966 World Cup — the only time he was on a losing Brazilian side — he bowed out. Garrincha had spells with Corinthians, Flamengo, Bangu and Portuguesa Santista, then brief periods in France and Italy. He had a few games for Brazilian club, Olaria, before being forced to retire. He died in January 1983, aged 50.

Chile's Compassionate Plea
Chile 1962

*A*T THE 1956 FIFA Congress in Lisbon, three nations formally applied to host the 1962 World Cup — Argentina, Chile and West Germany — but it was generally agreed that the competition could not be staged in Europe for a third successive tournament. Argentina, because of their footballing heritage, larger stadiums and the tremendous interest in the game amongst its people, were the favourites to be awarded the seventh World Cup, but in May 1960 Chile was rocked by dreadful earthquakes which claimed 5,000 lives. This tragedy, one would have thought, would have made Argentina even stronger candidates, but powerful pleading by the Chilean FA president, Carlos Dittborn, won the sympathy of FIFA and Chile were declared hosts for the 1962 tournament. Dittborn said: "We have nothing — that is why we must have the World Cup."

The Chileans set about building new grounds and the magnificent National Stadium in Santiago was completed in time for the start of the tournament. For a poor nation, Chile did not disappoint FIFA as World Cup hosts.

The National Stadium was magnificently located, with the snow-capped Andes acting as a breathtaking backdrop. The lovely coastal resort of Viña del Mar, near Valparaíso, was also a magnificent setting. However, the group based at Rancagua had to play their matches on the small ground of the Braden Copper company, whilst the other group was based at Arica, Dittborn's home town, in the far north of the country near to the Peruvian border.

The authorities were forced to charge high admission prices and hotel prices were inflated. Many impoverished Chileans in particular could not afford to attend the matches and it was fortunate that the tournament received global television coverage.

Alas, whilst the organization was acceptable, the football did not live up to expectations. The 'win at all costs' attitude had crept into the game and a lot of matches were defensive affairs. Even the majestic Brazilians adopted a 'defensive' 4-3-3 formation. And not only was the game becoming more defensive, the 1962 World Cup also saw some of the ugliest scenes ever witnessed on a football field and the Chile-Italy match was dubbed 'The Battle of Santiago'. It was reminiscent of 'The Battle of Berne' between Hungary and Brazil in 1954.

A record number of 52 countries took part in the qualifying competition, from an initial entry of 57. They were reduced to the 14 who eventually made the trip to join the hosts, Chile, and holders, Brazil. Colombia and Bulgaria made their World Cup debuts but absent were three of the four Home countries as only England qualified.

The 1958 runners-up, Sweden, were also missing. Still managed by George Raynor, they were eliminated by Switzerland after a play-off in Berlin. Their ageing team, which did them proud on home soil in 1958, had been forced to split up.

France, also one of the outstanding teams in 1958, were missing from the line-up in Chile but Mexico, whose goalkeeper Antonio Carbajal was appearing in a record fourth World Cup, were present. By the time they arrived in Chile, the Mexicans had already played eight qualifying matches.

The format was similar to 1958, with the 16 teams divided into four sections. For the first time they were officially called 'groups', as opposed to 'pools'. If any teams were level on points, they were to be separated by goal-average. There would be no more play-offs in the event of teams being level. This new rule was largely responsible for the defensive tactics and many group matches were drab, defensive affairs.

FIFA had been forced to reconsider the format after Northern Ireland, Wales and the Soviet Union had to play gruelling quarter-final matches in 1958, only two days after engaging in pool play-off matches. But if that was unacceptable, then so too was the new system, unless the soccer-watching public were prepared to tolerate defensive games.

Brazil were once again favourites. Pelé was now a 'mature' 21-year-old, and they had a new talent in the side. His name was Amarildo. And of course they still had Garrincha, Zagalo, Vavá, Didí, and the two Santos' in a side that had changed very little in the four years since they won the trophy on European soil. Now Brazil were playing on their home continent and the odds were stacked heavily in their favour.

Russia were also one of the fancied teams. They had won the inaugural European Championship in 1960 and impressive wins on their South American tour, over Uruguay, Argentina, and the World Cup hosts, Chile, confirmed they could beat the top Latin teams as well as their European counterparts.

Beyond Brazil and the Soviet Union, the pundits could see no further. Italy, England, Hungary and Argentina were no longer regarded as world forces. And the remainder of the pack looked as though they were simply there to make up the numbers. But Chile proved again, as Sweden did in 1958, that the host nation had a big advantage and they turned out to be the surprise team of the tournament.

Carlos Dittborn would have been proud of his team and the way the tournament was organized. Sadly, the 41-year-old died of a heart attack a month before the opening ceremony.

Chilean president Jorge Allesandri declares the 1962 tournament underway.

The opening ceremony of the 1962 World Cup.

1962 Qualifying Competition

UNQUESTIONABLY, the shock of the qualifying competition was the exit of Sweden, runners-up to Brazil in 1958 and a team which had beaten England at Wembley.

The Swedes' qualification looked assured when they were drawn with Switzerland and Belgium in their qualifying group. And after winning their first three matches, they seemed to be on their way to Chile before losing their final game to Switzerland, who ended the group with an identical record to the Swedes. Goal-average was not taken into account and a play-off was required in Berlin and to everyone's amazement the Swiss won 2-1, despite trailing at one stage.

Another shock saw France, who had finished in third place in Sweden four years earlier, dumped at the qualifying stage. They needed only to draw their final match with Bulgaria to qualify. The French went to Sofia intent on playing for that draw, but conceded a goal with less than a minute to go. Like Sweden, they lost a play-off, Bulgaria beating them, again 1-0, in Milan. It was the first time that the Bulgarians had qualified for the final stages of the World Cup.

Northern Ireland failed to reach their second successive Finals, despite a Billy McAdams hat-trick against West Germany, who won 4-3 in Belfast. The Germans won all four of their matches and qualified with ease.

The strong Hungarian side, which had won the bronze medal at the 1960 Rome Olympics, also had no problem in qualifying, but it was as well that the unplayed match between Holland and East Germany could not affect the eventual outcome, otherwise it would have caused FIFA some problems. The game could not go ahead because the Dutch authorities would not provide visas for the East German players.

Like West Germany, the Soviet Union also qualified for the final stages with a 100 per cent record, although they were not particularly impressive. England became the United Kingdom's only representative in the final stages, winning their group with something to spare, although their final match against Portugal could have proved vital, had it not been for the shock result of the qualifying tournament. In their penultimate match, Portugal surprisingly lost 4-2 to Luxembourg, who, prior to the game, had scored only one goal and conceded 19 in their three matches. It was certainly not a memorable international debut for Eusébio, the man who was to make such an impact on the 1966 tournament.

England's 9-0 beating of Luxembourg — with hat-tricks from Bobby Charlton and Jimmy Greaves — was the biggest win of the qualifying tournament. Playing for them that day was Bobby Robson — and the next time England won 9-0, Robson was the national manager.

Italy and Czechoslovakia both qualified comfortably. The Czechs did so at the expense of Scotland (after a play-off) and the Republic of Ireland. Britain's other representatives, Wales, still basking in their relative success in the 1958 tournament, were eliminated by Spain in an Africa-Europe pool. One of Spain's scorers in their 2-1 win at Cardiff was Real Madrid's Argentinian-born star, Alfredo di Stefano. Surprisingly, it was the only World Cup goal of his long and illustrious career.

Yugoslavia were the last European team to qualify, which they did from an Asian-European pool. In South America, Argentina came through their two matches against Ecuador with ease, scoring 11 goals on the way. However, Uruguay, the former champions, and Colombia both scraped through by odd-goal wins.

The final qualifiers were Mexico, who came through a complicated series of games against other CONCACAF nations before meeting Paraguay in the group final. To reach Chile, the Mexicans had to play eight games.

Results

EUROPE

Group One

19 Oct 1960 *Stockholm*	Sweden	2	Belgium 0
20 Nov 1960 *Brussels*	Belgium	2	Switzerland 4
20 May 1961 *Lausanne*	Switzerland	2	Belgium 1
28 May 1961 *Stockholm*	Sweden	4	Switzerland 0
4 Oct 1961 *Brussels*	Belgium	0	Sweden 2
29 Oct 1961 *Berne*	Switzerland	3	Sweden 2

Final Table

	P	W	D	L	F	A	Pts
Sweden	4	3	0	1	10	3	6
Switzerland	4	3	0	1	9	9	6
Belgium	4	0	0	4	3	10	0

Play-off
12 Nov 1961 *Berlin*   Switzerland ......2 Sweden 1
Switzerland qualified

Group Two

26 Sep 1960 *Helsinki*	Finland	1	France 2
11 Dec 1960 *Paris*	France	3	Bulgaria 0
16 Jun 1961 *Helsinki*	Finland	0	Bulgaria 2
28 Sep 1961 *Paris*	France	5	Finland 1
29 Oct 1961 *Sofia*	Bulgaria	3	Finland 1
12 Nov 1961 *Sofia*	Bulgaria	1	France 0

Final Table

	P	W	D	L	F	A	Pts
France	4	3	0	1	10	3	6
Bulgaria	4	3	0	1	6	4	6
Finland	4	0	0	4	3	12	0

Play-off
16 Dec 1961 *Milan*   Bulgaria ....1 France 0
Bulgaria qualified

Bulgaria's Kolev (10) scores the 89th-minute winner against France in Sofia which forced a play-off from which Bulgaria went into the finals in Chile.

There was bad feeling during the Greece-Northern Ireland game in Athens when Lukanides (on ground) was injured, but Israeli referee Eli Brisnel restored order and the game was completed.

Group Three

26 Oct	1960	*Belfast*	N. Ireland ....3 West Germany ...4
20 Nov	1960	*Athens*	Greece ....0 West Germany ...3
3 May	1961	*Athens*	Greece ....2 N. Ireland 1
10 May	1961	*Berlin*	West Germany ...2 N. Ireland 1
17 Oct	1961	*Belfast*	N. Ireland ....2 Greece 0
22 Oct	1961	*Augsburg*	West Germany ...2 Greece 1

Final Table

	P	W	D	L	F	A	Pts	
W.Germany	4	4	0	0	11	5	8	**West Germany**
N. Ireland	4	1	0	3	7	8	2	**qualified**
Greece	4	1	0	3	3	8	2	

Group Four

16 Apr	1961	*Budapest*	Hungary ....2 East Germany ...0
30 Apr	1961	*Rotterdam*	Holland ....0 Hungary 3
14 May	1961	*Leipzig*	East Germany ...1 Holland 1
10 Sep	1961	*Berlin*	East Germany ...2 Hungary 3
22 Oct	1961	*Budapest*	Hungary ....3 Holland 3

Holland v East Germany not played

Final Table

	P	W	D	L	F	A	Pts	
Hungary	4	3	1	0	11	5	7	**Hungary qualified**
Holland	3	0	2	1	4	7	2	
E.Germany	3	0	1	2	3	6	1	

Group Five

1 Jun	1961	*Oslo*	Norway...........0 Turkey...........1
18 Jun	1961	*Moscow*	Soviet Union ....1 Turkey...........0
1 Jul	1961	*Moscow*	Soviet Union ....5 Norway...........2
23 Aug	1961	*Oslo*	Norway...........0 Soviet Union 3
29 Oct	1961	*Istanbul*	Turkey...........2 Norway...........1
12 Nov	1961	*Istanbul*	Turkey...........1 Soviet Union 2

Final Table

	P	W	D	L	F	A	Pts	
Soviet Union	4	4	0	0	11	3	8	**Soviet Union**
Turkey	4	2	0	2	4	4	4	**qualified**
Norway	4	0	0	4	3	11	0	

Group Six

19 Oct	1960	*Luxembourg*	Luxembourg.....0 England 9
19 Mar	1961	*Lisbon*	Portugal..........6 Luxembourg.....0
21 May	1961	*Lisbon*	Portugal..........1 England 1
28 Sep	1961	*London*	England ....4 Luxembourg.....1
8 Sep	1961	*Luxembourg*	Luxembourg.....4 Portugal..........2
25 Oct	1961	*London*	England ....2 Portugal..........0

Final Table

	P	W	D	L	F	A	Pts	
England	4	3	1	0	16	2	7	**England qualified**
Portugal	4	1	1	3	9	7	3	
Luxembourg	4	1	0	3	5	21	2	

Brenner of Luxembourg heads clear from a Portuguese attack in Lisbon, but the home side still ran riot to win 6-0.

Group Seven
Round One
23 Nov 1960 *Nicosia*   Cyprus............1 Israel..............1
27 Nov 1960 *Tel Aviv*   Israel.............6 Cyrprus...........1
Round Two
14 Mar 1961 *Tel Aviv*   Israel.............1 Ethiopia..........0
19 Mar 1961 *Tel Aviv*   Ethiopia.........2 Israel..............3
Round Three
Israel progressed. Romania withdrew
Group Final
15 Oct 1961 *Tel Aviv*   Israel.............2 Italy..............4
 4 Nov 1961 *Turin*   Italy..............6 Israel.............0
Italy qualified

Group Eight
 3 May 1961 *Glasgow*   Scotland..........4 Rep of Ireland ...1
 7 May 1961 *Dublin*   Rep of Ireland ...0 Scotland..........3
14 May 1961 *Bratislava*   Czechoslovakia..4 Scotland..........0
26 Sep 1961 *Glasgow*   Scotland..........3 Czechoslovakia..2
 8 Oct 1961 *Dublin*   Rep of Ireland ...1 Czechoslovakia..3
29 Oct 1961 *Prague*   Czechoslovakia..7 Rep of Ireland ...1

Final Table   *P W D L F A Pts*
Czechoslovakia 4 3 0 1 16 5 6
Scotland   4 3 0 1 10 7 6
Rep of Ireland 4 0 0 4 3 17 0
Play-off
29 Nov 1961 *Brussels*   Czechoslovakia..4 Scotland..........2
Czechoslovakia qualified

Aerial battle during the Israel-Ethiopia qualifier in Tel Aviv.

AFRICA-EUROPE
Sub Group One
Egypt and Sudan both withdrew

Sub Group Two
30 Oct 1960 *Casablanca*   Morocco..........2 Tunisia...........1
13 Nov 1960 *Tūnis*   Tunisia...........2 Morocco..........1
Play-off
22 Jan 1961 *Palermo*   Morocco..........1 Tunisia...........1
Morocco qualified for semi-final after drawing lots

Sub Group Three
28 Aug 1960 *Accra*   Ghana............4 Nigeria 1
10 Sep 1960 *Lagos*   Nigeria ....2 Ghana 2
Ghana qualified for semi-final
Semi-final
 2 Apr 1961 *Accra*   Ghana ....0 Morocco..........0
28 May 1961 *Casablanca*   Morocco ....1 Ghana 0
Morocco qualified for Group Final

Sub Group Four
19 Apr 1961 *Cardiff*   Wales ....1 Spain 2
18 May 1961 *Madrid*   Spain ....1 Wales 1
Spain qualified for Group Final
Group Final
12 Nov 1961 *Casablanca*   Morocco..........0 Spain 1
23 Nov 1961 *Madrid*   Spain ....3 Morocco 2
Spain qualified

ASIA-EUROPE
Sub Group One
 6 Nov 1960 *Seoul*   South Korea .....2 Japan 1
11 Jun 1961 *Tōkyō*   Japan ....0 South Korea 2
South Korea qualified for Group Final

Sub Group Two
 4 Jun 1961 *Belgrade*   Yugoslavia ....2 Poland............1
25 Jun 1961 *Chorzów*   Poland............1 Yugoslavia 1
Yugoslavia qualified for Group Final

Group Final
 8 Oct 1961 *Belgrade*   Yugoslavia ....5 South Korea 1
26 Nov 1961 *Seoul*   South Korea .....1 Yugoslavia 3
Yugoslavia qualified

SOUTH AMERICA
Group One
 4 Dec 1960 *Guayaquil*   Ecuador ....3 Argentina 6
17 Dec 1960 *Buenos Aires* Argentina ....5 Ecuador 0
Argentina qualified

Group Two
15 Jul 1961 *La Paz*   Bolivia............1 Uruguay..........1
30 Jul 1961 *Montevideo*   Uruguay..........2 Bolivia............1
Uruguay qualified

Group Three
30 Apr 1961 *Bogotá*   Colombia ....1 Peru...............0
 7 May 1961 *Lima*   Peru...............1 Colombia 1
Colombia qualified

CONCACAF
(Central & North America)
Sub Group One
 6 Nov 1960 *Los Angeles*   United States ....3 Mexico............3
13 Nov 1960 *Mexico City*   Mexico............3 United States 0
Mexico qualified for second phase

Sub Group Two
21 Aug 1960 *San José*   Costa Rica ....3 Guatemala 2
28 Aug 1960 *Guatemala*   Guatemala ....4 Costa Rica 4
 4 Sep 1960 *Tegucigalpa*   Honduras ....2 Costa Rica 1
11 Sep 1960 *San José*   Costa Rica ....5 Honduras 0
25 Sep 1960 *Tegucigalpa*   Honduras ....1 Guatemala 1
Guatemala v Honduras abandoned with Honduras leading 2-0.
It was not replayed which resulted in Costa Rica and Honduras
engaging in a play-off.

Final Table *P W D L F A Pts*
Costa Rica   4 2 1 1 13 8 5
Honduras   3 1 1 1 3 7 3
Guatemala   3 0 2 1 7 8 2
Play-off
14 Jan 1961 *Guatemala*   Costa Rica ....1 Honduras 0
Costa Rica qualified for second phase

Sub Group Three
 2 Oct 1960 *Paramaribo*   Surinam ....1 Dutch Antilles ...2
27 Nov 1960 *Willemstad*   Dutch Antilles ...0 Surinam 0
Dutch Antilles qualified for second phase

Second Phase
22 Mar 1961 *San José*   Costa Rica ....1 Mexico............0
29 Mar 1961 *San José*   Costa Rica ....6 Dutch Antilles ...0
 5 Apr 1961 *Mexico City*   Mexico............7 Dutch Antilles ...0
12 Apr 1961 *Mexico City*   Mexico............4 Costa Rica 1
23 Apr 1961 *Willemstad*   Dutch Antilles ...2 Costa Rica 0
21 May 1961 *Willemstad*   Dutch Antilles ...0 Mexico............0

Final Table   *P W D L F A Pts*
Mexico   4 2 1 1 11 2 5   **Mexico qualified**
Costa Rica   4 2 0 2 8 6 4   **for Group Final**
Dutch Antilles 4 1 1 2 2 13 3

Group Final
29 Oct 1961 *Mexico City*   Mexico............1 Paraguay 0
 5 Nov 1961 *Asunción*   Paraguay ....0 Mexico............0
Mexico qualified

The band plays at the opening ceremony in Santiago.

Pedro Rocha of Uruguay.

1962 Tournament

Group One

URUGUAY 2   COLOMBIA 1 (Half-time 0-1)

Carlos Dittborn Stadium, Arica, 30 May
Attendance: 7,908

URUGUAY were no longer the feared team they were in the early days of the World Cup. Their struggle to qualify in 1962 confirmed this and in their opening match against World Cup debutants, Colombia, they were fortunate to scrape through after trailing at half-time.

The Colombians were given the lead in the 20th minute when Francisco Zuluaga converted a penalty, much against the run of play. The outsiders could have increased their lead when a Coll shot hit the post and it was not until the 57th minute that Uruguay equalized, through Luis Cubilla, and 17 minutes from time before José Sacia scored the winner. After that Uruguay played a boring, defensive game. Long before the final whistle many of the already small crowd had made their way home in the knowledge that neither of the two South American countries would be in contention for the seventh World Cup in 18 days time.

Uruguay: Sosa; Troche, Emilia Alvarez, Eliseo Alvarez, Mendez, Gonsalves, Cubilla, Rocha, Langon, Sacia, Perez.
Scorers: Cubilla, Sacia
Colombia: Sánchez; Zuluaga, J.González, López, Echeverri, Silva, Coll, Aceros, Klinger, Gamboa, Arias.
Scorer: Zuluaga (pen)
Referee: Albert Dorogy (Hungary)

Slava Metreveli of the USSR.

Igor Netto of the USSR.

Milan Galić of Yugoslavia.

SOVIET UNION 2   YUGOSLAVIA 0 (Half-time 0-0)

Carlos Dittborn Stadium, Arica, 31 May
Attendance: 9,622

TWO years earlier in Paris, the Soviets beat Yugoslavia to win the inaugural European Championship. Their meeting in the opening matches of the 1962 World Cup was a 'grudge' match which turned into a brutal encounter. Indeed, it was one of several matches of this tournament to be dogged by foul and vicious play.

Whilst both sides played skilful football, at times they allowed their temperament to get the better of them and Russian full-back Eduard Dubinski had his leg broken after a tackle by Mujić. The Yugoslav winger was sent home after the match and took no further part in the tournament.

Lev Yashin was outstanding in the Russian goal and thwarted many Yugoslav attacks. Unfortunately for Russia, one of the favourites to win the Jules Rimet Trophy, their world-class goalkeeper could not maintain this form throughout the tournament.

Both sides played attractive football in the first half. But after the Soviets opened the scoring through Ivanov in the second half, the Yugoslavs resorted to foul tactics which, in retrospect, were probably their downfall. They had been the better footballing side up to the time Russia took the lead.

Viktor Ponedelnik, scorer of the winner in the European Championship, had a hand in both of the Soviets' goals. The first was scored after his free-kick rebounded off the bar and was turned in by Valentin Ivanov after an hour. Five minutes from time, Ponedelnik scored the second goal.

Soviet Union: Yashin; Dubinski, Ostrovski, Voronin, Maslenkin, Netto, Metreveli, Ivanov, Ponedelnik, Kanevski, Meschki.
Scorers: Ivanov, Ponedelnik
Yugoslavia: Šoškić; Durković, Jusufi, Matus, Marković, Popović, Mujić, Šekularac, Jerković, Galić, Skoblar.
Referee: Albert Dusch (West Germany)

YUGOSLAVIA 3   URUGUAY 1 (Half-time 2-1)

Carlos Dittborn Stadium, Arica, 2 June
Attendance: 8,829

ALL Yugoslavia had to do to beat Uruguay was play the kind of football they had served up in the first half against Russia. That is what they did — and it reaped its just rewards.

Yugoslavia's inside-forward, Milan Galić, who had been the menace of the Russians, was again outstanding against the South Americans. But it was Uruguay who opened the scoring when Cabrera found the net after 18 minutes to give his team the lead after they had dominated the opening spell. Seven minutes later, Josip Skoblar levelled the scores when he struck the ball home from the penalty-spot. And in the 28th minute, Galić put the Slavs in front.

Jerković increased that lead two minutes after half-time and after that it was a 'stroll' for the Europeans, who showed they could defend with confidence as well as attack with force.

Alas, a bout of fisticuffs between Vladimir Popović and Ruben Cabrera resulted in Czech referee Karol Galba sending both players off the field.

Yugoslavia: Šoškić; Durković, Jusufi, Radaković, Marković, Popović, Melić, Šekularac, Jerković, Galić, Skoblar.
Scorers: Skoblar (pen), Galić, Jerković
Uruguay: Sosa; Troche, Emilia Alvarez, Eliseo Alvarez, Mendez, Gonsalves, Rocha, Bergara, Cabrera, Sacia, Perez.
Scorer: Cabrera
Referee: Karol Galba (Czechoslovakia)

SOVIET UNION 4   COLOMBIA 4 (Half-time 3-1)

Carlos Dittborn Stadium, Arica, 3 June
Attendance: 8,040

COLOMBIA made four changes for their match against the strong Russians, including the omission of Zuluaga, their scorer in the opening match against Uruguay. Many felt the changes were academic and the Russians would have no problem in sweeping aside the World Cup newcomers.

So it proved in the early stages. Russia's forwards were in superb form and three goals in three minutes saw them surge into a 3-0 lead with only 11 minutes gone. Ivanov (two) and Chislenko did the damage before Aceros pulled one back for Colombia after 20 minutes.

There were no further first-half goals and when Ponedelnik made it 4-1 ten minutes into the second half, the match seemed all over. But what a surprise the Colombians had in store as they threw everything into attack.

Ignacio Coll pulled one back in the 67th minute and four minutes later, the score was 4-3 when Antonio Rada beat Lev Yashin, who was having one of his worst games in the Russian goal. To complete a remarkable ten-minute spell for the South Americans, Marino Klinger, who had an outstanding game, made it 4-4. The Russians did not know what had hit them and were in disarray. They were lucky to hang on for the draw at the end of a remarkable 90 minutes play as Colombia brought off the shock of the tournament.

It was the first point Colombia ever obtained in the World Cup — but what a way to do it.

Soviet Union: Yashin; Tchokelli, Ostrovski, Netto, Maslenkin, Voronin, Chislenko, Ivanov, Ponedelnik, Kanevski, Meschki.
Scorers: Ivanov 2, Chislenko, Ponedelnik
Colombia: Sánchez; J.González, López, Alzate, Echeverri, Serrano, Coll, Aceros, Rada, Klinger, H.González.
Scorers: Aceros, Coll, Rada, Klinger
Referee: Jose Etzel Filho (Brazil)

SOVIET UNION 2 URUGUAY 1 (Half-time 1-0)
Carlos Dittborn Stadium, Arica, 6 June
Attendance: 9,973

AFTER poor showings against Colombia and Yugoslavia, the Uruguayans were given heart by the decline in the Soviets' form in their last match.

However, after their defensive lapses against the Colombians, Russia played a very tight game against Uruguay and seemed happy to play for the draw that would have been good enough to take them through to the next stage of the competition.

Eight minutes before the interval, Mamikin put the Soviets in front but José Sacia equalized eight minutes the other side of the break. But, thereafter, it was a dour defensive game with both sides hoping for a quick breakaway to score a second goal. That chance eventually fell to Russia. With Uruguay pushing forward, Ivanov broke away and scored a last-minute winner for the Soviets.

Soviet Union: Yashin; Tchokelli, Ostrovski, Netto, Maslenkin, Voronin, Chislenko, Ivanov, Ponedelnik, Mamikin, Khussainov.
Scorers: Mamikin, Ivanov
Uruguay: Sosa; Troche, Emilia Alvarez, Eliseo Alvarez, Mendez, Gonsalves, Cortes, Cubilla, Cabrera, Sacia, Perez.
Scorer: Sacia
Referee: Cesare Jonni (Italy)

YUGOSLAVIA 5 COLOMBIA 0 (Half-time 2-0)
Carlos Dittborn Stadium, Arica, 7 June
Attendance: 7,167

GOING into their final group game, underdogs Colombia still had a chance to qualify for the quarter-finals. However, they had to beat the Yugoslavs, whereas a draw was good enough for the Europeans. But after their result against the Soviets, who would say the Colombians would not bring off another shock result?

That was the theory. The reality was that their performance against Russia had drained the Colombian players and they were physically and mentally exhausted. Yugoslavia, meanwhile, continued to play good football and were technically superior to their opponents.

Jerković scored twice within five minutes midway through the first half as Yugoslavia built up a comfortable lead at the interval. Galić scored shortly after the start of the second half and Melić made it 4-0 in the 73rd minute. Galić netted for a second time three minutes from the final whistle as Yugoslavia sealed an emphatic win.

The result meant that both the European nations qualified for the quarter-finals, whilst the two South American countries were eliminated — just as many of those fans at the Carlos Dittborn Stadium eight days earlier had predicted.

Yugoslavia: Šoškić; Durković, Jusufi, Radaković, Marković, Popović, Anković, Šekularac, Jerković, Galić, Melić.
Scorers: Jerković 2, Galić 2, Melić
Colombia: Sánchez; Alzate, J.González, López, Echeverri, Serrano, Coll, Aceros, Klinger, Rada, H.González.
Referee: Carlos Robles (Chile)

Group One – Final Table						
	P	W	D	L	F	A	Pts
Soviet Union	3	2	1	0	8	5	5
Yugoslavia	3	2	0	1	8	3	4
Uruguay	3	1	0	2	4	6	2
Colombia	3	0	1	2	5	11	1

Dragoslav Šekularac of Yugoslavia.

Petar Radaković of Yugoslavia.

Group Two

CHILE 3 SWITZERLAND 1 (Half-time 1-1)
Estadio Nacional, Santiago, 30 May
Attendance: 65,006

THE host nation had the honour of kicking-off the seventh World Cup shortly after the opening ceremony which saw the two young sons of Carlos Dittborn raise the flags of Chile and Switzerland. Sadly, the message of welcome, friendship and unity of the opening ceremony was not to endure throughout the tournament and this particular group was to erupt and produce one of the most violent matches in the history of the World Cup.

More than 65,000 fans packed the National Stadium for Chile's opening game, but they were stunned into silence after only eight minutes when Rolf Wüthrich put Switzerland

Omar Sivori of Italy.

into the lead with a magnificent shot from over 30 yards. The Swiss held on to their slender lead until the last minute of the half, when Leonel Sánchez levelled the scores.

Ten minutes after the break, Ramírez put the home side into the lead and four minutes later, Sánchez scored his second goal, from the penalty-spot, to make it 3-1.

Chile: Escuti; Eyzaguirre, R.Sánchez, Contreras, Navarro, Toro, Rojas, Ramírez, Landa, Fouilloux, L.Sánchez.
Scorers: L.Sánchez 2 (1 pen), Ramírez
Switzerland: Elsener; Morf, Schneiter, Tacchella, Grobéty, Weber, Allemann, Pottier, Eschmann, Wüthrich, Antenen.
Scorer: Wüthrich
Referee: Ken Aston (England)

ITALY 0   WEST GERMANY 0 (Half-time 0-0)

Estadio Nacional, Santiago, 31 May
Attendance: 65,440

TWO Italian journalists covering the World Cup had made a scathing criticism of Chile. This enraged the home supporters and when the Italians took to the field for their first game against West Germany, they were jeered by the massive crowd, who were willing a German victory.

The game developed into a negative, defensive affair with both sides intent on not losing. Because of the defensive attitudes of the teams, the footballing world would not be treated

Goalkeeper Lorenzo Buffon makes a despairing effort to snatch the ball from Uwe Seeler's feet during the Italy-West Germany game.

Seeler gets between Luigi Radice (left) and Cesare Maldini to flash in a header on the Italian goal.

This time Buffon gets cleanly to the ball, although Seeler is still close by.

to the skills of opposing centre-forwards, Germany's Uwe Seeler and José Altafini of Italy. Altafini was a member of the Brazilian squad that won the World Cup four years earlier when known as Mazola, but he was now playing his League soccer in Italy.

There were many bad tempered incidents which the Italians carried over into their next game.

Helmut Haller of West Germany.

Italy: Buffon; Losi, Robotti, Salvadore, Maldini, Radice, Ferrini, Rivera, Altafini, Sivori, Menichelli.
West Germany: Fahrian; Nowak, Schnellinger, Schulz, Erhardt, Szymaniak, Sturm, Haller, Seeler, Brülls, Schäfer.
Referee: Bob Davidson (Scotland)

CHILE 2   ITALY 0 (Half-time 0-0)
Estadio Nacional, Santiago, 2 June
Attendance: 66,057

THIS was probably the blackest day in World Cup history as Chile and Italy took part in one of the most brutal games ever seen. It was, perhaps, unfortunate that the competition was receiving world-wide television coverage because it meant the scenes were flashed to all corners of the globe. What the viewers saw was the ugliest side of soccer.

Willibald Schulz of West Germany.

Sandro Salvadore is restrained as police come on to the pitch after yet another violent incident in the Italy-Chile game.

Referee Ken Aston has just sent off Giorgio Ferrini (in background, head bowed). It took nealy ten minutes to restore order.

Italy's Humberto Maschio nurses a broken nose after being on the receiving end of a punch from Leonel Sánchez of Chile. Remarkably, Sánchez escaped a sending-off.

Jorge Toro of Chile.

The teams were of Latin temperament and the Chileans were fired up by those articles written by the Italian journalists which criticized life in Chile, and Santiago in particular. The home fans jeered every move the Italians made. The atmosphere was electric, even before the start of the match.

It was only a matter of time before the game errupted and after only eight minutes, Giorgio Ferrini of Italy retaliated after being kicked from behind by Chile's centre-forward, Landa. Referee Ken Aston sent the Italian from the field, but he refused to leave. It took nearly ten minutes before FIFA officials and police got the Italian off the pitch.

With Italy down to ten men, they played a defensive game but the Chilean players were intimidating with their tackling. However, the Italians were also capable of violent tackling and five minutes before the interval, a bad tackle on Leonel Sánchez by Humberto Maschio resulted in the Chilean breaking the Argentine-born Italian's nose with a punch. The incident took place in front of the linesman and the Chilean was lucky to stay on the field.

Mario David became the second Italian to receive his marching orders following a tackle around Sánchez's neck.

Despite having a numerical advantage of two players it took Chile 74 minutes before they found the net, when Ramírez headed them into the lead following a free-kick. Two minutes from time, Toro assured the hosts of victory with a second goal.

When Aston blew the final whistle, he and the teams had to be escorted from the field by police. After studying film of the match, FIFA took immediate action and suspended Ferrini for one game and severely reprimanded Leonel Sánchez and David for their part in the violence.

Ken Aston said the match was 'uncontrollable'. He had considered abandoning it at one stage, but feared for his own and the players' safety. It turned out to be his last World Cup game.

Chile: Escuti; Eyzaguirre, Contreras, R.Sánchez, Navarro, Toro, Rojas, Ramírez, Landa, Fouilloux, L.Sánchez.
Scorers: Ramírez, Toro
Italy: Mattrel; David, Robotti, Salvadore, Janich, Tumburus, Maschio, Altafini, Ferrini, Menichelli.
Referee: Ken Aston (England)

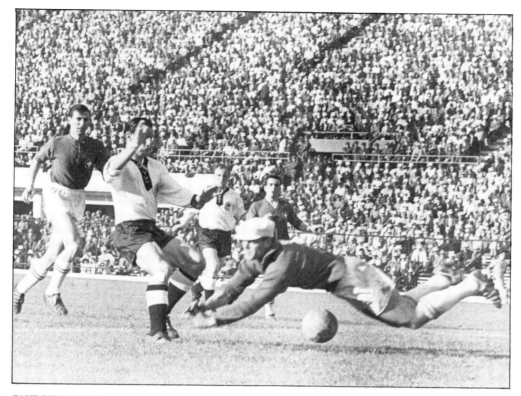

West Germany's Hans Schäfer slips the ball under the body of Swiss goalkeeper Charles Elsener.

WEST GERMANY 2   SWITZERLAND 1 (Half-time 1-0)

Estadio Nacional, Santiago, 3 June
Attendance: 64,922

THE day after the 'Battle of Santiago' West Germany took the field in the same stadium and showed the world that European soccer did not need to resort to violence.

The only black spot was the unfortunate injury to the skilful Swiss inside-forward, Eschmann, who received a fractured ankle in the first half. He played on bravely, albeit as a passenger.

West Germany, still managed by the legendary Sepp Herberger, took the lead right on the stroke of half-time, when Albert Brülls scored. Uwe Seeler put the Germans two goals in front after an hour, and 15 minutes from time, Schneiter scored a deserved consolation goal for the Swiss, whose defeat meant their exit from the competition.

Chilean Leonel Sánchez, who was severely reprimanded by FIFA after the 'Battle of Santiago'.

Seeler goes flying after a tackle from a Swiss defender.

West Germany: Fahrian; Nowak, Schnellinger, Schulz, Erhardt, Szymaniak, Koslowski, Haller, Seeler, Schäfer, Brülls.
Scorers: Brülls, Seeler
Switzerland: Elsener; Schneiter, Tacchella, Grobéty, Weber, Wüthrich, Antenen, Vonlanthen, Allemann, Eschmann, Dürr.
Scorer: Schneiter
Referee: Leo Horn (Holland)

West Germany's Brülls tries a shot at the Chilean goal.

Luis Eyzaguirre of Chile.

WEST GERMANY 2   CHILE 0 (Half-time 1-0)

Estadio Nacional, Santiago, 6 June
Attendance: 67,224

WITH Chile guaranteed a place in the last eight, they wanted to either win or draw to ensure they stayed in Santiago for the quarter-finals. But Sepp Herberger's team had other plans. The Germans could still be ousted if they lost to Chile and if Italy beat the Swiss by a big score. But all that was academic because Herberger's well-regimented team was too good for the Chileans and ran out winners in the best match of the group.

They took the lead midway through the first half when Horst Szymaniak converted a penalty. Chile were attacking well and it seemed a matter of time before they scored the equalizer. But it did not come and eight minutes from time, Seeler made the game safe for the Germans and Group Two was resolved, even before the final match. West Germany were top with Chile second. But the runners-up spot meant the hosts had to travel to Arica, whilst the Germans stayed in Santiago.

West Germany: Fahrian; Nowak, Schnellinger, Schulz, Erhardt, Giesemann, Kraus, Szymaniak, Seeler, Schäfer, Brülls.
Scorers: Szymaniak (pen), Seeler
Chile: Escuti; Eyzaguirre, Contreras, R.Sánchez, Navarro, Tobar, Rojas, Moreno, Landa, L.Sánchez, Ramírez.
Referee: Bob Davidson (Scotland)

Italy's Bruno Mora, opened the scoring against Switzerland after only three minutes.

Willibald Schulz (West Germany) seems to have the better of his Chilean opponent in the Estadio Nacional.

ITALY 3   SWITZERLAND 0 (Half-time 1-0)

Estadio Nacional, Santiago, 7 June
Attendance: 59,828

THE result of the final Group Two match was academic, for both teams were playing out time before packing their suitcases and making the trip back to Europe.

Italy won comfortably and seemed to be on their way to a big victory after opening the scoring through Mora in the third minute. But it was over an hour before they found the net again — and then Giacomo Bulgarelli scored twice within three minutes. Bulgarelli was one of eight new faces in the Italian team from the one which did 'battle' with Chile.

Switzerland suffered the set-back of an injury to their goalkeeper, Charles Elsener, and this proved to be the turning point of the game. The scoreline was certainly not a true reflection of Switzerland's overall performance.

Italy: Buffon; Losi, Robotti, Salvadore, Maldini, Radice, Mora, Bulgarelli, Sormani, Sivori, Pascutti.
Scorers: Bulgarelli 2, Mora
Switzerland: Elsener; Schneiter, Meier, Tacchella, Grobéty, Weber, Antenen, Vonlanthen, Wüthrich, Allemann, Dürr.
Referee: Nikolai Latychev (Soviet Union)

Group Three

BRAZIL 2   MEXICO 0 (Half-time 0-0)

Estadio Sausalito, Viña del Mar, 30 May
Attendance: 10,484

A VERY meagre crowd turned out at the beautiful Viña del Mar ground to see the defending champions start their seventh World Cup campaign. The Brazilian team was virtually unchanged since their triumph in Sweden four years earlier. Didí, Nilton Santos and Djalmar Santos were all appearing in their third World Cup finals, whilst the Mexican goalkeeper, Carbajal, was a veteran of a record fourth tournament going back to 1950.

Brazil's change of formation to 4-3-3 did not produce the flowing football they had displayed in Sweden and for the first half they were held by the defensively-minded Mexicans. The scoring was opened by Zagalo, after 56 minutes, and 18 minutes from time Pelé scored a magnificent solo effort to make it 2-0. Sadly, this was the only full match of the series for Pelé. He was injured in the next game and took no further part in the tournament.

In the end, Brazil coasted to a comfortable victory. Mexico, meanwhile, still awaited their first-ever victory in the final stages of the World Cup.

Brazil: Gilmar; D.Santos, Mauro, Zózimo, N.Santos, Zito, Garrincha, Didí, Vavá, Pelé, Zagalo.
Scorers: Zagalo, Pelé
Mexico: Carbajal; Del Muro, Cardenas, Sepúlveda, Villegas, Reyes, Najera, Del Aguila, H.Hernández, Jasso, Díaz.
Referee: Gottfried Dienst (Switzerland)

Group Two – Final Table						
	P	W	D	L	F	A	Pts
W.Germany	3	2	1	0	4	1	5
Chile	3	2	0	1	5	3	4
Italy	3	1	1	1	3	2	3
Switzerland	3	0	0	3	2	8	0

Antonio Carbajal, playing in his fourth World Cup tournament.

Pelé scored Brazil's second against Mexico.

Mexico abandon man-to-man marking and set eight players to look after Brazil's Garrincha.

The combined efforts of Jan Popluhár (3), Andrej Kvašnák (19) and Ladislav Novák of Czechoslovakia win the ball from Euloglo Martínez of Spain. Goalkeeper Vilam Schrojf looks to be in some agony as Martínez stands on his leg.

Djalma Santos of Brazil.

CZECHOSLOVAKIA 1   SPAIN 0 (Half-time 0-0)

Estadio Sausalito, Viña del Mar, 31 May
Attendance: 12,700

AFTER Brazil and Russia, the next most likely candidates to lift the Jules Rimet Trophy were Spain and Czechoslovakia. The Eastern Europeans had a team with flair, whilst the Spaniards had some great individuals, including Ferenc Puskás and José Santamaria, who appeared for Hungary and Uruguay respectively in the 1958 finals.

But the solid Czech defence, coupled with the absence of Alfredo di Stefano through injury, was too big a handicap for the Spaniards, who lost to a solitary goal scored by Štibrányi ten minutes from time, after Scherer had done all the work by beating Santamaria and making the telling pass.

It was a disappointing result for Spain, who did most of the attacking, but they failed to convert many chances which their Real Madrid stars, Puskás, Del Sol and Gento used to do regularly and with ease at club level.

Czechoslovakia: Schrojf; Lála, Novák, Pluskal, Popluhár, Masopust, Štibrányi, Scherer, Kvašnák, Adamec, Jelinek.
Scorer: Štibrányi
Spain: Carmelo; Rivilla, Reija, Segarra, Santamaria, Garay, Del Sol, Martínez, Puskás, Suárez, Gento.
Referee: Erich Steiner (Austria)

BRAZIL 0   CZECHOSLOVAKIA 0 (Half-time 0-0)

Estadio Sausalito, Viña del Mar, 2 June
Attendance: 14,903

WITH Masopust and Popluhár at the centre of their defence, the Czechs kept the Brazilian forwards at bay and withstood continual pressure.

In the end Brazil were content to play out the draw in the knowledge that Czechoslovakia were going to be a team to contend with if they were to retain the trophy.

The game, and tournament, was marred by an injury to Pelé who pulled a muscle while attempting a shot at goal. He was forced to leave the field for a while, but was little more than a limping passenger when he returned. He was so badly injured that he missed the remainder of the 1962 World Cup. But the Brazilians had an adequate replacement, who they were about to unleash on the footballing world. His name was Amarildo and he was to have an impact on the repeat game when these two sides met in the World Cup Final two weeks later.

Brazil: Gilmar; D.Santos, Mauro, Zózimo, N.Santos, Zito, Garrincha, Didí, Vavá, Pelé, Zagalo.
Czechoslovakia: Schrojf; Lála, Novák, Pluskal, Popluhár, Masopust, Štibrányi, Scherer, Kvašnák, Adamec, Jelinek.
Referee: Pierre Schwinte (France)

Zito of Brazil.

Garrincha (7) in action against Czechoslovakia's Kvašnák. The Czech forward was helping back in defence as his side forced a goalless draw against the World Champions.

Antonio Carbajal of Mexico.

Francisco Gento of Spain.

SPAIN 1   MEXICO 0 (Half-time 0-0)

Estadio Sausalito, Viña del Mar, 3 June
Attendance: 11,875

JUST as they had done against Czechoslovakia, Spain applied a great deal of pressure without getting any rewards and it was only a face-saving goal in the dying seconds, from inside-forward Peiró, which saved the Spaniards' blushes.

Spain were still in with an outside chance of qualifying for the quarter-finals, but they had to beat Brazil in their last game if they were going to achieve that. And the way they had played against Czechoslovakia and Mexico the odds on them achieving that must surely have been long.

Spain: Carmelo; Rodri, Gracia, Vérges, Santamaria, Pachín, Del Sol, Peiró, Puskás, Suárez, Gento.
Scorer: Peiró
Mexico: Carbajal; Del Muro, Cardenas, Sepúlveda, Jáuregui, Reyes, Najera, Del Aguila, H.Hernández, Jasso, Díaz.
Referee: Branko Tesanic (Yugoslavia)

BRAZIL 2   SPAIN 1 (Half-time 0-1)

Estadio Sausalito, Viña del Mar, 6 June
Attendance: 18,715

SPAIN'S manager Helenio Herrera, who was Milan coach at the time, made wholesale changes for the final game against Brazil and concentrated on youth rather than experience.

His new-look side rocked the Brazilians with a goal from Adelardo ten minutes before half-time. They clung on to this lead until the 71st minute, when Pelé's young replacement, Amarildo, celebrated his World Cup debut with the equalizer after a brilliant move by Garrincha, who had an outstanding tournament.

A draw would have been good enough for Brazil but they turned a possible defeat into

Luis Suárez of Spain.

Group Three - Final Table

	P	W	D	L	F	A	Pts
Brazil	3	2	1	0	4	1	5
Czechoslovakia	3	1	1	1	2	3	3
Mexico	3	1	0	2	3	4	2
Spain	3	1	0	2	2	3	2

Amarildo, who replaced the injured Pelé, is embraced by Brazilian officials after scoring both goals in the victory over Spain.

José Sanfilippo of Argentina.

Ivan Kolev of Bulgaria.

victory in the closing minute when Amarildo scored his second goal of the game. Again Garrincha had a hand in the goal.

Brazil: Gilmar; D.Santos, Mauro, Zózimo, N.Santos, Zito, Garrincha, Didí, Vavá, Amarildo, Zagalo.
Scorer: Amarildo 2
Spain: Araguistáin; Rodri, Gracia, Vérges, Echevarria, Pachín, Collar, Adelardo, Puskás, Peiró, Gento.
Scorer: Adelardo
Referee: Salvador Gonzales Bustamente (Chile)

MEXICO 3   CZECHOSLOVAKIA 1 (Half-time 2-1)

Estadio Sausalito, Viña del Mar, 7 June
Attendance: 10,648

THE final game of Group Three had no relevance in establishing the two qualifiers but it did have a bearing on who finished top of the group, Brazil or Czechoslovakia. The Europeans would have headed the South Americans had they won by three clear goals — but what a shock Mexico had in store for them.

Mexico had been one of the World Cup pioneers in 1930. Now, 32 years and 14 matches later, they were to win their first-ever game in the championship. Mexico's goalkeeper, Antonio Carbajal, was celebrating his 33rd birthday on the day of the match and what a birthday present it turned out to be for their star of the last four World Cups.

Czechoslovakia showed the Mexicans total respect by fielding a virtually full-strength team and it seemed as though Carbajal's birthday was going to turn into an unhappy event when Mašek scored for the Czechs in the first minute. But goals from Díaz, after ten minutes, and Del Aguila (29 minutes) gave the Mexicans a shock 2-1 lead at the interval.

They held on to that lead, despite continued Czech pressure and in the 89th minute were awarded a penalty which Héctor Hernández converted to give Mexico a memorable 3-1 victory.

Birthday boy Carbajal announced his retirement from international football after the tournament, but he was persuaded to change his mind and four years later he was in England for his fifth World Cup at the age of 37.

Mexico: Carbajal; Del Muro, Cardenas, Sepúlveda, Jáuregui, Reyes, Najera, Del Aguila, A.Hernández, H.Hernández, Díaz.
Scorers: Díaz, Del Aguila, H.Hernández (pen)
Czechoslovakia: Schrojf; Lála, Novák, Pluskal, Popluhár, Masopust, Štibrányi, Scherer, Kvašnák, Adamec, Mašek.
Scorer: Mašek
Referee: Gottfried Dienst (Switzerland)

Group Four

ARGENTINA 1   BULGARIA 0 (Half-time 1-0)

Braden Stadium, Rancagua, 30 May
Attendance: 7,134

THE tiny ground of the Braden Copper Company at Rancagua, near Valparaíso, was the venue for all Group Four matches. The small ground drew poor attendances and the opening game between Argentina and Bulgaria was watched by a crowd of only 7,134.

Bulgaria made their World Cup debut against the once-powerful Argentinians in a rather dull game, settled by one goal scored after only four minutes by Argentina's right winger Héctor Facundo. Indeed, he had the honour of scoring the first goal of the 1962 championship, but that was probably the most notable statistic in an otherwise drab game. Argentina 'put up the shutters' and prevented the Bulgarians playing creative football. The South Americans' tackling was aggressive at times and the small crowd were unimpressed with the way the Argentinians played.

The performance of these sides in the opening game indicated that Hungary and England would be the likely qualifiers from this group.

Argentina: Roma; Navarro, Páez, Saínz, Marzolini, Sacchi, Rossi, Facundo, Pagani, Sanfilippo, Belén.
Scorer: Facundo
Bulgaria: Naidenov; Rakarov, Kitov, A.Kostov, Dimitrov, Kovatchev, Diev, Velitchkov, Iliev, Yakimov, Kolev.
Referee: Juan Gardaezabal Garay (Spain)

HUNGARY 2   ENGLAND 1 (Half-time 1-0)

Braden Stadium, Rancagua, 31 May
Attendance: 7,938

IN contrast to the group's opening game, the Hungary-England meeting was one that had apparently been awaited with interest by local fans, yet less than 8,000 turned out at the tiny ground.

The result for England was a disappointing one. They were becoming predictable and although Johnny Haynes ran the midfield, his crossfield passes to his wingers were cut out time and again by the Hungarian defence.

Hungary had only one survivor from their team which reached the 1954 Final — goalkeeper Gyula Grosics — but in the place of Puskás and Hidegkuti were the exciting duo of Florian Albert and Lajos Tichy, who turned out to be two of the outstanding players of the group matches. Hungarian defender, Ernö Solymosi, was also outstanding and was regarded as one of the world's great defenders of the era.

It was Tichy who scored the only goal of the first half when his long-range shot beat Ron Springett after 15 minutes. Hungary started to play the sort of fluent football the world had seen from them in the early part of the 1950s, but the England defence, with Ron Flowers and newcomer Bobby Moore outstanding, was good enough to prevent further goals. Alas, England's forwards, with the exception of Bobby Charlton, showed little imagination and Gerry Hitchens, who played for Inter-Milan at the time, was surprisingly out of touch.

Ivan Dimitrov of Bulgaria.

Jimmy Armfield of England.

Ron Flowers of England slams home a penalty equalizer against Hungary.

Ernö Solymosi of Hungary.

János Göröcs.

England's Bryan Douglas.

England managed an equalizer from the penalty-spot after an hour when Ron Flowers converted the kick. But 15 minutes from time, Albert scored a magnificent solo goal to give Hungary a deserved win.

Hungary: Grosics; Mátrai, Sárosi, Solymosi, Mészöly, Sipos, Sándor, Rákosi, Albert, Tichy, Fenyvesi.
Scorers: Tichy, Albert
England: Springett; Armfield, Wilson, Moore, Norman, Flowers, Douglas, Greaves, Hitchens, Haynes, Charlton.
Scorer: Flowers (pen)
Referee: Leo Horn (Holland)

ENGLAND 3   ARGENTINA 1 (Half-time 2-0)

Braden Stadium, Rancagua, 2 June.
Attendance: 9,794

ENGLAND prepared themselves well for their second game. Having watched the defensive tactics of the Argentinians against Bulgaria, they made the necessary adjustments to the team although they made only one actual change, bringing in Alan Peacock for Gerry Hitchens.

On the other hand, Argentina made four changes and gave a World Cup debut to Antonio Rattín, who was to skipper the side in England four years later. And when the two sides next met in the World Cup he was involved in a sending-off which resulted in some unpleasant scenes at Wembley.

Peacock had a fine game at centre-forward, despite the close and often rough marking of Ruben Navarro. It was Flowers, again from the penalty-spot, who scored England's opening goal after 17 minutes. Three minutes before the interval, England's all-time top goalscorer, Bobby Charlton, made it 2-0 with a great shot.

England knew that they had to win in order to stay in contention for a quarter-final place and their attacks yielded another goal in the 65th minute when Jimmy Greaves opened his World Cup account. A defensive error allowed Sanfilippo to score a late goal for Argentina, but England registered their first win in the final stages since beating Switzerland 2-0 in 1954.

England: Springett; Armfield, Wilson, Moore, Norman, Flowers, Douglas, Greaves, Peacock, Haynes, Charlton.
Scorers: Flowers (pen), Charlton, Greaves
Argentina: Roma; Capp, Páez, Navarro, Marzolini, Sacchi, Rattín, Oleniak, Sosa, Sanfilippo, Belén.
Scorer: Sanfilippo
Referee: Nikolai Latychev (Soviet Union)

HUNGARY 6   BULGARIA 1 (Half-time 4-0)

Braden Stadium, Rancagua, 3 June
Attendance: 7,442

HUNGARY'S six goals against Bulgaria were the biggest haul of the 1962 World Cup finals. Albert and Tichy were outstanding and shared five goals between them, with Albert scoring the only hat-trick of the tournament.

Hungary really hit top form in this match and scored four goals before the game was 12 minutes old. Albert netted in the first minute and five minutes later added a second. Tichy made it 3-0 after eight minutes and then Solymosi scored a fourth.

Their lead was stretched to five goals when Albert completed his hat-trick in the 58th minute and the Chilean spectators, who were rooting for Bulgaria, were given some cheer when Sokolov scored six minutes later. Tichy scored his second and Hungary's sixth, 20 minutes from time.

Hungary: Ilku; Mátrai, Sárosi, Solymosi, Mészöly, Sipos, Sándor, Göröcs, Albert, Tichy, Fenyvesi.
Scorers: Albert 3, Tichy 2, Solymosi
Bulgaria: Naidenov; Rakarov, Kitov, A.Kostov, Dimitrov, Kovatchev, Sokolov, Velitchkov, Asparoukhov, Kolev, Dermendiev.
Scorer: Sokolov
Referee: Juan Gardeazabal Garay (Spain)

ARGENTINA 0   HUNGARY 0 (Half-time 0-0)

Braden Stadium, Rancagua, 6 June
Attendance: 7,945

HUNGARY'S four points from their first two games virtually assured them a place in the quarter-finals. Only a big defeat could now prevent their passage to the next stage. Understandably, they were content to play for a draw, which they achieved despite a set-back in the 12th minute when midfielder János Göröcs was injured.

Argentina's manager, Juan Carlos Lorenzo, made more changes in the hope of a better result than they had managed against England. The Argentinians needed to win. A draw would almost certainly have meant their exit.

Bulgarian goalkeeper Georgi Naidenov picks the ball out of the net again during the six-goal hammering by Hungary.

England's captain, Johnny Haynes.

England goalkeeper Ron Springett.

A youthful Bobby Moore gets the ball clear during the game against Hungary. It was Moore's first World Cup but the meagre crowd of less than 6,000 in Rancagua's Braden Stadium must have seemed a world away from the atmosphere of the English First Division.

Group Four – Final Table

	P	W	D	L	F	A	Pts
Hungary	3	2	1	0	8	2	5
England	3	1	1	1	4	3	3
Argentina	3	1	1	1	2	3	3
Bulgaria	3	0	1	2	1	7	1

Igor Netto of the USSR.

Following the injury to Göröcs, Hungary had no option but to play the defensive game which the Argentinians had mastered.

Argentina: Domínguez; Cap, Saínz, Delgado, Marzolini, Sacchi, Pando, Facundo, Pagani, Oleniak, González.
Hungary: Grosics; Mátrai, Sárosi, Solymosi, Mészöly, Sipos, Kuharszki, Göröcs, Monostroi, Tichy, Rákosi.
Referee: Arturo Maldonazdo Yamasaki (Peru)

BULGARIA 0   ENGLAND 0 (Half-time 0-0)

Braden Stadium, Rancagua, 7 June
Attendance: 5,700

SUCH was the lack of interest in this match that less than 6,000 fans flocked to the tiny Braden Stadium. England needed only to draw to go into the last eight because their goal-difference was superior to that of Argentina. Bulgaria, on the other hand, had no chance of progressing and many expected them to come out and play an open attacking 'nothing-to-lose' game. But they surprised the fans and England players by turning to defensive tactics right from the start.

England also played defensively but how close they came to letting the match slip away when Ivan Kolev got through and should have scored the goal that would have eliminated England. Those journalists who penned it as 'the most boring game of the tournament' were pretty accurate.

Bulgaria: Naidenov; Pentchev, Zechev, D.Kostov, Dimitrov, Kovatchev, A.Kostov, Velitchkov, Sokolov, Kolev, Dermendiev.
England: Springett; Armfield, Wilson, Moore, Norman, Flowers, Douglas, Greaves, Peacock, Haynes, Charlton.
Referee: Antoine Blavier (Belgium)

Quarter-finals

CHILE 2   SOVIET UNION 1 (Half-time 2-1)

Carlos Dittborn Stadium, Arica, 10 June
Attendance: 17,268

CHILE took the field in the World Cup quarter-finals on the day that the widow of Carlos Dittborn gave birth to a son. It would have been a great day indeed for Dittborn, who died shortly before the start of the series, for he would have seen two dreams fulfilled.

The tiny stadium was filled to capacity and across Chile the match was being listened to in every house and bar as radio and television sets relayed the game the length and breadth of this impoverished country.

After only 11 minutes, those watching and listening millions erupted with joy as Leonel Sánchez took Lev Yashin by surprise from a free-kick and put the home team in front. For Yashin it was yet another error in what turned out to be a disastrous tournament for the normally reliable Russian goalkeeper.

The non-stop chanting from the home fans came to an abrupt end in the 26th minute after Chislenko scored for Russia. But the silence lasted little more than a minute before wing-half Eladio Rojas spotted a gap in the Soviet defence and hit the ball from 30 yards. Again Yashin was possibly to blame as the ball shot into the corner of the net. The goal was just reward for Rojas, who was the outstanding player on the field.

After the pitch was eventually cleared of jubilant Chilean supporters, the match resumed and the hosts built a defensive wall which the Russians could not penetrate.

Chile: Escuti; Eyzaguirre, Contreras, R.Sánchez, Navarro, Toro, Rojas, Ramírez, Landa, Tobar, L.Sánchez.
Scorers: L.Sánchez, Rojas
Soviet Union: Yashin; Tchokelli, Ostrovski, Voronin, Maslenkin, Netto, Chislenko, Ivanov, Ponedelnik, Mamikin, Meschki.
Scorer: Chislenko
Referee: Leo Horn (Holland)

YUGOSLAVIA 1   WEST GERMANY 0 (Half-time 0-0)

Estadio Nacional, Santiago, 10 June
Attendance: 63,324

ALTHOUGH the National Stadium was filled with nearly 65,000 fans, they were not all that interested in what Yugoslavia and West Germany had to offer. Most of them were glued to radio sets listening to the Chile-Russia match at Arica. The 'ooohs and aaaghs', cheers and jeers' related to that match and bore little resemblance to play on the field in front of them.

Nevertheless, the European sides both played entertaining football considering the stakes and the defensive nature of football at the time. West Germany and Yugoslavia met at this

Victor Ponedelnik of the USSR.

Haller of West Germany wins the ball, despite the attentions of three Yugoslav defenders.

Hans Nowak of West Germany.

stage in the competition in 1954 and 1958 and on both occasions the Germans won without the Yugoslavs scoring.

This latest encounter seemed to be heading for extra-time before the 87th-minute goal scored from the edge of the penalty area by Peter Radaković, who was playing with his head swathed in bandages.

Yugoslavia: Šoškić; Durković, Jusufi, Radaković, Marković, Popović, Kovačević, Šekularac, Jerković, Galić, Skoblar.
Scorer: Radaković
West Germany: Fahrian; Nowak, Schnellinger, Schulz, Erhardt, Giesemann, Brülls, Haller, Seeler, Szymaniak, Schäfer.
Referee: Arturo Maldonado Yamasaki (Peru)

Uwe Seeler could not help West Germany's cause against the Yugoslavs.

Yugoslavia's players can hardly take it in – they are through to the World Cup semi-finals after an 87th-minute goal against West Germany.

Brazil's 1962 World Cup squad pictured at their hotel.

Bobby Charlton of England.

Nilton Santos fires in a shot against England at Viña del Mar.

BRAZIL 3   ENGLAND 1 (Half-time 1-1)

Estadio Sausalito, Viña del Mar, 10 June
Attendance: 17,736

IN the first half of their quarter-final clash with Brazil, England gave probably their finest World Cup performance since making their debut in 1950. But a six-minute spell by the Brazilians early in the second half, with Garrincha at his brilliant best, ended England's hopes of ousting the defending champions.

Garrincha opened the scoring with a cheeky header from a corner after half an hour. Then England nearly went 2-0 down when a back-pass by Flowers let in Amarildo, but Springett brought off a great save.

Gerry Hitchens was recalled to the side for the injured Alan Peacock and the Inter-Milan forward levelled the scores in the 38th minute when he followed up a Greaves header which rebounded off the bar. In an entertaining first half, England had done well and were holding the great Brazilians.

They fell behind after 53 minutes, however, when Vavá followed up a powerful free-kick from Garrincha. After the ball bounced off Springett's chest, the Brazilian had no difficulty in heading home.

Brazil were now playing magnificent football, with Garrincha outstanding. And it was Garrincha who scored Brazil's third goal six minutes later with a swerving chip from 20 yards.

England had played well, but the outstanding spells of the Brazilians proved decisive. The champions marched on and installed themselves as hot favourites to retain the title.

Brazil: Gilmar; D.Santos, Mauro, Zózimo, N.Santos, Zito, Garrincha, Didí, Vavá, Amarildo, Zagalo.
Scorers: Garrincha 2, Vavá
England: Springett; Armfield, Wilson, Moore, Norman, Flowers, Douglas, Greaves, Hitchens, Haynes, Charlton.
Scorer: Hitchens
Referee: Pierre Schwinte (France)

Garrincha, scored twice against England.

CZECHOSLOVAKIA 1   HUNGARY 0 (Half-time 1-0)

Braden Stadium, Rancagua, 10 June
Attendance: 11,690

HUNGARY went into their quarter-final with confidence. They were playing fluent football, like their predecessors of a decade earlier, and in Chile had shown they could score goals. The Czechs, on the other hand, had scored only two goals in qualifying for the semi-finals, but it was the well-organized Czechs who ran out winners.

The only goal of an excellent game was scored by Adolf Scherer, who latched on to a pass in the 12th minute and hammered the ball into the net from 20 yards. His shot sailed past Gyula Grosics and it was to be a sad end to his World Cup career, which had encompassed three tournaments.

Czechoslovakia turned out to be the surprise team of the tournament and their half-back line of Pluskal, Popluhár and Masopust was probably the best in the tournament and took a lot of beating — as Hungary had discovered as they sought an equalizer in the last 78 minutes of this game. Goalkeeper Schrojf was also in magnificent form and stopped everything the Magyars threw at him, with the exception of a Tichy effort which the Hungarians were unlucky to have disallowed for offside.

Czechoslovakia: Schrojf; Lála, Novák, Pluskal, Popluhár, Masopust, Pospichal, Scherer, Kvašnák, Kadraba, Jelinek.
Scorer: Scherer
Hungary: Grosics; Mátrai, Sárosi, Solymosi, Mészöly, Sipos, Sándor, Rákosi, Albert, Tichy, Fenyvesi.
Referee: Nikolai Latychev (Soviet Union)

Amarildo, whose shot was saved by Springett after a mistake by Flowers.

Semi-finals

BRAZIL 4   CHILE 2 (Half-time 2-1)

Estadio Nacional, Santiago, 13 June
Attendance: 76,594

WITH two South American nations opposing each other in the semi-final of the World Cup, one the hosts and the other the defending champions, it had to be the recipe for a fervent Latin clash. Add more than 76,000 spectators and the atmoshpere becomes electric. And that is what the seventh World Cup provided when Chile and Brazil met at Santiago's National Stadium on 13 June.

Most of the large crowd, the biggest of the tournament, were hoping for a 'home' win. But there are occasions when loyalty must give way to reality. Chile were lucky to be in the semi-finals and once more added fuel to the argument that the host nation has an advantage. Brazil, on the other hand, whilst not playing the sort of attractive football that won them

Miguel Escuti's despairing dive is in vain as Garrincha gives Brazil a ninth-minute lead over Chile.

Brazil's Zagalo gets in a shot against Chile.

Josef Masopust, stood firm as Yugoslavia mounted several raids on the Czech goal.

their first World Cup in Sweden four years earlier, were still the best team in what was really a poor tournament in terms of quality football.

Garrincha, who had been the unquestionable star of the tournament, put Brazil in front in the ninth minute with a great 20-yard left-footed drive. And he added a second after 31 minutes when he headed home a corner. Toro pulled one back for Chile four minutes before half-time, with a powerful shot from a free-kick, but three minutes after the break, Vavá restored Brazil's two-goal lead when he headed Garrincha's corner-kick into the net.

Leonel Sánchez brought Chile back into contention in the 61st minute with a goal from the penalty-spot and the Chilean fans were beginning to suspect there could be an upset, but Vavá ended all their dreams in the 77th minute with a fourth goal — another header, this time from a Zagalo cross.

Chile's Honorino Landa was sent off for a foul on Zito, and six minutes from time Garrincha was dismissed for kicking Rojas. His dismissal created a worrying time for Brazil and their supporters. FIFA were to discuss the case and rule whether he would be eligible for the Final. They knew that without him, and with no chance of Pelé returning, it would upset the fluency of the team. They faced an anxious overnight wait.

Brazil: Gilmar; D.Santos, Mauro, Zózimo, N.Santos, Zito, Garrincha, Didí, Vavá, Amarildo, Zagalo.
Scorers: Garrincha 2, Vavá 2
Chile: Escuti; Eyzaguirre, Contreras, R.Sánchez, Rodríguez, Toro, Rojas, Ramírez, Landa, Tobar, L.Sánchez.
Scorers: Toro, L.Sánchez (pen)
Referee: Arturo Maldonado Yamasaki (Peru)

CZECHOSLOVAKIA 3   YUGOSLAVIA 1 (Half-time 0-0)

Estadio Sausalito, Viña del Mar, 13 June
Attendance: 5,890

CZECHOSLOVAKIA returned to Viña del Mar where they played their preliminary matches, but the local fans remembered that they had not made a big impact on Group Three and less than 6,000 turned up to watch this semi-final.

Looking at Czechoslovakia's goalscoring record, one had to concede to the better judgement of the Viña del Mar fans. But for the first time, the Czechs produced a display of attacking football to go with their solid defence.

Despite a goalless first half they had the better of the strong Yugoslavs, although Yugoslavia made several raids on the Czech goal, only to be thwarted by the brilliant Schrojf, who had an outstanding tournament.

It did not take Czechoslovakia long after the start of the second half to penetrate the Yugoslavian defence. Josef Kadraba put them in front in the 49th minute and, although Drazan Jerković equalized in the 69th minute, continued Czech pressure paid off with two goals from Scherer in the last ten minutes, the second from the penalty-spot after Marković had handled.

The impressive Czechs had won themselves a place in the World Cup Final for the second time. The previous occasion was in 1934 when they pushed the powerful and fancied Italians to extra-time. Could they go one better and beat the powerful and fancied Brazilians in 1962?

Czechoslovakia: Schrojf; Lála, Novák, Pluskal, Popluhár, Masopust, Pospichal, Scherer, Kvašnák, Kadraba, Jelinek.
Scorers: Scherer 2 (1 pen), Kadraba
Yugoslavia: Šoškić; Durković, Jusufi, Radaković, Marković, Popović, Šijaković, Šekularac, Jerković, Galić, Skoblar.
Scorer: Jerković
Referee: Gottfried Dienst (Switzerland)

Milutin Šoškić of Yugoslavia.

Scherer beats Šoškić to score the crucial second goal for Czechoslovakia.

Third place play-off
CHILE 1   YUGOSLAVIA 0 (Half-time 0-0)

Estadio Nacional, Santiago, 16 June
Attendance: 66,697

CARLOS Dittborn said that Chile must have the 1962 tournament because it had nothing else in the aftermath of those dreadful earthquakes. His country was given the job of hosting the tournament and did not disappoint, even if the quality of football was not the best. Dittborn would have been proud of what the next three weeks held and he would have been even prouder of the way the hosts played in reaching the last four.

For the millions of Chilean football followers this third-place game with Yugoslavia was more important than the Final. And what scenes there were in the National Stadium when Eladio Rojas scored the only goal of the game with the last kick of the match. He collected a ball 30 yards out, beat two defenders and scored with a deflected shot. The stadium erupted and the celebrations started as the Chileans revelled in a marvellous victory and hailed their new hero, Rojas.

The fact that Brazil and Czechoslovakia had to do battle for the Jules Rimet Trophy the following day was irrelevant. The Chileans did not care — they'd won *their* World Cup.

Chile: Godoy; Eyzaguirre, Cruz, R.Sánchez, Rodríguez, Toro, Rojas, Ramírez, Campos, Tobar, L.Sánchez.
Scorer: Rojas
Yugoslavia: Šoškić; Durković, Svinjarević, Radaković, Marković, Popović, Kovačević, Šekularac, Jerković, Galić, Skoblar.
Referee: Juan Gardeazabal Gabay (Spain)

Drazan Jerković of Yugoslavia.

Final

BRAZIL 3   CZECHOSLOVAKIA 1 (Half-time 1-1)

Estadio Nacional, Santiago, 17 June
Attendance: 68,679

AFTER an anxious 24-hour wait, FIFA ruled that Garrincha could play in the World Cup Final. And Brazil could count themselves fortunate, for Garrincha was one of six players dismissed during the series. The others all received a one-match ban, yet 'The Little Bird' was let off with a reprimand. The Czechs, however, were ready for his presence, and kept him quiet throughout the game.

Despite the all-night long celebrations in Santiago, following Chile's capture of the third place, nearly 70,000 fans turned up for the Final. And what a surprise they received when Masopust put Czechoslovakia into a 15th-minute lead after racing on to a long pass from Scherer. But those who were familiar with their World Cup history knew that four of the six previous World Cup winners had fallen behind. And when Czechoslovakia were last in the Final, against Italy in 1934, they opened the scoring, yet still lost. History was about to repeat itself.

It took Brazil only two minutes to wipe out Masopust's goal, when Amarildo beat the outstanding Schrojf with a shot from an acute angle. The normally reliable 'keeper was to blame. He was expecting a cross and was slow to react to Amarildo's shot.

Czechoslovakia, who only went to Chile after beating Scotland in a play-off in the qualifiers, were not overawed and were a good match for the favourites. However, they allowed Brazil to take the lead for the first time in the 68th minute, when Zito started and finished a move, heading home an Amarildo centre. And 13 minutes from time the Czechs were completely demoralized when their normally dependable 'keeper fumbled a lob into the penalty area from Djalmar Santos. Vavá was on the spot to put the ball into the net.

Opposite page (top): Eladio Rojas celebrates his goal which earned Chile third place in the 1962 World Cup. *Opposite page (bottom):* Russian referee Nikolai Latychev prepares to toss the coin before the 1962 World Cup Final. The captains are Czechoslovakia's Ladislav Novák (left) and Brazil's Mauro.

> **WORLD CUP FACT**
>
> Brazil is the only nation to have been managed by brothers in the World Cup finals. Zeze Moreira was in charge in 1954, whilst his brother, Aimoré, was manager eight years later. Both were former Brazilian internationals.

Josef Masopust (second left) gives the Czechs a 15th-minute lead after racing on to a long pass from Scherer.

Amarildo (out of picture) beats Schrojf with a shot from an acute angle to level the scores two minutes later.

STATISTICS

Goalscorers:

4 — Valentin Ivanov (Soviet Union), Leonel Sánchez (Chile), Garrincha, Vavá (both Brazil), Florian Albert (Hungary), Drazan Jerković (Yugoslavia).

3 — Amarildo Tavares de Silveira (Brazil), Adolf Scherer (Czechoslovakia), Lajos Tichy (Hungary), Milan Galić (Yugoslavia).

2 — José Sacia (Uruguay), Victor Ponedelnik, Igor Chislenko (both Soviet Union), Jaime Ramírez, Jorge Toro, Eladio Rojas (all Chile), Uwe Seeler (West Germany), Giacomo Bulgarelli (Italy), Ron Flowers (England).

1 — Luis Cubilla, Ruben Cabrera (both Uruguay), Francisco Zuluaga, Germán Aceros, Ingacio Coll, Antonio Rada, Marino Klinger (all Colombia), Alexei Mamikov (Soviet Union), Josip Skoblar, Voijslav Melić, Peter Radaković (all Yugoslavia), Rolf Wüthrich, Heinz Schneiter (both Switzerland), Albert Brülls, Horst Szymaniak (both West Germany), Bruno Mora (Italy), Zagalo, Pelé, Zito (all Brazil), Josef Stibranyi, Vaclav Mašek, Josef Kadraba, Josef Masopust (all Czechoslovakia), Joaquin Peiró, Adelardo Sánchez (both Spain), Isidoro Díaz, Alfredo Del Aguila, Héctor Hernández (all Mexico), Hector Facundo, José Francisco Sanfilippo (all Argentina), Ernö Solymosi (Hungary), Bobby Charlton, Jimmy Greaves, Gerry Hitchens (all England), Georgi Sokolov (Bulgaria).

Own-goals
None

Hat-tricks
Florian Albert (Hungary v Bulgaria).

Fastest goal
1 minute — Florian Albert (Hungary v Bulgaria), Vaclav Mašek (Czechoslovakia v Mexico).

Most goals (team)
14 — Brazil

Teams failing to score
None

Total goals scored: 89
Average per game: 2.78

Top: Djalma Santos (left), Masopust, Didí and Jelinek (11) joust for the ball.

Middle: Gilmar makes a flying save.

Bottom: Didí watches Zagalo as he attempts to block the path of an opponent.

Brazil ran out winners and Mauro went up to collect the Jules Rimet Trophy as Brazil joined Uruguay and Italy as two-times winners.

Brazil: Gilmar do Santos Neves; Djalmar Santos, Mauro Ramos de Oliveira, Zózimo Alves Calazans, Nilton Santos, Zito, Garrincha, Didí, Vavá, Amarildo Tavares de Silveira, Zagalo.
Scorers: Amarildo, Zito, Vavá
Czechoslovakia: Viliam Schrojf; Jiri Tichy, Ladislav Novák, Svatopluk Pluskal, Jan Popluhár, Josef Masopust, Tomas Pospichal, Adolf Scherer, Andrej Kvašnák, Josef Kadraba, Jozef Jelinek II.
Scorer: Masopust
Referee: Nikolai Latychev (Soviet Union)

The victorious Brazilian team. Back row (left to right, players only): Djalma Santos, Zito, Gilmar, Nilton Santos, Zózimo, Mauro. Front row: Garrincha, Didí, Vavá, Amarildo, Zagalo.

Above and left: Brazilian skipper Mauro holds aloft the Jules Rimet Trophy.

Penalties
Scored: Francisco Zuluaga (Colombia v Uruguay) *Referee: Albert Dorogy (Hungary).* Josip Skoblar (Yugoslavia v Uruguay) *Referee: Karol Galba (Czechoslovakia).* Horst Szymaniak (West Germany v Chile) *Referee: Bob Davidson (Scotland).* Héctor Hernández (Mexico v Czechoslovakia) *Referee: Gottfried Dienst (Switzerland).* Ron Flowers (England v Hungary) *Referee: Leo Horn (Holland).* Ron Flowers (England v Argentina) *Referee: Nikolai Latychev (Soviet Union).* Leonel Sánchez (Chile v Brazil) *Referee: Arturo Maldonado Yamasaki (Peru).* Adolph Scherer (Czechoslovakia v Yugoslavia) *Referee: Gottfried Dienst (Switzerland).* Leonel Sánchez (Chile v Switzerland) *Referee: Ken Aston (England).*

Most appearances
6 — Djalma Santos, Didí, Garrincha, Gilmar do Santos Neves, Mauro Ramos de Oliveira, Nilton Santos, Vavá, Zagalo, Zito, Zózimo Alves Calazans (all Brazil), Luis Armando Eyzaguirre, Jaime Ramirez, Eladio Rojas, Leonel Sánchez, Raul Sánchez (all Chile), Andrej Kvašnák, Josef Masopust, Ladislav Novak, Svatopluk Pluskal, Jan Popluhár, Adolf Scherer, Viliam Schrojf (all Czechoslovakia), Vladimir Durković, Milan Galić, Drazan Jerković, Vlatko Marković, Vladimir Popović, Dragoslav Šekularac, Milutin Šoškić (all Yugoslavia).

Sendings-off
Vladimir Popović (Yugoslavia v Uruguay) *Referee: Karol Galba (Czechoslovakia).* Ruben Cabrera (Uruguay v Yugoslavia) *Referee: Karol Galba (Czechoslovakia).* Giorgio Ferrini (Italy v Chile) *Referee: Ken Aston (England).* Mario David (Italy v Chile) *Referee: Ken Aston (England).* Garrincha (Brazil v Chile) *Referee: Arturo Maldonado Yamasaki (Peru).* Honorino Landa (Chile v Brazil) *Referee: Arturo Maldonado Yamasaki (Peru).*

Most players used
20 — Italy
20 — Spain

Number of players used by Finalists
12 — Brazil
15 — Czechoslovakia

Top: Amarildo in action during the Final.

Middle: Santiago's national stadium packed with almost 69,000 spectators for the 1962 World Cup Final.

Bottom: The Czech team after the final whistle.

Top: Zito (number-four, arms raised) gives Brazil the lead in the 68th minute, heading home Amarildo's cross.

Middle: Vavá pounces on an error by the normally reliable Schrojf and puts the game beyond the Czechs' reach in the 77th minute.

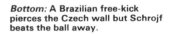

Bottom: A Brazilian free-kick pierces the Czech wall but Schrojf beats the ball away.

MEN WHO MADE THE HEADLINES - 1966

Geoff Hurst
(England)

GEOFF Hurst stands unique as the only man to have scored a hat-trick in a World Cup Final. He was born in Ashton-under-Lyne, Lancashire, in 1941 and turned professional with West Ham United. Between 1959 and 1972 he made over 400 League appearances and scored 180 goals, helping the Hammers win the FA Cup in 1964 and the European Cup-winners' Cup the following year. Both matches were at Wembley and Hurst made it a remarkable hat-trick in 1966, when England lifted the Jules Rimet Trophy. His second goal was one of the most controversial in World Cup history. Hurst had made his debut, against West Germany, only five months before the World Cup and it was an injury to Jimmy Greaves that saw him into the side in the finals, where he scored the winner against Argentina in the quarter-final. He also played in the 1970 finals and in 1972 moved to Stoke City before finishing his career at West Brom. Hurst won 49 caps and scored 24 goals for England. He managed Chelsea and Telford United and assisted Ron Greenwood with the national squad. His appearance for Essex against Lancashire means that he is the only first-class cricketer to have won a World Cup winners' medal at soccer.

Eusébio
(Portugal)

EUSÉBIO da Silva Ferreira was born at Lourenço Marques, Mozambique, in 1942 and in 1961 joined Benfica as a 19-year-old from his local club, for £7,500. In one of his first games for Benfica, in a Paris tournament, he scored a hat-trick against Pelé's Santos and became one of Europe's most lethal strikers. He scored twice in the 5-3 defeat of Real Madrid in the 1962 European Cup Final and gained runners-up medals in 1963 and 1968. Eusébio won the first of his 77 caps in 1961, but will be best remembered for his contribution to the 1966 World Cup. 'The Black Pearl' gave brilliant displays and scored some outstanding goals. Nine goals made him the tournament's top scorer and he netted four in Portugal's remarkable fight-back against North Korea. He was the 1965 European Footballer of the Year and in 1968 was the first winner of the Golden Boot Award, as Europe's leading scorer, a feat he repeated five years later. The Portuguese League's top scorer every year from 1964 to 1973, he helped Benfica to ten Championships and five Cup wins. Knee operations slowed him down and in 1975 he moved into the NASL. In 1976-7 he played for SC Beira Mar in Portugal and then had further spells in the USA and Mexico.

Uwe Seller
(West Germany)

UWE Seeler was West Germany's most prolific goalscorer until the arrival of Gerd Müller. Seeler, who was born at Hamburg in 1936, spent his entire professional career with his home-town club, despite many offers from Spanish and Italian clubs. He skippered SV Hamburg to the 1961 European Cup semi-final and the 1968 Cup-winners' Cup Final. His international career began as 17-year-old in October 1954, when he came on as a substitute against France for the first of 72 appearances which saw him score 43 goals. He played in the teams that reached the World Cup semi-finals (1958) and quarter-finals (1962) before skippering the side in the 1966 Final, bowing out of international soccer after West Germany clinched third place in the 1970 tournament. It was his 21st World Cup appearance and is still a record, since equalled by Poland's Zmuda. By 1970, Gerd Müller was the new German scoring sensation and Seeler played a deeper role, complementing Müller well. He played for Hamburg until 1972 and in his 18-year career made over 700 senior appearances, scored 551 goals and was the Bundesliga's leading goalscorer five times.

Ramsey's Wingless Wonders
England 1966

SINCE its launch in 1930, the World Cup had grown in stature to become the world's senior international soccer tournament. It was, then, only a matter of time before England, the birthplace of the game, hosted the tournament and that honour came in 1966, three years after the Football Association had celebrated its centenary.

As would be expected from the oldest football association in the world, the FA organized the tournament in an exemplary manner and the stadiums used for the group and knock-out matches were probably the best overall selection of grounds used for any World Cup celebration to date. The attendance figures were amongst the best ever recorded.

However, despite their organizational skills, the FA could not legislate for what happened four months before the start of the tournament, when the first drama of the eighth World Cup unfolded.

The Jules Rimet Trophy was on display, along with rare stamps, at an exhibition at Westminster's Central Hall. But on Sunday, 20 March 1966, to the horror of the FA and FIFA, the famous trophy was stolen. The theft was an embarrassment to officials, who faced the prospect of the World Cup starting without a trophy. However, there came to the rescue a black and white mongrel dog named Pickles. He did what Scotland Yard's best could not do — sniff out the cup, which was wrapped in newspaper in the garden of a house at Norwood, South London, one week after the theft. The FA's blushes were spared.

England and Uruguay eventually got the championship under way on 11 July, shortly after Her Majesty the Queen had performed the opening ceremony, but the 87,000 Wembley fans had to endure 90 minutes of negative, defensive football from the South Americans, who played with eight and even nine men in defence.

England manager Alf Ramsey had announced shortly after being appointed successor to Walter Winterbottom that "England would be world champions in 1966." Few believed him at the time and even fewer took him seriously after his team's failure to achieve anything against the defensive-minded Uruguayans. But, like so many world champions of the past, England followed the same pattern and improved with every game until, on 30 July 1966, Ramsey's heroes proved their boss right.

In retrospect, England were the best of what was really a rather poor selection of entrants. There was none of the dash that the 1954 Magyars exhibited. And gone was the flair of those magnificent 1958 Brazilians. Sadly, the game had become more defensive and individual skills had to make way for those of the tacticians.

Brazil arrived in England as favourites to win their third successive World Cup and thus retain the trophy. Alas, their ageing team was 'snuffed' and 'fouled' out of the tournament. Hungary, who promised so much in their group matches, also disappeared without trace thereafter.

After beating Argentina in a stormy match, England emerged as favourites along with Portugal, who had one of the game's most exciting players, Eusébio, in their ranks. It was unfortunate that these two teams met in the semi-final.

While the footballing world, including a global television audience of over 500 million, had their eyes on Pelé, Eusébio, Albert and Bobby Charlton, they could not help noticing a few lesser known players with wonderful names like Pak Do-ik, Pak Li-sup, Yan Soon-kook. They were the heroes of the North Korean side who, like Portugal, were making their debut in the final stages of the World Cup. And what an impact these diminutive Asians had on the tournament.

First they beat Italy 1-0, in one of the biggest-ever World Cup shocks, and then led Portugal 3-0 after little more than 20 minutes of their quarter-final clash. Defensively naïve, they eventually succumbed to the might of Eusébio, but their contribution to World Cup history will never be forgotten.

At the end of nearly three weeks of football, England became the first hosts since Italy in 1934 to win the trophy. The Final was one of the game's memorable matches and contained one of the World Cup's most controversial incidents, but England's victory did not stem from that one incident or one match. It stemmed from a series of professional performances. They had a good team spirit and believed in themselves. Most of all they had to thank Alf Ramsey's tactics. Once he realized that he had no world-class wingers at his disposal, Ramsey restructured the England team by packing the midfield and Ramsey's 'wingless wonders' were born.

Above (top): **Sir Stanley Matthews carries the FIFA flag in Westminster Abbey.** *Above (middle):* **Pickles, the dog that found the stolen World Cup.** *Above (bottom):* **England manager Alf Ramsey.**

Left (from left to right): **The World Cup on display in Central Hall, Westminster; Scotland Yard fingerprint expert is called in; Safe and sound. A police inspector displays the recovered trophy; Pickles gets his reward.**

1966 Qualifying Competition

OF the 70 teams entered for the qualifying competition, only 51 actually took part. Syria withdrew from the European Group Nine, which left the Republic of Ireland and Spain to fight it out, the Spaniards winning after a play-off. South Africa did not take part because they had been suspended by FIFA in 1964 for violating anti-discrimination codes in the FIFA charter. The other 17 withdrawals were in the Africa and Asia groups.

Aggrieved at FIFA's decision to allow only one qualifier from these groups, nations pulled out *en masse* with the exception of North Korea, who were left to play a two-legged match against the Oceania representatives, Australia. The Koreans duly qualified for their debut in the final stages. And what an impact they were to have there.

The other debutants were Portugal, who finally qualified after first trying in 1934. They came through a group which contained the 1962 runners-up, Czechoslovakia, who were one of three 1962 finalists not to make the trip to England. The others were Colombia, who finished bottom of their three-team group containing Chile and Ecuador, and Yugoslavia, eliminated by France. Yugoslavia had been semi-finalists in Chile four years earlier.

England, of course, automatically qualified as hosts, but there was to be no repeat of 1958 and none of the other Home Countries qualified. Northern Ireland came close, but a disappointing 1-1 draw in Albania in their final qualifier cost them the chance of a play-off match against Switzerland. It was Albania's only point of the qualifying competition.

Despite beating the Soviet Union 2-1 at Cardiff in their penultimate group match, Wales were no match in the return and the Russians had little difficulty in qualifying for the final stages. Scotland went to Naples for the final match of Group Eight, knowing they had to beat Italy to qualify. A draw would have given them another chance but it was Italy who ran out 3-0 winners and qualified for their sixth appearance in the finals, although they were to have an unhappy time in England.

Bulgaria qualified for their second successive finals after beating Belgium in a play-off, thanks to a late goal in a 2-1 win. West Germany were unbeaten as they qualified from Group Two at the expense of Sweden and Cyprus. Completing the European complement was Hungary, who also qualified without losing a game.

The three South American groups went true to form with Uruguay, Chile and Argentina all qualifying. Chile, however, had to survive a 2-1 play-off win over Ecuador to gain their place. The play-off was necessary after they lost 2-0 to Colombia in one of the shock results of the qualifiers. And that was after Chile had put seven goals past the Colombians in the first game.

Mexico qualified for their fifth successive finals and in goal for them again was Antonio Carbajal, who had been their 'keeper in the first post-war tournament in 1950. As usual, in qualifying from the Central-North American group, Mexico had to play more matches than any other qualifying nation.

Most people felt that North Korea, who qualified thanks only to the withdrawal of so many African and Asian nations, would simply be making up the numbers. And when they lost 7-0 to Hungary in a friendly *en route* to England, they were given no chance of surviving beyond the group games. But what surprises they had in store.

Results

EUROPE

Group One

9 May 1965 *Brussels*	Belgium	1 Israel	0
13 Jun 1965 *Sofia*	Bulgaria	4 Israel	0
26 Sep 1965 *Sofia*	Bulgaria	3 Belgium	0
27 Oct 1965 *Brussels*	Belgium	5 Bulgaria	0
10 Nov 1965 *Tel Aviv*	Israel	0 Belgium	5
21 Nov 1965 *Tel Aviv*	Israel	1 Bulgaria	2

Final Table

	P	W	D	L	F	A	Pts
Bulgaria	4	3	0	1	9	6	6
Belgium	4	3	0	1	11	3	6
Israel	4	0	0	4	1	12	0

Play-off
29 Dec 1965 *Florence, Italy* Bulgaria ....2 Belgium 1
Bulgaria qualified

Group Two

4 Nov 1964 *Berlin*	West Germany	1 Sweden	1
24 Apr 1965 *Karlsruhe*	West Germany	5 Cyprus	0
5 May 1965 *Norrköping*	Sweden	3 Cyprus	0
26 Sep 1965 *Stockholm*	Sweden	1 West Germany	2
7 Nov 1965 *Famagusta*	Cyprus	0 Sweden	5
14 Nov 1965 *Nicosia*	Cyprus	0 West Germany	6

Final Table

	P	W	D	L	F	A	Pts	
W.Germany	4	3	1	0	14	2	7	**West Germany**
Sweden	4	2	1	1	10	3	5	**qualified**
Cyprus	4	0	0	4	0	19	0	

Group Three

20 Sep 1964 *Belgrade*	Yugoslavia	3 Luxembourg	1
4 Oct 1964 *Luxembourg*	Luxembourg	0 France	2
8 Nov 1964 *Luxembourg*	Luxembourg	0 Norway	2
11 Nov 1964 *Paris*	France	1 Norway	0
18 Apr 1965 *Belgrade*	Yugoslavia	1 France	0
27 May 1965 *Trondheim*	Norway	4 Luxembourg	2
16 Jun 1965 *Oslo*	Norway	3 Yugoslavia	0
16 Sep 1965 *Oslo*	Norway	0 France	1
18 Sep 1965 *Luxembourg*	Luxembourg	2 Yugoslavia	5
9 Oct 1965 *Paris*	France	1 Yugoslavia	0
6 Nov 1965 *Marseille*	France	4 Luxembourg	1
7 Nov 1965 *Belgrade*	Yugoslavia	1 Norway	1

Final Table

	P	W	D	L	F	A	Pts	
France	6	5	0	1	9	2	10	
Norway	6	3	1	2	10	5	7	**France qualified**
Yugoslavia	6	3	1	2	10	8	7	
Luxembourg	6	0	0	6	6	20	0	

'The most important goal France ever scored,' according to a French reporter as the French beat Yugoslavia 1-0 in Paris. Defeat would almost certainly have denied France a place in the World Cup finals for the second time in succession.

Group Four

24 Jan 1965 *Lisbon*	Portugal..........5 Turkey...........1
19 Apr 1965 *Ankara*	Turkey...........0 Portugal..........1
25 Apr 1965 *Bratislava*	Czechoslovakia 0 Portugal..........1
2 May 1965 *Bucharest*	Romania.........3 Turkey...........0
30 May 1965 *Bucharest*	Romania.........1 Czechoslovakia 0
13 Jun 1965 *Lisbon*	Portugal..........2 Romania..........1
19 Sep 1965 *Prague*	Czechoslovakia 3 Romania.........1
9 Oct 1965 *Istanbul*	Turkey...........0 Czechoslovakia 6
23 Oct 1965 *Istanbul*	Turkey...........2 Romania.........1
31 Oct 1965 *Oporto*	Portugal..........0 Czechoslovakia 0
21 Nov 1965 *Brno*	Czechoslovakia 3 Turkey...........1
21 Nov 1965 *Bucharest*	Romania.........2 Portugal..........0

Final Table

	P	W	D	L	F	A	Pts	
Portugal	6	4	1	1	9	4	9	
Czechoslovakia	6	3	1	2	12	4	7	**Portugal qualified**
Romania	6	3	0	3	9	7	6	
Turkey	6	1	0	5	4	19	2	

Group Five

24 May 1964 *Rotterdam*	Holland..........2 Albania...........0
14 Oct 1964 *Belfast*	N. Ireland........1 Switzerland 0
25 Oct 1964 *Tiranë*	Albania...........0 Holland..........2
14 Nov 1964 *Lausanne*	Switzerland ......2 N. Ireland........1
17 Mar 1965 *Belfast*	N. Ireland........2 Holland..........1
7 Apr 1965 *Rotterdam*	Holland..........0 N. Ireland........0
11 Apr 1965 *Tiranë*	Albania...........0 Switzerland 2
2 May 1965 *Geneva*	Switzerland ......1 Albania...........0
7 May 1965 *Belfast*	N. Ireland........4 Albania...........1
17 Oct 1965 *Amsterdam*	Holland..........0 Switzerland 0
14 Nov 1965 *Berne*	Switzerland ......2 Holland..........1
24 Nov 1965 *Tiranë*	Albania...........1 N. Ireland........1

Final Table

	P	W	D	L	F	A	Pts	
Switzerland	6	4	1	1	7	3	9	
N. Ireland	6	3	2	1	9	5	8	**Switzerland**
Holland	6	2	2	2	6	4	6	**qualified**
Albania	6	0	1	5	2	12	1	

Group Six

25 Apr 1965 *Vienna*	Austria............1 East Germany ...1
23 May 1965 *Leipzig*	East Germany ...1 Hungary 1
13 Jun 1965 *Vienna*	Austria............0 Hungary 1
5 Sep 1965 *Budapest*	Hungary ....3 Austria............0
9 Oct 1965 *Budapest*	Hungary ....3 East Germany ...2
31 Oct 1865 *Leipzig*	East Germany ...1 Austria............1

Final Table

	P	W	D	L	F	A	Pts	
Hungary	4	3	1	0	8	5	7	**Hungary qualified**
E.Germany	4	1	2	1	5	5	4	
Austria	4	0	1	3	3	6	1	

Group Seven

21 Oct 1964 *Copenhagen*	Denmark ....1 Wales 0
29 Nov 1964 *Athens*	Greece ....4 Denmark 2
9 Dec 1964 *Athens*	Greece ....2 Wales 0
17 Mar 1965 *Cardiff*	Wales ....4 Greece 1
23 May 1965 *Moscow*	Soviet Union ....3 Greece 1
30 May 1965 *Moscow*	Soviet Union ....2 Wales 1
27 Jun 1965 *Moscow*	Soviet Union ....6 Denmark 0
3 Oct 1965 *Athens*	Greece ....1 Soviet Union 4
17 Oct 1965 *Copenhagen*	Denmark ....1 Soviet Union 3
27 Oct 1965 *Copenhagen*	Denmark ....1 Greece 1
27 Oct 1965 *Cardiff*	Wales ....2 Soviet Union 1
1 Dec 1965 *Wrexham*	Wales ....4 Denmark 2

Final Table

	P	W	D	L	F	A	Pts	
Soviet Union	6	5	0	1	19	6	10	
Wales	6	3	0	3	11	9	6	**Soviet Union**
Greece	6	2	1	3	10	14	5	**qualified**
Denmark	6	1	1	4	7	18	3	

Group Eight

21 Oct 1964 *Glasgow*	Scotland ....3 Finland 1
4 Nov 1964 *Genoa*	Italy...............6 Finland 1
18 Apr 1965 *Warsaw*	Poland............0 Italy...............0
23 May 1965 *Chorzów*	Poland............1 Scotland 1
27 May 1965 *Helsinki*	Finland ....1 Scotland 2
23 Jun 1965 *Helsinki*	Finland ....0 Italy...............2
26 Sep 1965 *Helsinki*	Finland ....2 Poland............0
13 Oct 1965 *Glasgow*	Scotland ....1 Poland............2
24 Oct 1965 *Szczecin*	Poland............7 Finland 0
1 Nov 1965 *Rome*	Italy...............6 Poland............1
9 Nov 1965 *Glasgow*	Scotland ....1 Italy...............0
7 Dec 1965 *Naples*	Italy...............3 Scotland 0

Scotland's goalkeeper Bill Brown looks back to see Poland's winner hit the back of his net. Only victory in Italy could now see Scotland join hosts England in the finals.

Final Table

	P	W	D	L	F	A	Pts	
Italy	6	4	1	1	17	3	9	
Scotland	6	3	1	2	8	8	7	Italy qualified
Poland	6	2	2	2	11	10	6	
Finland	6	1	0	5	5	20	2	

Group Nine

| 5 May 1965 *Dublin* | Rep of Ireland ...1 Spain ....0 |
| 27 Oct 1965 *Seville* | Spain ....4 Rep of Ireland ...1 |

Syria withdrew

Play-off
10 Nov 1965 *Paris, France* Spain ....1 Rep of Ireland ...0
Spain qualified

SOUTH AMERICA

Group One

16 May 1965 *Lima*	Peru...............1 Venezuela 0
23 May 1965 *Montevideo*	Uruguay..........5 Venezuela 0
30 May 1965 *Caracas*	Venezuela ....1 Uruguay..........3
2 Jun 1965 *Caracas*	Venezuela ....3 Peru...............6
6 Jun 1965 *Lima*	Peru...............0 Uruguay..........1
13 Jun 1965 *Montevideo*	Uruguay..........2 Peru...............1

Final Table

	P	W	D	L	F	A	Pts	
Uruguay	4	4	0	0	11	2	8	**Uruguay qualified**
Peru	4	2	0	2	8	6	4	
Venezuela	4	0	0	4	4	15	0	

Group Two

20 Jul 1965 *Barranquilla*	Colombia ....0 Ecuador 1
25 Jul 1965 *Guayaquil*	Ecuador ....2 Colombia 0
1 Aug 1965 *Santiago*	Chile.............7 Colombia 2
7 Aug 1965 *Barranquilla*	Colombia ....2 Chile.............0
15 Aug 1965 *Guayaquil*	Ecuador ....2 Chile.............2
22 Aug 1965 *Santiago*	Chile.............3 Ecuador 1

Final Table

	P	W	D	L	F	A	Pts
Chile	4	2	1	1	12	7	5
Ecuador	4	2	1	1	6	5	5
Colombia	4	1	0	3	4	10	2

Play-off
12 Oct 1965 *Lima, Peru*   Chile..............2 Ecuador 1
Chile qualified

Group Three

25 Jul 1965 *Asunción*	Paraguay ....2 Bolivia............0
1 Aug 1965 *Buenos Aires*	Argentina ....3 Paraguay 0
8 Aug 1965 *Asunción*	Paraguay ....0 Argentina 0
17 Aug 1965 *Buenos Aires*	Argentina ....4 Bolivia............1
22 Aug 1965 *La Paz*	Bolivia............2 Paraguay 1
29 Aug 1965 *La Paz*	Bolivia............1 Argentina 2

Final Table

	P	W	D	L	F	A	Pts	
Argentina	4	3	1	0	9	2	7	**Argentina qualified**
Paraguay	4	1	1	2	3	5	3	
Bolivia	4	1	0	3	4	9	2	

CONCACAF
(Central & North America)

Sub-Group One

16 Jan 1965 *Kingston*	Jamaica ....2 Cuba..............0
20 Jan 1965 *Kingston*	Nethlds Antilles 1 Cuba..............1
23 Jan 1965 *Kingston*	Jamaica ....2 Nethlds Antilles 0
30 Jan 1965 *Havana*	Cuba..............0 Nethlds Antilles 1
3 Feb 1965 *Havana*	Nethlds Antilles 0 Jamaica 0
8 Feb 1965 *Havana*	Cuba..............2 Jamaica 1

Final Table

	P	W	D	L	F	A	Pts	
Jamaica	4	2	1	1	4	2	5	**Jamaica qualified**
Cuba	4	2	0	2	3	3	4	**for Group Final**
Nethlds Antilles	4	1	1	2	1	3	3	

Sub-Group Two

7 Feb 1965 *Port of Spain*	Trinidad ....4 Surinam 1
12 Feb 1965 *San José*	Costa Rica ....1 Surinam 0
21 Feb 1965 *San José*	Costa Rica ....4 Trinidad 0
28 Feb 1965 *Paramaribo*	Surinam ....1 Costa Rica 3
7 Mar 1965 *Port of Spain*	Trinidad ....0 Costa Rica 1
14 Mar 1965 *Paramaribo*	Surinam ....6 Trinidad 1

Final Table

	P	W	D	L	F	A	Pts	
Costa Rica	4	4	0	0	9	1	8	**Costa Rica**
Surinam	4	1	0	3	8	9	2	**qualified for**
Trinidad	4	1	0	3	5	12	2	**Group Final**

Sub-Group Three

28 Feb 1965 *San Pedro Sula*	Honduras ....0 Mexico............1
4 Mar 1965 *Mexico City*	Mexico............3 Honduras 0
7 Mar 1965 *Los Angeles*	United States ....2 Mexico............2
12 Mar 1965 *Mexico City*	Mexico............2 United States 0
17 Mar 1965 *San Pedro Sula*	Honduras ....0 United States 1
21 Mar 1965 *Tegucigalpa*	United States ....1 Honduras 1

Final Table

	P	W	D	L	F	A	Pts	
Mexico	4	3	1	0	8	2	7	**Mexico qualified**
United States	4	1	2	1	4	5	4	**for Group Final**
Honduras	4	0	1	3	1	6	1	

Group Final

25 Apr 1965 *San José*	Costa Rica 0	Mexico...........0
3 May 1965 *Kingston*	Jamaica 2	Mexico...........3
7 May 1965 *Mexico City*	Mexico...........8	Jamaica 0
11 May 1965 *San José*	Costa Rica 7	Jamaica 0
16 May 1965 *Mexico City*	Mexico...........1	Costa Rica 0
22 May 1965 *Kingston*	Jamaica 1	Costa Rica 1

Final Table

	P	W	D	L	F	A	Pts	
Mexico	4	3	1	0	12	2	7	**Mexico qualified**
Costa Rica	4	1	2	1	8	2	4	
Jamaica	4	0	1	3	3	19	1	

ASIA-AFRICA

Algeria, Cameroon, Egypt, Ethiopia, Gabon, Ghana, Guinea, Liberia, Libya, Mali, Morocco, Nigeria, Senegal, South Korea, Sudan, Tunisia, United Arab Republic all withdrew which left North Korea as the sole survivors to play Australia in an Afro-Asian-Oceania final. South Africa had also originally entered but were subsequently suspended by FIFA and did not compete.

ASIA-AFRICA-OCEANIA

21 Nov 1965 *Phnom Penh*	North Korea 6	Australia 1
24 Nov 1965 *Phnom Penh*	Australia 1	North Korea 3

North Korea qualified

Grout's left-foot volley sails high over the Swiss crossbar as Holland and Switzerland fought out a goalless draw to give Northern Ireland hope. But the Irish could only manage a 1-1 draw in Tiranë – Albania's only point of the qualifying tournament – and it was Switzerland who made it to the finals.

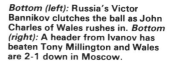

Bottom (left): Russia's Victor Bannikov clutches the ball as John Charles of Wales rushes in. *Bottom (right):* A header from Ivanov has beaten Tony Millington and Wales are 2-1 down in Moscow.

England's squad before the start of the tournament. Back row (left to right): George Cohen, Nobby Stiles, Joe Baker, Peter Thompson, Gordon Banks, George Eastham, Ron Springett, Gordon Milne, Ron Flowers, Ray Wilson, Paul Reaney, Jimmy Greaves, Gordon Harris, Norman Hunter, Roger Hunt, Harold Shepherdson (trainer). Front row: Jack Charlton, Keith Newton, Alan Ball, Geoff Hurst, Bobby Charlton, Bobby Moore.

Bobby Moore made his World Cup debut in Chile in 1962. Four years later he was on the threshold of a major triumph as England's skipper.

1966 Tournament

Group One

ENGLAND 0   URUGUAY 0 (Half-time 0-0)

Wembley Stadium, London, 11 July
Attendance: 87,148

THE opening match of the 1966 World Cup certainly did not live up to its showpiece image. Indeed, it was a boring, negative and dull game as the South Americans, with an eight, and sometimes nine-man defence, left with the draw they had sought.

England were by far the better team, but their 4-3-3 system, without conventional wingers, could not break through the Uruguayan defence. It was certainly a frustrating 90 minutes for England and their fans. Neither side came close to scoring and in the Uruguay goal, Mazurkiewicz earned the distinction of becoming the first foreign goalkeeper to prevent England from scoring at Wembley.

England: Banks; Cohen, Wilson, Stiles, J.Charlton, Moore, Ball, Greaves, R.Charlton, Hunt, Connelly.
Uruguay: Mazurkiewicz; Troche, Manicera, Ubiñas, Goncálves, Caetano, Cortés, Viera, Silva, Rocha, Pérez.
Referee: Istvan Zsolt (Hungary)

FRANCE 1   MEXICO 1 (Half-time 0-0)

Wembley Stadium, London, 13 July
Attendance: 69,237

A surprisingly large crowd turned up at Wembley to see these unfancied teams. France were expected to win easily, particularly after Mexico had lost a warm-up game to Tottenham Hotspur. But the lively Mexicans had a few surprises up their sleeves and, unlike their Latin rivals, Uruguay, did not bore the Wembley crowd with negative football.

After a goalless first half, Enrique Borja put the Mexicans in front in the 48th minute.

Goalmouth action from the England-Uruguay game which opened the tournament at Wembley.

WORLD CUP FACT

Over 40 nations have withdrawn from the World Cup for one reason or another. Egypt (1938, 1958, 1962 and 1966) have withdrawn most often.

Mexico's Wembley line-up.

Gordon Banks of England.

It was just reward for two earlier efforts which could have produced goals. One found the net but was ruled offside.

The Mexican forwards played with flair and imagination, but after an hour, their defence lapsed and allowed Gerard Hausser to equalize.

France: Aubour; Djorkaeff, Budzinski, Artelesa, de Michele, Bosquier, Herbin, Bonnel, Combin, Gondet, Hausser.
Scorer: Hausser
Mexico: Calderón; Chaires, Peña, Núñez, Hernández, Díaz, Mercado, Reyes, Borja, Fragoso, Padilla.
Scorer: Borja
Referee: Menachem Ashkenasi (Israel)

URUGUAY 2   FRANCE 1 (Half-time 2-1)

White City, London, 15 July
Attendance: 45,662

THIS was the only game of the 1966 tournament that was not played on a Football League ground, staged as it was at London's White City Stadium, which was then famous for its greyhound racing and athletics. Queen's Park Rangers later played on the ground, which has now made way for new developments.

England defender George Cohen.

The Uruguayan playing squad and coaching staff pictured at Wembley. Back row (left to right): Ondoni Veira, Juan López (manager), Dr Masliah, Pedro Rocha, Carlos Abate, Eliseo Alvarez, Hector Salva, Professor Omar Borras, Walter Taibo, Ladislao Mazurkiewicz, Hector Silva, Horacio Troche, Pablo Forlan. Middle row: Julio Cortés, José Urruzmendi, Nestor Gonçálves, Luis Ubiñas, Omar Caetano, Eliseo Alvarez, Dante Concito, José Sacia. Front row: Domingo Pérez, Victor Esparrago, Nelson Díaz, Jorge Manicera, Milton Viera, Luis Ramos, José Derude, Roberto Sosa.

Domingo Pérez of Uruguay.

Gabriel Núñez of Mexico.

A crowd of over 45,000 filled the stadium and, whilst it was the lowest attendance of Group One, it was still an indication of the popularity of the tournament with the English fans.

Mercifully, the Uruguayans were not as negative as they had been against England and, after France took the lead in the 15th minute, they were forced to come out and attack.

The French goal came from a hotly-disputed penalty, converted by de Bourgoing. The kick was awarded after Manicera brought down Herbet with a rugby tackle. There was no denying the foul but the Uruguayans felt it was outside the area.

Uruguay turned their thoughts to attacking and two goals — from Pedro Rocha and Julio Cortés — in five minutes towards the end of the first half gave them an interval lead.

The Uruguayans then turned to the tactics they knew best and defended solidly throughout the second half in the knowledge that victory would take them to the top of the group.

Uruguay: Mazurkiewicz; Troche, Ubiñas, Gonçálves, Manicera, Caetano, Viera, Cortés, Rocha, Sacia, Pérez.
Scorers: Rocha, Cortés
France: Aubour; Djorkaeff, Artelesa, Budzinski, Bosquier, Bonnel, Simon, Herbet, Gondet, de Bourgoing, Hausser.
Scorer: de Bourgoing (pen)
Referee: Karol Galba (Czechoslovakia)

ENGLAND 2   MEXICO 0 (Half-time 1-0)
Wembley Stadium, London, 16 July
Attendance: 92,570

IT was now Mexico's turn to play the defensive game against the host nation and, again, England were unimpressive as they struggled to break through.

Alf Ramsey brought in Martin Peters and Terry Paine as replacements for Alan Ball and John Connelly, but the new line-up was kept at bay until Bobby Charlton scored England's first goal of the tournament with a magnificent solo effort in the 37th minute. He picked up a pass in his own half, beat two defenders and then hammered the ball from 30 yards. Such was the magnificence of the goal that Charlton was suddenly being talked about in the same breath as Pelé.

It was Charlton who had a hand in England's second goal midway through the second half. He split the defence with a great pass to Jimmy Greaves, whose shot rebounded for Roger Hunt to put the ball in the net.

England now took over at the top of the group, but they were still far from impressive.

England: Banks; Cohen, Wilson, Stiles, J.Charlton, Moore, Paine, Greaves, R.Charlton, Hunt, Peters.
Scorers: R.Charlton, Hunt
Mexico: Calderón; Peña, Hernández, Chaires, Del Muro, Jáuregui, Díaz, Núñez, Borja, Reyes, Padilla.
Referee: Concetto Lo Bello (Italy)

MEXICO 0   URUGUAY 0 (Half-time 0-0)

Wembley Stadium, London, 19 July
Attendance: 61,112

IF Uruguay had any friends left after their first Wembley appearance on the opening day of the competition, they certainly did not have any after their next visit to the famous stadium. The Uruguayans played another defensive game in the knowledge that a draw was good enough to see them into the quarter-finals, but drawn games would hardly lift them the trophy.

Mexico, on the other hand, won some admirers because they took the game to the Uruguayans and attacked. Like England, though, they could not penetrate the solid defence.

In goal for Mexico was Antonio Carbajal, who was thus a veteran of five World Cups stretching back to 1950. No man has equalled his remarkable record and it was a pity that he had to bow out in such a drab match.

Uruguay: Mazurkiewicz; Troche, Ubiñas, Gonçálves, Manicera, Caetano, Viera, Rocha, Cortés, Sacia, Pérez.
Mexico: Carbajal; Chaires, Peña, Núñez, Hernández, Díaz, Mercado, Reyes, Cisneros, Borja, Padilla.
Referee: Bertil Lööw (Sweden)

ENGLAND 2   FRANCE 0 (Half-time 1-0)

Wembley Stadium, London, 20 July
Attendance: 98,270

IF France were to progress any further, then they had to attack and score lots of goals, but the England defence easily contained a forward line which had little to offer.

France were unfortunate that Robert Herbin was injured early in the game and he was a passenger for most of the match. The talents of one of their best players was sorely missed. Nevertheless, they did well to contain England until the 38th minute when a Jackie Charlton header rebounded off the crossbar and was turned in by Roger Hunt. The French appealed for offside, but the Peruvian referee allowed the goal to stand.

Hunt put England's victory beyond doubt in the 75th minute with his second goal when French goalkeeper Aubour, who seemed to have gathered the Liverpool forward's shot, suddenly let it slip through his hands.

At the time of the goal the French inside-left, Jacques Simon, was on the ground as a result of a heavy tackle from Nobby Stiles and France had to play the last 15 minutes with only nine fit men.

Stiles was heavily criticized for his tackling, particularly for the one which injured Simon, and Alf Ramsey came under pressure from FA officials to leave him out of the next match against the tough-tackling Argentinians. Ramsey refused and the matter was dropped.

Jimmy Greaves bid farewell to his World Cup career after being injured against the French, but England marched on. They topped Group One without conceding a goal. Yet they still had not produced their true form.

England: Banks; Cohen, Wilson, Stiles, J.Charlton, Moore, Callaghan, Greaves, R.Charlton, Hunt, Peters.
Scorer: Hunt 2
France: Aubour; Djorkaeff, Bosquier, Herbin, Artelesa, Budzinski, Herbet, Bonnel, Gondet, Simon, Hausser.
Referee: Arturo Yamasaki Maldonado (Peru)

Group Two

WEST GERMANY 5   SWITZERLAND 0 (Half-time 3-0)

Hillsborough, Sheffield, 12 July
Attendance: 36,127

WEST Germany were now managed by Sepp Herberger's former assistant, Helmut Schön, who was building a new national side around the experience of Brülls, Schnellinger and Seeler, the German skipper. This trio, together with Haller, were in the team which narrowly beat Switzerland 2-1 in a group match in Chile four years earlier. But at Sheffield in 1966, there was to be an easier victory for West Germany.

The Swiss made their task harder when they left out two of their key players, Jakob Kühn and Werner Leimgruber, for disciplinary reasons after they had broken a curfew.

West Germany gave a World Cup debut to Franz Beckenbauer and he responded with two goals.

Despite surviving an early scare, when they had to clear a dangerous Swiss cross from the face of the goal, the West German defence was hardly troubled. Held opened the scoring in the 16th minute after a Seeler shot rebounded to him. Haller made it 2-0 four minutes later and five minutes before the interval, Beckenbauer opened his World Cup account.

Seven minutes into the second half, Beckenbauer found the net again and 13 minutes

Group One – Final Table

	P	W	D	L	F	A	Pts
England	3	2	1	0	4	0	5
Uruguay	3	1	2	0	2	1	4
Mexico	3	0	2	1	1	3	2
France	3	0	1	2	2	5	1

England's Jimmy Greaves, one of football's greatest strikers, who was ultimately denied a place on the game's greatest stage.

Bobby Charlton, another England great.

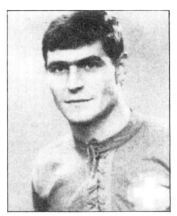

Ely Tacchella of Switzerland.

from time, Haller rounded off the biggest win of the 1966 World Cup when he converted a penalty.

Helmut Schön had moulded a good team. Whether they would be good enough to go all the way to the Final was hard to tell at this stage but their next two group matches, against Argentina and Spain, would both be severe tests.

West Germany: Tilkowski; Höttges, Schulz, Weber, Schnellinger, Beckenbauer, Haller, Brülls, Seeler, Overath, Held.
Scorers: Held, Haller 2 (1 pen), Beckenbauer 2
Switzerland: Elsener; Grobéty, Schneiter, Tacchella, Führer, Bäni, Dürr, Odermatt, Künzli, Hosp, Schindelholz.
Referee: Hugh Phillips (Scotland)

Siggy Held has given West Germany a 16th-minute lead and Switzerland are on their way to a 5-0 defeat.

ARGENTINA 2 SPAIN 1 (Half-time 0-0)

Villa Park, Birmingham, 13 July
Attendance: 47,982

PLAYING in heavy rain, these two well-matched Latin sides still managed to produce some good attacking moves in a first half which failed to yield a goal.

Argentina were looking the likely winners at the end of the first half and were certainly the more physical side, as Spain's Luís Suárez would confirm after coming in for some rough treatment from the Argentinian defenders.

The deadlock was eventually broken midway through the second half when Argentina's fine centre-forward, Luís Artime, scored. Five minutes later, Pirri restored the balance by heading an equalizer, but Spanish celebrations were short-lived and Artime put Argentina back in front in the 78th minute with a powerful 20-yard shot after a great pass from Onega.

The large crowd went home happy after watching an entertaining game which saw both sides play attractive, attacking football.

Action from Spain v Argentina.

Pirri (dark shirt) celebrates his goal for Spain as the Argentinian goalkeeper, Antonio Roma watches the ball nestle in his net. But Spain's joy was short-lived as Artime soon restored Argentina's lead.

Argentina celebrate after the victory over Spain.

Argentina: Roma; Perfumo, Marzolini, Ferreiro, Rattín, Albrecht, Solari, González, Artime, Onega, Mas.
Scorer: Artime 2
Spain: Iribar; Sanchís, Eladio, Pirri, Gallego, Zoco, Ufarte, del Sol, Peiró, Suárez, Gento.
Scorer: Pirri
Referee: Dimiter Rumentchev (Bulgaria)

Switzerland's Heinz Schneiter, played against West Germany but was left out for the game against Spain.

SPAIN 2 SWITZERLAND 1 (Half-time 0-1)

Hillsborough, Sheffield, 15 July
Attendance: 32,028

AFTER their 5-0 drubbing by West Germany, Switzerland made seven changes for their second game, including the recall of their two suspended stars, Kühn and Leimgruber. The changes nearly paid off and at the interval Switzerland led 1-0, thanks to a 28th-minute goal from Quentin.

Spain were not playing as well as in their opening match but still managed to equalize in the 57th minute, when it was left to full-back Sanchís to score a superb solo effort when he picked up the ball on the half-way line and dribbled through the defence. He showed his more illustrious forwards like Amancio, del Sol, Suárez and Gento, how it should have been done.

Robert Hosp of Switzerland.

The Swiss were unlucky not to regain the lead shortly afterwards, when a Quentin effort was disallowed. However, Spain prevented what would have been a memorable result for Switzerland when Amancio, one of five Real Madrid players in the team, scored with a brilliant header from a Gento cross in the 75th minute.

Spain's hopes of qualifying were still alive, but after a lacklustre performance against one of the tournament's weaker sides, they could hardly have expected to return to Spain with the Jules Rimet Trophy.

Spain: Iribar; Sanchís, Reija, Pirri, Gallego, Zoco, Amancio, del Sol, Peiró, Suárez, Gento.
Scorers: Sanchís, Amancio
Switzerland: Elsener; Brodmann, Führer, Leimgruber, Armbruster, Stierli, Bäni, Kühn, Gottardi, Hosp, Quentin.
Scorer: Quentin
Referee: Tofik Bakhramov (Soviet Union)

ARGENTINA 0 WEST GERMANY 0 (Half-time 0-0)

Villa Park, Birmingham, 16 July
Attendance: 51,419

THE knowledgeable Birmingham football fans filled Villa Park in the hope of seeing a classic match between the two best teams in Group Two. Alas, football came second best in what turned out to be an ugly, bruising display of ferocious tackling.

Both sides played defensively and West Germany utilized the otherwise magnificent midfield skills of Franz Beckenbauer in a deep-lying defensive role.

The severity of the tackling meant it was only a matter of time before a player received

Antonio Rattín of Argentina. He became the 'villain' of the 1966 World Cup.

Argentina's players greet the crowd before their game against West Germany.

Willy Schulz of West Germany.

his marching orders and in the 65th minute it was the Argentine defender, Jorge Albrecht, who was sent off following a high tackle on Weber. He had already been cautioned for a rugby-style tackle on Haller.

Argentina were subsequently reprimanded by FIFA for their violent play, but they had achieved their prime objective at Villa Park — to hold out for a draw.

Argentina: Roma; Perfumo, Marzolini, Ferreiro, Rattín, Albrecht, Solari, González, Artime, Onega, Mas.
West Germany: Tilkowski; Höttges, Schulz, Weber, Schnellinger, Beckenbauer, Haller, Brülls, Seeler, Overath, Held.
Referee: Konstantin Zecević (Yugoslavia)

ARGENTINA 2   SWITZERLAND 0 (Half-time 0-0)

Hillsborough, Sheffield, 19 July
Attendance: 31,443

ARGENTINA appeared to be a little subdued after the FIFA warning and the subsequent bad publicity following their performance against West Germany. Although they did not

West Germany's squad. Back row (left to right): Overath, Tilkowski, Krämer, Sieloff, Grabowski, Held, Schulz, Paul, Lattek (coach), Helmut Schön (manager), Bernard, Haller, physiotherapist, Schnellinger. Front row: Lutz, Weber, Beckenbauer, Emmerich, Hornig, physiotherapist, Höttges, Maier, Seeler, Patzke, Lorenz.

need to extend themselves to beat Switzerland, for long periods they struggled to make an impression.

The South Americans needed one point to qualify for the quarter-finals and after a goalless first half it looked as though they would be content to leave the score at that. But seven minutes into the second period, Artime scored his third goal of the tournament. Nine minutes from time, Onega made it 2-0 to guarantee Argentina's safe passage into the next phase.

Argentina: Roma; Perfumo, Marzolini, Ferreiro, Rattín, Calics, Solari, González, Artime, Onega, Mas.
Scorers: Artime, Onega
Switzerland: Eichmann; Führer, Brodmann, Kühn, Armbruster, Stierli, Bäni, Künzli, Gottardi, Hosp, Quentin.
Referee: Joaquim Fernandes Campos (Portugal)

WEST GERMANY 2   SPAIN 1 (Half-time 1-1)
Villa Park, Birmingham, 20 July
Attendance: 51,875

IF Spain wanted to join Argentina in the quarter-finals they had to beat West Germany, a draw was no good. They made changes to the forward line, which had failed to produce the style of play for which they had become recognized. Out went del Sol, Peiró, Gento and Suárez. The changes worked and, although the West Germans came for a draw, they also contributed to an attacking game after Spain opened the scoring.

Spain's chances of reaching the quarter-finals improved when Fusté, playing in his first match of the tournament, scored in the 23rd minute. Just before half-time, however, Emmerich, also playing his first game, hit a remarkable left-foot shot, from the narrowest of angles, which managed to find the net.

The game seemed to be heading for a draw when Seeler, appearing in his third World Cup, scored the winner for West Germany six minutes from time and ended the Spaniards' dreams. Not only was it Seeler's third World Cup, but it was also the third successive tournament in which he had scored. He was the second man, after Pelé, to achieve this distinction.

West Germany: Tilkowski; Höttges, Schulz, Weber, Schnellinger, Beckenbauer, Overath, Krämer, Seeler, Held, Emmerich.
Scorers: Emmerich, Seeler
Spain: Iribar; Sanchís, Reija, Glaría, Gallego, Zoco, Amancio, Adelardo, Marcelino, Fusté, Lapetra.
Scorer: Fusté
Referee: Armando Marques (Brazil)

Group Three

BRAZIL 2   BULGARIA 0 (Half-time 1-0)
Goodison Park, Liverpool, 12 July
Attendance: 52,847

GROUP Three was, by far, the best of the four World Cup sections in 1966 and the Merseyside fans were delighted when one of the tournament favourites, Brazil, were designated to play their three matches at Goodison Park.

The South Americans were aiming for their third successive win, but the team was beginning to look old. Vincente Feola was in charge again and he recalled two stars of his 1958 World Cup-winning team, Orlando and Bellini. They joined the already ageing Djalmar Santos and Garrincha. Admittedly Pelé was reaching his peak and there were other talented newcomers like 16-year-old Edu (who would have become the World Cup's youngest-ever player had he appeared in the final stages), Jairzinho, Gérson and Tostão.

Alas, opposing defences were intent on hacking down the Brazilian forwards, and Pelé in particular. Brazil were not allowed to play the attractive flowing football for which they had become renowned.

Pelé and the Bulgarian defender, Zhechev, engaged in a running battle throughout the group's opening match. Both subjected the other to some rough tackles and the 5,000 Brazilians amongst the large crowd were incensed at what they saw. Eventually Pelé was injured following a Zhechev tackle which put him out of the next game. The man expected to dominate the tournament spent much of the time either writhing in agony or nursing injuries.

However, he contributed the first goal of the 1966 World Cup when, after a quarter of an hour's play, he took a free-kick from just outside the penalty area and his swerving effort beat the Bulgarian 'keeper, Naidenov. The goal created World Cup history as Pelé became the first man to score in three successive tournaments.

Garrincha, like Pelé playing in his third successive finals, scored Brazil's other goal after

Group Two – Final Table

	P	W	D	L	F	A	Pts
W.Germany	3	2	1	0	7	1	5
Argentina	3	2	1	0	4	1	5
Spain	3	1	0	2	4	5	2
Switzerland	3	0	0	3	1	9	0

Spanish goalkeeper José Iribar is beaten by Lothar Emmerich's great left-foot shot for West Germany.

Pierre Quentin of Switzerland.

Hausruedi Führer of Switzerland.

Dimitar Yakimov of Bulgaria.

63 minutes. And like Pelé's opener, it was from a swerving free-kick. Despite opening their eighth World Cup campaign with a win, however, this was nothing like the Brazil of old.

Brazil: Gilmar; D.Santos, Bellini, Altair, Paulo Henrique, Denilson, Lima, Garrincha, Pelé, Alcindo, Jairzinho.
Scorers: Pelé, Garrincha
Bulgaria: Naidenov; Shalamanov, Vutzov, Gaganelov, Penev, Kitov, Zhechev, Yakimov, Dermendyev, Asparoukhov, Kolev.
Referee: Kurt Tschenscher (West Germany)

PORTUGAL 3   HUNGARY 1 (Half-time 1-0)
Old Trafford, Manchester, 13 July
Attendance: 37,311

PORTUGAL could not have wished for a better start to their first World Cup campaign when they were a goal up against the reigning Olympic champions after just 30 seconds.

Hungarian goalkeeper Antal Szentmihályi failed to gather a Simoës corner and Augusto rose to head home. Szentmihályi was injured early in the game and this eventually proved to be too great a handicap for the Magyars, who did well to overcome their early set-back.

Hungary, with Mátrai and Sipos, stalwarts of three World Cups, solid in defence, prevented any further Portuguese goals and in the 62nd minute they were back in the game when Bene equalized. The recovery was only temporary, though, and following another goalkeeping error, Augusto scored Portugal's second six minutes later. Torres made it 3-1 with a goal in injury time.

Portugal: Carvalho; Morais, Baptista, Vicente, Hilario, Graça, Coluña, Augusto, Eusébio, Torres, Simoës.
Scorers: Augusto 2, Torres
Hungary: Szentmihályi; Mátrai, Káposzta, Sóvári, Mészöly, Sipos, Bene, Nagy, Albert, Farkas, Rákosi.
Scorer: Bene
Referee: Leo Callaghan (Wales)

HUNGARY 3   BRAZIL 1 (Half-time 1-1)
Goodison Park, Liverpool, 15 July
Attendance: 57,455

HUNGARY replaced goalkeeper Szentmihályi with Gelei, whilst Brazil were forced to leave out Pelé and replace him with the exciting Tostão. Gérson also came into the revamped team.

This game was played in heavy rain, but the teams served up a classic encounter and the display of the Hungarians was reminiscent of the days of Puskás and Hidegkuti. Brazil also contributed to a magnificent match, but made the mistake of giving Florian Albert too much room. His mercurial runs and passes were the highlight of the game. One local supporter was so impressed with Albert's performance that he is reputed to have said to an adjacent spectator: 'If I went home and found that Albert was in bed with my wife I'd make him a cup of coffee and a hot water bottle'. That is how much they love their football on Merseyside.

Brazil got themselves into trouble as early as the third minute when Bene latched on to a wayward Brazilian pass, stormed through the defence and hit a great goal. Tostão equalized in the 14th minute, when he converted a Lima free-kick which rebounded to him, but the goal was much against the run of play.

Hungary's superiority was not reflected in the scoreline until the 64th minute when they took the lead again. Albert laid on a brilliant pass to Bene. The winger crossed and Farkas was there to volley the ball into the net. Eight minutes later the game was put beyond Brazil's reach when Mészöly converted a penalty after Henrique had brought down Bene.

It was Brazil's first World Cup defeat since 1954 when they were beaten in the much publicised 'Battle of Berne' when their conquerors were. . . Hungary. Between their two defeats, the South Americans had a record of 11 wins and two draws.

Albert's display at Goodison Park was one of the finest individual performances of the whole tournament and once again the football public had been captivated by a new breed of Magyars.

Hungary: Gelei; Káposzta, Mátrai, Sipos, Szepesi, Mathesz, Mészöly, Bene, Albert, Farkas, Rákosi.
Scorers: Bene, Farkas, Mészöly (pen)
Brazil: Gilmar; D.Santos, Bellini, Altair, Paulo Henrique, Lima, Gérson, Garrincha, Alcindo, Tostão, Jairzinho.
Scorer: Tostão
Referee: Ken Dagnall (England)

PORTUGAL 3   BULGARIA 0 (Half-time 2-0)
Old Trafford, Manchester, 16 July
Attendance: 33,355

PORTUGAL were never troubled as they chalked up their second successive win to make them one of the tournament's new favourites.

Jairzinho of Brazil.

Portugal took the lead in the sixth minute when Vutzov headed a spectacular own-goal, despite being under no pressure. The Portuguese did not need any help, though, and they made it 2-0 in the 38th minute when the new star of the world game, Eusébio, scored his first World Cup goal. It was the first of nine he was to score in 1966 as he ended the tournament as top scorer.

As Portugal coasted to an easy victory, without stretching themselves in the second half, Torres added a third goal ten minutes from time when he had the easiest of tasks in scoring from a bad back-pass.

Bulgaria were almost certainly out of the competition and Portugal knew that a draw in their final game with Brazil would be enough to advance them to the next stage.

Portugal: Pereira; Festa, Germano, Vincente, Hilario, Graça, Coluña, Augusto, Eusébio, Torres, Simoẽs.
Scorers: Vutzov (og), Eusébio, Torres
Bulgaria: Naidenov; Shalamanov, Vutzov, Gaganelov, Penev, Zhechev, Yakimov, Dermendyev, Zhekov, Asparoukhov, Kostov.
Referee: José Maria Codesal (Uruguay)

George Asparoukhov of Bulgaria.

PORTUGAL 3   BRAZIL 1 (Half-time 2-0)

Goodison Park, Liverpool, 19 July
Attendance: 62,204

IN an effort to stay in the competition, Brazil made nine changes from their match with Hungary and gave World Cup debuts to no fewer than seven players. Pelé returned to the side, even though he was not fully fit, and in goal Gilmar was replaced by Manga. But mistakes by the new 'keeper were instrumental in Portugal taking a 2-0 half-time lead.

The Portuguese forwards — Eusébio in particular — were so superior to those of the defending champions, but once again Pelé was subjected to some rough treatment and in the first half an hour had been hacked down by two vicious tackles. Then a foul by Morais made him a limping passenger.

Portugal opened the scoring in the 14th minute when the Brazilian 'keeper pushed out a Eusébio cross straight to Simoẽs, who had no trouble in heading home. Eusébio made

Alberto Festa of Portugal.

Hilário da Conceição of Portugal.

Referee George McCabe looks on as Pelé receives treatment after yet another brutal tackle. Portugal's Eusébio seems understandably sympathetic at the Brazilian star's plight.

Eusébio heads Portugal's second goal past Manga and World Champions Brazil are on their way out of the competition.

it 2-0 midway through the first half when he headed in a Coluña free-kick which had been glanced to him by Torres.

Rildo gave the Brazilian fans some hope in the 72nd minute, when he pulled a goal back, but five minutes from the end Eusébio drove in a powerful shot from a corner to seal an emphatic win and take the World Cup debutants into the quarter-finals.

The match could have offered an opportunity to compare the skills of Pelé and Eusébio, but Portugal were not prepared to let Pelé grace the same stage. After the match, Pelé threatened never to play in another World Cup game and announced: "I don't want to finish my life as an invalid."

Portugal: Pereira; Morais, Baptista, Vicente, Hilario, Graça, Coluña, Augusto, Eusébio, Torres, Simoẽs.
Scorers: Eusébio 2, Simoẽs
Brazil: Manga; Fidelis, Brito, Orlando, Rildo, Denilson, Lima, Jairzinho, Silva, Pelé, Paraná.
Scorer: Rildo
Referee: George McCabe (England)

Mário Coluña of Portugal.

HUNGARY 3   BULGARIA 1 (Half-time 2-1)

Old Trafford, Manchester, 20 July
Attendance: 22,064

HUNGARY needed only to draw to qualify alongside Portugal, but they received an almighty shock when Asparoukhov gave the Bulgarian's a great start when he scored their first — and only — goal of the tournament.

Strange as though it may have seemed, Bulgaria could still have qualified, despite losing their first two matches, but to achieve that they had to win 4-0 — and that was a tall order, despite their great start.

However, any such notions disappeared two minutes before the interval when, for the second successive match, Bulgaria conceded an own-goal when Davidov beat his own 'keeper. On the stroke of half-time, Mészöly put Hungary in the lead.

In the second half, Bulgaria succumbed to the skills of Albert, Bene and company and after 54 minutes, Bene made it 3-1, thus putting qualification out of the Bulgarians' reach.

Hungary: Gelei; Káposzta, Mátrai, Mészöly, Sipos, Szepesi, Mathesz, Albert, Rákosi, Bene, Farkas.
Scorers: Davidov (og), Mészöly, Bene
Bulgaria: Simeonov; Penev, Largov, Vutzov, Gaganelov, Zhechev, Davidov, Kotkov, Asparoukhov, Yakimov, Kolev.
Scorer: Asparoukhov
Referee: Roberto Goicoechea (Argentina)

Group Four

SOVIET UNION 3   NORTH KOREA 0 (Half-time 2-0)
Ayresome Park, Middlesbrough, 12 July
Attendance: 22,568

STANDING alongside the Soviet players, the tiny North Koreans (average height under 5ft 6in) looked no match for their European counterparts. The Koreans were lucky in the way they qualified for the final stages and many thought they were going to be easy opponents for Chile, Italy and the Russians — but appearances certainly deceived.

Whilst the Soviets were tactically and physically superior, the Koreans gave a display of endless running and fought bravely to the end. For half an hour they even managed to hold Russia, who were one of the fancied teams of this eighth World Cup.

Malafeev opened the scoring after 30 minutes and, two minutes later, the massive Banichevski was too powerful for the defence as he forced his way through for the second goal. The Middlesbrough fans, who were warming to the underdogs, suspected a barrage of goals but, surprisingly, the only other goal of the game came two minutes from time when Malafeev scored again.

Russia were one of the probable quarter-finalists from Group Four. North Korea were certainly not considered as one of the likely qualifiers. But this opening performance gave no indication of what they had in store as they became the dark horses of the 1966 World Cup, for what they lacked in size they certainly made up for with some enormously spirited performances.

Soviet Union: Kavasashvili; Ponomarev, Shesterniev, Khurtsilava, Ostrovski, Sabo, Sichinava, Chislenko, Malafeev, Banichevski, Khusainov.
Scorers: Malafeev 2, Banichevski
North Korea: Chan-myung; Li-sup, Yung-kyoo, Zoong-sun, Bong-chil, Seung-zin, Seung-hwi, Bong-jin, Doo-ik, Byong-woon, Seung-il.
Referee: Juan Gardeazabal Garay (Spain)

ITALY 2   CHILE 0 (Half-time 1-0)
Roker Park, Sunderland, 13 July
Attendance: 30,956

THE last time Chile and Italy met in the World Cup was four years earlier, in what became known as 'The Battle of Santiago'. Mercifully, Roker Park was not to witness repeat scenes as the teams played out a tame match in wet conditions.

Only four players, Fouilloux, Eyzaguirre and Leonel Sánchez of Chile, and Salvadore of Italy, remained from that infamous previous meeting and reprisals were not in any of the players' minds.

Whilst Italy were the more fancied of the two teams, they toiled for their win, despite scoring in the ninth minute. It was not until two minutes from time that they made their victory safe.

Their first goal was scored by Sandro Mazzola, whose father was one of Italy's leading strikers in 1949 and skipper of the national side. He lost his life in the air crash that wiped out the Torino team that year and would surely have led his country into the 1950 World Cup finals.

Italy settled the issue when Barison scored a late goal.

Italy: Albertosi; Burgnich, Facchetti, Rosato, Salvadore, Lodetti, Perani, Bulgarelli, Mazzola, Rivera, Barison.
Scorers: Mazzola, Barison
Chile: Olivares; Eyzaguirre, Cruz, Figueroa, Villanueva, Prieto, Marcos, Araya, Tobar, Fouilloux, Sánchez.
Referee: Gottfried Dienst (Switzerland)

CHILE 1   NORTH KOREA 1 (Half-time 1-0)
Ayresome Park, Middlesbrough, 15 July
Attendance: 15,887

THIS game was watched by the smallest attendance of the tournament. But there could

Giacinto Facchetti of Italy.

Lim Zoong-sun of North Korea.

Gianni Rivera of Italy.

Kim Seung-il of North Korea.

Tarcisio Burgnich of Italy.

Sandro Mazzola of Italy.

North Korea's goalkeeper Li Chan-myung punches the ball off the head of Chile's Ruben Marcos.

not have been many amongst the Ayresome Park crowd who were not willing a Korean victory. The local fans had really taken the tiny Orientals to heart with the typical English favouritism for the underdog.

However, they saw 'their' team fall behind midway through the first-half when Marcos scored from the penalty-spot after Sin Yung-kyoo had brought down Pedro Araya.

As the game approached the final whistle the Middlesbrough fans had resigned themselves to a second defeat for the Koreans and almost certain exit from the competition. Then, two minutes from time, Pak Seung-zin took advantage of a poor clearance from Elías Figueroa and scored North Korea's first-ever goal in the final stages of the World Cup. The fans went wild and were still cheering when the referee blew to end the match.

Chile: Olivares; Valentini, Cruz, Figueroa, Villanueva, Prieto, Marcos, Fouilloux, Landa, Araya, Sánchez.
Scorer: Marcos (pen)
North Korea: Chan-myung; Li-sup, Yung-kyoo, Zoong-sun, Yoon-kyung, Seung-zin, Seung-hwi, Bong-jin, Doo-ik, Dong-woon, Seung-il.
Scorer: Seung-zin
Referee: Alì Kandil (Egypt)

SOVIET UNION 1 ITALY 0 (Half-time 0-0)
Roker Park, Sunderland, 16 July.
Attendance: 31,989

ITALIAN team manager Edmondo Fabbri summed up the whole new thinking in football when he left out talented forward Gianni Rivera and replaced him with an extra defender. Fabbri was not concerned with winning. More important, he wanted to ensure that his team did not lose.

For nearly an hour, the Italians' ploy paid off, even though Chislenko had the freedom to run at the defence almost at will. Once he got there, he found a well-drilled unit that was difficult to penetrate, but in the 58th minute the Italians' plans were in disarray when Chislenko hit a powerful low shot past goalkeeper Albertosi.

Now Italy had to come forward and they could have done with Rivera. The Soviets thus made it two wins from two matches and guaranteed themselves a place in the quarter-finals.

Soviet Union: Yashin; Ponomarev, Shesterniev, Khurtsilava, Voronin, Danilov, Sabo, Chislenko, Malafeev, Banichevski, Khusainov.
Scorer: Chislenko
Italy: Albertosi; Burgnich, Facchetti, Rosato, Salvadore, Leoncini, Meroni, Lodetti, Mazzola, Bulgarelli, Pascutti.
Referee: Rudolf Kreitlein (West Germany)

NORTH KOREA 1 ITALY 0 (Half-time 1-0)
Ayresome Park, Middlesbrough, 19 July
Attendance: 18,727

ITALY made sweeping changes for their final group match. Back came Rivera in the hope that he would score goals. The star-studded Italians were, on paper, far superior to the Koreans. But, as the United States showed in 1950 when they beat an England team littered with the best-known names in world soccer, reputations sometimes count for nothing. The North

Group Four – Final Table						
	P	W	D	L	F	A	Pts
Soviet Union	3	3	0	0	6	1	6
North Korea	3	1	1	1	2	4	3
Italy	3	1	0	2	2	2	2
Chile	3	0	1	2	2	5	1

The hugely popular North Koreans (pictured left) caused a sensation by defeating Italy. It was the biggest World Cup upset since England lost to the USA in 1950.

Koreans were about to produce the biggest World Cup shock since that American win 16 years earlier.

They were tireless and tackled at every opportunity. Their forwards were too quick for the slow Italian defence. And, of course, they were spurred on by a totally biased local crowd.

Italy were reduced to ten men after 34 minutes when Bulgarelli went off after damaging his knee when he fouled Pak Seung-zin. Seven minutes later the Koreans scored the goal that ensured their place in World Cup folklore.

From a clearance, Seung-zin beat Rivera, who stood waiting for the ball, and headed back towards the Italian goal. Pak Doo-ik gathered the ball on the edge of the penalty area, moved forward and scored from 15 yards. It was a memorable goal.

The Koreans held on for their remarkable win, but had to endure a 24-hour wait to see if they would qualify for the last eight.

As for Italy, it was the ultimate humiliation. Twice winners of the trophy, they were sent packing and flew into Genoa airport in the early hours of the morning in the hope of avoiding irate fans. They were greeted with verbal abuse and a barrage of vegetables was thrown at them. For months afterwards, many of the Italian players were abused wherever they turned out across Italy. It took a long time for them to wipe out the memory of that day at Middlesbrough.

North Korea: Chan-myung; Zoong-sun, Yung-kyoo, Yung-won, Yoon-kyung, Seung-hwi, Bong-jin, Doo-ik, Seung-zin, Bong-hwan, Seung-kook.
Scorer: Doo-ik
Italy: Albertosi; Landini, Facchetti, Guarneri, Janich, Fogli, Perani, Bulgarelli, Mazzola, Rivera, Barison.
Referee: Pierre Schwinte (France)

SOVIET UNION 2   CHILE 1 (Half-time 1-1)

Roker Park, Sunderland, 20 July
Attendance: 22,590

FOLLOWING the outcome of the North Korea-Italy game, the Soviet Union were assured of topping Group Four and consequently they fielded nine reserves. One of them, Valeri Porkujan, scored both their goals as they ran out easy winners and, like Portugal, topped their group with a 100 per cent record. The Soviet victory also ensured that North Korea joined them in the quarter-finals.

Porkujan opened the scoring midway through the first-half, but Marcos levelled the scores after half an hour. Chile knew they had to attack and score goals if they wanted to remain in the tournament and they committed themselves to pushing players forward in the second-half. But, as often happens, it showed flaws in the defence and five minutes from time they forfeited a second goal when Porkujan scored again.

Soviet Union: Kavasashvili; Getmanov, Shesterniev, Afonin, Ostrovski, Voronin, Korneyev, Metreveli, Serebrianikov, Markarov, Porkujan.
Scorer: Porkujan 2
Chile: Olivares; Valentini, Cruz, Figueroa, Villanueva, Marcos, Prieto, Araya, Landa, Yavar, Sánchez.
Scorer: Marcos
Referee: John Adair (Northern Ireland)

Leonel Sánchez of Chile.

Top: FIFA referees' official Ken Aston tries to persuade Antonio Rattín to leave the field. *Middle:* Dejected Rattín sits it out. *Bottom:* Referee Rudolf Kreitlein is escorted from the Wembley pitch.

Right: England manager Alf Ramsey prevents George Cohen from exchanging shirts with an Argentinian. Ramsey called the Argentine players 'animals'.

Quarter-finals

ENGLAND 1 ARGENTINA 0 (Half-time 0-0)

Wembley Stadium, London, 23 July
Attendance: 90,584

WEMBLEY Stadium basked in glorious sunshine for England's quarter-final clash with Argentina. It was a great pity, then, that the South Americans' approach to the game was not as pleasing as the weather.

Right from the outset they were intent on over-zealous tackling which the West German referee, Rudolf Kreitlein, attempted to snuff out from the opening minutes by bringing out his notebook. This served only to incense the Argentinian captain, Rattín, who had a running argument with Kreitlein during the first half-hour. After 36 minutes the official's patience ran out and he ordered Rattín from the field. The player refused to go and there followed eight minutes of disgraceful scenes as police and FIFA officials came on to the pitch. Rattín eventually made the long walk back to the Wembley dressing-room, but at one time it looked as though the entire Argentinian team was going to walk off the field.

England left out Jimmy Greaves again, although many felt that he was fit enough to return. Into the team came the West Ham forward, Geoff Hurst. His introduction to the tournament was the turning point in England's eventual success, but he was a little fortunate to stay on the field after he brought down an Argentinian shortly after Rattín's dismissal. The Argentinians were certainly after retribution for their captain's sending-off.

However, it was Hurst who secured England's semi-final place with the only goal of the game, when he glanced home a 78th-minute cross from his West Ham teammate, Martin Peters. Argentina's agile goalkeeper, Roma, had at last been beaten after solidly defending his goal.

At the end of the game Alf Ramsey refused to let the England players exchange shirts with the South Americans, whom he subsequently described as "animals," a statement he later withdrew under FA pressure.

England: Banks; Cohen, Wilson, Stiles, J.Charlton, Moore, Ball, Hurst, R.Charlton, Hunt, Peters.
Scorer: Hurst
Argentina: Roma; Ferreiro, Marzolini, Rattín, Perfumo, Albrecht, Onega, Solari, Artime, González, Mas.
Referee: Rudolf Kreitlein (West Germany)

WEST GERMANY 4   URUGUAY 0 (Half-time 1-0)

Hillsborough, Sheffield, 23 July
Attendance: 33,751

DESPITE the scoreline, the Uruguayans were the equal of their European opponents until they allowed their temperament to get the better of them. Then their game fell apart.

Trailing to an 11th-minute goal after Held's shot was helped on its way by Haller, Uruguay seemed capable of levelling the scores. But the course of the game changed shortly before half-time when Uruguay had a penalty appeal turned down after Schnellinger appeared to handle the ball.

Uruguay no longer seemed intent on playing attacking football and instead wanted to 'take no prisoners'. As a result they paid heavily with two players dismissed early in the second half.

Skipper Troche was the first to go, when he retaliated after being kicked by Emmerich. He was given his marching orders after directing a kick at the German's stomach. Next to go was centre-forward Silva, after fouling Haller whose histrionics were definitely Oscar-winning material.

Down to nine men, the South Americans, could not cope and conceded three goals in the last 20 minutes when Beckenbauer, Seeler and Haller ensured West Germany's appearance in the semi-final.

West Germany: Tilkowski; Höttges, Weber, Schulz, Schnellinger, Beckenbauer, Haller, Overath, Seeler, Held, Emmerich.
Scorers: Held, Beckenbauer, Seeler, Haller
Uruguay: Mazurkiewicz; Troche, Ubiñas, Gonçálves, Manicera, Caetano, Salva, Rocha, Silva, Cortés, Pérez.
Referee: Jim Finney (England)

Above: Uruguay's Silva follows teammate Troche for an early bath, leaving his team down to nine men.

Below: Haller beats Uruguay's Mazurkiewicz to make it 4-0 for West Germany.

Seung-kook (bottom left) has been felled by a late challenge and cannot join in the celebrations for his goal which has just given North Korea a 3-0 lead over Portugal.

José Augusto of Portugal.

PORTUGAL 5   NORTH KOREA 3 (Half-time 2-3)

Goodison Park, Liverpool, 23 July
Attendance: 51,780

THIS game is immortalized in World Cup history as one of the truly memorable matches of the 14 tournaments since 1930.

The Koreans had already provided the shock of the tournament in beating Italy 1-0, but even the wildest of dreamers could not have envisaged another triumph over one of the new tournament favourites.

After 22 minutes, however, the scoreline read Portugal 0 North Korea 3. The football world could not believe what was happening. Portugal certainly couldn't — and neither could the Koreans.

It started in the very first minute when Pak Seung-zin scored with a left-foot shot from the edge of the penalty area. Twenty minutes later, Dong-woon had the easiest of tasks in scoring after the Portuguese goalkeeper, Pereira, misjudged a cross. In the 22nd minute, Seung-kook made it 3-0. The Goodison fans were stunned. The few thousand Middlesbrough fans who came to support 'their' team were deliriously happy. Portugal were shocked, but so too were the North Koreans, who did not know how to cope with the situation and kept attacking. That turned out to be their downfall and eventually the most gifted player in the tournament, Eusébio, took charge, and single-handedly demolished the Koreans.

Eusébio is on his way to a four-goal triumph against North Korea and a face-saving result for Portugal.

Eusébio goes flying over the outstretched legs of a North Korean defender.

Eusébio scored his first goal in the 27th minute and three minutes before the interval he had pulled another back from the penalty-spot. Ten minutes into the second half the scores were level after Eusébio hit a cracker from the edge of the six-yard box. And three minutes after that, Portugal took the lead for the first time when Eusébio scored his fourth goal, again from the penalty-spot, after he was brought down in the area during a great solo run.

The scoring spree ended 12 minutes from time when Augusto made it 5-3. Predictably, Eusébio had a hand in the goal, which came from a corner-kick taken by the four-goal hero.

So ended an amazing World Cup debut for the North Koreans. They will never be forgotten after their performances against Italy and Portugal. Neither will Eusébio be forgotten for the way he clawed his team back into the tournament with a fine individual performance.

Portugal: Pereira; Morais, Baptista, Vicente, Hilario, Graça, Coluña, Augusto, Eusébio, Torres, Simoẽs.
Scorers: Eusébio 4 (2 pens), Augusto
North Korea: Chan-myung; Zoong-sun, Yung-kyoo, Yung-won, Yoon-kyung, Seung-zin, Seung-hwi, Bong-jin, Doo-ik, Dong-woon, Seung-kook.
Scorers: Seung-zin, Dong-woon, Seung-kook
Referee: Menachem Ashkenasi (Israel)

Kálmán Mészöly of Hungary.

SOVIET UNION 2   HUNGARY 1 (Half-time 1-0)

Roker Park, Sunderland, 23 July
Attendance: 26,844

RUSSIA were the better and more powerful of the two teams and after taking a two-goal lead they showed they were capable of defending solidly, although they nearly came unstuck when the Hungarian forward, Rákosi, missed an easy chance late in the game.

The Soviets were fortunate to take the lead in the fifth minute when the Hungarian goalkeeper, Gelei, failed to hold a seemingly harmless shot from Malafeev and the ball dropped at the feet of Chislenko, who put it into the net. And when Russia made it 2-0 a couple of minutes into the second half, it was again thanks to a defensive error.

A shot from Malafeev appeared to be going wide and with the defence standing watching, Porkujan popped up to head home from close range near the post.

Bene immediately responded with a goal for the Magyars, but that is when the Soviets tightened up their defence, which was good enough to withstand 40 minutes of pressure from the Hungarian attack.

Soviet Union: Yashin; Ponomarev, Shesterniev, Voronin, Danilov, Sabo, Khusainov, Chislenko, Banichevski, Malafeev, Porkujan.
Scorers: Chislenko, Porkujan
Hungary: Gelei; Mátrai, Káposzta, Mészöly, Sipos, Szepesi, Nagy, Albert, Rákosi, Bene, Farkas.
Scorer: Bene
Referee: Juan Gardeazabal Garay (Spain)

Semi-finals

WEST GERMANY 2   SOVIET UNION 1 (Half-time 1-0)

Goodison Park, Liverpool, 25 July
Attendance: 43,921

THERE were fewer goals for the Goodison Park fans this time, and no excitement to match

Eduard Malafeev of the USSR.

Emmerich of West Germany is crowded out by three Russian defenders.

STATISTICS

Goalscorers:
9 — Eusébio Ferreira da Silva (Portugal).
5 — Helmut Haller (West Germany).
4 — Geoff Hurst (England), Franz Beckenbauer (West Germany), Valeri Porkujan (Soviet Union), Ferenc Bene (Hungary).
3 — Bobby Charlton, Roger Hunt (both England), José Augusto, José Torres (both Portugal), Eduard Malafeev (Soviet Union), Luis Artime (Argentina).
2 — Uwe Seeler, Sigfried Held (both West Germany), Igor Chislenko (Soviet Union), Kalman Mészöly (Hungary), Pak Seung-zin (North Korea), Ruben Marcos (Chile).
1 — Martin Peters (England), Lothar Emmerich, Wolfgang Weber (both West Germany), Antonio Simoês (Portugal), Anatoly Banichevski (Soviet Union), Ermindo Onega (Argentina), Janos Farkas (Hungary), Pak Doo-ik, Li Dong-woon, Yong Seung-kook (all North Korea), Pirri, Manuel Sanchís, Amaro Amancio, José Fusté (all Spain), Pelé, Manoel Garrincha dos Santos, Tostão, Rildo Costa Menezes (all Brazil), Pedro Rocha, Julio Cortés (both Uruguay), Sandro Mazzola, Paolo Barison (both Italy), Gerard Hausser, Héctor de Bourgoing (both France), Enrique Borja (Mexico), George Asparoukhov (Bulgaria), Pierre Quentin (Switzerland).

Own-goals
Ivan Vutzov (Bulgaria v Portugal).
Ivan Davidov (Bulgaria v Hungary).

Hat-tricks
Eusébio Ferreira da Silva (4 goals, Portugal v North Korea). Geoff Hurst (England v West Germany).

Fastest goal
1 minute — Pak Seung-zin, (North Korea v Portugal).

Most goals (team)
17 — Portugal

Teams failing to score
None

Total Goals Scored: 89
Average Per Game: 2.78

the quarter-final tie between Portugal and North Korea. Indeed, West Germany and the Soviet Union played the type of football that one had come to expect from 'everything to lose' semi-final clashes.

It was a poor game and often physical. Both sides tackled hard and Russia's Chislenko paid the penalty for kicking Held and was sent off.

The Russian defence was solid, with Shesterniev dominant and goalkeeper Lev Yashin in fine form. However, they conceded the first goal a minute before half-time when Haller scored after a great cross-field pass from Schnellinger.

Chislenko received his marching orders just before half-time and the Soviets spent most of the second half with only nine fit men after Sabo was injured after a failed attempt to foul Beckenbauer in the opening minutes of the game.

The Germans made it 2-0 after 68 minutes when a Beckenbauer shot deceived Yashin and spoilt an otherwise good day for the Soviet 'keeper.

Porkujan pulled one back two minutes from time when Tilkowski dropped a cross, and a minute later the Russian left winger came close to snatching a dramatic equalizer.

West Germany: Tilkowski; Lutz, Weber, Schulz, Schnellinger, Beckenbauer, Haller, Overath, Seeler, Held, Emmerich.
Scorers: Haller, Beckenbauer
Soviet Union: Yashin; Ponomarev, Shesterniev, Voronin, Danilov, Sabo, Khusainov, Chislenko, Banichevski, Malafeev, Porkujan.
Scorer: Porkujan
Referee: Concetto Lo Bello (Italy)

Franz Beckenbauer (not in picture) puts West Germany 2-0 ahead as Russian goalkeeper Lev Yashin is deceived by the ball's flight.

A desolate Eusébio after Portugal's defeat by England. Despite his nine goals in the tournament, the Portuguese went out in the semi-finals.

Penalties
Scored: Eusébio Ferreira da Silva 2 (Portugal v North Korea) *Referee: Jim Finney (England).* Eusébio Ferreira da Silva (Portugal v England) *Referee: Pierre Schwinte (France).* Eusébio Ferreira da Silva (Portugal v Soviet Union) *Referee: Ken Dagnall (England).* Helmut Haller (West Germany v Switzerland) *Referee: Hugh Phillips (Scotland).* Kalman Mészöly (Hungary v Brazil) *Referee: Ken Dagnall (England).* Héctor de Bourgoing (France v Uruguay) *Referee: Karol Galba (Czechoslovakia).* Ruben Marcos (Chile v North Korea) *Referee: Alì Kandil (Egypt).*

Most appearances
6 — Mario Coluña, Eusébio Ferreira da Silva, Hilario de Conceição, José Augusto, Antonio Simoës, José Torres, Jaime Graça (all Portugal); Franz Beckenbauer, Sigfried Held, Wolfgang Overath, Karl-Heinz Schnellinger, Willy Schulz, Uwe Seeler, Hans Tilkowski, Wolfgang Weber (all West Germany); Gordon Banks, Jackie Charlton, Bobby Charlton, George Cohen, Roger Hunt, Bobby Moore, Nobby Stiles, Ray Wilson (all England).

Sendings-off
Jorge Albrecht (Argentina v West Germany) *Referee: Konstatin Zecevic (Yugoslavia)* Horacio Troche (Uruguay v West Germany) *Referee: Jim Finney (England),* Héctor Silva (Uruguay v West Germany) *Referee: Jim Finney (England).* Antonio Rattín (Argentina v England) *Referee: Rudolf Kreitlein (West Germany).* Igor Chislenko (Soviet Union v West Germany) *Referee: Concetto Lo Bello (Italy).*

Most players used
21 — Soviet Union

Number of players used by Finalists
14 — West Germany
15 — England

ENGLAND 2 PORTUGAL 1 (Half-time 1-0)

Wembley Stadium, London, 26 July
Attendance: 94,493

AFTER the defensive tactics and violent tackling displayed by some teams in the eighth World Cup, it was refreshing to see two sides prepared to play 'good old fashioned football' and in a sporting atmosphere free from any major incident.

There was much newspaper hype given to a potentially heated clash between Nobby Stiles and Eusébio, but this did not materialize, as Stiles did an utterly professional job in curtailing the talent of the great Portuguese forward.

The game will be remembered for two Bobby Charlton goals, the second of which was one of the finest goals ever seen at Wembley. It was certainly one of Charlton's finest performances in an England jersey.

He scored his first after half an hour, when he side-footed the ball into the net from 20 yards after a shot from Hunt had been blocked by Pereira and rebounded to the waiting Manchester United star.

His second goal, 11 minutes from time, was a pure gem. Hurst pulled the ball back for Charlton to run in and hit it from just inside the penalty area. The 'keeper had no chance and even some of the Portuguese players shook Charlton's hand after the goal.

English hearts sank three minutes later, however, when Eusébio scored from the penalty-spot after Jackie Charlton was forced to handle the ball to prevent it entering the net.

The closing eight minutes were anxious moments for the England fans and Stiles did well to stop Simoës in front of goal. Then Banks made a great save from Coluña and England held out for their first appearance in a World Cup Final.

Eusébio in full flight.

Gordon Banks (on ground) saves a shot against Portugal with England teammates Wilson (left) and Peters watching.

England: Banks; Cohen, Wilson, Stiles, J.Charlton, Moore, Ball, Hurst, R.Charlton, Hunt, Peters.
Scorer: R.Charlton 2
Portugal: Pereira, Festa, Baptista, Carlos, Hilario, Graça, Coluña, Augusto, Eusébio, Torres, Simoẽs.
Scorer: Eusébio (pen)
Referee: Pierre Schwinte (France)

Third place play-off
PORTUGAL 2 SOVIET UNION 1 (Half-time 1-1)
Wembley Stadium, London, 28 July
Attendance: 87,696

AN unexpectedly large crowd turned up at Wembley for the third place play-off match and many of them probably wished they had not bothered. The game was played at half-pace, although it did produce the occasional moment of goalmouth excitement.

In the 12th minute, Eusébio scored his ninth goal of the tournament — and his fourth from the penalty-spot — after Khurtsilava handled unnecessarily.

Two minutes before half-time, Malafeev equalized after he latched on to a loose ball dropped by the Portuguese goalkeeper, Pereira. The game seemed to be fading into a draw and thousands of fans had left the stadium when Torres grabbed the winner for Portugal in the 88th minute, after Augusto headed down a Simoẽs cross.

Portugal: Pereira; Festa, Baptista, Carlos, Hilario, Graça, Coluña, Augusto, Eusébio, Torres, Simoẽs.
Scorers: Eusébio (pen), Torres
Soviet Union: Yashin; Ponomarev, Khurtsilava, Korneyev, Danilov, Voronin, Sichinava, Metreveli, Malafeev, Banichevski, Serebrianikov.
Scorer: Malafeev
Referee: Ken Dagnall (England)

Action from USSR v Portugal.

Final

ENGLAND 4 WEST GERMANY 2 (a.e.t.) (Half-time 1-1; 90 mins 2-2)
Wembley Stadium, London, 30 July
Attendance: 96,924

THE 1966 World Cup Final was the 200th match to be played in the final stages of the World Cup since its inauguration in 1930. And what a cracker it turned out to be.

Both sides were unchanged from their semi-final wins. England's Jimmy Greaves was definitely fit but Alf Ramsey still chose to sideline him. Helmut Schön, meanwhile, made a tactical change which many subsequently felt cost his side the 1966 Jules Rimet Trophy.

After Bobby Charlton's great game against Portugal, Schön thought it best to bring Franz

England (in unfamiliar red shirts) and West Germany line up before the 1966 World Cup Final at Wembley.

Beckenbauer deep into defence to mark the England forward. He did his job satisfactorily, but the German midfield suffered as a consequence.

England were playing their sixth game at Wembley and this was an obvious advantage. But, despite playing on home soil, they allowed West Germany to score first, in the 12th minute when a weak headed clearance from Ray Wilson dropped at the feet of Haller and his shot beat Gordon Banks. Six minutes later, however, England skipper Bobby Moore laid on the equalizer when he took a quick free-kick after being fouled. Moore spotted his West Ham colleague, Geoff Hurst, in the penalty area and crossed with pin-point accuracy on to the head of the striker, who rose to beat a flat-footed German defence.

Roared on by the large partisan crowd, England seemed to be the stronger of the two sides in the second half and in the 78th minute got a second goal. The tired legs of the ever-running Alan Ball launched a corner-kick from the right. The ball found Hurst and his shot was half-cleared by Höttges, only for the ball to roll to Martin Peters, who put England ahead.

As the minutes rolled by and socks were rolled down, the England fans were willing referee Dienst to blow the final whistle. In the dying seconds of injury time he did blow, but for a foul against Jack Charlton after he and Held had both jumped for a ball. Many thought the decision should have been in England's favour, but it was given the other way. Emmerich took the kick and the ball bobbled around in the six-yard box before reaching Weber on the right. His outstretched foot stabbed the ball past the despairing Gordon Banks from just six yards. It was his only goal of the tournament. The England team was stunned. The England fans were shattered. And then Dienst blew for the end of 90 minutes.

Alf Ramsey had to haul his tired players back into the game, telling them: "You've beaten them once this afternoon. Now go out and do it again."

Franz Beckenbauer, played deep in midfield to mark Bobby Charlton.

Geoff Hurst levels the scores as the German defence waits leaden-footed.

Martin Peters (16) wheels away after giving England a 2-1 lead.

Geoff Hurst, hat-trick hero.

Wolfgang Weber's last-minute equalizer for West Germany leaves England to do it all over again.

In the first period of extra-time, the tireless Ball pulled a ball back for Geoff Hurst to strike. What followed is probably the most controversial incident in World Cup history.

The West Ham striker's shot hit the underside of the bar, bounced down and returned into play. Hurst was adamant that it was a goal and so, too, was Roger Hunt, the nearest England player to the ball. The referee was not sure and consulted his Russian linesman, Tofik Bakhramov. After what seemed like an age, the referee pointed to the centre-spot and England were 3-2 ahead.

Was it a goal? Even to this day nobody is sure. After looking at the film from different angles countless times, it is still impossible to tell. The linesman was not up with the ball

Hurst cracks in the shot which brought England's third goal and was probably the most controversial in World Cup history.

Top and left: **Photographic evidence is inconclusive but after consulting his linesman (bottom) referee Dienst awards the goal.**

at the time of the incident, standing, as he was, some six or seven yards from the goal-line. So how could he have been so sure? Then again, Roger Hunt was adamant and the fact that he turned away immediately after the ball bounced, instead of attempting to stab it home, surely indicates that he really was convinced. The main point is, of course, it was a goal, the referee had allowed it.

England's win was sealed in the very last minute of the match when Hurst broke free to become the first and only man to score a hat-trick in a World Cup Final and England became the first hosts since Italy in 1934 to win the trophy. Once more the team scoring first in the Final ended up the beaten side.

Tears flowed freely from the England players after the match, notably from Bobby Charlton who, with Jack Charlton, had become the second pair of brothers after the Walters in 1954 to collect winners' medals. Nobby Stiles did a jig and Alf Ramsey, the man who had been telling the England fans all along that their team would be World Champions, took it all in his stride as Bobby Moore climbed Wembley's 39 steps to collect the Jules Rimet Trophy from Her Majesty the Queen.

England: Gordon Banks; George Cohen, Ray Wilson, Nobby Stiles, Jack Charlton, Bobby Moore, Alan Ball, Roger Hunt, Bobby Charlton, Geoff Hurst, Martin Peters.
Scorers: Hurst 3, Peters
West Germany: Hans Tilkowski; Horst-Dieter Höttges, Willy Schulz, Wolfgang Weber, Karl-Heinz Schnellinger, Helmut Haller, Franz Beckenbauer, Wolfgang Overath, Uwe Seeler, Sigfried Held, Lothar Emmerich.
Scorers: Haller, Weber
Referee: Gottfried Dienst (Switzerland)

Siggy Held gets past Jack Charlton.

Top: Geoff Hurst puts the result beyond doubt as he completes an historic hat-trick. *Middle:* Skipper Bobby Moore receives the Jules Rimet Trophy from Queen Elizabeth II. *Bottom:* England's winning team. Back row (left to right): Harold Shepherdson (trainer), Nobby Stiles, Roger Hunt, Gordon Banks, Jack Charlton, George Cohen, Ray Wilson, Alf Ramsey (manager). Front: Martin Peters, Geoff Hurst, Bobby Moore, Alan Ball, Bobby Charlton.

Opposite page: Bobby Moore, chaired aloft by Geoff Hurst and Ray Wilson, shows the World Cup trophy to England's deliriously happy fans.

MEN WHO MADE THE HEADLINES - 1970

Jairzinho
(Brazil)

JAIRZINHO was a worthy successor to Garrincha and his devastating bursts of speed combined with lethal shooting were one of the highlights of the great 1970 series. Born Jair Ventura Filho in 1944, he began on the left wing and at centre-forward with Botafogo and gained his chance on the right when Garrincha was injured. His international debut was against Portugal in the 1964 'Little World Cup' and two years later he appeared in the finals in England. With Garrincha recalled, though, Jairzinho switched to the left flank and was not as effective. In 1970, however, after recovering from a twice-broken right leg, he became the only player ever to score in every game including the Final. His seven goals were second only to Gerd Müller's ten and Jairzinho's came in many forms — delicate chips and powerful shooting. His winner against England was one of the tournament's most memorable goals but he was also a goalmaker and split defences with superb passing. He appeared in the 1974 World Cup, but without players like Pelé in support he was not as effective. He later played for Olympique of Marseille but soon returned to Río. Jairzinho won more than 80 caps, the last when he was in his 38th year.

Gerd Müller
(West Germany)

GERD Müller — 'Der Bomber' is the most prolific striker in World Cup history with a record 14 goals from two series. Gerhard Müller was born in November 1945, at Nördlingen, and began with his local club before joining Bayern Munich and helping them into the Bundesliga in 1965, only a season after signing. His international debut was in October 1966 against Turkey, West Germany's first match after their World Cup Final defeat. By the 1970 World Cup he was averaging around a goal for every international appearance and then hit ten in six matches, including successive hat-tricks, as the Germans reached the semi-finals. Müller scored four goals in the 1974 finals, including the winner in the Final, in his last international. He helped Bayern to many domestic and European honours, was European Footballer of the Year in 1970 and twice won the Golden Boot, scoring 365 goals in 628 senior games overall, including 69 in 62 internationals to pass Uwe Seeler's record. He never fully recovered from injury in 1978 and finished his career with Fort Lauderdale in the NASL, scoring 38 goals in 75 regular season games in three years.

Luigi Riva
(Italy)

IT was Luigi Riva's seven goals in the qualifying tournament which took Italy to the 1970 finals. Born at Leggiuno in November 1944, he began with Legnano in Serie C in 1962-3, joined Cagliari in 1963-4 and helped them into Serie A. Riva made his international debut as a substitute in Budapest in June 1965, but was inexplicably left out of the 1966 World Cup squad. He became established in 1967, then suffered a broken leg, but was soon back in action and finished as the League's top scorer. Originally a left winger, his deadly left foot combined with speed and courage to make him one of Italy's top strikers and best-loved players. In 1969-70 he helped Cagliari to their first Italian title and was the Italian League's top scorer for the third time in four seasons. Italy's top scorer in Mexico, he netted the crucial extra-time goal — his 22nd in 21 internationals — against West Germany in the semi-final. Soon afterwards, Riva again broke a leg, in a European Championship qualifier against Austria. He turned down a £1.5 million move to Juventus in 1973, at the age of 29, but had a bad 1974 World Cup and was dropped for the last game, against Poland. After retiring he became an executive with Cagliari.

Third Success For Brazil
Mexico 1970

THE choice of venue for the ninth World Cup was a two-nation contest between Argentina and Mexico and at a FIFA Congress during the 1964 Olympics in Tokyo, Mexico, already selected as hosts for the 1968 Olympic Games, were granted the tournament. Argentina was suffering from an unstable economy at the time and that, coupled with their track record of poor World Cup support over the years, were great influencing factors in taking the tournament to Central America for the first time.

However, there were many delegates, particularly from European nations, who were unhappy with the choice of venue, largely because of Mexico's high altitude and the problems it might cause. Fortunately, most teams soon acclimatized to the thin air but the intense heat, often up to 100°F during matches, was more of a problem and one that England players, in particular, were not relishing. But then England's problems started even before they arrived in Mexico.

Engaged on a tour of Ecuador and Colombia, the team was hit by a bombshell when skipper Bobby Moore was accused by shop assistant Clara Padilla of stealing a bracelet from the jewellery shop at the Tequendama Hotel in Bogotá, the team's headquarters. Moore was detained for four days whilst the rest of the team flew on to Mexico.

It was the kind of 'frame-up' to which other celebrities visiting the notorious city had been subjected and eventually the England skipper was released and cleared of all charges due to a lack of any evidence. But the Mexicans, who were building up a hate campaign against the English, used the incident to label Moore as 'a burglar, 'jewel thief' and a 'villain caught in the act'. Undeterred, Moore led England in true professional style and did not let the incident affect his play.

The format of the 1970 World Cup was exactly the same as when the tournament was held in England four years earlier, but now international soccer had become a '13-a-side game' following the introduction of substitutes. The only minor change to the format was the tossing of a coin to decide winners if teams were level after extra-time in quarter and semi-final matches. Thankfully, such a method of deciding a match was not necessary. FIFA made another ruling — any squad member designated the number-13 shirt did not have to wear it if he was superstitious.

Italy, Uruguay and Brazil were all taking part and, should one of them win the trophy for what would be a third time, then they would be allowed to retain it. Brazil and Italy eventually met in the Final and that marked the end of the Jules Rimet Trophy, which Brazil took home as their own property.

Notable absentees in Mexico were Portugal, one of the outstanding teams of the tournament in 1966, and Argentina, one of the toughest teams in England. Making their World Cup debuts were El Salvador, who survived the so-called 'football war', Morocco, the first African finalists since 1934, and Israel. Also making their first appearance since 1930 were Peru, now managed by the former Brazilian star, Didí.

Brazil, with Pelé fit again, played the beautiful attacking football people had come to expect from them since their performance in Sweden in 1958. Indeed, they were by far the best team in Mexico. Pre-tournament odds of 7/2 confirmed Brazil as favourites with England next at 4/1 followed by Italy at 7/1 and Uruguay and West Germany, both at 9/1.

The ninth World Cup opened in spectacular style in the magnificent Azteca Stadium, which had been built for the Olympic Games two years earlier. The stadium was filled with 112,000 fans for the opening ceremony which saw the release of 50,000 coloured balloons. It was the first of the spectacular opening ceremonies now associated with major international soccer events.

The tournament also became a major TV spectacle and to fit in with television companies requests, some matches kicked off at 12 noon. This was an unpopular decision with many players and managers because the heat in Mexico at that time of day was approaching 100°F.

With the defensive attitudes of coaching taking over from skills of the 1960s, many felt the heat and rarified atmosphere of Mexico would make the ninth World Cup even more negative. But they were in for a pleasant surprise as attacking football returned, notably from those talented Brazilians and the West Germans.

There was also none of the violence that had plagued the two previous competitions. The 1970 World Cup passed without a single player being sent off, equalling the 1950 World Cup record. Mexico 1970 is remembered as the World Cup when footballing skills returned.

FIFA president Sir Stanley Rous (far right) at the opening ceremony in Mexico City.

England skipper Bobby Moore looks pensive as unfounded accusations are made against him.

1970 Qualifying Competition

AWAR between two countries, a new World Cup record score and four of the 1966 quarter-finalists all eliminated — the qualifying competition for the ninth World Cup was certainly a lively one.

There were 71 entrants divided into 16 groups. Holders England and hosts Mexico were allocated groups although, of course, they did not have to play through the qualifying stages. The only withdrawal was North Korea, the footballing nation that won the hearts of millions in England four years earlier. Because of their refusal to meet Israel, they were forced to withdraw by FIFA.

Honduras and El Salvador played each other three times. And the third meeting sparked off a full-scale war between the two nations. After each side had won on home soil, a play-off was held in Mexico City and El Salvador triumphed 3-2 with an extra-time winner. This started clashes which spilled over to the two countries. Diplomatic relations were severed and war broke out.

Of course, the nations had been at loggerheads for months and their World Cup meeting was the spark which ignited a feud that had been going on for some time. The three-day war claimed a reported death toll in excess of 10,000, with many thousands more made homeless. It is the only instance when a soccer match has triggered off a war.

There were no such problems in the European qualifying groups, but there were certainly a few surprises. Portugal, third in 1966 and hailed as one of the rising teams of European soccer, were not only dumped out of their group but also finished bottom behind less-fancied nations, Romania, Greece and Switzerland. Portugal's great team was now ageing and Eusébio was not fully fit.

The Greeks were the surprise team of Group One and were eliminated only when Romania beat Switzerland in the last game, thanks to a Michaud own-goal.

Hungary were still a major force. They had retained their Olympic title in Mexico City in 1968 and, being used to the rarified atmosphere, were tipped as likely candidates to win the Jules Rimet Trophy in 1970. However, they never made the return trip to Mexico. A surprise 3-2 defeat by Denmark meant the Magyars had to play-off against their Eastern European neighbours, Czechoslovakia. The Czechs triumphed with a convincing 4-1 win and for the first time since 1950, Hungary were absent from the World Cup finals.

Italy, the reigning European champions, did not book their passage to Mexico until their last qualifying match, but then three first-half goals against East Germany, in front of 80,000 fans in Naples, ensured that the Italians would be taking part in their seventh tournament. They were desperately keen, of course, to make up for the disappointment and embarrassment of 1966.

Northern Ireland started their campaign with two wins and a home draw with the Soviets, but the return match against the Russians proved decisive and the Irish, without the injured George Best, lost 2-0. Russia thus had little problem in qualifying for the final stages.

Sweden were back in the finals after missing 1962 and 1966 but Yugoslavia, the 1968 European Championship runners-up, were missing after finishing second to Belgium, the first qualifiers for the 1970 tournament. It was Belgium's first appearance in the final stages since 1954. Finland were the 'whipping boys' in this group, conceding 28 goals, including nine against the Yugoslavs.

Cyprus were to hold the same 'title' in Group Seven and in the away match with West Germany were on the wrong end of a 12-0 defeat. Helped by four goals from Müller and three from Overath, the Germans established a new World Cup record score. Remarkably, six months earlier Cyprus had held the West Germans to a solitary Müller goal in Nicosia.

Group Eight was the closest of all European groups and Bulgaria leap-frogged above Holland and Poland to clinch top place after their 3-1 win over Luxembourg.

Argentina were another of the 1966 quarter-finalists to miss the trip to Mexico. Clear favourites to qualify from their three-team group, they opened their campaign with defeats at Bolivia and Peru, who were managed by the former Brazilian hero, Didí. It was Didí's team who qualified from this group. His old team, Brazil, had little trouble in qualifying, too, and were the only nation to do so with a 100 per cent record. Tostão was their top scorer with nine goals. The game between Brazil and Paraguay at the Maracana Stadium on 31 August 1969 attracted a crowd of 183,341, a record for a World Cup qualifying game.

Completing the South American complement were the reigning South American champions, Uruguay, who made rather heavy going of their group matches, yet came through unscathed after another display of defensive football for which they had become renowned in England four years earlier.

El Salvador, after ten matches and a war, came through the CONCACAF group after beating Haiti in a play-off to qualify for their first finals. Israel were also in their first finals, after beating Australia in the Asia-Oceania final. The third debutants in 1970 were Morocco, who became the first African nation since Egypt in 1934 to compete in the final stages.

Results

EUROPE

Group One

12 Oct 1968 Basle	Switzerland 1	Greece 0
27 Oct 1968 Lisbon	Portugal..........3	Romania 0
23 Nov 1968 Bucharest	Romania 2	Switzerland 0
11 Dec 1968 Athens	Greece 4	Portugal..........2
16 Apr 1969 Lisbon	Portugal..........0	Switzerland 2
16 Apr 1969 Athens	Greece 2	Romania 2
4 May 1969 Oporto	Portugal..........2	Greece 2
14 May 1969 Lausanne	Switzerland 0	Romania 1
12 Oct 1969 Bucharest	Romania 1	Portugal..........0
15 Oct 1969 Salonika	Greece 4	Switzerland 1
2 Nov 1969 Berne	Switzerland 1	Portugal..........1
16 Nov 1969 Bucharest	Romania 1	Greece 1

Final Table

	P	W	D	L	F	A	Pts	
Romania	6	3	2	1	7	6	8	
Greece	6	2	3	1	13	9	7	**Romania qualified**
Switzerland	6	2	1	3	5	8	5	
Portugal	6	1	2	3	8	10	4	

Group Two

25 Sep 1968 Copenhagen	Denmark 0	Czechoslovakia. .3
20 Oct 1969 Bratislava	Czechoslovakia. .1	Denmark 0
4 May 1969 Dublin	Rep of Ireland ...1	Czechoslovakia. .2
25 May 1969 Budapest	Hungary 2	Czechoslovakia. .0
27 May 1969 Copenhagen	Denmark 2	Rep of Ireland ...0

8 Jun 1969 *Dublin*	Rep of Ireland ...1 Hungary 2
15 Jun 1969 *Copenhagen*	Denmark ....3 Hungary 2
14 Sep 1969 *Prague*	Czechoslovakia. .3 Hungary 3
7 Oct 1969 *Prague*	Czechoslovakia. .3 Rep of Ireland ...0
15 Oct 1969 *Dublin*	Rep of Ireland ...1 Denmark 1
22 Oct 1969 *Budapest*	Hungary ....3 Denmark 0
5 Nov 1969 *Budapest*	Hungary ....4 Rep of Ireland ...0

Final Table

	P	W	D	L	F	A	Pts
Czechoslovakia	6	4	1	1	12	6	9
Hungary	6	4	1	1	16	7	9
Denmark	6	2	1	3	6	10	5
Rep of Ireland	6	0	1	5	3	14	1

Play-off

3 Dec 1969 *Marseille*   Czechoslovakia. .4 Hungary 1

Czechoslovakia qualified

Group Three

23 Oct 1968 *Cardiff*	Wales ....0 Italy.............1
29 Mar 1969 *Berlin*	East Germany ...2 Italy.............2
16 Apr 1969 *Dresden*	East Germany ...2 Wales 1
22 Oct 1969 *Cardiff*	Wales ....1 East Germany ...3
4 Nov 1969 *Rome*	Italy.............4 Wales 1
22 Nov 1969 *Naples*	Italy.............3 East Germany ...0

Final Table

	P	W	D	L	F	A	Pts
Italy	4	3	1	0	10	3	7
East Germany	4	2	1	1	7	7	5
Wales	4	0	0	4	3	10	0

Italy qualified

Group Four

23 Oct 1968 *Belfast*	N. Ireland ....4 Turkey............1
11 Dec 1968 *Istanbul*	Turkey...........0 N. Ireland 3
10 Sep 1969 *Belfast*	N. Ireland ....0 Soviet Union 0
15 Oct 1969 *Kiev*	Soviet Union ....3 Turkey............0
22 Oct 1969 *Moscow*	Soviet Union ....2 N. Ireland 0
16 Nov 1969 *Istanbul*	Turkey...........1 Soviet Union 3

Final Table

	P	W	D	L	F	A	Pts
Soviet Union	4	3	1	0	8	1	7
N. Ireland	4	2	1	1	7	3	5
Turkey	4	0	0	4	2	13	0

Soviet Union qualified

Northern Ireland's Jimmy Nicholson (right) is foiled by the USSR goalkeeper Rudakov in the goalless draw in Belfast. Derek Dougan is the Irish player in the background.

Group Five

9 Oct 1968 *Stockholm*	Sweden ....5 Norway...........0
5 Dec 1968 *Strasbourg*	France ....0 Norway...........1
19 Jun 1969 *Oslo*	Norway...........2 Sweden 5
10 Sep 1969 *Oslo*	Norway...........1 France 3
15 Oct 1969 *Stockholm*	Sweden ....2 France 0
2 Nov 1969 *Paris*	France ....3 Sweden 0

Final Table

	P	W	D	L	F	A	Pts
Sweden	4	3	0	1	12	5	6
France	4	2	0	2	6	4	4
Norway	4	1	0	3	4	13	2

Sweden qualified

Group Six

19 Jun 1968 *Helsinki*	Finland...........1 Belgium 2
25 Sep 1968 *Belgrade*	Yugoslavia ....9 Finland...........1
9 Oct 1968 *Waregem*	Belgium ....6 Finland...........1
16 Oct 1968 *Brussels*	Belgium ....3 Yugoslavia 0
27 Oct 1968 *Belgrade*	Yugoslavia ....0 Spain 0
11 Dec 1968 *Madrid*	Spain ....1 Belgium 0
23 Feb 1969 *Liège*	Belgium ....2 Spain 1
30 Apr 1969 *Barcelona*	Spain ....2 Yugoslavia 1
4 Jun 1969 *Helsinki*	Finland...........1 Yugoslavia 5
25 Jun 1969 *Helsinki*	Finland...........2 Spain 0
15 Oct 1969 *Cadiz*	Spain ....6 Finland...........0
19 Oct 1969 *Skopje*	Yugoslavia ....4 Belgium 0

Final Table

	P	W	D	L	F	A	Pts
Belgium	6	4	1	1	14	8	9
Yugoslavia	6	3	1	2	19	7	7
Spain	6	2	2	2	10	6	6
Finland	6	1	0	5	6	28	2

Belgium qualified

Group Seven

19 May 1968 *Vienna*	Austria............7 Cyprus............1
13 Oct 1968 *Vienna*	Austria............0 West Germany ...2
6 Nov 1968 *Glasgow*	Scotland ....2 Austria............1
23 Nov 1968 *Nicosia*	Cyprus............0 West Germany ...1
11 Dec 1968 *Nicosia*	Cyprus............0 Scotland 5

Above: Northern Ireland's George Best, arguably the greatest player never to have played in a World Cup finals, in action against the USSR in Belfast. *Left:* Alan Gilzean of Scotland is foiled by West Germany's Maier in Hamburg.

Pelé battles against the Paraguayan defence in the vital match which decided the South American Group Two. Brazil's victory in Río de Janeiro meant that Pelé could look forward to playing in his fourth World Cup finals.

16 Apr 1969 *Glasgow*	Scotland 1	West Germany ...1	
19 Apr 1969 *Nicosia*	Cyprus............1	Austria............2	
10 May 1969 *Nuremberg*	West Germany ...1	Austria............0	
17 May 1969 *Glasgow*	Scotland 8	Cyprus............0	
21 May 1969 *Essen*	West Germany .12	Cyprus............0	
22 Oct 1969 *Hamburg*	West Germany ...3	Scotland 2	
5 Nov 1969 *Vienna*	Austria............2	Scotland 0	

Final Table

	P	W	D	L	F	A	Pts	
West Germany	6	5	1	0	20	3	11	**West Germany**
Scotland	6	3	1	2	18	7	7	**qualified**
Austria	6	3	0	3	12	7	6	
Cyprus	6	0	0	6	2	35	0	

Group Eight

4 Sep 1968 *Rotterdam*	Luxembourg.....0	Holland 2	
27 Oct 1968 *Sofia*	Bulgaria 2	Holland 0	
26 Mar 1969 *Rotterdam*	Holland 4	Luxembourg.....0	
20 Apr 1969 *Kraków*	Poland............8	Luxembourg.....1	
23 Apr 1969 *Sofia*	Bulgaria 2	Luxembourg.....1	
7 May 1969 *Rotterdam*	Holland 1	Poland............0	
15 Jun 1969 *Sofia*	Bulgaria 4	Poland............1	
7 Sep 1969 *Chorzów*	Poland............2	Holland 1	
12 Oct 1969 *Luxembourg*	Luxembourg.....1	Poland............5	
22 Oct 1969 *Rotterdam*	Holland 1	Bulgaria 1	
9 Nov 1969 *Warsaw*	Poland............3	Bulgaria 0	
7 Dec 1969 *Luxembourg*	Luxembourg.....1	Bulgaria 3	

Final Table

	P	W	D	L	F	A	Pts	
Bulgaria	6	4	1	1	12	7	9	
Poland	6	4	0	2	19	8	8	**Bulgaria qualified**
Holland	6	3	1	2	9	5	7	
Luxembourg	6	0	0	6	4	24	0	

SOUTH AMERICA

Group One

27 Jul 1969 *La Paz*	Bolivia............3	Argentina 1	
3 Aug 1969 *Lima*	Peru...............1	Argentina 0	
10 Aug 1969 *La Paz*	Bolivia............2	Peru...............1	
17 Aug 1969 *Lima*	Peru...............3	Bolivia............0	
24 Aug 1969 *Buenos Aires*	Argentina 1	Bolivia............0	
31 Aug 1969 *Buenos Aires*	Argentina 2	Peru...............2	

Final Table

	P	W	D	L	F	A	Pts	
Peru	4	2	1	1	7	4	5	**Peru qualified**
Bolivia	4	2	0	2	5	6	4	
Argentina	4	1	1	2	4	6	3	

Group Two

27 Jul 1969 *Bogotá*	Colombia 3	Venezuela 0	
2 Aug 1969 *Caracas*	Venezuela 1	Colombia 1	
6 Aug 1969 *Bogotá*	Colombia 0	Brazil 2	
7 Aug 1969 *Caracas*	Venezuela 0	Paraguay 2	
10 Aug 1969 *Bogotá*	Columbia 0	Paraguay 1	
10 Aug 1969 *Caracas*	Venezuela 0	Brazil 5	
17 Aug 1969 *Asunción*	Paraguay 0	Brazil 3	
21 Aug 1969 *Río de Janeiro*	Brazil 6	Colombia 2	
21 Aug 1969 *Asunción*	Paraguay 1	Venezuela 0	
24 Aug 1969 *Río de Janeiro*	Brazil 6	Venezuela 0	
24 Aug 1969 *Asunción*	Paraguay 2	Colombia 1	
31 Aug 1969 *Río de Janeiro*	Brazil 1	Paraguay 0	

Final Table

	P	W	D	L	F	A	Pts	
Brazil	6	6	0	0	23	2	12	
Paraguay	6	4	0	2	6	5	8	**Brazil qualified**
Colombia	6	1	1	4	7	12	3	
Venezuela	6	0	1	5	1	18	1	

Group Three

6 Jul 1969 *Guayaquil*	Ecuador 0	Uruguay..........2	
13 Jul 1969 *Santiago*	Chile...............0	Uruguay..........0	
20 Jul 1969 *Montevideo*	Uruguay..........1	Ecuador 0	
27 Jul 1969 *Santiago*	Chile...............4	Ecuador 1	
3 Aug 1969 *Guayaquil*	Ecuador 1	Chile...............1	
10 Aug 1969 *Montevideo*	Uruguay..........2	Chile...............0	

Final Table

	P	W	D	L	F	A	Pts	
Uruguay	4	3	1	0	5	0	7	**Uruguay qualified**
Chile	4	1	2	1	5	4	4	
Ecuador	4	0	1	3	2	8	1	

CONCACAF
(Central & North America)

Sub Group One

27 Nov 1968 *San José*	Costa Rica 3	Jamaica 0	
1 Dec 1968 *San José*	Jamaica 1	Costa Rica 3	
5 Dec 1968 *Tegucigalpa*	Honduras 3	Jamaica 1	
8 Dec 1968 *Tegucigalpa*	Jamaica 0	Honduras 2	
22 Dec 1968 *Tegucigalpa*	Honduras 1	Costa Rica 0	
29 Dec 1968 *San José*	Costa Rica 1	Honduras 1	

Final Table

	P	W	D	L	F	A	Pts
Honduras	4	3	1	0	7	2	7
Costa Rica	4	2	1	1	7	3	5
Jamaica	4	0	0	4	2	11	0

Honduras qualified for second phase

Sub Group Two

17 Nov 1968	*Guatemala*	Guatemala ....4 Trinidad 0
20 Nov 1968	*Guatemala*	Trinidad ....0 Guatemala 0
23 Nov 1968	*Port au Prince*	Trinidad ....0 Haiti 4
25 Nov 1968	*Port au Prince*	Haiti ....2 Trinidad 4
8 Dec 1968	*Port au Prince*	Haiti ....2 Guatemala 0
23 Feb 1969	*Guatemala*	Guatemala ....1 Haiti 1

Final Table

	P	W	D	L	F	A	Pts
Haiti	4	2	1	1	8	4	5
Guatemala	4	1	2	1	4	2	4
Trinidad	4	1	1	2	4	10	3

Haiti qualified for second phase

Sub Group Three

24 Nov 1968	*Paramaribo*	Surinam ....6 Nethlds Antilles 0
1 Dec 1968	*San Salvador*	El Salvador.......6 Surinam 0
5 Dec 1968	*Aruba*	Nethlds Antilles 2 Surinam 0
12 Dec 1968	*San Salvador*	El Salvador.......1 Nethlds Antilles 0
15 Dec 1968	*San Salvador*	Nethlds Antilles 1 El Salvador.......2
22 Dec 1968	*Paramaribo*	Surinam ....4 El Salvador.......1

Final Table

	P	W	D	L	F	A	Pts
El Salvador	4	3	0	1	10	5	6
Surinam	4	2	0	2	10	9	4
Nethlds Antilles	4	1	0	3	3	9	2

El Salvador qualified for second phase

Sub Group Four

6 Oct 1968	*Toronto*	Canada ....4 Bermuda 0
13 Oct 1968	*Toronto*	Canada ....4 United States 2
20 Oct 1968	*Hamilton*	Bermuda ....0 Canada 0
26 Oct 1968	*Atlanta*	United States ....1 Canada 0
3 Nov 1968	*Kansas City*	United States ....6 Bermuda 2
11 Nov 1968	*Bermuda*	Bermuda ....0 United States 2

Final Table

	P	W	D	L	F	A	Pts
United States	4	3	0	1	11	6	6
Canada	4	2	1	1	8	3	5
Bermuda	4	0	1	3	2	12	1

United States qualified for second phase

Second Phase

20 Apr 1969	*Port au Prince*	Haiti ....2 United States 0
11 May 1969	*San Diego*	United States ....0 Haiti 1
8 Jun 1969	*Tegucigalpa*	Honduras ....1 El Salvador.......0
15 Jun 1969	*San Salvador*	El Salvador.......3 Honduras 0

Play-off

28 Jun 1969 *Mexico City* El Salvador.......3 Honduras 2
El Salvador and Haiti qualified for CONCACAF final

Final

| 21 Sep 1969 | *Port au Prince* | Haiti ....1 El Salvador.......2 |
| 28 Sep 1969 | *San Salvador* | El Salvador.......0 Haiti ....3 |

Play-off

8 Oct 1969 *Kingston* El Salvador.......1 Haiti 0
El Salvador qualified

ASIA-OCEANIA

Sub Group One

10 Oct 1969	*Seoul*	Japan ....1 Australia 3
12 Oct 1969	*Seoul*	South Korea .....2 Japan 2
14 Oct 1969	*Seoul*	Australia ....2 South Korea 1
16 Oct 1969	*Seoul*	Australia ....1 Japan 1
18 Oct 1969	*Seoul*	Japan ....0 South Korea 2
20 Oct 1969	*Seoul*	South Korea .....1 Australia 1

Final Table

	P	W	D	L	F	A	Pts
Australia	4	2	2	0	7	4	6
South Korea	4	1	2	1	6	5	4
Japan	4	0	2	2	4	8	2

Australia qualified for second phase

Second Phase

| 23 Nov 1969 | *Lourenço Marques* | Australia ....1 Rhodesia ....1 |
| 27 Nov 1969 | *Lourenço Marques* | Rhodesia ....0 Australia ....0 |

Play-off

1 Dec 1969 *Lourenço Marques* Australia ....3 Rhodesia 1
Australia qualified for Asia-Oceania final

Sub Group Two

| 28 Sep 1969 | *Tel Aviv* | Israel ....4 New Zealand .....0 |
| 1 Oct 1969 | *Tel Aviv* | New Zealand .....0 Israel ....2 |

Israel qualified for Asia-Oceania final
North Korea withdrew

Final

| 4 Dec 1969 | *Tel Aviv* | Israel ....1 Australia ....0 |
| 14 Dec 1969 | *Sydney* | Australia ....1 Israel ....1 |

Israel qualified

AFRICA

First Phase

| 17 Nov 1968 | *Algiers* | Algeria............1 Tunisia...........2 |
| 29 Dec 1968 | *Tunis* | Tunisia...........0 Algeria...........0 |

Tunisia qualified for second phase

| 3 Nov 1968 | *Casablanca* | Morocco ....1 Senegal ....0 |
| 1 Jan 1969 | *Dakar* | Senegal ....2 Morocco ....1 |

Play-off
13 Feb 1969 *Las Palmas* Morocco ....2 Senegal 0
Morocco qualified for second phase

| 26 Jan 1969 | *Tripoli* | Libya ....2 Ethiopia ....0 |
| 9 Feb 1969 | *Addis Adaba* | Ethiopia..........5 Libya ....1 |

Ethiopia qualified for second phase

| 27 Oct 1968 | *Ndola* | Zambia ....4 Sudan ....2 |
| 8 Nov 1968 | *Khartoum* | Sudan ....4 Zambia ....2 |

Sudan qualified for second phase because they scored more goals in the second game

| 7 Dec 1968 | *Lagos* | Nigeria ....1 Cameroon ....1 |
| 22 Dec 1968 | *Douala* | Camaroon........2 Nigeria ....3 |

Nigeria qualified for second phase
Ghana received a bye into the second phase

Second Phase

| 27 Apr 1969 | *Tunis* | Tunisia...........0 Morocco ....0 |
| 18 May 1969 | *Casablanca* | Morocco ....0 Tunisia...........0 |

Play-off
13 Jun 1969 *Marseille* Morocco ....2 Tunisia...........2
Morocco qualified for the third phase on toss of a coin

| 4 May 1969 | *Addis Adaba* | Ethiopia..........1 Sudan ....1 |
| 11 May 1969 | *Khartoum* | Sudan ....3 Ethiopia ....1 |

Sudan qualified for third phase

| 10 May 1969 | *Ibadan* | Nigeria ....2 Ghana ....1 |
| 18 May 1969 | *Accra* | Ghana ....1 Nigeria ....1 |

Nigeria qualified for third phase

Third Phase

13 Sep 1969	*Lagos*	Nigeria ....2 Sudan 2
21 Sep 1969	*Casablanca*	Morocco ....2 Nigeria 1
3 Oct 1969	*Khartoum*	Sudan ....3 Nigeria 3
10 Oct 1969	*Khartoum*	Sudan ....0 Morocco 0
26 Oct 1969	*Casablanca*	Morocco ....3 Sudan 0
8 Nov 1969	*Ibadan*	Nigeria ....2 Morocco 0

Final Table

	P	W	D	L	F	A	Pts
Morocco	4	2	1	1	5	3	5
Nigeria	4	1	2	1	8	7	4
Sudan	4	0	3	1	5	8	3

1970 Tournament

Group One

Vladimir Kaplichni of the USSR.

Right: Hernández (6) and Pérez (on ground) combine against the USSR's Muntian (far left), Shesterniev (14) and Asatiani (11) in the opening game of the 1970 World Cup.

Anatoli Bishovets of the USSR.

MEXICO 0   SOVIET UNION 0 (Half-time 0-0)

Azteca Stadium, Mexico City, 31 May
Attendance: 107,000

THE curtain-raiser of the 1970 World Cup turned out to be a tiresome affair, just as the opening match at Wembley had proved four years earlier.

Mexico went into the game without their great half-back Alberto Onofre, who broke a leg in a practice match four days before the start of the tournament. But they still had strength in depth and managed to play a defensive game and ensured they started their campaign without defeat. The Soviets also approached the game with the same attitude and the result was a drab, goalless draw.

The West German referee did not contribute to the flow of the game either, adhering to the letter of the law as directed by FIFA. They wanted no repeats of the vicious tackles that were seen in 1962 and 1966. And whilst the opening game of the tournament suffered because of the tight refereeing, the 16 nations took note of the officials' intentions in this tournament and it went through 32 matches without a player being sent off.

The best two chances of this match fell to López, in quick succession in the first-half, but it was only thanks to good goalkeeping that the Russian goal remained intact.

Pusatch made history when he replaced Shesterniev at half-time to become the World Cup's first substitute.

Mexico: Calderón; Vantolrá, Peña, Gúzman, Pérez, Hernández, Pulido, Velarde(Munguia), Valdivia, Fragoso, Lopéz.
Soviet Union: Kavasashvili; Kaplichni, Lovchev, Logofet, Shesterniev(Pusatch), Asatiani, Muntian, Serebrianikov, Bishovets, Evriuzhikan, Nodija(Khmelnitski).
Referee: Kurt Tschenser (West Germany)

BELGIUM 3   EL SALVADOR 0 (Half-time 1-0)

Azteca Stadium, Mexico City, 3 June
Attendance: 92,000

THE El Salvador team made up of part-time clerks, plumbers, students and accountants were no match for the more professional Belgian side. But the enthusiasm of the Central Americans was enormous and they won many friends in the Azteca Stadium with their non-stop display of running.

Despite the scoreline, Belgium made heavy going of their win and their captain, Paul

Van Himst, missed several chances. The El Salvador goalkeeper was, however, their hero and his performance kept the score to a respectable three goals.

Belgium's target-man, Van Moer, opened the scoring in the 12th minute but they had to wait more than 40 minutes for their second goal, when he found the net again. Lambert wrapped up the proceedings 13 minutes from time from the penalty-spot.

Belgium: Piot; Heylens, Thissen, Dewalque, Dockx, Semmeling(Poleunis), Van Moer, Devrindt, Van Himst, Lambert, Puis.
Scorers: Van Moer 2, Lambert (pen)
El Salvador: Magana; Rivas, Mariona, Osorio, Manzano(Cortés-Méndez), Quintanilla, Vásquez, Cabezas, Rodríguez, Martínez, Aparicio.
Referee: Andrei Radulescu (Romania)

SOVIET UNION 4   BELGIUM 1 (Half-time 1-0)

Azteca Stadium, Mexico City, 6 June
Attendance: 59,000

ANOTHER large crowd at the Azteca Stadium saw Russia go to the top of Group One with a powerful display. The Soviets took charge right from the onset and proved to be far too powerful for the Belgians. The Russian defence was well marshalled by Shesterniev and the Belgian forwards could not find a way through.

Bishovets scored with a 30-yard drive in the 15th minute, when his shot went under the 'keeper's body. The high altitude probably contributed to the goal.

It was not until the second half that the Russians showed their true worth when a three-goal feast destroyed Belgium. Asatiani made it 2-0 in the 56th minute and seven minutes later, Bishovets scored his second goal of the game. Khmelnitski made it 4-0 with 14 minutes remaining before Lambert scored a consolation goal four minutes from time.

The Soviets had always been renowned for their solid defence, but they had now found their way to goal and such was the impressive nature of their win that the bookmakers cut their odds dramatically.

Soviet Union: Kavasashvili; Afonin, Dzodzuashvili(Kiselev), Kaplichni(Lovchev), Khurtsilava, Shesterniev, Asatiani, Muntian, Bishovets, Evriuzhikan, Khmelnitski.
Scorers: Bishovets 2, Asatiani, Khmelnitski
Belgium: Piot; Heylens, Thissen, Dewalque, Jeck, Dockx, Semmeling, Van Moer, Van Himst, Puis, Lambert.
Scorer: Lambert
Referee: Rudolf Scheurer (Switzerland)

MEXICO 4   EL SALVADOR 0 (Half-time 1-0)

Azteca Stadium, Mexico City, 7 June
Attendance: 103,000

THIS game was marred by a controversial refereeing decision just before the interval and one had to sympathize with the El Salvador players.

Mexico attacked from the kick-off and an early goal looked assured. But they could not find the net and, as the first half wore on, their players and fans alike became frustrated.

With half-time only seconds away, the Egyptian referee blew for a foul to El Salvador. But it was the Mexican Padilla who took the kick and his pass found Valdivia, who scored. The El Salvador players were stunned and even more stunned when the referee allowed

Gustavo Peña of Mexico.

El Saldavor, one of the 'minnows' of the 1970 World Cup, line-up for a game prior to the tournament. Back row (left to right): Dr Romero, Magana, Vázquez, Mariona, Quintanilla, Rivas, Landaverde, José Santacolomba (assistant trainer). Front row: Rodríguez, Cabezas, Martínez, Monge, Acevedo.

Group One – Final Table

	P	W	D	L	F	A	Pts
Soviet Union	3	2	1	0	6	1	5
Mexico	3	2	1	0	5	0	5
Belgium	3	1	0	2	4	5	2
El Salvador	3	0	0	3	0	9	0

the goal to stand. They argued for at least four minutes and two players were booked, but referee Kandil would not change his decision.

El Salvador refused to retrieve the ball from the back of the net to restart the game and the referee had to place it on the centre-spot for the kick-off. He insisted on a player touching the ball and immediately blew for half-time. Had the incident happened at any other time than just before the interval, the entire El Salvador team would probably have walked off the pitch.

Many fans were indeed surprised to see El Salvador return for the second half, but they may as well have stayed in the dressing-room because they were so demoralized and had lost heart. A minute after the start of the second half, Valdivia increased Mexico's lead and ten minutes later, Fragoso stabbed the ball home to make it 3-0.

Basaguren made World Cup history seven minutes from time when he became the first substitute to score and to replace a substitute.

Mexico: Calderón; Vantolrá, Peña, Gúzman, Pérez, González, Munguia, Valdivia, Borja(Lopéz [Basaguren]), Fragoso, Padilla.
Scorers: Valdivia 2, Fragoso, Basaguren
El Salvador: Magana; Rivas, Mariona, Osorio, Cortés-Méndez(Monge), Quintanilla, Vásquez, Cabezas, Rodríguez, Martínez, Aparicio(Méndez).
Referee: Alì Kandil (Egypt/United Arab Republic)

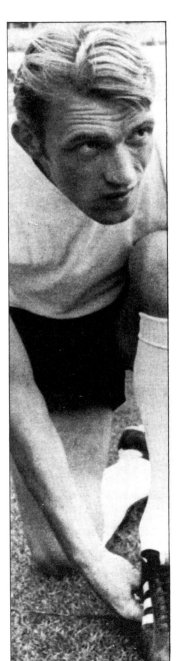
Paul Van Himst of Belgium.

SOVIET UNION 2   EL SALVADOR 0 (Half-time 0-0)
Azteca Stadium, Mexico City, 10 June
Attendance: 89,000

AFTER the experience of the Mexico game, when they were on the wrong end of a dreadful piece of refereeing, the El Salvadorians hauled themselves back for their daunting struggle against the Soviets. And what a show they gave as they held their more illustrious opponents for over 50 minutes.

The Russians once again showed what a good defence they had, but their forwards could not find the target in a goalless first half. Despite the half-time scoreline, one sensed a Russian victory would be the only result at the end of 90 minutes.

When their goals came, both were made by Muntian and scored by Bishovets, the first in the 51st minute and the second 16 minutes from time.

El Salvador went out of the tournament as the only team not to score a goal, but they certainly made friends along the way and manager Hernán Carrasco, called in to take charge of the team at the 11th hour, did a good job in the circumstances.

Soviet Union: Kavasashvili; Afonin, Dzodzuashvili, Khurtsilava, Shesterniev, Kiselev(Asatiani) Muntian, Serebrianikov, Bishovets, Pusatch(Evriuzhikan), Khmelnitski.
Scorer: Bishovets 2
El Salvador: Magana; Rivas, Mariona, Castro, Osorio, Vásquez, Portillo, Cabezas(Aparicio), Rodríguez(Sermeno), Méndez, Monge.
Referee: Ricardo Hormazabal Díaz (Chile)

MEXICO 1   BELGIUM 0 (Half-time 1-0)
Azteca Stadium, Mexico City, 11 June
Attendance: 105,000

WITH more than 100,000 fans displaying the utmost partisanship, it must have been an intimidating time for referee Coerezza and it would appear that the Argentinian official felt the pressure, as Mexico benefited from another dubious decision.

Mexico needed only to draw to qualify for the quarter-finals and Belgium, who had to win, seemed to be in low spirits. The hosts surprised their own fans by attacking from the start of what turned out to be a thrilling game.

The only goal came in the 15th minute, when Valdivia ran into the prostrate Jeck in the penalty area. Jeck had just made a clearance and was still on the ground. Remarkably, the referee awarded Mexico a penalty and Peña stepped up to strike the ball home.

Belgium, unlike El Salvador, did not give up, but at times they let their emotions get the better of them and this probably contributed to their downfall.

Mexico reached the quarter-finals for the first time in their history and, despite the dubious nature of the goal, the whole of Mexico City celebrated.

Mexico: Calderón; Vantolrá, Gúzman, Peña, Pérez, González, Munguia, Pulido, Padilla, Fragoso, Valdivia(Basaguren).
Scorer: Peña (pen)
Belgium: Piot; Heylens, Jeck, Dockx, Thissen, Dewalque, Poleunis(Devrindt), Semmeling, Van Moer, Van Himst, Puis.
Referee: Angel Norberto Coerezza (Argentina)

Group Two

URUGUAY 2   ISRAEL 0 (Half-time 1-0)

Cuauhtemoc Stadium, Puebla, 2 June
Attendance: 20,000

THE Israeli amateurs were no match for the powerful and well organized Uruguayans, who showed themselves as potential world champions after the opening game.

Luís Cubilla tormented the Israeli defence every time he got the ball and Esparrago and Maneiro were a constant threat. Only a fine performance by Israel's goalkeeper, Vissoker, prevented a barrage of goals.

Uruguay were without their classy winger, Júlio Morales, who was sidelined due to a knee operation but was hopeful of returning to the side before the end of the competition. Uruguay suffered another severe blow in the 13th minute when they lost Pedro Rocha with a groin injury. It was to be the end of the World Cup for him.

Maneiro headed Uruguay into the lead in the 23rd minute and five minutes into the second half, Mujica made it 2-0. The score could have been increased, but a Cubilla shot from six yards struck the crossbar.

Coached by the Argentine-born Eduardo Hohberg, who appeared in the 1954 finals, Uruguay served notice that they were a threat to the more fancied nations like Brazil and England.

Uruguay: Mazurkiewicz; Ubiñas, Mujica, Montero-Castillo, Ancheta, Matosas, Cubilla, Esparrago, Maneiro, Rocha(Cortés), Losada.
Scorers: Maneiro, Mujica
Israel: Vissoker; Rosen, Daniel, Talbi(Bar), Schwager, Rosenthal, Shum, Spiegler, Spiegel, Faygenbaum, Rom(Vollach).
Referee: Bob Davidson (Scotland)

ITALY 1   SWEDEN 0 (Half-time 1-0)

Luis Dosal Stadium, Toluca, 3 June
Attendance: 14,000

AT nearly 8,800 feet above sea level, the Toluca ground was the highest of all those used for the series and at the end of 90 minutes the high altitude had taken its toll on both sets of players.

The Italian skipper, Rivera, was left out of the team and his midfield role went to Mazzola. Rivera, not unnaturally, was far from happy at the decision.

Italy impressed in the first half and threw everything into attack in the first quarter of an hour and they were rewarded with the only goal of the game when Domenghini's shot was fortunate to find the net.

From a short corner of the left, Domenghini passed to Facchetti before taking the return and hitting the ball from outside the area. Sweden's reserve 'keeper, Hellström, seemed to have the shot covered but he let it slip under his body and into the goal.

Mordechai Spiegler of Israel.

Shamuel Rosenthal of Israel.

Luigi Riva of Italy.

Riva fires in a shot against Sweden.

Roberto Boninsegna of Italy.

Sweden made a spirited comeback in the second half but in the end both teams were beaten by the rarified atmosphere and heat and 22 pairs of legs played out the closing stages of the match without much conviction.

Italy: Albertosi; Burgnich, Facchetti, Cera, Niccolai(Rosato), Bertini, Domenghini, Mazzola, Boninsegna, de Sisti, Riva.
Scorer: Domenghini
Sweden: Hellström; Nordqvist, Grip, Svensson, Axelsson, B.Larsson(Niklasson), Grahn, Eriksson(Ejderstedt), Kindvall, Cronqvist, Olsson.
Referee: Jack Taylor (England)

URUGUAY 0   ITALY 0 (Half-time 0-0)

Cuauhtemoc Stadium, Puebla, 6 June
Attendance: 30,000

WITH one win to their credit, these sides were content in playing for the draw. Uruguay showed, as they had done in 1966, that they were masters of the defensive game. And the Italians were also adept at that side of the game.

What few chances were created were wasted in what was the most boring game of the tournament. Both sets of supporters booed their own players off the pitch at the end of 90 minutes and Luigi Riva commented: "It must have been bad to watch."

Uruguay: Mazurkiewicz; Ubiñas, Ancheta, Matosas, Mujica, Cortés, Montero-Castillo, Maneiro, Cubilla, Esparrago, Bareño(Zubia).
Italy: Albertosi; Burgnich, Cera, Rosato, Facchetti, de Sisti, Bertini, Mazzola, Domenghini (Furino), Boninsegna, Riva.
Referee: Rudolf Glockner (East Germany)

Uruguayan goalkeeper Ladislao Mazurkiewicz and Italy's Mario Bertini watch as defender Ubiñas clears in a rare goalmouth incident.

Ferruccio Valcareggi, manager of Italy.

Opposite page: Italy's Giancarlo de Sisti (left) and Ildo Maneiro of Uruguay battle for possession.

Uruguay's Bareño (17), Montero-Castillo (5) and Mujića (6) form a wall as Riva tries to break the goalless deadlock in Puebla.

Shraga Bar of Israel.

ISRAEL 1   SWEDEN 1 (Half-time 0-0)

Luis Dosal Stadium, Toluca, 7 June
Attendance: 9,000

SWEDEN made five changes from the side beaten by Italy, including the recall of their hitherto first-choice goalkeeper, Sven Larsson.

The first half was a one-sided affair with Sweden dominating proceedings. However, Israel were not pushovers and did well to hold their opponents to a goalless first half.

Israel played with more imagination than in their opening match and came out for the second half with more confidence, although they fell behind to a Turesson goal in the 57th minute. Sweden's lead lasted only three minutes, however, before Spiegler scored one of the best goals of the tournament. He picked up a loose ball in the middle of the field and strode through the defence before hitting the ball from 25 yards.

Sweden: G.Larsson; Selander, Axelsson, Grip, Svensson, B.Larsson, Nordahl, Turesson, Kindvall, Persson(Dalsson), Olsson.
Scorer: Turesson
Israel: Vissoker; Primo, Rosen, Bar, Rosenthal; Shum, Schwager, Spiegel, Vollach(Schuruk), Spiegler, Faygenbaum.
Scorer: Spiegler
Referee: Seyoun Tarrekegn (Ethiopia)

SWEDEN 1   URUGUAY 0 (Half-time 0-0)

Cuauhtemoc Stadium, Puebla, 10 June
Attendance: 18,000

SWEDEN had to win by two clear goals in order to qualify for the quarter-finals, but scoring against the Uruguayan defence was one of the hardest tasks of this tournament and finding two goals was something which only the very best attacks could manage.

Before the match there were rumours that the Brazilian referee, De Moraes, had been offered a bribe — which were later unfounded — and a replacement official was appointed.

Uruguay set about shutting out the Swedish attack and they certainly enhanced their reputation for destroying a game with their defensive tactics, preventing Sweden from playing attacking football.

The game was heading for another 0-0 scoreline when the Swedish substitute, Grahn, who had been on the pitch for little over five minutes, scored the only goal of the game with a header in the dying seconds.

Sweden: G.Larsson, Selander, Nordqvist, Axlesson, Grip, Svensson, B.Larsson, Eriksson, Kindvall(Turesson), Niklasson(Grahn), Persson.
Scorer: Grahn
Uruguay: Mazurkiewicz; Ubiñas, Ancheta, Matosas, Mujica, Montero-Castillo, Maneiro, Cortés, Esparrago(Fontes), Zubia, Losada.
Referee: Henry Landauer (United States)

Giacinto Facchetti, Italy's captain

ISRAEL 0   ITALY 0

Luis Dosal Stadium, Toluca, 11 June
Attendance: 9,000

ITALY might have considered themselves already into the quarter-finals — after all, only defeat at the hands of little Israel would stop them — but there was still the memory of their 1966 defeat by North Korea.

Ove Grahn turns away after scoring the winner against Uruguay.

Italy's Sandro Mazzola gets past an Israeli defender but the result was yet another goalless draw.

The threat of another embarrassing reverse seemed to prey on the Italian players' minds and they made a nervous start. Hardly prepared to play attacking football, they relied on their defence to carry them into the next phase of the competition. And when they did break out of defence, they were thwarted by Israel's outstanding goalkeeper, Vissoker.

Italy eventually gave their skipper, and reigning European Footballer of the Year, Gianni Rivera his first game when he came on as a second-half substitute for Domenghini, but his presence did little to change the Italian approach and they held out for a goalless draw.

The Italian style of football was borne out by the harsh statistic that they topped Group Two, yet had scored only one goal. They had not, of course, conceded any — and that was their aim.

Italy: Albertosi; Burgnich, Facchetti, Cera, Rosato, Bertini, Domenghini(Rivera), Mazzola, Boninsegna, de Sisti, Riva.
Israel: Vissoker; Primo, Bello, Bar, Rosenthal, Rosen, Shum, Spiegel, Faygenbaum(Rom), Spiegler, Schwager.
Referee: Antonio De Moraes (Brazil)

Group Three

ENGLAND 1   ROMANIA 0 (Half-time 0-0)
Jalisco Stadium, Guadalajara, 2 June
Attendance: 50,000

ENGLAND arrived in Mexico with a stronger squad than that which had lifted the Jules Rimet Trophy on home soil four years earlier and Alf Ramsey, the man who told the world that England would win the 1966 World Cup, said before the latest campaign: "We do not fear any team. We are going to be champions for the second time."

England's new 4-4-2 line-up took the field to catcalls and boos from the Mexican fans, who had been building a campaign of hate against the English. And when Ramsey criticized the Jalisco pitch, he did nothing to improve relations between the two countries.

Romania also gave England some rough treatment, but of a different kind. Mocanu, in particular, was responsible for some punishing tackles. After the way the Mexico-Russia match had been handled, it was perhaps surprising to see the Belgian referee, Loraux, allow so many fouls to go unpunished.

Dembrowski missed an easy chance to open the scoring in the first half when his effort hit the crossbar. Then Mocanu put Keith Newton out of the game after 50 minutes and his replacement, Tommy Wright, also received the same treatment from the tough Romanian.

The only goal of the game was scored by Geoff Hurst after 65 minutes. He carried on where he had left off four years earlier and scored with a well-taken left-foot shot low into the net.

England: Banks; Newton(Wright), Cooper, Mullery, Labone, Moore, Lee(Osgood), Ball, R.Charlton, Hurst, Peters.
Scorer: Hurst
Romania: Adamache; Salmareanu, Lupescu, Dinu, Mocanu, Dumitru, Nunweiler, Dembrowski, Tataru(Neagu), Dumitrache, Lucescu.
Referee: Vital Loraux (Belgium)

Roberto Rosato of Italy.

Alan Mullery of England is brought down by a Romanian defender in Guadalajara.

Geoff Hurst, hat-trick hero of the 1966 World Cup Final, opens his account in the 1970 tournament with a goal against Romania. Steve Adamache is the goalkeeper.

Martin Peters and Geoff Hurst are beaten by Romanian full-back Ludovic Salmareanu (2).

Gérson of Brazil.

Pelé and Tostão prepare to meet a centre against the Czechs. Defender Karel Dobias looks apprehensive.

Adamache clutches the ball as Hurst challenges.

Goalkeeper Felix of Brazil.

BRAZIL 4   CZECHOSLOVAKIA 1 (Half-time 1-1)

Jalisco Stadium, Guadalajara, 3 June
Attendance: 52,000

AFTER being hacked and chopped out of the 1966 tournament, Brazil were anxious to make a good start in the opening game of their ninth campaign, which was a repeat of the 1962 Final.

Now managed by one of the stars of the 1962 team, Mario Zagalo, who had replaced the controversial João Saldanha three months earlier, Brazil were again playing the kind of attractive, attacking football which had won them many admirers in the late 1950s and early 1960s. The personnel had changed, but the flair was the same.

Pelé was back, despite his threat to retire after the 1966 tournament, and he was now at his peak. In the four years since 1966, Brazil had developed many new talented players, like Carlos Alberto, Clodoaldo and Tostão, whose presence in Mexico was uncertain due to him undergoing an eye operation in the United States shortly before the start of the tournament.

Despite showing that great attacking flair, there was a question mark over the Brazilian defence and goalkeeper Felix was not regarded as one of the world's finest. Their defence showed its vulnerability after only 11 minutes, when they allowed Petras to open the scoring, but that goal was what the Brazilians needed and they proceded to take charge of the game.

Brazil equalized in the 24th minute from a free-kick when Jairzinho went on a 'dummy' run whilst Rivelino bent the ball around the defensive wall.

But the most spectacular piece of action came just before half-time — it was a Pelé shot which did not find the net. From inside his own half, and a full 60 yards from the opposing goal, the great Brazilian spotted the Czech 'keeper, Viktor, well out of his goal. Pelé sent a high ball goalwards and it bounced inches wide of the post with the goalkeeper frantically

Brazil's famous trainer, Americo.

Gérson bursts through the Czech defence as Brazil capture their old form to sweep aside their opponents, 4-1.

Pelé's goal against Czechoslovakia.

scrambling back to recover. It was a moment of sheer genius that only a player of Pelé's talent could improvise.

The Czechs had a couple of chances early in the second half, but once Pelé scored after taking Gérson's long pass on his chest in the 59th minute, it was one-way traffic. Pelé's goal meant that he had scored in four successive tournaments, something Uwe Seeler also achieved in 1970.

Jairzinho made it 3-1 just after the hour, when he took a pass from Gérson in what appeared to be an offside position. However, there was no disputing Jairzinho's second and Brazil's fourth goal, nine minutes from time when he beat four men before scoring.

Brazil opened their campaign with an emphatic win and clearly showed why they were favourites to become the permanent holders of the Jules Rimet Trophy.

Brazil: Felix; Carlos Alberto, Piazza, Brito, Everaldo, Clodoaldo, Gérson(Paulo Cesar), Jairzinho, Tostão, Pelé, Rivelino.
Scorers: Rivelino, Pelé, Jairzinho 2
Czechoslovakia: Viktor; Dobias, Migas, Horvath, Hagara, Hrdlicka(Kvašniák), Kuna, F.Vesely (B.Vesely), Petras, Adamec, Jokl.
Scorer: Petras
Referee: Ramón Barreto Ruiz (Uruguay)

Jairzinho, the exciting winger who scored in every game as Brazil won the World Cup in 1970.

Francis Lee gets in a goal-bound header but Felix prevented a score.

ROMANIA 2   CZECHOSLOVAKIA 1 (Half-time 0-1)

Jalisco Stadium, Guadalajara, 6 June
Attendance: 56,000

CZECHOSLOVAKIA found it necessary to make five changes after their opening defeat and there was a recall for Kvašniák, who had played in the 1962 Final. But the changes did little to improve the Czechs' performance and they offered little as Romania gave a polished display, which did not rely on the rough stuff they had served up in their opening game against England.

A diving header by Petras in the third minute gave the Czechs the lead but, as the game progressed, the Romanians became more dominant and in the 52nd minute Neagu managed to squeeze the ball between the post and goalkeeper from an acute angle after a run from the left. Fifteen minutes from time, Neagu was involved in Romania's second goal when he was rugby-tackled in the penalty area by Jan Zlocka. Dumitrache had no trouble with the spot-kick, sending the goalkeeper the wrong way.

The Czechs relied on Petras too much and in the end he burned himself out in the heat and rarified atmosphere. The Romanians, though, paced themselves well.

Romania: Adamache; Salmareanu, Lupescu, Dinu, Mocanu, Dumitru (Ghergheli), Nunweiler, Dembrowski, Neagu, Dumitrache, Lucescu(Tataru).
Scorers: Neagu, Dumitrache (pen)
Czechoslovakia: Vencel; Dobias, Migas, Horvath, Zlocka, Kuna, Kvašniák, B.Vesely, Petras, Jurkanin(Adamec), Jokl(F.Vesely).
Scorer: Petras
Referee: Diego de Leo (Mexico)

BRAZIL 1   ENGLAND 0 (Half-time 0-0)

Jalisco Stadium, Guadalajara, 7 June
Attendance: 66,000

THIS is the game that would have been a fitting finale to the tournament, but when the 1970 World Cup Final was staged two weeks later, England were no longer in the tournament and the expected final encounter between the 1962 and 1966 champions never materialized.

England were certainly a match for the South Americans and were unlucky to lose by a solitary goal. The Jalisco Stadium was full to capacity and the large crowd was to witness a classic game, played in intense heat which saw the England players each lose at least half a stone in weight.

The save they still talk about. Gordon Banks somehow scoops Pelé's header away from goal. Tostão is open-mouthed.

Jairzinho shoots Brazil ahead in the 59th minute after a brilliant pass from Pelé. England's players are Banks (1), Terry Cooper (11) and Brian Labone (15).

England were without Keith Newton, injured in the first game, whilst Brazil were missing the midfield skills of Gérson, also injured in his country's opening match.

For the England players there was the added disadvantage of having their night's sleep ruined by hundreds of Mexican fans chanting, honking car horns and generally making a lot of noise outside England's hotel, the Guadalajara Hilton. The actions of these fans went without intervention from the police.

England's attack was on top in the first quarter of an hour and came close to scoring, but the first half remained scoreless.

The only goal of the game came in the 59th minute, when Tostão worked the ball well on the left side of the penalty area. He crossed to Pelé, who brilliantly laid the ball off into the path of Jairzinho to blast past Gordon Banks. The England 'keeper had no chance with the shot and it was due only to his earlier magnificent save at the foot of the post, when he scooped a Pelé header off the line, that England were still in the match.

England went in search of an equalizer and shortly after coming on as substitute, Jeff

Paulo Cesar watches as a Bobby
Charlton shot sails goalwards.
England's Martin Peters is in
support.

Everaldo gets the better of Hurst.

Jairzinho, the flying winger, rounds
Terry Cooper.

Jairzinho again, this time getting
the better of Francis Lee.

Paulo Cesar of Brazil.

Astle had a perfect chance when the ball dropped to his feet after a defensive mistake. But the ball fell to his weaker left foot and he failed to hit the target. Shortly before, Astle had set up Alan Ball but the England midfielder miskicked.

Two more chances fell to Ball in the closing stages but he failed to convert either into a goal, although one of his efforts hit the bar.

Brazil: Felix; Carlos Alberto, Brito, Piazza, Everaldo, Clodoaldo, Rivelino, Paulo Cesar, Jairzinho, Tostão(Roberto), Pelé.
Scorer: Jairzinho
England: Banks; Wright, Cooper, Mullery, Labone, Moore, Lee(Astle), Ball, R.Charlton(Bell), Hurst, Peters.
Referee: Abraham Klein (Israel)

BRAZIL 3   ROMANIA 2 (Half-time 2-1)

Jalisco Stadium, Guadalajara, 10 June
Attendance: 50,000

ROMANIA exposed the weaknesses in the Brazilian defence which many had suspected but, despite the narrow scoreline, the result flattered the Europeans, who were not in the same class as their opponents.

Dumitrache was the lone hero of the Romanian forward line but his defence found it necessary to resort to rough tactics again and this time hard man Mocanu was joined in the role of villain by Dinu. Mocanu was certainly very lucky to stay on the field for the full 90 minutes.

Pelé put Brazil in front after 19 minutes, from a free-kick, and three minutes later, Jairzinho scored his fourth goal in three matches from close range.

After conceding the second goal, Romania withdrew goalkeeper Adamache and replaced

Top: Pelé scores one of his two goals against Romania. (bottom): Another Pelé effort against a gallant Romanian side that fought all the way before going down 3-2.

Edú of Brazil.

Rivelino, played against England but missed the game against Romania.

him with their normal first-choice 'keeper, Raducanu, who had been sidelined for disciplinary reasons after too many late-night returns to the team's hotel.

Romania pulled a goal back through Dumitrache in the 34th minute, but continual Brazilian pressure brought them another goal midway through the second half, when Pelé scored his second of the game to give his side maximum points. Dembrowski pulled one back for Romania five minutes from time.

Brazil: Felix; Carlos Alberto, Brito, Fontana, Everaldo(Marco Antonio), Clodoaldo(Edú), Piazza, Jairzinho, Tostão, Pelé, Paulo Cesar.
Scorers: Jairzinho, Pelé 2
Romania: Adamache(Raducanu); Salmareanu, Lupescu, Dumitru, Mocanu, Neagu, Dinu, Nunweiler, Dembrowski, Dumitrache(Tataru), Lucescu.
Scorers: Dumitrache, Dembrowski.
Referee: Ferdinand Marschall (Austria)

ENGLAND 1   CZECHOSLOVAKIA 0 (Half-time 0-0)

Jalisco Stadium, Guadalajara, 11 June
Attendance: 49,000

ENGLAND needed to draw to qualify for the quarter-finals and whilst they successfully progressed to the next stage of the competition, were unimpressive, particularly after their great showing against Brazil.

Bobby Charlton equalled Billy Wright's record of 105 England caps and his brother Jack was recalled to the reorganized England team. But the overall team performance left many wondering whether they were capable of holding on to the trophy.

England's goal came from the penalty-spot after Vladimir Hagara was penalized for handball in what looked like and accidental offence. The French referee later said that he had awarded the penalty for a foul on Colin Bell! Debutant Allan Clarke stepped up to stroke home the penalty.

England went shakily into the quarter-finals, whilst the Czechs packed their bags and went home. Upon their return, their manager was sacked and several players suspended because of their performance, poor attitude and fighting amongst themselves.

England: Banks; Newton, Cooper, Mullery, J.Charlton, Moore, Bell, Peters, Clarke, Astle (Osgood), R.Charlton(Ball).
Scorer: Clarke (pen)
Czechoslovakia: Viktor; Dobias, Migas, Hrivnak, Hagara, Pollak, Kuna, F.Vesely, Petras, Adamec, Capkovic(Jokl).
Referee: René Machin (France)

Group Three – Final Table

	P	W	D	L	F	A	Pts
Brazil	3	3	0	0	8	3	6
England	3	2	0	1	2	1	4
Romania	3	1	0	2	4	5	2
Czechoslovakia	3	0	0	3	2	7	0

Christo Bonev, put Bulgaria 2-0
ahead against Peru.

Goalkeeper Luis Rubinos, fumbled
to allow Bonev his chance.

Georgi Asparoukhov, who came on
for Bonev.

In what seemed the easiest group
of all, West Germany struggled and
had to wait until 12 minutes from
the end of their match against
Morocco before Gerd Müller (right)
snatched their winner.

Group Four

PERU 3   BULGARIA 2 (Half-time 0-1)
Guanajuato Stadium, León, 2 June
Attendance: 14,000

THE game started with a one-minute silence in memory of the 50,000 people who lost their lives in the Peruvian earthquake only two days before this match. The Peruvian players, wearing black armbands, were visibly affected by the tragedy, although mercifully, they had been able to make contact with close relatives who had survived one of the greatest disasters of modern times.

Peru were coached by Didí, one of the Brazilian stars of their 1958 and 1962 World Cup triumphs, and he had introduced Brazilian techniques into Peru's style which saw them regarded as the best of the outsiders. One would not have thought so after 49 minutes, however, when they trailed 2-0.

Bulgaria took the lead in the 12th minute when Dermendiev celebrated his 29th birthday by scoring the first goal of the tournament. It was the only goal of the first half, but four minutes after the start of the second period, Peru were in all sorts of trouble when their goalkeeper failed to hold a shot from Bonev. Six minutes later, however, the Peruvians were all-square after a remarkable comeback.

In the 50th minute, Gallardo, their tall outside-left, thumped home a shot off the underside of the crossbar and five minutes later, Peruvian skipper Chumpitaz scored from a free-kick after his shot found its way through the defensive wall which contained the then unusual sight of attacking players lined up with the defenders.

Then Peru's brilliant young inside-left Cubillas, one of the stars of the 1970 World Cup, dummied his way through the defence to score a brilliant solo goal in the 73rd minute to give Peru an emotional and dramatic win.

Peru: Rubinos; Campos(J.González), de la Torre, Chumpitaz, Fuentes, Cubillas, Mífflin, Challe, Baylon(Sotíl), León, Gallardo.
Scorers: Gallardo, Chumpitaz, Cubillas
Bulgaria: Simeonov, Shalamanov, Dimitrov, Davidov, Aladjov, Bonev(Asparoukhov), Penev, Yakimov, Popov(Maraschliev), Jekov, Dermendiev.
Scorers: Dermendiev, Bonev
Referee: Antonio Sbardella (Italy)

WEST GERMANY 2   MOROCCO 1 (Half-time 0-1)
Guanajuato Stadium, León, 3 June
Attendance: 9,000

WEST Germany, with established stars like Uwe Seeler and Franz Beckenbauer, together with their new goalscoring sensation Gerd Müller, were one of the favourites to win the

1970 World Cup. Morocco, on the other hand, were 500/1 outsiders. But what a shock they gave the Germans and held a 1-0 half-time lead.

Morocco were more skilful than many people expected and their goal, in the 21st minute, was fully deserved. A cross from Ghazouani caused all sorts of problems in the German defence and the ball fell to Houmane Jarir, who shot home.

The start of the second half produced one of the most amazing sights in World Cup history. When the referee signalled the start of the half, Morocco did not have a full complement of players on the pitch and goalkeeper Allal Ben Kassu was missing for nearly a minute whilst play continued. The Moroccan coach later complained bitterly that the referee had not called his players from the dressing-room.

There were no goals during this moment of confusion, but the Germans eventually equalized in the 56th minute, when Seeler found the net in his fourth consecutive World Cup. It came at the end of intense German pressure on the Moroccan goal.

Whilst a draw would have been a fair result, German embarrassment was saved 12 minutes from time when Gerd Müller added to his tally of ten goals in the qualifying competition to score the first of ten more goals in the final stages.

West Germany: Maier; Vogts, Schulz, Fichtel, Höttges(Löhr), Haller(Grabowski), Beckenbauer, Overath, Seeler, Müller, Held.
Scorers: Seeler, Müller
Morocco: Ben Kassu; Lamrani, Benkrief, Khanoussi, Slimani, Marroufi, Bamous(Faras), El Filali, Said, Ghazouani(El Kiati), Houmane Jarir.
Scorer: Houmane Jarir
Referee: Laurens Van Ravens (Holland)

Pedro León of Peru.

PERU 3   MOROCCO 0 (Half-time 0-0)
Guanajuato Stadium, León, 6 June
Attendance: 13,500

THE first half saw another magnificent display by the unfancied Moroccans as they held Peru to a goalless 45 minutes. They started the second half in the same mood and kept the South Americans at bay for a further 20 minutes before the brilliance of Cubillas turned the game in a ten-minute spell which produced all three goals.

The outstanding Peruvian forward had a hand in all three. He scored the first when he latched on to a bad clearance from the Moroccan goalkeeper in the 65th minute. Two minutes later he created the chance from which Challe scored. And in the 75th minute, Cubillas netted again with a magnificent effort.

Peru were establishing themselves as a useful team. Morocco, though, were virtually out of the tournament, but they had won a lot of friends with their enthusiasm.

Peru: Rubiños; P.González, de la Torre, Chumpitaz, Fuentes, Challe, Mífflin(Cruzado), Cubillas, Sotíl, León, Gallardo(Ramírez).
Scorers: Cubillas 2, Challe
Morocco: Ben Kassu; Lamrani, Benkrief(Fadili), Khanoussi, Slimani, Marroufi, Bamous, El Filali, Said(Alavi), Houmane Jarir, Ghazouani.
Referee: Tofik Bakhramov (Soviet Union)

WEST GERMANY 5   BULGARIA 2 (Half-time 2-1)
Guanajuato Stadium, León, 7 June
Attendance: 12,700

AFTER West Germany's fortunate win in the opening game against Morocco, Helmut Schön was forced to make changes to their team. In came Libuda — and what a difference he made as he teamed up with Müller to have a hand in all five German goals.

The Germans started with more resolution than against Morocco and attacked from the outset, yet surprisingly they found themselves trailing to a 12th-minute goal. Much against the run of play, Nikodimov broke away and caught the German defence flat-footed.

Libuda wiped out that lead in the 20th minute, when Simeonov in the Bulgarian goal misjudged his shot. Seven minutes later, Gerd Müller was on the end of a Libuda cross to make it 2-1.

The German lead was extended to 3-1 in the 52nd minute when Müller converted a penalty after Libuda had been brought down. Müller was also involved in the fourth goal, when he laid on the pass for Seeler to score.

Two minutes from time, Müller completed the first hat-trick of the series and a minute later, Kolev pulled back a late consolation goal for Bulgaria. The West Germans had at last shown the form which had established them as one of the pre-tournament favourites.

West Germany: Maier, Vogts, Schnellinger, Fichtel, Höttges, Beckenbauer(Weber), Overath, Libuda, Seeler, Müller, Löhr(Grabowski).
Scorers: Libuda, Müller 3 (1 pen), Seeler
Bulgaria: Simeonov; Gaidarski, Penev, Zhechev, Gaganelov(Shalamanov), Kolev, Bonev, Nikodimov, Dermendiev(Mitkov), Asparoukhov, Maraschliev.
Scorers: Nikodimov, Kolev
Referee: José Maria Ortiz de Mendibil (Spain)

Bertie Vogts of West Germany.

Peru attack the West German goal. The German players are (from left to right) Vogts (nearest ball), Fichtel, Schnellinger (3) and Beckenbauer. West Germany won 3-1 but both teams qualified for the quarter-finals.

Two fine German strikers, Uwe Seeler (left) and Gerd Müller.

WEST GERMANY 3   PERU 1 (Half-time 3-1)

Guanajuato Stadium, León, 10 June
Attendance: 18,000

THE Mexican fans really took to the Peruvians, who were playing attractive football. And when they entertained West Germany in their last group match, both teams had already qualified for the quarter-finals and there was the prospect of a good open game.

With nothing at stake, other than the right to stay at León or move to Guadalajara for the quarter-final, both teams attacked from the first whistle and the game was settled in the first half, with all four goals coming in a 25-minute spell.

Gerd Müller was the destroyer of Peru with his second successive hat-trick. All three goals came between the 19th and 39th minutes, Cubillas pulling one back for Peru a minute before half-time.

Despite a goalless second half, it was still an entertaining game and when the Germans started to tire, they were saved by their classy goalkeeper, Sepp Maier.

West Germany: Maier; Vogts, Fichtel, Schnellinger, Höttges(Patzke), Beckenbauer, Seeler, Overath, Libuda(Grabowski), Müller, Löhr.
Scorer: Müller 3
Peru: Rubinos; P.González, de la Torre, Chumpitaz, Fuentes, Mífflin, Challe(Cruzado), Sotíl, León(Ramírez), Cubillas, Gallardo.
Scorer: Cubillas
Referee: Arturo Aguilar Elizalde (Mexico)

BULGARIA 1   MOROCCO 1 (Half-time 1-0)

Guanajuato Stadium, León, 11 June
Attendance: 12,200

ALL that was to play for in the final game of Group Four was the 'wooden spoon'. That both teams went into the match without a point was evident from the way they played.

Bulgaria made wholesale changes and took their number of players used in the three matches to 20, but it made little difference as they, like Peru and West Germany before them, struggled against the Moroccans.

Zhechev gave the Europeans the lead five minutes before the interval but on the hour, Ghazouani equalized when a simple shot from outside the area was deflected past the Bulgarian goalkeeper by one of his own defenders.

Bulgaria: Yordanov; Shalamanov, Gaidarski, Zhechev, Penev(Dimitrov), Popov, Kolev, Yakimov(Bonev), Mitkov, Asparoukhov, Nikodimov.
Scorer: Zhechev
Morocco: Hazzaz; Fadili, Slimani, Khanoussi, Benkrief, Marroufi, Bamous(Chukri), El Filali, Said, Alavi(Faras), Ghazouani.
Scorer: Ghazouani
Referee: Antonio Saldanha Ribeiro (Portugal)

Group Four – Final Table

	P	W	D	L	F	A	Pts
W.Germany	3	3	0	0	10	4	6
Peru	3	2	0	1	7	5	4
Bulgaria	3	0	1	2	5	9	1
Morocco	3	0	1	2	2	6	1

Quarter-finals

WEST GERMANY 3   ENGLAND 2 (a.e.t.)   (Half-time 0-1; 90 mins 2-2)

Guanajuato Stadium, León, 14 June
Attendance: 24,000

IN a repeat of the 1966 Final, these teams had again to go into extra-time before producing a result. But this time it was in West Germany's favour as they gained revenge for their Wembley defeat of four years earlier.

England had to take the field without the world's number-one goalkeeper, Gordon Banks, who was taken ill on the morning of the match. Banks, who two days earlier learned that he had been awarded the OBE, was replaced by Peter Bonetti. Many people blamed the Chelsea 'keeper for England's defeat, although Bonetti accepted responsibility only for Germany's first goal.

Alan Mullery put England in front, with what was his only England goal, in the 31st minute. The defence were expecting a cross from Keith Newton, but he surprised them with a low ball to Mullery in the goalmouth.

Four minutes into the second half, Martin Peters scored and Newton again had a hand in the goal. England now appeared to be coasting into the semi-finals, but West Germany's manager, Helmut Schön, made a shrewd tactical substitution.

England were tiring and Schön brought on a fresh pair of legs in the form of winger Grabowski, who played a crucial part in his side's revival.

England's team, now on the defensive, were flagging, notably full-back Terry Cooper, but Alf Ramsey kept him on. Then Franz Beckenbauer gave the Germans hope with a right-foot shot from the edge of the penalty area. Shortly after the goal, Ramsey took off Bobby

'The Kaiser' – Franz Beckenbauer – who set the Germans on the road to recovery and eventual victory against England.

WORLD CUP FACT

In the qualifier between the USA and Bermuda in Kansas City on 3 November 1968, both goalkeepers were carried off injured before half-time. Sandy Feher (USA) was replaced by De Long and Granville Nusum (Bermuda) by Jennings.

Francis Lee (left) makes a desperate effort but West German goalkeeper Sepp Maier shepherds the ball out for a goal-kick.

WORLD CUP FACT

When Mario Zagalo managed Brazil to their 1970 triumph, he became the first man to play in and then manage a World Cup winning team. He was a member of the Brazilian sides which won the trophy in 1958 and 1962.

Wunderbar! Beckenbaur (left) rushes to join the celebrations as Vogts and Müller congratulate Uwe Seeler, who has just back-headed the equalizer against England.

Right and below: 'Der Bomber' –
Gerd Müller – volleys the winner
from close range and England's
dreams of retaining the World Cup
are in tatters. Stand-in goalkeeper
Peter Bonetti stands no chance of
stopping the shot.

Seeler and Mullery battle for the
ball.

Charlton, playing in a record 106th match for England. Many felt that Cooper should have been the man replaced and Ramsey's move was seen as a tactical blunder.

Then a long ball from Schnellinger found the head of Seeler and the veteran German back-headed the ball past Bonetti, who was out of position, to score a second German goal. With less than a quarter of an hour to go, the Germans had levelled the score and extra-time was necessary.

Geoff Hurst had a 'goal' disallowed in the extra period and three minutes into the second half of extra-time, Gerd Müller volleyed in from close range after Grabowski's cross was headed on to him by Löhr.

West Germany had staged a great comeback and the defeat marked the decline of English soccer at international level. They were not to qualify for the final stages of the World Cup again until 1982. Bobby Charlton, meanwhile, had played his last game for England.

West Germany: Maier; Schnellinger, Vogts, Fichtel, Höttges(Schulz), Beckenbauer, Overath, Seeler, Libuda(Grabowski), Müller, Löhr.
Scorers: Beckenbauer, Seeler, Müller
England: Bonetti; Newton, Cooper, Mullery, Labone, Moore, Lee, Ball, Hurst, R.Charlton (Bell), Peters(Hunter).
Scorers: Mullery, Peters
Referee: Angel Norberto Coerezza (Argentina)

West Germany line-up before the
kick-off. From left to right: Seeler,
Maier, Schnellinger, Beckenbauer,
Löhr, Müller, Fichtel, Libuda,
Overath, Höttges, Vogts.

ITALY 4　MEXICO 1 (Half-time 1-1)

Luis Dosal Stadium, Toluca, 14 June
Attendance: 24,000

AFTER early Italian pressure, the hosts eventually took charge and Italy began to look vulnerable. That was confirmed in the 13th minute when González scored after Fragoso had beaten three defenders. It was the first goal scored against Italy in the 1970 World Cup.

Although Italy equalized after 25 minutes, when a Domenghini shot was deflected into the goal by defender Peña, the first half still belonged to Mexico and the European champions went in at the interval with much to think about.

Their answer was to substitute Rivera for Mazzola and the presence of the Italian skipper transformed the game. He motivated his teammates into a stirring second half performance.

Luigi Riva, one of the stars of the tournament, put Italy in front in the 64th minute with a great left-foot shot. Five minutes later, Rivera finished a move which he had started in his own half by beating Calderón in the Mexican goal to make it 3-1.

Rivera was involved in Italy's fourth goal when he passed to Riva, who then rode two tackles before stabbing the ball past the goalkeeper at the second attempt.

After scoring only one goal in three group matches, Italy had now quadrupled their tally. More significantly, they had served a warning that they were improving as the tournament progressed.

Italy: Albertosi; Burgnich, Cera, Rosato, Facchetti, Bertini, Mazzola(Rivera), de Sisti, Domenghini(Gori), Boninsegna, Riva.
Scorers: Domenghini, Riva 2, Rivera
Mexico: Calderón; Vantolrá, Peña, Gúzman, Pérez, González(Borja), Pulido, Munguia(Díaz), Valdivia, Fragoso, Padilla.
Scorer: González
Referee: Rudolf Scheurer (Switzerland)

BRAZIL 4   PERU 2 (Half-time 2-1)
Jalisco Stadium, Guadalajara, 14 June
Attendance: 54,000

VINTAGE Brazil contributed most in an exciting game of attacking football which dashed the dreams of Peru, one of the surprise teams of the tournament. And for their coach, Didí, it was an unhappy reunion with his former colleagues.

Gérson returned for Brazil, but the man who did the most damage was Tostão, who had an outstanding game. He was responsible for Brazil's opening goal after 11 minutes, doing all the work before passing to Rivelino, who hit a low, swerving shot past the 'keeper.

Rivelino repaid the compliment four minutes later, when he laid on a ball for Tostão to hammer his shot into the net from an acute angle. With Felix out of position, Gallardo scored, also from the narrowest of angles, to reduce the arrears.

Seven minutes into the second half, Brazil restored their two-goal advantage when Tostão turned in a deflected Pelé shot. But the Peruvians would not give up and a fine run by substitute Sotíl was finished off by Cubillas, who found the net from 20 yards.

Brazil, though, had the final say when Jairzinho maintained his record of scoring in every game. He collected a defence-splitting pass from Tostão and had no trouble in rounding Rubinos to seal victory.

Brazil: Felix; Carlos Alberto, Brito, Piazza, Marco Antonio, Clodoaldo, Gérson(Paulo Cesar), Jairzinho(Roberto), Tostão, Pelé, Rivelino.
Scorers: Rivelino, Tostão 2, Jairzinho
Peru: Rubinos; Campos, Fernández, Chumpitaz, Fuentes, Mífflin, Challe, Baylon(Sotíl), León (Reyes), Cubillas, Gallardo.
Scorers: Gallardo, Cubillas
Referee: Vital Loraux (Belgium)

URUGUAY 1   SOVIET UNION 0 (a.e.t.) (Half-time 0-0; 90 mins 0-0)
Azteca Stadium, Mexico City, 14 June
Attendance: 45,000

THE Azteca Stadium was less than half full for this quarter-final clash, which many predicted

Italy's Gianni Rivera, came on and transformed the game against Mexico.

Sandro Mazzola, he made way for Rivera.

The USSR team which met Uruguay in the quarter-finals (left to right): Khurtsilava, Evriuzhikan, Dzodzuashvili, Bishovets, Khmelnitski, Muntian, Kaplichni, Afonin, Asatiani, Kavasashvili, Shesterniev.

Kakhi Asatiani of the USSR is in trouble with the referee.

would be a dour affair. Indeed it was, as the Uruguayans once more showed they were masters at shutting out the opposition.

Uruguay had Morales back for his first match after a knee operation but, as expected, it was the Soviets who did most of the attacking.

At the end of 90 minutes, Russia were showing more signs of tiring and in extra-time the game drifted away from them, despite having a Bishovets 'goal' ruled out for offside.

The only goal of the match came three minutes from the end and was surrounded by controversy. After spending more than 100 minutes on the substitutes' bench, Victor Esparrago was brought into the game and in the closing minutes got his head to a Cubilla cross to score. The Russians reckoned that the ball had gone out of play before Cubilla crossed but, despite their protests, the goal stood. Television replays of the incident subsequently vindicated the referee.

Uruguay: Mazurkiewicz; Ubiñas, Ancheta, Matosas, Mujica, Maneiro, Cortés, Montero-Castillo, Cubilla, Fontes(Esparrago), Morales(Gómez).
Scorer: Esparrago
Soviet Union: Kavasashvili; Afonin, Dzodzuashvili, Kaplichni, Khurtsilava(Logofet), Shesterniev, Asatiani(Kiselev), Muntian, Bishovets, Evriuzhikan, Khmelnitski.
Referee: Laurens Van Ravens (Holland)

Semi-finals

ITALY 4 WEST GERMANY 3 (a.e.t.) (Half-time 1-0; 90 mins 1-1)

Azteca Stadium, Mexico City, 17 June
Attendance: 80,000

THIS may not have been the most skilful game of the 1970 World Cup, but it was certainly the most memorable with five of the seven goals being scored in extra-time — and that was only made possible by a West German equalizer in injury time of normal play.

Italy opened the scoring in the seventh minute when Boninsegna hit home a left-foot shot after a fortunate rebound and, for the next 83 minutes, the Italians went on the defensive.

As the end approached, and with Italy seemingly on their way to their first Final since

Italian goalkeeper Enrico Albertosi.

Top: Gerd Müller scores his tenth goal of the tournament. *Below:* Italy soon reply through Rivera and the Germans are out.

1938, Schnellinger, a veteran of four World Cups, drove home a cross in the second minute of injury time to snatch a dramatic equalizer.

Germany's Franz Beckenbauer had been playing for half an hour with a dislocated shoulder, but he refused to leave the pitch and played on heavily strapped. It was a courageous display.

Five minutes into extra-time, the Germans took the lead for the first time when a harmless header from Seeler led to a defensive error. The ball came to Müller, whose goal sparked off a remarkable scoring spree over the next 16 minutes.

Burgnich made sure the German lead was short-lived when he netted after a defensive lapse from a Rivera free-kick. Two minutes before the interval, Domenghini broke on the right and passed to Riva. The classy forward hit a low shot into the far corner and Italy were back in front at 3-2.

With ten minutes to go, Müller scored his tenth goal of the tournament and the teams were level again. But virtually straight from the restart, Boninsegna went on another one of his runs and sent in a low cross for Rivera to side-foot the ball into the goal.

The large crowd in the Azteca had been treated to a marvellous extra-time period and were expecting more goals in the final nine minutes. But Rivera's goal signalled the end of the scoring in this remarkable semi-final.

West Germany's two-hour battle with England had taken more out of them than perhaps they realized and Helmut Schön put their defeat down to that match. The Italians, on the other hand, gave notice that their dull displays in the group matches served only to lull the other teams into a false sense of security. In reality they were a far better team than early results had indicated.

Italy: Albertosi; Cera, Burgnich, Bertini, Rosato(Poletti), Facchetti, Domenghini, Mazzola(Rivera), de Sisti, Boninsegna, Riva.
Scorers: Boninsegna, Burgnich, Riva, Rivera
West Germany: Maier; Schnellinger, Vogts, Schulz, Beckenbauer, Patzke(Held), Seeler, Overath, Grabowski, Müller, Löhr(Libuda).
Scorers: Schnellinger, Müller 2
Referee: Arturo Maldonado Yamasaki (Mexico)

BRAZIL 3   URUGUAY 1 (Half-time 1-1)

Jalisco Stadium, Guadalajara, 17 June
Attendance: 51,000

LIKE the other semi-final, this game was contested by two former winners of the trophy and was a repeat of the 1950 final game which Uruguay won.

Esparrago of Uruguay, who came on for Maneiro in the semi-final.

Tostão of Brazil.

Pelé tries to congratulate Clodoaldo, but the Brazilian is intent on a triumphal run after scoring Brazil's equalizer against Uruguay, right on half-time.

Mazurkiewicz dives at the feet of Jairzinho and the ball rolls towards the Uruguayan goal.

STATISTICS

Goalscorers:
10 — Gerhard Müller (West
      Germany).
7 — Jair Ventura Filho Jairzinho
      (Brazil).
5 — Teófilo Cubillas (Peru).
4 — Pelé (Brazil), Anatoliy
      Bishovets (Soviet Union).
3 — Roberto Rivelino (Brazil),
      Luigi Riva (Italy), Uwe Seeler
      (West Germany).
2 — Wilfried Van Moer, Raoul
      Lambert (both Belgium),
      Javier Valdivia Huerta
      (Mexico), Tostão (Brazil),
      Angelo Domenghini, Gianni
      Rivera, Roberto Boninsegna
      (all Italy), Ladislav Petras
      (Czechoslovakia), Florea
      Dumitrache (Romania),
      Alberto Gallardo (Peru).
1 — Emerich Dembrowski,
      Alexandru Neagu (both
      Romania), Kakhi Asatiani,
      Vitali Khmelnitski (both
      Soviet Union), Juan
      Basaguren, Javier Fragoso,
      Gustavo Peña, José Luís
      González (all Mexico),
      Mordechai Spiegler (Israel),
      Clodoaldo, Gérson, Carlos
      Alberto Torres (all Brazil),
      Ildo Maneiro, Juan Martín
      Mujica, Víctor Esparrago,
      Luís Cubilla (all Uruguay),
      Tarcisio Burgnich (Italy),
      Tom Turesson, Ove Grahn
      (both Sweden), Geoff Hurst,
      Allan Clarke, Alan Mullery,
      Martin Peters (all England),
      Reinhard Libuda, Franz
      Beckenbauer, Karl-Heinz
      Schnellinger, Wolfgang
      Overath (all West Germany),
      Héctor Chumpitaz, Roberto
      Challe (both Peru), Dinko
      Dermendiev, Dobromir
      Zechev, Christo Bonev,
      Asparuch Nikodimov, Bojil
      Kolev (all Bulgaria),
      Houmane Jakir, Mauhu
      Ghazouani (both Morocco).

Own-goals
None

Hat-tricks
Gerhard Müller (West Germany v
Bulgaria). Gerhard Müller (West
Germany v Peru).

Fastest goal
3 minutes — Ladislav Petras
(Czechoslovakia v Romania).

Most goals (team)
19 — Brazil

Teams failing to score
El Salvador

Total goals scored: 95
Average per game: 2.97

Penalties
Scored: Raoul Lambert (Belgium v
El Salvador) *Referee: Andrei
Radelescu (Romania)*. Gustavo
Peña (Mexico v Belgium) *Referee:
Angel Norberto Coerezza
(Argentina)*. Florea Dumitrache
(Romania v Czechoslovakia)
Referee: Diego de Leo (Mexico).
Allan Clarke (England v
Czechoslovakia) *Referee: René
Machin (France)*. Gerhard Müller
(West Germany v Bulgaria) *Referee:
José Maria Ortiz de Mendibil
(Spain)*.

Before the match, the Uruguayans complained to FIFA that Brazil were playing at Guadalajara once again and were benefiting from a near 'home advantage'. But their protests were to no avail.

The full house at the Jalisco Stadium saw the attacking flair of Brazil against the solid defence of Uruguay. Strangely, though, the Brazilians looked out of touch and once again found themselves trailing, when Morales laid on a pass for Cubilla to score from a narrow angle in the 19th minute with Felix out of position.

Brazil snatched their equalizer right on half-time, when Clodoaldo scored after Tostão had made the opening. The second half started with the Brazilians on top, although they nearly fell behind again when only a brilliant Felix save from a Cubilla header prevented a second Uruguayan goal.

But 14 minutes from the end, Jairzinho scored when he finished off a great move which he had started in his own half. He passed to Pelé, who in turn gave the ball to Tostão. He majestically laid the ball into the path of the marauding Jairzinho who hammered it into the net on the run.

Brazil sealed their place in the final when Rivelino crashed home a left-foot shot from a Pelé pass in the last minute.

Brazil: Felix; Carlos Alberto, Brito, Piazza, Everaldo, Clodoaldo, Gérson, Jairzinho, Tostão, Pelé, Rivelino.
Scorers: Clodoaldo, Jairzinho, Rivelino.
Uruguay: Mazurkiewicz; Ubiñas, Ancheta, Matosas, Mujica, Montero-Castillo, Cortés, Fontes, Cubilla, Maneiro(Esparrago), Morales.
Scorer: Cubilla
Referee: José Maria Ortiz de Mendibil (Spain)

Third place play-off
WEST GERMANY 1   URUGUAY 0 (Half-time 1-0)

Azteca Stadium, Mexico City, 20 June
Attendance: 104,000

THIS game broke with third place play-off tradition in that it produced some exciting football, although in the early stages it appeared that the large crowd was going to witness another drab affair. Only after Overath's goal, midway through the first half, did both teams push forward and thereafter the fans were treated to a good game, despite the fact that there were no more goals.

Overath had taken over the German midfield, marshalling the side in Beckenbauer's absence, and did a good job. Whilst Gerd Müller had a hand in making Overath's goal, the new scoring sensation failed to get on the score-sheet for the first time during West Germany's 1970 World Cup campaign, including the qualifying matches.

West Germany: Wolter; Schnellinger(Lorenz), Patzke, Fichtel, Weber, Vogts, Seeler, Overath, Libuda(Löhr), Müller, Held.
Scorer: Overath
Uruguay: Mazurkiewicz; Ubiñas, Ancheta, Matosas, Mujica, Montero-Castillo, Cortés, Fontes(Esparrago), Cubilla, Maneiro(Sandoval), Morales.
Referee: Antonio Sbardella (Italy)

Final

BRAZIL 4   ITALY 1 (Half-time 1-1)

Azteca Stadium, Mexico City, 21 June
Attendance: 107,000

AFTER analysing the performances of these teams in the semi-finals, the result was perhaps not as decisive as it might have been had they met two weeks earlier. Italy had certainly improved in front of goal; Brazil, whilst still a magnificent team going forward, were vulnerable at the back and Felix had let them down on a couple of occasions. The 1970 World Cup Final promised to be a game of contrasting styles.

The temperature in the Azteca Stadium was pleasantly cool, much to the relief of the players and the vast crowd, who eagerly awaited the clash which turned out to be a great advert for attacking football.

Mazzola was outstanding in the Italian midfield in the first half, whilst his opposite number, Gérson, controlled play in the second 45 minutes.

Whoever won would be the permanent holders of the Jules Rimet Trophy and it was Brazil who took the first step towards that aim when Pelé scored his country's 100th World Cup goal. He headed home a Rivelino lob from a Tostão throw-in and thus emulated Vavá by scoring in two World Cup Finals.

Eight minutes before half-time, Boninsegna levelled the scores when he took advantage of a defensive lapse and latched on to a lazy back-heel from Brito.

The well-regimented Italians were broken down in the second half by a great Gérson performance and it was his left-foot which put Brazil back in front in the 65th minute.

Azteca Stadium in Mexico City.

Brazil's Gérson, flanked by training staff, prays before the 1970 World Cup Final.

Pelé's looping header gives Brazil the lead over Italy.

He hit the ball on the turn from the edge of the penalty area, giving Italian 'keeper Albertosi no chance. It was the goal which Brazil needed to spark them into life and they started to produce the kind of football the Mexican fans had come to expect.

Twenty minutes from time Jairzinho created World Cup history by scoring in every round of the competition. The goal was made by Gérson, whose cross found the head of Pelé near the far post. Pelé refused to take the goal-scoring chance and instead headed the ball down for Jairzinho.

Brazil completely dominated the remainder of the match and four minutes from time their skipper, Carlos Alberto, scored after being fed by a brilliant ball from Pelé.

Millions of fans the world over revelled in the skills of the Brazilians as they won the trophy for the third time. For their manager, Mario Zagalo, it was a great addition to his two winners' medals as a player.

Brazil: Felix Mielli Venerando; Carlos Alberto Torres, Hercules Brito Ruas, Wilson Piazza da Silva, Everaldo Marques da Silva, Clodoaldo, Gérson Nunes de Olivéira, Jair Venutura Filho Jairzinho, Tostão, Pelé, Roberto Rivelino.
Scorers: Pelé, Gérson, Jairzinho, Carlos Alberto
Italy: Enrico Albertosi; Pierluigi Cera, Tarcisio Burgnich, Mario Bertini(Antonio Juliano), Roberto Rosato, Giacinto Facchetti, Angelo Domenghini, Alessandro Mazzola, Giancarlo de Sisti, Roberto Boninsegna(Gianni Rivera), Luigi Riva.
Scorer: Boninsegna
Referee: Rudolf Glöckner (East Germany)

Pelé celebrates the goal which meant that he had emulated Vavá by scoring in two World Cup Finals.

Top: Gérson scores Brazil's second to put them back in front. *Upper middle:* Jairzinho's gets Brazil's third, which means that he has scored in every game in the 1970 competition. *Lower middle:* Felix tips an Italian effort over the bar. *Bottom:* Tostão (falling) and Pelé (10) are involved in another attack in the Italian penalty area.

Most appearances

6 — *Hercules Brito Ruas, Carlos Alberto Torres,* Clodoaldo, *Felix Mielli Venerando,* Jair Ventura Filho Jairzinho, *Pelé, Wilson Piazza da Silva,* Tostão (all Brazil); *Enrico Albertosi,* Mario Bertini, Roberto Boninsegna, *Tarcisio Burgnich,* Pierluigi Cera, *Giancarlo de Sisti,* Angelo Domenghini, *Giacinto Facchetti,* Alessandro Mazzola, *Luigi Riva,* Roberto Rosato (all Italy); Johannes Löhr, *Gerhard Müller, Wolfgang Overath, Uwe Seeler, Hans-Hubert Vogts* (all West Germany); *Atilio Ancheta,* Víctor Esparrago, Ildo Maneiro, *Roberto Matosas, Ladislao Mazurkiewicz, Júlio Montero-Castillo, Juan Martín Mujica, Luis Ubiñas* (all Uruguay)

Those players in italics played in six complete games.

Sendings-off

None

Most players used

20 — Bulgaria

Number of players used by Finalists

16 — Brazil

17 — Italy

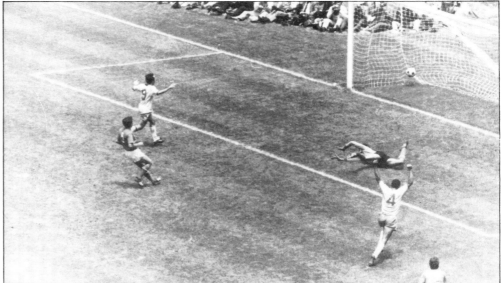

World Cup winner for the second time, Pelé complete with Mexican sombrero.

Top: Brazil's winning team. Back row (left to right, players only): Carlos Alberto, Brito, Felix, Wilson Piazza, Clodoaldo, Everaldo. Front row: Jairzinho, Gérson, Tostão, Pelé, Rivelino.

Beaten Finalists, Italy. Back row (left to right): Albertosi, Facchetti, Rosato, Domenghini, Boninsegna, Riva. Front row: Bertini, Cera, Mazzola, De Sisti, Burgnich.

In 1970, Brazil dazzled the soccer world with their remarkable free-kicks which they 'bent' around the defensive walls. Here, Rivelino (11) curls one around the Italian wall as Pelé watches.

MEN WHO MADE THE HEADLINES - 1974

Franz Beckenbauer
(West Germany)

ELEGANT Franz Beckenbauer was an outstanding captain, a great tactician and a revolutionary attacking sweeper. Born in Munich on 11 September 1945, he was in Bayern Munich's first team before his 18th birthday, won his first full cap after only 27 senior games and was West Germany's Footballer of the Year in 1966, the year he scored four goals in Germany's run to the World Cup Final. Many believed that Helmut Schön blundered by playing 'The Kaiser' out of position in the Final but he gave a great performance as England were eliminated in the 1970 quarter-finals. European Footballer of the Year in 1971 and 1976, he captained the 1972 European Champions and in 1974 at last gained a World Cup-winners' medal. He retired from international soccer in 1977 after winning 103 caps and inspiring Bayern Munich to many successes in domestic and European football. He teamed up with Pelé at New York Cosmos, in a $2 million move, and added two NASL championships to his collection before helping SV Hamburg to the Bundesliga title in 1982 and then playing a final season with the Cosmos. Appointed national coach in 1984, he steered West Germany to the 1986 and 1990 World Cup Finals and in the latter became only the second man, after Zagalo of Brazil, to achieve success as both a player — but the first as captain — and manager.

Grzegorz Lato
(Poland)

ALONG with Deyna and Szarmach, Grzegorz Lato was one of the stars of the Polish side which played such attractive football as they captured third place in the 1974 World Cup. Between them the trio scored 14 goals and Lato ended as top scorer with seven. Although stockily built, he was fast, had great acceleration and was an outstanding winger. He had a wonderful playing relationship with his fellow winger, Gadocha, on the left. Lato was born in 1950 and spent most of his senior career with Stal Mielec, helping them to the Polish title in 1973 and 1976. He made his international debut in 1971 and played his last and 104th game for Poland in 1984. His 45 international goals are second only to Lubanski's Polish record. It was Lato's run which made the goal which eliminated England at Wembley in 1973. However, his place in the World Cup squad was not assured until Lubanski dropped out. Lato turned out to be one of the stars of the tournament. Like Lubanski, he moved to KSC Lokeren in Belgium, in 1980 followed by spells in Mexico and Canada before his eventual retirement.

Johann Cruyff
(Holland)

A BRILLIANT if tempestuous star, Johann Cruyff's goals helped Holland into the 1974 World Cup Final, although the man who played a great part in 'total football' eventually finished with a losers' medal. Cruyff, one of the all-time greats, was born in Amsterdam in 1947 and at 19, and in his first season in Ajax's first team, was the Dutch League's top scorer and helped destroy Liverpool in the European Cup. In eight years, he won many domestic honours, a hat-trick of European Cup medals and was European Footballer of the Year three times. In 1973, Cruyff joined his old Ajax boss, Rinus Michels, for £922,000, and helped Barcelona win the Spanish League and Cup. In 1981, after three years in the NASL, with Los Angeles Aztecs and Washington Diplomats, he signed for Spanish Second Division club, Levante, but returned to Ajax in 1982, winning another League title with them and another with Feyenoord, whom he joined in 1984. As manager he took Ajax to a 1987 European Cup-winners' Cup Final win. In 1988 he rejoined Barcelona and led them to two Spanish Cup wins. His 48 games for Holland (33 goals) would have been more but for disputes with the Dutch FA and also his refusal to play in the 1978 World Cup.

The World of Total Football
West Germany 1974

AFTER the intense heat and high altitude of Mexico, it was to be the wet conditions of West Germany for the tenth World Cup. Munich had played host to the Olympic Games two years earlier, but the massacre of 11 Israeli athletes ruined one of the world's sporting spectacles. Consequently, security for the 1974 World Cup was tighter than ever before for soccer's greatest event.

Politics were now playing their role in football and when East and West Germany were paired together for their first-ever full international, security was at its visible highest.

Three days before the opening ceremony FIFA voted for its presidency and out went Sir Stanley Rous, after 13 years. For the first time in 70 years, the post was held by a non-European. The new president was João Havelange of Brazil, who is reputed to have spent thousands of pounds on his campaign to attain the highest post in world soccer.

Not only did FIFA have a new president in 1974, but they also had a new World Cup trophy. After their third win in Mexico, the Brazilians were allowed to retain the Jules Rimet Trophy, which has since been stolen and never recovered. The new trophy, designed by an Italian, stands 20 inches high, weighs around 11 pounds and is made of 18 carat gold. Brazil had originally offered to donate a new trophy, but FIFA commissioned the new one at a cost of £17,000. Names like the Stanley Rous Trophy and Churchill Cup were put forward, but FIFA called it the FIFA World Cup, thus reverting to its original name.

The format for the 1974 World Cup changed yet again. The 16 teams took part in four groups as they had been doing since 1950, but this time the top two teams in each group, instead of going through to a knock-out tournament, went into two further groups with the winners becoming the finalists and the runners-up meeting in the somewhat pointless third-place match. There were no semi-finals as such. For the first time goal-difference, as opposed to goal-average, was used to separate teams level on points in group matches and many coaches were mindful of the need to change tactics to fit this very important modification in the format.

West Germany, as reigning European champions and with home advantage, were clear favourites. The Soviets, who were runners-up to West Germany in the European Championships, were also expected to do well but they were not seen in Germany, having been expelled by FIFA after refusing, on political grounds, to play Chile in a qualifier.

Poland came to the finals with an exciting side, but Brazil resorted to rough defensive tactics which wiped out the memory of those heady days of beautiful, attacking football.

England's decline after elimination in the 1970 quarter-finals was highlighted when they failed to make the finals for the first time in 24 years. The responsibility of flying the flag for British soccer rested solely with Scotland but they went out of the competition in the first phase, despite being unbeaten.

With such well-known nations as England, Hungary, Portugal, Spain, Czechoslovakia and France all absent from the finals, it raised the question, yet again, about a qualifying competition which allowed lesser known and less talented nations like Australia, Zaïre and Haiti to qualify. But that is surely the magic of any cup competition — the mystery of the unknown. And Australia, the first Oceania representatives, were certainly not disgraced in Germany. Haiti and Zaïre were, admittedly, the 'whipping boys' in their respective groups but their lack of skill was compensated by unbounding enthusiasm and they both won lots of friends, if not matches.

Off the field the tenth World Cup was about money as teams became caught up in wranglings about bonuses. It was disappointing that financial undertones overtook football. By 1974, soccer had become an intensely commercial venture.

The two fancied teams, West Germany and Holland, were arguing with their officials right up to the last minute and the Germans came close to going on strike. Only the intervention of skipper Franz Beckenbauer prevented such action. Scotland, too, had their last-minute problems over cash with a football boot manufacturer.

Many nations were also sceptical about allowing the Press near their players. It was, therefore, refreshing to find a team like Yugoslavia offering an open door and not being involved in the off-the-field arguments over money, although perhaps, as a Communist country, they had little choice.

The tournament was well organized but the one thing the Germans got wrong was the weather. Having employed a computer to calculate the best days on which to play the games it turned out that many of the matches were played in atrocious conditions.

At the opening ceremony, two of the game's legends, Pelé and Uwe Seeler, stood in the middle of the pitch and showed the old and new World Cup trophies to the crowd. With both men retired from international soccer, the world's stage was ready for the next superstar to emerge and he did in the form of Holland's Johann Cruyff, who rightly succeeded Pelé as the world's number-one footballer.

His Dutch side was the most attractive of the tournament and went on to play the hosts in the Final. Both sides played what was dubbed 'Total Football' and the Germans won the trophy for the second time. Like their first success, 20 years earlier, they did so after losing a match on the way to the title.

The new World Cup trophy.

João Havelange, FIFA's new president.

Jules Rimet. The trophy named after him was now retained by the Brazilians.

1974 Qualifying Competition

FROM a list of 95 original entrants, a total of 89 nations played in the qualifying competition. West Germany and Brazil were exempt, of course, while Venezuela, Jamaica, Gabon and Madagascar withdrew after the draw for the qualifying matches was made in the summer of 1971.

Malta and Hungary got the competition underway at Valletta on 14 November 1971. Hungary won 2-0, but it was indicative of their continued demise that they failed to qualify for the second successive tournament. Their group was the closest in Europe with Austria, Sweden and Hungary all finishing level with eight points. The first two had identical goal-differences and thus engaged in a play-off. The game was staged at Gelsenkirchen on a snow-covered pitch, which should have suited both sides, and Sweden won 2-1, although they were saved when an Austrian shot hit the crossbar late in the game.

Italy reached their eighth finals without conceding a goal, but the Turks surprised the Italians by holding them to a goalless draw in Naples. In Group Three, Belgium never conceded a goal but were still eliminated. They were in the same group as Holland, whose 9-0 and 8-1 wins over Norway and Iceland respectively helped towards their overall goal-difference of 22, which was ten better than Belgium's. Belgium were certainly one team who had good cause to query the qualifying system.

East Germany clinched their first-ever appearance in the finals when they beat Albania 4-1 in the final match of Group Four and thus ousted Romania.

When England drew at home to Wales in Group Five it gave some indication that they could have problems in qualifying from their three-nation group. And, indeed, they failed to make the final stages for the first time since they first entered the World Cup in 1950. Despite continued second-half pressure by England in the final match of the group, Poland's goalkeeper, Jan Tomaszewski, had an outstanding game and secured a 1-1 draw for his team and a place in the finals. Sir Alf Ramsey was subsequently replaced as the England manager after this exit.

Another of the top sides from the 1966 tournament, Portugal, also continued with their decline and could finish only a poor second to Bulgaria in Group Six. Northern Ireland were in this group and, because of the troubles in Ulster, had to play all the 'home' matches in England. George Best was sent off in the 3-0 defeat by Bulgaria.

Yugoslavia were fortunate to qualify from Group Seven. Going into their final match against Greece in Athens, they needed to win by two clear goals to force a play-off with Spain. Their winning goal in a 4-2 victory came one minute from time amidst subsequent rumours — later proved unfounded — of bribery. In the play-off, a Katalinski goal gave the Slavs a 1-0 win in Frankfurt and earned their first place in the finals since 1962.

Czechoslovakia's 1-1 draw at Denmark proved to be the decisive match in Group Eight and by the time Scotland went to Prague for the final game of the three-team group, they had already clinched their place as Britain's only repre-

sentatives, thanks to a Joe Jordan winner against the Czechs at Hampden Park. It was Scotland's first jaunt into the finals since 1958 and in qualifying they had to endure a change of manager in mid-stream, when Tommy Docherty was lured away from the job to take charge at Manchester United. He was succeeded by Willie Ormond.

Despite losing to France in the opening match of Group Nine, the Soviet Union still headed the group by three points from their conquerors and the Republic of Ireland. But, such was the draw for the qualifying tournament, the Soviets had to play Chile, winners of the two-team South American group. After a goalless draw in Moscow, the Russians then refused to play in the National Stadium, Santiago, on the grounds that it had been used to house political prisoners during the recent coup. After lengthy meetings, FIFA ruled the match should go ahead and the Chileans took the field. Russia was nowhere to be seen and Chile went through to the finals. In readiness for the non-appearance of the Soviets, the Chilean FA had arranged a friendly for their national side against the top Brazilian club side, Santos — and the Brazilians won 5-0.

After losing at home to Colombia in their penultimate match, Uruguay had to beat Ecuador by two clear goals to secure their place in the finals. They duly won 4-0 and became the first of the qualifiers to book their ticket to West Germany.

Despite dropping only one point, Argentina assured themselves of a place in the finals only after beating Paraguay 3-1 in their final game. Both teams went into the match level on points and with identical goal-differences.

In the final South American group, consisting only of Peru and Chile after Venezuela's withdrawal, each team won a game 2-0 and met in a play-off in Montevideo. Chile won 2-1 and ousted one of the leading nations from the 1970 tournament. Chile, of course, eventually made the finals after their walk-over against the Soviet Union.

Jamaica withdrew from the CONCACAF group which required 33 matches before Haiti emerged as the first-time qualifiers from a final pool of 15 matches, all of which were played at Port au Prince over a 20-day period. Mexico were favourites to qualify but could only finish third in the final table. The biggest win of all the qualifying matches was recorded by Trinidad, who beat Antigua 11-1.

Even more matches were required to find the African representatives for Germany. Madagascar and Gabon both withdrew without kicking a ball and Nigeria were disqualified by FIFA on disciplinary grounds. The final match of the African group final, between Morocco and Zaïre, was not played because the Moroccans objected to a refereeing decision in the first match. However, it had no bearing on the outcome and after 45 matches Zaïre emerged as the first black African nation to qualify for the World Cup finals.

The final qualifiers were Australia, the first Oceania representatives to make the finals. They emerged from an Asian-Oceania series of groups which resulted in Australia beating South Korea 1-0 in a play-off after two drawn games. Australia's winning goal was scored by former Scottish League player, Jimmy McKay.

Results

EUROPE

Group One

14 Nov 1971 *Valletta*	Malta ....0 Hungary 2
30 Apr 1972 *Vienna*	Austria............4 Malta 0
6 May 1972 *Budapest*	Hungary ....3 Malta 0
25 May 1972 *Stockholm*	Sweden ....0 Hungary 0
10 Jun 1972 *Vienna*	Austria............2 Sweden 0
15 Oct 1972 *Gothenburg*	Sweden ....7 Malta 0

15 Oct	1972	*Vienna*	Austria............2 Hungary 2
25 Nov	1972	*Valletta*	Malta ....0 Austria............2
29 Apr	1973	*Budapest*	Hungary ....2 Austria............2
24 May	1973	*Gothenburg*	Sweden ....3 Austria............2
13 Jun	1973	*Budapest*	Hungary ....3 Sweden 3
11 Nov	1973	*Valletta*	Malta ....1 Sweden 2

Final Table

	P	W	D	L	F	A	Pts
Sweden	6	3	2	1	14	7	8
Austria	6	3	2	1	15	8	8
Hungary	6	2	4	0	12	7	8
Malta	6	0	0	6	1	20	0

Play-off
27 Nov 1973 *Gelsenkirchen* Sweden ....2 Austria............1
Sweden qualified

Group Two

8 Oct	1972	*Luxembourg*	Luxembourg .....0 Italy 4
21 Oct	1972	*Berne*	Switzerland ....0 Italy 0
22 Oct	1972	*Esch*	Luxembourg .....2 Turkey 0
10 Dec	1972	*Istanbul*	Turkey ....3 Luxembourg 0
13 Jan	1973	*Naples*	Italy ....0 Turkey 0
25 Feb	1973	*Istanbul*	Turkey ....0 Italy 1
31 Mar	1973	*Genoa*	Italy ....5 Luxembourg 0
8 Apr	1973	*Luxembourg*	Luxembourg .....0 Switzerland 1
9 May	1973	*Basle*	Switzerland ....0 Turkey 0
26 Sep	1973	*Lucerne*	Switzerland ....1 Luxembourg 0
20 Oct	1973	*Rome*	Italy ....2 Switzerland 0
18 Nov	1973	*Smyrna*	Turkey ....2 Switzerland 0

Final Table

	P	W	D	L	F	A	Pts
Italy	6	4	2	0	12	0	10
Turkey	6	2	2	2	5	3	6
Switzerland	6	2	2	2	2	4	6
Luxembourg	6	1	0	5	2	14	2

Italy qualified

Group Three

18 May	1972	*Liège*	Belgium..........4 Iceland 0
23 May	1972	*Brugge*	Iceland ....0 Belgium...........4
2 Aug	1972	*Oslo*	Norway ....4 Iceland 1
4 Oct	1972	*Oslo*	Norway ....0 Belgium...........4
1 Nov	1972	*Rotterdam*	Holland...........9 Norway 0
19 Nov	1972	*Anversa*	Belgium..........0 Holland...........0
2 Aug	1973	*Reykjavik*	Iceland ....0 Norway 4
22 Aug	1973	*Amsterdam*	Iceland ....0 Holland...........5
29 Aug	1973	*Deventer*	Holland...........8 Iceland 1
12 Sep	1973	*Oslo*	Norway ....1 Holland...........2
31 Oct	1973	*Brussels*	Belgium..........2 Norway 0
18 Nov	1973	*Amsterdam*	Holland...........0 Belgium...........0

Final Table

	P	W	D	L	F	A	Pts
Holland	6	4	2	0	24	2	10
Belgium	6	4	2	0	12	0	10
Norway	6	2	0	4	9	16	4
Iceland	6	0	0	6	2	29	0

Holland qualified

Group Four

21 Jun	1972	*Helsinki*	Finland ....1 Albania 0
20 Sep	1972	*Helsinki*	Finland ....1 Romania..........1
7 Oct	1972	*Dresden*	East Germany ....5 Finland 0
22 Oct	1972	*Bucharest*	Romania..........2 Albania 0
8 Apr	1973	*Magdeburg*	East Germany ....2 Albania 0
6 May	1973	*Tiranë*	Albania ....1 Romania..........4
27 May	1973	*Bucharest*	Romania..........1 East Germany 0
6 Jun	1973	*Tampere*	Finland ....1 East Germany 5
26 Sep	1973	*Leipzig*	East Germany ....2 Romania..........0
10 Oct	1973	*Tiranë*	Albania ....1 Finland 0
14 Oct	1973	*Bucharest*	Romania..........9 Finland 0
3 Nov	1973	*Tiranë*	Albania ....1 East Germany 4

Final Table

	P	W	D	L	F	A	Pts
East Germany	6	5	0	1	18	3	10
Romania	6	4	1	1	17	4	9
Finland	6	1	1	4	3	21	3
Albania	6	1	0	5	3	13	2

East Germany qualified

Group Five

15 Nov	1972	*Cardiff*	Wales ....0 England 1
24 Jan	1973	*London*	England ....1 Wales 1
28 Mar	1973	*Cardiff*	Wales ....2 Poland............0
6 Jun	1973	*Chorzów*	Poland............2 England 0
26 Sep	1973	*Chorzów*	Poland............3 Wales 0
17 Oct	1973	*London*	England ....1 Poland............1

Final Table

	P	W	D	L	F	A	Pts
Poland	4	2	1	1	6	3	5
England	4	1	2	1	3	4	4
Wales	4	1	1	2	3	5	3

Poland qualified

Above: John Toshack of Wales turns with arm raised after putting Wales 1-0 ahead against England at Wembley in a game which eventually ended in a 1-1 draw.
Left: Norman Hunter is consoled by Bobby Moore and Harold Shepherdson after being sent off in the 1-1 draw against Poland at Wembley. The dropped point cost England their place in the finals.

Group Six

29 Mar	1972	*Lisbon*	Portugal..........4 Cyprus............0
10 May	1972	*Nicosia*	Cyprus............0 Portugal 1
18 Oct	1972	*Sofia*	Bulgaria ....3 N. Ireland 0
19 Nov	1972	*Nicosia*	Cyprus............0 Bulgaria 4
14 Feb	1973	*Nicosia*	Cyprus............1 N. Ireland 0
28 Mar	1973	*Coventry*	N. Ireland ....1 Portugal 1
2 May	1973	*Sofia*	Bulgaria ....2 Portugal 1
8 May	1973	*London*	N. Ireland ....3 Cyprus............0
26 Sep	1973	*Sheffield*	N. Ireland ....0 Bulgaria 0
13 Oct	1973	*Lisbon*	Portugal..........2 Bulgaria 2
14 Nov	1973	*Lisbon*	Portugal..........1 N. Ireland 1
18 Nov	1973	*Sofia*	Bulgaria ....2 Cyprus............0

Final Table

	P	W	D	L	F	A	Pts
Bulgaria	6	4	2	0	13	3	10
Portugal	6	2	3	1	10	6	7
N. Ireland	6	1	3	2	5	6	5
Cyprus	6	1	0	5	1	14	2

Bulgaria qualified

Group Seven

19 Oct	1972	*Las Palmas*	Spain ....2 Yugoslavia 2
19 Nov	1972	*Belgrade*	Yugoslavia ....1 Greece 0
17 Jan	1973	*Athens*	Greece ....2 Spain 3
21 Feb	1973	*Malaga*	Spain ....3 Greece 1
21 Oct	1973	*Zagreb*	Yugoslavia ....0 Spain 0
12 Dec	1973	*Athens*	Greece ....2 Yugoslavia 4

Final Table

	P	W	D	L	F	A	Pts
Spain	4	2	2	0	8	5	6
Yugoslavia	4	2	2	0	7	4	6
Greece	4	0	0	3	5	11	0

Play-off
13 Feb 1974 *Frankfurt*   Yugoslavia ....1 Spain 0
Yugoslavia qualified

Scottish skipper Billy Bremner is chaired aloft by his celebrating teammates after the 2-1 victory over Czechoslovakia which qualified them for the finals.

Group Eight

18 Oct 1972 *Copenhagen* Denmark ....1 Scotland 4
15 Nov 1972 *Glasgow*   Scotland ....2 Denmark 0
 2 May 1973 *Copenhagen* Denmark ....1 Czechoslovakia ..1
 6 Jun 1973 *Prague*   Czechoslovakia ..6 Denmark 0
26 Sep 1973 *Glasgow*   Scotland ....2 Czechoslovakia ..1
17 Oct 1973 *Bratislava* Czechoslovakia ..1 Scotland 0

Final Table

	P	W	D	L	F	A	Pts
Scotland	4	3	0	1	8	3	6
Czechoslovakia	4	2	1	1	9	3	5
Denmark	4	0	1	3	2	13	1

Scotland qualified

Group Nine

13 Oct 1972 *Paris* France ....1 Soviet Union 0
18 Oct 1972 *Dublin* Rep of Ireland ...1 Soviet Union 2
15 Nov 1972 *Dublin* Rep of Ireland ...2 France 1
13 May 1973 *Moscow* Soviet Union ....1 Rep of Ireland ...0
19 May 1973 *Paris* France ....1 Rep of Ireland ...1
26 May 1973 *Moscow* Soviet Union ....2 France 0

Final Table

	P	W	D	L	F	A	Pts
Soviet Union	4	3	0	1	5	2	6
Rep of Ireland	4	1	1	2	4	5	3
France	4	1	1	2	3	5	3

Soviet Union qualified for play-off against South American Group Three winners (Chile)

SOUTH AMERICA

Group One

21 Jun 1973 *Bogotá*   Colombia ....1 Ecuador 1
24 Jun 1973 *Bogotá*   Colombia ....0 Uruguay..........0
28 Jun 1973 *Guayaquil* Ecuador ....1 Colombia 1
 1 Jul 1973 *Guayaquil* Ecuador ....1 Uruguay..........2
 5 Jul 1973 *Montevideo* Uruguay..........0 Colombia 1
 8 Jul 1973 *Montevideo* Uruguay..........4 Ecuador 0

Final Table

	P	W	D	L	F	A	Pts
Uruguay	4	2	1	1	6	2	5
Colombia	4	1	3	0	3	2	5
Ecuador	4	0	2	2	3	8	2

Uruguay qualified

The Irish Republic's Frank Stapleton in a heading duel with French defender Christian Lopez in Paris. The result was 1-1.

Group Two

 2 Sep 1973 *La Paz*   Bolivia............1 Paraguay 2
 9 Sep 1973 *Buenos Aires* Argentina ....4 Bolivia............0
16 Sep 1973 *Asunción*   Paraguay ....1 Argentina 1
23 Sep 1973 *La Paz*   Bolivia............0 Argentina 1
30 Sep 1973 *Asunción*   Paraguay ....4 Bolivia............0
 7 Oct 1973 *Buenos Aires* Argentina ....3 Paraguay 1

Final Table

	P	W	D	L	F	A	Pts
Argentina	4	3	1	0	9	2	7
Paraguay	4	2	1	1	8	5	5
Bolivia	4	0	0	4	1	11	0

Argentina qualified

Group Three

29 Apr 1973 *Lima*   Peru................2 Chile...............0
13 May 1973 *Santiago* Chile..............2 Peru...............0

Play-off
 5 Aug 1973 *Montevideo* Chile..............2 Peru...............1
Chile qualified for play-off against European Group Nine winners (Soviet Union)

Europe-South America Play-off
26 Sep 1973 *Moscow*   Soviet Union ....0 Chile..............0
Soviet Union refused to play second leg
Chile qualified

CONCACAF
(Central & North America)

Group One

20 Aug 1972 *Terranova*   Canada ....3 United States 2
24 Aug 1972 *Toronto*   Canada ....0 Mexico............1
29 Aug 1972 *Baltimore*   United States ....2 Canada 2
 3 Sep 1972 *Mexico City* Mexico............3 United States 1
 6 Sep 1972 *Mexico City* Mexico............2 Canada 1
10 Sep 1972 *Los Angeles* United States ....1 Mexico............2

Final Table

	P	W	D	L	F	A	Pts
Mexico	4	4	0	0	8	3	8
Canada	4	1	1	2	6	7	3
United States	4	0	1	3	6	10	1

Mexico qualified for Group Final

Group Two

 3 Dec 1972 *Guatemala*   Guatemala ....1 El Salvador.......0
10 Dec 1972 *San Salvador* El Salvador.......0 Guatemala 1
Guatemala qualified for Group Final

Group Three

3 Dec 1972 *Tegucigalpa* Honduras ....2 Costa Rica 1
10 Dec 1972 *San José*   Costa Rica ....3 Honduras 3
Honduras qualified for Group Final

Group Four

Netherlands Antilles qualified for Group Final, Jamaica withdrew

Group Five

15 Apr 1972 *Port au Prince* Haiti ....7 Puerto Rico 0
26 Sep 1972 *Puerto Rico* Puerto Rico ......0 Haiti 5
Haiti qualified for Group Final

Group Six

10 Nov 1972 *Port of Spain* Trinidad ....11 Antigua 1
19 Nov 1972 *Port of Spain* Antigua ....1 Trinidad 2
28 Nov 1972 *Paramaribo* Surinam ....1 Trinidad 2
30 Nov 1972 *Paramaribo* Trinidad ....1 Surinam 1
3 Dec 1972 *St John's* Antigua ....0 Surinam 6
10 Dec 1972 *St John's* Surinam ....3 Antigua 1

Final Table

	P	W	D	L	F	A	Pts
Trinidad	4	3	1	0	16	4	7
Surinam	4	2	1	1	11	4	5
Antigua	4	0	0	4	3	22	0

Trinidad qualified for Group Final

Group Final

29 Nov 1973 *Port au Prince* Honduras ....2 Trinidad 1
30 Nov 1973 *Port au Prince* Mexico............0 Guatemala 0
1 Dec 1973 *Port au Prince* Haiti ....3 Nethlds Antilles ...0
3 Dec 1973 *Port au Prince* Honduras ....1 Mexico............1
4 Dec 1973 *Port au Prince* Haiti ....2 Trinidad 1
5 Dec 1973 *Port au Prince* Guatemala ....2 Nethlds Antilles 2
7 Dec 1973 *Port au Prince* Haiti ....1 Honduras 0
8 Dec 1973 *Port au Prince* Mexico............8 Nethlds Antilles 0
10 Dec 1973 *Port au Prince* Trinidad ....1 Guatemala 0
12 Dec 1973 *Port au Prince* Honduras ....2 Nethlds Antilles 2
13 Dec 1973 *Port au Prince* Haiti ....2 Guatemala 1
14 Dec 1973 *Port au Prince* Trinidad ....4 Mexico............0
15 Dec 1973 *Port au Prince* Honduras ....1 Guatemala 1
17 Dec 1973 *Port au Prince* Trinidad ....4 Nethlds Antilles 0
18 Dec 1973 *Port au Prince* Mexico............1 Haiti 0

Final Table

	P	W	D	L	F	A	Pts
Haiti	5	4	0	1	8	3	8
Trinidad	5	3	0	2	11	4	6
Mexico	5	2	2	1	10	5	6
Honduras	5	1	3	1	6	6	5
Guatemala	5	0	3	2	4	6	3
Nethlds Antilles	5	0	2	3	4	19	2

Haiti qualified

ASIA

Preliminary Round
(to decide allocation of sub-group placements)

16 May 1973 *Seoul* South Vietnam . .1 Thailand 0
16 May 1973 *Seoul* Israel..............2 Japan 1
17 May 1973 *Seoul* Hong Kong ......1 Malaysia..........0
South Korea received a bye, Philippines withdrew

Group A – Sub Group One

20 May 1973 *Seoul* Japan ....4 South Vietnam . .0
22 May 1973 *Seoul* Hong Kong ......1 Japan 0
24 May 1973 *Seoul* Hong Kong ......1 South Vietnam . .0

Final Table

	P	W	D	L	F	A	Pts
Hong Kong	2	2	0	0	2	0	4
Japan	2	1	0	1	4	1	2
South Vietnam	2	0	0	2	0	5	0

Hong Kong and Japan qualified for Group A semi-finals

Group A – Sub Group Two

19 May 1973 *Seoul* South Korea .....4 Thailand 0
19 May 1973 *Seoul* Israel..............3 Malaysia..........0
21 May 1973 *Seoul* Israel..............6 Thailand 0
21 May 1973 *Seoul* South Korea .....0 Malaysia..........0

23 May 1973 *Seoul* Malaysia..........2 Thailand 0
23 May 1973 *Seoul* South Korea .....0 Israel..............0

Final Table

	P	W	D	L	F	A	Pts
Israel	3	2	1	0	9	0	5
South Korea	3	1	2	0	4	0	4
Malaysia	3	1	1	1	2	3	3
Thailand	3	0	0	3	0	12	0

Israel and South Korea qualified for Group A semi-finals

Group A – Semi-finals

26 May 1973 *Seoul* Israel..............1 Japan 0
26 May 1973 *Seoul* South Korea .....3 Hong Kong 1

Group A – Final

28 May 1973 *Seoul* South Korea .....1 Israel..............0
South Korea qualified for Group Final

Group B – Sub Group One

4 Mar 1973 *Auckland* New Zealand.....1 Australia 1
11 Mar 1973 *Sydney* Australia ....3 Iraq 1
11 Mar 1973 *Sydney* Indonesia.........1 New Zealand.....1
13 Mar 1973 *Sydney* Iraq ....2 New Zealand.....0
13 Mar 1973 *Sydney* Australia ....2 Indonesia.........1
16 Mar 1973 *Sydney* Iraq ....1 Indonesia.........1
16 Mar 1973 *Sydney* Australia ....3 New Zealand.....3
18 Mar 1973 *Melbourne* Indonesia.........1 New Zealand.....0
18 Mar 1973 *Melbourne* Australia ....0 Iraq 0
21 Mar 1973 *Sydney* Iraq ....3 Indonesia.........2
24 Mar 1973 *Sydney* Iraq ....4 New Zealand.....0
24 Mar 1973 *Sydney* Australia ....6 Indonesia.........0

Final Table

	P	W	D	L	F	A	Pts
Australia	6	3	3	0	15	6	9
Iraq	6	3	2	1	11	6	8
Indonesia	6	1	2	3	6	13	4
New Zealand	6	0	3	3	5	12	3

Australia qualified for Group B Final

Group B – Sub Group Two

4 May 1973 *Tehran* North Korea .....0 Iran 0
4 May 1973 *Tehran* Syria ....2 Kuwait............1
6 May 1973 *Tehran* Iran ....2 Kuwait............1
6 May 1973 *Tehran* North Korea .....1 Syria 1
8 May 1973 *Tehran* Iran ....1 Syria 0
8 May 1973 *Tehran* Kuwait............0 North Korea 0
11 May 1973 *Tehran* North Korea .....1 Iran 2
11 May 1973 *Tehran* Syria ....2 Kuwait............0
13 May 1973 *Tehran* Iran ....2 Kuwait............0
13 May 1973 *Tehran* North Korea .....3 Syria 0
15 May 1973 *Tehran* Syria ....1 Iran 0
15 May 1973 *Tehran* Kuwait............2 North Korea 0

Final Table

	P	W	D	L	F	A	Pts
Iran	6	4	1	1	7	3	9
Syria	6	3	1	2	6	6	7
North Korea	6	1	3	2	5	5	5
Kuwait	6	1	1	4	4	8	3

Iran qualified for Group B Final

Group B – Semi-finals

18 Aug 1973 *Sydney* Australia ....3 Iran 0
24 Aug 1973 *Tehran* Iran ....2 Australia 0
Australia qualified for Group Final

Group B – Final

28 Oct 1973 *Sydney* Australia ....0 South Korea 0
10 Nov 1973 *Seoul* South Korea .....2 Australia 2

Play-off
13 Nov 1973 *Hong Kong* Australia ....1 South Korea 0
Australia qualified

AFRICA

Group One

19 Nov 1972 *Agadir* Morocco ....0 Senegal 0
3 Dec 1972 *Dakar* Senegal ....1 Morocco 2
Morocco qualified for second round

Group Two

2 Mar 1972 *Algiers*   Algeria............1 Guinea 0
12 Mar 1972 *Conakry*   Guinea ....5 Algeria............1
Guinea qualified for second round

Group Three

8 Dec 1972 *Cairo*   Egypt ....2 Tunisia...........1
17 Dec 1972 *Tunis*   Tunisia...........2 Egypt 0
Tunisia qualified for second round

Group Four

15 Oct 1972 *Freetown*   Sierra Leone .....0 Ivory Coast.......1
29 Oct 1972 *Abidjan*   Ivory Coast.......2 Sierra Leone 0
Ivory Coast qualified for second round

Group Five

16 Jul 1972 *Nairobi*   Kenya.............2 Sudan.............0
23 Jul 1972 *Khartoum*   Sudan.............1 Kenya.............0
Kenya qualified for second round

Group Six

Mauritius qualified for second round, Madagascar withdrew

Group Seven

25 Nov 1972 *Addis Ababa* Ethiopia..........0 Tanzania 0
3 Dec 1972 *Dar es Salaam* Tanzania ....1 Ethiopia..........1

Play-off
10 Dec 1972 *Addis Ababa* Ethiopia..........3 Tanzania 0
Ethiopia qualified for second round

Group Eight

30 Apr 1972 *Maseru*   Lesotho...........0 Zambia 0
4 Jun 1972 *Ndola*   Zambia ....6 Lesotho...........1
Zambia qualified for second round

Group Nine

5 Aug 1972 *Ibadan*   Nigeria ....2 Congo Brazzaville..1
15 Aug 1972 *Brazzaville* Congo Brazzaville..1 Nigeria 1
Nigeria qualified for second round

Group Ten

18 Jun 1972 *Cotonou*   Dahomey ....0 Ghana 5
2 Jul 1972 *Accra*   Ghana ....5 Dahomey 1
Ghana qualified for second round

Group Eleven

6 Jun 1972 *Lome*   Togo..............0 Zaïre 0
20 Jun 1972 *Kinshasa*   Zaïre ....4 Togo..............0
Zaire qualified for second round

Group Twelve

Cameroon qualified for second round, Gabon withdrew

Second Round

10 Dec 1972 *Nairobi*   Kenya.............3 Mauritius 1
17 Dec 1972 *Port Louis*   Mauritius ....2 Kenya.............2
Kenya qualified for third round

11 Feb 1973 *Conakry*   Guinea ....1 Morocco 1
25 Feb 1973 *Rabat*   Morocco ....2 Guinea 0
Morocco qualified for third round

11 Feb 1973 *Tunis*   Tunisia...........1 Ivory Coast.......1
25 Feb 1973 *Abidjan*   Ivory Coast.......2 Tunisia...........1
Ivory Coast qualified for third round

10 Feb 1973 *Lagos*   Nigeria ....0 Ghana 2
(Game was abandoned in the 87th minute due to spectator
interference with Ghana leading 3-2. Following a FIFA inquiry
the game was awarded to Ghana 2-0)
25 Feb 1973 *Accra*   Ghana ....1 Nigeria 1
Ghana qualified for third round

4 Feb 1973 *Yaoundé*   Cameroon ....0 Zaïre 1
25 Feb 1973 *Donalda*   Zaïre ....0 Cameroon 1

Play-off
27 Feb 1973 *Kinshasa*   Zaïre ....2 Cameroon 0
Zaïre qualified for third round

1 Apr 1973 *Addis Adaba* Ethiopia..........0 Zambia 0
15 Apr 1973 *Lusaka*   Zambia ....4 Ethiopia..........2
Zambia qualified for third round

Third Round

20 May 1973 *Abidjan*   Ivory Coast.......1 Morocco 1
3 Jun 1973 *Tétouan*   Morocco ....4 Ivory Coast.......1
Morocco qualified for Group Final

5 Aug 1973 *Lusaka*   Zambia ....2 Kenya.............0
19 Aug 1973 *Nairobi*   Kenya.............2 Zambia 2
Zambia qualified for Group Final

5 Aug 1973 *Accra*   Ghana ....1 Zaïre 0
19 Aug 1973 *Kinshasa*   Zaïre ....4 Ghana 1
Zaïre qualified for Group Final

Group Final

21 Oct 1973 *Lusaka*   Zambia ....4 Morocco 0
4 Nov 1973 *Lusaka*   Zambia ....0 Zaïre 2
18 Nov 1973 *Kinshasa*   Zaïre ....2 Zambia 1
25 Nov 1973 *Rabat*   Morocco ....2 Zambia 0
9 Dec 1973 *Kinshasa*   Zaïre ....3 Morocco 0
                          Morocco ....0 Zaïre 2
(Last game not played but awarded 2-0 to Zaïre by FIFA)

Final Table

	P	W	D	L	F	A	Pts	
Zaïre	4	4	0	0	9	1	8	**Zaïre qualified**
Zambia	4	1	0	3	5	6	2	
Morocco	4	1	0	3	2	9	2	

**Zaïre, winners of the African Group Final.
Back row (left to right): Mwambi Kazadi,
Mafu, Ekofa, Boba, Ilunga, Mafuila, Tshimen,
Mokombo, Pombi. Front row: Malumba,
Mambwene, Jenbi, Mantantu, Mwepi, Etepe,
Maku.**

1974 Tournament

Group One

WEST GERMANY 1   CHILE 0 (Half-time 1-0)

Olympic Stadium, Berlin, 14 June
Attendance: 83,168

THE hosts and 2-1 favourites for the 1974 World Cup started with an unimpressive win against the very defensive Chileans.

There was a great deal of pressure on the Germans to do well and that pressure increased when they had to leave Günter Netzer out of their team. Netzer was one of their stars when they won the 1972 European Championship but, since his move to Real Madrid, had struggled to rediscover his form and there was no place for him in the starting line up.

The only goal of the game, and the first of the tournament, was a superb long-range effort from Paul Breitner in the 17th minute. The West Germans could not penetrate the Chilean defence any further and Breitner's goal was enough to enable the hosts to scrape through. Carlos Caszely of Chile was sent off after 67 minutes for kicking Bertie Vogts.

West Germany: Maier; Vogts, Breitner, Schwarzenbeck, Beckenbauer, Cullmann, Grabowski, Hoeness, Müller, Overath(Hölzenbein), Heynckes.
Scorer: Breitner
Chile: Vallejos; García, Quintano, Arias, Figueroa, Rodríguez(Lara), Caszely, Valdés(Véliz), Ahumada, Reinoso, Paez.
Referee: Dogan Babacan (Turkey)

EAST GERMANY 2   AUSTRALIA 0 (Half-time 0-0)

Volkspark Stadium, Hamburg, 14 June
Attendance: 17,000

BOTH these teams were making their World Cup debut and in the first half it was the Australian defence that proved defiant as the East Germans struggled in what was expected to be an easy match for them. Their frustration eventually boiled over and they had three players booked.

The Australian side was a multi-national team, moulded together by their Yugoslav manager, Zvonimir Rasic. And for the first 45 minutes at the Volkspark, they played well as a team, but in the second half, their defence succumbed to East German pressure and conceded two goals.

The first was an unfortunate own-goal in the 58th minute, when Colin Curran of the Western Suburbs club turned a Sparwasser shot past former Hibernian goalkeeper, Jack Reilly. The second goal came in the 72nd minute, a spectacular effort from Streich, who volleyed a left-wing cross into the roof of the net.

East Germany: Croy; Kische, Bransch, Weise, Wätzlich, Irmscher, Pommerenke, Sparwasser, Löwe(Hoffmann), Streich, Vogel.
Scorers: Curran (og), Streich
Australia: Reilly; Utjesenović, Wilson, Schaefer, Curran, Richards, Rooney, Mackay, Warren, Alston, Buljević.
Referee: Youssouf N'Diaye (Senegal)

Carlos Caszely of Chile was the first man to be sent off in the final stages of the World Cup using the red card method when he was dismissed against West Germany.

The Australians qualified from the Asia group. From left to right: Fraser, Curran, Baartz, Richards, Utjesenović, Mackay, Warren, Watkins, Alston, Abonyi, Wilson, Zvonimir Rasic (coach). By the time of the finals in West Germany, goalkeeper Fraser and midfielder Baartz had dropped from the scene.

Gerd Müller (third from left) heads home a Hoeness corner to put West Germany 3-0 up against Australia. Defenders are Schaefer (partly hidden), Reilly (1), and Utjesenović (2). The other West German is Hölzenbein (17), who came on for Heynckes.

Jurgen Croy of East Germany.

WEST GERMANY 3   AUSTRALIA 0 (Half-time 2-0)

Volkspark Stadium, Hamburg, 18 June
Attendance: 53,300

THE Australian defence once more proved very resilient, despite conceding two first-half goals. Overath put the Germans into the lead after 13 minutes, when he hammered in a half-clearance from outside the box. Five minutes later, Müller could have made it 2-0 but his powerful header rattled the crossbar.

Bernhard Cullmann eventually increased the score after 35 minutes, with a header from a right-wing cross, but the German fans were getting frustrated at their team's performance and they gave Franz Beckenbauer and his players a lot of verbal abuse.

One sensed that the Germans were conserving their energy for their tough final game against East Germany, but the fans did not see it that way. Müller made it 3-0 eight minutes into the second half, with a typical header at the near post from a Hoeness corner.

The final score was unjust on the Australians who again played well and had two good second-half chances to score, one of them when Abonyi's effort hit an upright.

West Germany: Maier; Vogts, Breitner, Schwarzenbeck, Beckenbauer, Cullmann(Wimmer), Grabowski, Heynckes(Hölzenbein), Overath, Müller, Hoeness.
Scorers: Overath, Cullmann, Müller
Australia: Reilly; Utjesenović, Wilson, Schaefer, Curran, Richards, Rooney, Mackay, Campbell (Abonyi), Alston, Buljević(Ollerton).
Referee: Mustafa Kamel (Egypt)

CHILE 1   EAST GERMANY 1 (Half-time 0-0)

Olympic Stadium, Berlin, 18 June
Attendance: 27,300

THE first 20 minutes was played in pouring rain, which should have suited the East Germans. But they failed to capitalize, despite two powerful Vogel shots which should have produced goals.

Martin Hoffmann opened the scoring in the 56th minute, when Ducke took a free-kick after he had been fouled and Hoffmann rose to meet the ball and head it past Vallejos.

A little over ten minutes later Ahumada diverted a cross from the right into the net to level the scores. East Germany had opportunities to go ahead, but Streich and Kische missed easy chances.

Chile: Vallejos; García, Figueroa, Quintano, Arias, Paez, Valdés(Yavar), Reinoso, Socías (Farías), Ahumada, Véliz.
Scorer: Ahumada
East Germany: Croy; Bransch, Kische, Weise, Wätzlich, Irmscher, Seguin(Kreische), Sparwasser, Hoffmann, Streich, Vogel(Ducke).
Scorer: Hoffmann
Referee: Aurelio Angonese (Italy)

EAST GERMANY 1   WEST GERMANY 0 (Half-time 0-0)

Volkspark Stadium, Hamburg, 22 June
Attendance: 60,200

AN emotive first-ever meeting between these two nations brought the inevitable tension and

Joachim Streich of East Germany.

Above: East German manager Georg Buschner celebrates his side's winning goal over West Germany.

Above, left: West Germany's Franz Beckenbauer (left) and East Germany's Bernd Bransch with Uruguayan referee Razmon Barreto Ruiz before the kick-off.

tight security. Some 3,000 East German fans had been granted permission to cross the border for the game, but only after strict security vetting.

Although West Germany were the reigning European champions, it was evident that the standard of the game in the East was improving, as was seen when FC Magdeburg beat AC Milan to win the 1974 European Cup-winners' Cup.

With four points from their two games, the West Germans were assured a place in the next phase, whereas the East Germans needed one point to progress further. Understandably, perhaps, they played a defensive game relying on breakaways.

The first half failed to produce a goal, although both sides came close. Kische missed a chance for the East Germans, whilst a West German effort struck a post.

West Germany dominated the second half and in the 69th minute they brought on Netzer as a replacement for Overath, for his first appearance of the tournament. But it was from one of the East German's breaks that the only goal of the game was scored ten minutes from time, when Sparwasser gathered a long ball from substitute Hamann, rounded a defender and beat Sepp Maier.

The result meant both German sides qualified for the next phase. By finishing second, West Germany went into the easiest second-phase group. Even so, Helmut Schön had to do something to improve his team's performance and he set about rebuilding his side.

Sparwasser (dark shirt, left) scores the historic goal that sank West Germany. Höttges (on ground), Vogts (2) and Maier are left floundering.

Group One – Final Table

	P	W	D	L	F	A	Pts
E.Germany	3	2	1	0	4	1	5
W.Germany	3	2	0	1	4	1	4
Chile	3	0	2	1	1	2	2
Australia	3	0	1	2	0	5	1

Defender Lobilo of Zaïre.

Willie Morgan of Scotland.

East Germany: Croy; Kurbjuweit, Bransch, Weise, Kreische, Wätzlich, Lauck, Sparwasser, Irmscher(Hamann), Kische, Hoffmann.
Scorer: Sparwasser
West Germany: Maier; Vogts, Schwarzenbeck(Höttges), Beckenbauer, Breitner, Hoeness, Overath(Netzer), Cullmann, Grabowski, Müller, Flohe.
Referee: Razmon Barreto Ruiz (Uruguay)

AUSTRALIA 0   CHILE 0 (Halft-time 0-0)

Olympic Stadium, Berlin, 22 June
Attendance: 14,000

AUSTRALIA knew they were out of the competition, whilst Chile still had an outside chance of qualifying, although one would not have thought so as the match petered out to a goalless draw.

The game was played in dreadful conditions and torrential rain forced play to be held up for a time. And this, despite the fact that the Germans had fed weather charts and records into a computer before calculating the best time to stage the World Cup matches.

The Australians won their first World Cup point and it was just reward for the 'Socceroos', who were far from disgraced. The only sad note from their final match was the dismissal of Raymond Richards, seven minutes from the end, for time-wasting. It was his second yellow card of the game but he stayed on the field for five minutes after his name was taken. It was only after a linesman pointed out the error that the referee had to send him off.

Australia: Reilly; Utjesenovic, Wilson, Schaefer, Curran(Williams), Richards, Rooney, Mackay, Abonyi, Alston(Ollerton), Buljevic.
Chile: Vallejos; García, Quintano, Figueroa, Arias, Paez, Valdés(Farías), Caszely, Ahumada, Reinoso, Véliz(Yavar).
Referee: Jafar Namdar (Iran)

Group Two

BRAZIL 0   YUGOSLAVIA 0 (Half-time 0-0)

Wald Stadium, Frankfurt, 13 June
Attendance: 62,000

FOR the third successive World Cup, the opening game ended goalless in yet another drab game which should have been one of the showpieces of the tournament.

Clodoaldo, Tostão, Pelé and Gérson were all missing from the great Brazilian team and how sad it was to see this once great attacking force resorting to a defensive game. Many described Brazil as 'cowards' for the way they played and at times they had ten and even 11 men behind the ball. Their style won them few friends in the Frankfurt crowd.

The heavy rain made good football practically impossible and the highlights of an uninspiring defensive game were near-misses from Rivelino, Oblak and Petkovic. Two minutes before half-time, the Yugoslavs could have counted themselves unlucky not to have been awarded a penalty, when Acimovic was chopped down in the box. The referee ignored their appeals and the defending champions held on for a draw.

Brazil: Leão; Nelinho, Luís Pereira, Mario Marinho, Francisco Marinho, Piazza, Rivelino, Paulo Cesar Lima, Valdomiro, Jairzinho, Leivinha.
Yugoslavia: Maric; Buljan, Katalinski, Bogicević, Hadziabdić, Muzinić, Oblak, Acimović, Petković, Surjak, Dzajić.
Referee: Rudolf Scheurer (Switzerland)

SCOTLAND 2   ZAÏRE 0 (Half-time 2-0)

Westfalen Stadium, Dortmund, 14 June
Attendance: 27,000

SCOTLAND manager Willie Ormond gambled on playing Denis Law in the hope that the ace goalscorer would find the net against Zaïre. But the one-time lethal striker did not get on the score-sheet and in the end, Scotland's inability to score more goals against one of the weakest teams in the competition contributed to their ultimate departure from the tournament.

The Africans were keen and fit but were no match for Scotland's organization. However, the Scots were enduring off-the-field problems with Jimmy Johnstone and skipper Billy Bremner coming close to being sent home for disciplinary reasons. These problems might have affected their form.

Scotland's first goal came in the 26th minute, when Peter Lorimer volleyed home a Joe Jordan header. Seven minutes later it was Jordan's turn to score when his header, from a Bremner free-kick, slipped through Kazadi's hands.

A five-minute floodlight failure early in the second half did not help the Scottish rhythm and they eased off during the closing stages. Although Scotland recorded their first win in the final stages of the World Cup, they would ultimately pay the penalty for not scoring more against one of the minnows of the 1974 competition.

Scotland: Harvey; Jardine, McGrain, Bremner, Holton, Blackley, Dalglish(Hutchison), Hay, Lorimer, Jordan, Law.
Scorers: Lorimer, Jordan
Zaïre: Kazadi; Mwepu, Mukombo, Buhanga, Lobilo, Kilasu, Mayanga(Kembo), Mana, N'daye, Kidumu(Kibonge), Kakoko.
Referee: Kurt Schulenburg (West Germany)

BRAZIL 0 SCOTLAND 0 (Half-time 0-0)

Wald Stadium, Frankfurt, 18 June
Attendance: 62,000

BRAZIL, with only Piazza, Rivelino and Jairzinho, remaining from the team which lifted the Jules Rimet Trophy in 1970, attacked for the first 20 minutes but the Scottish defence held out.

In the Scottish goal, David Harvey had an outstanding game, as did captain Billy Bremner, who received rave notices from Pelé, attending this World Cup as a spectator. In the second half Scotland were the better side and Bremner, Lorimer and Jordan all had chances to score as the Scots answered the critics, who had scant praise for them after their opening game against Zaïre.

Scotland finished the game the stronger side and, despite the goalless scoreline, theirs was a moral victory and one that delighted the 20,000 Scottish fans in the crowd.

Brazil: Leão; Nelinho, Luís Pereira, Mario Marinho, Francisco Marinho, Piazza, Rivelino, Paulo Cesar Lima, Jairzinho, Mirandinha, Leivinha(Paulo Cesar Carpegiani).
Scotland: Harvey; Jardine, McGrain, Holton, Buchan, Bremner, Hay, Dalglish, Morgan, Jordan, Lorimer.
Referee: Arie Van Gemert (Holland)

Dragan Dzajić of Yugoslavia.

Referee Arie Van Gemert watches as Brazil's Leivinha falls over the outstretched leg of Scottish defender Danny McGrain in the goalless draw in Frankfurt.

YUGOSLAVIA 9 ZAÏRE 0 (Half-time 6-0)

Park Stadium, Gelsenkirchen, 18 June
Attendance: 31,700

YUGOSLAVIA did to Zaïre what Scotland had failed to do — they scored a hatful of goals. And had they not eased off in the second half, the Yugoslavs could have added substantially to their tally of six from the first period.

A Bajević header in the sixth minute started the onslaught and in the 13th minute, a magnificent swerving free-kick from Dzajić made it 2-0. Surjak added the third five minutes later.

It was at this point that the Zaïre coach, Blagoje Vidinić, took off goalkeeper Kazadi and replaced him with Tubilandu. But the first time the new 'keeper touched the ball it was

Ivan Surjak of Yugoslavia.

Oblak celebrates as substitute Karasi (out of picture) heads past Harvey in the Scotland goal.

Yugoslavian goalkeeper Enver Maric makes a torpedo-like dive to try to stop Scotland's Joe Jordan. The other defenders are Bogicević (left) and Buljan.

Scotland skipper Billy Bremner.

Oblak (8) bears down on the Scottish goal. Jim Holton blocks his path.

to pick it out of the net after Katalinski scored. N'daye protested so much that he was eventually sent off for attacking the referee and Zaïre were reduced to ten men. Bajević made it 5-0 in the 29th minute and five minutes later, defender Bogicević joined in with goal number six.

Yugoslavia treated the second half like a training session and scored only three goals. Oblak, from another swerving free-kick, made it 7-0 on the hour and a couple of minutes later, Petković became the seventh different player to get his name on the score-sheet. Bajević, who was back in the Yugoslav team after suspension, completed his hat-trick shortly before the final whistle and rounded of a win which equalled Hungary's record score against South Korea in 1954. The South Korean goalkeeper that day, Hong, remains the only 'keeper to concede nine in a World Cup finals match, because the first Zaïre 'keeper was, of course, substituted,

Yugoslavia exposed the gap between the top teams and the 'also rans' and, perhaps understandably, the Zaïre players were so humiliated that they wanted to return home immediately after the defeat but were talked into staying on.

Yugoslavia: Maric; Buljan, Katalinski, Hadziabdić, Bogicević, Petković, Oblak, Acimović, Surjak, Bajević, Dzajić.
Scorers: Bajević 3, Dzajić, Surjak, Katalinski, Bogicević, Oblak, Petković.
Zaïre: Kazadi(Tubilandu), Mwepu, Mukombo, Buhanga, Lobilo, Kilasu, N'daye, Mana, Kembo, Kidumu, Kakoko(Mayanga).
Referee: Omar Delgado (Colombia)

SCOTLAND 1   YUGOSLAVIA 1 (Half-time 0-0)

Wald Stadium, Frankfurt, 22 June
Attendance: 56,000

SCOTLAND went into their final match knowing they had to win to be certain of progressing to the next phase. A draw would have sufficed, providing that Brazil won by only two clear goals.

Scotland had a couple of good chances to score in the first half but Jordan hit his shot against goalkeeper Maric, then Peter Lorimer beat the Yugoslav 'keeper, only to see Buljan clear off the line.

At half-time, Scotland received the news that Brazil were only one goal up against Zaïre and, if the scores at both games remained unaltered, then the Scots were still in the tournament.

As this match entered its final ten minutes, there was still no score but then Karasi, who had come on for top scorer Bajević in the hope of supporting the defence, headed past Harvey from a Dzajić cross. Scotland had to throw every man forward and in the last minute they were rewarded with a deserved equalizer when substitute Tommy Hutchison pulled the ball back for Joe Jordan to score with a left-footer from just inside the penalty area.

The game ended 1-1 and the Scottish players returned to their dressing-room and had to wait until the end of the Brazil-Zaïre match, an agonizingly long three minutes, before knowing their fate. Alas, they went out of the competition as the only team not to lose a game. They had certainly paid dearly for their failure to score more goals against Zaïre in their opening game.

Scotland: Harvey; Jardine, McGrain, Holton, Buchan, Bremner, Dalglish(Hutchison), Hay, Morgan, Jordan, Lorimer.
Scorer: Jordan
Yugoslavia: Maric; Buljan, Hadziabdić, Oblak, Katalinski, Bogicević, Petković, Acimović, Bajević(Karasi), Surjak, Dzajić.
Scorer: Karasi
Referee: Alfonso González Archundia (Mexico)

BRAZIL 3 ZAÏRE 0 (Half-time 1-0)
Park Stadium, Gelsenkirchen, 22 June
Attendance: 36,200

BRAZIL, needing to win by three clear goals to stay in the competition, made two changes from the side held to a goalless draw by Scotland. The established Paulo Cesar Lima was left out and replaced by his near-namesake, Paulo Cesar Carpegiani. Also into the team, for his first game, came the exciting Edú.

Jairzinho gave Brazil a great start by scoring in the 12th minute, when his low shot from a Luís Pereira pass beat the goalkeeper for Brazil's first goal of the tournament. Despite that great start, it was nearly an hour before Rivelino struck with a 25-yard drive to make it 2-0. It was the first time in the 1974 World Cup that memories of those great Brazilians of four years earlier came flooding back.

Brazil were still not through to the next stage of the tournament, however, for they still needed another goal. When it arrived, 11 minutes from time, it was a very fortunate one and a body-blow to Scotland's hopes of staying in the competition. A speculative shot from Valdomiro seemed to be covered by the goalkeeper, but he let the ball slip past him and into the net. Brazil had saved themselves by the skin of their teeth.

Brazil: Leão; Nelinho, Luís Pereira, Mario Marinho, Francisco Marinho, Piazza(Mirandinha), Rivelino, Leivinha(Valdomiro), Paulo Cesar Carpegiani, Jairzinho, Edú.
Scorers: Jairzinho, Rivelino, Valdomiro
Zaïre: Kazadi; Mwepu, Mukombo, Buhanga, Lobilo, Kibonge, Tshinabu(Kembo), Mana, N'tumba, Kidumu(Kilasu), Mayanga.
Referee: Nicolae Rainea (Romania)

Group Two – Final Table

	P	W	D	L	F	A	Pts
Yugoslavia	3	1	2	0	10	1	4
Brazil	3	1	2	0	3	0	4
Scotland	3	1	2	0	3	1	4
Zaïre	3	0	0	3	0	14	0

Zaïre's Yugoslavian-born manager Blagoje Vidinić.

Mayanga of Zaïre.

Zaïre team. Back row (left to right): Lobilo, Kibonge, Kazadi, Buhanga, Mwepu. Front row: Mayanga, Kidumu, Mana, Mbungu, Mukombo, Kakoko.

Ruud Krol of Holland.

Group Three

HOLLAND 2   URUGUAY 0 (Half-time 1-0)
Niedersachsen Stadium, Hanover, 15 June
Attendance: 55,000

DUTCH manager Rinus Michels brought together players with great individual skills and turned them into the most talented team in the tournament.

However, he had to make minor adjustments to the team when his powerful defender, Hulshoff, was injured before the start of the tournament and Michels moved Arie Haan from midfield into defence. Many questioned Michels' decision to play 33-year-old goalkeeper, Jan Jongbloed, but the manager's decision was soon to be justified.

Unfortunately Holland were not given the chance to display their enormous skills in their opening match because of some brutal tackling from the Uruguayans. It started in the fourth minute when Neeskens was left writhing on the touch-line after a tackle by Forlán. It was an all-too-familiar sight from the South Americans in 1974.

Holland took the lead as early as the seventh minute, when Rep headed home a right-wing chip from Suurbier. But their second goal did not come until three minutes from the end of the match, when Rensenbrink drew goalkeeper Mazurkiewicz out of position before laying a square ball for Rep to score his second of the game.

By then Uruguay had been reduced to ten men, perhaps predictably, when Júlio Montero-Castillo was sent off in the 70th minute for apparently punching Rensenbrink in the stomach.

Johann Cruyff, who had an outstanding game, said of the Uruguayans after the match: "They weren't hard, they were dirty. Hard is acceptable; dirty is dangerous."

So, 40 years after making their debut in the finals of the World Cup, Holland eventually won their first match.

Holland: Jongbloed; Suurbier, Rijsbergen, Haan, Krol, Jansen, Neeskens, van Hanegem, Rep, Cruyff, Rensenbrink.
Scorer: Rep 2
Uruguay: Mazurkiewicz; Jauregui, Masnik, Forlán, Pavoni, Esparrago, Montero-Castillo, Rocha, Cubilla(Milar), Morena, Mantegazza.
Referee: Karoly Palotai (Hungary)

Fernando Morena of Uruguay.

Cruyff in action against Uruguay.

Uruguay had a disappointing World Cup finals, scoring only one goal in their three games. Here they line-up for a friendly before the tournament. Back row (left to right): Santos, Masnik, Cardaccio, Mantegazza, Pavoni, González. Front row: Gimenez, De Simone, Morena, Gómez, Corbo.

BULGARIA 0 SWEDEN 0 (Half-time 0-0)

Rhein Stadium, Düsseldorf, 15 June
Attendance: 23,300

DESPITE the goalless scoreline, this was far from a dull game and both sides showed glimpses of attacking flair while both defended solidly. The Bulgarians, particularly, were a well-organized defensive outfit.

Sandberg and Edström, an outstanding header of the ball, were menacing for Sweden and posed the Bulgarians several problems. For Bulgaria, winger Denev had a great game and skipper Bonev showed why he was rated a world-class player, with some great passes which troubled the Swedish defence.

Sweden created the best chances, but a draw was probably the fairest result.

Bulgaria: Goranov; Velitchkov, Kolev, Penev, Voinov(Mikhailov), Bonev, Denev, Panov (M.Vassilev), Nikodimov, Z.Vassilev, Ivkov.
Sweden: Hellström; Olsson, Karlsson, Larsson, Andersson, Kindvall(Magnusson), Tapper, Grahn, Torstensson, Sandberg, Edström.
Referee: Edison Perez-Nunez (Peru)

Johann Cruyff of Holland.

HOLLAND 0 SWEDEN 0 (Half-time 0-0)

Westfalen Stadium, Dortmund, 19 June
Attendance: 53,700

SWEDEN'S second successive goalless draw was again far from drab and, had it not been for Cruyff's magnificent form in midfield, the Swedes could have sprung a surprise and beaten the fancied Dutch.

Cruyff created four good chances for his teammates but none were capitalized upon. After the match Rinus Michels praised the Swedes for the way they defended strongly and intelligently in holding out for the draw.

Holland: Jongbloed; Suurbier, Haan, Krol, Rijsbergen, Jansen, Neeskens, van Hanegem(de Jong), Rep, Cruyff, Keizer.
Sweden: Hellström; Olsson(Grip), Andersson, Karlsson, Nordqvist, Larsson, Ejderstedt, Tapper(Persson), Edström, Grahn, Sandberg.
Referee: Werner Winsemann (Canada)

BULGARIA 1 URUGUAY 1 (Half-time 0-0)

Niedersachsen Stadium, Hanover, 19 June
Attendance: 13,400

BULGARIA'S tall captain Bonev was again outstanding as he dominated the midfield and created plenty of openings. Based on the number of chances created, Bulgaria should have scored more than their solitary goal.

It was Bonev who scored the game's first goal after 75 minutes, when he flung himself full length to head home a Voinov cross. Three minutes from time, the Europeans seemed to be on their way to their first World Cup win but then Pavoni scored a gift goal for Uruguay after his shot sneaked under the body of goalkeeper Goranov.

Johnny Rep of Holland.

Cruyff in action against Bulgaria.

Uruguay were lucky to draw and they had been given a lesson in attacking football by Bulgaria. It was apparent that the South Americans were no longer the force they had been in the early days of World Cup soccer.

Bulgaria: Goranov; Velitchkov, Ivkov, Z.Vassilev, Penev, Kolev, Voinov, Bonev, Denev, Panov, Nikodimov(Mikhailov).
Scorer: Bonev
Uruguay: Mazurkiewicz; Jauregui, Forlán, Pavoni, Esparrago, Morena, Rocha, Garisto (Masnik), Mantegazza(Cardaccio), Milar, Corbo.
Scorer: Pavoni
Referee: Jack Taylor (England)

HOLLAND 4   BULGARIA 1 (Half-time 2-0)

Westfalen Stadium, Dortmund, 23 June
Attendance: 53,300

HOLLAND showed why they were one of the favourites to lift the new World Cup trophy when they gave a great performance against Bulgaria, who bowed out of their fourth World Cup still looking for their first win.

Cruyff, almost single-handedly, destroyed Bulgaria and after three games had established himself as one of the stars of the tournament. Another of Holland's outstanding players, Johannes Neeskens, put them in front with a fifth-minute penalty. One minute before half-time he made it 2-0, again from the penalty-spot.

Johnny Rep scored his third goal of the tournament in the 71st minute and seven minutes later, Bulgaria reduced the arrears when Krol put through his own goal in attempting to clear the ball over the bar.

Three minutes from time, de Jong headed home a Cruyff centre to make it 4-1 and ensure Holland's passage to the next phase.

Holland: Jongbloed; Suurbier, Hann, Rijsbergen, Krol, Neeskens(de Jong), van Hanegem (Israël), Jansen, Rep, Cruyff, Rensenbrink.
Scorers: Neeskens 2 (2 pens), Rep, de Jong
Bulgaria: Stoykov; Velitchkov, Ivkov, Penev, Z.Vassilev, Stoyanov(Mikhailov), Bonev, Kolev, Voinov, Panov(Borisov), Denev.
Scorer: Krol (og)
Referee: Anthony Bošković (Australia)

SWEDEN 3   URUGUAY 0 (Half-time 0-0)

Rhein Stadium, Düsseldorf, 23 June
Attendance: 28,300

SWEDEN needed a draw to stay in the competition, whereas Uruguay had to win. After two opening draws, the odds favoured the Europeans but at half-time there was still no score and after 225 minutes of football, Sweden were still looking for their first goal.

However, they did not have to wait long because a minute into the second half, their outstanding forward, Ralf Edström, opened their account. In the 74th minute, Sandberg made it 2-0 and the Uruguayan nightmare continued four minutes later as Edström scored his second.

Johannes Neeskens of Holland.

Sweden, like Brazil, thus qualified without conceding a goal. Uruguay, meanwhile, went out of the tournament and it was a sad exit for Pedro Rocha, who bowed out after his fourth tournament stretching back to 1962. When he got home, the Uruguay manager, 60-year-old Roberta Porta, resigned and at the same time apologized publicly for the disgraceful showing of Uruguay in the tenth World Cup.

Sweden: Hellström; Andersson, Grip, Karlsson, Nordqvist, Larsson, Grahn, Kindvall (Torstensson), Edström, Magnusson(Ahlström), Sandberg.
Scorers: Edström 2, Sandberg
Uruguay: Mazurkiewicz; Jauregui, Forlán, Pavoni, Garisto(Masnik), Esparrago, Rocha, Mantegazza, Milar, Morena, Corbo(Cubilla).
Referee: Erich Linemayr (Austria)

Group Four

ITALY 3   HAITI 1 (Half-time 0-0)

Olympic Stadium, Munich, 15 June
Attendance: 53,000

BEFORE the game, Haiti forward Emmanuel Sanon predicted that he would score two goals and added: "The Italian defence is too slow for me."

Sure enough, Sanon opened the scoring a minute into the second half and it not only looked as though his prediction might come true but it also revived Italian nightmares of their defeat by North Korea in 1966.

Sanon's goal was the first past Dino Zoff — who was celebrating his 32nd birthday — in 1,142 minutes of international football. But six minutes later, Gianni Rivera, playing in his fourth World Cup finals, equalized, much to the relief of the Italian camp.

Benetti, with a little help from a defender's deflection, shot Italy into the lead in the 66th minute but it was only after substitute Anastasi scored a third goal 12 minutes from time that Italy could relax a little.

Francillon had a great game in Haiti's goal and the gallant outsiders left the field having made a lot of friends with their style of play. It was unfortunate that full-back Ernst Jean-Joseph was later found to have taken an illegal substance and was banned from the rest of the tournament. He was the first player to be suspended from the World Cup for this reason.

Italy: Zoff; Spinosi, Morini, Burgnich, Facchetti, Mazzola, Capello, Rivera, Benetti, Chinaglia (Anastasi), Riva.
Scorers: Rivera, Benetti, Anastasi
Haiti: Francillon; Bayonne, Jean-Joseph, Nazaire, Auguste, Antoine, Desir, Vorbe, François, G.Saint-Vil(Barthelemy), Sanon.
Scorer: Sanon
Referee: Vicente Llobregat (Venezuela)

POLAND 3   ARGENTINA 2 (Half-time 2-0)

Neckar Stadium, Stuttgart, 15 June
Attendance: 32,700

AFTER some disgraceful performances in recent World Cups, it was nice to see Argentina no longer resorting to physical tactics in their quest for glory. Indeed, there were signs that they were on their way back as a top footballing nation. The fact that they had been awarded the 1978 World Cup probably had some bearing on them being 'good boys' in 1974.

Group Three – Final Table

	P	W	D	L	F	A	Pts
Holland	3	2	1	0	6	1	5
Sweden	3	1	2	0	3	0	4
Bulgaria	3	0	2	1	2	5	2
Uruguay	3	0	1	2	1	6	1

Tarcisco Burgnich of Italy.

Leslaw Cmikiewicz of Poland, substitute against Argentina.

Poland's team that beat Argentina. From left to right: Deyna, Tomaszewski, Gorgon, Zmuda, Szymanowski, Kasperczak, Szarmach, Musial, Lato, Gadocha, Maszczyk.

Jerzy Gorgon of Poland beats Mario Kempes of Argentina, watched by Szymanowski and Deyna in far background.

Poland's trainer Jacek Gmoch hugs Grzegorz Lato after the victory over Argentina.

Their opening match was a good, open contest which saw Poland race into a 2-0 lead in the first eight minutes. Kempes could have given Argentina an early lead but shortly afterwards Lato shot Poland in front after goalkeeper Carnevali dropped a corner. Two minutes later, it was Szarmach's turn to score after a Lato pass had pierced a slack defence.

Ruben Ayala, of Atlético Madrid, sent Mario Kempes on a run and his pass led to Heredia scoring in the 62nd minute to pull one back for the South Americans. But, two minutes later and after yet another error, Lato restored Poland's two-goal advantage after the 'keeper, Carnevali, threw the ball to the feet of the Polish forward. And this error was after Carnevali had just brought off a great save.

The scoring was completed when Babington netted the third goal in five minutes to pull back another, but it was to be the last goal of an entertaining game and Poland established themselves as one of the better teams in the tournament as they played the so-called 'Total Football'.

Poland: Tomaszewski; Gorgon, Szymanowski, Zmuda, Musial, Kasperczak, Deyna, Maszczyk, Lato, Szarmach(Domarski), Gadocha(Cmikiewicz).
Scorers: Lato 2, Szarmach
Argentina: Carnevali; Perfumo, Wolff, Heredia, Sá, Bargas(Telch), Babington, Brindisi (Houseman), Kempes, Ayala, Balbuena.
Scorers: Heredia, Babington
Referee: Clive Thomas (Wales)

ARGENTINA 1   ITALY 1 (Half-time 1-1)

Neckar Stadium, Stuttgart, 19 June
Attendance: 70,100

THIS all-Latin encounter could well have produced a dour defensive match but, on the contrary, it was a good game with both sides playing attractive football and with Argentina offering more in way of entertainment than their European opponents.

Carlos Babington, who nearly joined Stoke City in 1972, had a great game in marshalling the Argentine midfield and it was one of his many defence-splitting passes which led to the South Americans' first goal in the 19th minute. Babington's pass sent Houseman away and he smashed the ball past Zoff.

Italy's equalizer, 15 minutes later, was an own-goal by Perfumo. Benetti's pass was covered by the Argentine goalkeeper Carnevali, but Perfumo deflected the ball past him.

Argentina deserved to win, but the draw meant they had to emerge victorious from their last match to stand any chance of staying in the competition.

Argentina: Carnevali; Wolff(Glaría), Perfumo, Heredia, Sá, Telch, Houseman, Babington, Ayala, Kempes, Yazalde(Chazarreta).
Scorer: Houseman
Italy: Zoff; Spinosi, Facchetti, Benetti, Morini(Wilson), Burgnich, Mazzola, Capello, Anastasi, Rivera(Causio), Riva.
Scorer: Perfumo (og)
Referee: Pavel Kasakov (Soviet Union)

Roberto Boninsegna of Italy, was not used until the final game against Poland, when he came on as a substitute.

Poland's Lato (left) and Szarmach (on the ball) in action against Haiti.

POLAND 7   HAITI 0 (Half-time 5-0)

Olympic Stadium, Munich, 19 June
Attendance: 25,300

AFTER the great showing against Italy in the opening match, Haiti were taken apart by the Poles, who netted five times in the first-half.

The Haiti squad were in disarray following their off-field problems concerning Jean-Joseph's positive drug test and, yet again, it was thanks only to the heroics of goalkeeper Francillon that they kept the score down to seven.

Despite winning at a canter, Poland's first goal did not come until the 17th minute, when Lato netted. But a minute later Deyna made it 2-0 and then three goals in four minutes took Poland's first-half tally to five.

The 'old fashioned' style striker, Szarmach, added the third after half an hour and this was followed in quick succession by one from Gorgon and another from Szarmach.

Szarmach completed his hat-trick five minutes into the second half but the Poles did not find the net again until the 87th minute, when Lato, the man who opened the scoring, also completed it.

Ruben Ayala of Argentina.

Poland: Tomaszewski; Szymanowski, Gorgon, Zmuda, Musial(Gut), Deyna, Kasperczak, Lato, Maszczyk(Cmikiewicz), Szarmach, Gadocha.
Scorers: Lato 2, Deyna, Szarmach 3, Gorgon
Haiti: Francillon; Auguste, Bayonne, Vorbe, Nazaire, Antoine, André(Barthelemy), François, R.Saint-Vil(Racine), Desir, Sanon.
Referee: Suppiah Covindasamy (Singapore)

ARGENTINA 4   HAITI 1 (Half-time 2-0)

Olympic Stadium, Munich, 23 June
Attendance: 25,900

ARGENTINA had to win to stand a chance of remaining in the tournament — and even then they had to rely upon Poland beating Italy. The number of goals scored by Argentina and those conceded by Italy also had a bearing on who went forward to the next series of group matches.

Goals by Yazalde, in the 14th minute, and Houseman, three minutes later, set Argentina on their way to victory. Ayala added a third in the 58th minute before Sanon scored his second goal of the tournament for Haiti. Three minutes later, Yazalde netted Argentina's fourth and it proved to be an important goal as Argentina eventually qualified on goal-difference from Italy — by one goal.

Wilner Nazaire of Haiti.

Argentina: Carnevali; Wolff, Heredia, Perfumo, Sá, Babington, Telch, Houseman(Brindisi), Yazalde, Ayala, Kempes(Balbuena).
Scorers: Yazalde 2, Houseman, Ayala
Haiti: Francillon; Ducoste, Bayonne, Vorbe, Desir, Antoine, G.Saint-Vil(F.Leandre), Racine, Nazaire(M.Leandre), Sanon, Louis.
Scorer: Sanon
Referee: Pablo Sánchez-Ibáñez (Spain)

Philippe Vorbe of Haiti.

POLAND 2   ITALY 1 (Half-time 2-0)

Neckar Stadium, Stuttgart, 23 June
Attendance: 70,100

ITALY needed only to draw to stay in the competition and after a poor showing against

Group Four – Final Table

	P	W	D	L	F	A	Pts
Poland	3	3	0	0	12	3	6
Argentina	3	1	1	1	7	5	3
Italy	3	1	1	1	5	4	3
Haiti	3	0	0	3	2	14	0

Jan Tomaszewski of Poland.

Argentina they dropped two of their established players, Riva and Rivera. Two first-half goals by Poland, however, destroyed the Italians' chances.

Szarmach scored the first in the 39th minute with what was one of the goals of the tournament. The Polish forward raced a full 25 yards to meet a Kasperczak cross before beating Zoff with a header.

A minute before the interval Deyna inflicted the mortal blow by scoring Poland's second goal. Once more Kasperczak played a part in the goal when he dummied his way past two defenders before crossing to Deyna, one of the outstanding players of the tournament. Deyna's right-foot shot from the edge of the penalty area was as spectacular as Szarmach's opening goal.

Italy pushed forward and ten minutes from time nearly pulled a goal back, but Tomaszewski brought off a save from Facchetti at close range. Five minutes later Italy did score through Capello, but it was too late and with Argentina easily beating Haiti, the Italians were out of the tournament. They were, however, fortunate to lose by one goal, Poland were so superior.

After the tournament, back in Poland, the Polish team boss, Kazimierz Gorski, alleged that the Italians had offered his players bribes to ensure the right result for Italy. Gorski later withdrew the allegations.

Poland: Tomaszewski; Szymanowski, Gorgon, Musial, Zmuda, Kasperczak, Deyna, Maszczyk, Gadocha, Szarmach(Cmikiewicz), Lato.
Scorers: Szarmach, Deyna
Italy: Zoff; Spinosi, Facchetti, Benetti, Morini, Burgnich(Wilson), Causio, Mazzola, Capello, Anastasi, Chinaglia(Boninsegna).
Scorer: Capello
Referee: Hans Joachim Weyland (West Germany)

Group A

BRAZIL 1   EAST GERMANY 0 (Half-time 0-0)
Niedersachsen Stadium, Hanover, 26 June
Attendance: 59,700

FOR the first time in the tenth World Cup, the Brazilians showed their attacking flair, despite the fact that they managed only one goal.

The East Germans were tipped by many as potential Finalists and their defence was certainly one of the best left in the tournament. But, despite their many admirers, they were disappointing in their opening second phase match and Brazil deserved their win.

Zé Maria was recalled to the Brazilian defence and his presence certainly brought about an air of composure to a back line which gave a good all-round performance.

Brazil nearly opened the scoring in the fifth minute when a Valdomiro free-kick bounced up and hit East German 'keeper Croy on the head, but their attacking flair was eventually rewarded with a goal after an hour from a Rivelino free-kick, although it was not one of his 'benders' which defenders had come to expect.

Jairzinho joined the defensive wall and cleverly moved out of the way to allow Rivelino to blast a low, hard and straight drive through the wall for Brazil's match-winner.

Brazil: Leão; Zé Maria, Luís Pereira, Mario Marinho, Francisco Marinho, Paulo Cesar Carpegiani, Rivelino, Dirceu, Valdomiro, Jairzinho, Paulo Cesar Lima.
Scorer: Rivelino
East Germany: Croy; Kurbjuweit, Bransch, Weise, Streich, Wätzlich, Lauck(Löwe), Sparwasser, Hamann(Irmscher), Kische, Hoffmann.
Referee: Clive Thomas (Wales)

HOLLAND 4   ARGENTINA 0 (Half-time 2-0)
Park Stadium, Gelsenkirchen, 26 June
Attendance: 55,000

THE South Americans were harshly brought down to earth by a brilliant Dutch side with Johann Cruyff seemingly getting better with every game. Holland gave a display of breathtaking attacking football and destroyed Argentina with a tremendous first-half performance which saw them take a 2-0 lead.

Argentina were sorely missing the midfield skills of Carlos Babington, who was out through suspension after collecting his third booking. But even he would probably have been powerless against the mighty Cruyff.

It was Cruyff who scored Holland's first goal in the 11th minute. Van Hanegem stood on the ball, looked up and with several options, chose to chip the ball over the defence to Cruyff, who brilliantly rounded the 'keeper to score.

The Dutch constantly went forward and had two attempts cleared off the line before Ruud Krol made it 2-0 in the 25th minute, smashing home an unstoppable shot after Jansen's corner had been beaten out to him.

Johnny Rep rose high to head home Cruyff's cross to make it 3-0 after 72 minutes, and in the very last minute Cruyff completed the scoring with his second goal of the game.

After this performance Holland were the new favourites to win the World Cup and looked every bit like champions-elect.

Holland: Jongbloed; Suurbier(Israël), Haan, Rijsbergen, Krol, Jansen, Neeskens, van Hanegem, Rep, Cruyff, Rensenbrink.
Scorers: Cruyff 2, Krol, Rep
Argentina: Carnevali; Perfumo, Sá, Wolff(Glaría), Telch, Heredia, Balbuena, Yazalde, Ayala, Squeo, Houseman(Kempes).
Referee: Bob Davidson (Scotland)

HOLLAND 2   EAST GERMANY 0 (Half-time 1-0)

Park Stadium, Gelsenkirchen, 30 June
Attendance: 69,600

THE East Germans played a defensive game and used Konrad Weise to mark Johann Cruyff out of the game. Weise certainly did a better job than any other man had done so far in the tournament and the powerhouse of the Dutch team was kept very quiet. Nevertheless, Holland still looked dangerous and after they opened their account in the eighth minute, when Neeskens netted his fourth goal in five matches, a big score was anticipated. But it was not until 15 minutes into the second-half that Rensenbrink increased the lead with a superbly-taken goal.

Defeat for the East Germans meant they stood no chance of reaching the Final, but Holland still showed the signs that they had their minds on lifting the trophy.

Holland: Jongbloed; Suurbier, Haan, Rijsbergen, Krol, Jansen, Neeskens, van Hanegem, Rep, Cruyff, Rensenbrink.
Scorers: Neeskens, Rensenbrink
East Germany: Croy; Kische, Bransch, Weise, Kurbjuweit, Pommerenke, Schnupase, Lauck (Kreische), Löwe(Ducke), Sparwasser, Hoffmann.
Referee: Rudolf Scheurer (Switzerland)

Dino Zoff of Italy.

BRAZIL 2   ARGENTINA 1 (Half-time 1-1)

Niedersachsen Stadium, Hanover, 30 June
Attendance: 39,400

BRAZIL were back to the sort of form that had already won them three World Cups and in the second half took charge of the game and ran out comfortable winners, despite the closeness of the score.

It was the first World Cup meeting between these two South American neighbours and the honour of scoring the first goal went to Rivelino, who hammered home a thunderous effort after 31 minutes. But the Brazilian lead lasted a mere three minutes before Brindisi

Rivelino shoots for Brazil against Argentina.

Group A – Final Table

	P	W	D	L	F	A	Pts
Holland	3	3	0	0	8	0	6
Brazil	3	2	0	1	3	3	4
E.Germany	3	0	1	2	1	4	1
Argentina	3	0	1	2	2	7	1

Holland's Cruyff gets past yet another defender.

became the first man to score a goal past Brazil in this tournament when his free-kick over the defensive wall caught goalkeeper Leão out of position.

It was after conceding this goal that Brazil started to take charge and three minutes after the interval Jairzinho's header, from a Zé Maria cross on the right, turned out to be Brazil's winner. Despite dominating the remainder of the second half, Brazil failed to score again but went into their last match, against Holland, with two wins — like their European opponents.

Brazil: Leão; Zé Maria, Luís Pereira, Mario Marinho, Francisco Marinho, Paulo Cesar Carpegiani, Rivelino, Dirceu, Valdomiro, Jairzinho, Paulo Cesar Lima.
Scorers: Rivelino, Jairzinho
Argentina: Carnevali, Glaría, Heredia, Bargas, Sá(Carrascosa) Brindisi, Squeo, Babington, Balbuena, Ayala, Kempes(Houseman).
Scorers: Brindisi
Referee: Vital Loraux (Belgium)

HOLLAND 2   BRAZIL 0 (Half-time 0-0)

Westfalen Stadium, Dortmund, 3 July
Attendance: 53,700

HOLLAND had remained consistently brilliant throughout the tournament whilst Brazil had improved as it had progressed. This meeting was to be a 'winner take all' match with the victors progressing to the World Cup Final, although for Holland a draw would have been good enough.

Sadly, Brazil resorted to a series of ferocious tackles which had been seen from them early in the tournament. In the first two minutes, the referee had pulled them up for three fouls.

Holland, it must be said, were no angels and they dished out some rough treatment as well, although nothing as clinical as that served up by Brazil who were desperate to hold on to their title and would probably have stood more chance if they had played their attacking game.

Holland had the marginal advantage in a goalless first half, but were totally in command in the second period and managed to break down the Brazilian defence. After 50 minutes, Neeskens and Cruyff worked well before Neeskens took the return and, turning through nearly 180°, struck the ball over the top of the 'keeper.

It was only after going a goal down that Brazil pushed forward in search of the two goals now required to take them to the Final. But in the 65th minute, Cruyff volleyed home a Kroll cross from the right to make Brazil's task impossible.

In a game that had memories of the Chile-Italy 'Battle of Santiago' in 1962, Brazil's Luís Pereira was dismissed six minutes from the end for a high tackle on Neeskens. In addition to the sending-off, five other men were booked. Brazil not only surrendered their crown but also their good name.

Holland: Jongbloed; Suurbier, Haan, Rijsbergen, Krol, Neeskens(Israël), van Hanegem, Jansen, Rep, Cruyff, Rensenbrink(de Jong).
Scorers: Neeskens, Cruyff
Brazil: Leão; Zé Maria, Luís Pereira, Mario Marinho, Francisco Marinho, Paulo Cesar Carpegiani, Rivelino, Dirceu, Paulo Cesar Lima(Mirandinha), Jairzinho, Valdomiro.
Referee: Kurt Tschenscher (West Germany)

ARGENTINA 1   EAST GERMANY 1 (Half-time 1-1)

Park Stadium, Gelsenkirchen, 3 July
Attendance: 54,200

THE fact that neither side could progress any further was apparent in the performances of both teams in a dull match which was a disappointment for the large crowd.

The game's only two goals came in the first 20 minutes and thereafter the spectators were subjected to a stodgy diet of sterile football.

Streich gave East Germany the lead in the 14th minute but six minutes later, Houseman equalized for Argentina. Thereafter, there was nothing more of note to tell.

Argentina: Fillol; Wolff, Heredia, Bargas, Carrascosa, Brindisi, Telch, Babington, Houseman, Ayala, Kempes.
Scorer: Houseman
East Germany: Croy; Kurbjuweit, Bransch, Weise, Schnupase, Pommerenke, Löwe(Vogel), Streich(Ducke), Sparwasser, Kische, Hoffmann.
Scorer: Streich
Referee: Jack Taylor (England)

Arend Haan of Holland.

Group B

POLAND 1   SWEDEN 0 (Half-time 1-0)

Neckar Stadium, Stuttgart, 26 June
Attendance: 45,000

ON a wet Stuttgart pitch, Sweden were by far the better side in the early stages and defeat for the fancied Poles looked a distinct possibility, but Grahn and Tapper both missed first-half chances which were to cost the Swedes dearly.

The only goal of the game came two minutes before the interval when Szarmarch headed back a Gadocha cross from the right and leading scorer Lato was there to head the ball home. It was the first goal that Sweden had conceded in 313 minutes of football in the 1974 World Cup.

The Swedes came back well in the second half and in the 63rd minute were awarded a penalty after Gorgon pulled down Torstensson. But Tapper's kick was pushed around the post by Tomaszewski, the man who had defied England in the qualifying competition.

Sweden counted the cost of their misses and had severely damaged their chances of reaching the Final after this defeat.

Poland: Tomaszewski; Szymanowski, Gorgon, Zmuda, Gut, Deyna, Kasperczak, Maszczyk, Lato, Szarmach(Kmiecik), Gadocha.
Scorer: Lato
Sweden: Hellström; Karlsson, Grip, Nordqvist, Andersson(Augustsson), Grahn, Tapper (Ahlström), Larsson, Torstensson, Sandberg, Edström.
Referee: Ramón Barreto Ruíz (Uruguay)

WEST GERMANY 2   YUGOSLAVIA 0 (Half-time 1-0)
Rhein Stadium, Düsseldorf, 26 June
Attendance: 67,500

WEST Germany struggled to find their best form in the first half an hour and it was not

Rainer Bonhof of West Germany.

Action from West Germany's win over Yugoslavia in the Rhein Stadium, Düsseldorf.

Uli Hoeness of West Germany.

Georg Schwarzenbeck of West Germany in action against Yugoslavia.

Kazimierz Deyna of Poland.

until they scored their opening goal in the 39th minute that they started to play something like championship-winning football.

Beckenbauer was back to his best as he dominated midfield and, for the first time, the German fans were delighted with their team's performance.

Attacking full-back Paul Breitner scored the German's opening goal with a long-range shot. Gerd Müller, who had many scoring chances, eventually added his name to the score-sheet 13 minutes from time, when he was on the end of a good move involving Overath and Hoeness.

West Germany were second favourites behind Holland to win the World Cup, but at last their own fans were pleased with the way they played.

West Germany: Maier; Vogts, Schwarzenbeck, Beckenbauer, Breitner, Bonhof, Wimmer (Hoeness), Hölzenbein(Flohe), Overath, Müller, Herzog.
Scorers: Breitner, Müller
Yugoslavia: Maric; Buljan, Hadziabdić, Muzinić, Katalinski, Oblak(Jerković), Popivoda, Acimović, Surjak, Karasi, Dzajić(Petković).
Referee: Armando Marques (Brazil)

POLAND 2   YUGOSLAVIA 1 (Half-time 1-1)

Wald Stadium, Frankfurt, 30 June
Attendance: 53,200

POLAND maintained their 100 per cent record but, for the second successive match, were fortunate to come away with a win. Yugoslavia, meanwhile, played their best football of the tournament and showed themselves to be a very skilful side.

Deyna opened the scoring after 25 minutes, when he netted from the penalty-spot after an infringement by Karasi. But two minutes before half-time, the Yugoslav forward equalized to make amends for conceding the penalty. The goal came from a Bogicević run which led to substitute Jerković gliding the ball to Karasi, who rounded the 'keeper before scoring.

Lato never stopped running and his hard work was rewarded with yet another goal in the 62nd minute, when he beat the goalkeeper with a delicate header from Gadocha's corner. It turned out to be the winner and Poland remained the only unbeaten team in the tournament, albeit somewhat fortuitously.

Poland: Tomaszewski; Szymanowski, Gorgon, Zmuda, Musial, Kasperczak, Maszczyk, Deyna (Domarski), Lato, Szarmach(Cmikiewicz), Gadocha.
Scorers: Deyna (pen), Lato
Yugoslavia: Maric; Buljan, Hadziabdić, Bogicević, Katalinski, Oblak(Jerković), Petkovic (V.Petrović), Karasi, Bajević, Acimović, Surjak.
Scorer: Karasi
Referee: Rudolf Glöckner (East Germany)

WEST GERMANY 4   SWEDEN 2 (Half-time 0-1)

Rhein Stadium, Düsseldorf, 30 June
Attendance: 67,800

WEST Germany's improvement continued and the addition of Bonhof to the team coincided with their revival. His talents added more fire to the midfield and West Germany were now looking like potential world champions.

Despite their improved form, they still had to work hard to beat a good Swedish side, for whom Edström and Sandberg again proved to be a lethal strike force. And it was Edström who put them in front in the 26th minute with a well-timed left-foot volley after Schwarzenbeck's weak clearance. The goal came from one of Sweden's rare attacks in the first quarter of the game, which was played in torrential rain.

Six minutes after taking the lead, the Swedes lost Larsson through injury and his departure upset their rhythm. Nevertheless, they held on to their lead until the 50th minute when Overath hit a low drive from the edge of the box after Beckenbauer's shot had been punched out by the 'keeper.

A minute later, Germany were in the lead. Müller created an opening for Bonhof and his shot went into the net after rebounding off both uprights.

But the scoring was far from over. Sandberg made it 2-2 with the third goal in three minutes and in the closing stages, West Germany scored two late goals. The first was from substitute Grabowski, again after good work by Müller, and in the closing minutes, Hoeness converted a penalty after Müller had been brought down.

With two wins, a place in the Final was there for West Germany — if they could draw with Poland in the last match.

West Germany: Maier, Vogts, Schwarzenbeck, Beckenbauer, Breitner, Hoeness, Overath, Bonhof, Hölzenbein(Flohe), Müller, Herzog(Grabowski).
Scorers: Overath, Bonhof, Grabowski, Hoeness (pen)
Sweden: Hellström; Olsson, Augustsson, Karlsson, Nordqvist, Larsson(Ejderstedt), Torstensson, Tapper, Edström, Grahn, Sandberg.
Scorers: Edström, Sandberg
Referee: Pavel Kasakov (Soviet Union)

Gerhard Müller of West Germany.

SWEDEN 2 YUGOSLAVIA 1 (Half-time 1-1)

Rhein Stadium, Düsseldorf, 3 July
Attendance: 37,700

THIS game was purely academic. Neither team could reach the Final, or even qualify for the third place play-off.

Ivan Surjak put Yugoslavia ahead in the 27th minute, but Sweden levelled the scores three minutes later through Edström, who scored his fourth goal of the tournament. The game seemed destined for a draw but then Conny Torstensson scored the winner for Sweden four minutes from time.

Sweden: Hellström; Olsson, Karlsson, Nordqvist, Augustsson, Tapper, Grahn, Persson, Torstensson, Edström, Sandberg.
Scorers: Edström, Torstensson
Yugoslavia: Maric; Buljan, Hadziabdić, Katalinski, Bogicević, Pavlović(Peruzović), V.Petrović (Karasi), Jerković, Surjak, Acimović, Dzajić.
Scorer: Surjak.
Referee: Luis Pestarino (Argentina)

Ralf Edström, scored for Sweden.

WEST GERMANY 1 POLAND 0 (Half-time 0-0)

Wald Stadium, Frankfurt, 3 July
Attendance: 62,000

THE dreadful weather which had dogged the 1974 World Cup continued and the kick-off was delayed because of a cloudburst which turned the pitch into a quagmire. Despite the conditions, however, both sides played attractive football, although the Poles were slightly handicapped because the pitch did not allow them to play their usual fast, attacking game.

Left (top): Wolfgang Overath in action against Poland. *Left (bottom):* Jürgen Grabowski (centre) fends off the challenge of Poland's Jan Damarski.

Grzegorz Lato of Poland.

Group B – Final Table

	P	W	D	L	F	A	Pts
W.Germany	3	3	0	0	7	2	6
Poland	3	2	0	1	3	2	4
Sweden	3	1	0	2	4	6	2
Yugoslavia	3	0	0	3	2	6	0

STATISTICS

Goalscorers:
7 — Grzegorz Lato (Poland).
5 — Andrzej Szarmach (Poland), Johannes Neeskens (Holland).
4 — Gerhard Müller (West Germany), Ralf Edström (Sweden), Johannes Rep (Holland).
3 — Paul Breitner (West Germany), Roberto Rivelino (Brazil), Dusan Bajević (Yugoslavia), René Orlando Houseman (Argentina), Johannes Cruyff (Holland), Kazimierz Deyna (Poland).
2 — Wolfgang Overath (West Germany), Jair Ventura Filho Jairzinho (Brazil), Ivan Surjak, Stanislav Karasi (both Yugoslavia), Joachim Streich (East Germany), Joe Jordan (Scotland), Roland Sandberg (Sweden), Emmanuel Sanon (Haiti), Héctor Casimiro Yazalde (Argentina).
1 — Bernhard Cullmann, Reiner Bonhof, Jürgen Grabowski, Uli Hoeness (all West Germany), Valdomiro Vaz Franco (Brazil), Gianni Rivera, Romeo Benetti, Pietro Anastasi, Fabio Capello (all Italy), Sergio Ahumada (Chile), Dragan Dzajić, Josip Katalinski, Vladimir Bogicević, Branko Oblak, Ilja Petković (all Yugoslavia), Martin Hoffmann, Jürgen Sparwasser (both East Germany), Peter Lorimer (Scotland), Conny Torstensson (Sweden), Ramón Armando Heredia, Carlos Babington, Ruben Hugo Ayala, Miguel Angel Brindisi (all Argentina), Christo Bonev (Bulgaria), Ricardo Pavoni (Uruguay), Theo de Jong, Ruud Krol, Rob Rensenbrink (all Holland), Jerzy Gorgon (Poland).

Own-goals:
Colin Curran (Australia v East Germany), Ruud Krol (Holland v Bulgaria), Roberto Alfredo Perfumo (Argentina v Italy).

Hat-tricks
Dusan Bejević (Yugoslavia v Zaïre), Andrzej Szarmach (Poland v Haiti).

Fastest goal
80 seconds — Johannes Neeskens (Holland v West Germany).

Most goals (team)
16 — Poland

Teams failing to score
Australia and Zaïre

Total goals scored: 97
Average per game: 2.55

Top: Beckenbauer gets past two Polish defenders.

Right: Deyna (centre) in a midfield tussle with Brazilians Paulo Cesar Carpeggianai (17) and Jairzinho.

Although West Germany needed only a draw to reach the Final they still went on the attack and, despite the goalless first-half, the game was still an entertaining affair.

Lato had two good chances to put the Poles ahead in the first half and Maier brought off a remarkable save from him to keep Germany in the game.

When the only goal of the game came in the 76th minute, it was by Germany's lethal goalscorer, Gerd Müller. It followed good work from Bonhof, who moved into the penalty area and, as he was being tackled, passed to Müller. Surprisingly, this was the first scoring chance that Müller had all game and it was also the first lapse by the Polish defence. It was to prove costly, too, and they missed out on the chance of their first World Cup Final appearance.

West Germany: Maier, Vogts, Schwarzenbeck, Beckenbauer, Breitner, Bonhof, Overath, Hoeness, Grabowski, Müller, Hölzenbein.
Scorer: Müller
Poland: Tomaszewski; Szymanowski, Gorgon, Zmuda, Musial, Kasperczak(Cmikiewicz), Deyna, Maszczyk(Kmiecik), Lato, Domarski, Gadocha.
Referee: Erich Linemayr (Austria)

Third place play-off
POLAND 1   BRAZIL 0 (Half-time 0-0)

Olympic Stadium, Munich, 6 July
Attendance: 79,000

MANY people now felt that the third place play-off was a rather pointless fixture and this latest game was again a rather boring affair. With virtually nothing to play for, the game provided few thrills and at half-time the teams left the field to jeers from the surprisingly large crowd, who should have known that, by tradition, they were hardly likely to be treated to an entertaining game.

The only highlight of the first half was a missed chance by Jairzinho and it was not until the 76th minute that the tournament's top scorer, Grzegorz Lato, netted the only goal of the game, and his seventh of the tournament, when he hammered a low shot past Leão

after breaking clear on the right. The linesman had his flag up for offside, but the referee chose to ignore it. Jairzinho was convinced that the goal was offside and protested so much that he was booked.

   Lato missed an easy chance in the last minute, but the reigning Olympic champions scraped through 1-0 in a match that once again raised a question mark over its validity.

Poland: Tomaszewski, Szymanowski, Gorgon, Zmuda, Musial, Maszczyk, Deyna, Kasperczak (Cmikiewicz), Lato, Szarmach(Kapka), Gadocha.
Scorer: Lato
Brazil: Leão; Zé Maria, Alfredo, Mario Marinho, Francisco Marinho, Paulo Cesar Carpegiani, Rivelino, Ademir(Mirandinha), Valdomiro, Jairzinho, Dirceu.
Referee: Aurelio Angonese (Italy)

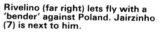

Rivelino (far right) lets fly with a 'bender' against Poland. Jairzinho (7) is next to him.

Final

WEST GERMANY 2   HOLLAND 1 (Half-time 2-1)

Olympic Stadium, Munich, 7 July
Attendance: 77,833

THESE talented teams provided an exhibition of 'total football' which thrilled a world-wide television audience of 1,000 million. The Dutch were the more skilful, but West Germany had a determination to win that even the talent of Johann Cruyff could do little about.

   The game opened in dramatic fashion. First, just before the start of the game it was noted the corner flags were missing. And with the game less than a minute old, and without a German player touching the ball, English referee Jack Taylor awarded Holland a penalty after Cruyff had been brought down by Hoeness. Neeskens scored from the spot, the first time that a penalty had been converted in a World Cup Final.

   Remarkably, the game saw a second penalty awarded in the 25th minute, but this time it was to the Germans after Hölzenbein had been brought down by Jansen. Breitner's well-placed kick into the corner of the net beat Jan Jongbloed.

   The German midfield of Bonhof and Beckenbauer was outstanding and it was Bonhof who made a move down the right two minutes before half-time before getting the ball into

Paul Breitner of West Germany.

Top: Neeskens' first-minute penalty for Holland in the 1974 World Cup Final. *Bottom:* Breitner (arms raised) celebrates his 25th-minute penalty equalizer for the Germans.

Penalties
Scored: Paul Breitner (West Germany v Holland) *Referee: Jack Taylor (England).* Johannes Neeskens (Holland v West Germany) *Referee: Jack Taylor (England).* Johannes Neeskens (Holland v Bulgaria) *Referee: Anthony Boslović (Australia).* Johannes Neeskens (Holland v Bulgaria) *Referee: Anthony Boslović (Australia).* Uli Hoeness (West Germany v Sweden) *Referee: Pavel Kasakov (Soviet Union).* Kazimierz Deyna (Poland v Yugoslavia) *Referee: Armando Marques (Brazil).*

Most Appearances
7 — *Emerson Leão, Mario Péres Ulibarri Marinho, Francisco das Chagas, Roberto Rivelino, Jair Ventura Filho Jairzinho* (all Brazil), *Josef Maier, Hans-Hubert Vogts, Paul Breitner,* Georg Schwarzenbeck, *Franz Beckenbauer, Uli Hoeness, Gerhard Müller,* Wolfgang Overath (all West Germany), *Jan Jongbloed,* Willem Suurbier, *Ruud Krol, Arend Haan,* Willem Rijsbergen, *Wilem Jansen, Johannes Rep,* Johannes Neeskens, *Johannes Cruyff,* Willem Van Hanegem (all Holland), *Jan Tomaszewski, Antoni Syzmanowski, Wladislaw Zmuda, Jerzy Gorgon,* Henryk Kasperczak, *Grzegorz Lato, Zygmunt Maszczyk, Kazimierz Deyna* (all Poland).
Players in italics played in 7 complete games.

Sendings-off
Raymond Richards (Australia v Chile) *Referee: Jafar Namdar (Iran).* Carlos Caszely (Chile v West Germany) *Referee: Dogan Babacan (Turkey).* Júlio Montero-Castillo (Uruguay v Holland) *Referee: Karoly Palotai (Hungary).* Luis Edmundo Pereira (Brazil v Holland) *Referee: Kurt Tschenscher (West Germany).* Mulamba N'daye (Zaïre v Yugoslavia) *Referee: Omar Delgado (Colombia).*

Most players used
19 — Argentina, East Germany and Haiti

Number of players used by Finalists
18 — West Germany
15 — Holland

the area, from where it was netted by Müller with a brilliant goal on the turn. It took Müller's overall tally of goals in World Cup finals to 14 and surpassed Juste Fontaine's previous record. It was Müller's last match in international football.

It turned out to be the goal which won West Germany the World Cup because the second half was the first-ever goalless second period in a World Cup Final. It was also another Final which was won by the side conceding the first goal.

Injuries to Rensenbrink and Rijsbergen did not help Holland's cause. Furthermore, Johann Cruyff was not allowed the freedom he had been used to and his frustration boiled over into a booking from referee Taylor.

The German fans soon forgot about their team's poor performances at the start of the tournament and praised their heroes after lifting the trophy on home soil. Like their last win, in 1954, they endured defeat on the way — but who cared?

Wolfgang Overath eventually added a winners' medal to his collection of one runners-up and one third-place medal. He is the only man in World Cup history to have collected all three.

West Germany: Josef Maier; Hans-Hubert Vogts, Georg Schwarzenbeck, Franz Beckenbauer, Paul Breitner, Rainer Bonhof, Uli Hoeness, Wolfgang Overath, Jürgen Grabowski, Gerhard Müller, Bernd Hölzenbein.
Scorers: Breitner (pen), Müller
Holland: Jan Jongbloed; Willem Suurbier, Willem Rijsbergen(Theo de Jong), Arend Haan, Ruud Krol, Willem Jansen, Willem van Hanegem, Johannes Neeskens, Johannes Rep, Johannes Cruyff, Rob Rensenbrink(René van de Kerkhof).
Scorer: Neeskens (pen)
Referee: Jack Taylor (England)

Wolfgang Overath (12) in a battle
with Johann Cruyff. Beckenbauer
(5) is in close attendance.

Jongbloed punches clear for
Holland, watched by Haan (2),
Overath (12) and Beckenbauer (5).

Above: A yellow card for Cruyff.

Right (top and middle): West Germany collect the World Cup and begin their celebrations.

Opposite page: West German skipper Franz Beckenbauer offers the World Cup trophy to goalkeeper Sepp Maier.

Holland line up before the 1974 World Cup Final. From left to right: Neeskens, Suurbier, Rijsbergen, Jansen, Krol, Rep, van Hanegem, Rensenbrink, Haan, Jongbloed, Cruyff.

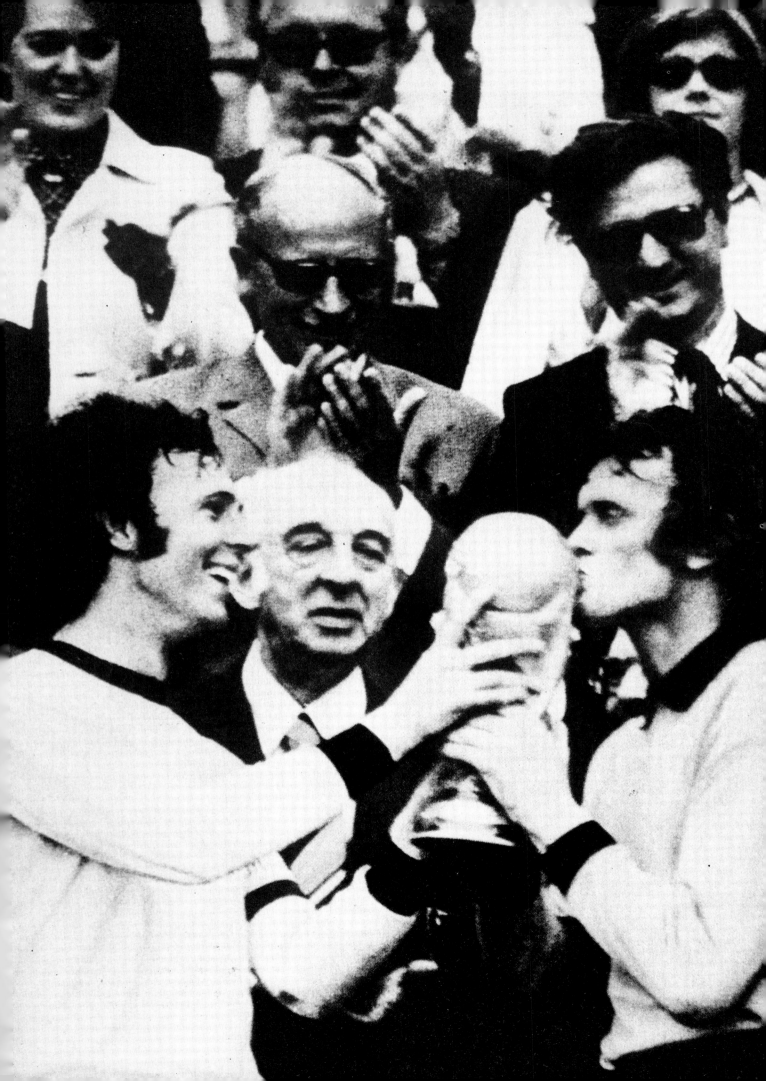

MEN WHO MADE THE HEADLINES - 1978

Mario Kempes
(Argentina)

MARIO Kempes compensated for failing to score in the 1974 World Cup by finishing top scorer with six goals in 1978, including two in the Final when he gained a winners' medal. Kempes was born at Belville, Córdoba, on 15 July 1954 and, after rejection by Boca Juniors, began with Instituto Córdoba and then Rosario Central before making his international debut in 1973, against Bolivia. In 1976, the man with great balance, speed and a powerful shot was transferred to Valencia. In his first full season against tight Spanish defences, he was the League's top scorer with 24 goals, the highest total for ten years. His 28 the following year was the highest total since Di Stefano's 31 in 1956-7. After a Spanish Cup-winners' medal in 1979, Kempes figured in Valencia's penalty decider in the 1980 European Cup-winners' Cup Final win over Arsenal. In March 1981, a million-pound deal took him to River Plate. In his third World Cup in 1982 he again failed to score and, after being substituted against Brazil, his World Cup career ended after 18 matches, three behind the record. Later that year he was back at Valencia and continued to delight Spanish fans with his goals before finishing his career in Austria.

Rob Rensenbrink
(Holland)

WHEN Johann Cruyff missed the 1978 World Cup, Rob Rensenbrink rose to the challenge and was his team's top scorer with five goals as they reached their second successive Final. Born at Oostzaan in 1947, he began with DWS (Amsterdam) before starring in Belgium, with Bruges, then Anderlecht. He made his international debut against Scotland in 1968 and by 1974 was an established international. He missed only one of Holland's games in the 1974 finals but manager Rinus Michels gambled on his fitness in the Final and Resenbrink took no part in the second half. He played in three successive European Cup-winners' Cup Finals, scoring two goals in each of Anderlecht's successes in 1976 and 1978. In Holland's opening game of the 1978 World Cup, he scored all three goals against Iran, including two penalties. Holland were beaten by Argentina after extra-time in the Final after a Rensenbrink shot hit a post in the last minute of normal time. His goal against Scotland was the 1,000th World Cup goal. He played his 46th and last international match in 1979 and in 1980 wound down his career with a spell at Portland Timbers in the NASL, followed by a brief stay with Toulouse in France in 1981.

Teofilio Cubillas
(Peru)

TEOFILIO Cubillas played in two tournaments eight years apart and scored five goals in each, making him one of the most prolific scorers in World Cup history. A virtually unknown 20-year-old in 1970, he was soon acknowledged after helping Peru to the quarter-finals. 'Nene' Cubillas was born at Lima in March 1949 and began with local team, Alianza. He liked to run at defences, was fast and had good close control and a fine shot. South American Footballer of the Year in 1972, the following year he joined FC Basle for £97,000. Six months later he signed for FC Porto, for £200,000, and settled into a midfield role. Peru did not qualify for the 1974 World Cup finals but 12 months later they were South American champions, Cubillas scoring twice in their 3-1 first-leg semi-final win over Brazil. When he helped Peru reach the second phase of the 1978 World Cup, he was an Alianza player again. In 1979, Cubillas joined George Best at Fort Lauderdale and in five seasons in the NASL scored 65 goals, including three in seven minutes against Los Angeles Aztecs in 1981. The 1982 World Cup failed to produce any more goals for him and he bowed out after 88 caps and 38 goals.

The Hosts Win Again
Argentina 1978

César Menotti, manager of the
victorious Argentinians.

ARGENTINA had been promised the 11th World Cup in 1966 but ten years later, a military junta headed by General Videla ousted Isabella Perón amidst charges of corruption. The country was under a state of siege and an estimated 5,000 people lost their lives with many more jailed and tortured.

With two years to the start of the World Cup, then, it was a worrying time for FIFA and some European countries, notably Holland, talked openly about boycotting the championships if they were staged in Argentina. But FIFA gave the go-ahead for the final stages to take place as planned. The new Argentinian regime had guaranteed a trouble-free tournament, but the delivery of such an undertaking looked unlikely when General Omar Actis, the president of the Argentina World Cup Organizing Committee, was assassinated by guerrillas. However, the tension was eased when the *Mononeros*, a left-wing terrorist movement, issued a statement to say there would be no violence or kidnappings because 'soccer is a game of the working class'. Happily, all the pre-tournament worries were unfounded and the 11th World Cup was to pass without a major incident.

A major rebuilding programme on Argentina's football stadiums was undertaken and, whilst most were ready in time for the start of the tournament, the state of some pitches left much to be desired and were well below standard for such an important event.

The cost of staging a World Cup competition had spiralled since the early days and in an effort to cut those costs, the Argentinian organizers engaged on a massive marketing campaign with the sale of every conceivable item bearing the competition's mascot or emblem.

The format for the 11th World Cup was identical to that of 1974 and from an initial entry of more than 100 nations, 16 teams made the journey to Argentina for South America's first finals since Chile in 1962. Because of their home advantage, Argentina were regarded as one of the fancied teams, along with their neighbours Brazil who, on a tour of Europe, had shown that they were back to their fluent best.

Argentina were managed by the chain-smoking 40-year-old César Luís Menotti. Many of his country's top players were earning their living in Europe and Menotti refused to call upon them for the tournament, with one exception — the brilliant Valencia striker, Mario Kempes. His recall from Europe as the only ex-patriot proved Menotti's shrewdness, for Kempes turned out to be the tournament's top scorer.

Brazil, on the other hand, were to endure problems on and off the field. Their fluent style was rarely evident in Argentina and problems between coach and players did not help. The Brazilian fans became increasingly frustrated at what they were witnessing and showed their dissent accordingly.

The Dutch, on paper, appeared to be past their best and were without Johann Cruyff, who refused to travel because of the political situation in Argentina. West Germany also appeared to be a fading nation and they, too, were missing the services of a key player, Franz Beckenbauer, who was playing his football in the United States with New York Cosmos. He had more pressing engagements in the North American Soccer League at the time of the 1978 World Cup.

Poland, Spain and France were three of the more fancied European teams and Britain's sole representatives, Scotland, were also tipped for the title — if only by their own army of fans and their manager Ally MacLeod. Alas, their squad of wonderfully gifted individuals did not blend as a team until it was too late.

Iran and Tunisia, who were to become the revelations of the tournament, were first-timers whilst there was a welcome return for Austria, France, Hungary, Spain, Mexico and Peru, all of whom had been missing in 1974. For Austria, it was their first finals since 1958.

The 11th World Cup was a colourful affair but still missed the talents of Cruyff, Pelé and Beckenbauer. It had its moments of magic and its ugly moments but, all in all, it was not a bad tournament. Nevertheless, one could not help but feel a sense of relief at Argentina's ultimate success. There was always a feverish undercurrent of tension in the country and one had to wonder what would have happened had the hosts not lifted the trophy.

FIFA president João Havelange.

The home of River Plate FC and
scene of the 1978 World Cup Final.

1978 Qualifying Competition

FOR the first time the number of entrants for the World Cup topped the 100 mark, although the tally of teams taking part in the preliminary tournament was reduced to double figures with the withdrawal of North Korea, United Arab Emirates, Central African Republic, Sudan, Tanzania and Zaïre.

Sierra Leone and Niger got the tournament underway on 7 March 1976 and, 21 months later, 14 teams qualified to join the holders, West Germany, and hosts, Argentina, for the final stages. There were two newcomers, Iran and Tunisia, the latter turning out to be the surprise team of the tournament as they showed how much the African game had developed.

Uruguay and England were the two previous winners who failed to qualify, while other notable absentees were Portugal, Czechoslovakia and the Soviet Union.

England's hopes disappeared when Italy, needing to win their final match against Luxembourg did so 3-0. England lost only one game, to Antognoni and Bettega goals in Rome, and it was that defeat which cost them a place in the finals. However, they had their preparations severely hindered with the resignation of manager Don Revie, midway through the qualifying tournament. He found the financial rewards offered by the United Arab Emirates too great a temptation.

Portugal were no match for Poland, who qualified undefeated, and Austria reached their first finals for 20 years by winning their last match, 1-0 away to Turkey. That victory took them above 1974 first-timers, East Germany.

Northern Ireland were unfortunate to find themselves in a group containing the 1974 runners-up, Holland, who qualified with ease, dropping only one point in the process.

The Republic of Ireland were also eliminated, despite beating France in Dublin, thanks to a Liam Brady goal. But the French went on to qualify from the three-team group by beating Bulgaria in the final match. Sweden also qualified, despite losing a match to second-placed Norway.

The best chance of a UK representative came from Group Seven. With Scotland and Wales being two of the three representatives, only Czechoslovakia stood in the way of a British team reaching the finals. The honour went to Scotland, who clinched victory in front of nearly 51,000 fans at Liverpool's Anfield Stadium, which Wales chose as their 'home' venue. Goals from Don Masson (penalty) and Kenny Dalglish ensured Scotland's second successive appearance in the finals.

Yugoslavia fared well in the 1974 finals, but were disappointing in the 1978 qualifiers, finishing third behind Romania and qualifiers, Spain. The Soviet Union lost to both Greece and Hungary in the final European group. Hungary finished top of the table but had to play a two-legged match against Bolivia. The Magyars won 9-2 on aggregate.

Brazil were held to draws by Colombia and Paraguay, but impressed in beating Colombia in the return match as they qualified for the South American group final — as did Bolivia, who came through their group at the expense of Venezuela and Uruguay. The Uruguayans suffered a severe set-back by failing to win either of their opening two matches. Also through to the South American group final was Peru, who topped Group Three after beating fellow contenders Chile in the final match.

Brazil, Bolivia and Peru played each other once at Cali, Colombia. The winners and runners-up both qualified for the finals, whilst the third-placed team had to meet Hungary for the right to progress to Argentina. Brazil made sure they did not have to play the Europeans with a convincing 8-0 win over Bolivia.

A complicated series of matches in the CONCACAF qualifiers resulted in six teams reaching a group final in Mexico. And after 15 more matches, Mexico eventually qualified. They had to play nine games to reach the finals and scored 23 goals. But they were fortunate to qualify out of their first group with a better goal-difference over the United States and Canada, after all three teams finished level on four points each. The Canada-USA match in Vancouver was the first World Cup game played on an artificial surface. The return at Seattle was the first World Cup match to be played indoors.

Iran were the Asian qualifiers from 17 entrants, winning ten of 12 matches in reaching their first finals. And in the African group, a complicated series of 45 matches saw Tunisia qualify after beating Egypt 4-1 in the final match; Egypt would have qualified for their first finals since 1934, had they drawn the match. Tunisia were perhaps fortunate to reach the final group matches because they survived a first-round penalty shoot-out against Morocco.

By the time Tunisia and Egypt met on 11 December 1977, 15 of the 16 finalists were known. Tunisia completed the line-up for the 11th World Cup.

Results

EUROPE

Group One

23 May 1976 *Limassol*	Cyprus	1 Denmark	5
16 Oct 1976 *Oporto*	Portugal	1 Poland	2
27 Oct 1976 *Copenhagen*	Denmark	5 Cyprus	0
31 Oct 1976 *Warsaw*	Poland	5 Cyprus	0
17 Nov 1976 *Lisbon*	Portugal	1 Denmark	0
5 Dec 1976 *Limassol*	Cyprus	1 Portugal	2
1 May 1977 *Copenhagen*	Denmark	1 Poland	2
15 May 1977 *Limassol*	Cyprus	1 Poland	3
21 Sep 1977 *Chorzów*	Poland	4 Denmark	1
9 Oct 1977 *Copenhagen*	Denmark	2 Portugal	4
29 Oct 1977 *Chorzów*	Poland	1 Portugal	1
16 Nov 1977 *Faro*	Portugal	4 Cyprus	0

Final Table

	P	W	D	L	F	A	Pts	
Poland	6	5	1	0	17	4	11	
Portugal	6	4	1	1	12	6	9	**Poland qualified**
Denmark	6	2	0	4	14	12	4	
Cyprus	6	0	0	6	3	24	0	

Group Two

13 Jun 1976 *Helsinki*	Finland	1 England	4
22 Sep 1976 *Helsinki*	Finland	7 Luxembourg	1
13 Oct 1976 *London*	England	2 Finland	1
16 Oct 1976 *Luxembourg*	Luxembourg	1 Italy	4
17 Nov 1976 *Rome*	Italy	2 England	0

England manager Don Revie points angrily as England go down 2-0 in Rome. Stan Bowles is the player on the ground, Mick Channon is extreme right.

30 Mar 1977 *London*   England ....5 Luxembourg.....0
26 May 1977 *Luxembourg* Luxembourg.....0 Finland...........1
8 Jun 1977 *Helsinki*   Finland..........0 Italy...............3
12 Oct 1977 *Luxembourg* Luxembourg.....0 England 2
15 Oct 1977 *Turin*   Italy...............6 Finland...........1
16 Oct 1977 *London*   England ....2 Italy...............0
3 Dec 1977 *Rome*   Italy...............3 Luxembourg.....0

Final Table

	P	W	D	L	F	A	Pts	
Italy	6	5	0	1	18	4	10	
England	6	5	0	1	15	4	10	**Italy qualified**
Finland	6	2	0	4	11	16	4	
Luxembourg	6	0	0	6	2	22	0	

Group Three

31 Oct 1976 *Izmir*   Turkey............4 Malta 0
17 Nov 1976 *Dresden*   East Germany ...1 Turkey............1
5 Dec 1976 *Gzira*   Malta ....0 Austria............1
2 Apr 1977 *Valletta*   Malta ....0 East Germany ...1
17 Apr 1977 *Vienna*   Austria............1 Turkey............0
30 Apr 1977 *Saltzburg* Austria............9 Malta 0
24 Sep 1977 *Vienna*   Austria............1 East Germany ...1
12 Oct 1977 *Leipzig*   East Germany ...1 Austria............1
29 Oct 1977 *Potsdam*   East Germany ...9 Malta 0
30 Oct 1977 *Izmir*   Turkey............0 Austria............1
16 Nov 1977 *Izmir*   Turkey............1 East Germany ...2
27 Nov 1977 *Valletta*   Malta ....0 Turkey............3

Final Table

	P	W	D	L	F	A	Pts	
Austria	6	4	2	0	14	2	10	
E.Germany	6	3	3	0	15	4	9	**Austria qualified**
Turkey	6	2	1	3	9	5	5	
Malta	6	0	0	6	0	27	0	

Group Four

5 Sep 1976 *Reykjavík*   Iceland............0 Belgium 1
8 Sep 1976 *Reykjavík*   Iceland............0 Holland 1
13 Oct 1976 *Rotterdam*   Holland ....2 N. Ireland 2
10 Nov 1976 *Liège*   Belgium ....2 N. Ireland 0
26 Mar 1977 *Antwerp*   Belgium ....0 Holland 2
11 Jun 1977 *Reykjavík*   Iceland............1 N. Ireland 0

Top left: A good start at Wembley as Dennis Tueart gives England a fourth-minute lead over Finland, but the result was only a narrow 2-1 win for the home side. ***Above:*** Belgium's Raoul Lambert heads his side's second goal against Northern Ireland with Hunter (left), Nicholl (centre) and Jennings (right) looking on.

31 Aug 1977 *Nijmegen*   Holland ....4 Iceland............1
4 Sep 1977 *Brussels*   Belgium ....4 Iceland............0
21 Sep 1977 *Belfast*   N. Ireland ....2 Iceland............0
12 Oct 1977 *Belfast*   N. Ireland ....0 Holland 1
26 Oct 1977 *Amsterdam*   Holland ....1 Belgium 0
16 Nov 1977 *Belfast*   N. Ireland ....3 Belgium 0

Final Table

	P	W	D	L	F	A	Pts	
Holland	6	5	1	0	11	3	11	
Belgium	6	3	0	3	7	6	6	**Holland qualified**
N. Ireland	6	2	1	3	7	6	5	
Iceland	6	1	0	5	2	12	2	

Group Five

9 Oct 1976 *Sofia*   Bulgaria ....2 France 2
17 Nov 1976 *Paris*   France ....2 Rep of Ireland ...0
30 Mar 1977 *Dublin*   Rep of Ireland ...1 France 0
1 Jun 1977 *Sofia*   Bulgaria ....2 Rep of Ireland ...1
12 Oct 1977 *Dublin*   Rep of Ireland ...0 Bulgaria 0
16 Nov 1977 *Paris*   France ....3 Bulgaria 1

Final Table

	P	W	D	L	F	A	Pts	
France	4	2	1	1	7	4	5	
Bulgaria	4	1	2	1	5	6	4	**France qualified**
Rep of Ireland	4	1	1	2	2	4	3	

Group Six

16 Jun 1976 *Stockholm*   Sweden ....2 Norway 0
8 Sep 1976 *Oslo*   Norway ....1 Switzerland 0
9 Jun 1976 *Basle*   Switzerland ......1 Sweden 2
8 Jun 1976 *Stockholm*   Sweden ....2 Switzerland 1
7 Sep 1976 *Oslo*   Norway ....2 Sweden 1
30 Oct 1977 *Berne*   Switzerland ......1 Norway 0

Final Table

	P	W	D	L	F	A	Pts	
Sweden	4	3	0	1	7	4	6	
Norway	4	2	0	2	3	4	4	**Sweden qualified**
Switzerland	4	1	0	3	3	5	2	

Group Seven

13 Oct 1976 *Prague*   Czechoslovakia ..2 Scotland 0
17 Oct 1976 *Glasgow*   Scotland ....1 Wales 0
30 Mar 1977 *Wrexham*   Wales ....3 Czechoslovakia ..0
21 Sep 1977 *Glasgow*   Scotland ....3 Czechoslovakia ..1
12 Oct 1977 *Liverpool*   Wales ....0 Scotland 2
16 Nov 1977 *Prague*   Czechoslovakia ..1 Wales 0

Final Table

	P	W	D	L	F	A	Pts	
Scotland	4	3	0	1	6	3	6	
Czechoslovakia	4	2	0	2	4	6	4	**Scotland qualified**
Wales	4	1	0	3	3	4	2	

Group Eight

10 Oct 1976 *Seville*	Spain 1	Yugoslavia 0
6 Apr 1977 *Bucharest*	Romania 1	Spain 0
8 May 1977 *Zagreb*	Yugoslavia 0	Romania 2
26 Oct 1977 *Madrid*	Spain 2	Romania 0
13 Nov 1977 *Bucharest*	Romania 4	Yugoslavia 6
30 Nov 1977 *Belgrade*	Yugoslavia 0	Spain 1

Final Table

	P	W	D	L	F	A	Pts	
Spain	4	3	0	1	4	1	6	**Spain qualified**
Romania	4	2	0	2	7	8	4	
Yugoslavia	4	1	0	3	6	8	2	

Group Nine

9 Oct 1976 *Pireus*	Greece 1	Hungary 1
24 Apr 1977 *Moscow*	Soviet Union 2	Greece 0
30 Apr 1977 *Budapest*	Hungary 2	Soviet Union 1
10 May 1977 *Salonika*	Greece 1	Soviet Union 0
18 May 1977 *Tbilisi*	Soviet Union 2	Hungary 0
25 May 1977 *Budapest*	Hungary 3	Greece 1

Final Table

	P	W	D	L	F	A	Pts	
Hungary	4	2	1	1	6	4	5	**Hungary qualified for**
Soviet Union	4	2	0	2	5	3	4	**play-off with third-**
Greece	4	1	1	2	2	6	3	**placed team in South American group final.**

SOUTH AMERICA

Group One

20 Feb 1977 *Bogota*	Colombia 0	Brazil 0
24 Feb 1977 *Bogota*	Colombia 0	Paraguay 1
6 Mar 1977 *Asunción*	Paraguay 1	Colombia 1
9 Mar 1977 *Río de Janeiro*	Brazil 6	Colombia 0
13 Mar 1977 *Asunción*	Paraguay 0	Brazil 1
20 Mar 1977 *Río de Janeiro*	Brazil 1	Paraguay 1

Final Table

	P	W	D	L	F	A	Pts	
Brazil	4	2	2	0	8	1	6	**Brazil qualified for**
Paraguay	4	1	2	1	3	3	4	**South American**
Colombia	4	0	2	2	1	8	2	**group final.**

Group Two

9 Feb 1977 *Caracas*	Venezuela 1	Uruguay..........1
27 Feb 1977 *La Paz*	Bolivia............1	Uruguay..........0
6 Mar 1977 *Caracas*	Venezuela 1	Bolivia............3
13 Mar 1977 *La Paz*	Bolivia............2	Venezuela 0
17 Mar 1977 *Montevideo*	Uruguay..........2	Venezuela 0
27 Mar 1977 *Montevideo*	Uruguay..........2	Bolivia............2

Final Table

	P	W	D	L	F	A	Pts	
Bolivia	4	3	1	0	8	3	7	**Bolivia qualified**
Uruguay	4	1	2	1	5	4	4	**for South American**
Venezuela	4	0	1	3	2	8	1	**group final.**

Scotland qualified for the finals after this European Group Seven game against Wales at Anfield. Don Masson beats Dai Davies from the penalty-spot to make it 1-0.

Group Three

20 Feb 1977 *Quito*	Equador 1	Peru...............1
27 Feb 1977 *Guayaquil*	Ecuador 0	Chile...............1
6 Mar 1977 *Santiago*	Chile...............1	Peru...............1
12 Mar 1977 *Lima*	Peru...............4	Ecuador 0
20 Mar 1977 *Santiago*	Chile...............3	Ecuador 0
26 Mar 1977 *Lima*	Peru...............2	Chile...............0

Final Table

	P	W	D	L	F	A	Pts	
Peru	4	2	2	0	8	2	6	**Peru qualified for**
Chile	4	2	1	1	5	3	5	**South American**
Ecuador	4	0	1	3	1	9	1	**group final.**

Group Final

10 Jul 1977 *Cali, Colombia*	Brazil 1	Peru...............0
14 Jul 1977 *Cali, Colombia*	Brazil 8	Bolivia............0
17 Jul 1977 *Cali, Colombia*	Peru...............5	Bolivia............0

Final Table

	P	W	D	L	F	A	Pts	
Brazil	2	2	0	0	9	0	4	**Brazil and Peru qualified.**
Peru	2	1	0	1	5	1	2	**Bolivia had to play-off**
Bolivia	2	0	0	2	0	13	0	**against Hungary, winners of the European Group Nine.**

Europe/South America play-off match

29 Oct 1977 *Budapest*	Hungary 6	Bolivia............0
30 Nov 1977 *La Paz*	Bolivia............2	Hungary 3

Hungary qualified

CONCACAF
(Central & North America)

Group One

24 Sep 1976 *Vancouver*	Canada 1	United States 1
3 Oct 1976 *Los Angeles*	United States 0	Mexico............0
10 Oct 1976 *Toronto*	Canada 1	Mexico............0
15 Oct 1976 *Puebla*	Mexico............3	United States 0
20 Oct 1976 *Seattle*	United States 2	Canada 0
27 Oct 1976 *Toluca*	Mexico............0	Canada 0

Final Table

	P	W	D	L	F	A	Pts
Mexico	4	1	2	1	3	1	4
United States	4	1	2	1	3	4	4
Canada	4	1	2	1	2	3	4

Play-off for second place
22 Dec 1976 *Port au Prince* Canada ....3 United States 0
Mexico and Canada qualified for group final.

Group Two

4 Apr 1976 *Panama City*	Panama 3	Costa Rica 2
2 May 1976 *Panama City*	Panama 1	El Salvador.......1

11 Jul	1976	*San José*	Costa Rica ....3 Panama 0
1 Aug	1976	*San Salvador*	El Salvador.......4 Panama 1
17 Sep	1976	*Panama City*	Panama ....2 Guatemala 4
26 Sep	1976	*Guatemala*	Guatemala ....7 Panama 0
1 Dec	1976	*San Salvador*	El Salvador.......1 Costa Rica 1
5 Dec	1976	*San José*	Costa Rica ....0 Guatemala 0
8 Dec	1976	*Guatemala*	Guatemala ....3 El Salvador.......1
12 Dec	1976	*Guatemala*	Guatemala ....1 Costa Rica 1
17 Dec	1976	*San José*	Costa Rica ....1 El Salvador.......1
19 Dec	1076	*San Salvador*	El Salvador.......2 Guatemala 0

Final Table

	P	W	D	L	F	A	Pts
Guatemala	6	3	2	1	15	6	8
El Salvador	6	2	3	1	10	7	7
Costa Rica	6	1	4	1	8	6	6
Panama	6	1	1	4	7	21	3

Guatemala and El Salvador qualified for group final.

Group Three

Extra Preliminary Round

| 2 Apr | 1976 | *Santo Domingo* | Dominican Rep. .0 Haiti..............3 |
| 17 Apr | 1976 | *Port au Prince* | Haiti..............3 Dominican Rep. .0 |

Haiti qualified for second round.

First Round

| 4 Apr | 1976 | *Georgetown* | Guyana...........2 Surinam ....0 |
| 29 Jun | 1976 | *Paramaribo* | Surinam ....3 Guyana...........0 |

Surinam qualified for third round.

| 31 Jul | 1976 | *Arubu* | Nethlds Antilles .1 Haiti..............2 |
| 14 Aug | 1976 | *Port au Prince* | Haiti..............7 Nethlds Antilles .0 |

Haiti qualified for third round.

| 15 Aug | 1976 | *Kingston* | Jamaica ....1 Cuba..............3 |
| 29 Aug | 1976 | *Havana* | Cuba..............2 Jamaica ....0 |

Cuba qualified for third round.

| 15 Aug | 1976 | *Bridgetown* | Barbados ....2 Trinidad & Tobago 1 |
| 31 Aug | 1976 | *Port of Spain* | Trinidad & Tobago 1 Barbados ....0 |

Play-off

| 14 Sep | 1976 | *Port of Spain* | Barbados ....1 Trinidad & Tobago 3 |

Trinidad & Tobago qualified for third round.

Second Round

| 14 Nov | 1976 | *Paramaribo* | Surinam ....1 Trinidad & Tobago 1 |
| 28 Nov | 1876 | *Port of Spain* | Trinidad & Tobago 2 Surinam ....2 |

Play-off

| 18 Dec | 1976 | *Cayenne* | Surinam ....3 Trinidad & Tobago 2 |

Surinam qualified for group final.

| 28 Nov | 1976 | *Havana* | Cuba..............1 Haiti..............1 |
| 11 Dec | 1976 | *Port au Prince* | Haiti..............1 Cuba..............1 |

Play-off

| 29 Dec | 1976 | *Panama City* | Cuba..............0 Haiti..............2 |

Haiti qualified for group final

Group Final

8 Oct	1977	*Monterrey*	Guatemala ....3 Surinam 2
8 Oct	1977	*Monterrey*	El Salvador.......2 Canada 1
9 Oct	1977	*Mexico City*	Mexico...........4 Haiti..............1
12 Oct	1977	*Mexico City*	Canada ....2 Surinam 1
12 Oct	1977	*Monterrey*	Haiti..............2 Guatemala 1
12 Oct	1977	*Mexico City*	Mexico...........3 El Salvador.......1
15 Oct	1977	*Monterrey*	Mexico...........8 Surinam 1
16 Oct	1977	*Mexico City*	Canada ....2 Guatemala 1
16 Oct	1977	*Mexico City*	Haiti..............1 El Salvador.......0
19 Oct	1977	*Mexico City*	Mexico...........2 Guatemala 1
20 Oct	1977	*Monterrey*	Canada ....1 Haiti..............1
20 Oct	1977	*Monterrey*	El Salvador.......3 Surinam 2
22 Oct	1977	*Monterrey*	Mexico...........3 Canada 1
23 Oct	1977	*Mexico City*	Haiti..............1 Surinam 0
23 Oct	1977	*Mexico City*	Guatemala ....2 El Salvador.......2

Final Table

	P	W	D	L	F	A	Pts
Mexico	5	5	0	0	20	5	10
Haiti	5	3	1	1	6	6	7
Canada	5	2	1	2	7	8	5
El Salvador	5	2	1	2	9	9	5
Guatemala	5	1	1	3	8	10	3
Surinam	5	0	0	5	6	17	0

Mexico qualified

AFRICA

Preliminary Round

| 7 Mar | 1976 | *Freetown* | Sierra Leone .....5 Niger ....1 |
| 21 Mar | 1976 | *Niamey* | Niger ....2 Sierra Leone .....1 |

Sierra Leone qualified for first round.

| 13 Mar | 1976 | *Ouagadougou* | Upper Volta .....1 Mauritania.......1 |
| 28 Mar | 1976 | *Nouakchott* | Mauritania.......0 Upper Volta .....2 |

Upper Volta qualified for first round.

First Round

| 1 Apr | 1976 | *Algiers* | Algeria............1 Libya ....0 |
| 16 Apr | 1976 | *Tripoli* | Libya ....0 Algeria............0 |

Algeria qualified for second round.

| 9 May | 1976 | *Lusaka* | Zambia ....4 Malawi ....1 |
| 30 May | 1976 | *Lilongwe* | Malawi ....0 Zambia ....1 |

Zambia qualified for second round.

| 4 Sep | 1976 | *Ouagadougou* | Upper Volta .....1 Ivory Coast.......1 |
| 25 Sep | 1976 | *Abidjan* | Ivory Coast.......2 Upper Volta .....0 |

Ivory Coast qualified for second round.

| 16 Oct | 1976 | *Freetown* | Sierra Leone .....0 Nigeria ....0 |
| 20 Oct | 1976 | *Lagos* | Nigeria ....6 Sierra Leone .....2 |

Nigeria qualified for second round.

| 17 Oct | 1976 | *Lomé* | Togo..............1 Senegal ....0 |
| 31 Oct | 1976 | *Dakar* | Senegal ....1 Togo..............1 |

Togo qualified for second round

| 17 Oct | 1976 | *Brazzaville* | Congo ....2 Cameroon ....2 |
| 31 Oct | 1976 | *Yaoundé* | Cameroon ....1 Congo ....2 |

Congo qualified for second round

| 29 Oct | 1976 | *Cairo* | Egypt ....3 Ethiopia ....0 |
| 14 Nov | 1976 | *Addis Adaba* | Ethiopia..........1 Egypt ....2 |

Egypt qualified for second round.

| 12 Dec | 1976 | *Casablanca* | Morocco..........1 Tunisia ....1 |
| 9 Jan | 1977 | *Tūnis* | Tunisia ....1 Morocco ....1 |

Tunisia won 4-2 on penalties and qualified for second round.

| 10 Oct | 1976 | *Accra* | Ghana ....2 Guinea ....1 |
| 24 Oct | 1976 | *Conakry* | Guinea ....2 Ghana ....1 |

Play-off

| 16 Jan | 1977 | *Lomé, Togo* | Guinea ....2 Ghana ....0 |

Guinea qualified for second round.

Zaïre, Kenya and Uganda also qualified for the second round following the withdrawal of their respective opponents; Central African Republic, Sudan and Tanzania.

Second Round

| 6 Feb | 1977 | *Tūnis* | Tunisia ....2 Algeria............0 |
| 28 Feb | 1977 | *Algiers* | Algeria............1 Tunisia ....1 |

Tunisia qualified for third round.

| 13 Feb | 1977 | *Lomé* | Togo..............0 Guinea ....2 |
| 27 Feb | 1977 | *Conakry* | Guinea ....2 Togo..............1 |

Guinea qualified for third round.

| 13 Feb | 1977 | *Abidjan* | Ivory Coast.......3 Congo ....2 |
| 27 Feb | 1977 | *Brazzaville* | Congo ....1 Ivory Coast.......3 |

Ivory Coast qualified for third round.

| 6 Feb | 1977 | *Nairobi* | Kenya.............0 Egypt ....0 |
| 27 Feb | 1977 | *Cairo* | Egypt ....1 Kenya.............0 |

Egypt qualified for third round.

13 Feb 1977 *Kampala*   Uganda...........1 Zambia 0
27 Feb 1977 *Lusaka*   Zambia ....4 Uganda...........2
Zambia qualified for third round.

Nigeria qualified for third round after withdrawal of Zaïre.

Third Round

 5 Jun 1977 *Conakry*   Guinea ....1 Tunisia..........0
19 Jun 1977 *Tūnis*   Tunisia..........3 Guinea 1
Tunisia qualified for group final.

10 Jul 1977 *Lagos*   Nigeria ....4 Ivory Coast.......0
24 Jul 1977 *Bouaké*   Ivory Coast.......2 Nigeria 2
Nigeria qualified for group final.

15 Jul 1977 *Cairo*   Egypt ....2 Zambia 0
31 Jul 1977 *Lusaka*   Zambia ....0 Egypt 0
Egypt qualified for group final.

Group Final

25 Sep 1977 *Tūnis*   Tunisia..........0 Nigeria 0
 8 Oct 1977 *Lagos*   Nigeria ....4 Egypt 0
21 Oct 1977 *Cairo*   Egypt ....3 Nigeria 1
12 Nov 1977 *Lagos*   Nigeria ....0 Tunisia..........1
25 Nov 1977 *Cairo*   Egypt ....3 Tunisia..........2
11 Dec 1977 *Tūnis*   Tunisia..........4 Egypt 1

Final Table

	P	W	D	L	F	A	Pts	
Tunisia	4	2	1	1	7	4	5	**Tunisia qualified**
Egypt	4	2	0	2	7	11	4	
Nigeria	4	1	1	2	5	4	3	

ASIA–OCEANIA GROUP

Oceania Group

13 Mar 1977 *Suva, Fiji*   Australia ....3 Taiwan 0
16 Mar 1977 *Suva, Fiji*   Taiwan ....1 Australia 2
20 Mar 1977 *Wellington*   New Zealand.....6 Taiwan 0
23 Mar 1977 *Wellington*   Taiwan ....0 New Zealand.....6
27 Mar 1977 *Canberra*   Australia ....3 New Zealand.....1
30 Mar 1977 *Wellington*   New Zealand.....1 Australia 1

Final Table

	P	W	D	L	F	A	Pts	
Australia	4	3	1	0	9	3	7	**Australia qualified**
New Zealand	4	2	1	1	14	4	5	**for group final.**
Taiwan	4	0	0	4	1	17	0	

Asian Group One

27 Feb 1977 *Singapore*   Singapore ....2 Thailand 0
28 Feb 1977 *Singapore*   Hong Kong .....4 Indonesia.........1
 1 Mar 1977 *Singapore*   Malaysia..........6 Thailand 4
 2 Mar 1977 *Singapore*   Hong Kong .....2 Singapore 2
 3 Mar 1977 *Singapore*   Indonesia.........0 Malaysia..........0
 5 Mar 1977 *Singapore*   Thailand ....1 Hong Kong 2
 6 Mar 1977 *Singapore*   Singapore ....1 Malaysia..........0
 7 Mar 1977 *Singapore*   Thailand ....3 Indonesia.........2
 8 Mar 1977 *Singapore*   Malaysia..........1 Hong Kong 1
 9 Mar 1977 *Singapore*   Indonesia.........4 Singapore 0

Final Table

	P	W	D	L	F	A	Pts
Hong Kong	4	2	2	0	9	5	6
Singapore	4	2	1	1	5	6	5
Malaysia	4	1	2	1	7	6	4
Indonesia	4	1	1	2	7	7	3
Thailand	4	1	0	3	8	12	2

Sub-group Final

12 Mar 1977 *Singapore*   Singapore ....0 Hong Kong 1
Hong Kong qualified for group final.

Asian Group Two

27 Feb 1977 *Tel Aviv*   Israel..............0 South Korea 0
 6 Mar 1977 *Tel Aviv*   Israel..............2 Japan 0
10 Mar 1977 *Tel Aviv*   Japan ....0 Israel..............2
20 Mar 1977 *Seoul*   South Korea .....3 Israel..............1
26 Mar 1977 *Tōkyō*   Japan ....0 South Korea 0
 3 Apr 1977 *Seoul*   South Korea .....1 Japan 0
North Korea withdrew

Final Table

	P	W	D	L	F	A	Pts	
South Korea	4	2	2	0	4	1	6	**South Korea**
Israel	4	2	1	1	5	3	5	**qualified for group**
Japan	4	0	1	3	0	5	1	**final.**

Asian Group Three

12 Nov 1977 *Riyadh*   Saudi Arabia.....2 Syria 0
26 Nov 1976 *Damascus*   Syria ....2 Saudi Arabia.....1
 7 Jan 1977 *Riyadh*   Saudi Arabia.....0 Iran 3
28 Jan 1977 *Damascus*   Syria ....0 Iran 1
 8 Apr 1977 *Tehrān*   Iran ....2 Syria 0
        (Syria withdrew, game awarded to Iran 2-0)
22 Apr 1977 *Tehrān*   Iran ....2 Saudi Arabia.....0

Final Table

	P	W	D	L	F	A	Pts	
Iran	4	4	0	0	8	0	8	**Iran qualified for**
Saudi Arabia	4	1	0	3	3	7	2	**group final.**
Syria	4	1	0	3	2	6	2	

Asian Group Four

11 Mar 1977 *Doha, Qatar* Kuwait............2 Bahrain...........0
13 Mar 1977 *Doha, Qatar* Qatar ....2 Bahrain...........0
15 Mar 1977 *Doha, Qatar* Qatar ....0 Kuwait............2
17 Mar 1977 *Doha, Qatar* Kuwait............2 Bahrain...........1
19 Mar 1977 *Doha, Qatar* Qatar ....0 Bahrain...........3
21 Mar 1977 *Doha, Qatar* Qatar ....1 Kuwait............4
United Arab Emirates withdrew.

Final Table

	P	W	D	L	F	A	Pts	
Kuwait	4	4	0	0	10	2	8	**Kuwait qualified**
Qatar	4	1	0	3	3	9	2	**for group final.**
Bahrain	4	1	0	3	4	6	2	

Group Final

19 Jun 1977 *Hong Kong*   Hong Kong ......0 Iran 2
26 Jun 1977 *Hong Kong*   Hong Kong ......0 South Korea 1
 3 Jul 1977 *Seoul*   South Korea .....0 Iran 0
10 Jul 1977 *Adelaide*   Australia ....3 Hong Kong 0
14 Aug 1977 *Melbourne*   Australia ....0 Iran 1
27 Aug 1977 *Sydney*   Australia ....0 South Korea 1
 2 Oct 1977 *Hong Kong*   Hong Kong ......1 Kuwait............3
 9 Oct 1977 *Seoul*   South Korea .....1 Kuwait............0
16 Oct 1977 *Sydney*   Australia ....1 Kuwait............2
23 Oct 1977 *Seoul*   South Korea .....0 Australia 0
28 Oct 1977 *Tehrān*   Iran ....1 Kuwait............0
30 Oct 1977 *Hong Kong*   Hong Kong ......2 Australia 5
 5 Nov 1977 *Kuwait*   Kuwait............2 South Korea 2
11 Nov 1977 *Tehrān*   Iran ....2 South Korea 2
12 Nov 1977 *Kuwait*   Kuwait............4 Hong Kong 0
18 Nov 1977 *Tehrān*   Iran ....3 Hong Kong 0
19 Nov 1977 *Kuwait*   Kuwait............1 Australia 0
25 Nov 1977 *Tehrān*   Iran ....1 Australia 0
 3 Dec 1977 *Kuwait*   Kuwait............1 Iran 2
 4 Dec 1977 *Pusan*   South Korea .....5 Hong Kong 2

Final Table

	P	W	D	L	F	A	Pts	
Iran	8	6	2	0	12	3	14	
South Korea	8	3	4	1	12	8	10	
Kuwait	8	4	1	3	13	8	9	**Iran qualified.**
Australia	8	3	1	4	11	8	7	
Hong Kong	8	0	0	8	5	26	0	

1978 Tournament

Group One

ITALY 2   FRANCE 1 (Half-time 1-1)

Estadio Mar del Plata, Mar del Plata, 2 June
Attendance: 42,373

ITALY and France kicked off what was widely regarded as the closest World Cup group since that which contained Brazil, the Soviet Union, England and Austria in 1958.

France, under the guidance of Michel Hidalgo, were once again a highly-respected European side and many people's tip as the outsiders to win the trophy. Their outstanding sweeper, Marius Trésor from Marseilles, passed a late fitness test and his presence bolstered the French defence. In midfield they had one of the superstars of the modern game in Michel Platini. Ironically, he was of Italian descent and his clash with Tardelli was eagerly awaited.

The French could not have wished for a better start. After only 31 seconds, Bernard Lacombe met a centre from Didier Six to net one of the quickest World Cup goals of all time.

Despite some unseemly off-the-ball tactics, Italy played the most open football seen from one of their national sides since the 1940s and they were rewarded with an equalizer from Paolo Rossi after 29 minutes.

Seven minutes into the second half, Zaccarelli, who came on as a substitute for Antognoni at the interval, completed an intricate move to give the Italians a victory which raised their morale, for they had arrived in Argentina without a great deal of confidence.

Italy: Zoff; Gentile, Bellugi, Scirea, Cabrini, Benetti, Tardelli, Antognoni(Zaccarelli), Causio, Rossi, Bettega.
Scorers: Rossi, Zaccarelli
France: Bertrand-Demanes; Janvion, Bossis, Rio, Trésor, Michel, Dalger, Guillou, Lacombe (Berdoll), Platini, Six(Rouyer).
Scorer: Lacombe
Referee: Nicolae Rainea (Romania)

Giancarlo Antognoni of Italy, substituted against France.

France's Michel Platini takes a tumble against Gaetano Scirea (8), Marco Tardelli (centre) and Renato Zaccarelli of Italy.

ARGENTINA 2   HUNGARY 1 (Half-time 1-1)

Estadio Antonio Liberti 'Monumental', Buenos Aires, 2 June
Attendance: 77,000

BOTH teams contributed to an exciting game which Argentina dominated through their outstanding array of individual talents. Kempes, Luque, Houseman and Valencia all starred for the hosts, whilst Nyilasi, Zombori and Torocsik had fine games for Hungary.

Thankfully, the Argentinians were nowhere near as physical as some of their predecessors, but they were still capable of dishing out the rough treatment when they felt it was required.

Csapo put Hungary in front with a superb goal after only ten minutes but five minutes

Tibor Nyilasi commits yet another foul on Agentina's Osvaldo Ardíles. Eventually, both Nyilasi and Andras Torocsik were sent off, leaving Hungary with only nine men.

Right (top): Leopoldo Luque equalizes for Argentina in the 14th minute against Hungary after evading Sandor Gujdar, who dives despairingly at his legs. Houseman (9), Kereki (centre), Kempes and Török look on. *Right (bottom):* Luque is sent crashing just outside the penalty area.

Roberto Bettega of Italy.

later, Luque scrambled the ball over the line for the equalizer after Gujdar failed to hold a powerful free-kick from Kempes. Argentina were on top in the second half, although Hungary were also capable of producing the unexpected.

The game deteriorated in the closing stages and ten minutes from time, Torocsik was dismissed for retaliation. Three minutes later, substitute Bertoni slid the ball home for the Argentinian winner after combining well with the other substitute, Alonso.

With the match lost and only one minute remaining, Hungary were reduced to nine men when Nyilasi also received his marching orders. The two Hungarians had paid the price for allowing themselves to be rattled by the Argentinians and the Magyars could ill-afford to be without them in the next match.

Argentina: Fillol; Olguín, Passarella, L.Galván, Tarantini, Ardíles, Gallego, Valencia(Alonso), Houseman(Bertoni), Luque, Kempes.
Scorers: Luque, Bertoni
Hungary: Gujdar; Török(Martos), Kereki, Kocsis, J.Toth, Nyilasi, Zombori, Pinter, Csapo, Torocsik, Nagy.
Scorers: Csapo
Referee: Antonio Garrido (Portugal)

ITALY 3   HUNGARY 1 (Half-time 2-0)

Estadio Mar del Plata, Mar del Plata, 6 June
Attendance: 32,000

HUNGARY sorely missed their two suspended stars. But it is doubtful whether they would have had any substantial bearing on a game dominated by Roberto Bettega.

The Italian forward gave one of the finest individual displays of the 11th World Cup. He scored one goal, made another and hit the woodwork three times.

Andras Toth scores Hungary's consolation goal against Italy, beating Dino Zoff from the penalty-spot.

Rossi put Italy in front after 34 minutes, when he turned a deflected Tardelli shot into the net. Almost immediately Bettega made it 2-0, when he brilliantly beat two defenders before scoring. Benetti made it three on the hour before Andras Toth scored a consolation goal for Hungary from the penalty-spot, nine minutes from time.

This win sent shock waves through many of the fancied teams because Italy had not been regarded as one of the favourites. But their performance confirmed they were on their way back to the top of world football.

Italy: Zoff; Gentile, Bellugi, Scirea, Cabrini(Cuccureddu), Benetti, Tardelli, Antognoni, Causio, Rossi, Bettega (Graziani).
Scorers: Rossi, Bettega, Benetti
Hungary: Meszaros; Martos, Kereki, Kocsis, J.Toth, Zombori, Pinter, Csapo, Pusztai, Fazekas (Halasz), Nagy(A.Toth).
Scorer: A.Toth (pen)
Referee: Ramón Baretto Ruíz (Uruguay)

Daniel Bertoni of Argentina.

ARGENTINA 2   FRANCE 1 (Half-time 1-0)

Estadio Antonio Liberti 'Monumental', Buenos Aires, 6 June
Attendance: 77,216

THIS French team must be have been one of the best sides ever to be eliminated from the first phrase of the World Cup — and one of the most unfortunate.

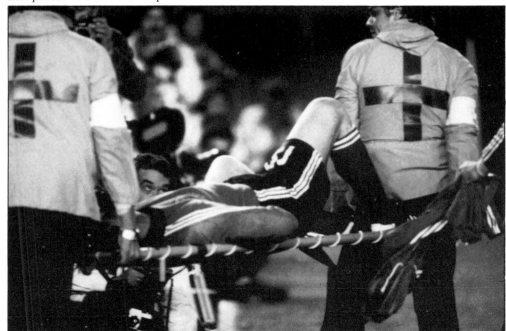

Daniel Passarella of Argentina.

French goalkeeper Jean-Paul Bertrand-Demanes is stretchered off after colliding with a goal-post after 55 minutes.

Argentina's Luque in full flight.

Not only did the French suffer a bizarre penalty decision against them, they were also deprived of a spot-kick themselves when Six was brought down in the penalty area. To add further to France's misfortune, goalkeeper Bertrand-Demanes was stretchered off ten minutes into the second half after colliding with a post.

France outplayed Argentina in the first half, with Platini outstanding, but still went in trailing 1-0 from a goal which came amidst much controversy in the very last seconds of the half.

After tackling Mario Kempes, French defender Trésor fell on the ball. There seemed no way that it was a deliberate foul, but referee Dubach of Switzerland awarded the spot-kick which Passarella converted. Remarkably, despite being close to the incident, the referee still had to consult with a linesman!

France got their just rewards on the hour when Platini converted a rebound after Rocheteau's shot came back off the bar. Platini and Six both had further near misses but, despite outplaying the hosts for most of the match, France fell behind again 18 minutes from time when Luque scored with a long-range shot much against the run of play. Argentina thus ran out the fortunate victors.

Argentina: Fillol; Olguín, Passarella, L.Galván, Tarantini, Ardíles, Gallego, Valencia(Alonso [Ortíz]), Houseman, Luque, Kempes.
Scorers: Passarella (pen), Luque
France: Bertrand-Demanes(Baratelli); Battiston, Bossis, Lopez, Trésor, Bathenay, Rocheteau, Michel, Lacombe, Platini, Six.
Scorer: Platini
Referee: Jean Dubach (Switzerland)

ITALY 1   ARGENTINA 0 (Half-time 0-0)

Estadio Antonio Liberti 'Monumental', Buenos Aires, 10 June
Attendance: 77,260

BOTH teams were assured of their passage to the next phase of the competition, which probably explained why the game developed into a scrappy affair, decided by a lone goal scored by Bettega after 67 minutes.

Italy relied heavily on Rossi up front, whilst Kempes looked like the only Argentinian capable of scoring past the solid Italian defence. The second half saw tempers flair and a clash between Italian hardman Benetti and Ardíles left the Argentinian holding his face. Minutes later, the Italian was booked for a dangerous tackle.

Bettega silenced the noisy home fans with his brilliant goal, crashed home from the edge of the penalty area after a superb one-two with Rossi.

The win meant Italy went to the top of the group, but the Argentinian fans were far from unhappy because their team had also qualified for the next stage.

Italy: Zoff; Gentile, Bellugi(Cuccureddu), Scirea, Cabrini, Benetti, Tardelli, Antognoni (Zaccarelli), Causio, Rossi, Bettega.
Scorer: Bettega
Argentina: Fillol; Olguín, Passarella, L.Galván, Tarantini, Ardíles, Gallego, Valencia, Bertoni, Kempes, Ortíz(Houseman).
Referee: Abraham Klein (Israel)

Osvaldo Ardíles, later to make a new reputation for himself in English League soccer.

Roberto Bettega slams home a 20-yard shot to give Italy a 1-0 victory over Argentina. Tarantini is the player on the ground and Bertoni and Olguín are the two nearest Argentinian players on the right of the picture.

FRANCE 3   HUNGARY 1 (Half-time 3-1)

Estadio Mar del Plata, Mar del Plata, 10 June
Attendance: 28,000

ONCE again the French showed what a talented and artistic side they were. It was unfortunate that the millions watching the competition world-wide would see no more of their talents in the 1978 World Cup.

Their final game was an exciting affair with all four goals coming in the first half, including three in a five-minute spell.

Lopez put France ahead with a 25-yard shot midway through the half and eight minutes before the interval, Berdoll beat off four tackles to increase the lead. Hungary pulled one back through Zombori in the 41st minute, but straight from the kick-off Rocheteau made it 3-1. The result ensured that Hungary finished bottom of the table.

France: Dropsy; Janvion, Bracci, Petit, Lopez, Trésor, Rouyer, Berdoll, Bathenay, Papi(Platini), Rocheteau(Six).
Scorers: Lopez, Berdoll, Rocheteau
Hungary: Gujdar; Martos, Kereki, Balint, J.Toth, Myilasi, Pinter, Zombori, Pusztai, Torocsik, Nagy(Csapo).
Scorer: Zombori
Referee: Arnaldo César Coelho (Brazil)

Group One – Final Table

	P	W	D	L	F	A	Pts
Italy	3	3	0	0	6	2	6
Argentina	3	2	0	1	4	3	4
France	3	1	0	2	5	5	2
Hungary	3	0	0	3	3	8	0

Argentina's Américo Gallego (striped shirt).

Group Two

POLAND 0   WEST GERMANY 0 (Half-time 0-0)

Estadio Antonio Liberti 'Monumental', Buenos Aires, 1 June
Attendance: 77,000

THE opening game of the 11th World Cup brought together the 1974 champions, West Germany, and third-placed Poland, who were out for revenge because it was the Germans who deprived them of their first-ever appearance in the Final four years earlier.

Alas, the opening game once again failed to provide any goals. Both teams obviously felt the pressure upon them as millions of television viewers watched them from all corners of the globe.

After dismal pre-tournament results against Brazil and Sweden, West German manager Helmut Schön dropped Karl-Heinz Rummenigge and recalled Hans Müller. The Poles included Lubanski, who missed the 1974 tournament.

Poland were the better side and made most of the running with Lato, Szarmach and Deyna an outstanding trio. West Germany, on the other hand, were disappointing. Their defence lacked understanding and after this performance there were many who doubted their ability to retain the trophy. The Germans desperately missed Gerd Müller and Franz Beckenbauer.

The best chances of the match fell to Poland in the second half, when Szarmach just failed to connect with a Deyna free-kick after 60 minutes. Fifteen minutes later, Lato did well to get a pass towards Deyna, but the ball fell just too far ahead of the Polish midfielder.

The match was only 25 minutes old when the crowd started jeering and, long before the final whistle, many empty seats were evident as the World Cup opener ended in a goalless draw for the fourth successive tournament.

Poland: Tomaszewski; Szymanowski, Makulewicz, Gorgon, Nawalka, Zmuda, Deyna, Lubanski(Boniek), Lato, Masztaler(Kasperczak), Szarmach.
West Germany: Maier; Vogts, Rüssmann, Kaltz, Zimmermann, Bonhof, H.Müller, Flohe, Abramczik, Fischer, Beer.
Referee: Angel Coerezza (Argentina)

TUNISIA 3   MEXICO 1 (Half-time 0-1)

New Rosario Stadium, Rosario, 2 June
Attendance: 25,000

TUNISIA were quoted as 1000/1 outsiders at the start of the tournament, but what a surprise they turned out to be, underlining the advancement made by African football in recent years.

The scoreline was a fair assessment of the play as the Tunisians trounced a side which had been expected to outplay them and, indeed, took the lead, even though it was Tunisia who dominated the first half. The Mexicans went ahead on the stroke of half-time, through an Ayala penalty. The awarding of the kick was unfortunate because a harmless shot from de la Torre struck Amor Jebali on the arm and the referee pointed to the spot.

Many thought this would have been a killer blow to the Tunisians, who had played with so much confidence and self-belief, but the goal acted as a spur and with the second half only ten minutes old, Kaabi equalized. In the 80th minute Ghommidh put the Tunisians in front and then Dhouieb secured a great victory with the third goal, three minutes from time. A minute later Khemais Labidi replaced Lahzami. It was his only World Cup appearance

Renato Zaccarelli of Italy.

Hans Müller of West Germany.

Klaus Fischer of West Germany.

Wlodzimierz Lubanski of Poland.

Sepp Maier of West Germany.

and, at two minutes, was the shortest career in the history of the World Cup finals until it was equalled by Trobbiani of Argentina in 1986.

Tunisia: Naili; Dhouieb, Moshen Labidi, Kaabi, Jebali, Ghommidh, Lahzami(Khemais Labidi), Ben Rehaiem, Akid, Dhiab, R.Ben Aziza(Karoui).
Scorers: Kaabi, Ghommidh, Dhouieb
Mexico: Reyes; Martínez, Teña, Ramos, Vázquez-Ayala, Mendizábal(Gómez), de la Torre, Cuellar, Rangel, Isiordia, Sánchez.
Scorer: Ayala (pen)
Referee: John Gordon (Scotland)

POLAND 1   TUNISIA 0 (Half-time 1-0)

New Rosario Stadium, Rosario, 6 June
Attendance: 15,000

THE Tunisians showed that their opening win against Mexico was no fluke, holding the powerful Poles to a solitary goal scored by Lato just before the interval.

Tunisia carried on where they had left off in their first game and played good football. It was only a momentary lapse three minutes from half-time which allowed Lato in.

Despite dominating long periods of the second half, Tunisia could not find the net but at least confirmed themselves as the best African nation ever to grace soccer's finest stage.

Poland: Tomaszewski; Szymanowski, Makulewicz, Gorgon, Nawalka, Zmuda, Deyna, Lubanski(Boniek), Lato, Kasperczak, Szarmach(Iwan).
Scorer: Lato
Tunisia: Naili; Dhouieb, Moshen Labidi, Gasmi, Kaabi, Ghommidh, Lhazami, Ben Rehaiem, Akid, Dhiab, Jebali.
Referee: Angel Martínez (Spain)

WEST GERMANY 6   MEXICO 0 (Half-time 4-0)

Estadio Córdoba, Córdoba, 6 June
Attendance: 46,000

HELMUT Schön was under pressure to make sweeping changes to his team and he responded by recalling Rummenigge and introducing Dieter Müller and Dietz. The changes certainly worked as Müller and Rummenigge between them contributed three goals as the Germans tore apart a weak Mexican side.

Dieter Müller started the avalanche in the 14th minute and after half an hour Hans Müller made it 2-0. Rummenigge added a third eight minutes from half-time and six minutes later, Flohe gave West Germany an unassailable lead.

They did not score again until the latter part of the second half when Rummenigge found the net for the second time and then Flohe added his second goal of the game.

The West German performance was considerably better than their opening match and it looked as though Schön had at last got the defending World Champions into top gear.

West Germany: Maier; Vogts, Dietz, Rüssmann, Kaltz, Bonhof, Fischer, Flohe, Rummenigge, D.Müller, H.Müller.
Scorers: Rummenigge 2, Flohe 2, H.Müller, D.Müller
Mexico: Reyes(Soto); Martínez, Teña, Ramos, Vázquez-Ayala, Mendizábal, Cuellar, de la Torre, Sánchez, Rangel, López-Zarza(Lugo).
Referee: Faruk Bouzo (Syria)

TUNISIA 0   WEST GERMANY 0 (Half-time 0-0)

Estadio Córdoba, Córdoba, 10 June
Attendance: 35,000

WEST Germany enjoyed renewed confidence after their six-goal romp against Mexico, but the harsh reality of the decline in their international football was painfully evident as they struggled against the plucky Tunisians.

Dhiab had an outstanding game for the Africans and gave his German counterparts a lesson in midfield dominance. The Tunisians tackled hard and always looked likely to snatch a goal that would eliminate the holders. That was not to happen but, although they were the team to go out, Tunisia's contribution to the 11th World Cup would not be forgotten.

Tunisia: Naili; Jebali, Dhouieb, Moshen Labidi, Kaabi, Ghommidh, Gasmi, Dhiab, Ben Rehaiem, Lahzami, Akid(R.Ben Aziza).
West Germany: Maier; Vogts, Rüssmann, Kaltz, Dietz, Bonhof, H.Müller, Flohe, D.Müller, Fischer, Rummenigge.
Referee: César Orosco Guerrero (Peru)

POLAND 3   MEXICO 1 (Half-time 1-0)

New Rosario Stadium, Rosario, 10 June
Attendance: 25,000

MEXICO's miserable World Cup ended with another sound defeat as Poland put three goals

Group Two - Final Table

	P	W	D	L	F	A	Pts
Poland	3	2	1	0	4	1	5
W.Germany	3	1	2	0	6	0	4
Tunisia	3	1	1	1	3	2	3
Mexico	3	0	0	3	2	12	0

Kazimierz Deyna of Poland.

West Germany and Poland both progressed to the next round. Here Fischer wins an aerial duel against four Polish defenders as the sides fought out a goalless draw.

past their defence to make it 12 goals conceded in three matches for the unhappy Central Americans.

After playing only as substitute in their first two games, Boniek started his first full match for Poland and two minutes before the interval celebrated with the opening goal. Seven minutes into the second half, Rangel equalized for Mexico but their moment of glory was short-lived as Poland's captain, Deyna, restored the lead four minutes later with his 45th international goal.

Although Poland now looked to be coasting to victory, they had a couple of lapses midway through the second half when two fine saves from Tomaszewski prevented Mexico equalizing. However, the game was put beyond Mexico's reach when Boniek scored his second goal of the game in the 84th minute.

Mexico had no points to show for their trip to Argentina and manager José Roca was reluctant to return home after his team's poor showing.

Poland: Tomaszewski; Szymanowski, Gorgon, Iwan(Lubanski), Kasperczak, Zmuda, Rudy (Makulewicz), Masztaler, Deyna, Lato, Boniek.
Scorers: Boniek 2, Deyna
Mexico: Soto; Gómez, Cisneros, Vázquez-Ayala, Cardeñas(Mendizábal), de la Torre, Cuellar, Sánchez, Flores, Ortega, Rangel.
Scorer: Rangel
Referee: Jafar Namdar (Iran)

WORLD CUP FACT

The quickest substitution in the finals came during the 1978 clash between Italy and Argentina when Mauro Bellugi of Italy was replaced by Antonello Cuccureddu after only six minutes.

Group Three

BRAZIL 1   SWEDEN 1 (Half-time 1-1)
Estadio Mar del Plata, Mar del Plata, 3 June
Attendance: 38,000

SWEDEN gave a workmanlike performance in taking their first point off Brazil in the World Cup. After defeats of 4-2, 7-1 and 5-2 in their previous meetings, it was a marked improvement for the Swedes.

Brazil, however, were disappointing and only Zico showed any of the traditional attacking flair for which the South Americans had become known. Rivelino, their only survivor from the 1970 winning team and their new captain, was particularly disappointing.

Rainer Bonhof of West Germany.

José Dirceu of Brazil.

Persistence saw Sjöberg put the Swedes in front in the 37th minute but in injury-time at the end of the first half, Reinaldo levelled the scores.

There were no second-half goals but Brazil came very close to snatching a last-gasp winner when Zico turned a corner into the net. Unfortunately for the Brazilians, Welsh referee Clive Thomas had blown his whistle to indicate the end of the match a split-second before the ball crossed the line. The game ended in confusion and Thomas was pelted with coins, but the score stood at 1-1.

Brazil: Leão; Amaral, Toninho, Oscar, Edinho, Cerezo(Dirceu), Zico, Rivelino, Gil(Nelinho), Reinaldo, Batista.
Scorer: Reinaldo
Sweden: Hellström; Borg, Roy Andersson, Nordqvist, Erlandsson, Tapper, Linderoth, L.Larsson(Edström), B.Larsson, Sjöberg, Wendt.
Scorer: Sjöberg
Referee: Clive Thomas (Wales)

AUSTRIA 2   SPAIN 1 (Half-time 1-1)
Estadio José Amalfitani, Buenos Aires, 3 June
Attendance: 49,317

ALTHOUGH Spain went into the tournament as one of the fancied teams, their manager Ladislav Kubala had been heavily criticized for his team's performance in drawing with Uruguay before the World Cup finals began.

The Spaniards have a poor record in the World Cup, despite competing in several tournaments with a team littered with individual stars. Their 1978 campaign was to be no different and they began with a shock defeat by the Austrians.

Schachner, a player from the Second Division of the Austrian League, rocked the Spaniards with a tenth-minute goal that still ranks amongst the best ever scored in the competition's 60-year history.

He picked up the ball on the half-way line, zig-zagged past two defenders, cut in from the right and beat Miguel Angel with a fierce, angled shot.

Spain drew level in the 21st minute when the Bilbao striker, Dani, saw his shot deflected past the Austrian 'keeper, Koncilia. But it was Hans Krankl who scored Austria's winner, 12 minutes from time when he thumped home a left-foot shot following a deflection.

The goal was a fitting way to celebrate Austria's return to the World Cup finals for the first time in 20 years. Incidentally, Krankl, who played for Austria Vienna, was Europe's leading goalscorer in 1977-8 with 41 goals.

Austria: Koncilia; Sara, Pezzey, Obermayer, Breitenberger, Kreuz, Prohaska, Hickersberger (Weber), Schachner(Pirkner), Krankl, Jara.
Scorers: Schachner, Krankl
Spain: Miguel Angel; Marcelino, Migueli, Pirri, de la Cruz, San José, Asensi, Cardenosa(Leal), Rexach(Quini), Ruben Cano, Dani.
Scorer: Dani
Referee: Karoly Palotai (Hungary)

AUSTRIA 1   SWEDEN 0 (Half-time 1-0)
Estadio José Amalfitani, Buenos Aires, 7 June
Attendance: 46,000

AUSTRIA kept themselves on course for an appearance in the second phase of the competition with this narrow win over Sweden. And it was that man Krankl who scored the winning goal for the second successive game, his 43rd-minute penalty being enough to secure victory.

Sweden, although they had been playing well up to the time of the goal, could not get back into the game but, with Spain and Brazil drawing, they still had a chance of staying in the tournament.

Austria: Koncilia; Sara, Pezzey, Obermayer, Breitenberger, Krieger(Weber), Prohaska, Hickersberger, Kreuz, Jara, Krankl.
Scorer: Krankl (pen)
Sweden: Hellström; Borg, Roy Andersson, Nordqvist, Erlandsson, B.Larsson, Linderoth (Edström), L.Larsson, Tapper(Torstensson), Sjöberg, Wendt.
Referee: Charles Corver (Holland)

BRAZIL 0   SPAIN 0 (Half-time 0-0)
Estadio Mar del Plata, Mar del Plata, 7 June
Attendance: 40,000

BRAZIL were without Rivelino, who was left out by Claudio Coutinho after the skipper had publicly voiced his opinions about the Brazilian team boss.

Rivelino's midfield skills were missed and Brazil could count themselves lucky to hold out for a draw. Indeed, had it not been for Cardenosa's indecision in the second half, when he had a chance to score what would surely have been the winner, they could have been in all sorts of trouble going into their last match, against Austria.

Batista of Brazil.

Taking the ball forward is Brazil's Cerezo. Dirceu is in support as another attack builds up against Spain.

Roberto Rivelino of Brazil.

Brazil: Leão; Nelinho(Gil), Oscar, Amaral, Edinho, Cerezo, Batista, Dirceu, Zico(Mendonça), Toninho, Reinaldo.
Spain: Miguel Angel; Uria(Guzman), Migueli(Biosca), Marcelino, Olmo, San José, Leal, Asensi, Cardenosa, Juanito, Santillana.
Referee: Sergio Gonella (Italy)

BRAZIL 1   AUSTRIA 0 (Half-time 1-0)
Estadio Mar del Plata, Mar del Plata, 11 June
Attendance: 40,000

AUSTRIA were already assured of their place in the semi-finals, but Brazil needed a win to make sure of their passage. A draw would have been far from certain to put them through.

Juanito of Spain.

Brazil's Gil is confronted by Pezzey (5) of Austria.

Group Three – Final Table

	P	W	D	L	F	A	Pts
Austria	3	2	0	1	3	2	4
Brazil	3	1	2	0	2	1	4
Spain	3	1	1	1	2	2	3
Sweden	3	0	1	2	1	3	1

Joe Jordan (Scotland) and Ruud Krol (Holland) in a heading duel.

Johannes Neeskens of Holland.

Rob Rensenbrink of Holland.

Thus, there was much pressure on the Brazilian manager, Coutinho, and in the end he was grateful for the solitary goal which squeezed them through.

Brazil lacked flair and imagination and gave poor value. Rivelino was still sidelined and Zico, who was to become one of the finest ever Brazilian players after Pelé, was on the substitute's bench for all but seven minutes.

The only goal of the game was scored five minutes from half-time, when the Austrian defender Pezzey misjudged a cross and Roberto was on hand to put the ball in the net.

Brazil: Leão; Toninho, Oscar, Amaral, Rodrígues Neto, Cerezo(Chicão), Batista, Dirceu, Mendonça(Zico), Gil, Roberto.
Scorer: Roberto
Austria: Koncilia; Sara, Pezzey, Obermayer, Breitenberger, Prohaska, Hickersberger(Weber), Krieger(Happich), Kreuz, Krankl, Jara.
Referee: Robert Wurtz (France)

SPAIN 1   SWEDEN 0 (Half-time 0-0)

Estadio José Amalfitani, Buenos Aires, 11 June
Attendance: 48,000

BOTH sides needed to win this game to stand any chance of remaining in the competition. In the end, that equation was academic because Brazil's win over Austria rendered the result of this match irrelevant.

Cardenosa had a brilliant second half for the Spaniards and certainly made up for his miss against Brazil. The game's only goal was scored by Asensi, 15 minutes from time, but the victory was worthless and what had proved the least entertaining of all the groups in Argentina ended with Brazil and Austria qualifying for the semi-final stage.

Spain: Miguel Angel; Marcelino, Biosca, Olmo(Pirri), San José, Leal, Asensi, Cardenosa, Uria, Juanito, Santillana.
Scorer: Asensi
Sweden: Hellström; Borg, Roy Andersson, Nordqvist, Erlandsson, B.Larsson, L.Larsson, Nilsson, Nordin, Sjöberg(Linderoth), Edström(Wendt)
Referee: Ferdinand Biwersi (West Germany)

Group Four

HOLLAND 3   IRAN 0 (Half-time 1-0)

Estadio Mendoza, Mendoza, 3 June
Attendance: 42,000

WHILST the Dutch lacked several key players, including Johann Cruyff, through either injury or refusal to play, their side still contained some of the best-known names in world soccer.

The role normally played by Cruyff was taken over by Rob Rensenbrink, who gave a remarkable performance and scored all Holland's goals, two of them from the penalty-spot.

Iran were physical at times but in skipper Ali Parvin, playing his 80th international, they had one of the great captains of this tournament.

Holland led by one goal at half-time, a 39th-minute Rensenbrink spot-kick after René van de Kerkhof had been upended, but they had already proved far too classy for their opponents and ran out comfortable winners.

A Rensenbrink header after 62 minutes made it 2-0 and he completed his hat-trick 11 minutes from time, when he scored his second penalty after Rep had been brought down.

Holland: Jongbloed; Suurbier, Krol, Haan, Rijsbergen, W.van de Kerkhof, Neeskens, Jansen, Rep, R.van de Kerkhof(Nanninga), Rensenbrink.
Scorer: Rensenbrink 3 (2 pens)
Iran: Hejazi; Nazari, Abdolahi, Kazerani, Eskandarian, Parvin, Ghassempour, Sadeghi, Nayebagha, Djahani, Faraki(Rowshan).
Referee: Alfonso Archundia (Mexico)

PERU 3   SCOTLAND 1 (Half-time 1-1)

Estadio Córdoba, Córdoba, 3 June
Attendance: 45,000

BECAUSE of their excellent team spirit, Scotland were heavily fancied as one of the best outsiders in this 11th World Cup tournament and the bookmakers made them 8/1 to lift the trophy. But after this game, the odds shot out to 66/1, following another disastrous World Cup match for the over-confident Scots who were without Gordon McQueen, who lost his battle to get fit.

Scotland treated Peru too lightly. But they should have realized that in the qualifiers, the Peruvians had lost only narrowly, 1-0, to Brazil. That should have served as an indication of their capabilities.

Scotland's Dalglish, Burns, Jordan and Gemmill look on in dismay as jubilant Peru celebrate Cubillas' 76th-minute free-kick which gave them a 3-1 lead.

Kenny Dalglish of Scotland.

Joe Jordan shot Scotland into the lead in the 15th minute, when he followed up a powerful Bruce Rioch shot which was pushed out to the Scottish striker. Then Cueto burst through in another of his many raids in the 42nd minute and his powerful left-foot shot beat Rough to level the scores.

Scotland had a chance to regain the lead in the 65th minute, when they were awarded a penalty after Bruce Rioch had been brought down, but Don Masson's spot-kick was saved by the goalkeeper. That was the turning point of the match and five minutes later, the outstanding Peruvian striker, Cubillas, strode through the defence to give his team a 2-1 lead.

Cubillas had wanted to retire before the tournament but was talked out of it. The Scots must have wished that he had not changed his mind, for he scored again in the 76th minute, when his free-kick was sliced past the defensive wall.

It was another World Cup disaster for Scotland and, to make matters worse, Willie Johnston failed a routine drugs test. He was subsequently banned from international football and immediately returned home.

Peru: Quiroga; Duarte, Manzo, Chumpitaz, Díaz, Velásquez, Cueto(P.Rojas), Cubillas, Muñante, La Rosa(Sotíl), Oblítas.
Scorers: Cubillas 2, Cueto
Scotland: Rough; Kennedy, Burns, Buchan, Forsyth, Rioch(Gemmill), Masson(Macari), Hartford, Dalglish, Jordan, Johnston.
Scorer: Jordan
Referee: Ulf Eriksson (Sweden)

HOLLAND 0   PERU 0 (Half-time 0-0)

Estadio Mendoza, Mendoza, 7 June
Attendance: 30,000

WITH this goalless draw, Peru and Holland virtually assured themselves a passage into the next phase of the World Cup, although the Dutch slumped badly after their opening performance. It was abundantly clear from early in the game that their 3-5-2 formation was ineffective against the Peruvian defence and, to make matters worse, Holland lost the services of Neeskens, who was forced to go off after 68 minutes with badly injured ribs.

The Dutch, who were quick to blame the state of the pitch for their poor display, put Peruvian goalkeeper Quiroga — not one of the world's best — under little pressure. Their best effort was a second-half shot from Rensenbrink and at one time it seemed that Peru might cause an upset and snatch victory.

Holland: Jongbloed; Suurbier, Krol, Rijsbergen, Poortvliet, Neeskens(Nanninga), Jansen, Hann, W.van de Kerkhof, R.van de Kerkhof(Rep), Rensenbrink.
Peru: Quiroga; Duarte, Manzo, Chumpitaz, Díaz, Velásquez, Cueto, Cubillas, Muñante, La Rosa(Sotíl), Oblítas.
Referee: Adolf Prokop (East Germany)

Peruvian goalkeeper Ramón Quiroga

Archie Gemmill of Scotland.

IRAN 1   SCOTLAND 1 (Half-time 0-1)

Estadio Córdoba, Córdoba, 7 June
Attendance: 8,000

THE thousands of Scottish fans who made the 7,000-mile journey to Argentina yelled abuse at their team during and after yet another dismal performance in which they were outwitted by the little-fancied Iranians.

Scotland took the lead, as they had done against Peru, when Eskandarian powered the ball into his own net from 15 yards for an absurd own-goal after Joe Jordan forced the error between the defender and his goalkeeper. The goal came two minutes from the interval and should have been a killer blow to the Iranians, but they came out raring to go in the second half and appeared not to have been unsettled by that ludicrous own-goal.

Thirteen minutes from time, Danaifar netted the equalizer after receiving a pass from Sadeghi, who got his cross in at the second attempt. Danaifar held off Gemmill and virtually ended Scotland's hopes of remaining in the tournament.

Iran: Hejazi; Nazari, Kazerani, Abdolahi, Eskandarian, Parvin, Ghassempour, Sadeghi, Danaifar(Nayebagha), Faraki(Rowshan), Djahani.
Scorer: Danaifar
Scotland: Rough; Jardine, Burns, Donachie, Buchan(Forsyth), Gemmill, Macari, Harford, Dalglish(Harper), Jordan, Robertson.
Scorer: Eskandarian (og)
Referee: Youssou N'Diaye (Senegal)

SCOTLAND 3   HOLLAND 2 (Half-time 1-1)

Estadio Mendoza, Mendoza, 11 June
Attendance: 40,000

MANY Scotland fans had been calling for Graeme Souness since the start of the tournament, but manager Ally MacLeod had ignored the Liverpool midfielder. Now, in a last-ditch attempt at salvaging some pride, MacLeod brought Souness into the team for his first game.

To stay in the tournament Scotland had to win by three clear goals but, as one Scottish wag put it, "Where are we going to find three Dutchmen prepared to score own-goals?"

Four pictures showing the build-up to Gemmill's brilliant goal against the Dutch.

He reckoned without Souness and the masterful Archie Gemmill, both of whom transformed the Scottish team. For the first time they played well together and yet, also for the first time, conceded the first goal when Kennedy brought down Rep in the penalty area and Rensenbrink converted the spot-kick to score the 1,000th goal in the World Cup finals.

Scotland were not undaunted and two minutes from half-time Souness floated a ball from the left and Joe Jordan headed it down for Kenny Dalglish to score. A minute after the start of the second half, Scotland found themselves in front when Gemmill converted a penalty after Souness had been chopped down in the area by Willy van de Kerkhof.

And half-way through the second half, Gemmill scored a great individual goal when he beat three defenders and then fooled the goalkeeper with a swerving shot into the far corner of the goal. It was one of the great goals of the 1978 World Cup.

Suddenly, Scotland were in sight of that three-goal margin which would have lifted their hopes, but those dreams of a miracle lasted only three minutes before Rep tore through the defence in the 71st minute and unleashed a shot from 25 yards to pull one back for Holland.

Scotland went out of the World Cup on goal-difference for the second successive tournament, but memories of their dismal performances against Peru and Iran were wiped out by this great win over the 1974 runners-up.

Scotland: Rough; Kennedy, Buchan, Donachie, Forsyth, Rioch, Gemmill, Hartford, Souness, Dalglish, Jordan.
Scorers: Gemmill 2 (1 pen), Dalglish
Holland: Jongbloed; Suurbier, Krol, Rijsbergen(Wildschut), Poortvliet, Neeskens(Boskamp), W.van de Kerkhof, Jansen, Rep, R.van de Kerkhof, Rensenbrink.
Scorers: Rensenbrink (pen), Rep
Referee: Erich Linemayr (Austria)

PERU 4 IRAN 1 (Half-time 3-1)

Estadio Córdoba, Córdoba, 11 June
Attendance: 25,000

PERU wound up their first phase with a convincing win over Iran and it was 29-year-old Teofilo Cubillas who did the damage with the second hat-trick of the tournament. Like the first, by Rob Rensenbrink, it contained two penalties.

Peru made known their intentions after two minutes when Velásquez rose high and, unchallenged, headed home a Muñante corner to give the South Americans the lead.

Cubillas scored his first goal in the 36th minute and three minutes later he converted the first of his two penalties. In the very next minute, Rowshan reduced the arrears with a fine volley from a left-wing cross.

Hejazi had a lot to do in the Iranian goal and in the 78th minute he conceded his fourth goal of the game when Cubillas completed his hat-trick from the penalty-spot. The win took Peru to the top of Group Four.

Peru: Quiroga; Duarte, Manzo(Leguia), Chumpitaz, Díaz, Velásquez, Cubillas, Cueto, Muñante, La Rosa(Sotíl), Oblítas.
Scorers: Cubillas 3 (2 pens), Velásquez
Iran: Hejazi; Nazari, Abdolahi, Kazerani, Allahvardi, Parvin, Ghassempour, Sadeghi, Danaifar, Faraki(Djahani), Rowshan(Fariba).
Scorer: Rowshan
Referee: Alojzi Jarguz (Poland)

Group Four - Final Table						
	P	W	D	L	F	A	Pts
Peru	3	2	1	0	7	2	5
Holland	3	1	1	1	5	3	3
Scotland	3	1	1	1	5	6	3
Iran	3	0	1	2	2	8	1

Holland's Peit Wildschut, came on as substitute for Rijsbergen against the Scots.

Scotland's Joe Jordan in aggressive mood.

Cubillas scores his second goal against Iran from the penalty-spot to put Peru 3-0 ahead. The same player scored again from the spot, earning Peru an eventual 4-1 victory.

Zoff collects a cross as his Italian teammate Bellugi fends off West Germany's Fischer. Vogts and Bettega are to the left. Gentile is number-five and Rummenigge is on the edge of the penalty area.

Group A

ITALY 0   WEST GERMANY 0 (Half-time 0-0)

Estadio Antonio Liberti 'Monumental', Buenos Aires, 14, June
Attendance: 60,000

PERHAPS unexpectedly it was the Germans, not the normally defensively-minded Italians, who went into the World Cup's 300th game with a negative attitude. And at the end of 90 minutes' play, the defending champions were relieved to escape with a draw, because the Italians had plenty of opportunities to emerge victorious.

Bettega squandered two first-half chances and Italy were unlucky not to be awarded a penalty when Rüssmann appeared to bundle Rossi over in the penalty area. At the other end, Dino Zoff brought off some fine saves from the German forwards, who relied on quick breakaways as their main form of attack.

Sepp Maier in the German goal was playing in his 16th game in a World Cup finals, surpassing the goalkeeping record previously held by Antonio Carbajal of Mexico. Maier also completed 449 minutes of continuous World Cup football without conceding a goal.

Italy: Zoff; Gentile, Bellugi, Scirea, Cabrini, Benetti, Antognoni(Zaccarelli), Tardelli, Causio, Rossi, Bettega.
West Germany: Maier; Vogts, Rüssmann, Zimmermann(Konopka), Dietz, Kaltz, Bonhof, Flohe (Beer), Rummenigge, Fischer, Hölzenbein.
Referee: Dusan Maksimovic (Yugoslavia)

HOLLAND 5   AUSTRIA 1 (Half-time 3-0)

Estadio Córdoba, Córdoba, 14 June
Attendance: 15,000

AFTER some indifferent performances in their opening group matches, Holland showed, in destroying Austria, that they were to be serious contenders for the title after all.

With three changes to the side beaten by Scotland, the Dutch simply tore the Austrians apart. Incidentally, Austria had lost only one of their previous 14 internationals — and the team to beat them on that occasion was Holland.

Ernie Brandts headed the Dutch into a sixth-minute lead and in the 35th minute, Rensenbrink

Dino Zoff, Italy's great goalkeeper.

converted his fourth penalty of the tournament. A minute later Rep gave Holland a 3-0 lead.

Rep scored his second goal after 53 minutes, before Obermayer netted a consolation goal for Austria ten minutes from time. But three minutes later, Willy van de Kerkhof scored Holland's fifth after Rensenbrink had set up the scoring chance.

Dutch manager Ernst Happel, who was born in Austria but managed the Belgian side Bruges had moulded together a fine new Dutch side. This latest win established them as one of the favourites for the title.

Holland: Schrijvers; Poortvliet, Krol, Brandts(van Kraay), Wildschut, Jansen, Hann, W.van de Kerkhof, R.van de Kerkhof(Schoenaker), Rep, Rensenbrink.
Scorers: Rep 2, Brandts, Rensenbrink (pen), W.van de Kerkhof.
Austria: Koncilia; Sara, Pezzey, Obermayer, Breitenberger, Hickersberger, Krieger, Prohaska, Kreuz, Krankl, Jara.
Scorer: Obermayer
Referee: John Gordon (Scotland)

HOLLAND 2 WEST GERMANY 2 (Half-time 1-1)

Estadio Córdoba, Córdoba, 18 June
Attendance: 46,000

THE West Germans came out of their defensive shell for this repeat of the 1974 Final and the result was a classic European encounter and one of the matches of the tournament.

Holland conceded an early goal when Schrijvers failed to hold a powerful shot from Bonhof and Abramczik was on hand to slot the ball home. That goal came in the third minute but Holland fought back and in the 26th minute, Haan became the first player to score past Sepp Maier since Neeskens's penalty in the Final four years earlier. Haan's shot from 30 yards left the experienced goalkeeper motionless.

West Germany re-established their lead 20 minutes from time when Dieter Müller's superb header from an Erik Beer cross sailed into the net. But seven minutes from the end, René van de Kerkhof deprived the Germans of a repeat of their victory four years earlier, when he scored after a brilliant dribble. Rüssmann handled the ball as it was going into the net but the referee allowed the goal to stand.

Sadly for Holland, Dick Nanninga, who had been on the field barely ten minutes, was dismissed two minutes from time for laughing derisively at a refereeing decision.

Holland: Schrijvers; Poortvliet, Krol, Brandts, Wildschut(Nanninga), Jansen, Hann, W.van de Kerkhof, R.van de Kerkhof, Rep, Rensenbrink.
Scorers: Haan, R.van de Kerkhof
West Germany: Maier; Vogts, Rüssmann, Kaltz, Dietz, Bonhof, Beer, Hölzenbein, Abramczik, D.Müller, Rummenigge.
Scorers: Abramczik, D.Müller
Referee: Ramón Barreto Ruíz (Uruguay)

Ruud Krol of Holland.

Much was expected of Italy's Antognoni in the 1978 finals but he disappointed.

Ruud Krol (second left) clears from West Germany's Dieter Müller (14). Ernie Brandts (22) is in attendance, Karl-Heinz Rummenigge looks on.

ITALY 1 AUSTRIA 0 (Half-time 1-0)

Estadio Antonio Liberti 'Monumental', Buenos Aires, 18 June
Attendance: 50,000

AFTER four tough matches, Italy were looking very jaded and it was thanks only to a moment of sheer magic from Paolo Rossi that they scraped home with a narrow victory.

Strässer appeals to the linesman as Rossi (left) gives Italy a 13th-minute lead over Austria. Goalkeeper Koncilia is the man in the middle.

Franco Causio of Italy.

The crowd jeered for much of the match, for they were expecting much more from the Italians. But it was Austria who finished the stronger side and deserved better for their efforts. They were denied two apparently valid penalty claims and in the second half, Krankl had the ball in the net but his effort was ruled out by a linesman.

The game's only goal came in the 13th minute and it momentarily checked the jeers as 21-year-old Rossi scored one of the outstanding goals of the tournament. After an interception, Rossi back-heeled the ball with a delicate flick to Causio and carried on running to take the return before scoring a memorable goal. But shortly afterwards the jeering started again.

Italy: Zoff; Gentile, Bellugi(Cuccureddu), Scirea, Cabrini, Benetti, Tardelli, Zaccarelli, Causio, Rossi, Bettega(Graziani).
Scorer: Rossi
Austria: Koncilia; Sara, Pezzey, Obermayer, Strässer, Prohaska, Kreuz, Hickersberger, Schachner (Pirkner), Krankl, Krieger.
Referee: Francis Rion (Belgium)

HOLLAND 2   ITALY 1 (Half-time 0-1)
Estadio Antonio Liberti 'Monumental', Buenos Aires, 21 June
Attendance: 70,000

HOLLAND went into their final match knowing a draw would probably be good enough to put them into their second successive World Cup Final. Italy, on the other hand, had to commit themselves to attack in the hope of winning and ensuring their place in the last two.

It was an ill-tempered match at times, but the best football came from Holland who gave a fine display of finishing as they played 'Total Football' — 1974 style.

It was Italy, though, who took a first-half lead when Brandts put through his own goal after 19 minutes. Rossi and Bettega had both beaten the offside trap and Brandts, rushing back to chase, connected with the ball and put it into his own net. At the same time he crashed into goalkeeper Schrijvers, who was stretchered off and replaced by the veteran Jongbloed, who had not played since the defeat by Scotland.

Brandts made amends for his first-half disaster five minutes into the second period, when his 20-yard shot beat Zoff after the Italians had reverted to their old ploy of 'holding on to their slender lead'.

Fifteen minutes from the end, Arie Hann scored the goal of the tournament when Zoff,

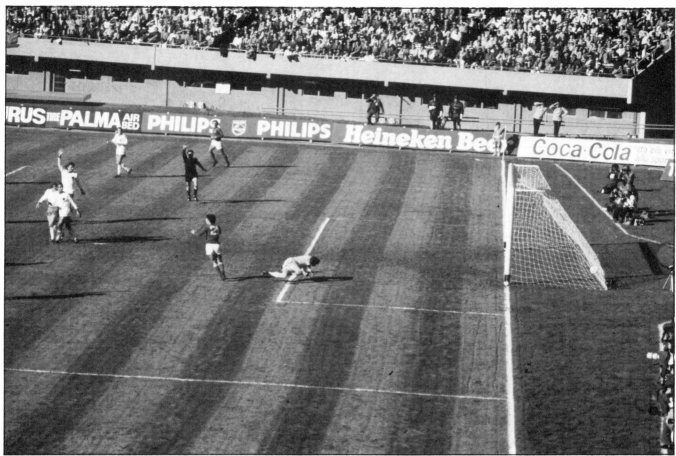

Rossi (21) turns after putting the ball in the net against Holland but Spanish referee Angel Martínez disallowed the goal for offside.

one of nine Juventus players in the Italian team, was beaten for the second time by a long-range shot, this time from 30 yards.

Holland held on to their lead and headed the all-European semi-final group by two points from Italy.

Holland: Schrijvers(Jongbloed); Brandts, Neeskens, Krol, Poortvliet, Jansen, Haan, R.van de Kerkhof, W.van de Kerkhof, Rep(van Kraay), Rensenbrink.
Scorers: Brandts, Haan
Italy: Zoff; Cuccureddu, Gentile, Scirea, Cabrini, Benetti(Graziani), Tardelli, Zaccarelli, Causio (C.Sala), Rossi, Bettega.
Scorer: Brandts (og)
Referee: Angel Martínez (Spain)

Paolo Rossi, who ended the 1978 World Cup with three goals to his name.

Arie Hann gives the victory sign after Holland's victory over Italy. Ernie Brandts looks equally pleased that the Dutch are through to the Final.

Group A – Final Table

	P	W	D	L	F	A	Pts
Holland	3	2	1	0	9	4	5
Italy	3	1	1	1	2	2	3
W.Germany	3	0	2	1	4	5	2
Austria	3	1	0	2	4	8	2

Krankl wrong-foots Kaltz (5) and goes on to put Austria ahead over the Germans. It was the Austrians' first victory over their neighbours in 47 years.

AUSTRIA 3   WEST GERMANY 2 (Half-time 0-1)

Estadio Córdoba, Córdoba, 21 June
Attendance: 20,000

WEST Germany still had an outside chance of reaching their second successive World Cup Final, but they required Holland and Italy to draw in Buenos Aires and at the same time had to beat Austria by five clear goals. It was certainly a tall order for a side that had been playing with less than its usual amount of flair and confidence. And in the end it was to be a sad exit for Germany and 62-year-old manager Helmut Schön, who bowed out after four tournaments in charge of the national team.

The Germans were given some hope after 19 minutes when Rummenigge opened the scoring, but there was no addition to the scoreline until the 60th minute when Bertie Vogts put through his own goal. Seven minutes later, Hans Krankl showed why he was one of the most lethal strikers in the world when he put Austria in front and destroyed Germany's chances of retaining the title.

Despite a Hölzenbein equalizer in the 72nd minute, all was lost for the Germans and Austria clinched their first victory over their arch rivals since they drubbed them 5-0 at Vienna in September 1931, when Krankl netted again two minutes from time. Little wonder Krankl was soon snapped up by Spanish club, Barcelona, for a £350,000 fee.

Austria: Koncilia; Sara, Pezzey, Obermayer, Strässer, Hickersberger, Prohaska, Kreuz, Krieger, Schachner(Oberacher), Krankl.
Scorers: Krankl 2, Vogts (og)
West Germany: Maier; Vogts, Rüssmann, Kaltz, Dietz, Bonhof, Beer(H.Müller), Hölzenbein, Abramczik, D.Müller(Fischer), Rummenigge.
Scorers: Rummenigge, Hölzenbein
Referee: Abraham Klein (Israel)

Group B

Hans Krankl, two-goal hero of Austria's historic win.

BRAZIL 3   PERU 0 (Half-time 2-0)

Estadio Mendoza, Mendoza, 14 June
Attendance: 40,000

WHILST Group A contained four European sides, Group B became known as the South American Group because of the presence of Peru, Brazil and Argentina. Poland were the exception.

Brazil and Argentina were clearly the favourites to fight out a place for the Final, but Brazil's manager Claudio Coutinho was under a lot of pressure and had to cope with abuse and effigies of him being burned by irate Brazilian supporters.

He brought top defender Zé Maria in for his first game of the tournament after recovering

Peru's Cueto battles with Roberto of Brazil.

César Cueto of Peru.

from injury and Brazil gave probably their best World Cup performance since the 1970 Final as they swept Peru aside with a stunning display of attacking football.

Muñante and La Rosa both missed chances for Peru, but the Brazilians certainly seized upon their chances and Dirceu confirmed his selection ahead of Rivelino when his 22-yard free-kick curved around the wall to give Brazil a 14th-minute lead.

Dirceu struck again after 27 minutes and the scoring was completed in the 70th minute when substitute Zico scored from the penalty-spot.

At last Brazil had contributed the kind of football for which the World Cup has become famous and suddenly they established themselves as favourites to reach their fifth Final.

Brazil: Leão; Toninho, Oscar, Amaral, Rodrígues Neto, Batista, Cerezo(Chicão), Dirceu, Mendonça, Gil(Zico), Roberto.
Scorers: Dirceu 2, Zico (pen)
Peru: Quiroga; Duarte, Manzo, Chumpitaz, Díaz(Navarro), Velásquez, Cueto, Cubillas, Muñante, La Rosa, Oblítas(P.Rojas).
Referee: Nicolae Rainea (Romania)

ARGENTINA 2   POLAND 0 (Half-time 1-0)

New Rosario Stadium, Rosario, 14 June
Attendance: 40,000

THE pre-tournament favourites, Argentina, went into this crucial match without striker Luque, who was suffering from a shoulder injury. But Mario Kempes managed quite nicely on his own, grabbing both goals.

For Kempes it was a return to his old stomping ground because he used to play for Rosario Central before his move to Spain. And he celebrated his return with the opening goal after a quarter of an hour, rising to head home powerfully past the experienced Polish 'keeper Tomaszewski. It was Kempes' first goal of the tournament but he was to finish leading scorer.

Kaz Deyna, playing his 100th game for Poland, missed a penalty after a handling offence when his weak shot was comfortably saved by Fillol. Had he scored, the game may well have taken on a different complexion.

However, Argentina scraped home and sealed the victory with another Kempes goal 20 minutes from time when he struck a well-hit shot after a good run by Ardíles.

Argentina: Fillol; Olguín, L.Galván, Passarella, Tarantini, Ardíles, Gallego, Valencia(Villa), Houseman(Ortíz), Kempes, Bertoni.
Scorer: Kempes 2
Poland: Tomaszewski; Szymanowski, Zmuda, Kasperczak, Makulewicz, Nawalka, Deyna, Boniek, Masztaler(Mazur), Lato, Szarmach.
Referee: Ulf Eriksson (Sweden)

POLAND 1   PERU 0 (Half-time 0-0)

Estadio Mendoza, Mendoza, 18 June
Attendance: 35,000

THIS was the worst match of Group B and the busiest man on the field was England referee Pat Partridge, who booked four players, including the Peru goalkeeper Quiroga for a foul on Lato. . . in the Polish half of the field!

Zbigniew Boniek of Poland.

STATISTICS

Goalscorers:
6 — Mario Kempes (Argentina).
5 — Teófilo Cubillas (Peru), Rob Rensenbrink (Holland).
4 — Leopoldo Luque (Argentina), Hans Krankl (Austria).
3 — Carlos Roberto de Oliveira, José Guimaraes Dirceu (both Brazil), Karl-Heinz Rummenigge (West Germany), Johannes Rep (Holland), Paolo Rossi (Italy).
2 — Daniel Bertoni (Argentina), Nelinho (Brazil), Dieter Müller, Heinz Flohe (West Germany), Roberto Bettega (Italy), Zbigniew Boniek, Grzegorz Lato (both Poland), Arie Haan, Ernie Brandts (both Holland), Archie Gemmill (Scotland).
1 — Renato Zaccarelli, Romeo Benetti, Franco Causio (all Italy), Hans Müller, Rudiger Abramcyzk, Bernd Hölzenbein (all West Germany), Reinaldo, Zico (both Brazil), Wille van de Kerkhof, René van de Kerkhof, Dick Nanninga (all Holland), Daniel Passarella, René Houseman, Alberto Tarantini (all Argentina), Kazimierz Deyna, Andrezej Szarmach (both Poland), Walter Schachner, Erich Obermayer (both Austria), César Cueto, José Valásquez (both Peru), Bernard Lacombe, Michel Platini, Christian Lopez, Marc Berdoll, Dominique Rocheteau (all France), Mokhtar Dhouieb, Ali Kaabi, Nejib Ghommidh (all Tunisia), Juan Manuel Asensi, Dani (both Spain), Joe Jordan, Kenny Dalglish (both Scotland), Andras Toth, Sandor Zombori, Karoly Csapo (all Hungary), Arturo Vázquez-Ayala, Victor Rangel (both Mexico), Thomas Sjöberg (Sweden), Iraj Danaifar, Hassan Rowshan (both Iran).

Own-goals
Andranik Eskandarian (Iran v Scotland), Ernie Brandts (Holland v Italy), Hans-Hubert Vogts (West Germany v Austria).

Hat-tricks
Rob Rensenbrink (Holland v Iran).
Teófilo Cubillas (Peru v Iran).
NB. Both included two penalties.

Fastest goal
31 seconds — Bernard Lacombe (France v Italy).

Most goals (team)
15 — Argentina and Holland

Teams failing to score
None

Total goals scored: 102
Average per game: 2.68

Poland kept alive their slim hopes of reaching the Final with a rare header from Szarmach in the 64th minute. For Peru it was to be the end of their hopes of reaching the Final.

Poland: Kukla; Szymanowski, Gorgon, Zmuda, Makulewicz, Masztaler(Kasperczak), Nawalka, Deyna, Boniek(Lubanski), Lato, Szarmach.
Scorer: Szarmach
Peru: Quiroga; Duarte, Manzo, Chumpitaz, Navarro, Cueto, Quesada, Cubillas, Muñante (P.Rojas), La Rosa(Sotíl), Oblítas.
Referee: Pat Partridge (England)

ARGENTINA 0   BRAZIL 0 (Half-time 0-0)

New Rosario Stadium, Rosario, 18 June
Attendance: 46,000

WITH emotions running high in a fixture guaranteed to keep players and fans on their toes, it was hardly surprising that four players were booked and four more went off injured in a game full of wild and occasionally savage tackles.

With the need to remain unbeaten the overriding factor, it was hardly surprising that the game remained goalless at the end of 90 gruelling minutes and Argentina maintained their fine record against their neighbours.

The packed Rosario ground was full of fervent fans who witnessed no fewer than six fouls in the first three minutes. That set the pattern of the game.

Brazil controlled midfield, despite Menotti's decision to play Mario Kempes in the middle of the park, but the move did not work for the Argentinians.

The best chance of the first half fell to Ortíz, but he ruined a good opportunity to put the hosts in front when he shot wide from eight yards. After half an hour Argentina lost Ardíles, who went off injured and was replaced by Ricky Villa. They both joined Tottenham Hotspur shortly after the end of the tournament.

The goalless scoreline left the group wide open with one of these two powerful nations almost certain to make the Final. But which one depended on their respective goalscoring powers in their final matches.

Argentina: Fillol; Olguín, L.Galván, Passarella, Tarantini, Ardíles(Villa), Gallego, Kempes, Bertoni, Luque, Ortíz(Alonso).
Brazil: Leão; Toninho, Oscar, Amaral, Rodrígues Neto(Edinho), Chicão, Batista, Dirceu, Mendonça(Zico), Gil, Roberto.
Referee: Karoly Palotai (Hungary)

BRAZIL 3   POLAND 1 (Half-time 1-1)

Estadio Mendoza, Mendoza, 21 June
Attendance: 44,000

THE Brazilians were annoyed that their final match kicked off before Argentina's. Consequently, the hosts knew exactly what they had to do to reach the Final. It was certainly an unfair advantage but all Argentina's matches kicked off later because the organizers felt that people would not attend the other matches if they kicked off at the same time. Instead, they would watch them on television.

Nevertheless, Brazil knew one thing — they had to beat Poland, and score as many goals as possible. But at half-time, with the score 1-1, things were not looking too good for the South American favourites.

Brazil again played exciting football but received a severe set-back when Zico went off injured after seven minutes. Five minutes later, however, they took the lead from a Nelinho free-kick. A minute before the interval Lato equalized for the Europeans.

Boniek and Deyna had outstanding games for Poland as they threatened to upset the Brazilian plans. But Brazil took charge and in the 57th minute, Roberto followed up Toninho's cross which hit the post and put them back in front from the rebound. Five minutes later, Roberto netted again after the ball had rebounded off post and crossbar with the Polish defence in disarray.

Brazil won and temporarily headed the group with five points and a goal-difference of five. They were in the Final unless Argentina could score at least four against Peru and win by at least three clear goals.

Brazil: Leão; Toninho, Oscar, Amaral, Nelinho, Batista, Cerezo(Rivelino), Dirceu, Gil, Roberto, Zico(Mendonça).
Scorers: Nelinho, Roberto 2
Poland: Kukla; Maculewicz, Zmuda, Gorgon, Szymanowski, Boniek, Nawalka, Deyna, Kasperczak(Lubanski), Lato, Szarmach.
Scorer: Lato
Referee: Juan Silvagno (Chile)

ARGENTINA 6   PERU 0 (Half-time 2-0)

New Rosario Stadium, Rosario, 21 June
Attendance: 40,567

ARGENTINA knew exactly what they had to do to reach the 1978 World Cup Final —

score four goals and win by three clear goals. And they made their intentions clear from the first whistle as they attacked the Peruvian goal guarded by the Argentine-born Quiroga.

However, despite Argentina having five men up front for most of the time — and the encouragement of a capacity crowd — the first 20 minutes passed without a goal. But then Mario Kempes struck with his third goal of the tournament.

After taking a pass from Passarella, some 20 yards out, the striker beat the defence and hit a left-foot shot past the 'keeper. The floodgates were open and Argentina should have had three more goals before Tarantini finally scored their second two minutes from half-time, when his low header from a Bertoni corner found its way into the net.

Kempes and Luque worked a free-kick well before Kempes took the return to make it 3-0 in the 48th minute. One minute later Luque, nursing a black eye from the Brazilian game, made sure Argentina reached their target when he headed home from Bertoni's header into the goalmouth.

The hosts were in the Final, but they wanted to take no chances and sought more goals. In the 66th minute, two minutes after coming on for Bertoni, Houseman finished off a dazzling run by Ortíz.

To complete the celebrations, Luque added a sixth goal in the 72nd minute after a fine move created by Larrossa, the stand-in for the injured Osvaldo Ardíles.

The win put Argentina in their first Final since 1930 and as one Brazilian reporter wrote: 'If Brazil had won 50-0 against Poland, Argentina would have won 52-0!' A bit of an exaggeration, perhaps, but the point was taken.

Argentina: Fillol; Olguín, L.Galván, Passarella, Tarantini, Larrosa, Gallego(Oviedo), Kempes, Bertoni(Houseman), Luque, Ortíz.
Scorers: Kempes 2, Luque 2, Tarantini, Houseman
Peru: Quiroga; Duarte, Manzo, Chumpitaz, R.Rojas, Velásquez(Gorriti), Cubillas, Cueto, Muñante, Quesada, Oblítas.
Referee: Robert Wurtz (France)

Third place play-off
BRAZIL 2   ITALY 1 (Half-time 0-1)
Estadio Antonio Liberti 'Monumental', Buenos Aires, 24 June
Attendance: 76,609

THE Brazilians took the field amidst jeers and boos from the Argentinian fans after claims of drug-taking by Mario Kempes and bribes offered to Peru to 'throw' the last match of Group B.

Italy, meanwhile, ran out without Benetti and Tardelli, both sidelined after receiving two cautions. However, they took the lead seven minutes before half-time when Causio scored with a far-post header from a Rossi centre.

The second half, though, belonged to Brazil and they won the match with two spectacular goals. The first came after 63 minutes when Nelinho's 35-yard shot swerved both ways, completely deceiving Dino Zoff who, yet again, let in a long-range effort.

A minute later Rivelino came on as substitute for Cerezo and had a hand in Brazil's winner on his final World Cup appearance. His cross was chested down by Mendonça for Dirceu to volley into the net from 20 yards. For the second successive game, Dino Zoff, one of the world's best goalkeepers, had conceded two long-range shots.

Tempers frayed after Brazil's second goal and the game ended with Brazil going home

Group B – Final Table

	P	W	D	L	F	A	Pts
Argentina	3	2	1	0	8	0	5
Brazil	3	2	1	0	6	1	5
Poland	3	1	0	2	2	5	2
Peru	3	0	0	3	0	10	0

Penalties
Scored: Andras Toth (Hungary v Italy) *Referee: Ramón Barreto Ruíz (Uruguay).* Daniel Passarella (Argentina v France) *Referee: Jean Dubach (Switzerland).* Arturo Vázquez-Ayala (Mexico v Tunisia) *Referee: John Gordon (Scotland).* Hans Krankl (Austria v Sweden) *Referee: Charles Corver (Holland).* Rob Rensenbrink (Holland v Iran) *Referee: Alfonso Archundia (Mexico).* Rob Rensenbrink (Holland v Iran) *Referee: Alfonso Archundia (Mexico).* Archie Gemmill (Scotland v Holland) *Referee: Erich Linemayr (Austria).* Rob Rensenbrink (Holland v Scotland) *Referee: Erich Linemayr (Austria).* Teófilo Cubillas (Peru v Iran) *Referee: Alojzi Jarguz (Poland).* Teófilo Cubillas (Peru v Iran) *Referee: Alojzi Jarguz (Poland).* Rob Rensenbrink (Holland v Austria) *Referee: John Gordon (Scotland).* Zico (Brazil v Peru) *Referee: Nicolae Rainea (Romania).*

Most appearances
7 — *Ubaldo Matildo Fillol, Jorge Olguín, Luís Galván, Daniel Passarella, Alberto Tarantini,* Américo Gallego, *Mario Kempes* (all Argentina); *Emerson Leão, José Oscar Bernardi, João Amaral Santos, João Batista Da Silva, José Guimaraes Dirceu, Gil* (all Brazil); *Dino Zoff, Claudio Gentile,* Antonio Cabrini, Gaetano Scirea, Franco Causio, Roberto Bettega, *Paolo Rossi* (all Italy); *Ruud Krol, Willy van de Kerkhof,* Willem Jansen, Johannes Rep, *Rob Rensenbrink,* René van de Kerkhof (all Holland).
Those players in italics appeared in seven full games.

Sendings-off
Andras Torocsik (Hungary v Argentina) *Referee: Antonio Garrido (Portugal).* Tibor Nyilasi (Hungary v Argentina) *Referee: Antonio Garrido (Portugal).* Dick Nanninga (Holland v West Germany) *Referee: Ramón Barreto Ruíz (Uruguay).*

Most players used
22 — France

Number of players used by Finalists
17 — Argentina
19 — Holland

Antognoni (9) fires in a free-kick against Brazil but goalkeeper Leão is behind the ball and the Brazilians went on to win the third place game 2-1 to remain unbeaten in the tournament.

Luque (left) and Haan battle for the ball in the Final.

The Dutch side which finished runners-up in the 1978 World Cup. Back row (left to right): Rep, Jongbloed, Haan, Brandts, Neeskens, Krol. Front row: Jansen, Poortvliet, Willy van de Kerkhof, René van de Kerkhof, Rensenbrink.

in the knowledge that they were the only unbeaten team in the 11th World Cup — and all they had to show for it was third place.

Brazil: Leão; Nelinho, Oscar, Amaral, Rodrígues Neto, Cerezo(Rivelino), Batista, Dirceu, Gil(Reinaldo), Roberto, Mendonça.
Scorers: Nelinho, Dirceu
Italy: Zoff; Cuccureddu, Gentile, Scirea, Cabrini, P.Sala, Antognoni(C.Sala), Maldera, Causio, Rossi, Bettega.
Scorer: Causio
Referee: Abraham Klein (Israel)

Final

ARGENTINA 3   HOLLAND 1 a.e.t. (Half-time 1-0; 90mins 1-1)

Estadio Antonio Liberti 'Monumental', Buenos Aires, 25 June
Attendance: 77,260

THE capacity crowd at the home of the River Plate club greeted Argentina with the now customary ticker-tape welcome as thousands of pieces of paper were thrown from all parts of the ground and littered the goalmouths.

The match was beamed by television to 90 countries, including China and South Africa, and they were to witness a contest between a host nation who had received their share of good fortune in reaching the Final, and a Dutch side who had improved as the tournament went along and proved themselves to be the best of the European nations.

It was Holland's second successive appearance in the World Cup Final and for the second tournament in succession the kick-off was delayed. This time Argentina were slightly late coming on to the pitch and then they objected to a lightweight cast on the injured arm of René van de Kerkhof. The game eventually started ten minutes late.

Italian bank official Sergio Gonella was the referee, although Abraham Klein of Israel was the first choice but had been replaced when Argentinian officials complained because of Holland's political ties with Israel. It was sad that one of the game's leading referees should miss out on such an occasion because of politics. Politics and sport were now no longer divorced from each other.

Strangely, Holland resorted to tough tackling from the outset and in the 14th minute their captain, Ruud Krol, was booked for a brutal foul. He was one of four players — two from each side — cautioned by the referee.

Mario Kempes and Leopoldo Luque were menacing and posed the Dutch defence all sorts of problems in the first half, so it was not surprising that Kempes was on hand to open

Above: **Mario Kempes stretches out to poke a shot past Jongbloed in the 38th minute of the 1978 World Cup Final. The other players pictured are Bertoni of Argentina and Dutch skipper Krol.**

Left: **Dutch substitute Dick Nanninga heads home to level the scores, beating Galván, Passarella and goalkeeper Fillol. The other Dutch player is Jan Poortvliet.**

Fillol (foreground) and Tarantini of Agentina.

the scoring in the 38th minute after Luque and Ardíles, now fit again, set up the move on the left before Kempes met a cross.

Dick Nanninga had been telling reporters all week: "I shall come on in the last ten minutes and I shall take a goal." In fact, he came on as a 59th-minute substitute for Johnny Rep and as the game went into the last ten minutes, Holland had still not scored and Argentina were holding on to their slim lead. But then the forecast was proved partially correct when René van de Kerkhof beat the offside trap and floated a cross in from the right for Nanninga to score.

With the game heading for extra-time, Rob Rensenbrink, who had enjoyed an outstanding tournament, saw a shot hit the post. It was the nearest Holland had ever come to winning the World Cup.

In the final minute of the first period of extra-time, Kempes struck again with his sixth goal of the tournament, when he beat three men to drive the ball past Jongbloed. Five minutes from the end, Kempes opened up the defence again but this time he created the opening for Bertoni to score. Argentina thus became the fifth host nation to win the World Cup.

Argentina's chain-smoking manager, César Menotti, at last took the World Cup to Argentina, after having to watch neighbours Uruguay and Brazil win it five times between them.

And so came the end of a successful tournament which was well supported. It had its moments of brilliance. It had its less memorable moments. But without the likes of Beckenbauer, Pelé and Cruyff, perhaps one could not have expected too much.

Argentina: Ubaldo Matildo Fillol; Jorge Olguín, Luís Galván, Daniel Passarella, Alberto Tarantini, Osvaldo Ardíles(Omar Larrosa), Américo Gallego, Mario Kempes, Daniel Bertoni, Leopoldo Luque, Oscar Ortíz(René Houseman).
Scorers: Kempes 2, Bertoni
Holland: Jan Jongbloed; Willem Jansen(Willem Suurbier), Ernie Brandts, Ruud Krol, Jan Poortvliet, Arie Haan, Willy van de Kerkhof, Johannes Neeskens, René van de Kerkhof, Johannes Rep(Dick Nanninga), Rob Rensenbrink.
Scorer: Nanninga
Referee: Sergio Gonella (Italy)

Above: Kempes (striped shirt nearest goal) raises his arms to celebrate his and Argentina's second goal in extra-time. Other Argentinians are (from left to right): Bertoni, Houseman (9) and Luque.

Right: Bertoni fires home Argentina's third goal in the 24th minute of extra-time and the South Americans are World Cup winners at last, after taking part in the first-ever Final in 1930.

Argentinian skipper Daniel Passerella holds aloft the World Cup.

Poortvliet is sent crashing by Argentinian substitute, Omar Larrosa.

Mario Kempes, leading scorer in the 1978 World Cup finals with six goals.

Argentina line up before the Final.

Passarella with the trophy, surrounded by his joyful teammates.

MEN WHO MADE THE HEADLINES - 1982

Paolo Rossi
(Italy)

PAOLO Rossi's career lay in tatters in 1980, after he was suspended for three years following an alleged 'fixing' scandal. Rossi continually protested his innocence and the ban was commuted to two years. Born in September 1956, knee problems dogged him with Juventus' junior side and they loaned him to Como, then to Serie B club, Lanerossi Vicenza, who converted him from a winger to centre-forward. Rossi became an instant sensation and his 21 goals helped them to promotion and the club paid £1.5 million to take him permanently. After being relegated, however, Lanerossi transfer-listed him at £3 million, but he refused to join Naples and went to Perugia on loan. It was as a result of their game with Avellino in 1980 that he was accused of taking a bribe after the match ended 2-2 and Rossi scored both Perugia's goals. In 1981, whilst still suspended, Juventus bought him for £500,000. His suspension ended on 29 April 1982 and he was immediately recalled to international football in the 1982 World Cup. His marvellous hat-trick against Brazil secured a semi-final place and he netted two against Poland in the semi-final and the opening goal of the Final as Italy won the trophy for the third time.

Karl-Heinz Rummenigge
(West Germany)

KARL-HEINZ Rummenigge was another in the German line that produced Helmut Rahn, Uwe Seller and Gerd Müller. Born in Westphalia in 1955, he played locally for Borussia Lippstadt before giving up his job as a bank clerk to join Bayern Munich as an 18-year-old. Having won a European Cup medal with Bayern in 1976, he was looking forward to a good run in the 1978 World Cup but, despite his three goals, the Germans had a poor tournament. Two years later there was glory, though, as West Germany became European Champions. In the Final, against Belgium, Rummenigge laid on the winning goal for Hrubesch and was named Player of the Tournament. He was also European Footballer of the Year and repeated that performance in 1981. In the 1982 World Cup he scored five goals, including a hat-trick against Chile, and skippered West Germany to the Final. But he was not fully fit and was substituted after 69 minutes as Italy ran out easy winners. In 1984 he became West Germany's most expensive footballer when he joined Inter-Milan for £2.5 million. He made his 19th World Cup appearance in the memorable 1986 Final, when Argentina beat West Germany. Altogether he won 95 caps and scored 45 international goals.

Zico
(Brazil)

ZICO, born Artur Antunes Coimbra at Río in 1953, was the youngest of five footballing brothers. He made his League debut for Flamengo in 1973 and his international debut in 1976, against Uruguay, scoring with one the dead-ball shots for which he became famous. Zico netted over 100 goals in his first two seasons and was South American Footballer of the Year in 1977 (and in 1981 and 1982). In the 1978 World Cup he suffered niggling injuries and was unhappy with coach Claudio Coutinho's defensive game. In 1982, however, Brazil returned to the attacking style which suited Zico's change of pace, body-swerves and dynamic shooting. His hat-trick against Bolivia clinched a place in the finals and in Spain his four goals, including the equalizer against Scotland, took his total for Brazil past 50. In 1983, after 650 goals and four Brazilian championship medals, he made a £2.5million move to Udinese, returning to Flamengo in the summer of 1985. He played in three games in the 1986 World Cup, all as a substitute. His last match was the quarter-final against France when Brazilian fans chanted for him. Alas, minutes later he missed a penalty. It was a sad end for one of Brazil's most popular players. After 1,047 senior games, including 74 for Brazil, he eventually retired in 1990 and was appointed his country's Sports Minister.

The Italian Job
Spain 1982

*I*N April 1970, Sir Stanley Rous stated the World Cup finals would be better balanced with 24 teams. Now, 12 years later, there was the opportunity to see if he was right because, at the FIFA Congress before the 1978 tournament, it was agreed to increase the teams from 16 to either 20 or 24, depending upon the host nation's ability to cater for the extra matches. In 1982, the number was to be Sir Stanley's magical 24.

Spain played host to the 12th World Cup and laid on a spectacular opening ceremony, Alas, with a few isolated exceptions, the football certainly did not live up to the glamour of the opening scene.

Because of the increased number of entrants, there was yet another new format. The 24 teams were divided into six groups of four. The top two teams then went into four further groups of three with the group winners progressing to a semi-final knock-out stage.

However, before all that got underway there were many who doubted Spain's ability to stage such a spectacular event. And those who did doubt their organizational ability had their fears confirmed at the draw in Madrid on 16 January 1982 — it was absolute chaos.

First, there had been a lot of bickering about the decision to make England one of the six seeded teams, notably from France and Belgium, who had every right to complain. After all, England had finished second in their qualifying group and struggled to qualify for the finals. Nevertheless, FIFA decided that England would be one of the seeds along with Italy, West Germany, Argentina, Brazil and Spain.

But that was only the start of the debacle at the draw. To ensure that Peru and Chile would not be included in the same group as their South American rivals, Argentina and Brazil, the miniature footballs containing their names were supposed to be left out of the cage until after the first two names drawn out had been placed in Argentina and Brazil's groups. But someone forgot to remove them and Peru and Chile were in from the start. To add to the confusion, Scotland were placed in Argentina's group and then it was realized that Belgium should have been in that group, so Scotland were transferred to Brazil's group. . . confusion reigned.

And it did not stop there. The giant cage containing the footballs jammed and one of the miniature balls split in half. All-in-all it was a comedy of errors and one that must have left the millions watching on television wondering what the Spaniards had in store five months later when the competition was due to get underway. One should add, in fairness to the Spanish officials, that certain aspects of the draw must have been handled by FIFA themselves but, whatever, it hardly augered well.

Spain spent £40 million revamping their stadiums, which were in excellent condition by the time the series got underway, and a further £60 million on organizational costs. And it has to be said that after the embarrassment of the draw, the tournament was successful from the administrative viewpoint. It was just a pity the organizers had no control over the standard of football.

There were always worries about the security arrangements in Spain because of the troubles surrounding the Basque separatist movement. There was the added problem of England possibly meeting Argentina at some stage of the competition, only months after the start of the Falklands War. Fortunately that did not happen.

Argentina, Brazil and Spain were considered likely champions but it was Brazil who became clear favourites after coach Telê Santana showed the 1,500 million fans watching on television that he had produced another Brazilian side capable of doing what they enjoy best — playing attacking football. It was Brazil's finest side since 1970 and players, coach and fans were confident of a fourth triumph. In Zico they had the next in a long line of outstanding Brazilian footballers. He had scored a goal a game for his club, Flamengo, and many Brazilians regard him as their best-ever player after Pelé.

Argentina still had the cigarette-smoking César Menotti at the helm, but he was to pay the price for falling into the same trap as Sir Alf Ramsey by keeping his winning side together too long.

The increase in the number of teams to 24 meant there was more of a true world-wide representation of nations with Kuwait, Cameroon, Honduras, Algeria and New Zealand all going in with the big boys for the first time. And the little football nations were far from the cannon fodder many expected. West Germany, Poland, Peru, Italy, Chile, Czechoslovakia, Spain and Northern Ireland would all testify to that, for they were each held to a draw by one or other of the so-called 'minnows'.

Initially, increasing the number of teams was seen as a controversial move and many felt that it would produce more defensive games. Indeed, some of the games were tedious and negative affairs, but at the end of the day the average number of goals per game was at its highest since 1970 and the new format had won its admirers before the end of the tournament.

King Juan Carlos performed the opening ceremony on 13 June and shortly afterwards Belgium beat Argentina 1-0 in the first opening match since 1962 to see a goal scored. That should have been significant but this was not to be one of the best World Cups and, despite the presence of stars like Platini, Zico, Rossi, Socrates and Junior, it was a disappointing tournament, especially for the new 'superstar' of world soccer, Diego Maradona. His day was still to come.

Enzo Bearzot, manager of the 1982 World Cup winners, Italy.

1982 Qualifying Competition

WHEN the closing date for entrants arrived in March 1980, a total of 109 teams had entered the 12th World Cup. As usual there was a spate of withdrawals and Ghana, Uganda, Libya and Iran all pulled out without kicking a ball. The Central African Republic also failed to take part, because they did not pay their entry fee on time.

The Irish got the qualifying tournament underway, with the Republic beating Cyprus 3-2 in Nicosia on 26 March and on the same day, Northern Ireland drew 0-0 with Israel in Tel Aviv. These were the first of more than 300 matches which would eventually decide the 22 teams to join the host nation, Spain, and the holders, Argentina, in the final stages more than two years later.

Six of the seven European groups contained five teams and each produced two qualifiers. The only exception was the three-team Group Seven, which was won by Poland.

Britain had its best representation since 1958, with three qualifiers. Missing were Wales, who paid dearly for a home draw with Iceland. It meant that Czechoslovakia needed only to draw their final match against Russia to qualify on goal-difference. They managed a 1-1 scoreline and the Welsh went out, leaving the two Eastern European nations to go through to the finals.

West Germany qualified with a 100 per cent record and 33 goals from eight games, including a seven-goal haul against Finland and eight against Albania. Having conceded only three goals from their first seven matches, West Germany had to let in five against Bulgaria if the latter team was to qualify ahead of Austria. The Germans won 4-0.

The Republic of Ireland came close to qualifying for their first finals but lost out on an inferior goal-difference to France. The group winners were Belgium, who reached their first finals since 1970, but in fourth place, and behind the Republic of Ireland, were the 1974 and 1978 runners-up, Holland. They started their campaign disastrously with defeats by both the Republic and Belgium and failed to recover.

When the draw was made, England seemed to have an easy passage into the finals. But what problems they caused for themselves as they suffered defeats in Romania, Switzerland and Norway. The last two were particularly embarrassing reverses. England faced the possibility of failing to qualify yet again, but were saved when Romania suffered a home defeat by Switzerland. It meant England had to beat Hungary, who had already qualified, in the final match of Group Four to join the Magyars in Spain.

In a dour match at Wembley, England secured their win through a solitary Paul Mariner goal and thus successfully, if not impressively, came through the qualifying round for the first time since 1962.

Yugoslavia and Italy qualified from their group as anticipated but Italy stumbled along the way, being held to a home draw by Greece and then beating Luxembourg at home by a single goal. On this form Italy were not considered as one of the favourites in Spain.

Scotland and Northern Ireland both qualified from the lowest scoring of all the European groups. And, despite losing to Portugal in their last match, Scotland had already assured themselves of first place. On the same night, Northern Ireland booked their trip to Spain after beating Israel 1-0 at Belfast, thanks to an Armstrong goal after 27 minutes. Portugal were disappointing in this group and lost twice to Switzerland and once to Israel and Northern Ireland.

Poland completed the European complement by winning all

four matches to qualify ahead of rivals, East Germany and Malta.

Thanks to new manager Telê Santana, Brazil reverted to the sort of attacking team that the soccer public had enjoyed so much. The manager was anxious to wipe away the memory of their defensive attitude in Argentina four years earlier and if their performance in the qualifying rounds was anything to go by, he had succeeded. They swept aside Bolivia and Venezuela without dropping a point to qualify with ease.

Despite opening with a 3-2 win over Colombia, Uruguay did not win another game and trailed in second place to qualifiers Peru. Uruguay, therefore, were the only former champions not to reach the finals.

The reigning South American champions, Paraguay, finished bottom of their group which was won by Chile, whose only blemish was a 0-0 draw against Ecuador at Quito.

The CONCACAF groups were split into three zones: Northern, Central and Caribbean which, in turn, was split into two groups. Despite its complex nature, two teams from each zone eventually qualified for the CONCACAF finals which produced two qualifiers, Honduras and El Salvador, who both came from the Central Zone — happily, there was no 'football war' this time. Mexico were deprived of a place in the finals after a goalless draw with Honduras in their last match.

The African group was played on a series of two-legged knock-out matches before the number of teams was reduced to four semi-finalists, with the two winners qualifying for Spain.

Egypt were fortunate to go through to the third round without kicking a ball, thanks to the withdrawal of their respective opponents, Ghana and Libya. But when they were eventually called upon to play, they lost at the first attempt to Morocco.

Cameroon clinched a place in the finals in front of 120,000 fervent fans with a 2-1 win over Morocco, whilst Algeria won both their matches against Nigeria. Cameroon and Algeria became the next two countries, following in the footsteps of Morocco, Zaïre and Tunisia, to show the soccer public just what an emerging soccer continent Africa was. Both fared well in the finals in Spain, and Algeria were desperately unlucky not to qualify for the second phase.

The final qualifying group, Asia/Oceania, was divided into a series of sub-groups which eventually brought together four group finalists with Kuwait emerging at the head of the table. China looked set for the second qualifying place because New Zealand went into their last match, away to Saudi Arabia, needing to win by six clear goals to qualify and by five to force a play-off. Despite the Saudis being bottom of the table, it was still a tall order for the Kiwis, who could only manage to draw 2-2 in the home match. But there was a remarkable turnabout as the New Zealanders won 5-0 and forced a play-off against China.

That game was in Singapore on 10 January 1982, only six days before the draw for the finals, and the New Zealanders won 2-1, thanks to Wynton Rufer's winning goal. And so, after 15 matches, New Zealand qualified for their first World Cup finals. On their way to qualifying they had established a new World Cup record score when they beat Fiji 13-0. But spare a thought for the Fijians, two days earlier Australia put ten goals past them.

In Spain, there were to be no such scoring exploits for New Zealand but, like the other newcomers, Algeria, Cameroon and Kuwait, they were not the push-overs many had expected.

Results

EUROPE

Group One

4 Jun 1980	*Helsinki*	Finland.............0 Bulgaria..........2
3 Sep 1980	*Tiranë*	Albania............2 Finland...........0
24 Sep 1980	*Helsinki*	Finland............0 Austria...........2
19 Oct 1980	*Sofia*	Bulgaria..........2 Albania...........1
15 Nov 1980	*Vienna*	Austria.............5 Albania..........0
3 Dec 1980	*Sofia*	Bulgaria..........1 West Germany...3
6 Dec 1980	*Tiranë*	Albania............0 Austria............1
1 Apr 1981	*Tiranë*	Albania............0 West Germany...2
29 Apr 1981	*Hamburg*	West Germany...2 Austria............0
13 May 1981	*Sofia*	Bulgaria..........4 Finland...........0
24 May 1981	*Lahti*	Finland............0 West Germany...4
28 May 1981	*Vienna*	Austria.............2 Bulgaria..........0
17 Jun 1981	*Linz*	Austria.............5 Finland...........1
2 Sep 1981	*Kotka*	Finland............2 Albania...........1
23 Sep 1981	*Bochum*	West Germany...7 Finland...........1
14 Oct 1981	*Vienna*	Austria.............1 West Germany...3
14 Oct 1981	*Tiranë*	Albania............0 Bulgaria..........2
11 Nov 1981	*Sofia*	Bulgaria..........0 Austria............0
18 Nov 1981	*Dortmund*	West Germany...8 Albania...........0
22 Nov 1981	*Düsseldorf*	West Germany...4 Bulgaria..........0

Final Table

	P	W	D	L	F	A	Pts	
W.Germany	8	8	0	0	33	3	16	
Austria	8	5	1	2	16	6	11	**West Germany and**
Bulgaria	8	4	1	3	11	10	9	**Austria qualified**
Albania	8	1	0	7	4	22	2	
Finland	8	1	0	7	4	27	2	

Group Two

26 Mar 1980	*Nicosia*	Cyprus.............2 Rep of Ireland...3
10 Sep 1980	*Dublin*	Rep of Ireland...2 Holland...........1
11 Oct 1980	*Limassol*	Cyprus.............0 France.............7
15 Oct 1980	*Dublin*	Rep of Ireland...1 Belgium..........1
28 Oct 1980	*Paris*	France.............2 Rep of Ireland...0
19 Nov 1980	*Brussels*	Belgium..........1 Holland...........0
19 Nov 1980	*Dublin*	Rep of Ireland...6 Cyprus............0
21 Dec 1980	*Nicosia*	Cyprus.............0 Belgium..........2
18 Feb 1981	*Brussels*	Belgium..........3 Cyprus............2
22 Feb 1981	*Groningen*	Holland..........3 Cyprus............0
25 Mar 1981	*Rotterdam*	Holland..........1 France.............0
25 Mar 1981	*Brussels*	Belgium..........1 Rep of Ireland...0
29 Apr 1981	*Paris*	France.............3 Belgium..........2
29 Apr 1981	*Nicosia*	Cyprus.............0 Holland...........1
9 Sep 1981	*Rotterdam*	Holland..........2 Rep of Ireland...2
9 Sep 1981	*Brussels*	Belgium..........2 France.............0
14 Oct 1981	*Rotterdam*	Holland..........3 Belgium..........0
14 Oct 1981	*Dublin*	Rep of Ireland...3 France.............2
18 Nov 1981	*Paris*	France.............2 Holland...........0
5 Dec 1981	*Paris*	France.............4 Cyprus............0

Final Table

	P	W	D	L	F	A	Pts	
Belgium	8	5	1	2	12	9	11	
France	8	5	0	3	20	8	10	
Rep of Ireland	8	4	2	2	17	11	10	**Belgium and France**
Holland	8	4	1	3	11	7	9	**qualified**
Cyprus	8	0	0	8	4	29	0	

Group Three

2 Jun 1980	*Reykjavíc*	Iceland.............0 Wales..............4
3 Sep 1980	*Reykjavíc*	Iceland.............1 Soviet Union....2
24 Sep 1980	*İzmir*	Turkey.............1 Iceland............3
15 Oct 1980	*Cardiff*	Wales..............4 Turkey............0
15 Oct 1980	*Moscow*	Soviet Union....5 Iceland............0
19 Nov 1980	*Cardiff*	Wales..............1 Czechoslovakia..0
3 Dec 1980	*Prague*	Czechoslovakia..2 Turkey............0
25 Mar 1981	*Ankara*	Turkey.............0 Wales..............1
15 Apr 1981	*Istanbul*	Turkey.............0 Czechoslovakia..3
27 May 1981	*Bratislava*	Czechoslovakia..6 Iceland............1
30 May 1981	*Wrexham*	Wales..............0 Soviet Union....0
9 Sep 1981	*Reykjavíc*	Iceland.............2 Turkey............0
9 Sep 1981	*Prague*	Czechoslovakia..2 Wales..............0
23 Sep 1981	*Reykjavíc*	Iceland.............1 Czechoslovakia..1
23 Sep 1981	*Moscow*	Soviet Union....4 Turkey............0
7 Oct 1981	*İzmir*	Turkey.............0 Soviet Union....3
14 Oct 1981	*Swansea*	Wales..............2 Iceland............2
28 Oct 1981	*Tbilisi*	Soviet Union....2 Czechoslovakia..0
18 Nov 1981	*Tbilisi*	Soviet Union....3 Wales..............0
29 Nov 1981	*Bratislava*	Czechoslovakia..1 Soviet Union....1

Final Table

	P	W	D	L	F	A	Pts	
Soviet Union	8	6	2	0	20	2	14	
Czechoslovakia	8	4	2	2	15	6	10	**Soviet Union and**
Wales	8	4	2	2	12	7	10	**Czechoslovakia**
Iceland	8	2	2	4	10	21	6	**qualified**
Turkey	8	0	0	8	1	22	0	

Alain Giresse (dark shirt) of France gets past a Cypriot defender as the French sweep to a 4-0 victory in Paris in the final match of European Group Two.

Left: Paul Mariner on his knees after scoring the goal which sent England to Spain.

Group Four

10 Sep 1980 *London*	England ....4 Norway 0
24 Sep 1980 *Oslo*	Norway...........1 Romania 1
15 Oct 1980 *Bucharest*	Romania ....2 England 1
29 Oct 1980 *Berne*	Switzerland ......1 Norway...........2
19 Nov 1980 *London*	England ....2 Switzerland 1
28 Apr 1981 *Lucerne*	Switzerland ......2 Hungary 2
29 Apr 1981 *London*	England ....0 Romania 0
13 May 1981 *Budapest*	Hungary ....1 Romania 0
20 May 1981 *Oslo*	Norway...........1 Hungary 2
30 May 1981 *Basle*	Switzerland ......2 England 1
3 Jun 1981 *Bucharest*	Romania ....1 Norway...........0
6 Jun 1981 *Budapest*	Hungary ....1 England 3
17 Jun 1981 *Oslo*	Norway...........1 Switzerland 1
9 Sep 1981 *Oslo*	Norway...........2 England 1
23 Sep 1981 *Bucharest*	Romania ....0 Hungary 0
10 Oct 1981 *Bucharest*	Romania ....1 Switzerland 2
14 Oct 1981 *Bucharest*	Hungary ....3 Switzerland 0
31 Oct 1981 *Budapest*	Hungary ....4 Norway...........1
11 Nov 1981 *Berne*	Switzerland ......0 Romania 0
18 Nov 1981 *London*	England ....1 Hungary 0

Final Table

	P	W	D	L	F	A	Pts
Hungary	8	4	2	2	13	8	10
England	8	4	1	3	13	8	9
Romania	8	2	4	3	5	5	8
Switzerland	8	2	3	3	9	12	7
Norway	8	2	2	4	8	15	6

Hungary and England qualified

Group Five

10 Sep 1980 *Luxembourg*	Luxembourg.....0 Yugoslavia 5
27 Sep 1980 *Ljubljana*	Yugoslavia ....2 Denmark 1
11 Oct 1980 *Luxembourg*	Luxembourg.....0 Italy...............2
15 Oct 1980 *Copenhagen*	Denmark ....0 Greece 1
1 Nov 1980 *Rome*	Italy...............2 Denmark 0
15 Nov 1980 *Turin*	Italy...............2 Yugoslavia 0
19 Nov 1980 *Copenhagen*	Denmark ....4 Luxembourg....0
6 Dec 1980 *Athens*	Greece ....0 Italy...............2
28 Jan 1981 *Salonika*	Greece ....2 Luxembourg....0
11 Mar 1981 *Luxembourg*	Luxembourg.....0 Greece 2
29 Apr 1981 *Split*	Yugoslavia ....5 Greece 1
1 May 1981 *Luxembourg*	Luxembourg.....1 Denmark 2
3 Jun 1981 *Copenhagen*	Denmark ....3 Italy...............1
9 Sep 1981 *Copenhagen*	Denmark ....1 Yugoslavia 2
14 Oct 1981 *Salonika*	Greece ....2 Denmark 3
17 Oct 1981 *Belgrade*	Yugoslavia ....1 Italy...............1
14 Nov 1981 *Turin*	Italy...............1 Greece 1
21 Nov 1981 *Novi Sad*	Yugoslavia ....5 Luxembourg.....0
29 Nov 1981 *Athens*	Greece ....1 Yugoslavia 2
5 Dec 1981 *Naples*	Italy...............1 Luxembourg.....0

Final Table

	P	W	D	L	F	A	Pts
Yugoslavia	8	6	1	1	22	7	13
Italy	8	5	2	1	12	5	12
Denmark	8	4	0	4	14	11	8
Greece	8	3	1	4	10	13	7
Luxembourg	8	0	0	8	1	23	0

Yugoslavia and Italy qualified

Veteran goalkeeper Dino Zoff rescues Italy in their game against Yugoslavia in Belgrade. Vahidin Halilhodzić reaches for the ball but cannot make contact. The teams drew 1-1 and both eventually qualified for the finals.

Group Six

26 Mar 1980 *Tel Aviv*	Israel	0 N. Ireland	0
18 Jun 1980 *Stockholm*	Sweden	1 Israel	1
10 Sep 1980 *Stockholm*	Sweden	0 Scotland	1
15 Oct 1980 *Belfast*	N. Ireland	3 Sweden	0
15 Oct 1980 *Glasgow*	Scotland	0 Portugal	0
12 Nov 1980 *Tel Aviv*	Israel	0 Sweden	0
19 Nov 1980 *Lisbon*	Portugal	1 N. Ireland	0
17 Dec 1980 *Lisbon*	Portugal	3 Israel	0
25 Feb 1981 *Tel Aviv*	Israel	0 Scotland	1
25 Mar 1981 *Glasgow*	Scotland	1 N. Ireland	1
28 Apr 1981 *Glasgow*	Scotland	3 Israel	1
29 Apr 1981 *Belfast*	N. Ireland	1 Portugal	0
3 Jun 1981 *Stockholm*	Sweden	1 N. Ireland	0
24 Jun 1981 *Stockholm*	Sweden	3 Portugal	0
9 Sep 1981 *Glasgow*	Scotland	2 Sweden	0
14 Oct 1981 *Lisbon*	Portugal	1 Sweden	2
14 Oct 1981 *Belfast*	N. Ireland	0 Scotland	0
28 Oct 1981 *Tel Aviv*	Israel	4 Portugal	1
18 Nov 1981 *Belfast*	N. Ireland	1 Israel	0
18 Nov 1981 *Lisbon*	Portugal	2 Scotland	1

Final Table

	P	W	D	L	F	A	Pts	
Scotland	8	4	3	1	9	4	11	
N. Ireland	8	3	3	2	6	3	9	
Sweden	8	3	2	3	7	8	8	**Scotland and**
Portugal	8	3	1	4	8	11	7	**Northern Ireland**
Israel	8	1	3	4	6	10	5	**qualified**

Group Seven

7 Dec 1980 *Valletta*	Malta	0 Poland	2
4 Apr 1981 *Valletta*	Malta	1 East Germany	2
2 May 1981 *Chorzów*	Poland	1 East Germany	0
10 Oct 1981 *Leipzig*	East Germany	2 Poland	3
11 Nov 1981 *Jena*	East Germany	5 Malta	1
15 Nov 1981 *Wrocław*	Poland	6 Malta	0

Final Table

	P	W	D	L	F	A	Pts	
Poland	4	4	0	0	12	2	8	**Poland qualified**
E.Germany	4	2	0	2	9	6	4	
Malta	4	0	0	4	2	15	0	

SOUTH AMERICA

Group One

8 Feb 1981 *Caracas*	Venezuela	0 Brazil	1
15 Feb 1981 *La Paz*	Bolivia	3 Venezuela	0
22 Feb 1981 *La Paz*	Bolivia	1 Brazil	2
15 Mar 1981 *Caracas*	Venezuela	1 Bolivia	0
22 Mar 1981 *Río de Janeiro*	Brazil	3 Bolivia	1
29 Mar 1981 *Goiânia*	Brazil	5 Venezuela	0

Final Table

	P	W	D	L	F	A	Pts	
Brazil	4	4	0	0	11	2	8	**Brazil qualified**
Bolivia	4	1	0	3	5	6	2	
Venezuela	4	1	0	3	1	9	2	

Group Two

26 Jul 1981 *Bogotá*	Colombia	1 Peru	1
9 Aug 1981 *Montevideo*	Uruguay	3 Colombia	2
16 Aug 1981 *Lima*	Peru	2 Colombia	0
23 Aug 1981 *Montevideo*	Uruguay	1 Peru	2
6 Sep 1981 *Lima*	Peru	0 Uruguay	0
13 Sep 1981 *Bogotá*	Colombia	1 Uruguay	1

Final Table

	P	W	D	L	F	A	Pts	
Peru	4	2	2	0	5	2	6	**Peru qualified**
Uruguay	4	1	2	1	5	5	4	
Colombia	4	0	2	2	4	7	2	

Group Three

17 May 1981 *Quito*	Ecuador	1 Paraguay	0
24 May 1981 *Quito*	Ecuador	0 Chile	0
31 May 1981 *Asunción*	Paraguay	3 Ecuador	1
7 Jun 1981 *Asunción*	Paraguay	0 Chile	1
14 Jun 1981 *Santiago*	Chile	2 Ecuador	0
21 Jun 1981 *Santiago*	Chile	3 Paraguay	0

Final Table

	P	W	D	L	F	A	Pts	
Chile	4	3	1	0	6	0	7	**Chile qualified**
Ecuador	4	1	1	2	2	5	3	
Paraguay	4	1	0	3	3	6	2	

AFRICA

First Round

18 May 1980 *Addis Ababa*	Ethiopia	0 Zambia	0
1 Jun 1980 *Ndola*	Zambia	4 Ethiopia	0

Zambia qualified for Second Round

31 May 1980 *Freetown*	Sierra Leone	2 Algeria	2
13 Jun 1980 *Oran*	Algeria	3 Sierra Leone	1

Algeria qualified for Second Round

8 May 1980 *Tripoli*	Libya	2 Gambia	1
6 Jul 1980 *Banjul*	Gambia	0 Libya	0

Libya qualified for Second Round

22 Jun 1980 *Conakry*	Guinea	3 Lesotho	1
6 Jul 1980 *Maseru*	Lesotho	1 Guinea	1

Guinea qualified for Second Round

22 Jun 1980 *Dakar*	Senegal	0 Morocco	1
6 Jul 1980 *Casablanca*	Morocco	0 Senegal	0

Morocco qualified for Second Round

29 Jun 1980 *Tūnis*	Tunisia	2 Nigeria	0
12 Jul 1980 *Lagos*	Nigeria	2 Tunisia	0

Nigeria won 4-3 on penalties and qualified for Second Round

5 Jul 1980 *Nairobi*	Kenya	3 Tanzania	1
19 Jul 1980 *Dar es Salaam*	Tanzania	5 Kenya	0

Tanzania qualified for Second Round

29 Jun 1980 *Yaoundé*	Cameroon	3 Malawi	0
20 Jul 1980 *Camusua*	Malawi	1 Cameroon	1

Cameroon qualified for Second Round

13 Jul 1980 *Kinshasa*	Zaïre	5 Mozambique	2
27 Jul 1980 *Maputo*	Mozambique	1 Zaïre	2

Zaïre qualified for Second Round

16 Jul 1980 *Niamey*	Niger	0 Somalia	0
27 Jul 1980 *Mogadishu*	Somalia	1 Niger	1

Niger qualified for Second Round
Egypt and Madagascar qualified for the Second Round following the withdrawal of Ghana and Uganda. Zimbabwe, Sudan, Liberia and Togo all had byes into the Second Round.

Second Round

12 Oct 1980 *Douala*	Cameroon	2 Zimbabwe	0
16 Oct 1980 *Salisbury*	Zimbabwe	1 Cameroon	0

Cameroon qualified for Third Round

16 Nov 1980 *Fès*	Morocco	2 Zambia	0
30 Nov 1980 *Lusaka*	Zambia	2 Morocco	0

Morocco won 5-4 on penalties and qualified for Third Round

6 Dec 1980 *Lagos*	Nigeria	1 Tanzania	1
20 Dec 1980 *Dar es Salaam*	Tanzania	0 Nigeria	2

Nigeria qualified for Third Round

16 Nov 1980 *Antananarivo*	Madagascar	1 Zaire	1
21 Dec 1980 *Kinshasa*	Zaïre	3 Madagascar	2

Zaïre qualified for Third Round

7 Dec 1980 *Monrovia*	Liberia	0 Guinea	0
21 Dec 1980 *Conakry*	Guinea	1 Liberia	0

Guinea qualified for Third Round

12 Dec 1980 *Constantine*	Algeria	2 Sudan	0
28 Dec 1980 *Khartoum*	Sudan	1 Algeria	1

Algeria qualified for Third Round

14 Dec 1980 *Niamey*   Niger ....0 Togo..............1
28 Dec 1980 *Lomé*   Togo...............1 Niger 2
Niger qualified for Third Round
Egypt qualified for Third Round because of Libya's withdrawal.

Third Round

12 Apr 1981 *Conakry*   Guinea ....1 Nigeria 1
25 Apr 1981 *Lagos*   Nigeria ....1 Guinea 0
Nigeria qualified for Group Finals

12 Apr 1981 *Kinshasa*   Zaïre ....1 Cameroon 0
26 Apr 1981 *Yaoundé*   Cameroon ....6 Zaïre 1
Cameroon qualified for Group Finals

26 Apr 1981 *Casablanca* Morocco ....1 Egypt 0
8 May 1981 *Cairo*   Egypt ....0 Morocco 0
Morocco qualified for Group Finals

1 May 1981 *Constantine* Algeria............4 Niger 0
31 May 1981 *Niamey*   Niger ....1 Algeria............0
Algeria qualified for Group Finals

Group Finals

10 Oct 1981 *Lagos*   Nigeria ....0 Algeria............2
30 Oct 1981 *Algiers*   Algeria............2 Nigeria 1
Algeria qualified

15 Nov 1981 *Kenitra*   Morocco ....0 Cameroon 2
29 Nov 1981 *Yaoundé*   Cameroon ....2 Morocco 1
Cameroon qualified

CONCACAF
(Central & North America)

Northern Zone

18 Oct 1980 *Toronto*   Canada ....1 Mexico.............1
25 Oct 1980 *Ft Lauderdale*   United States ....0 Canada 0
1 Nov 1980 *Vancouver*   Canada ....2 United States 1
9 Nov 1980 *Mexico City*   Mexico.............5 United States 1
16 Nov 1980 *Mexico City*   Mexico.............1 Canada 1
23 Nov 1980 *Ft Lauderdale*   United States ....2 Mexico.............1

Final Table

	P	W	D	L	F	A	Pts	
Canada	4	1	3	0	4	3	5	**Canada and Mexico**
Mexico	4	1	2	1	8	5	4	**qualified for Group**
United States	4	1	1	2	4	8	3	**Final**

Central Zone

2 Jul 1980 *Panama City* Panama ....0 Guatemala 2
30 Jul 1980 *Panama City* Panama ....0 Honduras 2
10 Aug 1980 *Panama City* Panama ....1 Costa Rica 1
24 Aug 1980 *Panama City* Panama ....1 El Salvador.......3
1 Oct 1980 *San José*   Costa Rica ....2 Honduras 3
5 Oct 1980 *San Salvador* El Salvador.......4 Panama 1
12 Oct 1980 *Guatemala*   Guatemala ....0 Costa Rica 0
26 Oct 1980 *Tegucigalpa* Honduras ....0 Guatemala 0
26 Oct 1980 *San Salvador* El Salvador.......2 Costa Rica 0
             Costa Rica forfeited match, awarded 2-0 to El Salvador
5 Nov 1980 *San José*   Costa Rica ....2 Panama 0
9 Nov 1980 *Guatemala*   Guatemala ....0 El Salvador.......0
16 Nov 1980 *Guatemala*   Guatemala ....5 Panama 0
16 Nov 1980 *Tegucigalpa* Honduras ....1 Costa Rica 0
23 Nov 1980 *San Salvador* El Salvador.......2 Honduras 1
26 Nov 1980 *San José*   Costa Rica ....0 Guatemala 3
30 Nov 1980 *Tegucigalpa* Honduras ....2 El Salvador.......0
7 Dec 1980 *Guatemala*   Guatemala ....0 Honduras 1
10 Dec 1980 *San José*   Costa Rica ....0 El Salvador.......0
14 Dec 1980 *Tegucigalpa* Honduras ....5 Panama 0
21 Dec 1980 *San Salvador* El Salvador.......1 Guatemala 0

Final Table

	P	W	D	L	F	A	Pts	
Honduras	8	5	2	1	15	5	12	**Honduras and El**
El Salvador	8	5	2	1	12	5	12	**Salvador qualified**
Guatemala	8	3	3	2	10	2	9	**for Group Final**
Costa Rica	8	1	4	3	6	10	6	
Panama	8	0	1	7	3	24	1	

Caribbean Zone – Preliminary Round

30 Mar 1980 *Georgetown* Guyana ....5 Grenada 2
13 Apr 1980 *St George's* Grenada ....2 Guyana 3
Guyana qualified for Group A

Caribbean Zone – Group A

17 Aug 1980 *Havana*   Cuba ....3 Surinam 0
7 Sep 1980 *Paramaribo* Surinam ....0 Cuba 0
28 Sep 1980 *Georgetown* Guyana ....0 Surinam 1
12 Oct 1980 *Paramaribo* Surinam ....4 Guyana 0
9 Nov 1980 *Havana*   Cuba ....1 Guyana 0
30 Nov 1980 *Linden*   Guyana ....0 Cuba 3

Final Table

	P	W	D	L	F	A	Pts	
Cuba	4	3	1	0	7	0	7	**Cuba qualified for**
Surinam	4	2	1	1	5	3	5	**Group Final**
Guyana	4	0	0	4	0	9	0	

Caribbean Zone – Group A

1 Aug 1980 *Port au Prince* Haiti ....2 Trinidad & Tobago 0
17 Aug 1980 *San Fernando*   Trinidad & Tobago 1 Haiti 0
12 Sep 1980 *Port au Prince* Haiti ....1 Nethlds Antilles 0
9 Nov 1980 *Port of Spain*   Trinidad & Tobago 0 Nethlds Antilles 0
29 Nov 1980 *Curaçao*   Nethlds Antilles 0 Trinidad & Tobago 0
12 Dec 1980 *Curaçao*   Nethlds Antilles 1 Haiti 1

Final Table

	P	W	D	L	F	A	Pts	
Haiti	4	2	1	1	4	2	5	**Haiti qualified for**
Trinidad & Togago	4	1	2	1	1	2	4	**Group Final**
Nethlds Antilles	4	0	3	1	1	2	3	

Group Final

1 Nov 1981 *Tegucigalpa* Mexico............4 Cuba 0
2 Nov 1981 *Tegucigalpa* Canada ....1 El Salvador.......0
3 Nov 1981 *Tegucigalpa* Honduras ....4 Haiti 0
6 Nov 1981 *Tegucigalpa* Haiti ....1 Canada 1
6 Nov 1981 *Tegucigalpa* Mexico.............0 El Salvador.......1
8 Nov 1981 *Tegucigalpa* Honduras ....2 Cuba 0
11 Nov 1981 *Tegucigalpa* El Salvador.......0 Cuba 0
11 Nov 1981 *Tegucigalpa* Mexico.............1 Haiti 1
12 Nov 1981 *Tegucigalpa* Honduras ....2 Canada 1
15 Nov 1981 *Tegucigalpa* Haiti ....0 Cuba 2
15 Nov 1981 *Tegucigalpa* Mexico.............1 Canada 1
16 Nov 1981 *Tegucigalpa* Honduras ....0 El Salvador.......0
19 Nov 1981 *Tegucigalpa* Haiti ....0 El Salvador.......1
21 Nov 1981 *Tegucigalpa* Cuba ....2 Canada 2
22 Nov 1981 *Tegucigalpa* Honduras ....0 Mexico.............0

Final Table

	P	W	D	L	F	A	Pts	
Honduras	5	3	2	0	8	1	8	
El Salvador	5	2	2	1	2	1	6	
Mexico	5	1	3	1	6	3	5	
Canada	5	1	3	1	6	6	5	**Honduras and El**
Cuba	5	1	2	2	4	8	4	**Salvador qualified**
Haiti	5	0	2	3	2	9	2	

ASIA/OCEANIA

Group One

25 Apr 1981 *Auckland*   New Zealand .....3 Australia 3
3 May 1981 *Suva*   Fiji ....0 New Zealand 4
7 May 1981 *Taipei*   Taiwan ....0 New Zealand 2
11 May 1981 *Jakarta*   Indonesia.........0 New Zealand 2
16 May 1981 *Sydney*   Australia ....0 New Zealand 2
20 May 1981 *Melbourne* Australia ....2 Indonesia.........0
23 May 1981 *Auckland*   New Zealand .....5 Indonesia.........0
30 May 1981 *Auckland*   New Zealand .....2 Taiwan 0
31 May 1981 *Suva*   Fiji ....0 Indonesia.........0
6 Jun 1981 *Suva*   Fiji ....2 Taiwan 1
10 Jun 1981 *Adelaide*   Australia ....3 New Zealand 2
15 Jun 1981 *Jakarta*   Indonesia.........1 Taiwan 0
28 Jun 1981 *Taipei*   Taiwan ....2 Indonesia.........0
26 Jul 1981 *Suva*   Fiji ....1 Australia 4
4 Aug 1981 *Taipei*   Taiwan ....0 Fiji 0
10 Aug 1981 *Jakarta*   Indonesia.........3 Fiji 3

14 Aug 1981 *Melbourne* Australia ....10 Fiji 0
16 Aug 1981 *Auckland* New Zealand ...13 Fiji 0
30 Aug 1981 *Jakarta* Indonesia........1 Australia 0
 6 Sep 1981 *Taipei* Taiwan ....0 Australia 0

Final Table

	P	W	D	L	F	A	Pts	
New Zealand	8	6	2	0	31	3	14	**New Zealand**
Australia	8	4	2	2	22	9	10	**qualified for Group**
Indonesia	8	2	2	4	5	14	6	**Final**
Taiwan	8	1	3	4	5	8	5	
Fiji	8	1	3	4	6	35	5	

Group Two

18 Mar 1981 *Riyadh* Qatar ....0 Iraq 1
19 Mar 1981 *Riyadh* Syria ....0 Bahrain..........1
21 Mar 1981 *Riyadh* Iraq ....0 Saudi Arabia.....1
22 Mar 1981 *Riyadh* Qatar ....3 Bahrain..........0
24 Mar 1981 *Riyadh* Syria ....0 Saudi Arabia.....2
25 Mar 1981 *Riyadh* Iraq ....2 Bahrain..........0
27 Mar 1981 *Rihadh* Qatar ....2 Syria 1
28 Mar 1981 *Riyadh* Bahrain..........0 Saudi Arabia.....1
30 Mar 1981 *Riyadh* Iraq ....2 Syria 1
31 Mar 1981 *Riyadh* Qatar ....0 Saudi Arabia.....1

Final Table

	P	W	D	L	F	A	Pts	
Saudi Arabia	4	4	0	0	5	0	8	**Saudi Arabia**
Iraq	4	3	0	1	5	2	6	**qualified for Group**
Qatar	4	2	0	2	5	3	4	**Final**
Bahrain	4	1	0	3	1	6	2	
Syria	4	0	0	4	2	7	0	

Group Three

21 Apr 1981 *Kuwait City* Malaysia..........1 South Korea 2
22 Apr 1981 *Kuwait City* Kuwait............6 Thailand 0
24 Apr 1981 *Kuwait City* South Korea .....5 Thailand 1
25 Apr 1981 *Kuwait City* Kuwait............4 Malaysia..........0
27 Apr 1981 *Kuwait City* Malaysia..........2 Thailand 2
29 Apr 1981 *Kuwait City* Kuwait............2 South Korea 0

Final Table

	P	W	D	L	F	A	Pts	
Kuwait	3	3	0	0	12	0	6	
South Korea	3	2	0	1	7	4	4	**Kuwait qualified**
Malasia	3	0	1	2	3	8	1	**for Group Final**
Thailand	3	0	1	2	3	13	1	

Group Four – Preliminary Round

21 Dec 1980 *Hong Kong* Hong Kong ......0 China.............1
22 Dec 1980 *Hong Kong* North Korea .....3 Macao 0
22 Dec 1980 *Hong Kong* Singapore ....0 Japan 1
China and Japan qualified for Sub-Group A, North Korea qualified for Sub-Group B.

Group Four – Sub-Group A

24 Dec 1980 *Hong Kong* China.............3 Macao 0
26 Dec 1980 *Hong Kong* China.............1 Japan 0
28 Dec 1980 *Hong Kong* Japan ....3 Macao 0

Final Table

	P	W	D	L	F	A	Pts	
China	2	2	0	0	4	0	4	**China qualified for**
Japan	2	1	0	1	3	1	2	**Sub-Group semi-**
Macao	2	0	0	2	0	6	0	**finals**

Group Four – Sub-Group B

24 Dec 1980 *Hong Kong* Hong Kong ......1 Singapore 1
26 Dec 1980 *Hong Kong* Singapore ....0 North Korea 1
28 Dec 1980 *Hong Kong* Hong Kong ......2 North Korea 2

Final Table

	P	W	D	L	F	A	Pts	
North Korea	2	1	1	0	3	2	3	**North Korea and**
Hong Kong	2	0	2	0	3	3	2	**Hong Kong**
Singapore	2	0	1	1	1	2	1	**qualified for Sub-Group semi-finals**

The two nations to qualify from the complicated Asia/Oceania group were New Zealand (*top picture*) and Kuwait (*bottom*). The Kuwaitis finished top of the final table but the Kiwis finished level on points with China and had to overcome them in a play-off game in Singapore before booking their passage to Spain.

Sub-Group semi-finals

30 Dec 1980 *Hong Kong* North Korea .....1 Japan 0
31 Dec 1980 *Hong Kong* China.............0 Hong Kong 0
China won 5-4 on penalties

Sub-Group Final

 4 Jan 1981 *Hong Kong* China.............4 North Korea 2
China qualified for Group Final

Group Final

24 Sep 1981 *Peking* China.............0 New Zealand.....0
 3 Oct 1981 *Auckland* New Zealand.....1 China.............0
10 Oct 1981 *Auckland* New Zealand.....1 Kuwait............2
18 Oct 1981 *Peking* China.............3 Kuwait............0
 4 Nov 1981 *Riyadh* Saudi Arabia.....0 Kuwait............1
12 Nov 1981 *Kuala Lumpur* Saudi Arabia.....2 China.............4
19 Nov 1981 *Kuala Lumpur* China.............2 Saudi Arabia.....0
28 Nov 1981 *Auckland* New Zealand.....2 Saudi Arabia.....2
30 Nov 1981 *Kuwait City* Kuwait............1 China.............0
 7 Dec 1981 *Kuwait City* Kuwait............2 Saudi Arabia.....0
14 Dec 1981 *Kuwait City* Kuwait............2 New Zealand.....2
19 Dec 1981 *Riyadh* Saudi Arabia.....0 New Zealand.....5

Final Table

	P	W	D	L	F	A	Pts
Kuwait	6	4	1	1	8	6	9
New Zealand	6	2	3	1	11	6	7
China	6	3	1	2	9	4	7
Saudi Arabia	6	0	1	5	4	16	1

Play-off for second qualifying place

10 Jan 1982 *Singapore* New Zealand.....2 China.............1
Kuwait and New Zealand qualified

1982 Tournament

Group One

Antonio Cabrini of Italy.

ITALY 0   POLAND 0 (Half-time 0-0)

Balaidos Stadium, Vigo, 14 June
Attendance: 33,000

ITALY kicked off their tenth World Cup campaign in the knowledge that they had won their last four opening matches. But they were not to record their fifth successive win after coming up against a resilient and well-organized Polish defence.

Italy had the reliable Dino Zoff in goal for his 100th international, and back in the team was Paolo Rossi after his two-year suspension following a bribes scandal. But Rossi was off form and the opening game proved to be a worrying time for the Italian boss, Enzo Bearzot.

Both teams were equally matched with neither wanting to take chances. Poland began to take charge in the second half with Boniek, who played for Italian club Juventus, outstanding. But the best scoring chance fell to Italy ten minutes from time, when Tardelli followed up a clearance off the line, only to see his shot strike the bar.

Italy: Zoff; Gentile, Collovati, Scirea, Cabrini, Antognoni, Marini, Tardelli, Conti, Graziani, Rossi.
Poland: Mlynarczyk; Janas, Jalocha, Matysik, Zmuda, Majewski, Smolarek, Buncol, Lato, Iwan(Kusto), Boniek.
Referee: Michel Vautrot (France)

Guillermo La Rosa of Peru made three appearances, two as a substitute, and scored one goal as the Peruvians finished bottom of Group One.

CAMEROON 0   PERU 0 (Half-time 0-0)

Riazor Stadium, La Coruña, 15 June
Attendance: 11,000

DESPITE the goalless scoreline this was a lively game, thanks largely to the Africans who played well against a less well-organized Peruvian team, who struggled to contain the Cameroon midfielders.

Both sides had chances to open the scoring in the first half. First, a Roger Milla goal was ruled offside for Cameroon and then, just before the interval, Julio César Uríbe's shot went narrowly wide.

For Cameroon's manager Jean Vincent, one of the stars of the 1958 French World Cup team, it was a satisfactory baptisim for his team. For Peru's 71-year-old Brazilian-born manager, 'Tim', it was probably a disappointing start, although he was grateful for the draw at the end of 90 minutes.

Peru: Quiroga; Duarte, Díaz, Salguero, Olaechea, Leguía(Barbadillo), Cueto, Velásquez, Oblítas, Cubillas(La Rosa), Uríbe.
Cameroon: N'Kono; Kaham, Kunde, Onana, N'djeya, M'Bom, Abega, M'Bida, Aoudou, N'guea (Bahoken), Milla(Tokoto).
Referee: Franz Wohrer (Austria)

Poland's Grzegorz Lato. At 32, he made seven appearances in what was his third World Cup tournament.

ITALY 1   PERU 1 (Half-time 1-0)

Balaidos Stadium, Vigo, 18 June
Attendance: 25,000

AFTER struggling in their opening game, Italy again gave their fans a worrying time as they failed to beat Peru, who were unlucky to be denied a penalty by referee Eschweiler.

Conti scored the first goal of the group after 189 goalless minutes when he shot Italy into the lead in the 19th minute following a well-worked move down the left by Cabrini and Antognoni. Peru were then unlucky not to have been awarded that penalty after Gentile tripped Oblítas, clearly in the area.

Rossi was substituted at half-time by Causio and as he left the field at the interval it was impossible to imagine that he would have such an impact on the tournament in its later stages.

Peru were the stronger team in the second half and they were rewarded six minutes from time, when a Díaz shot was turned into the Italian goal by defender Collovati.

Italy: Zoff; Gentile, Collovati, Scirea, Cabrini, Antognoni, Marini, Tardelli, Conti, Graziani, Rossi(Causio).
Scorer: Conti
Peru: Quiroga; Duarte, Díaz, Salguero, Olaechea, Cubillas, Cueto, Velásquez, Barbadillo(La Rosa), Uríbe(Leguía), Oblítas.
Scorer: Díaz
Referee: Walter Eschweiler (West Germany)

CAMEROON 0　POLAND 0 (Half-time 0-0)

Riazor Stadium, La Coruña, 19 June
Attendance: 19,000

CAMEROON once again showed what a well-disciplined and organized team they were as their defence held out against the Polish attack in the first half. But in the second period the Africans ventured forward and their midfielders created many chances which were squandered by their forwards.

Poland did most of the attacking with Boniek and Lato both going close. The goalkeeping of Thomas N'Kono, who had an outstanding game, kept the scoreline goalless at the interval.

The Cameroon counter-attacks certainly exposed the Polish defence at times and had their forwards been on target they may have snatched a winner. Roger Milla was particularly effective and made some piercing runs.

Despite a storming finish, which could have produced a goal, the game ended as the third goalless draw in this group.

Cameroon: N'Kono; Kaham, Onana, N'djeya, M'Bom, Aoudou, Abega, Kunde, M'Bida, Milla, N'guea(Tokoto).
Poland: Mlynarczyk; Majewski, Janas, Zmuda, Jalocha, Matysik, Lato, Boniek, Buncol (Szarmach), Palasz(Kusto), Smolarek.
Referee: Alexis Ponnet (Belgium)

POLAND 5　PERU 1 (Half-time 0-0)

Riazor Stadium, La Coruña, 22 June
Attendance: 25,000

AT last, Group One came alive as the goal famine came to a spectacular end. But it was nearly an hour before the fans at La Coruña saw their first goal of the tournament.

Despite the Polish avalanche of goals, it was Peru who were the more lively of the sides in the first ten minutes and only two good saves from Mlynarczyk prevented the South Americans taking the lead. But thereafter, Poland took charge and a Boniek 'goal' was ruled out in the 16th minute. He also saw one of his shots hit the bar, whilst a Buncol effort hit the post.

After a blank first half, Peru made two tactical substitutions by taking off Cubillas and Oblítas in an effort to tighten up their defence. But the move backfired because Poland took the lead after 55 minutes when Smolarek scored after a Peruvian pass went astray in midfield. Three minutes later, Boniek created a chance for Lato to score his tenth World Cup goal stretching over three tournaments. And in the 61st minute, Boniek was rewarded with a goal after Buncol created the opening.

Poland went further ahead with their fourth goal in 13 minutes when Buncol scored. Substitute Ciolek netted in the 76th minute after being on the pitch only three minutes; and seven minutes from time La Rosa got a consolation goal for Peru, who kept running right to the end.

Poland: Mlynarczyk; Majewski, Janas, Zmuda, Jalocha(Dziuba), Buncol, Boniek, Matysik, Kupcewicz, Lato, Smolarek(Ciolek).
Scorers: Smolarek, Lato, Boniek, Buncol, Ciolek
Peru: Quiroga; Duarte, Díaz, Salguero, Olaechea, Cubillas(Uríbe), Velásquez, Cueto, Leguía, La Rosa, Oblítas(Barbadillo).
Scorer: La Rosa
Referee: Mario Rubio Vazquez (Mexico)

CAMEROON 1　ITALY 1 (Half-time 0-0)

Balaidos Stadium, Vigo, 23 June
Attendance: 20,000

CAMEROON had to win to stay in the tournament, whereas a draw was good enough for the Italians. Both teams were level on two points, but Italy's one goal to Cameroon's none was proving decisive in a low-scoring group.

Italy appeared very nervous but still had the better of the first half and paid dearly for not capitalizing on their many chances. Graziani worked hard and made several openings but Italy squandered some easy chances, notably Conti's 11th-minute effort when he missed the target with an open goal at his mercy.

N'Kono, in the Cameroon goal, had another outstanding game and was unlucky when he conceded Italy's goal on the hour. He stumbled and was unable to get to Graziani's header.

However, a minute later, M'Bida levelled the score with a goal that had a suspicion of offside about it. The celebrations that greeted the Cameroon goal was reminiscent of a side which had just won the World Cup. Surprisingly, though, Cameroon went on the defensive when they needed another goal to stay in the tournament. Perhaps their World Cup climax was in holding Italy to a draw.

The Italians held on for the point and went through to the next phase, even though they did not win any of their three group matches. The Africans, on the other hand, were out of the tournament, despite being undefeated. But what a lot of friends they made in Spain as they became one of the charismatic teams of the 1982 World Cup, both on and off the field.

Group One – Final Table

	P	W	D	L	F	A	Pts
Poland	3	1	2	0	5	1	4
Italy	3	0	3	0	2	2	3
Cameroon	3	0	3	0	1	1	3
Peru	3	0	2	1	2	6	2

Cameroon midfield player Théophile Abega, a key member of the side that finished third in Group One after a creditable performance against the Italians.

Julio César Uribe, ever-present for Peru.

As for Italy, they looked anything but champions after another poor performance.

Italy: Zoff; Gentile, Collovati, Scirea, Cabrini, Tardelli, Conti, Antognoni, Graziani, Rossi, Oriali.
Scorer: Graziani
Cameroon: N'Kono; Kaham, Onana, N'djeya, M'Bom, Aoudou, Kunde, Abega, M'Bida, Milla, Tokoto.
Scorer: M'Bida
Referee: Bogdan Dotchev (Bulgaria)

Group Two

ALGERIA 2   WEST GERMANY 1 (Half-time 0-0)

El Molinón Stadium, Gijón, 16 June
Attendance: 42,000

WEST Germany, under new manager Jupp Derwall, had won the 1980 European Championship and were showing signs of re-emerging as one of the leading soccer nations. But their opening game at Gijón saw them brought down to earth with one almightly bump as Algeria brought off a World Cup shock to rival the United States' win over England in 1950 and North Korea's victory over Italy in 1966.

Before the match, West Germany were the 3/1 second favourites to win the World Cup; Algeria were 1,000/1. But those odds were made to look a nonsense as Algeria, masterminded by the African Footballer of the Year, Lakhdar Belloumi, gained a memorable win.

Despite dominating the game for most of the 90 minutes, the German forwards let their side down and they were obviously suffering far more from the heat than their opponents.

Madjer gave the Africans the lead in the 54th minute when he followed up Belloumi's shot which rebounded off Schumacher. And then Karl-Heinz Rummenigge, who was having a surprisingly quiet game, made his contribution in the 68th minute when he scored after taking a pass from Magath.

The Germans were really suffering from the effects of the heat by now, but nevertheless thought that their goal would quell the fire in the Algerians. Yet any thoughts they had of being able to ease off were dispelled a minute later when Assad started the move which led to a second Algerian goal, by Belloumi. It gave the Africans their second successive win over West Germany. The previous one had been in a friendly in 1964.

After the match Derwall said: "I still can't believe it. It's beyond my understanding." But, if it was any consolation for the German team boss, on each occasion that West Germany had won the World Cup, they had lost in a group match. . .

Algeria: Cerbah, Merzekane, Kourichi, Guendouz, Dahleb, Mansouri, Fergani, Belloumi, Madjer(Larbes), Zidane(Bensaoula), Assad.
Scorers: Madjer, Belloumi
West Germany: Schumacher; Kaltz, K-H.Förster, Stielike, Briegel, Dremmler, Breitner, Magath (Fischer), Littbarski, Hrubesch, Rummenigge.
Scorer: Rummenigge
Referee: Ravoredo Enrique Labo (Peru)

Lakhdar Belloumi, grabbed the winner for Algeria - 1,000/1 outsiders - to give them a sensational start to the 1982 World Cup finals.

Algeria's flying winger, Djamel Zidane.

Belloumi acknowledges the crowd in the El Molinón Stadium after his memorable goal. It was the second time that Algeria had beaten West Germany.

AUSTRIA 1   CHILE 0 (Half-time 1-0)

Carlos Tartiere Stadium, Oviedo, 17 June
Attendance: 22,500

AUSTRIA came into their first match having wound up their preparations with a 17-1 win over Candas, a local village team based near Gijón. But now it was the real thing.

And they were far too good for the Chileans who, despite having some good individual players, were not as well-organized as their European opponents.

Austrian midfielder Prohaska had an outstanding game and it was little surprise when his side took the lead in the 21st minute after Schachner headed home a Krauss centre. Four minutes later, Krauss brought down Carlos Caszely in the penalty area. The same player took the spot-kick, which was wide of its target. It proved to be a costly miss as Austria ran out winners by that solitary first-half goal.

Austria: Koncilia; Krauss, Obermayer, Pezzey, Degeorgi(Baumeister), Hattenberger, Prohaska, Hintermaier, Schachner, Krankl, Weber(Jurtin).
Scorer: Schachner
Chile: Osbén; Garrído, Valenzuela, Figueroa, Bigorra, Dubó, Yáñez, Neira(Rojas), Bonvallet, Caszely, Moscoso(Gamboa).
Referee: Juan Daniel Cardellino (Uruguay).

Uli Stielike, a tough competitor for the West Germans but he could not prevent humiliation at the hands of the Algerians.

WEST GERMANY 4   CHILE 1 (Half-time 1-0)

El Molinón Stadium, Gijón, 20 June
Attendance: 42,000

WEST German skipper Karl-Heinz Rummenigge passed a fitness test only an hour before the kick-off and he went on to have an outstanding game as he played his part in restoring German pride after the humiliation of their defeat by Algeria.

West Germany were well in control and Rummenigge scored after only nine minutes to underline the Germans' determination that there should be no repeat result from the Algeria match. The opening goal had a shade of luck about it when the German skipper's shot from 22 yards slipped under Osbén's body.

Germany seemed content to hold on to their lead and allowed Chile to come back at them for the remainder of the first half. But in the second they opened up and ran out easy winners.

Rummenigge scored his second goal after 56 minutes, when he rose to head powerfully into the goal off the post and again via the 'keeper's body. Ten minutes later the German captain completed his hat-trick after working a good one-two with Felix Magath.

Nine minutes from time, West Germany helped improve their goal-difference when Reinders scored less than two minutes after coming on for Littbarski.

Chile got a consolation goal right on time when Moscoso scored a magnificent solo goal after wrong-footing Manny Kaltz before releasing a fierce shot.

West Germany: Schumacher; Kaltz, K-H.Förster, Stielike, Briegel, Dremmler, Breitner (Matthäus), Magath, Littbarski(Reinders), Hrubesch, Rummenigge.
Scorers: Rummenigge 3, Reinders
Chile: Osbén; Garrído, Valenzuela, Figueroa, Bigorra, Dubó, Bonvallet, Soto(Letelier), Gamboa(Neira), Yáñez, Moscoso.
Scorer: Moscoso
Referee: Bruno Galler (Switzerland)

AUSTRIA 2   ALGERIA 0 (Half-time 0-0)

Carlos Tartiere Stadium, Oviedo, 21 June
Attendance: 22,000

THE Algerian dream survived for another 56 minutes at Oviedo before Walter Schachner scored his second goal of the tournament to put the Austrians in front. The Africans could not respond and eventually fell to a second goal.

Yet Austria looked unsettled for long periods and seemed likely candidates to be on the end of another Algerian surprise as the Africans took the initiative from the start. It was only a solid Austrian defence and two good saves from Koncilia which prevented an Algerian goal in the first 45 minutes. Austria were perhaps a little unlucky not to be awarded a penalty when Krankl was tripped.

Austria changed their tactics in the second half and, after employing three front runners, they looked more dangerous. Schachner scored the first in the 56th minute, after a Welzl shot rebounded off the Algerian defence. Eleven minutes later Hans Krankl drove a left-foot shot into the net to make it 2-0 and that was to prove the end of Algeria's ambitions, although they still had a chance of qualifying for the next phase.

Austria: Koncilia; Krauss, Obermayer, Pezzey, Degeorgi, Hattenberger, Prohaska(Weber), Hintermaier, Schachner, Krankl, Baumeister(Welzl).
Scorers: Schachner, Krankl
Algeria: Cerbah; Merzekane, Guendouz, Kourichi, Mansouri, Fergani, Dahleb(Tlemcani), Belloumi(Bensaoula), Madjer, Assad, Zidane.
Referee: Tony Bosković (Australia)

West Germany's Paul Breitner, a member of the team defeated by Algeria.

Group Two - Final Table

	P	W	D	L	F	A	Pts
W.Germany	3	2	0	1	6	3	4
Austria	3	2	0	1	3	1	4
Algeria	3	2	0	1	5	5	4
Chile	3	0	0	3	3	8	0

Karl-Heinz Förster, another player with whom West German manager Jupp Derwall kept faith after the shock of the opening game.

Mario Kempes of Argentina. His side lost the curtain-raiser to Belgium.

ALGERIA 3   CHILE 2 (Half-time 3-0)

Carlos Tartiere Stadium, Oviedo, 24 June
Attendance: 16,000

ALGERIA did it again. And it was their attacking first-half flair which produced a second win, a victory which was this time anything but a fluke.

Algeria scored three first-half goals but the way Chile played, they could have had a lot more. The Chileans lacked organization and the Algerian forwards were rampant, despite missing the skills of Belloumi.

After a fine move from Bensaoula in the eighth minute, Assad found the net for Algeria's first goal. It was Assad who scored the second after half an hour, when his shot was turned into the net by defender Figueroa. Four minutes later, Bensaoula made it 3-0 with a powerful shot from just outside the area.

Having run for every ball in the first half, the Algerians paid the penalty in the second period and soon tired. This gave Chile the opportunity to get back into the game and after an hour, Neira scored from the penalty-spot after Guendouz brought down Yáñez. Sixteen minutes from time, Letelier beat three defenders and then rounded the 'keeper to make it 3-2 and suddenly Chile were back in the game. But the Algerians then tightened up their defence and held on for another win. Alas, despite two wins, four points and one of the shock results of all time, they were eliminated because of a contrived result between West Germany and Austria in the final match.

Algeria: Cerbah; Larbes, Merzekane, Kourichi, Guendouz, Fergani, Bourrebou(Yahi), Bensaoula, Mansouri(Dahleb), Assad, Madjer.
Scorers: Assad 2, Bensaoula
Chile: Osbén; Gallindo, Figueroa, Valenzuela, Bigorra, Dubó, Neira, Yáñez, Bonvallet(Soto), Caszely(Letelier), Moscoso.
Scorers: Neira (pen), Letelier
Referee: Romulo Mendez (Guatemala)

WEST GERMANY 1   AUSTRIA 0 (Half-time 1-0)

El Molinón Stadium, Gijón, 25 June
Attendance: 41,000

THIS was one of the most distasteful matches in World Cup history. No, it was not a dirty game — there was not enough physical contact for that — but the teams heaped disgrace upon the competition by the way they contrived the result after the Germans had scored the first goal.

Because of the format of the tournament, a 1-0 win to West Germany meant that both these European neighbours would proceed to the next phase at the expense of Algeria. How sad it was that the game of soccer should be reduced to this sort of farce.

For the first ten minutes, West Germany played good attacking football in search of the goal they needed to guarantee them victory. But after Hrubesch headed home a Littbarski cross, the game lost any meaning. The Algerian supporters amongst the crowd constantly shouted, booed and heckled both sides, claiming that the result had been fixed. They tried to get on to the pitch to halt proceedings — and one German supporter was so disgusted that he set fire to his national flag on the terraces.

The following day, Algeria protested to FIFA that the game was fixed and called for both teams to be disqualified on the grounds that they had violated the principles of sportsmanship. Unfortunately, their protest was rejected.

West Germany: Schumacher; Kaltz, K-H.Förster, Stielike, Briegel, Dremmler, Breitner, Magath, Littbarski, Hrubesch(Fischer), Rummenigge(Matthäus).
Scorer: Hrubesch
Austria: Koncilia; Krauss, Obermayer, Pezzey, Degeorgi, Hattenberger, Prohaska, Hintermaier, Schachner, Krankl, Weber.
Referee: Bob Valentine (Scotland)

Group Three

BELGIUM 1   ARGENTINA 0 (Half-time 0-0)

Nou Camp Stadium, Barcelona, 13 June
Attendance: 95,000

THE opening game of the 1982 World Cup produced something which the previous four openers had failed to provide — a goal. It may have been only one goal, but it ended the spate of goalless draws in World Cup curtain-raisers.

Belgium were returning to the World Cup fold for the first time since 1970, whilst Argentina had very much the same side which lifted the trophy on home soil four years earlier. Manager Menotti was to eventually pay the price of not changing his squad, just as Sir Alf Ramsey had done with the England team after their 1966 triumph.

There was one very noticeable newcomer in the Argentina team. He was the man hailed

as the new superstar of world soccer, Diego Maradona, and he made his World Cup debut on his new home ground after his £4 million move to Barcelona.

Argentina gave a brilliant display for the first ten minutes but were surprised by Belgium's cynical and defensive tactics and Maradona was chopped down and crowded out by the Europeans, who at times had 11 men back in defence

Ardíles kept pushing forward for Argentina but to no avail and the 1978 top scorer, Mario Kempes, had little success up front. Just after the hour mark, and with the game seemingly heading towards another goalless scoreline, Vandenbergh collected a cross from Vercauteren and struck a left-foot shot from just outside the penalty area. Argentina were the first defending champions to lose their opening game since Italy in 1950.

Belgium: Pfaff; Gerets, L.Millecamps, Baecke, De Schrijver, Coeck, Vercauteren, Vandersmissen, Vandenbergh, Czerniatynski, Ceulemans.
Scorer: Vandenbergh
Argentina: Fillol; Olguín, Galvan, Passarella, Tarantini, Ardíles, Maradona, Gallego, Bertoni, Díaz(Valdano), Kempes.
Referee: Vojtech Christov (Czechoslovakia)

HUNGARY 10   EL SALVADOR 1 (Half-time 3-0)

Nuevo Estadio, Elche, 15 June
Attendance: 23,000

FOR those critics who campaigned for more European and/or South American teams at the expense of the lesser-known nations, this game added fuel to their argument. El Salvador should not have been on the same pitch as Hungary and were the only one of the minnows to let their 'side' down.

Hungary took the lead as early as the third minute when Nyilasi was allowed a free header at goal. And that was to be the pattern of the game — Hungary scoring whenever they wanted.

Pölöskei had the second goal on the score-board after ten minutes and Fazekas scored the only other first-half goal after 23 minutes.

Toth and Fazekas added two more before Ramírez Zapata scored for the Central Americans in the 64th minute. Laszlo Kiss, who came on as a substitute for Torocsik in the 55th minute, found the net for goal number-six with 20 minutes to go. Seven minutes later he had completed his hat-trick (the only one by a substitute in the final stages of the World Cup) and, with a goal from Szentes in between, made it 9-1. Nyilasi, who had an outstanding game, took the score into double figures for the biggest win in the final stages of the World Cup. And Hungarian boss, Kalman Meszöly, was still angry with his players for conceding a goal!

Daniel Bertoni slams a free-kick towards the Belgian goal as goalkeeper Jean-Marie Pfaff takes off.

Daniel Passarella of Argentina.

El Salvador (*pictured right*) had a unique baptism in the 1982 World Cup finals, going down 10-1 against Hungary. Thereafter, however, they proved more difficult to beat, conceding only three more goals in two games.

Hungary: Mészáros; Balint, Martos, Garaba, Toth, Müller(Szentes), Nyilasi, Sallai, Fazekas, Torocsik(L.Kiss), Pölöskei.
Scorers: Kiss 3, Nyilasi 2, Fazekas 2, Toth, Pölöskei, Szentes
El Salvador: Guevara Mora; Castillo, Cruz Jovel, Rodríguez, Recinos, Huezo, Rugamas (Ramírez Zapata), Ventura, Rivas, Hernández, González.
Scorer: Ramírez Zapata
Referee: Ebrahim Al Doy (Bahrain)

ARGENTINA 4   HUNGARY 1 (Half-time 2-0)

José Rico Perez Stadium, Alicante, 18 June
Attendance: 32,093

HUNGARY certainly had to cope with a lot more pressure than in their opening game and it was fortunate for them that goalkeeper Mészáros had an outstanding game, otherwise they could have been on the receiving end of a real hammering.

Diego Maradona was at last given the chance to show why he was being tagged 'the world's greatest footballer', although he was finding it hard to live with this label at times. Nevertheless, he gave a dazzling display and contributed two great goals to a decisive win.

Argentina applied pressure from the first whistle but did not score until the 26th minute, when Maradona headed down a Passarella free-kick for Bertoni to steer home. Two minutes later, Maradona scored his first World Cup goal when he pounced on a rebound after Bertoni's shot was only half saved by Mészáros.

After further pressure, Argentina scored their third goal ten minutes into the second half when a great Maradona drive beat the 'keeper. Ardíles made it 4-0 on the hour and 14 minutes from time, Pölöskei scored a consolation goal for the Magyars.

After their poor opening performance, this was more like the Argentina of 1978 and suddenly their fans began to believe in their team's ability to retain the trophy.

Argentina: Fillol; Olguín, Galvan, Passarella, Tarantini(Barbas), Gallego, Ardíles, Maradona, Valdano(Calderón), Bertoni, Kempes.
Scorers: Maradona 2, Bertoni, Ardíles
Hungary: Mészáros; Martos(Fazekas), Balint, Toth, Varga, Garaba, Nyilasi, Sallai, Rab, L.Kiss (Szentes), Pölöskei.
Scorer: Pölöskei
Referee: Belaid Lacarne (Algeria)

BELGIUM 1   EL SALVADOR 0 (Half-time 1-0)

Nuevo Estadio, Elche, 19 June
Attendance: 15,000

EL SALVADOR put their ten-goal nightmare behind them and tightened up their defence to frustrate the Belgians, who were expecting an easy game. Instead, they were constantly faced by an El Salvador penalty area packed tight with defenders.

The Central Americans' goalkeeper, Guevara Mora, had a great game and made some excellent saves. At the other end, Belgium's goalkeeper, Jean-Marie Pfaff of Bayern Munich, had little to do but he was fortunate to be playing in this match at all because he was saved from possibly drowning after an accident in the team's hotel swimming-pool shortly before the match.

The only goal of the game was scored by Coeck, from a free-kick after 25 minutes, and the small crowd were expecting a barrage of goals thereafter. They were disappointed.

Argentina's Diego Maradona, scored twice in the 4-1 defeat of Hungary.

Belgium: Pfaff; Gerets, L.Millecamps, Meeuws, Baecke, Vandersmissen(Van der Elst), Coeck, Vercauteren, Czerniatynski, Ceulemans(Van Moer), Vandenbergh.
Scorer: Coeck
El Salvador: Guevara Mora; Osorto(Díaz Arevalo), Cruz Jovel, Rodríguez, Recinos, Fagoaga, Ventura, Huezo, Ramírez Zapata, González, Rivas.
Referee: Malcolm Moffat (Ireland)

Group Three – Final Table

	P	W	D	L	F	A	Pts
Belgium	3	2	1	0	3	1	5
Argentina	3	2	0	1	6	2	4
Hungary	3	1	1	1	12	6	3
El Salvador	3	0	0	3	1	13	0

BELGIUM 1   HUNGARY 1 (Half-time 0-1)
Nuevo Estadio, Elche, 22 June
Attendance: 37,000

DESPITE a 10-1 win to their credit, Hungary still needed to win their final game to ensure their place in the next round. But wasted chances cost them dearly and they came away with one point.

Hungary scored first after 28 minutes, when Varga netted, and they looked like holding on to the slender lead which would have taken them through. Fourteen minutes from time, however, Czerniatynski saved the day for Belgium and made sure they gained the point they needed to head the group.

Hungary still had a chance of remaining in the competition but they depended upon El Salvador taking a point off Argentina. Even Hungary knew that was an impossible task.

Belgium: Pfaff; Gerets(Plessers), L.Millecamps, Baecke, Coeck, Meeuws, Vercauteren, Vandersmissen(Van Moer), Czerniatynski, Vandenbergh, Ceulemans.
Scorer: Czerniatynski
Hungary: Mészáros; Martos, Kerekes, Garaba, Varga, Nyilasi, Müller(Sallai), Pölöskei, Fazekas, Torocsik, L.Kiss(Csongradi).
Scorer: Varga
Referee: Clive White (England)

Alberto Tarantini of Argentina.

ARGENTINA 2   EL SALVADOR 0 (Half-time 1-0)
José Rico Perez Stadium, Alicante, 23 June
Attendance: 32,000

ARGENTINA had to win their final match to go through to the next phase and, like Belgium, they found themselves up against a packed El Salvador defence.

At times the game became an ill-tempered affair as Argentina were frustrated at not being able to score the hatful of goals they had promised.

Midway through the first half, Argentina were awarded a hotly-disputed penalty which Passarella converted. But they could not add to that score in the first half, despite constantly pushing forward. A second goal eventually came after 52 minutes, when Bertoni completed a fine individual effort.

Argentina scraped through but on this performance they hardly looked capable of holding on to the World Cup. Maradona was expected to score goals against the Central Americans but he left one commentator reflecting the views of many when he asked: "If he can't score against them, what chance has he got against the likes of Brazil?" There would be chance to find the answer to that question before the tournament was over.

Argentina: Fillol; Olguín, Galvan, Passarella, Tarantini, Ardíles, Gallego, Maradona, Bertoni (Díaz), Kempes, Calderón(Santamaria).
Scorers: Passarella (pen), Bertoni
El Salvador: Guevara Mora; Osorto(Díaz Arevalo), Rodríguez, Cruz Jovel, Recinos, Rugamas, Ventura(Alfaro), Huezo, Ramírez Zapata, González, Rivas.
Referee: Luis Barrancos (Bolivia)

Group Four

ENGLAND 3   FRANCE 1 (Half-time 1-1)
San Mamés Stadium, Bilbao, 16 June
Attendance: 44,172

FOR their first game in the World Cup finals since 1970, England were without established stars Trevor Brooking and captain Kevin Keegan. In Keegan's absence, manager Ron Greenwood, who was celebrating his 50th game in charge of the England team, gave the captaincy to Mick Mills.

Playing in a temperature of more than 100°F, England got off to a remarkable start when Bryan Robson scored after 27 seconds to record the fastest-ever World Cup goal.

It came from a set-piece throw-in and Robson was on hand to volley home a Mariner cross. France equalized after 25 minutes, when Larios intercepted a pass. He pushed the ball to Giresse, who laid on a perfect scoring chance for Soler, who shot across the face of the goal and beat the diving Peter Shilton.

Robson restored the English lead in the 66th minute, when he towered above the defence

Erwin Vandenbergh of Belgium.

France's Christian Lopez and goalkeeper Jean-Luc Ettori are beaten by this header from England skipper Bryan Robson, who made the score 2-0.

Bryan Robson (left) again dominant in the air gets the better of an aerial battle with Ettori.

Zdenek Nehoda of Czechoslovakia.

to meet a Trevor Francis cross and headed powerfully into the net. And a good England performance was rounded off eight minutes from time when Mariner scored the third goal from close range after Francis' shot had rebounded off defender Trésor. It was the fifth successive international in which Mariner had scored.

England: Shilton; Butcher, Mills, Sansom(Neal), Thompson, Coppell, Robson, Wilkins, Francis, Mariner, Rix.
Scorers: Robson 2, Mariner
France: Ettori, Battiston, Bossis, Trésor, Lopez, Larios(Tigana), Girard, Giresse, Rocheteau (Six), Platini, Soler.
Scorer: Soler
Referee: Antonio Garrido (Portugal)

CZECHOSLOVAKIA 1   KUWAIT 1 (Half-time 1-0)

Nuevo Estadio José Zorrilla, Valladolid, 17 June
Attendance: 25,000

CZECHOSLOVAKIA, like England, were playing in their first finals since 1970. But, unlike England, they found life tough in their opening match and came up against a well-prepared Kuwait side, who fully deserved to draw.

Kuwait were coached by the Brazilian, Carlos Alberto Perreira, who succeeded Mario Zagalo in 1978, and he blended together a talented team who approached the game in a fresh and lively manner.

The Europeans were under pressure from the start and must have been relieved when they were awarded a dubious penalty in the 21st minute, after Vizek appeared to fall over in the penalty area. Panenka made no mistake with the kick. Despite this set-back, Kuwait kept pushing forward and after 58 minutes they got their deserved equalizer through Al Dakhil, who scored with a powerful 30-yard drive which deceived Hruska in the Czech goal.

Kuwait had plenty of chances to take both points and a Kuwaiti win would have been a fair reflection of the way the teams played.

Czechoslovakia: Hruska; Barmos, Jurkemić, Fiala, Kukucka, Panenka(Bicovsky), Berger, Kriz, Janečka(Petrzela), Nehoda, Vizek.
Scorer: Panenka (pen)
Kuwait: Al Tarabulsi; Naeem Saed, Ma'Yoof, Mubarak, Jasem, Al Buloushi, Al Houti, Ahmed Karam(Kameel), Al Anbari, Yaqoub, Al Dakhil.
Scorer: Al Dakhil
Referee: Benjamin Dwomoh (Ghana)

England's 1982 World Cup squad. Back row (left to right): Robson, Woodcock, Foster, Hoddle, Withe, Anderson, Brooking. Middle row: Coppell, Rix, Thompson, Clemence, Corrigan, Shilton, Butcher, Francis, Wilkins. Front row: Sansom, McDermott, Mariner, Keegan, Mills, Neal.

Trevor Francis, scored against Czechoslovakia and Kuwait.

ENGLAND 2   CZECHOSLOVAKIA 0 (Half-time 0-0)

San Mamés Stadium, Bilbao, 20 June
Attendance: 41,123

ENGLAND did a 'professional' job in winning their second successive match, but it was not until the second half that they converted their chances. In reality they should have gone in at half-time leading by three or four goals.

Bryan Robson had several scoring opportunities before he failed to appear for the second half after suffering a groin injury. He was replaced by Hoddle, whose long passes posed all sorts of problems for the Czechs.

England's first goal, after 63 minutes, came after a goalkeeping error when Seman could not hold a Wilkins cross and Francis was on hand to slam the ball home from five yards. Three minutes later, Barmos scored an own-goal when he deflected Mariner's low cross into the net.

England may have been slightly lucky with their two goals but, all the same, their superiority was worth more than that.

England: Shilton; Mills, Thompson, Butcher, Sansom, Coppell, Robson(Hoddle), Wilkins, Francis, Mariner, Rix.
Scorers: Francis, Barmos (og)
Czechoslovakia: Seman (Stromsik); Barmos, Radimec, Vojacek, Fiala, Chaloupka, Berger, Jurkemić, Janečka(Masny), Nehoda, Vizek.
Referee: Charles Corver (Holland)

Saad Al Houti of Kuwait.

Francis (8) slams the ball home from five yards to give England the lead over the Czechs. Terry Butcher is the other England player.

Gérard Soler of France in a tussle with Kuwait's Mahboub Mubarak.

Michel Hidalgo, the French manager, is restrained by police during the uproar surrounding his side's fourth 'goal' against Kuwait. The game was held up for eight minutes when the Kuwaitis protested that they had heard a whistle and stopped playing. Eventually the goal was disallowed, hence Hidalgo's anger.

Marius Trésor of France.

FRANCE 4   KUWAIT 1 (Half-time 2-0)

Nuevo Estadio José Zorrilla, Valladolid, 21 June
Attendance: 30,034

AFTER their impressive opening draw with Czechoslovakia, it looked as though the big financial investment in Kuwait football was paying dividends. One man responsible for the nation's emergence as a growing power in the world game was Prince Fahid, but he was to be at the centre of a remarkable protest against the Soviet referee in the second half which resulted in play being held up for eight minutes.

At the time of the incident, France were 3-1 ahead. Their first goal was scored by Genghini after half an hour, when his swerving free-kick beat the defensive wall. Michel Platini stamped his mark on this World Cup with a second goal three minutes before the interval, with a well-taken shot from the edge of the goal area after a great pass from Giresse.

Three minutes after the interval, the French were three goals ahead when Six converted a great volley from a free-kick after taking the ball on his chest.

Kuwait scored their solitary goal 15 minutes from time, when Al Buloushi netted from a free-kick. But a minute later came that explosive incident.

Russian referee Miroslav Stupar, who did not have the best of games, awarded France a fourth goal when Giresse blasted home from close range with the Kuwaiti defenders rooted to the spot. They maintained that they had stopped upon hearing a whistle. The Kuwaiti FA president, Prince Fahid, came on to the pitch from his seat in the stands and protested long and hard. At one stage it looked as though the entire Kuwaiti team would be taken off the pitch. Stupar eventually reversed his decision which, understandably, then annoyed the French.

However, play was eventually resumed and France scored a fourth goal in the 90th minute, when Bossis netted to make up for the disappointment of having a 69th-minute goal disallowed.

For Prince Fahid's interference, an £8,000 fine was imposed on the Kuwaitis by FIFA. It would not have made much of a dent in the Prince's wallet, however, for he was one of the world's richest men.

France: Ettori; Amoros, Janvion(Lopez), Trésor, Bossis, Giresse, Platini(Girard), Genghini, Soler, Lacombe, Six.
Scorers: Genghini, Platini, Six, Bossis
Kuwait: Al Tarabulsi; Naeem Saed, Ma'Yoof, Mubarak, Jasem(Al Shemmari), Al Buloushi, Al Houti, Ahmed Karam(Kameel), Al Anbari, Yaquob, Al Dakhil.
Scorer: Al Buloushi
Referee: Miroslav Stupar (Soviet Union)

CZECHOSLOVAKIA 1   FRANCE 1 (Half-time 0-0)

Nuevo Estadio José Zorrilla, Valladolid, 24 June

FRANCE needed only to draw to qualify for the next phase, whilst the Czechs had to win. And in the first half, both sides had chances to find the net with Vizek and Janečka having Czechoslovakia's best chances and Lacombe going close for the French.

The first half remained goalless but the deadlock was broken in the 66th minute when Didier Six scored from close range after Lacombe had done well before making the crucial pass.

Czechoslovakia were now up against it and had to find the resources to score two goals.

They pushed forward but France had by now pulled themselves together and were solid in defence, although goalkeeper Ettori looked shaky at times. The Czechs' pressure was rewarded six minutes from time when they won a penalty and Panenka converted his second spot-kick of the tournament.

The last five minutes provided high drama with Czechoslovakia searching for a second goal. However, they had Vizek dismissed for apparently kicking Platini and in the closing minutes a Nehoda effort was headed off the line as France scraped through.

Czechoslovakia: Stromsik; Barmos, Fiala, Vojacek, Stambacher, Radimec, Bicovsky, Kriz (Masny), Nehoda, Vizek, Janecka(Panenka).
Scorer: Panenka (pen)
France: Ettori; Amoros, Trésor, Janvion, Bossis, Giresse, Platini, Genghini, Soler(Girard), Lacombe(Couriol), Six.
Scorer: Six
Referee: Paolo Casarin (Italy)

ENGLAND 1   KUWAIT 0 (Half-time 1-0)

San Mamés Stadium, Bilbao, 25 June
Attendance: 39,700

DESPITE giving their poorest display of the tournament so far, England still managed to win their group with a 100 per cent record, something only Brazil could match.

Kuwait were perhaps a little over-eager, whilst England eased off far too much in the knowledge that they had already topped Group Four, no matter what the outcome of this game.

They were caught offside many times and in the second half wasted a lot of scoring chances. The only goal of the game was netted by Trevor Francis after 27 minutes. A long kick downfield from Peter Shilton found Paul Mariner, who back-heeled the ball to Francis, leaving him plenty of room to crack home an angled shot.

England: Shilton; Neal, Mills, Foster, Thompson, Coppell, Hoddle, Wilkins, Mariner, Francis, Rix.
Scorer: Francis
Kuwait: Al Tarabulsi; Naeem Saed, Ma'Yoof, Mubarak, Jasem(Al Shemmari), Al Buloushi, Al Houti, Kameel, Al Anbari, Al Dakhil, Al Suwaayed.
Referee: Gilberto Aristizabal (Colombia)

Group Five

HONDURAS 1   SPAIN 1 (Half-time 1-0)

Luis Casanova Stadium, Valencia, 16 June
Attendance: 49,562

THE host nation went into their opening match at odds of 5/1 to win the trophy, whereas Honduras were 500/1 outsiders. As it turned out, the Spaniards could not cope with the immense pressure heaped upon them as one of the favourites on their own soil.

King Juan Carlos was amongst the Valencia crowd but what a sad day it turned out to be as he watched his team fall behind to a seventh-minute goal from Zelaya.
That stunned the large crowd and for nearly an hour Spain found themselves trailing. It looked as though another World Cup shock was on the cards but in the 65th minute, the hosts were awarded a penalty and López-Ufarte put away the kick to spare the King, the players and the fans any further embarrassment.

It was a poor start for Spain and their team of highly-talented individuals once more showed that they had problems playing together at the highest level.

Honduras: Arzu; Gutiérrez, Villegas, Costly, Bulñes, Maradiaga, Yearwood, Zelaya, Norales (Caballero), Betancourt, Figueroa.
Scorer: Zelaya
Spain: Arconada; Camacho, Tendillo, Alexanco, Gordillo, Joaquín(Sánchez), Alonso, Zamora, Juanito(Saura), Satrustegui, López-Ufarte.
Scorer: López-Ufarte (pen)
Referee: Arturo Ithurralde (Argentina)

NORTHERN IRELAND 0   YUGOSLAVIA 0 (Half-time 0-0)

La Romereda Stadium, Zaragoza, 17 June
Attendance: 25,000

IT was a welcome return to the World Cup finals for Northern Ireland after an absence of 24 years. On that occasion one of their players was Billy Bingham. Now he was the manager who was to make them one of the surprise packages of this tournament.

Bingham introduced Norman Whiteside who, at 17 years and 41 days, became the World

Group Four – Final Table

	P	W	D	L	F	A	Pts
England	3	3	0	0	6	1	6
France	3	1	1	1	6	5	3
Czechoslovakia	3	0	2	1	2	4	2
Kuwait	3	0	1	2	2	6	1

Michel Platini of France.

Heads high as Spain and Honduras fight out a 1-1 draw in the opening match.

Cup's youngest-ever debutant, surpassing the record of the great Pelé. Also in the Irish team was the veteran goalkeeper Pat Jennings, who made his international debut before Whiteside was born.

The game itself was not all that inspiring, although Northern Ireland gave a tireless display and did well to hold the more talented Yugoslavs.

The goalless draw meant the group was thrown wide open and, unlike the other groups, there was now no such thing as an outsider.

Northern Ireland: Jennings; J.Nicholl, C.Nicholl, McClelland, Donaghy, McIlroy, M.O'Neill, McCreery, Armstrong, Hamilton, Whiteside.
Yugoslavia: Pantelić; Zajec, Jovanović, Stojković, Hrstić, Slijvo, Gudelj, Surjak, Petrović, Vujović, Susić.
Referee: Erik Fredriksson (Sweden)

SPAIN 2   YUGOSLAVIA 1 (Half-time 1-1)

Luis Casanova Stadium, Valencia, 20 June
Attendance: 48,000

SPANISH fans went home somewhat happier after this match, although their team struggled and had to come back from a tenth-minute Yugoslav goal.

Gudelj put the Slavs in the lead, but two minutes later came a controversial penalty decision in favour of the Spaniards. The Yugoslavian players maintained that Zajec's foul on Alonso was outside the area. Danish referee Herning Lund-Sörensen was unmoved, however, and pointed to the spot. Even then, there was more controversy to follow.

López-Ufarte, who scored from the spot in the opening game, missed the target completely but the referee ordered the kick to be retaken because the goalkeeper had moved. Juanito then stepped up for the second attempt and scored. It seemed, once more, that the referee had been subjected to the sort of pressure imposed on predecessors officiating host nation matches.

Yugoslavia looked the better of the sides in the second half but, following a defensive error which led to a corner, Saura got the ball into the net. He had only been on the field for three minutes, but his goal turned out to be Spain's winner.

Spain: Arconada; Camacho, Tendillo, Alexanco, Gordillo, Sánchez(Saura), Alonso, Zamora, Juanito, Satrustegui(Quini), López-Ufarte.
Scorers: Juanito (pen), Saura
Yugoslavia: Pantelić; Krmpotić, Zajec, Stojković, Jovanović(Halilhodzić), Gudelj, Petrović, Slijvo, Vujović(Sestić), Surjak, Susić.
Scorer: Gudelj
Referee: Herning Lund-Sörenson (Denmark)

Luís Miguel Arconada, Spain's goalkeeper.

HONDURAS 1   NORTHERN IRELAND 1 (Half-time 0-1)

La Romereda Stadium, Zaragoza, 21 June
Attendance: 15,000

THESE sides were well-matched and if the run of the ball was slightly more in Honduras' favour, then Northern Ireland must have reflected on the missed chances that should have given them their first win.

Armstrong had a great game for Ireland and it was the clever winger who opened the scoring after two minutes when he followed up a McIlroy free-kick which rebounded off the bar.

After scoring so early in the game, it appeared that the Irish would achieve a sizeable victory but Honduras kept coming forward and on the hour scored a deserved equalizer when Laing beat Jennings.

Northern Ireland's Norman Whiteside, broke Pelé's record as the youngest player to appear in a World Cup finals tournament.

Honduras (*pictured right*) finished bottom of Group Five but did well to draw with Northern Ireland and Spain and suffer only a single-goal defeat at the hands of Yugoslavia.

Northern Ireland: Jennings; J.Nicholl, C.Nicholl, McClelland, Donaghy, Armstrong, M.O'Neill(Healy), McCreery, McIlroy, Hamilton, Whiteside(Brotherston).
Scorer: Armstrong
Honduras: Arzu; Gutiérrez, Villegas, Costly, Cruz, Maradiaga, Yearwood, Figueroa, Zelaya, Betancourt, Norales(Laing).
Scorer: Laing
Referee: Sun Cham Tan (Hong Kong)

YUGOSLAVIA 1   HONDURAS 0 (Half-time 0-0)
La Romereda Stadium, Zaragoza, 24 June
Attendance: 25,000

HONDURAS, who had given Spain and Northern Ireland headaches, now posed similar problems for Yugoslavia, who went into this group as one of the fancied teams and yet had to apply their greater international experience to secure this win. Indeed, it was earned only with a last-gasp winner three minutes from time.

Honduras maintained their high standard of play and certainly left this tournament with a lot of admirers, although they tarnished their reputation a little by having Gilberto Yearwood sent off after protesting against the refereeing decision which allowed Petrović to score the winner from the penalty-spot in the 87th minute.

Yugoslavia's survival hung by a thread as their fate now rested with Spain and Northern Ireland. As it turned out, the Eastern Europeans made an early exit from the 12th World Cup.

Yugoslavia: Pantelić; Krmpotić, Zajec, Stojković, Jovanović(Halilhodzić), Gudelj, Slijvo, Surjak, Petrović, Vujović(Sestić), Susić.
Scorer: Petrović (pen)
Honduras: Arzu; Drummond, Costly, Villegas, Bulñes, Yearwood, Cruz(Laing), Zelaya, Maradiaga, Betancourt, Figueroa.
Referee: Gastón Castro (Chile)

NORTHERN IRELAND 1   SPAIN 0 (Half-time 0-0)
Luis Casanova Stadium, Valencia, 25 June
Attendance: 49,562

NORTHERN Ireland needed a win to make sure they topped Group Five and go through to the next round. Spain, on the other hand, could afford the luxury of defeat, although by no more than one goal.

The pressure on Spain as hosts had been telling from the start, but it was never more evident than in this match and after Northern Ireland scored early in the second half, there was the very real possibility of the hosts making an early departure from the tournament.

Pat Jennings had an outstanding game as the Irish made the Spaniards look very mediocre. Indeed, this was surely Northern Ireland's finest-ever World Cup performance, eclipsing even their appearance in the 1958 quarter-finals.

It was a physical game with three bookings and a sending-off, but the Irish refused to be intimidated either by the Spanish team or the home supporters, who whipped up an electric atmosphere.

In the first minute of the second half, Billy Hamilton sent over a cross from the right. Spain's goalkeeper, Arconada, was caught in two minds and eventually pushed the ball out to Gerry Armstrong, who hammered home the goal of his career from around the penalty-spot.

Ireland defended their lead stoutly but suffered a set-back after an hour when Mal Donaghy was given his marching orders after a set-to with José Camacho, after the Spanish full-back had brought him down.

Despite their defeat, Spain still went through to the next round along with the group's top team, Northern Ireland, who completed a fairy-tale for manager Billy Bingham.

Northern Ireland: Jennings; J.Nicholl, C.Nicholl, McCreery, Donaghy, M.O'Neill, McIlroy (Cassidy), McClelland, Hamilton, Armstrong, Whiteside(Nelson).
Scorer: Armstrong
Spain: Arconada; Camacho, Tendillo, Alexanco, Gordillo, Sánchez, Alonso, Saura, Juanito, Satrustegui(Quini), López-Ufarte(Gallego).
Referee: Héctor Ortiz (Paraguay)

Group Six

BRAZIL 2   SOVIET UNION 1 (Half-time 0-1)
Sánchez Pizjuán Stadium, Seville, 14 June
Attendance: 68,000

BRAZIL had thrown away their defensive tactics and reverted to the style of play which

Group Five – Final Table

	P	W	D	L	F	A	Pts
N. Ireland	3	1	2	0	2	1	4
Spain	3	1	1	1	3	3	3
Yugoslavia	3	1	1	1	2	2	3
Honduras	3	0	2	1	2	3	2

Jesús María Satrustegui of Spain.

Luisinho of Brazil.

Alexander Chivadze, the Soviet Union's highly-rated defender.

Socrates (arm raised) celebrates after giving Brazil a 75th-minute equalizer against the Soviets. It was a magnificent goal, one of the greatest in World Cup history.

won them the 1970 World Cup. Nevertheless, the Soviets were a good match for the South Americans before eventually succumbing to continued Brazilian pressure.

The game was played with the kind of skill and sportsmanship that was reminiscent of the 1958 World Cup in Sweden. And for excitement, flair and ability, there was probably as much in this one match as there was in the whole of the 1978 tournament put together.

The game was played to a constant Samba beat from the Brazilian fans, albeit silenced temporarily in the 33rd minute when Bal scored a freak goal for Russia after goalkeeper Waldir Peres allowed the ball to squeeze through his arms. The Soviets, playing in their first World Cup since 1970, held on to that lead until 15 minutes from the end, when the Brazilian captain, Socrates, scored a magnificent goal.

After picking up a poor Russian pass, he side-stepped two defenders before hitting an unstoppable shot from outside the penalty area. It was one of the great goals of the World Cup.

Two minutes from time, Eder made sure that Brazil opened their account with a win and sent the unfortunate Soviets away with nothing to show for their contribution to an excellent game.

Brazil: Waldir Peres; Leandro, Oscar, Luisinho, Junior, Socrates, Dirceu(Paulo Isidoro), Zico, Falcão, Serginho, Eder.
Scorers: Socrates, Eder
Soviet Union; Dasaev; Sulakvelidze, Chivadze, Baltacha, Demianenko, Bessonov, Gavrilov (Susloparov), Bal, Daraselia, Shengelia(Andreyev), Blokhin.
Scorer: Bal
Referee: Augusto Lamo Castillo (Spain)

SCOTLAND 5   NEW ZEALAND 2 (Half-time 3-0)

La Rosaleda Stadium, Málaga, 15 June
Attendance: 36,000

HAVING travelled more than 60,000 miles in qualifying for their first finals, New Zealand, the 50th nation to compete in the finals, were determined to put up a good show in Spain. But, whilst they gave an honest and hard-working performance, they were no match for the more experienced Scots.

Scotland put a lot of pressure on themselves, despite the apparent ease of their victory which the scoreline suggests. Lapses of concentration allowed New Zealand to score twice and those goals ultimately cost Scotland a place in the next round.

Kenny Dalglish put Scotland ahead in the 18th minute and then two goals by John Wark, in the 29th and 32nd minutes, gave the Scots a comfortable 3-0 lead at the interval.

But ten minutes into the second half came that first lapse when Steve Sumner took advantage of a defensive mix-up between goalkeeper Alan Rough and captain Danny McGrain. Ten minutes later New Zealand were only a goal behind after Steve Wooddin scored.

The Scottish fans must have been casting their minds back to the disastrous finals of 1978 but John Robertson eased their worries when his chip shot found the net in the 73rd minute. Ten minutes from time, the three-goal lead was restored through Steve Archibald.

Scotland: Rough; McGrain, Hansen, Evans, Gray, Souness, Strachan(Narey), Dalglish, Wark, Brazil(Archibald), Robertson.
Scorers: Wark 2, Dalglish, Archibald, Robertson
New Zealand: Van Hattum; Hill, Malcolmson(Cole), Elrick, Almond(Herbert), Sumner, McKay, Cresswell, Boath, Rufer, Wooddin.
Scorers: Sumner, Wooddin
Referee: David Socha (United States)

Socrates of Brazil.

BRAZIL 4   SCOTLAND 1 (Half-time 1-1)

Benito Villamarín Stadium, Seville, 18 June
Attendance: 47,379

THIS game was played in a carnival atmosphere as both sets of fervent fans mixed on the terraces to help make it a memorable occasion and serve as a reminder of what football used to be like. On the pitch Brazil outplayed the Scots with sheer skill, which also reminded us of how the game used to be played.

Yet it was Scotland who took the lead in the 18th minute, after coping with early Brazilian pressure. Full-back David Narey powered home a swerving right-foot shot from the edge of the penalty area. It was the sort of goal of which his Brazilian counterparts would have been proud.

Brazil were technically superior and once they scored they had Scotland at their mercy. The outstanding Zico put an end to the Scottish dream in the 33rd minute, when his 25-yard free-kick swerved past the wall of defenders who remained rooted to the spot as the ball flew into the net.

Three minutes after the interval, Oscar headed home a curling Junior corner to put Brazil in front and a marvellous chip over goalkeeper Alan Rough from Eder in the 64th minute

John Robertson's (11) free-kick, a delicate chip over New Zealand's defensive wall, evades goalkeeper Frank Van Hattum to restore the Scots' two-goal lead.

This time Scotland are on the wrong end of a chip-shot as Eder gives Brazil a 3-1 lead.

Oleg Blokhin of the Soviet Union.

Junior of Brazil.

put the game beyond Scotland's reach. Brazil sealed a memorable performance with yet another great goal four minutes from time, when Falcão hit a tremendous shot from 25 yards which sailed past the Scottish 'keeper.

Brazil's win was efficient and impressive and must have sent shock waves through the other fancied nations. At this early stage of the tournament the South Americans were justifying their tag as favourites.

Brazil: Waldir Peres; Leandro, Oscar, Luisinho, Junior, Falcão, Cerezo, Zico, Socrates, Eder, Serginho(Paulo Isidoro).
Scorers: Zico, Oscar, Eder, Falcão
Scotland: Rough; Narey, Miller, Hansen, Gray, Wark, Souness, Strachan(Dalglish), Hartford (McLeish), Archibald, Robertson.
Scorer: Narey
Referee: Luis Siles Calderón (Costa Rica)

SOVIET UNION 3   NEW ZEALAND 0 (Half-time 1-0)
La Rosaleda Stadium, Málaga, 19 June
Attendance: 19,000

DESPITE a brave performance, which did not disgrace them, New Zealand lost to a much fitter, faster and stronger Soviet team, who coasted to victory. The New Zealanders played a defensive game in the first half but they responded to the support of the Scottish fans in the stadium and attacked more in the second period after falling 2-0 behind.

Gavrilov was on hand to open the scoring from close range in the 24th minute, after a Bal shot across the area rebounded to him.

Oleg Blokhin increased the Soviets' lead three minutes into the second half but he was fortunate to have a scoring chance after Shengelia's first attempt at a shot was completely mis-kicked. Blokhin was there to power home a left-foot shot from the edge of the box.

Baltacha rammed home a square pass from Blokhin in the 69th minute and the spirited New Zealanders were down and out of the tournament.

Soviet Union: Dasaev; Sulakvelidze, Chivadze, Baltacha, Demianenko, Bessonov, Shengelia, Bal, Daraselia(Oganesian), Gavrilov(Rodionov), Blokhin.
Scorers: Gavrilov, Blokhin, Baltacha
New Zealand: Van Hattum; Dods, Herbert, Elrick, Boath, Cole, Sumner, McKay, Cresswell, Rufer, Wooddin.
Referee: Yousef El Ghoul (Libya)

SCOTLAND 2   SOVIET UNION 2 (Half-time 1-0)
La Rosaleda Stadium, Málaga, 22 June
Attendance: 45,000

SCOTLAND knew that a draw would be no good to them in their final match because of their inferior goal-difference to the Soviets. So they committed themselves to attack and in the 15th minute, Joe Jordan scored the crucial first goal.

Despite a good first-half showing, however, Scotland could not increase their lead and in the second half the Russians eventually wore them down before Chivadze scored the equalizer on the hour. Six minutes from time Scotland's hopes were dashed when Shengelia broke clear after an awful mix-up by Hansen and Miller which left the Russian with an easy scoring chance.

Souness gave the Scots a glimmer of hope with three minutes left, but it was too late and the promise of a comfortable Scottish win, based on their first-half performance, fizzled out. For the second successive World Cup tournament, Scotland were eliminated on goal-difference.

Scotland: Rough; Gray, Hansen, Miller, Strachan(McGrain), Narey, Souness, Jordan(Brazil), Wark, Robertson, Archibald.
Scorers: Jordan, Souness
Soviet Union: Dasaev; Sulakvelidze, Chivadze, Baltacha, Demianenko, Shengelia(Andreyev), Bessonov, Bal, Borovsky, Gavrilov, Blokhin.
Scorers: Chivadze, Shengelia
Referee: Nicolae Rainea (Romania)

Group Six – Final Table	P	W	D	L	F	A	Pts
Brazil	3	3	0	0	10	2	6
Soviet Union	3	1	1	1	6	4	3
Scotland	3	1	1	1	8	8	3
New Zealand	3	0	0	3	2	12	0

BRAZIL 4   NEW ZEALAND 0 (Half-time 2-0)

Benito Villamarín Stadium, Seville, 23 June
Attendance: 43,000

BRAZIL wound up their group matches in a blaze of glory with another exhilarating display of attacking football. New Zealand went out in awe of their masters, in what was the biggest game in the country's soccer history.

The New Zealanders, playing less defensively than in their previous games, managed to get close enough to have a couple of chances at the Brazilian goal. But all the goals, and classy ones they were, came from the South Americans.

Zico started it all off with a spectacular bicycle-kick in the 29th minute to connect with a Leandro cross. Two minutes later the same players were involved in the second goal. Zico met a Leandro cross and powered the ball into the corner of the net.

Zico laid on the third goal for Falcão after 55 minutes and also had a hand in the fourth, scored by Serginho in the 70th minute.

Brazil: Waldir Peres; Leandro, Oscar(Edinho), Luisinho, Junior, Falcão, Cerezo, Socrates, Zico, Serginho (Paulo Isidoro), Eder.
Scorers: Zico 2, Falcão, Serginho
New Zealand: Van Hattum; Dods, Herbert, Elrick, Boath, Sumner, McKay, Cresswell(Cole), Almond, Rufer(B.Turner), Wooddin.
Referee: Damar Matovinović (Yugoslavia)

Group A

POLAND 3   BELGIUM 0 (Half-time 2-0)

Nou Camp Stadium, Barcelona, 28 June
Attendance: 65,000

POLAND continued were they left off and followed up their 5-1 win over Peru by soundly beating Belgium, thanks to a magnificent display from Zbigniew Boniek, who scored all three goals.

Belgium had to reorganize their defence after losing key players through injury, but were forced to attack after Boniek struck in the fourth minute, when he latched on to a ball pulled back by Lato and thundered it into the net.

With Belgium pushing forward, this gave Lato the opportunity to set up counter-attacks from midfield as he gave another majestic display. Boniek made it 2-0 in the 26th minute, when he finished off a good move with a header.

Belgium's misery continued seven minutes after half-time when Boniek strode through the advancing defence to score with ease and complete his hat-trick.

Boniek had been seeking to join an English club, but none seemed interested in him. Juventus, however, had agreed to take him and how those English clubs must have been regretting their decision after this great solo performance.

Poland: Mlynarczyk; Dziuba, Majewski, Zmuda, Janas, Lato, Buncol, Matysik, Kupcewicz (Ciolek), Boniek, Smolarek.
Scorer: Boniek 3
Belgium: Custers; Renquin, L.Millecamps, Meeuws, Plessers(Baecke), Van Moer(Van der Elst), Coeck, Vercauteren, Ceulemans, Vandenbergh, Czerniatynski.
Referee: Luis Siles Calderón (Costa Rica)

SOVIET UNION 1   BELGIUM 0 (Half-time 0-0)

Nou Camp Stadium, Barcelona, 1 July
Attendance: 45,000

BELGIUM made four changes to the side beaten by Poland, including the introduction of their third goalkeeper in successive matches when they gave a first outing to Jacques Munaron.

The Russians proved sterner opposition than the Poles but, despite playing well, Belgium were unable to find the net.

The only goal of the game was scored by Oganesyan four minutes after half-time, when he half-connected with a volley. It was a sloppy goal but one good enough to send Belgium packing, despite piling on late pressure. Once again, their inability to finish let them down.

Zico of Brazil.

Group A - Final Table

	P	W	D	L	F	A	Pts
Poland	2	1	1	0	3	0	3
Soviet Union	2	1	1	0	1	0	3
Belgium	2	0	0	2	0	4	0

England full-back Kenny Sansom goes flying after a tackle by a West German defender.

Kevin Keegan, along with Trevor Brooking, made his first appearance of the tournament against Spain. He fluffed a simple chance with a header and was clearly out of touch.

West Germany's Uwe Reinders (13) shoots wide from a free-kick in the drab encounter with England.

Soviet Union: Dasaev; Borovsky, Chivadze, Baltacha, Demianenko, Bessonov, Bal(Daraselia), Gavrilov, Shengelia(Rodionov), Oganesian, Blokhin.
Scorers: Oganesyan
Belgium: Munaron; Renquin, L.Millecamps, Meeuws, De Schrijver(M.Millecamps), Coeck, Verheyen, Vercauteren, Vandersmissen(Czerniatynski), Vandenbergh, Ceulemans.
Referee: Michel Vautrot (France)

POLAND 0   SOVIET UNION 0 (Half-time 0-0)

Nou Camp Stadium, Barcelona, 4 July
Attendance: 65,000

POLAND needed only to draw to qualify for the semi-finals and they obtained it with a clever defensive game.

The Soviets lacked variety up front and could not penetrate the Polish defence. And the more the Poles defended, the more they grew in confidence and consequently started pushing forward. Indeed, they could well have snatched a winner.

The Soviets had three clear first-half chances but Blokhin, Oganesian and Sulakvelidze all failed to take advantage. The Soviets were eliminated and Poland reached the semi-final for the second time in their history.

Poland: Mlynarczyk; Dziuba, Zmuda, Janas, Majewski, Kupcewicz(Ciolek), Buncol, Matysik, Lato, Boniek, Smolarek.
Soviet Union: Dasaev; Borovsky, Chivadze, Baltacha, Sulakvelidze, Demianenko, Bessonov, Gavrilov(Daraselia), Shengelia(Andreyev), Oganesian, Blokhin.
Referee: Bob Valentine (Scotland)

Group B

ENGLAND 0   WEST GERMANY 0 (Half-time 0-0)

Santiago Bernabéu Stadium, Madrid, 29 June
Attendance: 75,000

IN a stadium that has seen some of the world's finest football from some of the world's greatest teams, it was a shame that its knowledgeable fans should be treated to a drab and boring affair between sides who have so often dished up World Cup treats.

The Germans seemed frightened of the English, whilst England seemed to lack inventiveness. Bryan Robson had a good header well saved but England's only other decent chances fell to Ray Wilkins, with a 20-yard shot, and Steve Coppell, who also had a long-range effort. But that was about it and Robson's 38th-minute shot was the last time the German goal was seriously threatened.

West Germany launched a final assault in the hope of snatching a winner and came very close when a Rummenigge shot rattled the bar five minutes from time. A goalless draw was the right result for such a disappointing match.

England: Shilton; Butcher, Mills, Thompson, Sansom, Coppell, Robson, Wilkins, Francis (Woodcock), Mariner, Rix.
West Germany: Schumacher; Kaltz, K-H.Förster, Stielike, Briegel, Dremmler, B.Förster, Breitner, H.Müller(Fischer), Reinders(Littbarski), Rummenigge.
Referee: Arnaldo César Coelho (Brazil)

WEST GERMANY 2   SPAIN 1 (Half-time 0-0)

Santiago Bernabéu Stadium, Madrid, 2 July
Attendance: 90,089

DURING their group matches, Spain had given plenty of indication that they were unlikely

to reach the semi-final and this defeat by West Germany in their first second-phase match confirmed their exit from a tournament which they had high hopes of winning before the start. But that has happened many times to the Spaniards over the years, high hopes followed by bitter disappointments.

Once again, nerves seemed to be Spain's biggest opponents as they carried the burden of the host nation and allowed the Germans to outclass them. The elegant Paul Breitner had an outstanding game and gave one of the finest individual performances of the 12th World Cup.

West Germany created more chances in the first 15 minutes than they did in the whole of their match against England, but they must have gone in at the interval frustrated at not having taken the lead.

They lost the injured Rummenigge at half-time, but five minutes into the second half came the goal they had been threatening. Littbarski, who had been left out of the starting line-up against England, was on hand to follow up a loose ball after the Spanish goalkeeper, Arconada, failed to hold a long-range shot from Dremmler.

Littbarski was also involved in the second German goal after 75 minutes when, following a good Breitner move, he rounded the Spanish 'keeper before passing to Fischer, who had the easiest of tasks to put the ball into the empty net.

After a lapse in concentration by the German defence, Zamora headed home a Sánchez cross to score for the hosts nine minutes from time, but by then Spain were out of their 'own' World Cup.

West Germany: Schumacher; Kaltz, Stielike, K-H.Förster, Briegel, Dremmler, Breitner, B.Förster, Littbarski, Fischer, Rummenigge(Reinders).
Scorers: Littbarski, Fischer
Spain: Arconada; Urquiaga, Tendillo, Alexanco, Gordillo, Camacho, Alonso, Zamora, Juanito (López-Ufarte), Quini(Sánchez), Santillana.
Scorer: Zamora
Referee: Paolo Casarin (Italy)

ENGLAND 0   SPAIN 0 (Half-time 0-0)

Santiago Bernabéu Stadium, Madrid, 5 July
Attendance: 75,000

ENGLAND knew that they had to win either 2-0 or by scoring three goals or more against Spain in the final match. But they found their task a hard one on a night of near-misses in the Santiago Bernabéu Stadium.

Ironically, it was the first time in the tournament that Spain had kept a clean sheet, thanks to a good display by goalkeeper Arconada. Once again, England struggled against a Continental defence.

England's own defence was solid enough, but their forwards could not find the goals that their side required. A desperate substitution 27 minutes from time — when Ron Greenwood brought on Kevin Keegan and Trevor Brooking for their first games of the tournament after being injured — added more power to the England front line. But it also added to the frustration as both newcomers missed easy chances. Keegan fluffed a simple header with the goal beckoning 20 minutes from time. On almost any other occasion he would have scored with ease.

The game ended goalless and it was a sad exit for England, who went out of the competition despite not losing. It was also a sad farewell for manager Greenwood, who was in charge of the team for the last time before handing over to his successor, Bobby Robson.

England: Shilton; Mills, Butcher, Thompson, Sansom, Wilkins, Robson, Mariner, Rix (Brooking), Francis, Woodcock(Keegan).
Spain: Arconada; Urquiaga, Tendillo(Maceda), Alexanco, Gordillo, Saura(Uralde), Alonso, Zamora, Camacho, Satrustegui, Santillana.
Referee: Alexis Ponnet (Belgium)

Group C

ITALY 2   ARGENTINA 1 (Half-time 0-0)

Sarria Stadium, Barcelona, 29 June
Attendance: 43,000

IF there is anything likely to get Latin emotions running high, it is an Argentina-Italy soccer match. This game was no exception and, like many before it, was a very physical encounter.

The first half was goalless with Italy 'sorting out' Argentina and Gentile shadowing Maradona every where he went. The little Argentinian was kept out of the game by the tough, but experienced, Italian defender. Like Pelé in 1966, the Argentine star was chopped down time and time again.

While Italy won the 'physical' first-half battle, they beat Argentina in the second by coming

Group B – Final Table

	P	W	D	L	F	A	Pts
W.Germany	2	1	1	0	2	1	3
England	2	0	2	0	0	0	2
Spain	2	0	1	1	1	2	1

Trevor Brooking, came into the side against Spain. Both he and Keegan had been injured and both missed chances as England struggled to a goalless draw.

Phil Thompson (left) and Ray Wilkins trudge to the dressing-room after the draw against Spain saw England eliminated.

Jorge Olguín of Argentina.

Zico (partly hidden by Argentinian goalkeeper Ubaldo Fillol) follows up Eder's brilliant free-kick to put Brazil into a 12th-minute lead in the Sarria Stadium.

out and playing good football. After the match, Argentina's manager, Menotti commented: "Italy surprised us by playing attacking football. We failed to adjust to their unusual approach."

The Argentine attack lacked any orthodox wingers and, consequently, the Italian defence had no problems mastering the attacks thrown at them. It was from a 68th-minute counter-attack that Marco Tardelli finished off a classic move after Conti had opened up the defence.

Italy played a more defensive game after taking the lead. Maradona hit a post from a free-kick, but after 68 minutes Italy went further ahead after Rossi broke clear, amidst Argentinian claims for offside. His shot was blocked by Fillol, the ball ran free and Tardelli laid it off for Cabrini to hammer home a powerful left-foot shot from just inside the penalty area.

Passarella pulled one back for Argentina six minutes from the end, when his 25-yard free-kick went in whilst the referee was still pushing back the defensive wall. The goal stood, but it was not enough.

Italy: Zoff; Gentile, Cabrini, Collovati, Scirea, Tardelli, Antognoni, Oriali(Marini), Conti, Rossi(Altobelli), Graziani.
Scorers: Tardelli, Cabrini
Argentina: Fillol; Olguín, Galvan, Passarella, Tarantini, Gallego, Ardíles, Maradona, Bertoni, Díaz(Calderón), Kempes(Valencia).
Scorer: Passarella
Referee: Nicolae Rainea (Romania)

BRAZIL 3   ARGENTINA 1 (Half-time 1-0)

Sarria Stadium, Barcelona, 2 July
Attendance: 44,000

IF there is one match likely to get the Latin emotions running even higher than an Italy-Argentina clash, it is the all-South American encounter between Brazil and Argentina. But this latest in the series proved to be a one-sided affair with Brazil in total command.

For Maradona, it was a chance to compare his skills with the masters. But sadly, his World Cup was to end with a sending-off and he left the world's greatest stage a fallen idol. His day, of course was yet to come.

Brazil ridiculed Argentina with their brilliant one-touch football which, at times, was better than that of their 1970 side. Zico put them in the lead after 12 minutes, when a brilliant Eder free-kick swerved both ways and also dipped on its way around the defensive wall before hitting the bar. Zico was on hand to follow up the rebound.

Running off the ball and taking advantage of space was a major feature of the Brazilian play as they left Argentina struggling. In particular, Maradona was disappointing and an insignificant figure.

It was, therefore, perhaps, surprising that Brazil's second goal did not come until the 67th minute, when Serginho headed home a Falcão cross at the far post. Five minutes later, Junior made it 3-0 with one of the best goals of the tournament when he appeared around the back of the defence to finish off a move which involved five men.

Maradona's frustration at making no impact on the game and at having a penalty appeal turned down took its toll in the closing minutes, when the studs of his boots found the groin of Batista. Referee Rubio Vázquez had no hesitation in sending the 21-year-old off the field.

In the final minute, Díaz scored for Argentina but it was to no avail. They had failed in their bid to hold on to the World Cup trophy.

Brazil: Waldir Peres; Leandro(Edevaldo), Oscar, Luisinho, Junior, Cerezo, Zico(Batista), Falcão, Serginho, Socrates, Eder.
Scorers: Zico, Serginho, Junior
Argentina: Fillol; Olguín, Galvan, Passarella, Tarantini, Barbas, Maradona, Ardíles, Bertoni (Santamaria), Kempes(Díaz), Calderón.
Scorers: Díaz
Referee: Mario Rubio Vázquez (Mexico)

ITALY 3   BRAZIL 2 (Half-time 2-1)

Sarria Stadium, Barcelona, 5 July
Attendance: 44,000

WHAT a climax to the final match of Group C! Brazil could afford the luxury of a draw to reach the semi-final, whereas Italy had to win. And although nobody had managed to do that against Brazil in this tournament, Paolo Rossi was about to burst back on to the scene with a hat-trick.

Italy attacked from the outset and after five minutes took the lead when a Carbrini centre left the defence standing and Rossi was there to head home his first goal of the competition.

Brazil had come from behind to beat the Soviet Union and Scotland, so they were not unduly worried and in the 12th minute they were level when Socrates took a pass from Zico and raced through for a great solo goal. It came only minutes after Serginho had missed an easy chance.

For most of the game Zico was well-guarded by Gentile, who did a good job in subduing the star Brazilian, just as he had done with Maradona in the previous game.

Rossi restored the Italian lead after 25 minutes, when another defensive blunder, this time by Cerezo, allowed the Italian forward to score his second goal. Italy then had two more good chances to increase their lead but failed to do so and suddenly, from being in the driving seat, they found themselves struggling again as Falcão levelled the scores.

Falcão, who was playing his League soccer in Italy with Roma, wrong-footed the defence before scoring with his left foot and with 22 minutes remaining, Brazil were looking favourites to go through to the semi-finals. But they paid the price for pushing forward when they should have been holding on for a draw.

They allowed Italy to snatch the winner 15 minutes from time, when Rossi completed his hat-trick after Junior had headed weakly away from a corner.

In the dying minutes, Dino Zoff brought off a great save when the Brazilians claimed that the ball was over the line. The referee did not share their view and a magnificent game ended with Italy the victors.

Brazil had been the most outstanding and attractive team of the tournament. Their exit was a sad one for them and the World Cup in general.

Italy: Zoff; Gentile, Collovati(Bergomi), Scirea, Cabrini, Tardelli(Marini), Antognoni, Oriali, Graziani, Conti, Rossi.
Scorer: Rossi 3
Brazil: Waldir Peres; Leandro, Oscar, Luisinho, Junior, Cerezo, Socrates, Zico, Falcão, Serginho (Paulo Isidoro), Eder.
Scorers: Socrates, Falcão
Referee: Abraham Klein (Israel)

Group C - Final Table

	P	W	D	L	F	A	Pts
Italy	2	2	0	0	5	3	4
Brazil	2	1	0	1	5	4	2
Argentina	2	0	0	2	2	5	0

Osvaldo Ardíles of Argentina, now had the added experience of four seasons of English League soccer.

Italy's Paolo Rossi (second left) completes his hat-trick with the winner against Brazil as Italy go through to the semi-final.

Gérard Soler of France.

Group D

FRANCE 1   AUSTRIA 0 (Half-time 1-0)

Vicente Calderón Stadium, Madrid, 28 June
Attendance: 37,000

DESPITE the closeness of the scoreline, France were vastly superior to the lethargic Austrians, who would have been well beaten had France taken just some of their many second-half chances.

The French had plenty of space in midfield and Rocheteau tormented the Austrian defence after coming on as a 14th-minute substitute for Bernard Lacombe. Rocheteau was involved in the move which led to the only goal, six minutes before the interval.

The French substitute was brought down and Genghini's 20-yard free-kick fooled Austrian 'keeper, Koncilia, who completely misjudged the flight and pace of the ball.

France had given some indifferent performances in getting to this stage of the tournament but it was apparent, even in their opening defeat by England, that they had a lot of skill and they showed that they could play well as a team, even without Michel Platini, who missed this match through injury.

France: Ettori; Battiston, Janvion, Trésor, Bossis, Giresse, Tigana, Genghini(Girard), Soler, Lacombe(Rocheteau), Six.
Scorer: Genghini
Austria: Kocilia; Krauss, Obermayer, Pezzey, Degeorgi(Baumeister), Prohaska, Hintermaier, Hattenberger, Schachner, Jara(Welzl), Krankl.
Referee: Karoly Palotai (Hungary)

AUSTRIA 2   NORTHERN IRELAND 2 (Half-time 0-1)

Vicente Calderón Stadium, Madrid, 1 July
Attendance: 20,000

AUSTRIA made five changes to their side, including the axing of top goalscorer Hans Krankl. They were anxious to salvage something after their poor showing in the opening match against France. Whilst neither side achieved the victory each was seeking, a draw was a fair result.

Hamilton and Armstrong gave non-stop performances at the spearhead of the Irish attack and it was Hamilton who scored both Irish goals.

The match was played in intense heat and the stadium was less then one-third full as the Spanish fans opted out of a clash between the probable 'also rans' of Group D.

Hamilton opened the scoring in the 27th minute, when McCreery sent a sweeping crossfield pass to Armstrong, who beat two defenders before crossing to the head of Hamilton.

Austria equalized five minutes into the second half, after a Schachner shot was blasted against the post. Baumeister picked up the loose ball and hit it past Northern Ireland's replacement goalkeeper, Jim Platt, who was standing in for the injured Pat Jennings.

Six minutes later, Schachner had the ball in the Irish net again, but the goal was disallowed following an infringement. In the 67th minute, however, the Austrians took the lead for the first time when Hintermaier's 22-yard free-kick flew past Platt.

Hamilton and Armstrong kept on running and in the 74th minute, Hamilton brought Northern Ireland back into the game with a header from a well-judged lob from Jimmy Nicholl. It was a goal which eliminated Austria and kept Ireland's hopes alive. But what an uphill task they had against France.

Austria: Koncilia; Krauss, Obermayer, Pezzey, Pregersbauer(Hintermaier), Prohaska, Pichler, Baumeister, Schachner, Hagmayr(Welzl), Jurtin.
Scorers: Pezzey, Hintermaier
Northern Ireland: Platt; J.Nicholl, C.Nicholl, McIlroy, Nelson, M.O'Neill, McClelland, Armstrong, Hamilton, Whiteside(Brotherston), McCreery.
Scorer: Hamilton 2
Referee: Adolf Prokop (East Germany)

Billy Hamilton celebrates after giving Northern Ireland the lead over Austria.

Hamilton (extreme left) outjumps the Austrian defence to score one of his two headed goals.

FRANCE 4   NORTHERN IRELAND 1 (Half-time 1-0)

Vicente Calderón Stadium, Madrid, 4 July
Attendance: 37,000

PAT Jennings was back in the Northern Ireland goal but, alas, the Irish luck eventually ran out as France, with Rocheteau and Platini outstanding, outclassed them.

Rocheteau, reminiscent of vintage George Best, gave a great individual performance and scored two of France's four goals as the French were barely troubled by the Irish attack.

Seven minutes after Martin O'Neill had a goal disallowed for offside, the outstanding midfielder, Giresse, put France ahead in the 33rd minute when he received a ball pulled back to him by Platini. Two minutes after the break, Rocheteau ran at the defence from the half-way line before scoring a great solo goal. And after a brilliant piece of close control, the same player scored again in the 63rd minute after beating two defenders.

By the time Armstrong pulled one back for Ireland, after Ettori failed to hold a Whiteside cross in the 75th minute, the required victory was well out of their reach and France capped a comfortable win with a goal ten minutes from time, by the man who started it all, when Alain Giresse headed home a Tigana pass.

Northern Ireland went to Spain as complete outsiders but left having been one of the revelations of the tournament. They had given a better account of themselves than many expected.

France: Ettori; Amoros, Bossis, Janvion, Trésor, Genghini, Platini, Giresse, Tigana, Rocheteau (Couriol), Soler(Six).
Scorers: Giresse 2, Rocheteau 2
Northern Ireland: Jennings; J.Nicholl, C.Nicholl, Donaghy, McCreery(J.O'Neill), McIlroy, McClelland, M.O'Neill, Armstrong, Hamilton, Whiteside.
Scorer: Armstrong
Referee: Alojzi Jarguz (Poland)

Giancarlo Antognoni went off injured after Italy took the lead against Poland.

Semi-finals

ITALY 2   POLAND 0 (Half-time 1-0)

Nou Camp Stadium, Barcelona, 8 July
Attendance: 50,000

BOTH sides were missing key players, who were sidelined after receiving two cautions. Italy were without hard man Gentile, whilst Poland sorely missed the goalscoring talents of Boniek.

The Poles, like Brazil, could not cope with Italy, who had been transformed following Rossi's return to form and he completed his remarkable scoring run with two more goals to take his tally to five in two matches.

The teams had met in their opening group matches and that game ended goalless. But Italy had now found their true form and Poland, uncharacteristically, resorted to rough tactics as a substitute for their lack of fire-power.

Playing in temperatures well in excess of 100°F, Italy came close to scoring in the opening minutes and eventually found the net midway through the first half when Rossi, swivelling as he shot, turned in a free-kick. Five minutes later, Italy suffered the loss of Antognoni through injury.

Lato troubled the Italian defence as the Poles went looking for the equalizer and after 35 minutes, a Kupcewicz free-kick hit the woodwork. Poland came out for the second half

Rossi's second goal against the Poles, a 72nd-minute header from a far-post cross.

Italy take the lead over Poland as Rossi swivels to turn in a free-kick.

STATISTICS

Goalscorers:
6 — Paolo Rossi (Italy).
5 — Karl-Heinz Rummenigge (West Germany).
4 — Zbigniew Boniek (Poland), Zico (Brazil).
3 — Laszlo Kiss (Hungary), Alain Giresse (France), Paulo Roberto Falcão (Brazil), Gerry Armstrong (Northern Ireland).
2 — Marco Tardelli (Italy), Salah Assad (Algeria), Bryan Robson, Trevor Francis (both England), Pierre Littbarski, Klaus Fischer (both West Germany), Laszló Fazekas, Tibor Nyilasi, Gabor Pölöskei (all Hungary), Bernard Genghini, Michel Platini, Didier Six, Dominique Rocheteau (all France), Walter Schachner (Austria), Antonin Panenka (Czechoslovakia), Diego Maradona, Daniel Bertoni, Daniel Passarella (all Argentina), Socrates, Sergio Bernardino Serginho, Aleixo de Assis Eder (all Brazil), Billy Hamilton (Northern Ireland), John Wark (Scotland).
1 — Antonio Cabrini, Allesandro Altobelli, Bruno Conti, Francesco Graziani (all Italy), Rabah Madjer, Lakhdar Belloumi, Tedj Bensaoula (all Algeria), Erwin Vandenbergh, Ludo Coeck, Alex Czerniatynski (all Belgium), Paul Mariner (England), Guillermo La Rosa, Rubén Díaz (both Peru), Uwe Reinders, Horst Hrubesch, Paul Breitner (all West Germany), Jozsef Toth, Lázár Szentes, Jozsef Varga (all Hungary), Gérard Soler, Maxime Bossis, Marius Trésor, René Girard, Alain Couriol (all France), Janusz Kupcewicz, Stefan Majewski, Wlodzimierz Smolarek, Wlodzimierz Ciolek, Grzegorz Lato, Andrzej Szarmach, Andrzej Buncol (all Poland), Hans Krankl, Bruno Pezzey, Reinhold Hintermaier (all Austria), Ramírez Zapata (El Salvador), Gregoire M'Bida (Cameroon), Juan Carlos Letelier, Gustavo Moscoso, Miguel Angel Neira (all Chile), Osvaldo Ardíles, Ramón Díaz (both Argentina), Abdullah Al Buloushi, Faisad Al Dakhil (both Kuwait), Héctor Zelaya, Tony Laing (both Honduras), José Oscar Bernardi, Junior (both Brazil), Juanito, Jesús María Zamora, Roberto López-Ufarte, Enrique Saura (all Spain), Kenny Dalglish, Steve Archibald, John Robertson, David Narey, Joe Jordan, Graeme Souness (all Scotland), Ivan Gudelj, Vladimir Petrović (both Yugoslavia), Steve Wooddin, Steve Sumner (both New Zealand), Alexander Chivadze, Sergej Baltacha, Ramaz Shengelia, Yuri Gavrilov, Khoren Oganesian, Andrej Bal, Oleg Blokhin (all Soviet Union).

trailing by that lone Rossi goal and were soon on the attack. They were unfortunate not to have been awarded a penalty in the 58th minute when Smolarek appeared to have been brought down in the area.

In the 70th minute, Graziani was stretchered off following a foul and two minutes later, Rossi struck the decisive goal in a counter-attack as Poland pushed forward. He headed home a perfect far-post cross from Conti to inflict upon Poland their second semi-final defeat in eight years.

Once more Paolo Rossi was the inspiration behind the Italians, who had reached their fourth World Cup Final. Since his return to form, Italy had been transformed from a team looking incapable of scoring into possible world champions.

Italy: Zoff; Cabrini, Collovati, Bergomi, Scirea, Antognoni(Marini), Conti, Oriali, Tardelli, Rossi, Graziani(Altobelli).
Scorer: Rossi 2
Poland: Mlynarczyk; Dziuba, Zmuda, Janas, Majewski, Matysik, Kupcewicz, Buncol, Lato, Ciolek(Palasz), Smolarek(Kusto).
Referee: Juan Daniel Cardellino (Uruguay)

WEST GERMANY 3   FRANCE 3 a.e.t. (Half-time 1-1; 90 mins 1-1)
West Germany won 5-4 on penalties
Sánchez Pizjuán Stadium, Seville, 8 July
Attendance: 63,000

WEST Germany and France provided a feast of pulsating football in the best match of the 1982 World Cup, and one of the all-time great games which was reminiscent of the 1970 West Germany-Italy semi-final. It was a shame that penalties should eventually decide the winners and it was the first time that a match in the World Cup finals was decided in this way. World soccer's heavy fixture schedule made a play-off match a virtual impossibility.

Platini was in sparkling form for the French, who had already proved to be one of the most attractive teams of the tournament. Their one possible weak link was goalkeeper Ettori and it was his failure to hold a shot in the 18th minute which allowed Littbarski in to score the opening goal. But nine minutes later, France equalized from the penalty-spot after Rocheteau had been held back by Bernd Förster. Before placing the ball on the spot, Platini kissed it — then duly rammed it home.

There were no further goals during the next 63 minutes of normal time, although both sides had chances to win the match in the closing minutes and Stielike's clearance off the line kept Germany in the game.

Only two minutes into extra-time, Trésor volleyed home France's second goal from the edge of the penalty area after a Giresse free-kick. In the 98th minute, Giresse completed a fine move with a great shot from the edge of the 18-yard box to put France 3-1 ahead and seemingly on their way to the Final.

Manager Juup Derwall took a gamble when he sent on the half-fit Rummenigge just two minutes before France's third goal, but the German captain was to turn the game in their favour.

Rummenigge had been on the field for only six minutes when he pulled a goal back in the 102nd minute with a finely taken near-post effort from a Littbarski centre.

The French were now beginning to look tired and the Germans capitalized in the 17th minute of extra-time when Hrubesch headed back a centre for Fischer to score with an overhead kick. West Germany had equalized.

Referee Charles Corver of Holland signalled the end of 120 exciting minutes — and there was more to come with the penalty competition.

Giresse scored for France: Kaltz did likewise for West Germany. Amoros and Breitner each scored. Rocheteau put France ahead at 3-2 before Stielike shot straight at Ettori and France were in with a great chance — but then Didier Six missed from the spot. Littbarski levelled

Karl-Heinz Rummenigge's scores from a Littbarski cross to reduce the deficit to 3-2 against France. Rummenigge is partly hidden by the French number-five.

it at 3-3, Platini and Rummenigge made it 4-4. It was now sudden-death and Bossis' kick was saved by Schumacher. Horst Hrubesch had the responsibility of putting West Germany into the World Cup Final and kept his cool to do so.

The West German hero, though, was goalkeeper Harald Schumacher, but an hour earlier he was the villain and should not have been allowed to stay on the field after an appalling foul on Battiston which left the Frenchman unconscious for three minutes before being carried off. The French substitute had been on the pitch for only eight minutes and that incident was a turning point of the game. It was the only unsavoury incident in an exciting match in which, sadly, there had to be a loser.

West Germany: Schumacher; Kaltz, K-H.Förster, Stielike, Briegel(Rummenigge), B.Förster, Dremmler, Breitner, Littbarski, Magath(Hrubesch), Fischer.
Scorers: Littbarski, Rummenigge, Fischer.
France: Ettori; Amoros, Janvion, Bossis, Tigana, Trésor, Genghini(Battiston[Lopez]), Giresse, Platini, Rocheteau, Six.
Scorers: Platini (pen), Trésor, Giresse
Referee: Charles Corver (Holland)

Third place play-off
POLAND 3   FRANCE 2 (Half-time 2-1)

José Rico Perez Stadium, Alicante, 10 July
Attendance: 28,000

THE 1982 World Cup outshone recent competitions on two important counts: First, the opening match produced a goal and second, the third place play-off match was not boring.

Poland used their normal first-team squad and had Boniek back in action after his suspension. And what a difference he made. France, however, used the match to introduce new faces and made seven changes from the side that lost in the semi-final. The changes were necessary due to injury and exhaustion after such a mentally demanding game.

All the early pressure was on the Polish goal and a fierce left-foot shot from Girard went in off the post to put France ahead in the 13th minute. A minute later they should have extended their lead but Soler missed a good chance after doing the hard work in beating the defenders.

With five minutes to the half-time whistle, the Poles must have been relieved at being only one goal behind. But then came a remarkable transformation as they struck twice in three minutes. The first goal, in the 41st minute, came from the left boot of Szarmach after a great pass from Boniek. His shot, like Girard's, went in off the post.

Three minutes later, French goalkeeper, Castaneda, misjudged Kupcewicz's corner and Majewski was on hand to make it 2-1.

One minute the other side of the interval, Poland were further ahead when Kupcewicz's curling free-kick confused the goalkeeper. France kept coming forward and in the 73rd minute, Couriol latched on to a long pass from Tigana to make it 3-2, despite Polish claims that it was offside.

Poland hung on to repeat their best-ever World Cup final placing of third in 1974. Zmuda, Lato and Szarmach played in both winning teams.

Poland: Mlynarczyk; Dziuba, Janas, Zmuda, Majewski, Matysik(Wójcicki), Kupcewicz, Buncol, Lato, Boniek, Szarmach.
Scorers: Szarmach, Majewski, Kupcewicz
France: Castaneda; Amoros, Mahut, Trésor, Janvion(Lopez), Girard, Larios, Tigana(Six), Couriol, Soler, Bellone.
Scorers: Girard, Couriol
Referee: Antonio Garrido (Portugal)

Manny Kaltz evades Alessandro
Altobelli, the substitute who scored
Italy's third goal and then was
himself replaced by Franco Causio.

Paolo Rossi celebrates his opening
goal of the 1982 World Cup Final.

West Germany, the 1982 runners-
up. Back row (left to right):
Breitner, Stielike, Schumacher,
Briegel, Rummenigge, Fischer.
Front row: Littbarski, Bernd
Förster, Kaltz, Dremmler, Karl-
Heinz Förster.

Final

ITALY 3   WEST GERMANY 1 (Half-time 0-0)

Santiago Bernabéu Stadium, Madrid, 11 July
Attendance: 90,000

ITALY were the most improved team in the tournament and they were now clear favourites
to win their third world title. But they went into the Final without injured midfielder,
Antognoni, and when the game was only eight minutes old they suffered another set-back
when Graziani went off with an injured shoulder after colliding with Stielike.

To make matters even worse, Antonio Cabrini wrote his name into the World Cup record
books by becoming the first man to miss a penalty in a Final. His 25th-minute spot-kick
came as a result of Conti being brought down, but Cabrini's kick was wide of the goal.

Despite all these handicaps and set-backs, Italy were marginally better in a first half
dominated by fouls from both sides. There were arguably 20 bookable fouls in the first
hour, yet only two yellow cards were shown by the Brazilian official, Coelho, the first non-
European to referee a Final.

Both sides spent the first 45 minutes testing each other out as they lacked any real shape.
Some of the tackling, meanwhile, could only be described as shameful at times.

The second half started the same as the first, with a series of fouls, but the game came
to life after 57 minutes when Rossi scored his sixth goal of the tournament. He was one

Italy, the 1982 World Champions.
Back row (left to right): Zoff,
Graziani, Bergomi, Scirea,
Collovati, Gentile. Front row:
Conti, Rossi, Oriali, Cabrini,
Tardelli.

Paolo Rossi opens the scoring for Italy in the Final and takes his tally to six goals in his last three games, diving to head past Schumacher.

Above: Marco Tardelli clenches his fist after scoring the goal that put Italy 2-0 ahead. *Left:* Tardelli lets fly his brilliant left-foot shot, watched by Rossi (20). Schumacher stood no chance as the ball flew into the net.

Briegel's tackle on Conti (16) resulted in a penalty for Italy, but Cabrini became the first man to miss from the spot in a World Cup Final.

Karl-Heinz Rummenigge, no winning medal for him.

of three men who went for the ball from a Gentile cross and it was his head which got there first. Italy were one up.

After 68 minutes, Tardelli made it 2-0 with a brilliant left-foot shot from the edge of the penalty area. Nine minutes from time, the Italians made sure of victory when Altobelli hammered home a Conti cross from the right.

Paul Breitner pulled one back two minutes later, with a powerful shot from the edge of the box, but it was only a token reward as Italy went on to win their third world title, thanks to the efforts of Paolo Rossi who completely transformed the team once he had rediscovered his form.

Italy: Dino Zoff; Antonio Cabrini, Gaetano Scirea, Claudio Gentile, Fulvio Collovati, Gabriele Oriali, Giuseppe Bergomi, Marco Tardelli, Bruno Conti, Paolo Rossi, Francesco Graziani (Alessandro Altobelli[Franco Causio]).
Scorers: Rossi, Tardelli, Altobelli
West Germany: Harald Schumacher; Manfred Kaltz, Uli Stielike, Karl-Heinz Förster, Bernd Förster, Wolfgang Dremmler(Horst Hrubesch), Paul Breitner, Hans-Peter Briegel, Pierre Littbarski, Klaus Fischer, Karl-Heinz Rummenigge(Hans Müller).
Scorer: Breitner
Referee: Arnaldo César Coelho (Brazil)

Italy's third goal, scored by
Altobelli.

Dino Zoff cannot prevent Breitner's
consolation goal for West
Germany.

Italy's Marco Tardelli plants a kiss
on the World Cup trophy. Bruno
Conti follows him on the Italians'
lap of honour around the Santiago
Bernabéu Stadium.

Forty-year-old Dino Zoff played a major role in taking the World Cup to Italy after 40 years' absence. *Left:* Zoff makes a fine save from Fischer in the Final. *Above and below:* Zoff celebrates with the trophy.

MEN WHO MADE THE HEADLINES - 1986

Jan Ceulemans
(Belgium)

BELGIUM have long been over-shadowed by their more illustrious European neighbours, but in the 1980s they emerged as strong challengers and one of their stars, Jan Ceulemans, was undoubtedly of world class. Resisting pressure to move to Spanish or Italian football, Ceulemans has remained loyal to his homeland, where he was born in Lier in 1957. He won his first full cap in 1977 and is now heading towards the 100 mark, way past Paul Van Himst's Belgian record of 81. Ceulemans began as a striker — hardly surprising as he is 6ft 2in — but in recent years converted into a midfielder. He started his professional career with Lierse SK before a move to Club Brugge in 1978, for a then Belgian record fee of £250,000. Injury saw him miss Brugge's European Cup Final against Liverpool and the club has not appeared in a European final since, although he has won three Belgian League medals and a Cup-winners' medal. When Belgium reached the 1980 European Championship Final, he was one of the tournament's outstanding players. Ceulemans was in both the 1982 and 1986 World Cup squads but Belgium did not live up to expectations, although he was again outstanding. Ceulemans was Belgian Footballer of the Year in 1980, 1985 and 1988.

Michel Platini
(France)

MICHEL Platini, grandson of an Italian immigrant, was born at Joeuf in 1955 and began with Nancy, where his father was coach. He played in the 1976 Olympics and that year made his full international debut, against Czechoslovakia. In 1979, after scoring 98 goals in seven years with Nancy, Platini moved to AS Saint-Etienne. In 1982, Juventus paid £1.2 million for him and his goals helped them win three Italian titles in four years as well as European honours. He skippered France to the 1984 European Championship, his nine goals, including two hat-tricks, taking him past Fontaine's overall French record. In 1985 he won his third successive European Footballer of the Year award and converted the penalty which beat Liverpool in the ill-fated European Cup Final. Platini played in three World Cups from 1978. In 1982 he helped France to fourth place and in 1986, they finished third and Platini at last showed his true class. In August 1987 he played for the Rest of the World against the Football League at Wembley and then retired, after 72 caps and 41 goals, to concentrate on his vast business empire. However, after France failed to qualify for the 1990 World Cup, Platini took over as team manager. It was his first coaching job in football.

Diego Maradona
(Argentina)

DIEGO Armando Maradona, now regarded as the world's greatest footballer was born at Lanus on 30 October 1960 and played for Los Cebollitos (The Little Onions) before joining Argentinos Juniors. At 16 he was Argentina's youngest-ever international when he played against Hungary. Two years later he captained the World Youth Cup winners and was soon transferred to Boca Juniors for £1 million. South American Footballer of the Year in 1979 and 1980, in 1982 Maradona joined Barcelona for a world record £5 million. His World Cup debut was on his new home ground at the Nou Camp Stadium but his tournament ended with a sending-off against Brazil. In his first season at Barcelona, they won the League, League Cup and Super Cup. Two years later, another world record fee of £6.9 million took him to success-starved Napoli and in 1987 they won a League and Cup double. A year earlier Maradona had captained Argentina to a second World Cup win. He was involved in a controversial goal against England but also gave some majestic displays, weaving his way through tightly-packed defences. Maradona won a UEFA Cup-winners' medal in 1989 and in 1990, despite early-season differences, he guided Napoli to a second League title. In 1990, although not the great player of four years earlier, he again skippered Argentina to the Final but failed to become the first captain to lift the World Cup twice.

'The Hand of God'
Mexico 1986

Diego Maradona, the man whose name became synonymous with the 1986 World Cup.

THE 13th World Cup was awarded to Mexico, who thus became the first country to host the competition on two occasions. However, the Mexicans were selected only as replacement hosts after the original choice, Colombia, announced in 1983 that they could no longer afford to stage soccer's greatest tournament.

After Colombia's withdrawal, Brazil, Canada, the United States and Mexico all staked claims to be the 1986 hosts. Canada and the United States were discounted because of the lack of World Cup tradition, but Brazil and Mexico were likely candidates, having both staged successful events in the past. But Brazil suddenly dropped out of the running. The reasons were never made clear and were certainly hard to comprehend, considering that FIFA president João Havelange was from Brazil.

The series was organized by Televisa, a radio and television network whose president was 57-year-old Amilio Azcarraga, a friend of Havelange. One of Televisa's senior executives was Guillermo Canedo, president of the World Cup organizing committee and a vice-president of FIFA. The public were left to deduce the machinations behind it all.

Azcarraga had persuaded the new Mexican president, Miguel de la Madrid Hurtado, that the nation's struggling economy needed a prestige event like the World Cup and he agreed. But Mexico was going through its worst financial crisis for 50 years and was unable to pay its foreign debts, whilst unemployment was at a critical level.

Their problems did not end there. Eight months before the first ball was kicked, an earthquake devastated Mexico City and three coastal states, killing an estimated 25,000 people. It was an alarming situation for the players, supporters and media representatives who were scheduled to make the trip to Mexico. Indeed, there was speculation that a last-minute replacement host nation would have to be found, but FIFA were advised immediately after the disaster that none of the designated grounds had suffered any damage and consequently played down the rumours and fears. Thereafter they were adamant that the 13th World Cup would remain with Mexico.

The South Americans, especially Brazil and Argentina, were much-fancied teams, while the best European challenge seemed to come from France and the new European pace-setters, Denmark. Poland, Hungary and the Soviet Union were also strong entrants from the Eastern bloc, and Algeria qualified for the second time thus showing that the gap between the leading nations and those from the Third World was narrowing all the time.

Canada, Iraq and Denmark were the only debutants but none disgraced themselves on football's finest stage, which produced one of the strongest gatherings of footballers for a long time.

The draw, which took place in Mexico City on 15 December 1985, saw the 24 teams seeded, with six nations in each of four categories. Hosts Mexico, Argentina, West Germany, France, Poland and Brazil constituted the top-seeded group.

Mexican army tanks were in evidence amidst fears of political violence during the tournament.

Whilst the draw brought together four teams in each of six groups, there was yet another significant change in format because the second phase reverted to a knock-out tournament. The top two in each group qualified for the knock-out stage, together with the four best third-placed teams. Therefore, in four of the groups, only one team would be eliminated.

To ensure there would be no repeat of the West Germany-Austria farce of 1982, the final matches in each group were played simultaneously, to ensure that the results could not be contrived.

The Mexican stadiums were ideal for such a major event, with the Azteca Stadium in Mexico City still a magnificent showpiece. The organizers reckoned that its 100,000-plus capacity could be emptied in only 12 minutes if needed. Although the grounds were up to standard, the altitude was to become a big problem for many teams and again many matches were played at mid-day to allow for television schedules. Consequently the heat posed problems.

Because of its massive unemployment, many Mexicans could not afford to attend live matches, but television coverage was ample and in poorer districts of Mexico City, giant TV screens were installed. They also served as a deterrent to those seeking to gain admission without a ticket.

To add to Mexico's seemingly never-ending problems, political or otherwise, the United States Senate was told of drug-trafficking amongst top Mexican government officials, just weeks before the start of the World Cup. This led to angry denials by the Mexicans and a strained relationship between the two nations. And to make matters even worse, a couple of weeks before the start of the tournament, bombs were found outside the US Embassy and one of Mexico City's top hotels. Suddenly there were fears of a repeat of the Munich Olympic massacre.

With all these problems, Mexico **had** to provide a football spectacle to restore some of its pride and credibility. They did not do a bad job, although some aspects of the TV coverage left a lot to be desired and technicians from other countries were eventually called in to help iron out the problems.

The opening ceremony was grand and colourful, even if the Mexican fans drowned speeches by their political leaders as a way of expressing their dissent.

Lighter side of the World Cup – Pique, the mascot of the 1986 finals.

1986 Qualifying Competition

A RECORD 121 teams entered the 13th World Cup by the time the closing date for entries arrived in October 1983. Hosts Mexico and holders Italy were exempt but the other 119 teams went into the draw for the qualifying matches which got underway on 2 May 1984, when Cyprus lost 2-1 at home to Austria. Ironically, neither of these two teams qualified for the final stages.

Because of withdrawals, the number of teams who played in the qualifying matches was 110 and, for one reason or another, the following teams withdrew: Barbados, Grenada, Oman, Lebanon, Iran, Lesotho, Niger and Toga. Jamaica were expelled by FIFA.

Europe had the most representatives in the qualifiers, with 32 nations battling for final places. Four of the seven European groups each provided two finalists, whilst the remaining three sent only one team to Mexico. However, there was a lifeline for the second-placed teams in those three groups because they were given a second chance of qualifying via play-offs. Belgium and Scotland duly took their chances.

Belgium lost out on automatic qualification after finishing second to Poland in Group One. They had the same points and identical goal-difference but Poland had scored three more goals and automatically qualified for the finals. Belgium, however, beat Holland in a play-off to earn a trip to Mexico.

West Germany scored 22 goals in reaching their ninth successive finals and were joined by Portugal, who qualified for the second time. Their only other appearance was in those great days of Eusébio, during the 1966 World Cup in England.

When they lost 1-0 at home to Portugal on 16 October 1985, it was the first time the West Germans had lost a qualifying match in the World Cup.

England and Northern Ireland were paired together in Group Three and both qualified. Northern Ireland lost the group's opening game to Finland. It was the Finns' first international win for 23 matches, but the Irish got into winning ways in their next match, at home to Romania. The game was watched by FIFA president João Havelange, who opened a new stand at Windsor Park.

England had some big wins and remained unbeaten in their eight qualifying matches, the only European side to go to Mexico without a defeat. Bryan Robson was top scorer with five goals and scored a hat-trick in their 8-0 win in Turkey, — England's biggest away win for 24 years.

A Gary Lineker hat-trick in the 5-0 home win over Turkey secured England's place in the finals and on the same night, Northern Ireland kept their hopes alive with a 1-0 victory in Romania, thanks to a Jimmy Quinn goal. A goalless draw at Wembley the following month was good enough to guarantee them a place in the finals.

Bulgaria and France finished top of Group Four with the same records but the French just edged in with a slightly better goal-difference. Both sides qualified but France, the reigning European champions, had to get at least a point off Yugoslavia in their last match to book their place. Two goals from Michel Platini in front of 50,000 Paris fans made sure.

Successive defeats by Hungary, at home, and Austria cost Holland dearly and they finished three points adrift of the Magyars, who qualified for their ninth finals. But Holland were not completely out; they had to play Belgium in a two-legged play-off. A 1-0 away defeat was not too ominous for the Dutch but Belgium's one goal in Holland's 2-1 win in the return match was good enough to send them through to Mexico on the away-goals rule, whilst Holland failed to reach the finals for the second successive tournament.

Denmark had been earning a reputation as an attractive side and, despite losing to Switzerland, headed Group Six, one point ahead of the Soviet Union. Their leading scorer, Elkjaer-Larsen, scored eight goals. The Republic of Ireland, who had a good 1-0 win over the Soviets, briefly topped this group, as did Switzerland, but in the end the two strongest teams emerged.

The final European group contained the two remaining British representatives, Scotland and Wales. But, despite being only a four-team group, neither topped the table. That honour belonged to Spain, runners-up in the 1984 European Championship.

Scotland played inconsistent football. Mo Johnston scored twice in nine minutes as they beat Spain 3-1, but the Scots then lost at home to Wales, who won with an Ian Rush goal. It was Scotland's first home defeat by Wales since 1951 and their first home defeat in the World Cup qualifiers since losing to Poland in 1965. Wales, though, had damaged their chances of qualifying after an embarrassing defeat by Iceland.

By the time Wales and Scotland met for their last match at Cardiff, both had a chance of booking an automatic place in the finals. But a draw at Ninian Park ultimately meant that Wales were out and Scotland went through to a play-off match against Australia. The match in Cardiff, however, was marred by the death of Scotland manager Jock Stein who collapsed and died in the tunnel on the way back to the dressing-room.

South America's three past winners, Uruguay, Brazil and Argentina, all qualified but not with the ease they expected. Brazil, after winning away at Bolivia and Paraguay, were held to draws at home by the same two teams. Uruguay, the reigning South American champions, had to beat Chile in their final match to gain an automatic place in the finals. Chile would have booked that place with a draw, but a 2-1 win was good enough for the former champions.

The second and third-placed clubs in the South American Group One, plus the runners-up in the other two groups, then engaged in a knock-out tournament to find one more South American representative. That place went to Paraguay, who reached their first finals since 1958.

The African matches were divided into their usual host of sub-groups and there was also the usual quota of withdrawals before the remaining teams, after the first round, engaged in a knock-out tournament designed to find two qualifiers, which turned out to be Morocco and Algeria, both stalwarts of recent World Cup finals and two teams who had shocked a lot of the more powerful soccer nations.

Asia's qualifying groups were even more complicated with sub-groups 2A, 2B and so on. But at the end of 64 matches, South Korea qualified for their first finals since 1954 and Iraq reached their first-ever finals. The Koreans were the first Asian side to appear in two finals. Iraq did well to reach the finals because they could not play home matches due to the political situation with Iran. But spare a thought for China. They were eliminated in the first round after finishing second in their group behind Hong Kong – yet they scored a staggering 23 goals.

South Korea's coach, Kim Sung-nam, went into the finals with complete optimism. He said that his side would be the big surprise of the finals and feared no one. "Fame doesn't win games," he added. Whilst they failed to progress beyond the first phase, his optimism was not unfounded because they were not disgraced and caused Argentina and Italy a few problems.

Canada, coached by the former England goalkeeper Tony Waiters, reached their first finals after winning the

CONCACAF group ahead of Honduras and Costa Rica. Their fellow member of the Commonwealth, Australia, topped the Oceania/Asia group. But they did not gain automatic entry into the finals, having instead to meet Scotland over two legs to decide which nation made the trip.

Scotland won the first leg 2-0 in Glasgow, with Frank McAvennie scoring on his international debut. Two weeks later, a goalless draw in Melbourne was good enough to take Scotland into their fourth successive finals. It was the last match of a qualifying competition, which had started over 18 months earlier.

Results

EUROPE

Group One

17 Oct 1984 *Brussels*	Belgium 3	Albania 1
17 Oct 1984 *Zabrze*	Poland............3	Greece 1
31 Oct 1984 *Mielec*	Poland............2	Albania 2
19 Dec 1984 *Athens*	Greece 0	Belgium 0
22 Dec 1984 *Tiranë*	Albania...........2	Belgium 0
27 Feb 1985 *Athens*	Greece 2	Albania 0
27 Mar 1985 *Brussels*	Belgium 2	Greece 0
1 Mar 1985 *Brussels*	Belgium 2	Poland............0
19 May 1985 *Athens*	Greece 1	Poland............4
30 May 1985 *Tiranë*	Albania...........0	Poland............1
11 Sep 1985 *Chorzów*	Poland............0	Belgium 0
30 Oct 1985 *Tiranë*	Albania...........1	Greece 1

Final Table

	P	W	D	L	F	A	Pts	
Poland	6	3	2	1	10	6	8	**Poland qualified for**
Belgium	6	3	2	1	7	3	8	**Finals, Belgium qualified**
Albania	6	1	2	3	6	9	4	**for European play-off**
Greece	6	1	2	3	5	10	4	**against the runners-up in**
								Group Five (Holland)

Group Two

23 May 1984 *Norrköping*	Sweden 4	Malta 0
12 Sep 1984 *Stockholm*	Sweden 0	Portugal..........1
14 Oct 1984 *Oporto*	Portugal.........2	Czechoslovakia ..1
17 Oct 1984 *Cologne*	West Germany...2	Sweden 0
31 Oct 1984 *Prague*	Czechoslovakia ..4	Malta 0
14 Nov 1984 *Lisbon*	Portugal..........1	Sweden 3
16 Dec 1984 *Valletta*	Malta 2	West Germany...3
10 Feb 1985 *Valletta*	Malta 1	Portugal.........3
24 Feb 1985 *Lisbon*	Portugal..........1	West Germany...2
27 Mar 1985 *Saarbrücken*	West Germany...6	Malta 0
21 Apr 1985 *Valletta*	Malta 0	Czechoslovakia ..0
1 May 1985 *Prague*	Czechoslovakia ..1	West Germany...5
5 Jun 1985 *Stockholm*	Sweden 2	Czechoslovakia ..0
25 Sep 1985 *Stockholm*	Sweden 2	West Germany...2
25 Sep 1985 *Prague*	Czechoslovakia ..1	Portugal..........0
12 Oct 1985 *Lisbon*	Portugal.........3	Malta 2
16 Oct 1985 *Prague*	Czechoslovakia ..2	Sweden 1
16 Oct 1985 *Stuttgart*	West Germany...0	Portugal..........1
17 Nov 1985 *Munich*	West Germany...2	Czechoslovakia ..2
17 Nov 1985 *Valletta*	Malta 1	Sweden 2

Final Table

	P	W	D	L	F	A	Pts	
W.Germany	8	5	2	1	22	9	12	
Portugal	8	5	0	3	12	10	10	
Sweden	8	4	1	3	14	9	9	**West Germany and**
Czechoslovakia	8	3	2	3	11	12	8	**Portugal qualified**
Malta	8	0	1	7	6	25	1	

Group Three

27 May 1984 *Pori*	Finland...........1	N. Ireland 0
12 Sep 1984 *Belfast*	N. Ireland 3	Romania 2
17 Oct 1984 *London*	England 5	Finland 0
31 Oct 1984 *Antalya*	Turkey............1	Finland 2
14 Nov 1984 *Belfast*	N. Ireland 2	Finland 1
14 Nov 1984 *Istanbul*	Turkey............0	England 8
27 Feb 1985 *Belfast*	N. Ireland 0	England 0
3 Apr 1985 *Craiova*	Romania 3	Turkey............0
1 May 1985 *Belfast*	N. Ireland 2	Turkey............0
1 May 1985 *Bucharest*	Romania 0	England 0
22 May 1985 *Helsinki*	Finland...........1	England 1
6 Jun 1985 *Helsinki*	Finland...........1	Romania 1
28 Aug 1985 *Timişoara*	Romania 2	Finland 0
11 Sep 1985 *İzmir*	Turkey............0	N. Ireland 0
11 Sep 1985 *London*	England 1	Romania 1
25 Sep 1985 *Tampere*	Finland...........1	Turkey............0
16 Oct 1985 *Bucharest*	Romania 0	N. Ireland 1
16 Oct 1985 *London*	England 5	Turkey............0
13 Nov 1985 *London*	England 0	N. Ireland 0
13 Nov 1985 *İzmir*	Turkey............1	Romania 3

Final Table

	P	W	D	L	F	A	Pts	
England	8	4	4	0	21	2	12	
N. Ireland	8	4	2	2	8	5	10	**England and**
Romania	8	3	3	2	12	7	9	**Northern Ireland**
Finland	8	3	2	3	7	12	8	**qualified**
Turkey	8	0	1	7	2	24	1	

Group Four

29 Sep 1984 *Belgrade*	Yugoslavia 0	Bulgaria 0
13 Oct 1984 *Luxembourg*	Luxembourg.....0	France 4
20 Oct 1984 *Leipzig*	East Germany ...2	Yugoslavia 3
17 Nov 1984 *Esch*	Luxembourg.....0	East Germany ...5
21 Nov 1984 *Paris*	France 1	Bulgaria 0
5 Dec 1984 *Sofia*	Bulgaria 4	Luxembourg.....0
8 Dec 1984 *Paris*	France 2	East Germany ...0
27 Mar 1985 *Zenica*	Yugoslavia 1	Luxembourg.....0
3 Apr 1985 *Sarajevo*	Yugoslavia 0	France 0
6 Apr 1985 *Sofia*	Bulgaria 1	East German 0
1 May 1985 *Luxembourg*	Luxembourg.....0	Yugoslavia 1
2 May 1985 *Sofia*	Bulgaria 2	France 0
18 May 1985 *Babelsberg*	East Germany ...3	Luxembourg.....1
1 Jun 1985 *Sofia*	Bulgaria 2	Yugoslavia 1
11 Sep 1985 *Leipzig*	East Germany ...2	France 0
25 Sep 1985 *Luxembourg*	Luxembourg.....1	Bulgaria 3
28 Sep 1985 *Belgrade*	Yugoslavia 1	East Germany ...2
30 Oct 1985 *Paris*	France 6	Luxembourg.....0
16 Nov 1985 *Paris*	France 2	Yugoslavia 0
16 Nov 1985 *Karl-Marx Stadt*	East Germany ...2	Bulgaria 1

Final Table

	P	W	D	L	F	A	Pts	
France	8	5	1	2	15	4	11	
Bulgaria	8	5	1	2	13	5	11	
E.Germany	8	5	0	3	16	9	10	**France and**
Yugoslavia	8	3	2	3	7	8	8	**Bulgaria qualified**
Luxembourg	8	0	0	8	2	27	0	

Group Five

2 May 1984 *Nicosia*	Cyprus............1	Austria............2
26 Sep 1984 *Budapest*	Hungary 3	Austria............1
17 Oct 1984 *Rotterdam*	Holland 1	Hungary 2
14 Nov 1984 *Vienna*	Austria............1	Holland 0
17 Nov 1984 *Limassol*	Cyprus............1	Hungary 2
23 Dec 1984 *Nicosia*	Cyprus............0	Holland 1
27 Feb 1985 *Amsterdam*	Holland 7	Cyprus............1
3 Apr 1985 *Budapest*	Hungary 2	Cyprus............0
17 Apr 1985 *Vienna*	Austria............0	Hungary 3
1 May 1985 *Rotterdam*	Holland 1	Austria............1
7 May 1985 *Graz*	Austria............4	Cyprus............0
14 May 1985 *Budapest*	Hungary 0	Holland 1

Final Table

	P	W	D	L	F	A	Pts	
Hungary	6	5	0	1	12	4	10	**Hungary qualified for**
Holland	6	3	1	2	11	5	7	**Finals, Holland qualified**
Austria	6	3	1	2	9	8	7	**for European play-off**
Cyprus	6	0	0	6	3	18	0	**against runners-up in**
								Group One (Belgium)

Group Six

12 Sep 1984 *Dublin*	Rep of Ireland ...1	Soviet Union 0
12 Sep 1984 *Oslo*	Norway..........0	Switzerland 1

26 Sep 1984 *Copenhagen*	Denmark	1	Norway	0
10 Oct 1984 *Oslo*	Norway	1	Soviet Union	1
17 Oct 1984 *Oslo*	Norway	1	Rep of Ireland	...0
17 Oct 1984 *Berne*	Switzerland	1	Denmark	0
14 Nov 1984 *Copenhagen*	Denmark	3	Rep of Ireland	...0
17 Apr 1985 *Berne*	Switzerland	2	Soviet Union	2
1 May 1985 *Dublin*	Rep of Ireland	...0	Norway	0
2 May 1985 *Moscow*	Soviet Union	4	Switzerland	0
2 Jun 1985 *Dublin*	Rep of Ireland	...3	Switzerland	0
5 Jun 1985 *Copenhagen*	Denmark	4	Soviet Union	2
11 Sep 1985 *Berne*	Switzerland	0	Rep of Ireland	...0
25 Sep 1985 *Moscow*	Soviet Union	1	Denmark	0
9 Oct 1985 *Copenhagen*	Denmark	0	Switzerland	0
16 Oct 1985 *Oslo*	Norway	1	Denmark	5
19 Oct 1985 *Moscow*	Soviet Union	2	Rep of Irealnd	...0
30 Oct 1985 *Moscow*	Soviet Union	1	Norway	0
13 Nov 1985 *Lucerne*	Switzerland	1	Norway	1
13 Nov 1985 *Dublin*	Rep of Ireland	...1	Denmark	4

Final Table

	P	W	D	L	F	A	Pts	
Denmark	8	5	1	2	17	6	11	
Soviet Union	8	4	2	2	13	8	10	**Denmark and**
Switzerland	8	2	4	2	5	10	8	**Soviet Union**
Rep of Ireland	8	2	2	4	5	10	6	**qualified**
Norway	8	1	3	4	4	10	5	

Group Seven

12 Sep 1984 *Reykjavík*	Iceland	1	Wales	0
17 Oct 1984 *Seville*	Spain	3	Wales	0
17 Oct 1984 *Glasgow*	Scotland	3	Iceland	0
14 Nov 1984 *Glasgow*	Scotland	3	Spain	1
14 Nov 1984 *Cardiff*	Wales	2	Iceland	1
27 Feb 1985 *Seville*	Spain	1	Scotland	0
27 Mar 1985 *Glasgow*	Scotland	0	Wales	1
30 Apr 1985 *Wrexham*	Wales	3	Spain	0
28 May 1985 *Reykjavík*	Iceland	0	Scotland	1
12 Jun 1985 *Reykjavík*	Iceland	1	Spain	2
10 Sep 1985 *Cardiff*	Wales	1	Scotland	1
25 Sep 1985 *Seville*	Spain	2	Iceland	1

Teammates Steve Nicol (left) and Ian Rush, of English club giants Liverpool, on opposite sides as Scotland and Wales clash in a World Cup qualifying match in Cardiff. The Welsh had earlier scored a surprise victory in Glasgow but the 1-1 draw in the return game meant that they failed to capitalize and were eliminated. Spain topped the group after beating Iceland and Scotland eventually went through after beating Oceania winners, Australia, in a play-off.

Final Table

	P	W	D	L	F	A	Pts	
Spain	6	4	0	2	9	8	8	**Spain qualified for Finals,**
Scotland	6	3	1	2	8	4	7	**Scotland qualified for**
Wales	6	3	1	2	7	6	7	**play-off against the**
Iceland	6	1	0	5	4	10	2	**Oceania winners (Australia)**

European Play-off

16 Oct 1985 *Brussels*	Belgium	1	Netherlands	0
20 Nov 1985 *Rotterdam*	Netherlands	2	Belgium	1

Belgium qualified (on away goals rule)

SOUTH AMERICA

Group One

26 May 1985 *Bogotá*	Colombia	1	Peru	0
26 May 1985 *San Cristóbal*	Venezuela	2	Argentina	3
2 Jun 1985 *Bogotá*	Colombia	1	Argentina	3
2 Jun 1985 *San Cristóbal*	Venezuela	0	Peru	1
9 Jun 1985 *Buenos Aires*	Argentina	3	Venezuela	0
9 Jun 1985 *Lima*	Peru	0	Colombia	0
16 Jun 1985 *Buenos Aires*	Argentina	1	Colombia	0
16 Jun 1985 *Lima*	Peru	4	Venezuela	1
23 Jun 1985 *Lima*	Peru	1	Argentina	0
23 Jun 1985 *San Cristóbal*	Venezuela	2	Colombia	2
30 Jun 1985 *Buenos Aires*	Argentina	2	Peru	2
30 Jun 1985 *Bogotá*	Colombia	2	Venezuela	0

Final Table

	P	W	D	L	F	A	Pts	
Argentina	6	4	1	1	12	6	9	**Argentina qualified for**
Peru	6	3	2	1	8	4	8	**Finals, Peru and**
Colombia	6	2	2	2	6	6	6	**Colombia qualified for**
Venezuela	6	0	1	5	5	15	1	**South American play-offs**

The Argentinian team that battled it out with Peru to reach the finals. Back row (left to right): Passarella, Clausen, Garré, Trossero, Russo, Fillol. Front row: Burruchaga, Giusti, Pasculli, Maradona, Valdano.

Group Two

3 Mar 1985 *Quito*	Ecuador	1	Chile	1
10 Mar 1985 *Montevideo*	Uruguay	2	Ecuador	1
17 Mar 1985 *Santiago*	Chile	6	Ecuador	2
24 Mar 1985 *Santiago*	Chile	2	Uruguay	0
31 Mar 1985 *Quito*	Ecuador	0	Uruguay	2
7 Apr 1985 *Montevideo*	Uruguay	2	Chile	1

Final Table

	P	W	D	L	F	A	Pts	
Uruguay	4	3	0	1	6	4	6	**Uruguay qualified**
Chile	4	2	1	1	10	5	5	**for Finals, Chile**
Equador	4	0	1	3	4	11	1	**qualified for South American play-offs**

Uruguay were the first South Americans to qualify. This team beat Chile. Back row (left to right): Rodríguez, Acevedo, Montelongo, Bossio, Gutiérrez, Diogo, unknown. Front row: Aguilera, Barrios, Francescoli, Santin, Cabrera, trainer.

Group Three

26 May 1985 *Santa Cruz*	Bolivia............1	Paraguay 1	
2 Jun 1985 *Santa Cruz*	Bolivia............0	Brazil 2	
9 Jun 1985 *Asunción*	Paraguay 3	Bolivia 0	
16 Jun 1985 *Asunción*	Paraguay 0	Brazil 2	
23 Jun 1985 *Río de Janeiro*	Brazil 1	Paraguay 1	
30 Jun 1985 *Río de Janeiro*	Brazil 1	Bolivia............1	

Final Table

	P	W	D	L	F	A	Pts	
Brazil	4	2	2	0	6	2	6	**Brazil qualified for Finals,**
Paraguay	4	1	2	1	5	4	4	**Paraguay qualified for**
Bolivia	4	0	2	2	2	7	2	**South American play-offs**

South American Play-offs

27 Oct 1985 *Asunción*	Paraguay 3	Colombia 0	
3 Nov 1985 *Cali*	Colombia 2	Paraguay 1	

Paraguay qualified for final

27 Oct 1985 *Santiago*	Chile..............4	Peru...............2	
3 Nov 1985 *Lima*	Peru...............0	Chile..............1	

Chile qualified for final

Final

10 Nov 1985 *Asunción*	Paraguay 3	Chile..............0	
17 Nov 1985 *Santiago*	Chile..............2	Paraguay 2	

Paraguay qualified

CONCACAF
(Central & North America)

Canada qualified for Round Two following the expulsion of Jamaica

Round One – Group One

29 Jul 1984 *San Salvador*	El Salvador.......5	Puerto Rico 0	
5 Aug 1984 *San Juan*	Puerto Rico 0	El Salvador.......3	

El Salvador qualified for Round Two

29 Sep 1985 *Curaçao*	Nethlds Antilles 0	United States 0	
6 Oct 1984 *St Louis*	United States 4	Nethlds Antilles 0	

United States qualified for Round Two

Round One – Group Two

Costa Rica qualified for Round Two following the withdrawal of Barbados. Guatemala had a walk-over into Round Two.

15 Jun 1984 *Colón*	Panamá 0	Honduras 3	
24 Jun 1984 *Tegucigalpa*	Honduras 1	Panama 0	

Honduras qualified for Round Two

Round One – Group Three

Trinidad & Tobago qualified for Round Two following the withdrawal of Granada

4 Aug 1984 *Port au Prince*	Antigua 0	Haiti..............4	
7 Aug 1984 *Port au Prince*	Haiti...............1	Antigua 2	

Haiti qualified for Round Two

15 Aug 1984 *Paramaribo*	Surinam 1	Guyana...........0	
29 Aug 1984 *Georgetown*	Guyana...........1	Surinam 1	

Surinam qualified for Round Two

Round Two – Group One

24 Feb 1985 *San Salvador*	Surinam 0	El Salvador.......3	
27 Feb 1985 *San Salvador*	El Salvador.......3	Surinam 0	
3 Mar 1985 *Tegucigalpa*	Surinam 1	Honduras 1	
6 Mar 1985 *Tegucigalpa*	Honduras 2	Surinam 1	
10 Mar 1985 *San Salvador*	El Salvador.......1	Honduras 2	
14 Mar 1985 *Tegucigalpa*	Honduras 0	El Salvador.......0	

Final Table

	P	W	D	L	F	A	Pts	
Honduras	4	2	2	0	5	3	6	**Honduras qualified**
El Salvador	4	2	1	1	7	2	5	**for CONCACAF**
Surinam	4	0	1	3	2	9	1	**Final**

Round Two – Group Two

13 Apr 1985 *Vancouver*	Canada 2	Haiti..............0	
20 Apr 1985 *Vancouver*	Canada 2	Guatemala 1	
26 Apr 1985 *Port au Prince*	Haiti..............0	Guatemala 1	
5 May 1985 *Guatemala*	Guatemala 1	Canada 1	
8 May 1985 *Port au Prince*	Haiti..............0	Canada 2	
15 May 1985 *Guatemala*	Guatemala 4	Haiti..............0	

Final Table

	P	W	D	L	F	A	Pts	
Canada	4	3	1	0	7	2	7	**Canada qualified**
Guatemala	4	2	1	1	7	3	5	**for CONCACAF**
Haiti	4	0	0	4	0	9	0	**Final**

Round Two – Group Three

24 Apr 1985 *San José*	Trinidad & Tobago 0	Costa Rica 3	
28 Apr 1985 *San José*	Costa Rica 1	Trinidad & Tobago 1	
15 May 1985 *St Louis*	Trinidad & Tobago 1	United States 2	
19 May 1985 *Los Angeles*	United States 1	Trinidad & Tobago 0	
26 May 1985 *San José*	Costa Rica 1	United States 1	
31 May 1985 *Los Angeles*	United States 0	Costa Rica 1	

Final Table

	P	W	D	L	F	A	Pts	
Costa Rica	4	2	2	0	6	2	6	**Costa Rica**
United States	4	2	1	1	4	3	5	**qualified for**
Trinidad & Tobago	4	0	1	3	2	7	1	**CONCACAF Final**

Final

10 Aug 1985 *San José*	Costa Rica 2	Honduras 2	
17 Aug 1985 *Toronto*	Canada 1	Costa Rica 1	
25 Aug 1985 *Tegucigalpa*	Honduras 0	Canada 1	
1 Sep 1985 *San José*	Costa Rica 0	Canada 0	
8 Sep 1985 *Tegucigalpa*	Honduras 3	Costa Rica 1	
14 Sep 1985 *St Johns*	Canada 2	Honduras 1	

Final Table

	P	W	D	L	F	A	Pts	
Canada	4	2	2	0	4	2	6	**Canada qualified**
Honduras	4	1	1	2	6	6	3	
Costa Rica	4	0	3	1	4	6	3	

ASIA

Round One – Group 1A

Oman withdrew

12 Apr 1985 *Riyadh*	Saudi Arabia.....0	Utd Arab Emirates 0	
19 Apr 1985 *Dubai*	Utd Arab Emirates 1	Saudi Arabia.....0	

United Arab Emirates qualified for Round Two

Round One – Group 1B

Lebanon withdrew

15 Mar 1985 *Amman*	Jordan............1	Qatar 0	
29 Mar 1985 *Amman*	Jordan............2	Iraq 3	
5 Mar 1985 *Doha*	Qatar 3	Iraq 0	
12 Apr 1985 *Doha*	Qatar 2	Jordan 0	
19 Apr 1985 *Kuwait*	Iraq 2	Jordan 0	
5 May 1985 *Calcutta*	Iraq 2	Qatar 1	

Final Table

	P	W	D	L	F	A	Pts	
Iraq	4	3	0	1	7	6	6	**Iraq qualified for**
Qatar	4	2	0	2	6	3	4	**Round Two**
Jordan	4	1	0	3	3	7	2	

Round One – Group 2A

22 Mar 1985 *Damascus*	Syria 1	Kuwait............0	
29 Mar 1985 *Sana'a'*	North Yemen 0	Syria 1	
5 Apr 1985 *Kuwait*	Kuwait...........5	North Yemen 0	
12 Apr 1985 *Kuwait*	Kuwait...........0	Syria 0	
19 Apr 1985 *Damascus*	Syria 3	North Yemen 0	
26 Apr 1985 *Sana'a'*	North Yemen 1	Kuwait............3	

Final Table

	P	W	D	L	F	A	Pts	
Syria	4	3	1	0	5	0	7	**Syria qualified for**
Kuwait	4	2	1	1	8	2	5	**Round Two**
North Yemen	4	0	0	4	1	12	0	

Round One - Group 2B

Iran withdrew
29 Mar 1985 *Aden*   South Yemen ....1 Bahrain...........4
12 Apr 1985 *Bahrain*   Bahrain...........3 South Yemen 3
Bahrain qualified for Round Two

Round One - Group 3A

2 Mar 1985 *Katmandu*   Nepal ....0 South Korea 2
10 Mar 1985 *Kuala Lumpur* Malaysia..........1 South Korea 0
16 Mar 1985 *Katmandu*   Nepal ....0 Malaysia..........0
31 Mar 1985 *Kuala Lumpur* Malaysia..........5 Nepal 0
6 Apr 1985 *Seoul*   South Korea .....4 Nepal 0
19 May 1985 *Seoul*   South Korea .....2 Malaysia..........0

Final Table

	P	W	D	L	F	A	Pts	
South Korea	4	3	0	1	8	1	6	**South Korea**
Malaysia	4	2	1	1	6	2	5	**qualified for Round**
Nepal	4	0	1	3	0	11	1	**Two**

Round One - Group 3B

15 Mar 1985 *Jakarta*   Indonesia.........1 Thailand 0
18 Mar 1985 *Jakarta*   Indonesia.........2 Bangladesh.......0
21 Mar 1985 *Jakarta*   Indonesia.........2 India 1
23 Mar 1985 *Bangkok*   Thailand ....3 Bangladesh.......0
26 Mar 1985 *Bangkok*   Thailand ....0 India 0
29 Mar 1985 *Bangkok*   Thailand ....0 Indonesia.........1
30 Mar 1985 *Dacca*   Bangladesh.......1 India 2
2 Apr 1985 *Dacca*   Bangladesh.......2 Indonesia.........1
5 Apr 1985 *Dacca*   Bangladesh.......1 Thailand 0
6 Apr 1985 *Calcutta*   India ....1 Indonesia.........1
9 Apr 1985 *Calcutta*   India ....1 Thailand 1
12 Apr 1985 *Calcutta*   India ....2 Bangladesh.......1

Final Table

	P	W	D	L	F	A	Pts	
Indonesia	6	4	1	1	8	4	9	
India	6	2	3	1	7	6	7	**Indonesia qualified**
Thailand	6	1	2	3	4	4	4	**for Round Two**
Bangladesh	6	2	0	4	5	10	4	

Round One - Group 4A

17 Feb 1985 *Macao*   Macao...........2 Brunei 0
17 Feb 1985 *Hong Kong*   Hong Kong ....0 China 0
20 Feb 1985 *Macao*   Macao...........0 China 4
23 Feb 1985 *Hong Kong*   Hong Kong ....8 Brunei 0
26 Feb 1985 *Macao*   China ....8 Brunei 0
1 Mar 1985 *Hong Kong*   Brunei ....0 China 4
6 Apr 1985 *Bandar Seri Begawan* Brunei ....1 Hong Kong 5
13 Apr 1985 *Bandar Seri Begawan* Brunei ....1 Macao...........2
28 Apr 1985 *Macao*   Macao...........0 Hong Kong 2
4 May 1985 *Hong Kong*   Hong Kong ....2 Macao...........0
12 May 1985 *Beijing*   China ....6 Macao...........0
19 May 1985 *Beijing*   China ....1 Hong Kong 2

Final Table

	P	W	D	L	F	A	Pts	
Hong Kong	6	5	1	0	19	2	11	
China	6	4	1	1	23	2	9	**Hong Kong**
Macao	6	2	0	4	4	15	4	**qualified for Round**
Brunei	6	0	0	6	2	29	0	**Two**

Round One - Group 4B

19 Jan 1985 *Singapore*   Singapore ....1 North Korea 1
23 Feb 1985 *Singapore*   Singapore ....1 Japan 3
21 Mar 1985 *Tōkyō*   Japan ....1 North Korea 0
30 Apr 1985 *P'yŏngyang*   North Korea .....0 Japan 0
18 May 1985 *Tōkyō*   Japan ....5 Singapore 0
25 May 1985 *P'yŏngyang*   North Korea .....2 Singapore 0

Final Table

	P	W	D	L	F	A	Pts	
Japan	4	3	1	0	9	1	7	**Japan qualified for**
North Korea	4	1	2	1	3	2	4	**Round Two**
Singapore	4	0	1	3	2	11	1	

Round Two

20 Sep 1985 *Dubai*   Utd Arab Emirates 2 Iraq 3
27 Sep 1985 *At Ṭā'if*   Iraq ....1 Utd Arab Emirates 2
Iraq qualified for Round Three on away goals rule

6 Sep 1985 *Bahrain*   Bahrain...........1 Syria 1
20 Sep 1985 *Damascus*   Syria ....1 Bahrain...........0
Syria qualified for Round Three

21 Jul 1985 *Seoul*   South Korea .....2 Indonesia.........0
30 Jul 1985 *Jakarta*   Indonesia.........1 South Korea 4
South Korea qualified for Round Three

11 Aug 1985 *Kōbe*   Japan ....3 Hong Kong 0
22 Sep 1985 *Hong Kong*   Hong Kong ......1 Japan 2
Japan qualified for Round Three

Semi-final

26 Nov 1985 *Tōkyō*   Japan ....1 South Korea 2
3 Nov 1985 *Seoul*   South Korea .....1 Japan 0
South Korea qualified

15 Nov 1985 *Damascus*   Syria ....0 Iraq 0
29 Nov 1985 *At Ṭā'if*   Iraq ....3 Syria 1
Iraq qualified

AFRICA

Round One - Zone A

**Madagascar qualified for Round Two because Lesotho refused
to play them.**

15 Jul 1984 *Curepipe*   Mauritius ....0 Malawi 1
28 Jul 1984 *Lilongwe*   Malawi ....4 Mauritius 0
Malawi qualified for Round Two

29 Jul 1984 *Ndola*   Zambia ....3 Uganda 0
25 Aug 1984 *Kampala*   Uganda ....1 Zambia 0
Zambia qualified for Round Two

28 Aug 1984 *Cairo*   Egypt ....1 Zimbabwe 0
30 Sep 1984 *Harare*   Zimbabwe ....1 Egypt 1
Egypt qualified for Round Two

13 Oct 1984 *Mwanza*   Tanzania ....1 Sudan 1
27 Oct 1984 *Khartoum*   Sudan ....0 Tanzania 0
Sudan qualified for Round Two on away goals rule.

13 Oct 1984 *Nairobi*   Kenya.............2 Ethiopia..........1
28 Oct 1984 *Addis Ababa* Ethiopia..........3 Kenya.............3
Kenya qualified for Round Two

Round One - Zone B

Libya qualified for Round Two following Niger's withdrawal
30 Jun 1984 *Freetown*   Sierra Leone .....0 Morocco..........1
15 Jul 1984 *Rabat*   Morocco..........4 Sierra Leone 0
Morocco qualified for Round Two

28 Oct 1984 *Cotonou*   Benin ....0 Tunisia...........2
13 Nov 1984 *Tūnis*   Tunisia...........4 Benin 0
Tunisia qualified for Round Two

Round One - Zone C

Guinea qualified for Round Two after Toga withdrew
1 Jul 1984 *Luanda*   Angola............1 Senegal 0
15 Jul 1984 *Dakar*   Senegal ....1 Angola............0
Angola won 4-3 on penalties and qualified for Round Two

21 Oct 1984 *Abidjan*   Ivory Coast.......4 Gambia...........0
4 Nov 1984 *Banjul*   Gambia...........3 Ivory Coast.......2
Ivory Coast qualified for Round Two

20 Oct 1984 *Lagos*   Nigeria ....3 Liberia............0
4 Nov 1984 *Monrovia*   Liberia............0 Nigeria 1
Nigeria qualified for Round Two
Algeria, Cameroon and Ghana all received byes into Round Two

Round Two

10 Feb 1985 *Conakry*   Guinea ....1 Tunisia 0
24 Feb 1985 *Tūnis*   Tunisia ....2 Guinea 0
Tunisia qualified for quarter-final

22 Feb 1985 *Khartoum* Sudan ....0 Libya 0
8 Mar 1985 *Tripoli*   Libya ....4 Sudan 0
Libya qualified for quarter-final

31 Mar 1985 *Luanda*   Angola............0 Algeria............0
19 Apr 1985 *Algiers*   Algeria............3 Angola............2
Algeria qualified for quarter-final

6 Feb 1985 *Nairobi*   Kenya ....0 Nigeria 3
20 Apr 1985 *Lagos*   Nigeria ....3 Kenya.............1
Nigeria qualified for quarter-final

7 Apr 1985 *Lusaka*   Zambia ....4 Cameroon 1
21 Apr 1985 *Yaoundé*   Cameroon ....1 Zambia 1
Zambia qualified for quarter-final

7 Apr 1985 *Rabat*   Morocco ....2 Malawi 0
21 Apr 1985 *Lilongwe* Malawi ....0 Morocco 0
Morocco qualified for quarter-final

5 Apr 1985 *Cairo*   Egypt ....1 Madagascar 0
21 Apr 1985 *Antananarivo* Madagascar ......1 Egypt 0
Egypt won 4-2 on penalties and qualified for quarter-final

7 Apr 1985 *Abidjan*   Ivory Coast.......0 Ghana 0
21 Apr 1985 *Accra*   Ghana ....2 Ivory Coast.......0
Ghana qualified for quarter-final

Quarter-finals

6 Jul 1985 *Lagos*   Nigeria ....1 Tunisia...........0
20 Jul 1985 *Tūnis*   Tunisia ....2 Nigeria 0
Tunisia qualified for semi-final

14 Jul 1985 *Accra*   Ghana ....0 Libya 0
26 Jul 1985 *Benghazi* Libya ....2 Ghana 0
Libya qualified for semi-final

13 Jul 1985 *Algiers* Algeria............2 Zambia 0
28 Jul 1985 *Lusaka*   Zambia ....0 Algeria............1
Algeria qualified for semi-final

12 Jul 1985 *Cairo*   Egypt ....0 Morocco 0
28 Jul 1985 *Casablanca* Morroco ....2 Egypt 0
Morocco qualified for semi-final

Semi-finals

6 Oct 1985 *Tūnis*   Tunisia ....1 Algeria............4
18 Oct 1985 *Algiers*   Algeria............3 Tunisia 0
Algeria qualified

6 Oct 1985 *Rabat*   Morocco ....3 Libya ...:.........0
18 Oct 1985 *Benghazi* Libya ....1 Morocco 0
Morocco qualified

OCEANIA/ISRAEL

3 Sep 1985 *Tel Aviv*   Israel ....6 Taiwan 0
8 Sep 1985 *Tel Aviv*   Taiwan ....0 Israel 5
21 Sep 1985 *Auckland* New Zealand.....0 Australia 0
5 Oct 1985 *Auckland* New Zealand.....5 Taiwan 1
8 Oct 1985 *Tel Aviv*   Israel ....1 Australia 2
12 Oct 1985 *Christchurch* Taiwan ....0 New Zealand.....5
20 Oct 1985 *Melbourne* Australia ....1 Israel 1
23 Oct 1985 *Adelaide* Australia ....7 Taiwan 0
26 Oct 1985 *Auckland* New Zealand.....3 Israel 1
27 Oct 1985 *Sydney*   Taiwan ....0 Australia 8
3 Nov 1985 *Sydney*   Australia ....2 New Zealand.....0
10 Nov 1985 *Tel Aviv*   Israel ....3 New Zealand.....3

Final Table

	P	W	D	L	F	A	Pts	
Australia	6	4	2	0	20	2	10	**Australia qualified for**
Israel	6	3	1	2	17	6	7	**play-off against the**
New Zealand	6	3	1	2	13	7	7	**runners-up in European**
Taiwan	6	0	0	6	1	36	0	**Group Seven (Scotland).**

Europe/Oceania Play-off

20 Nov 1985 *Glasgow*   Scotland ....2 Australia 0
4 Dec 1985 *Melbourne* Australia ....0 Scotland 0
Scotland qualified

Scotland created a record by travelling the furthest ever to qualify for a World Cup finals when they met Australia in Melbourne. Here Australia's O'Connor and Scotland's Nicol tussle for the ball. Scotland's 2-0 win in the first leg at Hampden eventually proved enough to see them through with a goalless draw on the other side of the world.

Below : The last two qualifiers, pictured before their final squads were selected. *Left:* Morocco. Back row (left to right): José Faria (coach), Bouyahyaoui, El Biaz, Bouderbala, Fadili, Haddaoui, Zaki, Merry. Front row: Labied, Timoumi, Lamriss, Dolmy, Krimau. *Right*: Scotland (from left to right): Speedie, Gough, McLeish, Cooper, Bett, Nicol, Strachan, Malpas, Aitken, Leighton, Miller.

1986 Tournament

Group A

Fernando De Napoli of Italy.

BULGARIA 1   ITALY 1 (Half-time 0-1)

Azteca Stadium, Mexico City, 31 May
Attendance: 95,000

THESE teams approached their opening match with troubled times behind them. Despite beating Uruguay in their final warm-up game, the Bulgarian national team had been decimated after the Bulgarian Cup Final scandal of 1985 which resulted in the Communist Party disbanding the offending clubs and banning leading players for life. One of them, goalkeeper Borislav Mikhailov, however, was reinstated and lined up as Bulgaria started their fifth World Cup campaign still seeking their first win.

Italy, the defending champions, had been struggling to score goals in their build up to the finals and suffered pre-World Cup defeats by Norway and Poland.

More than 10,000 police officers were in and around the Azteca Stadium for the opening match but there were no problems amongst the fans, although the estimated 100,000 cars in the surrounding area posed a major problem and the Bulgarian players were stuck in a traffic jam for 20 minutes on their way to the stadium.

Italy left out Paolo Rossi but his replacement, Galderisi, had a good game as Italy created enough chances to win comfortably. Scirea and Cabrini, both playing in their third tournaments, had excellent games in the Italian defence and it was from a Scirea free-kick, two minutes from the interval, that Altobelli gave Italy the lead. However, they were restricted to one goal thanks to good goalkeeping by Mikhailov.

Italy's frustration at not scoring in the second half clearly showed and, five minutes from time, Sirakov glanced a header past Galli from an acute angle to equalize for Bulgaria. Some commentators felt that Dino Zoff's successor was slow to react.

Bulgaria did not wilt in the intense heat, as they had done in Mexico in 1970, and they picked up a valuable point from their opening game which, whilst it was not a classic, was a good spectacle in comparison with some openers in recent years. It was excellently handled by Swedish referee Erik Fredriksson.

Italy: Galli; Bergomi, Vierchowod, Scirea, Cabrini, De Napoli, Bagni, Di Gennaro, Conti (Vialli), Galderisi, Altobelli.
Scorer: Altobelli
Bulgaria: Mikhailov; Zdravkov, Dimitrov, Arabov, A.Markov, Sadkov, Sirakov, Getov, Gospodinov(Yeliazkov), Iskrenov(Kostadinov), Mladenov.
Scorer: Sirakov
Referee: Erik Fredriksson (Sweden)

Alexander Markov of Bulgaria.

Italy's new goalkeeper, Giovanni Galli, is beaten by this 85th-minute header from Sirakov which saw Bulgaria claw their way back to a 1-1 draw.

ARGENTINA 3   SOUTH KOREA 1 (Half-time 2-0)

Estadio Olimpico '68, Mexico City, 2 June
Attendance: 60,000

DIEGO Maradona responded quickly to the succession of fouls inflicted on him by destroying the South Koreans in the first 20 minutes. Thus, they had little chance of emulating their Northern counterparts in England 20 years earlier, by reaching the quarter-finals.

Argentina started the game without their 1978 captain, Daniel Passarella, who was suffering from a stomach injury. Indeed, fate was to decree that he did not appear in the latest campaign as he subsequently injured a calf in training. Nevertheless, the new Argentine side did very nicely without him and Maradona showed that he had come of age since his sad sending-off in Spain four years earlier.

Maradona had a hand in the opening goal after only five minutes, when he was brought down. From the free-kick the ball rebounded off the defensive wall and was played by Maradona to Real Madrid striker Valdano, who hit the ball from an angle past the unsighted Korean goalkeeper.

Another foul on Maradona in the 17th minute produced goal number-two, when the Argentine skipper floated the free-kick to Ruggeri, who had an easy task in heading into the net.

After half an hour, the South Americans had the game won and thereafter only Maradona performed with any conviction. His teammates played at a strolling pace.

Kim Pyung-suk, the man given the task of marking the world's outstanding footballer, had been taken off in disgrace after 20 minutes.

Argentina extended their lead a minute after the interval and, yet again, Maradona had a hand in it. His cross caused all sorts of panic amongst the Korean defence and Valdano had an easy tap in for the third goal. Later in the tournament, that phrase 'Maradona had a hand in the goal' was to take on a new meaning.

Fifteen minutes from time, Chang-sun scored a consolation goal from 25 yards, but South Korea had proved no match for the Argentinians and Maradona, in particular, showed the football world how much he had matured in the last four years.

Argentina: Pumpido; Clausen, Brown, Ruggeri, Garré, Giusti, Batista(Olarticoechea), Burruchaga, Pasculli(Tapia), Maradona, Valdano.
Scorers: Valdano 2, Ruggeri
South Korea: Yung-kyo; Kyung-hoon, Yong-hwan, Min-kook, Yong-se(Byung-ok), Jung-moo, Pyung-suk(Kwang-rae), Chang-sun, Joo-sung, Soon-hoo, Bum-keun.
Scorer: Chang-sun
Referee: Victoriano Sánchez Arminio (Spain)

Diego Maradona of Argentina.

South Korea's Jung-moo launches himself into the tackle against Néstor Clausen of Argentina.

ARGENTINA 1   ITALY 1 (Half-time 1-1)

Cuauhtemoc Stadium, Puebla, 5 June
Attendance: 32,000

THIS was the fourth World Cup meeting between these two Latin sides, who had won the trophy four times between them. To date one match had been drawn, whilst Italy had won the other two. But on the showing of their respective opening matches, Argentina looked to have a good chance of recording their first World Cup win over the Italians.

Gianluca Vialli of Italy.

But they received a set-back after only five minutes, when they had a penalty awarded against them after Brown cleared a ball which struck teammate Garré on the arm. Despite long and heated protests, referee Keizer was not moved and Altobelli sent Pumpido the wrong way with the kick.

Maradona had another outstanding first half and in the 34th minute he shook off his marker and Napoli teammate, Bagni, in the penalty area, after a great long ball from Valdano. From an acute angle, Maradona beat Galli.

Just before the interval, the game looked like erupting as many had feared, but things quietened down and the second half it became an intense midfield battle as both sides seemed happy to settle for a draw. Conti, who posed the Argentina defence all sorts of problems, was unlucky not to put his side in front when his effort hit the post shortly after half-time. But the game ended with Argentina still seeking their first World Cup win over Italy.

Argentina: Pumpido; Cuciuffo, Ruggeri, Brown, Garré, Giusti, Batista(Olarticoechea), Burruchaga, Maradona, Borghi(Enrique), Valdano.
Scorer: Maradona
Italy: Galli; Bergomi, Vierchowod, Scirea, Cabrini, Bagni, De Napoli(Baresi), Di Gennaro, Conti(Vialli), Galderisi, Altobelli.
Scorer: Altobelli (pen)
Referee: Jan Keizer (Holland)

BULGARIA 1   SOUTH KOREA 1 (Half-time 1-0)
Estadio Olimpico '68, Mexico City, 5 June
Attendance: 45,000

AFTER their disappointing opening game against Argentina, South Korea came out and played attacking football in torrential rain at the Estadio Olimpico '68, against a Bulgarian side who must have expected to pick up both points.

The Koreans did well to come back after conceding an 11th-minute goal, which was well taken by Getov after a goalkeeping error. But the Asians constantly came forward and were unfortunate not to get an equalizer when a Kim Joo-sung shot hit a post.

Their well-deserved leveller eventually came in the 68th minute, when Kim Jong-boo, a second-half substitute for Soo-jin, scored from close range and South Korea collected their first-ever point in a World Cup finals.

Bulgaria: Mikhailov; Arabov, Zdravkov, Dimitrov, Sadkov, Petrov, Sirakov, Gospodinov, Mladenov, Getov(Yeliazkov), Iskrenov(Kostadinov).
Scorer: Getov
South Korea: Yung-kyo; Jung-moo, Young-jeung, Kyung-hoon, Yong-hwan, Kwang-rae(Min-kook), Chang-sun, Soo-jin(Jong-boo), Byung-joo, Joo-sung, Bum-keun.
Scorer: Jong-boo
Referee: Fallaj Al-Shanar (Saudi Arabia)

ARGENTINA 2   BULGARIA 0 (Half-time 1-0)
Estadio Olimpico '68, Mexico City, 10 June
Attendance: 65,000

AFTER two games featuring the brilliance of Maradona, this was a dull match with only occasional flashes of genius from their star performer. The Argentinian defence was well organized but the insignificant Bulgarians posed few problems and goalkeeper Pumpido was a virtual onlooker for most of the game.

A Cuciuffo cross from the right found the head of Valdano at the far post in the third minute and Argentina were one up. Surprisingly, they did not score again until the 78th minute, when Burruchaga's head was on the end of a pin-point accurate left-wing cross from Maradona.

Argentina booked their place in the last 16, but the Bulgarians had to wait a few days to learn their fate. Eventually, as one of the four best third-placed teams, they also qualified, although they still had not won a game in the World Cup finals.

Argentina: Pumpido; Cuciuffo, Brown, Ruggeri, Garré, Giusti, Batista(Olarticoechea), Burruchaga, Maradona, Valdano, Borghi(Enrique).
Scorers: Valdano, Burruchaga
Bulgaria: Mikhailov; Sirakov(Zdravkov), A.Markov, Dimitrov, Yeliazkov, Sadkov, Petrov, Yordanov, P.Markov, Mladenov(Velitchkov), Getov.
Referee: Morera Berny Ulloa (Costa Rica)

ITALY 3   SOUTH KOREA 2 (Half-time 1-0)
Cuauhtemoc Stadium, Puebla, 10 June
Attendance: 20,000

MENTION the word 'Korea' to any Italian soccer fan and he immediately casts his mind back to that dreadful day in the 1966 World Cup, when North Korea beat Italy 1-0. But there was to be no repeat 20 years later, as the Italians won with ease, despite the apparent closeness of the score.

Altobelli put them in front in the 18th minute, when he received the ball from a Di Gennaro cross and dummied the goalkeeper before scoring. Altobelli had a chance to make it 2-0 in the 36th minute but his penalty-kick hit the post.

Argentina's Ricardo Giusti.

It was a bad-tempered game at times and four players received cautions. The Koreans upset the Italians with an equalizer just after the hour mark, when Choi Soon-ho scored a great goal from 25 yards. But it was much against the run of play and came after a period of intense Italian pressure.

However, the Italian advantage was restored in the 73rd minute, when Altobelli scored his second goal, from a free-kick, and in the 82nd minute the same player took the credit for the third Italian goal, although FIFA subsequently credited it as an own-goal to Kwang-rae. Altobelli and De Napoli had opened the defence before the ball was turned into the goal by the Korean defender.

The Koreans pulled one back in the last minute when Cha Bum-keun, who played for Bayer 04 Leverkusen in the Bundesliga and was reputed to have more than 140 full international appearances to his name, headed down for Jung-moo to score.

Italy won but the scoreline does not indicate the superiority of the defending champions.

Italy: Galli; Collovati, Vierchowod, Scirea, Cabrini, De Napoli, Conti, Bagni(Baresi), Di Gennaro, Galderisi(Vialli), Altobelli.
Scorers: Altobelli 2, Kwang-rae (og)
South Korea: Yung-kyo; Kyung-hoon, Kwang-rae, Yong-hwan, Jung-moo, Young-jeung, Soon-ho, Chang-sun, Byung-joo(Jong-boo), Bum-keun, Joo-sung(Jong-soo).
Scorers: Soon-ho, Jung-moo
Referee: David Socha (United States)

Group B

MEXICO 2   BELGIUM 1 (Half-time 2-1)
Azteca Stadium, Mexico City, 3 June
Attendance: 110,000

THE passion of the home fans was as intense as it had been when Mexico hosted the tournament 16 years earlier. And again they were expecting success for their team. In Hugo Sánchez, the Real Madrid striker, they certainly had one of the world's outstanding players. The home fans were pinning high hopes on him.

The Mexicans played good possession football, whilst Belgium struggled to get Ceulemans involved fully in the game. Indeed, the Europeans were disappointing.

One can perhaps imagine the noise made by 110,000 Mexican fans when Quirarte gave them the lead midway through the first half, after he met a Boy free-kick and beat the Belgian 'keeper, Pfaff, who was late going down for the ball. The noise had hardly died down when their hero, Sánchez, made it 2-0 seven minutes before the interval. Again Boy was involved, as his corner to the near post was flicked on by Múñoz and Sánchez was on hand to head the ball into the net.

Vandenbergh had a free header a minute before half-time, when a Gerets long throw confused Larios in the Mexican goal, and he made it 2-1. There were no further goals, even though Mexico pushed forward in the second half in search of adding to their tally. But they nearly

Group A – Final Table

	P	W	D	L	F	A	Pts
Argentina	3	2	1	0	6	2	5
Italy	3	1	2	0	5	4	4
Bulgaria	3	0	2	1	2	4	2
South Korea	3	0	1	2	4	7	1

Hugo Sánchez, dominant in the air for Mexico against Belgium.

Pablo Larios, whose mistake allowed Erwin Vandenbergh a free header for the Belgians.

This deep cross eluded the Belgian defence and Sánchez was on hand to head home Mexico's second goal.

Top: Paraguay's goalkeeper Roberto Fernández is congratulated by teammate Jorge Núñez after saving Sánchez's penalty-kick. *Below:* Sánchez holds his head in disbelief.

Pablo Larios collects a cross during an attack on the Mexican goal in the Azteca Stadium.

paid the price for their constant attacking in the last minute, when Ceulemans had a half-chance but failed to convert it into a goal.

Mexico: Larios; Trejo, Felix Cruz, Quirarte, Servin, Aguirre, Negrete, Múñoz, Boy(España), Flores(Javier Cruz), Sánchez.
Scorers: Quirarte, Sánchez
Belgium: Pfaff; Gerets, Broos, F.Van der Elst, De Wolf, Vercauteren, Vandereycken, Scifo, Ceulemans, Vandenbergh(Demol), Desmet(Claesen).
Scorer: Vandenbergh
Referee: Carlos Esposito (Argentina)

PARAGUAY 1   IRAQ 0 (Half-time 1-0)
Bombonera Stadium, Toluca, 4 June
Attendance: 24,000

PARAGUAY were still managed by the ageing Cayetano Re, who had been sacked and reinstated in 1985. He managed to pull his side through the qualifiers and built a team around Julio Cesar Romero, the South American Footballer of the Year in 1985, who played his football with Fluminense of Brazil.

Iraq, playing in their first finals, were the more adventurous in the first half, with Hussein Said outstanding. But they fell behind to a Romero goal ten minutes before the interval, when the clever midfielder chipped the ball over the Iraq goalkeeper.

Iraq had the ball in the net right on the stroke of half-time, when Ahmed Amaiesh Rhadi headed in from a corner, but the referee blew his whistle a fraction of a second before the ball went into the net, in an incident reminiscent of Brazil's 'goal' against Sweden in 1978. But, despite the protests, the goal was not allowed and the incident unsettled the Iraq players in the second half.

Paraguay had plenty of chances to increase their score in the second period and Zabala and Mendoza both had attempts which hit the woodwork.

Paraguay: Fernández; Torales, Zabala, Schettina, Delgado, Núñez, Ferreira, Romero, Cabañas, Cañete, Mendoza(Guasch).
Scorer: Romero
Iraq: Raad Hammoudi; Khalil Allawi, Mahmoud Samir, Salim Nadhum, Al-Roubai Ghanim, Hassan Haris(Aufi Abdul), Abidoun Natik, Hanna Basil(Kassim Basim), Shihab Ali Hussein, Ahmed Amaiesh Rhadi, Hussein Said.
Referee: Edwin Pikon-Ackong (Mauritius)

MEXICO 1   PARAGUAY 1 (Half-time 1-0)
Azteca Stadium, Mexico City, 7 June
Attendance: 114,600

PARAGUAY were being fancied by many as a good outside bet, but it was hard to assess the potential of either side in a match dominated by fouls. There was no way either team was allowed to play good football as the foul count was a staggering 77, 45 of which were commited by Mexico. Remarkably there were no dismissals, although referee George Courtney of England put five names into his notebook, including that of Hugo Sánchez, who was also booked in the opening game and was now forced to miss Mexico's third match.

Mexico got off to a great start when Boy, the man involved in both their goals against Belgium, sent Servin away down the left flank and his cross was chested down by Flores,

who shot in the far corner of the goal. The game was only two minutes old and those Mexican fans went wild once more.

After that, though, the game degenerated into an ill-tempered series of fouls and the match offered little more entertainment until the closing ten minutes. In the 84th minute, Paraguay got the equalizer they deserved when Romero, known as 'Romerito' by the Paraguayan fans, rose high to powerfully head home a perfect cross from Cañete.

It looked as though the game was going to be taken away from the South Americans when Courtney awarded a last-minute penalty, after Sánchez had been brought down seemingly outside the area. The Mexican forward picked himself up to take the kick, but saw Fernández turn the ball on to the post. Justice was done and Mexico's 'hero' was now a villain. The large crowd made their feelings very clear to Hugo Sánchez.

Mexico: Larios; Trejo, Felix Cruz, Quirarte, Servin, Negrete, Aguirre, Múñoz, Boy(España), Flores(Javier Cruz), Sánchez.
Scorer: Flores
Paraguay: Fernández; Torales(Hicks), Delgado, Schettina, Zabala, Romero, Cañete, Núñez, Ferreira, Cabañas, Mendoza(Guasch).
Scorer: Romero
Referee: George Courtney (England)

Belgian celebrations after Scifo scores his side's first goal against Iraq.

BELGIUM 2   IRAQ 1 (Half-time 2-0)
Bombonera Stadium, Toluca, 8 June
Attendance: 20,000

AFTER opening defeats, both sides needed a win to stand any realistic chance of staying in the tournament and whilst the odds were tipped in Belgium's favour, Iraq were unlucky to lose and had to play most of the second half with ten men.

Belgium scored with the second shot of the game — after 15 minutes. The goal was scored by Vincenzo Scifo, the Italian player with Belgian parentage, when he drove powerfully past the goalkeeper from a good pass by Ceulemans. Five minutes later, a Nico Claesen penalty, after Vercauteren was brought down, seemed to set Belgium on their way to a comfortable win and, indeed, they grew in confidence. But in a tough game, which resulted in six bookings and a sending-off, Iraq never gave up.

Hanna Basil was the man sent off for a foul on De Wolf, but shortly before his 52nd-minute dismissal he forced Pfaff to make a full-length save and left the Belgians in no doubt that they still had a fight on their hands. When Ahmed Amaiesh Rhadi scored for Iraq in the 58th minute, it brought them right back into the game, but Belgium held on for their win against a tough, and occasionally physical side.

Belgium: Pfaff; Gerets, F.Van der Elst, Demol(Grün), De Wolf, Vandereycken, Scifo(Clijsters), Ceulemans, Vercauteren, Desmet, Claesen.
Scorers: Scifo, Claesen (pen)
Iraq: Raad Hammoudi; Khalil Allawi, Mahmoud Samir, Salim Nadhum, Al-Roubai Ghanim, Hassan Haris, Abidoun Natik, Hanna Basil, Shihab Ali Hussein, Ahmed Amaiesh Rhadi, Minshid Kerim Saddam(Aufi Abdul).
Scorer: Ahmed Amaiesh Rhadi
Referee: Palacio Jesus Diaz (Colombia)

Roberto Cabañas of Paraguay dives after the ball against Belgium.

BELGIUM 2   PARAGUAY 2 (Half-time 1-0)
Bombonera Stadium, Toluca, 11 June
Attendance: 16,000

THIS was undoubtedly the best match of a poor group. There had been a lot of discontent in the Belgian camp leading up to the game but they still managed to produce their best performance of the tournament so far.

Belgium had three scoring chances in the first ten minutes and in the 24th minute, Cañete

Belgium's Jan Ceulemans (11) and Stéphane Demol (21) are calmed down after a foul on Demol by a Paraguayan defender.

Group B - Final Table

	P	W	D	L	F	A	Pts
Mexico	3	2	1	0	4	2	5
Paraguay	3	1	2	0	4	3	4
Belgium	3	1	1	1	5	5	3
Iraq	3	0	0	3	1	4	0

Belgian goalkeeper Jean-Marie Pfaff.

Another unpleasant incident in the Belgium-Paraguay game, this time involving Pfaff.

had a shot deflected narrowly past Pfaff's post as Paraguay also had a good chance to take the lead. But the honour of getting the first goal eventually fell to Vercauteren in the 31st minute, when he beat Fernández with a lob after a breakaway by Ceulemans following a Paraguayan attack.

Five minutes later, Pfaff was beaten by a lob at the other end but he was saved by a spectacular clearance by Renquin on the line. Paraguay's eventual equalizer came five minutes into the second half, when Cabañas scored after a bad back-pass by Broos. Ten minutes later Belgium were back in front when Veyt slotted the ball past the goalkeeper after a well-timed run.

Another Belgian defensive error in the 76th minute allowed Cabañas to beat the Belgian offside trap, which had proved largely ineffective, to score his second goal. The draw was good enough to take both teams through to the next round, Paraguay as runners-up and Belgium as one of the best third-placed teams.

Belgium: Pfaff; Broos, Grün(L.Van der Elst), Renquin, Demol, Vervoort, Scifo, Vercauteren, Ceulemans, Veyt, Claesen.
Scorers: Vercauteren, Veyt
Paraguay: Fernández; Torales, Guasch, Delgado, Zabala, Núñez, Romero, Ferreira, Cañete, Cabañas, Mendoza(Hicks).
Scorer: Cabañas 2
Referee: Bogdan Dotchev (Bulgaria)

MEXICO 1   IRAQ 0 (Half-time 0-0)

Azteca Stadium, Mexico City, 11 June
Attendance: 103,762

MEXICO were almost certain of a place in the next round but their fans wanted to make sure of their place in style. Iraq, though, prevented another carnival in Mexico City, although the hosts managed to scrape through by a solitary goal.

Mexico were without the suspended Hugo Sánchez, whilst the Iraqi team contained several new faces as a result of injuries and suspensions.

Most of the attacking came from the home side as Iraq were penned in their own half for most of the game. Despite the constant pressure, the first half remained goalless.

Mexico did not have anybody capable of converting their chances, or of piercing the tight Iraq defence. Not only was Sánchez missing, but the Mexican boss, Milutinović, also left out Múñoz and Trejo, each of whom had already collected one yellow card. He did not want to risk them picking up another, with a place in the next round almost guaranteed.

The Mexicans' frustration eventually came to an end in the 54th minute, when a Negrete free-kick over the defensive wall appeared to be going out for a goal-kick. But then Quirarte popped up, to head into the net from an acute angle.

Mexico gained the win that took them to the top of the group, but the way they struggled to get the two points was far from impressive. The large crowd hardly cared, of course, they just wanted to see their side win.

Mexico: Larios; Amador(Domínguez), Quirarte, Felix Cruz, Servin, De los Cobos(Javier Cruz), España, Negrete, Aguirre, Boy, Flores.
Scorer: Quirarte
Iraq: Jassim Abdul Fattah; Khalil Allawi, Maod Ibrahim, Salim Nadhum, Al-Roubai Ghanim, Tweresh Ainid(Hamzi Shaker), Abidoun Natik(Aufi Abdul), Kassim Basim, Shihab Ali Hussein, Ahmed Amaiesh Rhadi, Minshid Kerim Saddam.
Referee: Zoran Petrović (Yugoslavia)

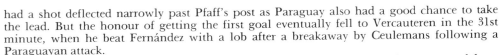

Group C

FRANCE 1   CANADA 0 (Half-time 0-0)

Nou Camp Stadium, León, 1 June
Attendance: 65,000

FRANCE, the reigning European champions, against World Cup newcomers Canada — it had the look of a very one-sided affair. But one statistic had been overlooked — France had not won on foreign soil since beating Luxembourg in a qualifying match nearly two years earlier.

And this game was far from being a one-sided affair, even though the French created most of the chances. Canada, managed by former England goalkeeper Tony Waiters, defended well and kept the 1982 semi-finalists at bay for 78 minutes.

Battiston, Bossis and Platini were all appearing in their third finals, whilst this was a new experience for the Canadians, who had exciting winger Carl Valentine, formerly of Oldham Athletic and West Bromwich Albion, in their line up.

Canada had the two best chances of a goalless first half, through Vrablić and Sweeney, but the only goal of the game was scored by Papin 12 minutes from time, when he made up for earlier missed chances. For France, though, there were few celebrations, just relief at scraping through their opening match.

France: Bats; Amoros, Battiston, Bossis, Tusseau, Fernández, Tigana, Platini, Giresse, Papin, Rocheteau(Stopyra).
Scorer: Papin
Canada: Dolan; Lenarduzzi, Samuel, Bridge, Wilson, Ragan, James(Segota), Norman, Sweeney (Lowery) Valentine, Vrablić.
Referee: Hernán Silva Arce (Chile)

Vladimir Bessonov of the Soviet Union.

SOVIET UNION 6   HUNGARY 0 (Half-time 3-0)
Irapuato Stadium, Irapuato, 2 June
Attendance: 16,600

BOTH these teams were fancied outsiders before the start of the tournament. But after this match, Hungary's dreams of emulating their 1954 predecessors and reaching the Final lay in tatters after they had been taken apart by a rampant Soviet attack which was without Oleg Blokhin.

The Soviets varied their attacks and caused mayhem in the Hungarian defence. With only two minutes played, Yakovenko shot the Russians in front. Two minutes later, Aleinikov blasted one from 25 yards and caught Disztl unawares in the Hungarian goal. With less than five minutes gone, the Soviets were two up.

After being brought down in the penalty area midway through the first half, Belanov picked himself up to convert the resulting spot-kick. There wasn't another goal until the 66th minute, when Yaremchuk seized on a pass from Yakovenko and walked the ball around the goalkeeper. Dajka scored an own-goal in the 74th minute, when he turned the ball into his own net after a chase with Yaremchuk, who is given credit for the goal by FIFA. Four minutes later, Yevtushenko shot high over the bar from the penalty-spot but in the next minute Belanov's replacement, Rodionov, made amends when he scored after a breakaway by Aleinikov. Hungary's misery was complete as they suffered their biggest-ever World Cup defeat.

Soviet boss, Valeri Lobanovski, had been appointed only three weeks before the start of the tournament. He was manager of the successful Dinamo Kiev side and his winning World Cup team contained eight of their players. It was a move that paid off, because they played good, fluent football and performed as a unit. However, Russian goalkeeper Dasaev was perhaps fortunate that he had very little to do. Shortly before the game he spent five hours in hospital, suffering from food poisoning.

Soviet Union: Dasaev; Larionov, Bessonov, Kuznetsov, Demianenko, Yaremchuk, Aleinikov, Yakovenko(Yevtushenko), Rats, Belanov(Rodionov), Zavarov.
Scorers: Yakovenko, Aleinikov, Belanov (pen), Yaremchuk 2, Rodionov
Hungary: Disztl; Sallai, Garaba, Péter(Dajka), Kardos, Bognár, Nagy, Détári, Róth(Burcsa), Kiprich, Esterhazy.
Referee: Luigi Agnolin (Italy)

Sergei Aleinikov (20) blasts home the Soviets' second goal after only five minutes of the game against Hungary and set his side further along the road to a humiliating 6-0 defeat of their Iron Curtain neighbours.

Pavel Yakovenko (Soviet Union) and Michel Platini of France.

Oleg Blokhin of the Soviet Union.

Alain Giresse of France.

FRANCE 1   SOVIET UNION 1 (Half-time 0-0)

Nou Camp Stadium, León, 5 June
Attendance: 36,540

THESE fancied teams provided a feast of attacking football in a thrilling game. The Soviets looked slightly more dangerous in attack but at the other end, Michel Platini posed the Russian defence plenty of problems.

The first half failed to yield a goal, although a Platini thunderbolt from 30 yards struck an upright. But the Russians increased the pace in the second period and were rewarded with the first goal after 53 minutes. And what a goal it was, as a Rats shot from fully 30 yards found its way through a ruck of defenders for one of the best goals of the tournament.

Eight minutes later, the French Footballer of the Year, Fernández, levelled the scores. After a lot of pressure on the Soviet goal, a clever lob by Tigana found Fernández in the area and after controlling the ball well, he stabbed it into the net.

A draw was a fair result and meant that the Soviet Union moved to the top of the group on goal-difference.

France: Bats; Ayache, Bossis, Battiston, Amoros, Giresse(Vercruysse), Fernández, Platini, Tigana, Stopyra, Papin(Bellone).
Scorer: Fernández
Soviet Union: Dasaev; Bessonov, Demianenko, Larionov, Yaremchuk, Yakovenko(Radionov), Kuznetsov, Zavarov(Blokhin), Aleinikov, Rats, Belanov.
Scorer: Rats
Referee: Romualdo Arppi Filho (Brazil)

HUNGARY 2   CANADA 0 (Half-time 1-0)

Irapuato Stadium, Irapuato, 6 June
Attendance: 13,800

HUNGARY kept alive their hopes of reaching the second round after finding Canada an easier proposition than the more fancied French had done in the opening match. The Magyars' confidence was boosted through an Esterhazy goal after only two minutes.

Both sides chose new goalkeepers after losing their opening matches, but it was Canada's new 'keeper, Tino Lettieri, who was first called upon for duty — and that was to pick the ball out of the net after Esterhazy's early goal, from an acute angle after a Kiprich cross.

Canada were not demoralized, though, and came back well to create three good chances, each of which should have brought the equalizer. But Hungary were the better side and fully deserved their second goal 15 minutes from time, when Détári was on hand to score after a Kiprich shot had been fumbled by the goalkeeper.

Mike Sweeney, who came on as a 41st-minute substitute, received his marching orders five minutes from time after grabbing at Bognár. It was Sweeney's second yellow card and he earned the unwanted distinction of being the first man to be sent off in this tournament.

Hungary: Szendrei; Sallai, Varga, Kardos, Garaba, Kiprich, Nagy(Dajka), Détári, Esterhazy, Burcsa(Róth), Bognár.
Scorers: Esterhazy, Détári
Canada: Lettieri; Wilson(Sweeney), Samuel, Bridge, Lenarduzzi, Norman, Gray, Ragan, James (Segota), Vrablić, Valentine.
Referee: Jamal Al Sharif (Syria)

FRANCE 3   HUNGARY 0 (Half-time 1-0)

Nou Camp Stadium, León, 9 June
Attendance: 31,420

HUNGARY were looking for the win that would guarantee them a place in the second round. France, meanwhile, could afford the luxury of a draw or perhaps even defeat. They knew that their three points would probably be enough to take them through. That did not mean, though, that they were prepared to take any chances and so it proved.

Hungary applied a lot of pressure on the French goal but just could not score. They sorely missed the talents of Nyilasi. France were the better side, both in attack and midfield, where Platini was again an outstanding and inspirational figure.

After continued French pressure, a cross from the right by full-back Ayache was met by Stopyra, who headed home from six yards to put France in to the lead four minutes from half-time.

Hungary were unlucky not to equalize just after the break, when a Détári shot hit the bar. Hungary continued to pressurize but after 62 minutes, France increased their lead when Rocheteau, despite being surrounded by defenders, laid the ball into the path of Tigana, who hammered his shot low into the corner of the net.

Six minutes from time, Rocheteau added the third after a delicate pass from Platini across the face of the goal. France ran out easy winners and established themselves as one of the tournament favourites.

France: Bats; Ayache, Battiston, Bossis, Amoros, Fernández, Tigana, Giresse, Platini, Papin (Rocheteau), Stopyra(Ferreri).
Scorers: Stopyra, Tigana, Rocheteau
Hungary: Disztl; Sallai, Róth, Kardos, Varga, Garaba, Dajka, Détári, Hannich(Nagy), Kovács (Bognár), Esterhazy.
Referee: Carlos Antonio Silva Valente (Portugal)

Group C – Final Table

	P	W	D	L	F	A	Pts
Soviet Union	3	2	1	0	9	1	5
France	3	2	1	0	5	1	5
Hungary	3	1	0	2	2	9	2
Canada	3	0	0	3	0	5	0

Soviet substitute Igor Belanov appears to be beaten to the ball by Canada's Randy Samuel, although everyone else has their gaze fixed elsewhere.

SOVIET UNION 2   CANADA 0 (Half-time 0-0)

Irapuato Stadium, Irapuato, 9 June
Attendance: 14,200

KNOWING that they were assured of a second-round place, the Soviets fielded a team consisting mainly of reserves, but they were still far too good for the plucky Canadians.

Russia rested nine regular first-teamers but their replacements showed little flair in a first half which failed to produce a goal. It was only after the more experienced Belanov came on as second-half substitute that the Soviets looked capable of scoring.

It was down to one of the veterans, Oleg Blokhin, holder of more than 100 international caps, to open the scoring after 58 minutes when he got on the end of pass from Belanov to net from close range. It was virtually Belanov's first kick of the match.

In scoring the goal, though, Blokhin was injured and had to go off. He was replaced by Zavarov, who scored the second Soviet goal 15 minutes from time. Again it came from a Belanov through-ball into the penalty area.

The Soviets topped the group on goal-difference ahead of France and both qualified for the next phase. Hungary and Canada were both eliminated but Tony Waiters' team went out with dignity and were far from disgraced in what was a very tough group.

Soviet Union: Chanov; Morozov, Bubnov, Kuznetsov, Bal, Blokhin(Zavarov), Litovchenko, Yevtushenko, Aleinikov, Rodionov, Protasov(Belanov).
Scorers: Blokhin, Zavarov
Canada: Lettieri; Lenarduzzi, Wilson, Ragan, Bridge, Valentine, Gray(Pakos), Samuel, Mitchell, James(Segota), Norman.
Referee: Idriss Traore (Mali)

Group D

BRAZIL 1   SPAIN 0 (Half-time 0-0)

Jalisco Stadium, Guadalajara, 1 June
Attendance: 35,748

BRAZIL started their latest World Cup campaign as favourites, just as they had done for most post-war tournaments. But defeats by West Germany and Hungary on their pre-World Cup tour of Europe had some commentators doubting their ability to win the trophy for the fourth time. The Brazilians were the most famous World Cup nation, though, and could never be discounted.

They were managed by Telê Santana, who was recalled from Saudi Arabia for his second spell in charge of the squad, and the 53-year-old guided them through the qualifying tournament. Spain were managed by one of their former players, Miguel Múñoz, and he insisted on his team doing all their training behind closed doors to prevent Brazilian television cameras spying on them.

Even before the kick-off, the Brazilians were unhappy because the Mexicans did not play the Brazilian national anthem. Instead they played *Song of the Flag* which was a patriotic tune played at political meetings.

Whether this had anything to do with the fact that Brazil lacked conviction once play got under way, or whether the discontent in their camp spilled over on to the field, was not known. Either way, they did not start as though they were likely champions.

The two sets of fans created a carnival atmosphere on the terraces but on the pitch it turned into an aggressive game and in the fourth minute Julio Alberto was booked for a bad foul on Edinho.

Emilio Butragueño of Spain.

Northern Ireland's Pat Jennings ended his career against Brazil with 119 full international caps, a world record until passed by England's Peter Shilton in the 1990 finals.

There was a controversial incident in the Brazil-Spain game when a shot from Míchel hit the crossbar and bounced down on to the goal-line (*top picture*). Despite Spanish protests (*bottom picture*) Australian referee Chris Bambridge ruled that the ball had not wholly crossed the line.

Spain were impressive in defence and nearly caught Brazil with their breakaways. The Spaniards were certainly relieved to have the pressure of being hosts taken away from them, a burden which they found too great in 1982.

Spain were most unfortunate not to have gone ahead in the 55th minute when a Míchel shot hit the underside of the bar and clearly bounced over the line. But referee Bambridge waved play on. Five minutes later, Socrates netted from a corner but the goal was disallowed for 'hands'. In the 63rd minute, however, Socrates, the doctor of medicine with an interest in politics, turned the ball into the net after a Careca shot rebounded to him. The goal had a suspicion of offside about it.

Socrates was one of the world's most creative midfield players but his chance of playing in the World Cup must have been in jeopardy after breaking an ankle in training in 1985, shortly after his return from Italian football with Fiorentina.

His goal separated the two teams but Spain could count themselves a little unfortunate not to have come out of the game with a point.

Brazil: Carlos; Branco, Edinho, Julio Cesar, Edson, Junior(Falcão), Socrates, Alemão, Elzo, Casagrande(Muller), Careca.
Scorer: Socrates
Spain: Zubizarreta; Tomás, Maceda, Goicoechea, Camacho, Víctor, Míchel, Francisco(Señor), Julio Alberto, Butragueño, Salinas.
Referee: Chris Bambridge (Australia)

ALGERIA 1   NORTHERN IRELAND 1 (Half-time 0-1)

Trez de Marzo Stadium, Guadalajara, 3 June
Attendance: 22,000

THESE teams were both revelations in Spain four years earlier, as they shocked more fancied nations, and Algeria's win against West Germany was one of the all-time World Cup shocks. Northern Ireland had produced their own surprise by beating the hosts, Spain.

Alas, there were many off-the-ball incidents which turned this match into a violent affair at times. The Algerian players made some intimidating tackles and were seen to spit at Irish players. It was all very unsavoury. Surprisingly, of the four bookings issued by referee Butenko, three were of Northern Ireland players but Algeria were fortunate to finish the game with 11 men.

Northern Ireland got off to a great start when Penney was brought down on the edge of the penalty area and Whiteside's free-kick was deflected into the net by Guendouz. But, despite such a great start and their dominance of midfield, the Irish forwards were negative and could not capitalize, although a Whiteside header was cleared off the line and Hamilton wasted a good chance.

The Algerians looked dangerous only after Notts County's Rachid Harkouk came on as a 30th-minute substitute for Madjer, who went off after a clash of heads with Mal Donaghy. And after 58 minutes, the over-cautious Irish conceded the equalizer when Guendouz took a short free-kick to Zidane, who beat Pat Jennings with a low shot from 25 yards. The Africans then seemed content to hold out for the draw.

Algeria: Larbi El Hadi; Medjadi, Kourichi, Guendouz, Mansouri, Kaci-Saïd, Ben Mabrouk, Maroc, Madjer(Harkouk), Zidane(Belloumi), Assad.
Scorer: Zidane
Northen Ireland: Jennings; J.Nicholl, O'Neill, McDonald, Donaghy, Penney(Stewart), McIlroy, McCreery, Worthington, Hamilton, Whiteside(Clarke).
Scorer: Whiteside
Referee: Valeri Butenko (Soviet Union)

BRAZIL 1   ALGERIA 0 (Half-time 0-0)

Jalisco Stadium, Guadalajara, 6 June
Attendance: 48,000

AS the scoreline suggests, Brazil struggled to overcome Algeria as they gave one of their most subdued World Cup performances ever.

Algeria were honourable in defeat and had two efforts, from Belloumi and Assad, cleared off the line as they could easily have shocked the Brazilians with the first goal. But this is probably what the South Americans needed to motivate them.

Brazil also had many first-half chances and the Algerians were lucky when the referee ruled out Casagrande's 'goal' after it was alleged that he had made contact with the goalkeeper in the process.

The Brazilians were relieved when Careca scored the only goal after 66 minutes, but the strike had a piece of good fortune about it. Muller's low cross from the right caused a mis-kick and as the Algerian defence hesitated, Careca was there to snap up the chance from close range.

Brazil had maximum points from their first two games and became the first team to book their place in the second round. But they had been far from impressive.

Brazil: Carlos; Edson(Falcão) Julio Cesar, Edinho, Branco, Junior, Alemão, Elzo, Socrates, Careca, Casagrande(Muller).
Scorer: Careca

Algeria: Drid; Medjadi, Mansouri, Megharia, Guendouz, Kaci-Saïd, Assad(Bensaoula), Ben Mabrouk, Menad, Belloumi(Zidane), Madjer.
Referee: Romulo Méndez Molina (Guatemala)

SPAIN 2   NORTHERN IRELAND 1 (Half-time 2-0)

Trez de Marzo Stadium, Guadalajara, 7 June
Attendance: 28,00

A sunbaked Trez de Marzo Stadium saw these teams renew their acquaintanceship from four years earlier, when Northern Ireland rocked the hosts with a 1-0 victory. But revenge was to be sweet for the Spaniards, who sealed their success within 20 minutes.

The Irish defence was in disarray in that opening spell and conceded two goals before eventually settling down. Butragueño was sent through by Míchel with the defence caught 'cold' and after 63 seconds the Spanish striker had the ball in the net. It was the fastest goal in the series.

Salinas finished well to score from just inside the penalty area after 18 minutes, after the Irish had given the ball away. The goal ended a sequence of 14 games in which Northern Ireland had not conceded more than one goal.

The Irish now settled and two minutes into the second half brought themselves back into the match when Clarke headed into an empty net from 18 yards after a mix-up between Galego and goalkeeper Zubizarreta.

The outcome remained in doubt until the final whistle, which seemed to come early because the referee added very little injury-time, even though Gordillo suffered a bad leg injury which was later confirmed as a break. It took time to sort out, but the referee did not add time on for the stoppage and Northern Ireland now faced the huge task of having to beat Brazil in their last match if they were to keep their hopes alive.

Spain: Zubizarreta; Tomás, Goicoechea, Gallego, Camacho, Míchel, Víctor, Francisco, Gordillo (Calderé), Butragueño, Salinas(Señor).
Scorers: Butragueño, Salinas
Northern Ireland: Jennings; J.Nicholl, McDonald, O'Neill, Donaghy, Penney(Stewart), McIlroy, McCreery, Worthington(Hamilton), Clarke, Whiteside.
Scorer: Clarke
Referee: Horst Brummeier (Austria)

BRAZIL 3   NORTHERN IRELAND 0 (Half-time 2-0)

Jalisco Stadium, Guadalajara, 12 June
Attendance: 51,000

PAT Jennings was playing in his 119th and last international match. It was also his 41st birthday, but the Brazilians made sure there would be no happy returns for the outstanding goalkeeper as they gave their best performace of the tournament so far.

Playing in brilliant sunshine, the Brazilians' fluency was rewarded with a 15th-minute goal when a simple, but classy, move was completed by Careca.

Muller pulled back a low cross to Careca, who struck the ball majestically from nine yards and left Jennings motionless. Four minutes from half-time, Brazil increased their lead

Socrates, ran the midfield for Brazil.

Zico, came on for his first game of the tournament against the Irish.

Brazil's Edinho (4) is crowded out by the Irish defence.

Group D – Final Table

	P	W	D	L	F	A	Pts
Brazil	3	3	0	0	5	0	6
Spain	3	2	0	1	5	2	4
N. Ireland	3	0	1	2	2	6	1
Algeria	3	0	1	2	1	5	1

when Branco laid a pass into the path of Josimar, who hammered the ball inside the left post from 30 yards.

Socrates and Junior were magnificent in the Brazilian midfield and when Zico came on for Socrates he carried on where the master left off as they dominated this part of the field, even though the Irish dedicated themselves to all-out attack in the second half. By then, Northern Ireland were doomed and three minutes from time, Careca scored from ten yards after Zico, playing in his third tournament, back-heeled the ball to him.

It was a sad end to a magnificent career for the Irish goalkeeper and respectful of his contribution to world football, the Brazilian players signed the match-ball and presented it to him after the game.

Brazil: Carlos; Edinho, Josimar, Julio Cesar, Branco, Elzo, Alemão, Junior, Socrates(Zico), Muller(Casagrande), Careca.
Scorers: Careca 2, Josimar
Northern Ireland: Jennings; J.Nicholl, Donaghy, O'Neill, McDonald, McCreery, McIlroy, Whiteside(Hamilton), Campbell(Armstrong), Stewart, Clarke.
Referee: Sigfried Kirschen (East Germany)

SPAIN 3   ALGERIA 0 (Half-time 1-0)

Tecnológico Stadium, Monterrey, 12 June
Attendance: 23,980

SPAIN needed to win or draw to make sure of their second-round place, although in retrospect they would have gone through with a narrow defeat. But they spared all the 'ifs and buts' with a three-goal victory.

Both sides were rather physical at times and Spain were less impressive than in their other two group matches. Indeed, had Algeria played with more than one front runner, Rachid Harkouk, they could have come away from their final match with a better result.

Algeria were unlucky to lose goalkeeper Drid, who was injured in a clash with Goicoechea. The brave 'keeper stayed on the field for a few more minutes but after conceding the first goal, in the 18th minute, he eventually went off.

The opening goal was scored by Calderé, who ran on to a pass inside from Salinas. After that Spain did most of the attacking but it was not until the 68th minute that they increased their lead when second-half substitute Eloy beat the offside trap to lay on the scoring chance for Calderé. And three minutes later, with the Algerian defence exposed, Eloy made it 3-0.

Spain had to overcome injuries and illnesses in their three group matches and did well to come out with the one narrow defeat by Brazil. Algeria, however, were unable to repeat their giantkilling exploits of 1982 and a couple of days after their elimination, coach Rabah Saadane was dismissed.

Spain: Zubizarreta; Tomás, Gallego, Goicoechea, Camacho, Víctor, Míchel(Señor), Francisco, Calderé, Butragueño(Eloy), Salinas.
Scorers: Calderé 2, Eloy
Algeria: Drid(Larbi El Hadi); Megharia, Mansouri, Kourichi, Guendouz, Kaci-Saïd, Harkouk, Maroc, Belloumi, Madjer, Zidane(Menad).
Referee: Shizuo Takada (Japan)

Group E

WEST GERMANY 1   URUGUAY 1 (Half-time 0-1)

La Corregidora Stadium, Querétaro, 4 June
Attendance: 30,500

WEST Germany ended 1985 with a run of six internationals without a win, but went to Mexico with an impressive record in more recent times, including wins over Italy, Brazil and Holland. And once more they were one of the fancied teams, particularly with that record and their World Cup tradition behind them. In the build-up to the tournament, manager Franz Beckenbauer said his team would not win the World Cup, but a few days before their opening match, he retracted the comments, saying that they were made in haste and he now felt his team had as good a chance as any other side in the competition.

Uruguay also had a World Cup tradition, but in recent years they had done little to remind us of what a once-great team they were.

West Germany did the early attacking but the Uruguayan defence employed its customary intimidating tactics and twice hacked down Brehme in the opening minutes. The game was played in intense heat which suited the Uruguayans more. They took the lead in the fourth minute when a poor back-pass from Berthold allowed Alzamendi to thump the ball in off the underside of the crossbar.

Predictably, after taking the lead, Uruguay resorted to their defensive tactics with eight men often packing the their own third of the field. The attacking football came largely from the Germans and they caused some anxious moments for Uruguayan goalkeeper, Alvez. Littbarski was brought on as a second-half substitute for Brehme and he added extra power

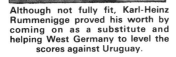

Although not fully fit, Karl-Heinz Rummenigge proved his worth by coming on as a substitute and helping West Germany to level the scores against Uruguay.

Antonio Alzamendi, Uruguay's scorer against West Germany, in a midfield scrap with Karl-Heinz Förster.

to the attack. But it was not until after Rummenigge, playing in his third finals, was brought on in the 73rd minute that West Germany got their equalizer.

It came six minutes from time and Rummenigge was involved in the move which resulted in Allofs scoring with an angled shot from outside the penalty area. Thus, the 'Group of Death' ended with the former champions each getting a point.

Despite the cynical nature of some of the Uruguayan fouls, there was one nice touch from them. After a German player went down injured, a Uruguayan kicked the ball into touch immediately so he could receive treatment. When the Germans eventually took the throw-in, they reciprocated by throwing the ball directly over the goal-line for a goal-kick to Uruguay. It is a feature which, happily, is now common in British domestic football.

Uruguay: Alvez; Diogo, Acevedo, Gutiérrez, Batista, Bossio, Barrios(Saralegui), Santin, Francescoli, Alzamendi(Ramos), Da Silva.
Scorer: Alzamendi
West Germany: Schumacher; Berthold, Förster, Eder, Briegel, Matthäus(Rummenigge), Magath, Brehme(Littbarski), Augenthaler, Völler, Allofs.
Scorer: Allofs
Referee: Vojtech Christov (Czechoslovakia)

DENMARK 1   SCOTLAND 0 (Half-time 0-0)

Neza 86 Stadium, Nezahualcoyotl, Toluca, 4 June
Attendance: 18,000

SCOTLAND'S new boss, Alex Ferguson, was faced with a major problem a few weeks before the tournament, when the country's most capped player, Kenny Dalglish, was forced to pull out with a knee injury. The Scots were to miss his goalscoring skills.

Denmark were making their World Cup debut and looked tense in a first half dominated by Scotland, who had two good chances to take the lead. First, Nicholas was a split-second late in getting to the ball and then Gough hurried his shot.

Denmark were much improved in the second half and seemed to pace themselves better in the heat and humid atmosphere. In the 58th minute, Elkjaer-Larsen scored after an Arnesen pass had split the defence. Scotland were not out of it, though, and they had an Aitken 'goal' ruled out for offside. Five minutes from time, Frank McAvennie went close with a spectacular effort.

Denmark held on for victory and Scotland were to pay the price of not capitalizing on their chances in the first half. Indeed, it was a familiar story in the Scots' World Cup history.

Denmark: Rasmussen; Busk, M.Olsen, Nielsen, Lerby, J.Olsen(Mölby), Berggren, Bertelsen, Arnesen(Sivebaek), Laudrup, Elkjaer-Larsen.
Scorer: Elkjaer-Larsen
Scotland: Leighton; Gough, Malpas, McLeish, Miller, Souness, Aitken, Nicol, Nicholas, Strachan(Bannon), Sturrock(McAvennie).
Referee: Lajos Nemeth (Hungary)

WEST GERMANY 2   SCOTLAND 1 (Half-time 1-1)

La Corregidora Stadium, Querétaro, 8 June
Attendance: 30,000

SCOTLAND went into the match without McLeish, who had to withdraw at the last minute suffering from the dreaded 'Montezuma's Revenge'. But, despite having to reorganize their team, they played well, although still lacking fire-power in attack.

The Germans hit a post in the opening minutes of a game played at a surprisingly fast pace, despite the heat which saw some of the Scottish players shed seven pounds during the game.

It was the Scots who gained the early advantage with a 17th-minute goal, when a Nicol cross was turned to Strachan by Aitken and the Manchester United midfielder's powerful

West Germany's Lothar Matthäus, who made way for Rummenigge with the Germans trailing 1-0.

Denmark's left-sided midfielder, Sören Lerby.

Rudi Völler wins this aerial battle as
Graeme Souness (4) of Scotland
watches and waits.

shot was deflected past Schumacher. Alas, Scotland's moment of joy lasted only five minutes — again a familiar story.

Allofs cut into the defence and crossed from the touch-line. Völler was there with an easy chance to make it 1-1 and Scotland paid the price for failing to contain the Germans after taking the lead.

West Germany went ahead five minutes after the half-time interval, when Völler made the opening in the penalty area before the ball ran away to Allofs, who scored from close range.

West Germany were always in control thereafter and only fine goalkeeping by Jim Leighton prevented further goals. Scotland, however, had two chances to equalize but Gough and substitute Frank McAvennie failed with their attempts.

Two successive defeats meant that Scotland were almost certainly going to exit from the 13th World Cup. Yet, despite their failure to gain any points, they were probably playing the best football seen by a Scottish side in the World Cup.

West Germany: Schumacher; Berthold, Förster, Augenthaler, Briegel(Jakobs), Matthäus, Magath, Eder, Littbarski(Rummenigge), Völler, Allofs.
Scorers: Völler, Allofs
Scotland: Leighton; Gough, Narey, Miller, Malpas, Nicol(McAvennie), Bannon(Cooper), Souness, Strachan, Aitken, Archibald.
Scorer: Strachan
Referee: Ioan Igna (Romania)

DENMARK 6   URUGUAY 1 (Half-time 2-1)

Neza 86 Stadium, Nezahualcoyotl, Toluca, 8 June
Attendance: 26,500

GONE were the nerves of their World Cup debut as Denmark destroyed the South American champions with a great display of imaginative football which yielded six goals.

The goalscoring spree started in the tenth minute when Laudrup made space on the right of the penalty area and laid the ball off to Elkjaer-Larson, who split the defence before scoring.

Ten minutes later Uruguay were down to ten men when Bossio received his marching orders after tripping Arnesen. Six minutes earlier, he had recieved his first booking for kicking Laudrup. Despite the Uruguayans well-tried tactics, they failed to intimidate the Danes and four minutes from the interval Lerby started and finished a move which began in his own half of the field.

But right on the stroke of half-time, Francescoli was checked by Busk in the area and the offended player converted the kick to keep the South Americans in the game.

However, the ten-man Uruguayans could not contain the Danes and in the 52nd minute Laudrup scored a great goal after picking up the ball 20 yards out and beating two defenders before scoring. Elkjaer-Larsen pounced for the fourth goal in the 68th minute, when he picked up a loose ball after more good work from Laudrup. And ten minutes from time

Tough-tackling Dane, Klaus
Berggren.

Denmark's hat-trick hero Preben Elkjaer-Larsen nets past Uruguay's Fernando Alvez.

the Danish striker completed his hat-trick when he collected the ball in his own half and tore through the Uruguayan defence, which was pushing up.

Six minutes after coming on as a substitute for Laudrup, Jesper Olsen scored Denmark's sixth and last goal with two minutes remaining.

Denmark's performance won them a lot of acclaim and many friends and they were likened to the sparkling Dutch side of the 1970s. Like those Dutch masters, they were also talked about as potential world champions.

Denmark: Rasmussen; Nielsen, M.Olsen, Busk, Andersen, Berggren, Arnesen, Lerby, Bertelsen (Mölby), Laudrup(J.Olsen), Elkjaer-Larsen.
Scorers: Elkjaer-Larsen 3, Lerby, Laudrup, J.Olsen
Uruguay: Alvez; Diogo, Gutiérrez, Acevedo, Batista, Saralegui, Bossio, Santin(Salazar), Francescoli, Alzamendi(Ramos), Da Silva.
Scorers: Francescoli (pen)
Referee: Antonio Ramirez Marquez (Mexico)

DENMARK 2   WEST GERMANY 0 (Half-time 1-0)
La Corregidora Stadium, Querétaro, 13 June
Attendance: 36,000

WITH both sides assured of a place in the second round, the spectators were left wondering at what pace the game would be played, particularly after Franz Beckenbauer rested some of his more experienced players. But Denmark wanted to win and stay in Querétaro for their second-round match against Spain, and from the outset they attacked.

Sivebaek had a shot scrambled off the line in the sixth minute and a minute later, Lerby forced a fine save from Schumacher. Laudrup then had the ball in the net but the 'goal' was ruled out following an offside decision. But then West Germany had the opportunity to take the lead when Allofs (twice), Berthold, Jakobs and Brehme all missed chances.

Despite the West German dominance in the closing half of the first period, the first goal fell to Denmark two minutes from half-time. Morten Olsen was upended in the area by Rolff and Jesper Olsen stroked the penalty-kick in the opposite direction to Schumacher's dive.

Eriksen, a second-half substitute for Elkjaer-Larsen, scored Denmark's second goal after 63 minutes when he side-footed a low cross from Arnesen into the net, after Lerby and Mölby had combined well on the right.

Denmark maintained their 100 per cent record and headed the group, but the match was marred two minutes from the end when Frank Arnesen was sent off for taking a swing at Matthäus. The Danish midfielder had been dismissed a couple of weeks earlier, in a warm-up game against Paraguay.

Denmark: Høgh; Busk, M.Olsen, Sivebaek, Andersen, Arnesen, Mölby, J.Olsen(Simonsen), Lerby, Elkjaer-Larsen(Eriksen), Laudrup.
Scorers: J.Olsen (pen), Eriksen
West Germany: Schumacher; Berthold, Förster(Rummenigge), Eder, Herget, Brehme, Matthäus, Jakobs, Rolff(Littbarski), Völler, Allofs.
Referee: Alexis Ponnet (Belgium)

SCOTLAND 0   URUGUAY 0 (Half-time 0-0)
Neza 86 Stadium, Nezahualcoyotl, Toluca, 13 June
Attendance: 20,000

URUGUAY went into the final game of the 'Group of Death' needing a win to guarantee a place in the second round or, at worst, a draw to keep their slim hopes alive. Scotland had to win to stand any chance of staying in the competition.

Yet the headstrong Uruguayans hardly improved their chances when, in the first minute, Batista was given his marching orders for hacking down Strachan.

Despite being reduced to ten men for the second successive match, the South Americans

Eduardo Acevedo (3) of Uruguay lunges at the ball with Steve Nicol of Scotland.

Uruguay's José Batista (on ground) is shown the red card after only one minute of the game against Scotland as French referee Joël Quiniou stamps his authority on a potentially explosive game.

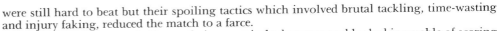

Group E – Final Table

	P	W	D	L	F	A	Pts
Denmark	3	3	0	0	9	1	6
W.Germany	3	1	1	1	3	4	3
Uruguay	3	0	2	1	2	7	2
Scotland	3	0	1	2	1	3	1

were still hard to beat but their spoiling tactics which involved brutal tackling, time-wasting and injury faking, reduced the match to a farce.

Scotland could not capitalize on their numerical advantage and looked incapable of scoring as the Uruguayans pulled every player back in a blanket wall of defence. And the best chance of the match fell to Uruguay, when Cabrera went close with a second-half header.

Uruguay achieved their aim of progressing into the second round, but they had tarnished their image in the progress.

Scotland: Leighton; Gough, Miller, Nairey, Albiston, Strachan, Aitken, McStay, Nicol(Cooper), Sharp, Sturrock(Nicholas).
Uruguay: Alvez; Batista, Gutiérrez, Diogo, Acevedo, Pereya, Barrios, Santin, Francescoli (Alzamendi), Ramos(Saralegui), Cabrera.
Referee: Joël Quiniou (France)

Group F

MOROCCO 0   POLAND 0 (Half-time 0-0)

Universitario Stadium, Monterrey, 2 June
Attendance: 19,000

PLAYING in their fourth successive tournament, Poland were amongst the top seeds but were brought down to earth by a Morocco side which created the first big shock of the series by holding the fancied Europeans to a goalless draw.

The Mexican fans remembered the Moroccans from the 1970s, when they took the lead against the West Germans. Now they came close to bringing off another major shock.

The Moroccan performance was not one of good fortune but was achieved by a disciplined and skilful display of football. The renowned Polish attack, with Boniek now playing deep, did little to put pressure on Morocco's goalkeeper, Zaki, who was tested only once, by Urban in the second half. The same player could have won the match for the Poles five minutes from time but his shot hit a post. A Polish goal then would have been an injustice to the Africans.

Just before half-time, a 25-yard shot from Timoumi, who had recovered from a broken leg just in time to play in the finals, was saved at the second attempt by Mlynarczyk. The Poles were jeered by the Mexican fans as they left the field at half-time.

Boniek moved forward more in the second half but the Polish performance was far from polished and they did little to justify their seeding.

Morocco: Zaki; Khalifi, El Biaz, Bouyahyaoui, Lamriss, Dolmy, El Haddaoui(Souleymani), Timoumi(Khairi), Mustapha Merry, Bouderbala, Krimau.
Poland: Mlynarczyk; Kubicki(Przybys), Wójcicki, Majewski, Ostrowski, Matysik, Buncol, Komornicki, Boniek, Smolarek, Dziekanowski(Urban).
Referee: José Luis Martinez (Uruguay)

PORTUGAL 1   ENGLAND 0 (Half-time 0-0)

Tecnológico Stadium, Monterrey, 3 June
Attendance: 23,000

THE last time these teams met in the World Cup was in the 1966 semi-final, when England won 2-1. Twenty years later, Portugal had their chance for revenge.

But the Portuguese went into the game having only just resolved a dispute over bonuses which nearly saw their entire squad go on strike. The Portuguese FA had applied to FIFA for permission to fly out 22 reserves if such action was taken. Fortunately for them, and perhaps unfortunately for England, the strike was called off.

England had problems of their own and on the eve of the game, team doctor Dr Vernon Edwards was admitted to hospital after suffering a heart attack.

Mark Hateley fluffed a chance to give England a 25th-minute lead but most of the time they were stifled by the Portuguese midfield, which often numbered four and even five players. The Portuguese were happy to contain the English attack and rely on breakaways but their first real scoring chance did not come until the 75th minute.

Diamantino got past Sansom on the right and his low cross beat the defence before Carlos Manuel tapped in at the far post. It was the first World Cup goal conceded by Peter Shilton since the opening game of the 1982 tournament and he had gone a record 499 minutes with a clean sheet, surpassing Sepp Maier's record.

England had plenty of chances in the second half but could only reflect on what might have been.

Portugal: Bento; Álvaro, Frederico, Oliveira, Inacio, Diamantino(José Antonio), Pacheco, André, Sousa, Carlos Manuel, Gomes(Futre).
Scorer: Carlos Manuel
England: Shilton; G.M.Stevens, Fenwick, Butcher, Sansom, Hoddle, Robson(Hodge), Wilkins, Waddle(Beardsley), Hateley, Lineker.
Referee: Volker Roth (West Germany)

Sergio Santin of Uruguay.

Mohamed Timoumi of Morocco.

ENGLAND 0   MOROCCO 0 (Half-time 0-0)

Tecnológico Stadium, Monterrey, 6 June
Attendance: 20,200

ENGLAND'S World Cup dream looked to be in tatters after they were held to a goalless draw by the Moroccans, who gained their second point of the tournament.

England were awful in the first half and in the closing minutes of the half they lost two key players, Ray Wilkins and captain Bryan Robson.

Robson went off after dislocating his shoulder in the 41st minute and one minute later Wilkins was dismissed after throwing the ball at the referee to show his disgust at a decision. It was Wilkins' second bookable offence and he became the first English player to be dismissed in a World Cup finals.

England pulled themselves together in the second half but found the Moroccan defence impossible to penetrate. In the end, England were perhaps a little grateful not to see a repeat of the 1950 scoreline when they lost 1-0 to the United States. The fans who had made the long journey to Mexico were far from happy and made their feelings known to the team as they left the stadium.

England: Shilton; G.M.Stevens, Fenwick, Butcher, Sansom, Hoddle, Robson(Hodge), Wilkins, Hateley(G.A.Stevens), Lineker, Waddle.
Morocco: Zaki; Khalifi, El Biaz, Bouyahyaoui, Lamriss(Oudani), Dolmy, Mustapha Merry (Souleymani), Bouderbala, Timoumi, Khairi, Krimau.
Referee: Gabriel Gonzalez (Paraguay)

Zaki, Morocco's goalkeeper, whose real name is Ezaki Badou.

POLAND 1   PORTUGAL 0 (Half-time 0-0)

Universitario Stadium, Monterrey, 7 June
Attendance: 19,915

PORTUGAL had to call up replacement goalkeeper Damas after their regular 'keeper, Bento, broke a leg in training after the England match. Instead of playing the defensive game, as they did against England, the Portuguese forwards were more ambitious but this time they came up against a defensively-minded Polish side.

The first half was strewn with errors but in the second half the Portuguese midfield dominated. However, Boniek was an inspiration for the Poles and he was involved in the move which led to Smolarek scoring the only goal in the 63rd minute.

Poland resorted to excessive spoiling tactics when under pressure and substitute Futre was crudely checked by the Polish sweeper, Wójcicki, less than a minute after the start of the second half.

Portugal played the better football and the result was much against the run of play. But the outcome left England bottom of the group, which was now wide open as all four teams were capable of qualifying for the second round.

Poland: Mlynarczyk; Majewski, Ostrowski, Pawlak, Wójcicki, Matysik, Komornicki(Karaś), Urban, Boniek, Smolarek(Zgutczynski), Dziekanowski.
Scorer: Smolarek
Portugal: Damas; Álvaro, Frederico, Oliveira, Inacio, Carlos Manuel, André(J.Magalhães), Pacheco, Sousa, Gomes(Futre), Diamantino.
Referee: Alì Bennaceur (Tunisia)

ENGLAND 3   POLAND 0 (Half-time 3-0)

Universitario Stadium, Monterrey, 11 June
Attendance: 22,700

AFTER the loss of Wilkins and Robson as a result of events in the Morocco match, one would have thought that England's chances of staying in the tournament were slim. But

England's fine goalscorer Gary Lineker.

Lineker (centre) finishes off a magnificent move and beats Polish goalkeeper Jozef Mlynarczyk. Lineker's hat-trick saw the Poles beaten 3-0.

Group F – Final Table

	P	W	D	L	F	A	Pts
Morocco	3	1	2	0	3	1	4
England	3	1	1	1	3	1	3
Poland	3	1	1	1	1	3	3
Portugal	3	1	0	2	2	4	2

England's Trevor Steven.

Aziz Bouderbala of Morocco.

the changes which had to be made were like a breath of fresh air to the England team and suddenly they played to their capabilities and with an air of enthusiasm and confidence that had been missing from earlier performances.

In came Reid and Hodge, as replacements for the missing stars, and starting their first game were Trevor Steven and Peter Beardsley. Suddenly England showed speed and skill and played some attractive football. Lineker and Beardsley destroyed the Polish defence, whilst Glenn Hoddle was outstanding in midfield.

By half-time England had hauled themselves back from the brink of an exit and had destroyed Poland with a Gary Lineker hat-trick.

The first goal came after eight minutes and concluded a fine move started by Hoddle in his own half and finished when Lineker scored from close range after a Stevens' cross. And it was from a Hodge cross, five minutes later, that Lineker scored his second goal with a half-volley.

Shortly afterwards, Hodge had an effort disallowed for offside but then Lineker completed his hat-trick, the first by an England player in the World Cup finals since Geoff Hurst in 1966. Polish goalkeeper Mlynarczyk misjudged a Trevor Steven corner and Lineker was on hand to score from close-in yet again.

England's win took them to second place in the group and Poland also qualified as one of the best third-placed teams. It had seemed hardly likely, though, before this match.

England: Shilton; G.M.Stevens, Butcher, Fenwick, Sansom, Hoddle, Steven, Reid, Hodge, Lineker(Dixon), Beardsley(Waddle).
Scorer: Lineker 3
Poland: Mlynarczyk; Pawlak, Majewski, Wójcicki, Ostrowski, Komornicki(Karaś), Matysik (Buncol), Urban, Dziekanowski, Boniek, Smolarek.
Referee: André Daina (Switzerland)

MOROCCO 3   PORTUGAL 1 (Half-time 2-0)

Jalisco Stadium, Guadalajara, 11 June
Attendance: 28,000

AFTER holding Poland and England to goalless draws, the Moroccans feared nobody, not even Portugal with their excellent record. And at Guadalajara, the Africans completely outclassed their more illustrious European opponents.

Portugal applied all the early pressure and in the opening 15 minutes they should have taken the lead. But gradually, through being allowed more freedom, the Moroccans got into the game and after 18 minutes Khairi put them in front when he picked up a loose ball and beat the 'keeper from 25 yards. Nine minutes later, he scored his second goal of the game when his low shot, after a pass from Khalifi, again beat Damas.

Krimau made it 3-0 after 63 minutes, when he fired home a Timoumi cross, and the most improbable win of the group was assured. Portugal pulled back a late consolation goal ten minutes from time but there were none of the exploits which the 1966 Portuguese had displayed when up against those North Koreans. This time they went out of the tournament and coach José Torres resigned a few days after the match.

Morocco: Zaki; Khalifi, El Biaz, Bouyahyaoui, Lamriss, Dolmy, El Haddaoui(Souleymani), Timoumi, Khairi, Bouderbala, Krimau.
Scorers: Khairi 2, Krimau
Portugal: Damas; Álvaro(Águas), Frederico, Oliveira, Inacio, J.Magalhães, Carlos Manuel, Pacheco, Sousa(Diamantino), Gomes, Futre.
Scorer: Diamantino
Referee: Alan Snoddy (Northern Ireland)

Round Two

MEXICO 2   BULGARIA 0 (Half-time 1-0)

Azteca Stadium, Mexico City, 15 June
Attendance: 114,580

THE noise in the Azteca Stadium was deafening as more than 100,000 Mexican fans willed their team on to a quarter-final appearance and thus repeat their feat of 16 years earlier, when they were the host nation.

Bulgaria had reached the second round without a win to their credit and, apart from Getov's 25th-minute chance, they never looked like chalking up their first success.

Hugo Sánchez was back after suspension and he nearly made amends shortly after Getov's blunder, but was deprived by a fine save from Mikhailov. However, the hosts did take the lead in the 35th minute when Negrete and Aguirre played a neat one-two before the former volleyed the ball into the net.

On the hour Servin made it 2-0 when he timed his run perfectly to meet Negrete's corner and score with a powerful header.

Bulgaria offered little to the game, whereas Mexico were well-organized without being outstanding. It was good enough to earn them a quarter-final place.

Manuel Negrete (22) scores one of the finest goals ever to grace a World Cup finals with this spectacular overhead kick for Mexico against Bulgaria. It showed that Hugo Sánchez was not the only Mexican capable of scoring spectacular goals on the world stage.

Mexico: Larios; Amador, Quirarte, Felix Cruz, Servin, Múñoz, Negrete, España, Boy(De los Cobos), Aguirre, Sánchez.
Scorers: Negrete, Servin
Bulgaria: Mikhailov; Zdravkov, Arabov, Petrov, Dimitrov, Sadkov, Yordanov, Kostadinov, Gospodinov, Paschev(Iskrenov), Getov(Sirakov).
Referee: Romualdo Arppi Filho (Brazil)

BELGIUM 4   SOVIET UNION 3 a.e.t. (Half-time 0-1; 90 mins 2-2)

Nou Camp Stadium, León, 15 June
Attendance: 32,277

THE Soviet Union came to the second round having easily headed their group, whereas Belgium struggled to qualify from third place. But what a great game these sides provided at León. And what a surprise the result turned out to be.

After a lively opening few minutes, during which both teams created chances, the game quietened down for a spell before coming back to life in the 27th minute, when the Soviet Union opened the score with a brilliant solo effort from Belanov, who shot from 25 yards into the top corner of the net.

Belgium had been threatening an equalizer for half an hour and in the end they were rewarded when Scifo met Vercauteren's cross at the far post to score. But Belanov put the Russians back in front in the 70th minute, when Zavarov crossed from the right after an error by the otherwise mercurial Ceulemans. The cross was met by Belanov, who steered the ball under Pfaff's body.

Six minutes later, Belgium were level again and Ceulemans was rewarded for his excellent play with a goal. He gathered a long ball from Vervoort and scored on the turn, despite pleas from the Soviet defenders that he was offside.

Both sides had chances to clinch victory in the closing minutes. A Rodionov shot hit the bar, whilst Dasaev brought off a brilliant save from a Veyt header.

And so the game went into extra-time and after another ten minutes play, Belgium took the lead for the first time when a Demol header from a Vercauteren centre beat the goalkeeper. Belgium increased their lead in the second half of extra-time when Claesen volleyed a superb goal.

The excitement was still not over. A minute later, Belanov scored from the penalty-spot after he had been brought down in the area and so became the first Soviet player to score a hat-trick in the final stages of the World Cup. The Russians still did not give up and in the dying seconds, Pfaff tipped a Yevtushenko lob over the bar.

The whistle eventually blew time on one of the best games of the 1986 tournament and one of the most gripping end-to-end matches in World Cup history. It was sad that there had to be a loser.

Belgium: Pfaff; Grün(Clijsters), Gerets(L.Van der Elst), Renquin, Vervoort, Scifo, Demol, Ceulemans, Vercauteren, Claesen, Veyt.
Scorers: Scifo, Ceulemans, Demol, Claesen
Soviet Union: Dasaev; Bessonov, Demianenko, Kuznetsov, Bal, Zavarov(Rodionov), Aleinikov, Yakovenko(Yevtushenko), Yaremchuk, Belanov, Rats.
Scorer: Belanov 3 (1 pen)
Referee: Erik Fredriksson (Sweden)

Michel Renquin of Belgium.

Vincenzo Scifo equalizes against the Soviet Union and suddenly the Belgians are being taken seriously with their attacking football.

Josimar is congratulated by teammate Elzo after scoring Brazil's second goal with a spectacular drive against Poland. The Brazilians went on to win 4-0.

Wilmar Cabrera of Uruguay.

BRAZIL 4   POLAND 0 (Half-time 1-0)

Jalisco Stadium, Guadalajara, 16 June
Attendance: 45,000

AT last Brazil played open, attacking football. But how close Poland came to scoring in the opening ten minutes when the Brazilian goal was saved only by the woodwork.

Boniek was menacing and he posed problems for the Brazilian defence as Poland monopolized the first 25 minutes. But then Brazil crept back into the game and after half an hour they opened the scoring when Socrates converted a hotly-disputed penalty after Careca had been brought down by Tarasiewicz.

As the second half unfolded, Brazil became even more dominant and Poland missed several good chances. Ten minutes into the second half, Josimar danced through the Polish defence and with awesome power, fired a shot into the net to make it 2-0.

Brazil were pacing themselves in the heat far better than the Poles, who were beginning to wilt, and in the 78th minute Edinho, who played his League soccer in Italy with Udinese, scored after a back-heel from Careca. The goal heralded the return of the Brazilians' true skills.

Zico, on as a substitute for Socrates, was brought down in the 82nd minute and Careca slotted home the spot-kick to complete Poland's anguish. A minute later the Poles brought on Wladislav Zmuda, who equalled Uwe Seeler's record of 21 World Cup appearances, although his contribution to this game was purely academic.

Brazil: Carlos; Josimar, Julio Cesar, Edinho, Branco, Elzo, Alemão, Socrates(Zico), Junior, Careca, Muller(Silas).
Scorers: Socrates (pen), Josimar, Edinho, Careca (pen)
Poland: Mlynarczyk; Przybys(Furtok), Ostrowski, Tarasiewicz, Karaś, Wójcicki, Majewski, Urban(Zmuda), Boniek, Dziekanowski, Smolarek.
Referee: Volker Roth (West Germany)

ARGENTINA 1   URUGUAY 0 (Half-time 1-0)

Cuauhtemoc Stadium, Puebla, 16 June
Attendance: 26,000

THIS second-round match was a repeat of the very first World Cup Final 56 years earlier and, indeed, was the first time these two South American neighbours had met in the World Cup since that day. It was also the World Cup's 400th game.

The match was expected to be a tough and tight defensive game, and a potentially explosive affair was superbly handled by the Italian referee, Luigi Agnolin. Despite seven bookings, the game was not a brutal one — simply, it was played by two Latin sides with equally volatile temperaments.

Maradona created two excellent chances for Argentina in the first half. First, he laid on a perfect cross for Valdano, then he curled a tremendous free-kick against the bar from at least 30 yards. But, apart from those two efforts, the two defences were troubled very little in the opening period until Pasculli struck for the game's only goal four minutes from half-time, when he took advantage of a poor clearance from Acevedo.

Despite a thunderstorm, Argentina dominated the second half, with Maradona magnificent and creating chance after chance for both himself and his colleagues. But once the pitch became sticky, the two teams seemed to get bogged down and there was no further score.

Argentina: Pumpido; Cuciuffo, Ruggeri, Brown, Garré, Giusti, Batista(Olarticoechea), Burruchaga, Pasculli, Maradona, Valdano.
Scorer: Pasculli
Uruguay: Alvez; Gutiérrez, Acevedo(Paz), Rivero, Santin, Ramos, Bossio, Barrios, Pereira, Cabrera(Da Silva), Francescoli.
Referee: Luigi Agnolin (Italy)

Jorge Barrios of Uruguay.

FRANCE 2   ITALY 0 (Half-time 1-0)
Estadio Olimpico '68, Mexico City, 17 June
Attendance: 70,000

A WORLD Cup meeting between the reigning World and European Champions did, on paper, promise so much. But in reality it was nowhere near the close match many expected and France won easily.

The French were now at the peak of their maturity and, with their midfield outstanding, played like potential World Champions.

Michel Platini again confirmed his status as one of the world's top players and it was his goal in the 14th minute which set France on their way to victory.

The move which led to the goal was started by Fernández, who passed to Rocheteau. He, in turn, stroked the ball to Platini, who casually lifted it over Galli in the Italian goal.

After half an hour, Fernández nearly increased the lead but his 35-yard shot hit the bar with Galli off his line and well beaten.

The Italian attack offered little more than a token gesture and the French were never troubled by the Latin forwards.

France got a deserved second goal after 57 minutes, following a great move which started deep in their own half. It ended with Rocheteau laying the ball off for Stopyra to score from a narrow angle.

France had been promising so much in recent World Cups. Was this to be their year at last?

France: Bats; Ayache, Battiston, Bossis, Amoros, Giresse, Tigana, Fernández(Tusseau), Platini (Ferreri), Rocheteau, Stopyra.
Scorers: Platini, Stopyra
Italy: Galli; Bergomi, Vierchowod, Scirea, Cabrini, Baresi(Di Gennaro), De Napoli, Bagni, Conti, Altobelli, Galderisi(Vialli).
Referee: Carlos Esposito (Argentina)

Klaus Allofs of West Germany.

WEST GERMANY 1   MOROCCO 0 (Half-time 0-0)
Universitario Stadium, Monterrey, 17 June
Attendance: 19,800

WEST Germany had struggled to beat Morocco when the teams last met in the World Cup in 1970, also in Mexico. And 16 years later it was the same story. Only a last-gasp winner saved the Germans from embarrassment.

The favourites struggled for large parts of the match and the Moroccan defence coped well with the unimaginative German attack, particularly in the first-half. A minute from half-time, the Europeans nearly took the lead but were thwarted by a great save from Zaki in the Moroccan goal, after he saved point-blank from Rummenigge.

Whilst Morocco defended well, they offered very little in attack and it was fortunate for them the Germans were not better organized up front.

However, with extra-time looming, the Moroccans paid a high price for failing to organize their defensive wall when the Germans were awarded a free-kick 25 yards out and Matthäus scored the face-saving winner.

West Germany: Schumacher; Berthold, Förster, Jakobs, Briegel, Eder, Matthäus, Magath, Rummenigge, Allofs, Völler(Littbarski).
Scorer: Matthäus
Morocco: Zaki; Khalifi, Bouyahyaoui, Oudani, Lamriss, Dolmy, El Haddaoui, Bouderbala, Timoumi, Khairi, Krimau.
Referee: Zoran Petrović (Yugoslavia)

ENGLAND 3   PARAGUAY 0 (Half-time 1-0)
Azteca Stadium, Mexico City, 18 June
Attendance: 98,728

A WEEK earlier, England were on the verge of packing for home. Now their fans were optimistic of them winning the World Cup for the second time. The cliché is that 'football

Left: Peter Beardsley pounces on a rebound to put England 2-0 ahead against Paraguay. *Above:* Alvin Martin (left) and Glenn Hoddle (4) mob Beardsley after his goal.

French goalkeeper Jöel Bats has every reason to be pleased, for he has just saved a penalty-kick from Brazil's Zico. There was, of course, more penalty drama at the end of extra-time.

Jesper Olsen gave Denmark a 33rd-minute lead from the penalty-spot but the Danes' joy was short-lived as Spain went on to win 5-1.

Michel Platini holds his head in despair after missing from the spot in the penalty competition against Brazil, but he could breathe again after France went through 4-3.

is a funny game' and so it proved when one looked at how England's fortunes changed in a matter of seven days.

There was no recall for Ray Wilkins, whilst Bryan Robson was still out injured. But the two were not missed as England continued their transformation.

Peter Shilton was again outstanding in the England goal and on the half-hour he pulled off two crucial saves. First, he made amends for a weak clearance which was driven back by Cañete. And a minute later, the same player forced Shilton to bring off another fine save. But in the next attack England scored when Gary Lineker notched his fourth goal of the tournament from a Glenn Hoddle cross which was pushed on by Steve Hodge.

Paraguay started dishing out some rough treatment in the second half but ten minutes after the break, Peter Beardsley pounced on a rebound after a Terry Butcher shot came off the 'keeper's chest. Beardsley, one of England's bright new stars, put the ball away to make it 2-0.

Lineker met a Gary Stevens (Spurs) cross to score the third goal in the 72nd minute and his total of five took him to the top of the goalscoring list. England's win also set up their first meeting with Argentina since the Falklands conflict.

England: Shilton; G.M.Stevens, Martin, Butcher, Sansom, Steven, Reid(G.A.Stevens), Hoddle, Hodge, Lineker, Beardsley(Hateley).
Scorers: Lineker 2, Beardsley
Paraguay: Fernández; Torales(Guasch), Schettina, Delgado, Zabala, Cañete, Romero, Núñez, Ferreira, Cabañas, Mendoza.
Referee: Jamal Al Sharif (Syria)

SPAIN 5   DENMARK 1 (Half-time 1-1)

La Corregidora Stadium, Querétaro, 18 June
Attendance: 38,500

DENMARK had been one of the revelations of the opening matches and their goalscoring exploits were winning them many admirers. Spain, on the other hand, had done well to overcome adversity in terms of injury and illness. But there could not have been anybody — including the Spaniards — who would have envisaged the above scoreline.

Everything was going in Denmark's favour as they led with half-time approaching. But then came a dreadful blunder which probably cost them the match.

Jesper Olsen had given Denmark the lead in the 33rd minute, when he scored from the penalty-spot after Berggren had been brought down in the area by Gallego. But two minutes from the interval, Denmark's goalscorer turned villain when his dreadful pass across the face of his own goal allowed the Real Madrid striker, Emilio Butragueño, to intercept and score with ease.

This unsettled the Danes and in the 56th minute, Butragueño was again on the score-sheet when he headed home from a Victor corner. Spain were now playing with confidence and after 69 minutes they went further ahead when Goicoechea scored from a penalty after Butragueño had been brought down by Busk.

Ten minutes from time, Butragueño completed his hat-trick after the Danes had been caught going forward. In the last minute the same player was brought down in the box by Morten Olsen. He got up to score from the kick and became the first man since Eusébio in 1966 to score four goals in one game in the final stages of the World Cup.

Spain played their best football of the tournament, but one could not help but wonder at what the outcome would have been, had Jesper Olsen not made that suicidal pass at the end of the first half.

Spain: Zubizarreta; Tomás, Gallego, Goicoechea, Camacho, Julio Alberto, Víctor, Míchel (Francisco), Calderé, Butragueño, Salinas(Eloy).
Scorers: Butragueño 4 (1 pen), Goicoechea (pen)
Denmark: Høgh; Busk, M.Olsen, Nielsen, Andersen(Eriksen), Berggren, J.Olsen(Mölby), Bertlesen, Lerby, Laudrup, Elkjaer-Larsen.
Scorer: J.Olsen (pen)
Referee: Jan Keizer (Holland)

Quarter-finals

FRANCE 1   BRAZIL 1 a.e.t. (Half-time 1-1; 90 mins 1-1)
France won 4-3 on penalties

Jalisco Stadium, Guadalajara, 21 June
Attendance: 65,777

FRANCE had been playing like potential world champions but to turn dreams into reality one has to beat the best, and there was no finer test of France's ability than this meeting with Brazil. If the French were ever going to get the better of their South American opponents, there would be no better chance than in this meeting.

It was a fine game, played in typically hot Mexican midday heat. It was the Europeans who turned on the early pressure, but Brazil took the lead in the 18th minute when Careca finished off a clever move, involving Muller and Junior, to score from 15 yards.

Both sides continued to attack and after half an hour the French goal survived when a Muller shot hit a post. But in the 41st minute, France drew level when the Brazilian goalkeeper, Carlos, conceded his first goal in 401 minutes' football. Midfielder Giresse sent Rocheteau away and his cross fooled the defence before falling to Michel Platini, who prodded the ball home.

The end-to-end action continued in the second half but if failed to produce any further goals and after 70 minutes the Brazilian fans were calling for Zico. Coach Telê Santana brought him on in place of Muller and four minutes later, Zico was given the responsibility of putting Brazil in front from the penalty-spot after Branco had been brought down by Bats. But the Brazilian superstar's kick was saved by the French 'keeper.

Twenty-two pairs of tired legs were subjected to extra-time, during which the best chance fell to Bellone four minutes from the end, but he was fouled by Carlos outside the penalty area. The referee played the advantage rule, but Bellone was off-balance and there turned out to be no advantage.

So the game went to a penalty competition and the French must have had memories of their semi-final defeat by West Germany in similar circumstances in 1982.

Socrates missed the first kick and then Stopyra converted his to put France ahead. They always remained with their noses slightly in front and Bellone gained compensation, for being brought down by Carlos, by scoring his spot-kick which went in off a post.

Platini missed for France when the score was 3-3 but with the next kick, Julio Cesar did the same and it was down to Luis Fernández to put France into the semi-finals. He wrong-footed Carlos and the Brazilian carnival was over.

West German goalkeeper Harald Schumacher celebrates after Mexico's Raul Servin misses a penalty.

France: Bats; Battiston, Amoros, Bossis, Tusseau, Giresse(Ferreri), Tigana, Platini, Fernández, Stopyra, Rocheteau(Bellone).
Scorer: Platini
Brazil: Carlos; Josimar, Julio Cesar, Edinho, Branco, Alemão, Socrates, Junior(Silas), Elzo, Muller(Zico), Careca.
Scorer: Careca
Referee: Ioan Igna (Romania)

WEST GERMANY 0   MEXICO 0 a.e.t. (Half-time 0-0; 90 mins 0-0)
West Germany won 4-1 on penalties
Universitario Stadium, Monterrey, 21 June
Attendance: 44,386

WEST Germany had been making life tough for themselves and this quarter-final match was yet another near thing for the former champions, although even the hosts felt the effects of the intense heat.

It was a drab game and the worst of the four quarter-final clashes, made worse by the fact that the fans had to be subjected to 120 minutes football because of the extra-time which was required after a goalless 90 minutes. Even then, no goals resulted and another penalty competition was required.

Allofs, Brehme, Matthäus and Littbarski all scored for the Germans, whilst only Negrete scored for the hosts, who found it difficult to get the ball home, either from open play or from the penalty-spot. And so Germany reached a record eighth World Cup semi-final.

West Germany: Schumacher; Berthold, Förster, Jakobs, Briegel, Brehme, Eder(Littbarski), Matthäus, Magath, Allofs, Rummenigge(Hoeness).
Mexico: Larios; Servin, Felix Cruz, Quirarte, Amador(Javier Cruz), Múñoz, Aguirre, Negrete, España, Boy(De los Cobos), Sánchez.
Referee: Palacio Jesus Diaz (Colombia)

ARGENTINA 2   ENGLAND 1 (Half-time 0-0)
Azteca Stadium, Mexico City, 22 June
Attendance: 114,580

THIS was the third World Cup meeting between these sides and on each of the previous occasions, England had emerged victorious. But this latest clash had a special significance because it was the first meeting between the two sides since the Falklands War in 1982, four years after Argentina first won the World Cup.

Argentina gave a very professional performance and probably deserved to win, even though their first goal was surrounded with controversy.

England's spearhead attack of Beardsley and Lineker was snuffed out by the revamped Argentinian defence and the difference between the sides was the sheer brilliance of Diego Maradona, who seemed to scare the England defenders every time he came near the penalty area.

Maradona's first goal is probably one of the World Cup's most talked about incidents, after England's third goal in the 1966 Final.

This 1986 goal was scored after 51 minutes, when Maradona pushed forward and then passed to Valdano on the right. But he lost the ball to Hodge, who sliced a back-pass to Peter Shilton. Maradona rose to meet the ball with his head and in an instant the ball was in the net. Shilton knew that the Argentinian had put the ball in with his hand and

Michel Platini scored twice in the 1986 tournament. He became manager of the French team in 1990.

Diego Maradona (dark shirt, second right) rounds Peter Shilton to score a magnificent second goal against England in the quarter-final. It was a superb effort and left England's defenders trailing in his wake. Strangely, it was only after this goal that Bobby Robson's team began to attack and almost pulled off a draw.

'The Hand of God' beats Peter Shilton and Maradona scores one of the most controversial goals in World Cup history.

Pfaff looks happy, as well he might, for he has just saved a penalty from Spanish substitute, Eloy, and Belgium are through to the semi-final.

subsequent television replays confirmed this to be the case. In all fairness to the Tunisian referee it looked a perfectly good goal on the spur of the moment and he allowed it to stand.

Despite this blatant piece of cheating by the world's greatest footballer, there was no denying the brilliance of Maradona four minutes later, when he made Stevens, Butcher and Fenwick look like amateur players as he waltzed through them before scoring a remarkable solo goal. All three seemed frightened of tackling Maradona for fear of conceding a penalty.

It was only after going two goals in arrears that England really got on the attack. Manager Bobby Robson brought on John Barnes as a 74th-minute substitute for Trevor Steven. Not only did Barnes make history as England's 100th player in the World Cup finals, but he also added much-needed fuel to the England attack and it was from one of his crosses in the 81st minute that Lineker headed in at the far post for his sixth goal of the tournament.

Lineker had a great chance to level the scores three minutes from time, but just failed to connect with a Barnes cross and Argentina ran out 2-1 winners.

Maradona later said, tongue in cheek no doubt, that his goal was from 'The Hand of God'. There was also an interesting comment from Pelé. He said of the incident: "It is certain that if the Argentines or Uruguayans had been in the same spot as the English, they would have trampled the referee."

Argentina: Pumpido; Cuciuffo, Brown, Ruggeri, Olarticoechea, Batista, Giusti, Burruchaga (Tapia), Enrique, Valdano, Maradona.
Scorer: Maradona 2
England: Shilton; G.M.Stevens, Butcher, Fenwick, Sansom, Hoddle, Steven(Barnes), Reid (Waddle), Hodge, Lineker, Beardsley.
Scorer: Lineker
Referee: Ali Bennaceur (Tunisia)

BELGIUM 1   SPAIN 1 a.e.t. (Half-time 1-0; 90 mins 1-1)
Belgium won 5-4 on penalties
Cuauhtemoc Stadium, Puebla, 22 June
Attendance: 45,000

BASED on the respective quarter-final results of Spain and Belgium, this game was wide open, for both sides had beaten well-fancied teams in getting to this stage of the finals. And at the end of 120 minutes' play and a penalty competition, the two sides were separated by only one penalty miss.

Spain were now being tipped as likely champions, but had to go into this game without the 'Butcher of Bilbao', Goicoechea, who was suspended after receiving a second yellow card in his previous game. And with Belgium improving all the time, the scales were probably tipped in their favour.

All the early attacking came from the Spaniards, who took advantage of a surprisingly poor Belgium midfield. Their defence, though, was on top form and, despite the early pressure and an unsuccessful penalty appeal by Butragueño, it was Belgium who opened the scoring in the 34th minute.

Vercauteren sent in a low cross from the left and Ceulemans flung himself at it to connect with a header at the near post. It was a good goal, if against the run of the play.

Veyt should have sewn it up for Belgium shortly after the start of the second half but his shot was touched past the post by Zubizarreta. Pfaff in the Belgium goal also saved his side on several occasions as Spain continued to do most of the second-half attacking. But it was not until the 85th minute that their pressure was rewarded with a goal, when Señor, a second-half substitute, scored with a 25-yard free-kick which was deflected past Pfaff who was going the wrong way.

Extra-time failed to produce any further goals and so a third quarter-final went to a penalty

383

competition. Belgium scored all five of their spot-kicks, whilst Eloy was the unfortunate Spaniard to miss. Belgium's winning kick was scored by Leo Van der Elst.

Belgium had qualified for the finals only after being given a second chance in the qualifying tournament. And they only came through their opening group in Mexico as one of the best third-placed teams. Suddenly, though, they found themselves only one game away from the World Cup Final.

Belgium: Pfaff; Gerets, Renquin, Demol, Vervoort, Vercauteren(L.Van der Elst), Scifo, Grün, Ceulemans, Claesen, Veyt(Broos).
Scorer: Cuelemans
Spain: Zubizarreta; Tomás(Señor), Gallego, Chendo, Camacho, Julio Alberto, Víctor, Míchel, Calderé, Butragueño, Salinas(Eloy).
Scorer: Señor
Referee: Sigfried Kirschen (East Germany)

Semi-finals

José Antonio Camacho of Spain.

WEST GERMANY 2 FRANCE 0 (Half-time 1-0)
Jalisco Stadium, Guadalajara, 25 June
Attendance: 45,000

THIS was a repeat of the 1982 semi-final which the West Germans won in a penalty competition. It was also a return meeting of Harald Schumacher and Patrick Battiston, who was seriously injured in that infamous collision with the German 'keeper. And to serve as a reminder to those who had forgotten, an effigy of Schumacher was seen hanging by a rope behind the German's goal.

Happily, there was no repeat of the incident. But there was also none of the excitement of that classic 1982 match in Seville.

The French midfield was not firing on all cylinders and Michel Platini was kept out of the game by Rolff. Matthäus and Allofs also gave great performances for West Germany as Franz Beckenbauer's team at last silenced their critics.

The Germans took the lead in the eighth minute, from a free-kick after Rummenigge was brought down with a touch of the theatricals. Brehme's kick went under the diving body of goalkeeper Bats, who was to later make amends for the mistake with some fine first-half saves.

France started pushing forward more after falling behind, but they did not get into their stride until the second half. Stopyra made a good run, but his shot hit Schumacher's legs, and in a frantic last five minutes, France had three other scoring chances. But the only other goal fell to Völler, from a breakaway a minute from time, as West Germany reached their fifth World Cup Final.

West Germany: Schumacher; Brehme, Förster, Jakobs, Briegel, Eder, Matthäus, Magath, Rolff, Allofs, Rummenigge(Völler).
Scorers: Brehme, Völler
France: Bats; Ayache, Battiston, Bossis, Amoros, Tigana, Giresse(Vercruysse), Platini, Fernández, Stopyra, Bellone(Xuereb).
Referee: Luigi Agnolin (Italy)

Harald Schumacher of West Germany.

STATISTICS

Goalscorers:
6 — Gary Lineker (England).
5 — Emilio Butragueño (Spain), Careca (Brazil), Diego Armando Maradona (Argentina).
4 — Preben Elkjaer-Larsen (Denmark), Igor Belanov (Soviet Union), Jorge Valdano (Argentina), Alessandro Altobelli (Italy).
3 — Rudi Völler (West Germany), Jesper Olsen (Denmark), Nico Claesen, Jan Ceulemans (both Belgium)
2 — Klaus Allofs (West Germany), Abdelrazak Khairi (Morocco), Ramón Calderé (Spain), Julio César Romero, Roberto Cabañas (both Paraguay), Socrates, Josimar Pereira (both Brazil), Jean-Pierre Papin, Yannick Stopyra, Michel Platini (all France), Jorge Burruchaga (Argentina), Fernando Quirarte (Mexico), Vincenzo Scifo (Belgium), Ivan Yaremchuk (Soviet Union).
1 — Nasko Sirakov, Plamen Getov (both Bulgaria), Oscar Ruggeri, Pedro Pablo Pasculli, José Luis Brown (all Argentina), Park Chang-sun, Kim Jong-boo, Choi Soon-ho, Huh Jung-moo (all South Korea), Hugo Sánchez, Luis Flores, Manuel Negrete, Raul Servin (all Mexico), Erwin Vandenbergh, Frank Vercauteran, Danny Veyt, Stéphane Demol (all Belgium), Ahmed Amaiesh Rhadi (Iraq), Lajos Détári, Marton Esterhazy (both Hungary), Edinho (Brazil), Manuel Amoros, Luis Fernández, Jean-Marc Ferreri, Bernard Genghini, Jean Tigana, Dominique Rocheteau (all France), Pavel Yakovenko, Alexandr Zavarov, Oleg Blokhin, Sergei Rodionov, Sergei Aleinikov, Vassiliy Rats (all Soviet Union), Norman Whiteside, Colin Clarke (both Northern Ireland), Djamel Zidane (Algeria), Andreas Brehme, Karl-Heinz Rummenigge, Lothar Matthäus (all West Germany), Gordon Strachan (Scotland), Krimau (Morocco), Santos Carlos Manuel, Diamantino Miranda (both Portugal), Julio Salinas, Eloy Olaya Prendes, Andoni Goicoechea, Juan Antonio Señor (all Spain), Antonio Alzamendi, Enzo Francescoli (both Uruguay), Sören Lerby, Michael Laudrup, John Eriksen (all Denmark), Wlodzimierz Smolarek (Poland), Peter Beardsley (England).

ARGENTINA 2   BELGIUM 0 (Half-time 0-0)

Azteca Stadium, Mexico City, 25 June
Attendance: 110,420

THIS was also a repeat of a 1982 World Cup meeting. On that occasion, these teams met in the opening match and Belgium won 1-0, in the process keeping Diego Maradona out of the game by means, foul or otherwise. But there was no stopping Maradona this time as he single-handedly took the Europeans apart with a magnificent solo performance which also earned him two more goals.

In the opening minutes, Vercauteren reminded Maradona about their last meeting when he brought the Argentinian down, but Maradona was too clever and quick for the Belgian defence most of the time.

Belgium defended solidly in the first half and as the game wore on it became a scrappy and somewhat tedious affair. Valdano had the ball in the net in the ninth minute but his effort was disallowed because he steered the ball into the net with his arm. The Argentinians protested, no doubt spurred on by their successful 'Hand of God' goal against England in the quarter-finals.

Belgium's attack lacked fluency and if a goal was going to come, the South Americans looked more likely to score and, indeed, they found the net after 51 minutes. Enrique crossed from the right, Maradona cleverly took the ball, beat two defenders and then shot past Pfaff in the Belgian goal. Ten minutes later, Maradona scored another of his specials when he left three defenders trailing in his wake before slotting the ball home. It was reminiscent of his second goal against England and underlined the solo role he had played in taking Argentina to their third World Cup Final.

Argentina: Pumpido; Cuciuffo, Ruggeri, Brown, Olarticoechea, Giusti, Enrique, Batista, Burruchaga(Bochini), Maradona, Valdano.
Scorer: Maradona 2
Belgium: Pfaff; Gerets, Grün, Demol, Renquin(Desmet), Vervoort, Scifo, Vercauteren, Ceulemans, Claesen, Veyt.
Referee: Antonio Ramirez Marquez (Mexico)

Third place play-off
FRANCE 4   BELGIUM 2 a.e.t. (Half-time 2-1; 90 mins 2-2)

Cuauhtemoc Stadium, Puebla, 28 June
Attendance: 21,000

DUE to injuries and tiredness, France fielded only three regular first-choice players, Amoros, Tigana and Battiston. Belgium, however, fielded a full-strength team and were expected to take third place.

Belgium's Nico Claesen makes it
2-2 in the 73rd minute and, again,
extra-time is required. This time,
however, there was no penalty
competition as France scored twice
more to equal their best-ever
placing in the World Cup.

The French, of course, had to overcome the severe disappointment of losing a second successive World Cup semi-final, but they managed it in some style.

That did not look likely after ten minutes, when Belgium took the lead through Ceulemans after France had missed a golden opportunity at the other end. However, the French pulled level in the 27th minute, after a defensive mix-up allowed Ferreri to score. And three minutes from half-time, France went in front when Papin finished of a good move inspired by Tigana.

Despite trailing at half-time, Belgium had already had plenty of chances to wrap up a victory and in the 73rd minute, Claesen made it 2-2 and the game went into extra-time. It was Belgium's third game of the series to require an extra half-hour's play.

Two minutes before the interval, Genghini put France ahead once more after another defensive error. And right on time, Amoros completed the scoring with a spot-kick after he had been brought down by Gerets.

France equalled their best World Cup finish and whilst Belgium had to be content with fourth place, they won a special place in Mexican hearts after setting up a fund out of their bonuses to go to the underprivileged children of Mexico City, who were roaming the streets. It was heartening to know that footballers have a sense of responsibility beyond scoring goals, winning matches and collecting big pay-cheques.

France: Rust; Le Roux(Bossis), Battiston, Bibard, Amoros, Tigana(Tusseau), Genghini, Vercruysse, Ferreri, Bellone, Papin.
Scorers: Ferreri, Papin, Genghini, Amoros (pen)
Belgium: Pfaff; Renquin(F.Van der Elst), Gerets, Demol, Grün, Vervoort, Scifo(L. Van der Elst), Veyt, Mommens, Ceulemans, Claesen.
Scorers: Ceulemans, Claesen
Referee: George Courtney (England)

Final

ARGENTINA 3   WEST GERMANY 2 (Half-time 1-0)

Azteca Stadium, Mexico City, 29 June
Attendance: 114,590

UNLIKE the 1982 Final, which was one-sided and not a particularly good match, the 13th World Cup Final was a good one which had plenty of individual skills, excitement, drama and five goals. Furthermore, the result was in doubt until the final whistle.

Maradona had his usual good game for Argentina but the South Americans showed that they were not just a one-man team and their midfield, notably Burruchaga, was outstanding. West Germany, for their part, showed little imagination until they went two goals down.

The Germans had very few chances in a tense first half and midway through the first period, in one of Argentina's first serious assaults on the German goal, a Burruchaga free-kick was floated over Schumacher, who missed the ball, leaving Brown with the easiest of headers at the far post.

West Germany brought on Völler for Allofs in the second half and, whilst Brown was off the field injured, the Germans pushed forward to try to capitalize on their advantage. But it was Argentina who broke away and Maradona found Enrique on the left. His pass to Valdano was calmly put into the net by the Argentine forward and West Germany were 2-0 down.

The Germans now showed more inventiveness and attacked with some conviction. In the 73rd minute, Brehme's corner to the near post was headed in by Rummenigge, who was scoring in his third successive tournament.

Eight minutes later, and from another Brehme corner, Berthold headed on for Völler to score and the teams were all square. But, just as West Germany looked as though they could become the first European team to win the World Cup in the Americas, Maradona took

Own-goals:
Cho Kwang-rae, South Korea v Italy.

Hat-tricks
Preben Elkjaer-Larsen (Denmark v Uruguay), Gary Lineker (England v Poland), Igor Belanov (Soviet Union v Belgium), Emilio Butragueño (4 goals) (Spain v Denmark).

Fastest goal
63 seconds — Emilio Butragueño (Spain v Northern Ireland).

Most goals (team)
14 — Argentina

Teams failing to score
Canada

Total goals scored: 132
Average per game: 2.54

Penalties
Scored: Alessandro Altobelli (Italy v Argentina) *Referee: Jan Keizer (Holland)*, Nico Claesen (Belgium v Iraq) *Referee: Palacio Jesus Diaz (Colombia)*, Igor Belanov (Soviet Union v Hungary) *Referee: Luigi Agnolin (Italy)*, Enzo Francescoli (Uruguay v Denmark) *Referee: Antonio Ramirez Marquez (Mexico)*, Jesper Olsen (Denmark v West Germany) *Referee: Alexis Ponnet (Belgium)*, Igor Belanov (Soviet Union v Belgium) *Referee: Erik Fredriksson (Sweden)*, Socrates (Brazil v Poland) *Referee: Volker Roth (West Germany)*, Careca (Brazil v Poland) *Referee: Volker Roth (West Germany)*, Jesper Olsen (Denmark v Spain) *Referee: Jan Keizer (Holland)*, Andoni Goicoechea (Spain v Denmark) *Referee: Jan Keizer (Holland)*, Emilio Butragueño (Spain v Denmark) *Referee: Jan Keizer (Holland)*, Manuel Amoros (France v Belgium) *Referee: George Courtney (England)*.

Most appearances
7 — Sergio Daniel Batista, *José Luis Brown*, Jorge Burruchaga, *Diego Armando Maradona, Jorge Valdano*, Ricardo Giusti, Julio Jorge Olarticoechea, *Nery Pumpido, Oscar Ruggeri* (all Argentina); *Jean-Marie Pfaff*, Vincenzo Scifo, *Jan Ceulemans*, Nico Claesen, Stéphane Demol (all Belgium); *Manuel Amoros, Patrick Battiston*, Maxime Bossis (all France); *Harald Schumacher*, Karl-Heinz Förster, Norbert Eder, Lothar Matthäus, Karl-Heinz Rummenigge, Klaus Allofs (all West Germany).
Those players in italics played in seven full games.

Argentina and West Germany line up before the 1986 World Cup Final. From left to right are Argentinian players Burruchaga, Valdano, Giusti, Olarticoechea, Enrique, Batista, Brown, Ruggeri, Cuciuffo, Pumpido, Maradona, then officials Erik Fredriksson (linesman), Romualdo Arppi Filho (referee) and Morera Berny Ulloa (linesman) and the West Germans, Rummenigge, Schumacher, Briegel, Jakobs, Berthold, Förster, Eder, Allofs, Brehme, Magath and Matthäus.

charge, kept cool and laid on a well-timed pass over the half-way line. The ball beat the West German offside trap and found Burruchaga, who gave Schumacher no chance with a powerful shot. The Germans had been on level terms for only two minutes.

Maradona almost crowned another great performance with a goal, but Harald Schumacher turned his low free-kick away from danger in the closing minutes. With two minutes to go, Argentina brought on Trobbiani for his World Cup debut. And at two minutes, his appearance equalled the shortest-ever World Cup finals career of Khemais Labidi (Tunisia) in 1978.

It was a second successive loser's medal for Förster, Briegel, Rummenigge and Schumacher and afterwards the German goalkeeper said: "We lost because I was so bad." In truth, Argentina won because they were probably the the best side in the tournament. They certainly had the star of the tournament in Diego Maradona, who had now established himself as one of the all-time World Cup greats.

Below: Argentina's three goals which won the World Cup. In descending order: Brown outjumps the German defence to make it 1-0; Valdano beats Schumacher and the score is 2-0; Burruchaga, having accepted Maradona's pass, regains the lead for Argentina. *Below right:* Karl-Heinz Rummenigge and Oscar Ruggeri battle it out. Rummenigge scored the Germans' first goal.

Argentina: Nery Pumpido; José Luis Cuciuffo, José Luis Brown, Oscar Ruggeri, Julio Jorge Olarticoechea, Sergio Daniel Batista, Ricardo Giusti, Héctor Adolfo Enrique, Jorge Burruchaga (Marcelo Trobbiani), Diego Armando Maradona, Jorge Valdano.
Scorers: Brown, Valdano, Burruchaga
West Germany: Harald Schumacher; Thomas Berthold, Dittmar Jakobs, Karl-Heinz Förster, Hans-Peter Briegel, Andreas Brehme, Lothar Matthäus, Felix Magath(Dieter Hoeness), Norbert Eder, Karl-Heinz Rummenigge, Klaus Allofs(Rudi Völler).
Scorers: Rummenigge, Völler
Referee: Romualdo Arppi Filho (Brazil)

Berthold's flick is headed in by Völler (partly hidden by the Argentinian number 5) and West Germany are level. The Germans, who were appearing in their fifth World Cup Final, had little time to celebrate, though. Two minutes later, Burruchaga scored the winner for Argentina.

Sendings-off
Michael Sweeney (Canada v Hungary) *Referee: Jamal Al Sharif (Syria)*, Ray Wilkins (England v Morocco) *Referee: Gabriel Gonzalez (Paraguay)*, Basil Gorgis (Iraq v Belgium) *Referee: Palacio Jesus Diaz (Colombia)*, Miguel Bossio (Uruguay v Denmark) *Referee: Antonio Ramirez Marquez (Mexico)*, José Batista (Uruguay v Scotland) *Referee: Joël Quiniou (France)*, Frank Arnesen (Denmark v West Germany) *Referee: Alexis Ponnet (Belgium)*, Thomas Berthold (Mexico v West Germany) *Referee: Palacio Jesus Diaz (Colombia)*, Javier Aguirre (Mexico v West Germany) *Referee: Palacio Jesus Diaz (Colombia)*.

Most players used
21 — France

Number of players used by Finalists
18 — Argentina
17 — West Germany

Skipper Maradona (right) and goalkeeper Pumpido gaze at the FIFA World Cup trophy as Argentina are crowned champions.

MEN WHO MADE THE HEADLINES - 1990

Roger Milla
(Cameroon)

ROGER Milla, at 38, was the star of the Cameroon team in 1990, scoring four goals as they became the first African side to reach a World Cup quarter-final. Born at Yaoundé, the capital of Cameroon, Milla began with Eclair Douala, then played for Leopards of Douala. With his next club, Tonnerre of Yaoundé, he won Cameroon League and Cup medals. Africa's Footballer of the Year in 1976, he moved to France in 1977 and spent two seasons at Valenciennes before being transferred to Monaco. He had four seasons with Bastia and between 1984 and 1987 was with Saint-Etienne before a move to Montpellier. He won the French Cup with Monaco in 1980 and with Bastia in 1981 and collected a French Second Division championship medal with Saint-Etienne. After 152 goals in the French League, he retired to the French Reunion Islands to play for Saint Pierre, helping them win the local league title in 1990. After 81 full caps, Milla was tempted out of retirement for his second World Cup, returning after the coach got the nod of approval from the other players. In five games, all as a 'super sub', Milla scored the two goals which beat Romania and the two that beat Colombia. In the quarter-final against England he was involved in Cameroon's two goals. Milla, who changed his name from Miller to sound more African, is the oldest man to score in the final stages of a World Cup.

Salvatore Schillaci
(Italy)

ITALIAN fans have had a long line of scoring aces to cheer, but they were unaware that another was about to be unleashed during Italia '90. Salvatore Schillaci of Juventus arrived at the championships with only two full caps to his name, but in the opening match he came on as substitute for Carnevale and four minutes later scored the only goal of the game against Austria. Schillaci went on to become the tournament's top scorer with six goals and only in the game against the USA did he fail to score. He comes from a poor background and his mother was always against him becoming a footballer, wanting him to get a 'proper job' instead. Born at Palermo in 1964, Schillaci started his senior career in 1982, in the Italian Serie 'C' with local team, Messina, whom he helped to promotion in 1986-7. In 1988-9, his last season with Messina, he was top scorer in Serie 'B' with 23 goals. Next season he was playing for Juventus in Serie 'A', ending the campaign with 15 goals, the highest tally by a Juventus player in his debut season since 1946-7. Schillaci's memorable season was crowned with UEFA and Italian Cup-winners' medals and in March 1990 he made his international debut, against Switzerland. Ironically, he was the last member of the Italian squad to be pencilled-in for the World Cup.

Paul Gascoigne
(England)

IN football terms, Paul Gascoigne came of age during Italia '90, only five years after making his Football League debut as a 17-year-old with Newcastle United. Truly, Gascoigne was the inspiration behind an England team whose performances improved dramatically as the tournament progressed. Born in 1967, like teammate Chris Waddle in Gateshead, he began with Newcastle and soon won Under-21 honours. In 1988, he became England's most expensive footballer when he joined Tottenham Hotspur for £2 million. Two months later he made his full England debut, coming on as substitute for his former Newcastle teammate, Peter Beardsley, against Denmark at Wembley. 'Gazza' has a reputation for being the England team's practical joker but, as Bobby Robson said, this is only one side of a 'precocious talent'. That talent was never more evident than during England's World Cup run. Gascoigne chased every ball from his midfield role and showed great defensive skills as well as being involved in most of England's goalscoring moves. When he received his second yellow card of the tournament, during the semi-final, it meant he would have missed the World Cup Final, should England have qualified. But Gascoigne showed tremendous character and, although visibly shaken and upset, he knuckled down and played magnificently in trying to send his country through.

Argentina Pay the Penalty
Italy 1990

*E*NGLAND, the Soviet Union, Greece and Italy were the final four candidates bidding to stage the 14th World Cup, but when FIFA made their choice, only the Italians and the Soviets were left in the running. Italy had their fine World Cup tradition to call upon, but the Soviets had harmed their claim by announcing their boycott of the 1984 Olympic Games to be held in Los Angeles. On 19 May 1984, Italy were unanimously chosen as hosts for the 1990 World Cup, only the second nation, after Mexico, to be awarded two tournaments.

The Italian FA, like many before them, caused some anxious moments with rebuilding programmes well behind schedule. The huge cost of the work was not only counted in millions of lire, but also in human lives as workers died in the quest to turn Italy's stadiums into some of the finest in the world.

For the second successive tournament all the previous champions took part. Newcomers Costa Rica and the United Arab Emirates gave hope to lesser soccer nations. The Republic of Ireland were also competing in the finals for the first time and Egypt returned after an absence of 56 years. For the USA there was the chance to repeat their giantkilling act of 1950, the last time they had appeared in the finals.

Colombia reached the finals for only the second time, 28 years after their debut, whilst former World Cup Finalists Czechoslovakia, Sweden, and Holland returned. Cameroon were also back and turned out to be one of surprises of the series.

England were named as one of the top six seeds, despite finishing runners-up to Sweden in their qualifying group. This upset some who felt that the English had gained their status because of their unruly fans. England were based in Cagliari, on the island of Sardinia, and, as one of the seeded teams, were to play all their group matches at one venue. This reduced the amount of travelling by their supporters but the good intentions went astray when Holland, one of the second seeded teams and whose fans also had a bad reputation, were drawn in the same group.

The format was the same as 1986 with the 24 finalists divided into six groups. The top two in each went through to the second phase and were joined by the four best third-placed teams. England's group was not resolved until the final games. FIFA had to draw lots between Holland and the Republic of Ireland to decide second and third place. After the opening group matches, the competition became a knock-out affair. Again, the unsatisfactory penalty competitions were used to resolve matches that were still level after extra-time.

Over 73,000 people packed the Stadio Giuseppe Meazza in Milan for the opening ceremony which was beamed to more than 500 million people in 100 countries. They saw a parade of women dressed in national costumes and were then treated to excerpts from Verdi's opera *Nabucco* which was shown live on giant TV screens from La Scala. By the time the 14th World Cup ended, Italian tenor, Luciano Pavarotti, was as well-known to soccer fans as Zenga, Schillaci, Maradona, and 'Gazza' himself.

Argentina and Cameroon got the tournament underway and the game was to be indicative of two notable features of Italia '90 — giantkilling and dismal refereeing. The Africans showed how they had narrowed the gap between themselves and the recognized giants of world soccer and Cameroon began by beating the defending champions.

There was much pre-tournament publicity surrounding the England fans and occasional skirmishes did break out. But it was poor and inconsistent refereeing that really threatened Italia '90. Officials were under a FIFA directive to stick to the letter of the law but few applied commonsense. Players were ordered to pull up their socks and tuck in their shirts but scant regard was paid to players play-acting in the hope of getting an opponent cautioned or sent off. The World Cup Final itself was to be a classic example of this.

A TV audience of 26 billion people watched the 52 matches, nearly double the 1986 figure, and the main sponsors had to pay around £10 million each to have their names flashed around the world for four weeks.

It was a World Cup that promised so much. There were the 'samba footballers' from Brazil, but they lost their way and were but a shadow of the Brazilians of old. There were the Dutch, immensely talented but apparently suffering from dressing-room unrest. And there were the Italians, who found the strain of being favourites and hosts too great.

There were some memorable moments. After an indifferent start, England were unlucky not to reach the Final, the Cameroons brightened up the tournament and the Costa Ricans produced some shocks. The Republic of Ireland highlighted that the format meant it was not necessary to win matches to progress They reached the quarter-final without winning any of their five games, moving to the last eight on penalties.

It was left to two teams with great World Cup traditions to fight out the Final. Both were searching for their third victory and West Germany, by far the outstanding team in the tournament, were favourites. Argentina, fielding one of their poorest national sides of the last decade, reached the Final, thanks largely to good fortune rather than skill. West Germany won the World Cup but, with the odd exception, the game summed up Italia '90.

There were fears that hordes of travelling fans would create mayhem at Italia '90, but the majority of supporters were well-behaved and created a carnival atmosphere that was perhaps the highlight of the tournament. *Top:* An Irish supporter in fancy dress. *Middle:* Fans from the United Arab Emirates. *Bottom:* A Brazilian lovely and her friend cheer the South Americans.

1990 Qualifying Competition

WHEN the draw for the qualifying tournament was made at Zurich on 12 December 1987, a total of 109 names went into the hat. Missing, of course, were the 1990 hosts, Italy, and defending champions, Argentina, but also absent was Mexico, who had been banned from international football for two years by FIFA after fielding over-age players in an Under-20 tournament. The ban also cost Mexico a place in the 1988 Seoul Olympics.

Seven nations — Lesotho, Rwanda, Togo, Bahrain, South Yemen, India and Nepal — eventually withdrew without kicking a ball, whilst Libya played two matches against Burkina Faso and one game against the Ivory Coast, losing 1-0, before withdrawing.

The remaining 101 were left to fight out the 22 places for the finals and the honour of getting the qualifying tournament underway went to Guyana and Trinidad & Tobago, the latter winning 4-0 on 17 April 1988. Ironically, Trinidad were engaged in the very last game of the series 19 months later and narrowly missed out on their first finals.

With competition so fierce for those final places, some of the games were heated at times, but there was no more disgraceful incident than at Río on 3 September 1989, when Chilean players and officials engaged in one of the most blatant attempts at cheating in which they tried to deceive FIFA, who, thankfully, saw through the ruse.

It happened in the final game of the South American qualifying Group Three. Chile had to beat Brazil by two clear goals to qualify. With 69 minutes played and Brazil leading 1-0, a flare was thrown from the crowd into the Chilean goalmouth, where captain and goalkeeper Robert Antonio Rojas was standing. After a short delay, Rojas fell to the ground writhing in agony, but television film later showed that the flare had not made contact with him.

The Chilean team maintained that they were neither mentally nor physically capable of continuing with the match and refused to play on. Chilean FA officials and medical advisors went along with Rojas' acting and all received either life or long-term bans from football. Furthermore, Chile were barred from the 1994 World Cup and fined $100,000.

Brazil qualified for their 14th finals, whilst former holders, Uruguay, and Colombia, appearing in their first finals since 1962, made up the South American contingent.

England and West Germany were the only other two former World Cup winners to have to play in the qualifying tournament and went through, thus ensuring that all previous winners of the trophy assembled in Italy.

The European qualifiers were divided into seven groups of either four or five teams. All the group winners automatically qualified, as did the runners-up in the five-team groups. The two best second-placed teams in the three four-team groups also qualified: West Germany and England were the two best runners-up in those groups but Denmark, one of the most attractive teams in the 1986 tournament, missed out on the chance of qualifying.

Defeat by Romania in their final match cost Denmark a place, although a home draw with Bulgaria had already all but dashed their hopes. If it was any consolation to the Danes, their 7-1 win over Greece was the highest score of the European qualifying matches.

England qualified from Group Two without conceding a goal, yet still finished second to Sweden, who held the English to draws in both matches. In third place was Poland, who had qualified for the last four finals.

Group Three was wide open until the last matches, with four teams still capable of qualifying. The Soviet Union and

Austria successfully came through their final matches, whilst the two unsuccessful aspirants were Turkey and East Germany.

West Germany, however, had little trouble in qualifying, along with Holland, from Group Four at the expense of Wales and Finland. The two former finalists came through their six matches undefeated, as did Yugoslavia, winners of Group Five. Accompanying the Slavs were another British representative, Scotland, who qualified for their fifth successive tournament, a British record. A 1-1 draw with Cyprus in their second match cost France a place in the finals. That lost point would have put them level with Scotland and the French would have qualified through a superior goal-difference.

Hungary once again missed out when they trailed behind Spain and the Republic of Ireland. The Irish thus followed their debut in the 1988 European Championship finals by qualifying for their first World Cup finals. It was, though, at the expense of Northern Ireland, heroes of the 1982 World Cup.

The final European group wound up with Belgium guaranteed their place in Italy, whilst Portugal had to beat Czechoslovakia by four goals in their last match if they were to overtake the Czechs. The task was beyond the Portuguese, who were still searching for another Eusébio, and the goalless draw meant that Czechoslovakia qualified for their eighth finals.

The African qualifying tournament was marred by the deaths of seven fans during the Nigeria-Angola game in Lagos — the crowd in the 80,000 capacity stadium was 20,000 over that limit — and of the 24-year-old Nigerian player, Sam Okwaraji, who collapsed and died during the match.

At the end of 56 qualifying matches, Egypt, appearing in only their second finals and first since 1934, and Cameroon, unbeaten in their three games in the 1982 series, emerged at the top of the pile.

Oceania had no representative in the finals. After a series of qualifying matches, Israel topped the group but had to play a two-legged play-off match against Colombia, winners of the South American Group Two. It was the Colombians who won their ticket to Italy.

After being sustained for so many years by the memory of their sensational win over England in 1950, the United States got another chance at the world's greatest soccer tournament when they qualified from the CONCACAF group, although their achievement attracted as few lines in the *New York Times* as it did in the London *Daily Telegraph*. Of course, the presence of the USA in Italy gave a much-needed boost to their plans as hosts for the 1994 tournament.

Their qualification, though, was largely due to Mexico's enforced absence. The Americans clinched victory in the last match of the qualifying series at Port of Spain on 18 November 1989, when they defied the odds to beat fancied Trinidad & Tobago. The Trinidad & Tobago players and their fanatical supporters were gracious in defeat and earned great praise from FIFA.

Joining the United States in the finals from the CONCACAF group were Costa Rica, first-time qualifiers, who went to Italy with a new boss, Velibor Milutinovic, who was in charge of the host nation, Mexico, in the 1986 finals. Milutinovic was Costa Rica's fifth manager since the start of their 1990 World Cup campaign and the man who guided them to the finals, Marvin Rodríguez, was sacked shortly after his success. In addition to their succession of managers, the Costa Rican FA also had three different presidents during the same period.

South Korea and the surprise package, the United Arab Emirates, qualified from the Asian group but China, like

Trinidad, came agonizingly close to their first finals and were only minutes away from qualifying. Needing to beat Qatar in their last match, the Chinese led 1-0 with four minutes to go but then conceded two goals to experience the agony which, coupled with the ecstacy, makes the FIFA World Cup the most compelling of all truly global sporting events.

Results

EUROPE

Group One

19 Oct 1988 *Athens*	Greece 1	Denmark 1
19 Oct 1988 *Sofia*	Bulgaria 1	Romania 3
2 Nov 1988 *Bucharest*	Romania 3	Greece 0
2 Nov 1988 *Copenhagen*	Denmark 1	Bulgaria 1
26 Apr 1989 *Athens*	Greece 0	Romania 0
26 Apr 1989 *Sofia*	Bulgaria 0	Denmark 2
17 May 1989 *Copenhagen*	Romania 1	Bulgaria 0
17 May 1989 *Bucharest*	Denmark 7	Greece 1
11 Oct 1989 *Varna*	Bulgaria 4	Greece 0
11 Oct 1989 *Copenhagen*	Denmark 3	Romania 0
15 Nov 1989 *Athens*	Greece 1	Bulgaria 0
15 Nov 1989 *Bucharest*	Romania 3	Denmark 1

Final Table

	P	W	D	L	F	A	Pts	
Romania	6	4	1	1	10	5	9	
Denmark	6	3	2	1	15	6	8	**Romania qualified**
Greece	6	1	2	3	3	15	4	
Bulgaria	6	1	1	4	6	8	3	

Group Two

19 Oct 1988 *London*	England 0	Sweden 0
19 Oct 1988 *Chorzów*	Poland...........1	Albania...........0
5 Nov 1988 *Tiranë*	Albania...........1	Sweden 2
8 Mar 1989 *Tiranë*	Albania...........0	England 2
26 Apr 1989 *London*	England 5	Albania...........0
7 May 1989 *Stockholm*	Sweden 2	Poland...........1
3 Jun 1989 *London*	England 3	Poland...........0
6 Sep 1989 *Stockholm*	Sweden 0	England 0
8 Oct 1989 *Stockholm*	Sweden 3	Albania...........1
11 Oct 1989 *Katowice*	Poland...........0	England 0
25 Oct 1989 *Chorzów*	Poland...........0	Sweden 2
15 Nov 1989 *Tiranë*	Albania...........1	Poland...........2

Final Table

	P	W	D	L	F	A	Pts	
Sweden	6	4	2	0	9	3	10	
England	6	3	3	0	10	0	9	**Sweden and**
Poland	6	2	1	3	4	8	5	**England qualified**
Albania	6	0	0	6	3	15	0	

Sweden's Pritz takes a tumble as he is tackled by England skipper Bryan Robson (right) with Gary Stevens in the background, during the opening game of European Group Two. The game at Wembley ended in a goalless draw, as did the return in Stockholm. Both teams qualified for the finals in Italy.

Group Three

31 Aug 1988 *Reykjavík*	Iceland...........1	Soviet Union 1
12 Oct 1988 *Istanbul*	Turkey...........1	Iceland...........1
19 Oct 1988 *Kiev*	Soviet Union 2	Austria...........0
19 Oct 1988 *East Berlin*	East Germany ...2	Iceland...........0
2 Nov 1988 *Vienna*	Austria...........3	Turkey...........2
30 Nov 1988 *Istanbul*	Turkey...........3	East Germany ...1
12 Apr 1989 *Magdeburg*	East Germany ...0	Turkey...........2
26 Apr 1989 *Kiev*	Soviet Union 3	East Germany ...0
10 May 1989 *Istanbul*	Turkey...........0	Soviet Union 1
20 May 1989 *Leipzig*	East Germany ...1	Austria...........1
31 May 1989 *Moscow*	Soviet Union 1	Iceland...........1
14 Jun 1989 *Reykjavíc*	Iceland...........0	Austria...........0
23 Aug 1989 *Salzburg*	Austria...........2	Iceland...........1
6 Sep 1989 *Vienna*	Austria...........0	Soviet Union 0
6 Sep 1989 *Reykjavíc*	Iceland...........0	East Germany ...3
20 Sep 1989 *Reykjavíc*	Iceland...........2	Turkey...........1
8 Oct 1989 *Karl-Marx-Stadt*	East Germany ...2	Soviet Union 1
25 Oct 1989 *Istanbul*	Turkey...........3	Austria...........0
15 Nov 1989 *Simferopol'*	Soviet Union 2	Turkey...........0
15 Nov 1989 *Vienna*	Austria...........3	East Germany ...0

Final Table

	P	W	D	L	F	A	Pts	
Soviet Union	8	4	3	1	11	4	11	
Austria	8	3	3	2	9	9	9	
Turkey	8	3	1	4	12	10	7	**Soviet Union and**
E.Germany	8	3	1	4	9	13	7	**Austria qualified**
Iceland	8	1	4	3	6	11	6	

Group Four

31 Aug 1988 *Helsinki*	Finland...........0	West Germany ...4
14 Sep 1988 *Amsterdam*	Holland 1	Wales 0
19 Oct 1988 *Swansea*	Wales 2	Finland...........2
19 Oct 1988 *Munich*	West Germany ...0	Holland 0
26 Apr 1989 *Rotterdam*	Holland 1	West Germany ...1
31 May 1989 *Cardiff*	Wales 0	West Germany ...0
31 May 1989 *Helsinki*	Finland...........0	Holland 1
6 Sep 1989 *Helsinki*	Finland...........1	Wales 0
4 Oct 1989 *Dortmund*	West Germany ...6	Finland...........1
11 Oct 1989 *Wrexham*	Wales 1	Holland 2
15 Nov 1989 *Cologne*	West Germany ...2	Wales 1
15 Nov 1989 *Rotterdam*	Holland 3	Finland...........0

Final Table

	P	W	D	L	F	A	Pts	
Holland	6	4	2	0	8	2	10	
W.Germany	6	3	3	0	13	3	9	**Holland and West**
Finland	6	1	1	4	4	16	3	**Germany qualified**
Wales	6	0	2	4	4	8	2	

Group Five

14 Sep 1988 *Oslo*	Norway...........1	Scotland 2
28 Sep 1988 *Paris*	France 1	Norway...........0
19 Oct 1988 *Glasgow*	Scotland 1	Yugoslavia 1
22 Oct 1988 *Nicosia*	Cyprus...........1	France 1
2 Nov 1988 *Limassol*	Cyprus...........0	Norway...........3
19 Nov 1988 *Belgrade*	Yugoslavia 3	France 2
11 Dec 1988 *Rijeka*	Yugoslavia 4	Cyprus...........0
8 Feb 1989 *Limassol*	Cyprus...........2	Scotland 3
8 Mar 1989 *Glasgow*	Scotland 2	France 0
26 Apr 1989 *Glasgow*	Scotland 2	Cyprus...........1
29 Apr 1989 *Paris*	France 0	Yugoslavia 0
21 May 1989 *Oslo*	Norway...........3	Cyprus...........1
14 Jun 1989 *Oslo*	Norway...........1	Yugoslavia 2
5 Sep 1989 *Oslo*	Norway...........1	France 1
6 Sep 1989 *Zagreb*	Yugoslavia 3	Scotland 1
11 Oct 1989 *Sarajevo*	Yugoslavia 1	Norway...........0
11 Oct 1989 *Paris*	France 3	Scotland 0

Eventual qualifiers, Scotland and Yugoslavia, drew 1-1 at Hampden Park in European Group Five. Here, Scotland's Richard Gough is held off by Ziatko Vujovic.

28 Nov 1989 *Athens*	Cyprus 1	Yugoslavia 2
15 Nov 1989 *Glasgow*	Scotland 1	Norway 1
18 Nov 1989 *Toulouse*	France 2	Cyprus 0

Final Table

	P	W	D	L	F	A	Pts	
Yugoslavia	8	6	2	0	16	6	14	
Scotland	8	4	2	2	12	12	10	
France	8	3	3	2	10	7	9	**Yugoslavia and**
Norway	8	2	2	4	10	9	6	**Scotland qualified**
Cyprus	8	0	1	7	6	20	1	

Group Six

21 May 1988 *Belfast*	N. Ireland 3	Malta 0
14 Sep 1988 *Belfast*	N. Ireland 0	Rep of Ireland ...0
19 Oct 1988 *Budapest*	Hungary 1	N. Ireland 0
16 Nov 1988 *Seville*	Spain 2	Rep of Ireland ...0
11 Dec 1988 *Valletta*	Malta 2	Hungary 2
21 Dec 1988 *Seville*	Spain 4	N. Ireland 0
22 Jan 1989 *Valletta*	Malta 0	Spain 2
8 Feb 1989 *Belfast*	N. Ireland 0	Spain 2
8 Mar 1989 *Budapest*	Hungary 0	Rep of Ireland ...0
23 Mar 1989 *Seville*	Spain 4	Malta 0
12 Apr 1989 *Budapest*	Hungary 1	Malta 1
26 Apr 1989 *Valletta*	Malta 0	N. Ireland 2
26 Apr 1989 *Dublin*	Rep of Ireland ...1	Spain 0
28 May 1989 *Dublin*	Rep of Ireland ...2	Malta 0
4 Jun 1989 *Dublin*	Rep of Ireland ...2	Hungary 0
6 Sep 1989 *Belfast*	N. Ireland 1	Hungary 2
11 Oct 1989 *Budapest*	Hungary 2	Spain 2
11 Oct 1989 *Dublin*	Rep of Ireland ...3	N. Ireland 0
15 Nov 1989 *Seville*	Spain 4	Hungary 0
15 Nov 1989 *Valletta*	Malta 0	Rep of Ireland ...2

Final Table

	P	W	D	L	F	A	Pts	
Spain	8	6	1	1	20	3	13	
Rep of Ireland	8	5	2	1	10	2	12	
Hungary	8	2	4	2	8	12	8	**Spain and Republic**
N. Ireland	8	2	1	5	6	12	5	**of Ireland qualified**
Malta	8	0	2	6	3	18	2	

Group Seven

1 Sep 1988 *Luxembourg*	Luxembourg.....1	Switzerland 4
18 Oct 1988 *Esch*	Luxembourg.....0	Czechoslovakia ..2

19 Oct 1988 *Brussels*	Belgium 1	Switzerland 0
16 Nov 1988 *Bratislava*	Czechoslovakia ..0	Belgium 0
16 Nov 1988 *Oporto*	Portugal 1	Luxembourg.....0
15 Feb 1989 *Lisbon*	Portugal 1	Belgium 1
26 Apr 1989 *Lisbon*	Portugal 3	Switzerland 1
29 Apr 1989 *Brussels*	Belgium 2	Czechoslovakia ..1
9 May 1989 *Prague*	Czechoslovakia ..4	Luxembourg.....0
1 Jun 1989 *Lille*	Luxembourg.....0	Belgium 5
7 Jun 1989 *Berne*	Switzerland 0	Czechoslovakia ..1
6 Sep 1989 *Brussels*	Belgium 3	Portugal 0
20 Sep 1989 *Neuchâtel*	Switzerland 1	Portugal 2
6 Oct 1989 *Prague*	Czechoslovakia ..2	Portugal 1
11 Oct 1989 *Saarbrücken*	Luxembourg.....0	Portugal 3
11 Oct 1989 *Basel*	Switzerland 2	Belgium 2
25 Oct 1989 *Prague*	Czechoslovakia ..3	Switzerland 0
25 Oct 1989 *Brussels*	Belgium 1	Luxembourg.....1
15 Nov 1989 *Lisbon*	Portugal 0	Czechoslovakia ..0
15 Nov 1989 *St Gallen*	Switzerland 2	Luxembourg.....1

Final Table

	P	W	D	L	F	A	Pts	
Belgium	8	4	4	0	15	5	12	
Czechoslovakia	8	5	2	1	13	3	12	**Belgium and**
Portugal	8	4	2	2	11	8	10	**Czechoslovakia**
Switzerland	8	2	1	5	10	14	5	**qualified**
Luxembourg	8	0	1	7	3	22	1	

SOUTH AMERICA

Group One

20 Aug 1989 *La Paz*	Bolivia............2	Peru...............1
27 Aug 1989 *Lima*	Peru...............0	Uruguay..........2
3 Sep 1989 *La Paz*	Bolivia............2	Uruguay..........1
10 Sep 1989 *Lima*	Peru...............1	Bolivia............2
17 Sep 1989 *Montevideo*	Uruguay..........2	Bolivia............0
24 Sep 1989 *Montevideo*	Uruguay..........2	Peru...............0

Final Table

	P	W	D	L	F	A	Pts	
Uruguay	4	3	0	1	7	2	6	**Uruguay qualified**
Bolivia	4	3	0	1	6	5	6	
Peru	4	0	0	4	2	8	0	

Group Two

20 Aug 1989 *Barranquilla*	Colombia 2	Ecuador 0
27 Aug 1989 *Asunción*	Paraguay 2	Colombia 1
3 Sep 1989 *Guayaquil*	Ecuador 0	Colombia 0
10 Sep 1989 *Asunción*	Paraguay 2	Ecuador 1
17 Sep 1989 *Barranquilla*	Colombia 2	Paraguay 1
24 Sep 1989 *Asunción*	Ecuador 3	Paraguay 1

Final Table

	P	W	D	L	F	A	Pts	
Colombia	4	2	1	1	5	3	5	**Colombia qualified to**
Paraguay	4	2	0	2	6	7	4	**meet the Oceania winners,**
Ecuador	4	1	1	2	4	5	3	**Israel, for a place in the**
								finals

Group Three

30 Jul 1989 *Caracas*	Venezuela 0	Brazil 4
6 Aug 1989 *Caracas*	Venezuela 1	Chile...............3
13 Aug 1989 *Santiago*	Chile...............1	Brazil 1
20 Aug 1989 *São Paulo*	Brazil 6	Venezuela 0
27 Aug 1989 *Mendoza, Arg*	Chile...............5	Venezuela 0
3 Sep 1989 *Rio de Janeiro*	Brazil 2	Chile...............0

Game awarded 2-0 to Brazil by FIFA after it was abandoned after 65 minutes following Chile's walk-out with Brazil 1-0 ahead.

Final Table

	P	W	D	L	F	A	Pts	
Brazil	4	3	1	0	13	1	7	**Brazil qualified**
Chile	4	2	1	1	9	4	5	
Venezuela	4	0	0	4	1	18	0	

OCEANIA

Group One

11 Dec 1988 *Taipei*	Taiwan 0	New Zealand.....4
15 Dec 1988 *Aukland*	New Zealand.....4	Taiwan 1

New Zealand qualified for Oceania final

Group Two

26 Nov 1988 *Nadi*   Fiji ....1 Australia 0
 3 Dec 1988 *Newcastle*   Australia ....5 Fiji 1
Australia qualified for Oceania final

Final

 5 Mar 1989 *Tel Aviv*   Israel ....1 New Zealand.....0
12 Mar 1989 *Sydney*   Australia ....4 New Zealand.....1
19 Mar 1989 *Tel Aviv*   Israel ....1 Australia 1
 2 Apr 1989 *Auckland*   New Zealand.....2 Australia 0
 9 Apr 1989 *Auckland*   New Zealand.....2 Israel 2
16 Apr 1989 *Sydney*   Australia ....1 Israel 1

Final Table

	P	W	D	L	F	A	Pts	
Israel	4	1	3	0	5	4	5	**Israel qualified to meet**
Australia	4	1	2	1	6	5	4	**Colombia in play-off for a**
New Zealand	4	1	1	2	5	7	3	**place in the finals**

South America/Oceania Play-off

15 Oct 1989 *Barranquilla* Colombia ....1 Israel 0
30 Oct 1989 *Tel Aviv*   Israel ....0 Colombia 0
Colombia qualified

AFRICA

First Round - Group One

16 Jul 1988 *Kampala*   Uganda...........1 Malawi 0
30 Jul 1988 *Blantyre*   Malawi ....3 Uganda...........1
Malawi qualified for Second Round
 7 Aug 1988 *Luanda*   Angola............0 Sudan.............0
11 Nov 1988 *Khartoum*   Sudan.............1 Angola............2
Angola qualified for Second Round
Zimbabwe and Zambia qualified for Second Round following withdrawals of Lesotho and Rwanda

First Round - Group Two

 3 Jun 1988 *Tripoli*   Libya ....3 Burkina Faso 0
 3 Jul 1988 *Ouagadougou* Burkina Faso ....2 Libya 0
Libya qualified for Second Round
 7 Aug 1988 *Accra*   Ghana ....0 Liberia............0
21 Aug 1988 *Monrovia*   Liberia............2 Ghana 0
Liberia qualified for Second Round
 5 Aug 1988 *Tūnis*   Tunisia...........5 Guinea 0
21 Aug 1988 *Conakry*   Guinea ....3 Tunisia...........0
Tunisia qualified for Second Round. Gabon qualified for Second Round following withdrawal of Togo.

Second Round - Group A

 6 Jan 1989 *Annaba*   Algeria............3 Zimbabwe 0
22 Jan 1989 *Harare*   Zimbabwe ....0 Ivory Coast.......0
11 Jun 1989 *Abidjan*   Ivory Coast.......0 Algeria............0
25 Jun 1989 *Harare*   Zimbabwe ....1 Algeria............2
13 Aug 1989 *Abidjan*   Ivory Coast.......5 Zimbabwe 0
25 Aug 1989 *Annaba*   Algeria............1 Ivory Coast.......0
Libya played one match, losing 1-0 to Ivory Coast at Abidjan on 8 Jan 1989, but then refused to meet Algeria and withdrew.

Final Table

	P	W	D	L	F	A	Pts	
Algeria	4	3	1	0	6	1	7	**Algeria qualified**
Ivory Coast	4	1	2	1	5	1	4	**for Africa final**
Zimbabwe	4	0	1	3	1	10	1	

Second Round - Group B

 6 Jan 1989 *Cairo*   Egypt ....2 Liberia............0
 7 Jan 1989 *Nairobi*   Kenya............1 Malawi 1
21 Jan 1989 *Lilongwe*   Malawi ....1 Egypt 1
22 Jan 1989 *Monrovia*   Liberia............0 Kenya 0
10 Jun 1989 *Nairobi*   Kenya............0 Egypt 0
11 Jun 1989 *Monrovia*   Liberia............1 Malawi 0
24 Jun 1989 *Lilongwe*   Malawi ....1 Kenya 0
25 Jun 1989 *Monrovia*   Liberia............1 Egypt 0

11 Aug 1989 *Cairo*   Egypt ....1 Malawi 0
12 Aug 1989 *Nairobi*   Kenya ....1 Liberia............0
26 Aug 1989 *Cairo*   Egypt ....2 Kenya 0
26 Aug 1989 *Lilongwe*   Malawi ....0 Liberia............0

Final Table

	P	W	D	L	F	A	Pts	
Egypt	6	3	2	1	6	2	8	
Liberia	6	2	2	2	2	3	6	**Egypt qualified for**
Malawi	6	1	3	2	3	4	5	**Africa final**
Kenya	6	1	3	2	2	4	5	

Second Round - Group C

 7 Jan 1989 *Enugu*   Nigeria ....1 Gabon 0
 8 Jan 1989 *Yaoundé*   Cameroon ....1 Angola............1
22 Jan 1989 *Libreville* Gabon ....1 Cameroon 3
22 Jan 1989 *Luanda*   Angola............2 Nigeria 2
10 Jun 1989 *Ibadan*   Nigeria ....2 Cameroon 0
11 Jun 1989 *Luanda*   Angola............2 Gabon 0
25 Jun 1989 *Luanda*   Angola............1 Cameroon 2
25 Jun 1989 *Libreville* Gabon ....2 Nigeria 1
12 Aug 1989 *Lagos*   Nigeria ....1 Angola............0
13 Aug 1989 *Yaoundé*   Cameroon ....2 Gabon 1
27 Aug 1989 *Yaoundé*   Cameroon ....1 Nigeria 0
27 Aug 1989 *Libreville* Gabon ....1 Angola............0

Final Table

	P	W	D	L	F	A	Pts	
Cameroon	6	4	1	1	9	6	9	
Nigeria	6	3	1	2	7	5	7	**Cameroon qualified**
Angola	6	1	2	3	6	7	4	**for Africa final**
Gabon	6	2	0	4	5	9	4	

Second Round - Group D

 8 Jan 1989 *Rabat*   Morocco ....1 Zambia 0
 8 Jan 1989 *Kinshasa*   Zaïre ....3 Tunisia 1
22 Jan 1989 *Tūnis*   Tunisia ....2 Morocco 1
22 Jan 1989 *Lusaka*   Zambia ....4 Zaïre 2
11 Jun 1989 *Kinshasa*   Zaïre ....0 Morocco 0
11 Jun 1989 *Lusaka*   Zambia ....1 Tunisia 0
25 Jun 1989 *Lusaka*   Zambia ....2 Morocco 1
25 Jun 1989 *Tūnis*   Tunisia ....1 Zaïre 0
13 Aug 1989 *Casablanca* Morocco ....0 Tunisia 0
13 Aug 1989 *Kinshasa*   Zaïre ....1 Zambia 0
27 Aug 1989 *Tūnis*   Tunisia ....1 Zambia 0
27 Aug 1989 *Kenitra*   Morocco ....1 Zaïre 1

Final Table

	P	W	D	L	F	A	Pts	
Tunisia	6	3	1	2	5	5	7	
Zambia	6	3	0	3	7	6	6	**Tunisia qualified**
Zaïre	6	2	2	2	7	7	6	**for Africa final**
Morocco	6	1	3	2	4	5	5	

Final

 8 Oct 1989 *Algiers*   Algeria............0 Egypt 0
17 Nov 1989 *Cairo*   Egypt ....1 Algeria............0
 8 Oct 1989 *Yaoundé*   Cameroon ....2 Tunisia 0
19 Nov 1989 *Tūnis*   Tunisia ....0 Cameroon 1
Egypt and Cameroon qualified

ASIA

Group One

 6 Jan 1989 *Khalifa*   Qatar ....1 Jordan 0
 6 Jan 1989 *Muscat*   Oman..............1 Iraq 1
13 Jan 1989 *Muscat*   Oman..............0 Qatar 0
13 Jan 1989 *'Ammān*   Jordan ....0 Iraq 1
20 Jan 1989 *'Ammān*   Jordan ....2 Oman.............0
20 Jan 1989 *Doha*   Qatar ....1 Iraq 0
27 Jan 1989 *'Ammān*   Jordan ....1 Qatar 1
27 Jan 1989 *Baghdād*   Iraq ....3 Oman.............1
 3 Feb 1989 *Doha*   Qatar ....3 Oman.............0
 3 Feb 1989 *Baghdād*   Iraq ....4 Jordan 0
10 Feb 1989 *Muscat*   Oman..............0 Jordan 2
10 Feb 1989 *Baghdād*   Iraq ....2 Qatar 2

Final Table

	P	W	D	L	F	A	Pts	
Qatar	6	3	3	0	8	3	9	
Iraq	6	3	2	1	11	5	8	**Qatar qualified for**
Jordan	6	2	1	3	5	7	5	**Asia final**
Oman	6	0	2	4	2	11	2	

Group Two

10 Mar 1989 *Sana'ā'*   North Yemen ....0 Syria 1
15 Mar 1989 *Jedda*   Saudi Arabia .....5 Syria 4
20 Mar 1989 *Sana'ā'*   North Yemen ....0 Saudi Arabia 1
25 Mar 1989 *Latakia*   Syria ....2 North Yemen 0
30 Mar 1989 *Latakia*   Syria ....0 Saudi Arabia 0
 5 Apr 1989 *Jedda*   Saudi Arabia ....1 North Yemen 0
Bahrain withdrew

Final Table

	P	W	D	L	F	A	Pts	
Saudi Arabia	4	3	1	0	7	4	7	**Saudi Arabia**
Syria	4	2	1	1	7	5	5	**qualified for Asia**
North Yemen	4	0	0	4	0	5	0	**final**

Group Three

 6 Jan 1989 *Islamabad* Pakistan ....0 Kuwait............1
13 Jan 1989 *Kuwait*   Kuwait............3 Utd Arab Emirates 2
20 Jan 1989 *Sharjah*   Utd Arab Emirates 5 Pakistan 0
27 Jan 1989 *Kuwait*   Kuwait............2 Pakistan 0
 3 Feb 1989 *Sharjah*   Utd Arab Emirates 1 Kuwait............0
10 Feb 1989 *Islamabad* Pakistan ....1 Utd Arab Emirates 4
South Yemen withdrew

Final Table

	P	W	D	L	F	A	Pts	
Utd Arab Emirates	4	3	0	1	12	4	6	**United Arab**
Kuwait	4	3	0	1	6	3	6	**Emirates qualified**
Pakistan	4	0	0	4	1	12	0	**for Asia final**

Group Four

23 May 1989 *Seoul*   Malaysia..........2 Nepal 0
23 May 1989 *Seoul*   Singapore ....0 South Korea 3
25 May 1989 *Seoul*   Malaysia..........1 Singapore 0
25 May 1989 *Seoul*   Nepal ....0 South Korea 9
27 May 1989 *Seoul*   Singapore ....3 Nepal 0
27 May 1989 *Seoul*   South Korea .....3 Malaysia..........0
 3 Jun 1989 *Singapore* Singapore ....2 Malaysia..........2
 3 Jun 1989 *Singapore* South Korea .....4 Nepal 0
 5 Jun 1989 *Singapore* Malaysia..........0 South Korea 3
 5 Jun 1989 *Singapore* Nepal ....0 Singapore 7
 7 Jun 1989 *Singapore* Singapore ....0 South Korea 3
 7 Jun 1989 *Singapore* Malaysia..........3 Nepal 0
India withdrew

Final Table

	P	W	D	L	F	A	Pts	
South Korea	6	6	0	0	25	0	12	
Malaysia	6	3	1	2	8	8	7	**South Korea**
Singapore	6	2	1	3	12	9	5	**qualified for Asia**
Nepal	6	0	0	6	0	28	0	**final**

Group Five

19 Feb 1989 *Bangkok*   Thailand ....1 Bangladesh.......0
23 Feb 1989 *Guangzhou* China............2 Bangladesh.......0
23 Feb 1989 *Bangkok*   Thailand ....0 Iran 3
27 Feb 1989 *Dacca*   Bangladesh.......1 Iran 2
28 Feb 1989 *Bangkok*   Thailand ....0 China............3
 4 Mar 1989 *Dacca*   Bangladesh.......0 China............2
 8 Mar 1989 *Dacca*   Bangladesh.......3 Thailand 1
17 Mar 1989 *Teherān*   Iran ....1 Bangladesh.......0
30 Mar 1989 *Teherān*   Iran ....3 Thailand 0
15 Jul 1989 *Shenyang*   China............2 Iran 0
22 Jul 1989 *Teherān*   Iran ....3 China............2
29 Jul 1989 *Shenyang*   China............2 Thailand 0
Nepal withdrew

Final Table

	P	W	D	L	F	A	Pts	
China	6	5	0	1	13	3	10	
Iran	6	5	0	1	12	5	10	**China qualified for**
Bangladesh	6	1	0	5	4	9	2	**Asia final**
Thailand	6	1	0	5	2	14	2	

Group Six

21 May 1989 *Jakarta*   Indonesia........0 North Korea 0
22 May 1989 *Hong Kong*   Hong Kong ......0 Japan 0
27 May 1989 *Hong Kong*   Hong Kong ......1 North Korea 2
28 May 1989 *Jakarta*   Indonesia.........0 Japan 0
 4 Jun 1989 *Hong Kong*   Hong Kong ......1 Indonesia.........1
 4 Jun 1989 *Tōkyō*   Japan ....2 North Korea 1
11 Jun 1989 *Tōkyō*   Japan ....5 Indonesia.........0
18 Jun 1989 *Kōbe*   Japan ....0 Hong Kong 0
25 Jun 1989 *P'yŏngyang* North Korea .....2 Japan 0
25 Jun 1989 *Jakarta*   Indonesia.........3 Hong Kong 2
 2 Jul 1989 *P'yŏngyang* North Korea .....4 Hong Kong 1
 9 Jul 1989 *P'yŏngyang* North Korea .....2 Indonesia........1

Final Table

	P	W	D	L	F	A	Pts	
North Korea	6	4	1	1	11	5	9	
Japan	6	2	3	1	7	3	7	**North Korea**
Indonesia	6	1	3	2	5	10	5	**qualified for Asia**
Hong Kong	6	0	3	3	5	10	3	**final**

Final

12 Oct 1989 *Singapore*   Utd Arab Emirates 0 North Korea 0
12 Oct 1989 *Singapore*   China.............2 Saudi Arabia 1
13 Oct 1989 *Singapore*   South Korea .....0 Qatar 0
16 Oct 1989 *Singapore*   Qatar ....1 Saudi Arabia 1
16 Oct 1989 *Singapore*   South Korea .....1 North Korea 0
17 Oct 1989 *Singapore*   Utd Arab Emirates 2 China.............1
20 Oct 1989 *Singapore*   China.............0 South Korea 1
20 Oct 1989 *Singapore*   North Korea .....2 Qatar 0
21 Oct 1989 *Singapore*   Utd Arab Emirates 0 Saudi Arabia 0
24 Oct 1989 *Singapore*   Utd Arab Emirates 1 Qatar 1
24 Oct 1989 *Singapore*   North Korea .....0 China.............1
25 Oct 1989 *Singapore*   Saudi Arabia ....0 South Korea 2
28 Oct 1989 *Singapore*   Utd Arab Emirates 1 South Korea 1
28 Oct 1989 *Singapore*   Saudi Arabia .....2 North Korea 0
28 Oct 1989 *Singapore*   Qatar ....2 China.............1

Final Table

	P	W	D	L	F	A	Pts	
South Korea	5	3	2	0	5	1	8	
Utd Arab Emirates	5	1	4	0	4	3	6	
Qatar	5	1	3	1	4	5	5	**South Korea and**
China	5	2	0	3	5	6	4	**United Arab**
Saudi Arabia	5	1	2	2	4	5	4	**Emirates qualified**
North Korea	5	1	1	3	2	4	3	

CONCACAF
(Central & North America)

First Round

17 Apr 1988 *Georgetown*   Guyana..........0 Trinidad & Tobago 4
 8 May 1988 *Port of Spain*   Trinidad & Tobago 1 Guyana...........0
Trinidad & Tobago qualified for Second Round

30 Apr 1988 *Havana*   Cuba..............0 Guatemala 1
15 May 1988 *San Marcos* Guatemala ....1 Cuba 1
Guatemala qualified for Second Round

12 May 1988 *Kingston*   Jamaica ....1 Puerto Rico 0
29 May 1988 *San Juan*   Puerto Rico ......1 Jamaica 2
Jamaica qualified for Second Round

19 Jun 1988 *St John's*   Antigua ....0 Nethlds Antilles 1
29 Jul 1988 *Curaçao*   Nethlds Antilles 3 Antigua 1
Netherlands Antilles qualified for Second Round

17 Jul 1988 *Alajuela*   Costa Rica ....1 Panama 1
31 Jul 1988 *Panama City*   Panama ....0 Costa Rica 2
Costa Rica qualified for Second Round

Second Round

24 Jul 1988 *Kingston*   Jamaica ....0 United States 0
13 Aug 1988 *St Louis*   United States ....5 Jamaica 1
United States qualified for CONCACAF final

 9 Oct 1988 *Guatemala* Guatemala ....1 Canada 0
15 Oct 1988 *Burnaby*   Canada ....3 Guatemala 2
Guatemala qualified for CONCACAF final on away-goals rule

 1 Oct 1988 *Curaçao*   Nethlds Antilles 0 El Salvador.......1
16 Oct 1988 *San Salvador* El Salvador.......5 Nethlds Antilles 0
El Salvador qualified for CONCACAF final

30 Oct 1988 *Port of Spain*   Trinidad & Tobago 0 Honduras 0
13 Nov 1988 *Tegucigalpa* Honduras ....1 Trinidad & Tobago 1
Trinidad & Tobago qualified for CONCACAF final on away-goals rule
Costa Rica qualified for CONCACAF final following Mexico's disqualification by FIFA

Final

19 Mar 1989 *Guatemala*   Guatemala ....1 Costa Rica 0
 2 Apr 1989 *San José*   Costa Rica ....2 Guatemala 1
16 Apr 1989 *San José*   Costa Rica ....1 United States 0
30 Apr 1989 *Fenton*   United States ....1 Costa Rica 0
13 May 1989 *Torrance*   United States ....1 Trinidad & Tobago 1
28 May 1989 *Port of Spain* Trinidad & Tobago 1 Costa Rica 1
11 Jun 1989 *San José*   Costa Rica ....1 Trinidad & Tobago 0
17 Jun 1989 *New Britain* United States ....2 Guatemala 1
25 Jun 1989 *San Salvador* El Salvador.......2 Costa Rica 4
16 Jul 1989 *San José*   Costa Rica ....1 El Salvador.......0
30 Jul 1989 *Port of Spain* Trinidad & Tobago 2 El Salvador.......0
13 Aug 1989 *Tegucigalpa* El Salvador.......0 Trinidad & Tobago 0
20 Aug 1989 *Guatemala*   Guatemala ....0 Trinidad & Tobago 1
 3 Sep 1989 *Port of Spain* Trinidad & Tobago 2 Guatemala 1
17 Sep 1989 *Tegucigalpa* El Salvador.......0 United States 1
 8 Oct 1989 *Guatemala*   Guatemala ....0 United States 0
 5 Nov 1989 *Fenton*   United States ....0 El Salvador.......0
18 Nov 1989 *Port of Spain* Trinidad & Tobago 0 United States 1
The two games between Guatemala and El Salvador were not played due to the domestic situation in El Salvador

Final Table

	P	W	D	L	F	A	Pts
Costa Rica	8	5	1	2	10	6	11
United States	8	4	3	1	6	3	11
Trinidad & Tobago	8	3	3	2	7	5	9
Guatemala	6	1	1	4	4	7	3
El Salvador	6	0	2	4	2	8	2

Costa Rica and United States qualified

Dreadlocked Trinidad and Tobago star, Brian Williams, is manhandled by the USA's Brian Bliss during the final CONCACAF game in Port of Spain. The Americans pulled off a surprise 1-0 win to join group leaders, Costa Rica, in Italy.

Frank Stapleton watches as Tony Cascarino wrestles a defender out of the way during the Republic of Ireland's European Group Six game against Spain in Dublin. A crowd of 49,160 saw Míchel put through his own goal after 15 minutes to give the Irish a 1-0 win.

1990 Tournament

Group A

Lubomír Moravčik of
Czechoslovakia.

ITALY 1   AUSTRIA 0 (Half-time 0-0)

Stadio Olimpico, Rome, 9 June
Attendance: 72,303

WHEN Italy first staged the World Cup in 1934 they were under tremendous pressure to win the trophy, not least because Mussolini used the tournament as a propaganda platform for his country. Of course, there was no such dictatorial interference 56 years later — but the pressure on the hosts was just as great as it had been in that second tournament.

Italian supporters do not take kindly to failure. Indeed, they demand success from their team. But how agonizing it must have been for the majority of the 72,000 spectators inside Rome's Olympic Stadium — a venue that was practically rebuilt for the 1990 World Cup — as they endured 78 minutes of attacking football from their team without it yielding a goal.

The Italians played some of their most attractive football for a long time and combined well as a team and from the kick-off they attacked the Austrian goal in an almost rampaging style not normally associated with Latin footballers.

Vialli, Ancelotti and Carnevale, who missed an easy chance from six yards, all had opportunities to send the Italians into the half-time break with a comfortable lead, yet the first half remained goalless.

Italian hearts fluttered when Herzog, the 'White Gullit', struck a well-timed volley in the opening minute of the second half but the ball went wide. Then Italian frustrations returned when Giannini headed wide with an open goal beckoning. It seemed as though nothing was going right for the host nation, despite their attractive, attacking football.

Vialli missed narrowly with a shot from the edge of the penalty area and then De Agostini forced Lindenberger into a good save. The Italians could count themselves unlucky not to have been awarded a penalty when Donadoni was brought down in the box after a piece of skilful football. But, shortly afterwards, Schillaci, who had been on the field for only four minutes, headed home the winner when he met a Vialli cross.

There were 12 minutes remaining and the stadium erupted. Flags and banners were waved and Italian supporters breathed sighs of relief.

The scoreline may have looked close but the way the Italians played must have sent shock waves through their rivals. It was a good team performance with Vialli outstanding. Italy were surely now hot favourites in their own land.

Italy: Zenga; Baresi, Bergomi, Ferri, Maldini, Ancelotti(De Agostini), De Napoli, Giannini, Donadoni, Carnevale(Schillaci), Vialli.
Scorer: Schillaci
Austria: Lindenberger; Russ, Pecl, Aigner, Streiter, Schötell, Linzmaier(Hörtnagl), Artner (Zsak), Herzog, Polster, Ogris.
Referee: José Ramiz Wright (Brazil)

CZECHOSLOVAKIA 5   UNITED STATES 1 (Half-time 2-0)

Stadio Comunale, Florence, 10 June
Attendance: 33,266

WITH typical American bravado the US coach, Bob Gansler, said before the start of the tournament that his team was not good enough to win the World Cup — they would probably lose to Italy on penalties in the Final. Of course, Gansler knew that his players were no match for European professional teams but, as Baron de Coubertin, founder of the modern Olympics decreed, it is not the winning but the taking part that is important. And the fact that the United States were playing in their first World Cup finals for 40 years was success in itself.

Unlike their last appearance, when they humbled the mighty England team of the day with a side largely made up of soccer mercenaries, the USA team now comprised home-grown players, who succumbed to the thrusting efficiency of the Czechs.

For 15 minutes the Americans showed signs that another shock may be on its way but, thereafter, it was one-way traffic and after the unmarked Skuhravý opened the scoring in the 25th minute, one suspected a barrage of goals once the inexperienced American defence had been exposed. Perhaps surprisingly, the goals did not come as frequently as the Czech dominance might have reflected and they scored only one more before half-time, when Bílek netted from the penalty-spot after Windischmann brought down Hašek.

Hašek had the easiest of chances to score with a near-post header in the 50th minute and three minutes later, the US team was reduced to ten men when the Swiss referee sent off Wynalda for what appeared a push on a Czech player at a throw-in. The decision seemed absurd and highlighted even further the inconsistency of refereeing at these championships. Wynalda later claimed that the Czech had first stamped on his foot

Tomáš Skuhravý of
Czechoslovakia.

Despite being down to ten men, the United States gain some slim hope as Caligiuri rounds Czech goalkeeper Stéjskal to pull his side back to 3-1. However, Czechoslovakia scored twice more to win with ease and even missed a penalty.

Nevertheless, with 37 minutes to go and down to ten men, the Americans broke away and reduced the arrears to 3-1 when Caligiuri scored a well-taken individual goal. Skuhravý, however, reconfirmed the Czech advantage with his second goal in the 78th minute. Every time he had the goal in his sights thereafter, he shot in search of his hat-trick. And when Czechoslovakia were awarded a second penalty in the closing minutes it looked as though he would get the chance. But the kick was taken by Bílek, who mysteriously tried to chip the ball over goalkeeper Meola. The USA 'keeper, perhaps the one man in their side capable of making a living in European football, saved with ease.

Luhový completed the scoring in injury time but the Czechs had eased off in the closing stages and should have added further to the scoreline.

Czechoslovakia: Stéjskal; Straka, Kadlec, Kocian, Hašek, Kubíc, Bílek, Chovanec, Moravčik(Weiss), Skuhravý, Knofliček(Luhový).
Scorers: Skuhravý 2, Bílek (pen), Hašek, Luhový
United States: Meola; Trittschuh, Windischmann, Armstrong, Wynalda, Caligiuri, Ramos, Harkes, Stollmeyer(Balboa), Murray(Sullivan), Vermes.
Scorer: Caligiuri
Referee: Kurt Roethlisberger (Switzerland)

Bílek, scored one penalty and missed another as the Czechs hammered the United States.

ITALY 1   UNITED STATES 0 (Half-time 1-0)
Stadio Olimpico, Rome, 14 June
Attendance: 73,423

IN boxing parlance this would have been described as a 'mismatch'. And as Mike Downey of the *Los Angeles Times* wrote before the game: "A calf stands a better chance to win a rodeo."

Everybody — even their own fans — had the United States team written off. On paper it was going to be a walk-over and there was much speculation about Italy creating a new World Cup record score. Fortunately for the Americans, though, the Italians have never been all that interested in setting records, simply in winning matches.

When Vialli brilliantly dummied for Giannini to run on to the ball and put Italy ahead after only 11 minutes, it looked as though the floodgates were open and that the Italians would indeed score a hatful of goals. Despite continued pressure from the hosts, however, they could not find the net again, although they had a great chance when the Mexican referee awarded them a penalty — the third conceded by the Americans in this tournament — after Berti was upended in the box. Although Vialli sent Meola the wrong way, his shot struck an upright and rebounded to safety.

In the second half the United States nearly brought off the 'impossible' and came close to drawing level when a fine free-kick from Murray beat the defensive wall. Goalkeeper Zenga could not hold the shot and Vermes followed up. Zenga smothered his attempt but the ball was still heading for the net when Ferri cleared, almost off the line.

Italy thus achieved their main objective of maximum points but they were disappointing and seemed to lack conviction. The Americans, however, had tightened up their game after their 5-1 beating by the Czechs and they came out of this 'mismatch' with credit and respectability.

Italy: Zenga; Baresi, Bergomi, Ferri, Maldini, Berti, De Napoli, Giannini, Donadoni, Carnevale (Schillaci), Vialli.
Scorer: Giannini
United States: Meola; Doyle, Banks(Stollmeyer), Windischmann, Armstrong, Balboa, Harkes, Ramos, Caligiuri, Vermes, Murray(Sullivan).
Referee: Edgardo Codesal Mendez (Mexico)

Tony Polster of Austria.

Czech goalkeeper, Jan Stéjskal.

Miroslav Kadlec of Czechoslovakia.

CZECHOSLOVAKIA 1   AUSTRIA 0 (Half-time 1-0)
Stadio Comunale, Florence, 15 June
Attendance: 38,962

CZECHOSLOVAKIA emerged as a real threat to the established teams when they beat Austria by a solitary goal to go to the top of Group A and qualify for the next round. Austria, on the other hand, were disappointing and some of their tackling bordered upon the cynical as Scottish referee George Smith booked five of their players.

Skuhravý and Knofliček posed the Austrian defence problems all afternoon and it was thanks largely to the goalkeeping skills of Klaus Lindenberger that the scoreline was still goalless after the first half-hour. But then Lindenberger turned villain when he brought down Chovanec, who had latched on to a bad back pass from Pfeffer. It was Czechoslovakia's third penalty in two games.

Chovanec took no further part in the game after damaging his thigh in the incident, but his effort did not go unrewarded because Michal Bílek — Czechoslovakia's 1989 Footballer of Year — converted the spot-kick.

Even though they failed to add any further goals, Czechoslovakia were superior to the once-fancied Austrians, whose only chance of survival was to score a hatful of goals against the United States in their last match.

Czechoslovakia: Stéjskal; Kadlec, Kocian, Hašek, Bílek, Chovanec(Bielik), Kubíc, Moravčik, Němeček, Skuhravý, Knofliček(Weiss).
Scorer: Bílek (pen)
Austria: Lindenberger; Aigner, Pecl, Pfeffer, Schötell(Ogris), Russ(Streiter), Zsak, Hörtnagl, Herzog, Polster, Rodax.
Referee: George Smith (Scotland)

ITALY 2   CZECHOSLOVAKIA 0 (Half-time 1-0)
Stadio Olimpico, Rome, 19 June
Attendance: 73,303

IN previous tournaments, Italy showed themselves to be slow starters and Italia '90 was no different. But in their third group match they gave their best performance to date and displayed the kind of form which had made them clear pre-tournament favourites.

For their first World Cup meeting with the Czechs since the 1934 Final, Italy introduced the £7.7 million striker, Roberto Baggio, into their starting line-up and his new partnership with Schillaci was to be a major reason for the Italians' improved form.

Constant Italian pressure was rewarded in the tenth minute when Schillaci headed the ball brilliantly between the goalkeeper and a defender to open the scoring following Giannini's volley.

Whilst most of the pressure came from the hosts, the East Europeans contributed to an entertaining game and midway through the second half they were unlucky not to equalize when Griga headed home, only to be ruled offside. Then Baggio produced a piece of sheer magic which partly answered the question of whether he was worth his huge transfer fee.

He gathered the ball on the half-way line, played a one-two with Giannini and then strode through the defence to score one of the finest individual goals of the tournament.

Suddenly he became the Italians' new 'favourite son' as the fans celebrated Italy's first win over Czechoslovakia in any match for 37 years and qualification for the second phase as the only team not to concede a goal.

For Italian boss Azeglio Vicini it was a pleasing performance and, considering that Schillaci and Baggio had not played together before, Vicini could be doubly pleased that he had unleashed such a lethal strike force which left rivals pondering on the remainder of the tournament.

Italy: Zenga; Baresi, Bergomi, Ferri, Maldini, Berti, De Napoli(Vierchowod), Giannini, Baggio, Donadoni(De Agostini), Schillaci.
Scorers: Schillaci, Baggio
Czechoslovakia: Stéjskal; Kadlec, Kinier, Hašek, Bílek, Chovanec, Moravčik, Weiss(Griga), Němeček (Bielik), Skuhravý, Knofliček.
Referee: Joël Quiniou (France)

AUSTRIA 2   UNITED STATES 1 (Half-time 0-0)
Stadio Comunale, Florence, 19 June
Attendance: 34,857

THE Americans learned a lot from their 5-1 defeat by Czechoslovakia in their opening game and wound up their programme with two satisfying results, even though neither game yielded a point. But it did give hope for their players, who would be reaching maturity by the time the 1994 World Cup came around.

Alas, the Americans' farewell game of the 1990 tournament was a dreadful advertisement for soccer, with the Austrians indulging in some crude tackling in a bad-tempered match which saw nine players booked and one, Peter Artner of Austria, sent off.

Both sides went into the game without a point and Austria's only chance of survival was a big win. But a goalless first half gave every indication that they, like the Americans, were on their way out of the tournament. In the US goal, Meola had a fine game and frustrated the Austrian forwards several times. However, he was eventually beaten in the 51st minute when his defence showed its naïvety in allowing Ogris to steal the ball near the half-way line. The Austrian put his head down, raced for goal and blasted the ball past Meola.

Twelve minutes later, another defensive lapse allowed Streiter to find a way through before passing to Rodax, who had an easy job in scoring. The Americans, who had a numerical advantage since the 33rd minute when Artner was sent off for an awful tackle on Vermes, failed to use the extra man to their advantage, but they scored a consolation goal eight minutes from time when Bruce Murray's shot went through Lindenberger's legs.

Austria's narrow win gave them a slim mathematical chance of staying in the tournament. But with a record of 12 yellow cards and one dismissal in their first three games, one had to wonder whether they had anything positive to contribute to Italia '90.

Austria: Lindenberger; Aigner, Pecl, Pfeffer, Artner, Streiter, Zsak, Herzog, Polster(Reisinger), Ogris, Rodax(Glatzmeyer).
Scorers: Ogris, Rodax
United States: Meola; Doyle, Banks(Wynalda), Windischmann, Armstrong, Balboa, Harkes, Ramos, Caligiuri(Bliss), Vermes, Murray.
Scorer: Murray
Referee: Jamal Al Sharif (Syria)

Group B

CAMEROON 1   ARGENTINA 0 (Half-time 0-0)
Stadio Giuseppe Meazza (San Siro), Milan, 8 June
Attendance: 73,780

WORLD Cup opening games have traditionally produced few goals, but never before has the opener provided a greater shock than when Cameroon, reduced to nine men at the end of 90 minutes play, beat defending champions Argentina.

Cameroon went into the game with a record of never having lost in the final stages of the World Cup.

After a glittering 40-minute opening ceremony, the 1986 champions, complete with Diego Maradona, set about retaining the trophy and in the first ten minutes they looked as though they would swamp the Africans.

Some of the Cameroon players resorted to rough tactics and Maradona was subjected to the sort of treatment which some of the world's greatest players have suffered over the years. But French referee Vautrot stood no nonsense and brought out the yellow card at the first opportunity.

Argentina, though, were a shadow of their winning team of four years earlier and, whilst Maradona showed glimpses of brilliance, his teammates did not seem to be on the same wavelength. As the game wore on, it was the Africans who showed more creativity. Indeed, had they been able to finish, they would have gone into the interval with a comfortable lead.

The second half began with Maradona being chopped down again, although it seemed that he took advantage of the referee's over-protective nature. In fact, the refereeing left a

Group A - Final Table

	P	W	D	L	F	A	Pts
Italy	3	3	0	0	4	0	6
Czechoslovakia	3	2	0	1	6	3	4
Austria	3	1	0	2	2	3	2
United States	3	0	0	3	2	8	0

Klaus Lindenberger of Austria.

Left: Opening game of Italia '90 in the magnificent Stadio Giuseppe Meazza at San Siro, Milan. The Cameroons are attacking the Argentinian goal.

Cyril Makanaky of Cameroon.

Argentine goalkeeper Pumpido watches the ball nestle in the net after Omam Biyik's header had given the ten-man Cameroon team the lead.

Emile M'Bouh of Cameroon.

bit to be desired and when Vautrot sent off Kana Biyik in the 60th minute, it seemed obvious, even before the action replays started rolling, that he had not committed a foul. It was simply that Caniggia's heel had made contact with the Cameroon defender during a run.

Yet Kana Biyik's dismissal spurred Cameroon on and five minutes later his brother, Omam Biyik, rose high to meet a cross from the left. He headed the ball down hard but Pumpido in the Argentinian goal should have stopped it. Instead, he let the ball slip under his body and into the net. Pumpido, one of five survivors from the 1986 winning team, could only hang his head in shame.

Cameroon held on bravely, but two minutes from time they were reduced to nine men when Massing was sent off for a crude tackle on Caniggia. This time the dismissal was fully justified, for Caniggia was flattened in full flight with the African making absolutely no attempt to get the ball.

Whilst Cameroon fully deserved their victory, the result must go down in World Cup history as one of the biggest shocks, alongside the United States' win over England in 1950, North Korea's humbling of Italy in 1966 and West Germany's demise against Algeria in 1982. For a team whose only contact with their Russian coach, Valeri Nepomniaschi, is via an interpreter, it was a remarkable achievement.

Cameroon: N'Kono; Ebwelle, Massing, Kunde, Akem N'Dip, Tataw, M'Bouh, Kana Biyik, Makanaky(Milla), M'Fede(Libiih), Omam Biyik.
Scorer: Omam Biyik
Argentina: Pumpido; Simón, Ruggeri(Caniggia), Fabbri, Sensini(Calderón), Lorenzo, Batista, Burruchaga, Basualdo, Maradona, Balbo.
Referee: Michel Vautrot (France)

François Omam Biyik, scored against Argentina.

The Cameroon players swarm around each other after pulling off a major World Cup shock.

ROMANIA 2 SOVIET UNION 0 (Half-time 1-0)

Stadio Sant Nicola, Bari, 9 June
Attendance: 42,960

ROMANIA arrived in Italy as one of the fancied outsiders but, after their second-half performance against the Soviets in the new Bari stadium, they won a lot of admirers and became favourites to qualify from Group B.

The Soviets, runners-up to Holland in the 1988 European Championships, dominated the opening period as both sides played skilful football. Had it not been for some excellent goalkeeping from the experienced Lung, then the Soviets could have led by three or four goals inside the first 35 minutes. Protasov, Kuznetsov, Litovchenko, Aleinikov and Zavarov all had chances to open the scoring but it was Lăcătus, the star of the Romanian side, who scored the first goal four minutes from half-time when, following a poor goal-kick by Dasaev, he cut in from the right and beat the Soviet 'keeper at the near post.

There were no further goals in the first half, although Lăcătus came close to adding a second within a minute of his opening goal.

Romania took charge in a second half of continuous end-to-end football. They looked more dangerous on the break and in the 54th minute scored their second goal, although it was a somewhat fortuitous affair.

Romania were awarded a penalty after Khidiyatullin handled the ball. The offence was clearly a yard outside the penalty area but the referee Cardellino, who was well behind play, pointed to the spot without consulting the linesman who was much nearer to the offence. Lăcătus converted the penalty and in the closing minutes the same player missed an easy chance to complete his hat-trick from six yards.

The Romanians deserved their victory and now felt confident of getting beyond the initial stage for the first time in their history.

Romania: Lung; Rednic, Klein, Andone, G.Popescu, Rotariu, Sabău, Timofte, Lupescu, Lăcătus(Dumitrescu), Răducioiu(Balint).
Scorer: Lăcătus 2 (1 pen)
Soviet Union: Dasaev; Bessonov, Khidiyatullin, Kuznetsov, Gorlukovich, Rats, Aleinikov, Litovchenko(Yaremchuk), Zavarov, Protasov, Dobrovolsky(Borodyuk).
Referee: Juan Daniel Cardellino (Uruguay)

Jorge Burruchaga of Argentina, scorer of the winning goal in the 1986 Final, 1990 was not a good year for him.

ARGENTINA 2 SOVIET UNION 0 (Half-time 1-0)

Stadio San Paolo, Naples, 13 June
Attendance: 55,759

ACCORDING to the Argentinian coach, Carlos Bilardo, this match was 'the first final of the championships'. With both sides losing to less fancied teams in their opening match, pressure was certainly on the two sets of players. Defeat meant almost certain elimination, whereas victory was probable salvation.

Both teams made several changes from their opening embarrassments and the Soviets dropped Rinat Dasaev — not much of a 31st-birthday present for their experienced goalkeeper.

After only ten minutes, Argentina were dealt a cruel blow when they lost their goalkeeper, Pumpido, with a double fracture of a leg after he collided with teammate, Olarticoechea. Shortly afterwards the Soviets nearly took the lead but were deprived by the 'Hand of God,' when, following a corner, Maradona blatantly handled a goal-bound header from Kuznetsov. Referee Erik Fredriksson stood only ten feet from the incident, yet did not penalize the Argentinian captain. It was certainly a strange decision by the tournament's most experienced referee, who was officiating in his third World Cup finals, and it subsequently earned him criticism from FIFA and an early flight home.

After being on top, Argentina eventually took the lead in the 27th minute with a goal which stemmed from a piece of Maradona magic. A brilliant piece of ball-control led to a corner on the left. Maradona took the kick himself and the ball was eventually cleared to Olarticoechea, who raced through the defence and crossed from the goal-line. His centre was met by Troglio, who was unmarked in the penalty area, and his powerful header beat the stand-in Soviet 'keeper, Uvarov.

Argentina relaxed a little after the goal and allowed the Soviets to get back into the game, forcing Goycochea to bring off some fine saves.

The second half was only three minutes old when Bessonov was dismissed after tugging at Caniggia's shirt when the player was through. Surprisingly, though, Argentina struggled against ten men and the Soviets looked more likely to equalize. Eventually, however, their legs began to tire and in the 79th minute the Argentinians increased their lead.

The South Americans might have been awarded a free-kick after a heavy tackle, but the referee waved play on. A split-second later, Kuznetsov was guilty of a sloppy back-pass which Burruchaga intercepted to score easily.

The South Americans deserved their victory but how different it might have been if Fredriksson had penalized Maradona for his handling offence. Then again, what uproar there would have been in the Naples Stadium, adopted home of Diego Maradona, if he had been penalized, although it had to be said that he was eventually booked — one of several yellow cards in the match — for standing near the ball at a Soviet free-kick.

Julio Jorge Olarticoechea of Argentina.

Argentina: Pumpido(Goycochea); Batista, Basualdo, Burruchaga, Caniggia, Maradona, Monzon(Lorenzo), Olarticoechea, Serrizuela, Simón, Troglio.
Scorers: Troglio, Burruchaga
Soviet Union: Uvarov; Bessonov, Khidiyatullin, Kuznetsov, Aleinikov, Zavarov(Liuty), Protasov(Litovchenko), Dobrovolsky, Zygmantovich, Shalimov, Gorlukovich.
Referee: Erik Fredriksson (Sweden)

WORLD CUP FACT

No captain has ever lifted the World Cup trophy twice. Diego Maradona skippered the 1986 winners and was captain of the 1990 runners-up and Karl-Heinz Rummenigge has led two losing teams in the Finals.

As Argentina struggled to qualify for the second round, Maradona, the man they relied on most, seemed out of touch. His theatrical approach to opponents' challenges also won him few friends.

André Kana Biyik of Cameroon.

CAMEROON 2   ROMANIA 1 (Half-time 0-0)

Stadio Sant Nicola, Bari, 14 June
Attendance: 38,687

HAVING sprung surprises in their opening matches, these teams would probably have settled for the draw which would have enhanced both their chances of qualifying for the second phase. And that seemed to be the probable outcome with 15 minutes remaining, but then 38-year-old Roger Milla changed the whole course of the game.

The first 75 minutes were, to say the least, a dull affair and the only real scoring chance fell to Hagi, whose 21st-minute free-kick was tipped over the bar by N'Kono. Cameroon were the better side in the second half but the game did not come alive until Milla pounced to put the Africans in front.

A member of Cameroon's 1982 squad, Milla came out of semi-retirement for this latest campaign and, despite his ageing legs, he got past Andone before driving the ball into the net in the 76th minute to become the oldest man ever to score in the World Cup finals.

The Africans increased the pressure and ten minutes later Milla showed finishing skills of which even the Brazilians would have been proud. He picked up a loose ball on the right of the penalty area and drove it past Lung in the Romanian goal.

As they seemed to be coasting to a comfortable win, the Africans allowed the Romanian substitute, Gavrila Balint, to score a minute later, although the goal had a suspicion of offside about it. Despite being only one minute left on the clock, there was enough injury-time to make it a nervy closing few moments for the African players.

When the draw for the 1990 finals was made, this group appeared to be one of the toughest. Certainly nobody would have imagined that Cameroon would emerge at the top of the pile after two matches and become the first qualifiers for the second round.

Cameroon: N'Kono; Tataw, Kunde(Pagal), Akem N'Dip, Ebwelle, Onana, M'Bouh, Omam Biyik, Makanaky, M'Fede, Maboang(Milla).
Scorer: Milla 2
Romania: Lung; Rednic, Klein, Andone, Rotariu, G.Popescu, Sabău, Timofte, Hagi (Dumitrescu) Lăcătus, Răducioiu(Balint).
Scorer: Balint
Referee: Hernán Arce Silva (Chile)

SOVIET UNION 4   CAMEROON 0 (Half-time 2-0)

Stadio Sant Nicola, Bari, 18 June
Attendance: 37,307

WHILST a place in the second phase was only an outside possiblity for the Soviets, they still had their pride to play for and for the first time in this tournament they showed their true class, destroying the Africans with a display of football which yielded four goals. And that total could well have been seven or eight. Alas, it was still not enough to send the Soviets through to the next phase.

After missing several early chances, the Soviet Union eventually took the lead in the 21st minute. A low cross into the area by Litovchenko was met by Protasov, who beat goalkeeper N'Kono and a defender to the ball before pushing it over the line.

Eight minutes later, Aleinikov finished off a clever piece of work by striking a shot against the bar for Zygmantovich to slam the rebound into the net.

Seven minutes into the second half, Zavarov, a half-time substitute for Shalimov, soon made his mark by increasing the Russian lead when he raced on to a defence-splitting pass from Dobrovolsky and finished well to make it 3-0.

A cross from Gorlukovich in the 63rd minute found Dobrovolsky at the far post and his header beat N'Kono to increase the Soviet lead even further. The Soviets' slim chance of success depended on them scoring lots of goals and on a definite result from the Argentina-Romania game the same evening. They did their bit, but with the others playing out a draw in Naples, the Soviet Union were eliminated at the first stage for the first time in their history.

Soviet Union: Uvarov; Gorlukovich, Khidiyatullin, Kuznetsov, Demianenko, Zygmantovich, Aleinikov, Litovchenko(Yaremchuk), Shalimov(Zavarov), Protasov, Dobrovolsky.
Scorers: Protasov, Zygmantovich, Zavarov, Dobrovolsky
Cameroon: N'Kono; Onana, Ebwelle, Kunde(Milla), Tataw, Akem N'Dip, M'Bouh, Kana Biyik, M'Fede, Makanaky(Pagal), Omam Biyik.
Referee: José Ramiz Wright (Brazil)

ARGENTINA 1   ROMANIA 1 (Half-time 0-0)

Stadio San Paolo, Naples, 18 June
Attendance: 52,733

BOTH sides were fully aware that if they could pick up a point from their remaining match, then both would qualify for the second phase.

Diego Maradona, again playing in his 'home' stadium, showed little of his true class in an end-to-end first half which entertained, despite some bad fouls and, of course, the usual spate of histrionics. Several times Romania exposed Argentina down the right and the Eastern Europeans looked the more dangerous in the first period.

Lăcătus, for Romania, and Caniggia for Argentina, both had first-half chances to give their respective side the lead, but 60 minutes had elapsed before a Maradona corner found

Monzon at the near post and the Argentinian defender scored with a glancing header. The Romanians had paid the price of not having a second defender on the goal-line marking the far post.

Five minutes later the Romanians got a deserved equalizer when a Lăcătuş cross from the right was headed back to Balint, who made up for two early misses by directing a good header over the defence and into the net. The original cross was so well directed that poor Goycochea in the Argentinian goal was left stranded, well out of position, as the equalizing header went in.

As the final whistle neared, the Romanians took a more cautious approach, whilst the Argentinians went in search of another goal. But referee Valente eventually signalled the end of the match and the Romanians progressed beyond the first stage for the first time in their history.

One feature of the match had again been the refereeing. Maradona's theatrical reaction to almost any challenge saw several Romanians booked, whilst at least two Argentinians could count themselves fortunate not to have been shown a yellow card after cynical tackles.

Argentina: Goycochea; Monzon, Serrizuela, Simón, Batista, Basualdo, Burruchaga(Dezotti), Maradona, Olarticoechea, Troglio(Giusti), Caniggia.
Scorer: Monzon
Romania: Lung; Rednic, Klein, Andone, G.Popescu, Rotariu, Sabău(Mateuţ), Hagi, Lupescu, Lăcătuş, Balint(Lupu).
Scorer: Balint
Referee: Carlos Antonio Silva Valente (Portugal)

Group B - Final Table

	P	W	D	L	F	A	Pts
Cameroon	3	2	0	1	3	5	4
Romania	3	1	1	1	4	3	3
Argentina	3	1	1	1	3	2	3
Soviet Union	3	1	0	2	4	4	2

Marius Lăcătuş of Romania.

Group C

BRAZIL 2   SWEDEN 1 (Half-time 1-0)
Stadio Delle Alpi, Turin, 10 June
Attendance: 62,628

BRAZIL and Sweden have met several times in the World Cup and those with long memories will remember that classical Brazilian performance in the 1958 Final, when they ran out 5-2 winners. Alas, the fans packed inside the new Delle Alpi Stadium were not treated to a repeat performance as the South Americans played a cautious game in opening their 14th campaign with a narrow win.

The South Americans created plenty of chances with some wonderful defence-splitting passes in the first half, but they missed the goalscoring talents of some of their stars of the past. However, their latest goalscoring sensation, Careca, who plays his league soccer alongside Diego Maradona at Napoli, opened the scoring with a magnificent goal in the 40th minute when he latched on to a marvellous ball from Branco which split the Swedish defence. Careca scored in typical Brazilian fashion, after rounding the 'keeper.

Brazil's slender half-time lead was nearly erased in the early minutes of the second half when Brolin's shot from a corner caused chaos in the Brazilian defence, once more underlining the one possible flaw in the South Americans' game.

However, shortly after Brazil had been let off the hook, Muller was sent away on a run down the right. He reached the by-line and pulled the ball back to Careca, who was waiting unmarked at the far post. He had the easiest of chances, tapping the ball in for the second goal in the 62nd minute.

Sweden, who had worked hard and did not deserve to be two goals in arrears, were rewarded when the industrious 21-year-old, Tomas Brolin, maintained his record of scoring in every international in which he had played, when he turned his marker, Mozer, in the box to score a clever goal and give the scoreline a more respectable look.

Brazil: Taffarel; Jorginho, Ricardo Gomes, Branco, Mozer, Galvão, Dunga, Alemão, Valdo (Silas), Careca, Muller.
Scorer: Careca 2
Sweden: Ravelli; R.Nilsson, Larsson, Ljung(Strömberg), Schwarz, Ingesson, Limpár, J.Nilsson, Thern, Brolin, Magnusson(Pettersson).
Scorer: Brolin
Referee: Tullio Lanese (Italy)

Jim Leighton, Scotland's unhappy goalkeeper.

COSTA RICA 1   SCOTLAND 0 (Half-time 0-0)
Stadio Luigi Ferraris, Genoa, 11 June
Attendance: 30,867

SCOTLAND qualified for their fifth successive World Cup finals, a British record, but in their previous four championships they failed to progress beyond the first phase because of their inexplicable desire to press the 'self destruct' button. World Cup '90 appeared to be no different.

Costa Rica, appearing in their first finals, thanks largely to the ban on Mexico, were 1000/1 outsiders to lift the trophy, whilst Scotland were 50/1. But, as often happens, the

Careca of Brazil.

Mo Johnston of Scotland.

Careca of Brazil (centre) and Conejo, Costa Rica's goalkeeper, face each other in the penalty area. Also in the picture is Gómez (12), left, and Muller (15), right.

favourites in a two-horse race failed. Scotland's disorganized team fell to the only goal of the game, scored by Juan Cayasso.

Scotland showed their Central American opponents respect from the start and, whilst they had most of the first 45 minutes play, they lacked inventiveness and were unable to finish what chances they created.

Scottish ambitions were shattered five minutes into the second half when Claudio Jara back-heeled a Ramirez pass into the path of Cayasso, who blasted the ball past Jim Leighton. It was only after going a goal behind that the Scots raised their game and continually raided the Costa Rican goal. Yet they could still not find enough conviction to put the ball in the net. Goalkeeper Conejo had an outstanding game and brought off a magnificent save when he blocked a Mo Johnston shot from close range. Continued raids were just as fruitless as Costa Rica clung on for a memorable World Cup debut win.

Meanwhile, the estimated 10,000 Scots in the crowd voiced their dissent at their manager and team in no uncertain manner. And the Scots' cup of misfortune seemed to be overflowing when it was announced that Richard Gough's foot injury was serious enough to see him fly home the next day. One of Scotland's classiest defenders would take no further part in the 1990 World Cup.

Costa Rica: Conejo; Flores, Gonzalez, Montero, Chávez, Chavarria, Ramirez, Gómez, Cayasso, Marchena, C. Jara(Medford).
Scorer: Cayasso
Scotland: Leighton; Gough(McKimmie), McLeish, McPherson, Malpas, Aitken, McStay, Bett(McCoist), McCall, Johnston, McInally.
Referee: Juan Carlos Loustau (Argentina)

BRAZIL 1   COSTA RICA 0 (Half-time 1-0)

Stadio Delle Alpi, Turin, 16 June
Attendance: 58,007

BRAZIL, playing in their 14th consecutive World Cup finals, against Costa Rica, newcomers to the world's biggest soccer tournament, seemed on paper to be the biggest David versus Goliath confrontation of the whole series. But, as earlier results had shown, reputations counted for nothing in Italia '90. And this match further highlighted the struggles that the more established teams were enduring against the so-called 'minnows'.

Brazil came out believing it would be easy. Admittedly, they bombarded the Costa Rican goal from the onset and that was the pattern for most of the match. But in harsh reality, the Brazilians could not convert their countless chances into goals.

This was not the Brazil of old. They were playing more to the European style and long gone was their great attacking flair. Their only goal did not even have any of the old Brazilian magic about it. Muller pounced on a loose ball in the 33rd minute and, with the aid of a couple of deflections, the ball found itself in the back of the net. That was the extent of the scoring, although an avalanche of goals had threatened. Brazil hit the woodwork four times, whilst Taffarel was rarely troubled by the Costa Rican attack. But this game underlined Brazil's inability to put the ball in the net and, after this performance, they no longer looked like one of the championship favourites.

Brazil: Taffarel; Jorghino, Ricardo Gomes, Branco, Mozer, Galvão, Dunga, Alemão, Valdo (Silas), Careca(Bebeto), Muller.
Scorer: Muller
Costa Rica: Conejo; Flores, Gonzalez, Montero, Chávez, Chavarria, Ramirez, Gómez, Cayasso (Guimaraes), Marchena, C. Jara(Mayers)
Referee: Naji Jouini (Tunisia)

SCOTLAND 2   SWEDEN 1 (Half-time 1-0)

Stadio Luigi Ferraris, Genoa, 16 June
Attendance: 31,823

THIS was a crucial game for both sides after losing their opening games. Defeat meant almost certain elimination, whereas victory would provide a lifeline.

From the start, Scotland, without Richard Gough who had returned home with a foot injury and with his career in jeopardy, showed a spirit that was not evident in their opening match. The Scots now played as a team and were rewarded with a tenth-minute goal when McPherson headed on a MacLeod corner and Stuart McCall was on hand to stab the ball over the line for his first international goal.

Scotland looked as though they wanted to win and their players gave maximum effort in that quest. They were not content in holding on to a one-goal lead and went in search of an all-important second. But they had to wait until seven minutes from time when they were awarded a penalty after Roy Aitken, following up his own shot, was tripped in the area by Roland Nilsson. Under pressure, Mo Johnston struck the ball hard and well and easily beat Ravelli in the Swedish goal.

A defensive lapse two minutes later allowed Strömberg, who read a floated cross into the area, to side-foot the ball past Leighton. This set up a frantic last five minutes, but Scotland held on to gain a vital win and help to erase the memory of the Costa Rica defeat.

Scotland: Leighton; McLeish, Malpas, McPherson, Levein, Aitken, MacLeod, Durie(McStay), McCall, Johnston, Fleck(McCoist).
Scorers: McCall, Johnston (pen)
Sweden: Ravelli; R.Nilsson, Hysén, Larsson(Strömberg), Schwarz, Limpár, Thern, Ingesson, Brolin, J.Nilsson, Pettersson(Ekström).
Scorer: Strömberg
Referee: Carlos Maciel (Paraguay)

COSTA RICA 2   SWEDEN 1 (Half-time 0-1)

Stadio Luigi Ferraris, Genoa, 20 June
Attendance: 30,223

IN a World Cup full of surprise results, Costa Rica became the unlikeliest qualifiers from Group C, ahead of Scotland and Sweden. But their three performances gave every indication that their passage to the next phase would make them tough opponents. And in coming from behind to beat Sweden, they showed tremendous character.

The Swedes, clear favourites, took the lead in the 31st minute when Conejo, one of the tournament's best goalkeepers, could only parry a 20-yard Schwarz free-kick to Ekström, who had little difficulty in opening the scoring. But the game took on a different appearance after the Costa Ricans brought on substitute Hernán Medford in the 62nd minute.

Within a couple of minutes, Medford might have levelled the scores and his presence added to the fluency of the Central Americans' attacks. In the 75th minute their skipper, Roger Flores, took advantage of poor Swedish marking to head home a Gonzalez free-kick.

Three minutes from time, the Swedish defenders were again not up to their task, allowing Medford to run fully 40 yards before he pushed the ball past goalkeeper Ravelli for a memorable goal. It gave the Costa Ricans a remarkable win as Italia '90 continued to produce shocks. And it was the first time in the series that a team had come from behind to win.

Costa Rica: Conejo; Flores, Montero, Gonzalez, Marchena, Ramirez, Chávez, Chavarria (Guimaraes), Gómez(Medford), Cayasso, C.Jara.
Scorers: Flores, Medford
Sweden: Ravelli; R.Nilsson, Hysén, Schwarz, Pettersson, Larsson, Ingesson, Strömberg (Engqvist), J.Nilsson, Brolin(Gren), Ekström.
Scorer: Ekström
Referee: Zoran Petrović (Yugoslavia)

BRAZIL 1   SCOTLAND 0 (Half-time 0-0)

Stadio Delle Alpi, Turin, 20 June
Attendance: 62,502

EIGHT minutes from time in the rain-soaked Delle Alpi stadium, Scotland's fans saw their team's chances of reaching the second phase of the World Cup for the first time vanish when Brazilian substitute Muller scored the goal which maintained the South Americans' 100 per cent record in the tournament.

The Brazilians had the better of the first half, although some of their supporters were not too pleased with the way they played. Scotland, however, were pushing forward but, shortly before the interval, they were pushed back on the defensive and this ultimately proved to be their downfall.

Scotland had a chance to take the lead when an Aitken header from a McCall corner was kicked off the line by Branco with the 'keeper beaten. A draw would have guaranteed them a place in the second phase but it was only after going 1-0 behind that they created their only other real chance.

With the game heading towards a goalless draw, McStay gave the ball away and Alemão got in a shot from outside the penalty area. Jim Leighton could not hold the ball and Muller stormed in to put it into the net from an acute angle.

Romario of Brazil.

Branco of Brazil and McKimmie of Scotland.

Group C – Final Table

	P	W	D	L	F	A	Pts
Brazil	3	3	0	0	4	1	6
Costa Rica	3	2	0	1	3	2	4
Scotland	3	1	0	2	2	3	2
Sweden	3	0	0	3	3	6	0

After failing to hold a shot from Alemão, Scotland goalkeeper Jim Leighton can only watch as Muller storms in to put Brazil ahead.

Scotland frantically went in search of an equalizer but their only real chance came in the dying seconds, when Gillespie headed the ball across the goal to Johnston, whose effort was magnificently saved by goalkeeper Taffarel from point-blank range.

Defeat for Scotland meant their future lay in the hands of other teams. Unfortunately, the 'buts' outnumbered the 'ifs'.

Brazil: Taffarel; Jorginho, Ricardo Gomes, Branco, Rocha, Galvão, Dunga, Alemão, Valdo, Careca, Romario(Muller).
Scorer: Muller
Scotland: Leighton; McKimmie, McLeish, McPherson, Aitken, Malpas, McStay, McCall, MacLeod(Gillespie), Johnston, McCoist(Fleck).
Referee: Helmut Kohl (Austria)

Group D

COLOMBIA 2   UNITED ARAB EMIRATES 0 (Half-time 0-0)
Stadio Renato Dall'Ara, Bologna, 9 June
Attendance: 30,791

COLOMBIA made a welcome return to the World Cup fold after an absence of 28 years, whilst the United Arab Emirates were gracing the world's finest soccer stage for the first time. The game, however, was disappointing as the Arabs played disorganized football and were prone to many mistakes. It was largely due to these errors that Colombia were made to look the better side.

The Emirates offered little in attack, although they defended solidly. Nevertheless, they nearly stole the lead in the closing minutes of the first half when Ali Thani Jumaa intercepted a back pass from Escobar. Thani Jumaa's effort was blocked and the rebound was put just wide.

Colombia's superiority was rewarded when Redin headed them into the lead in the 50th minute, when he was on the end of a good cross from Leonel Alvarez. The Arabs had only one chance of equalizing, when Adnan Khamis Al Talyani raced clear, but 'keeper Higuita, renowned for his antics outside the penalty area, made one of his excursions to rob the Emirates attacker.

The South Americans first World Cup win was sealed three minutes from time when Valderrama, the red-headed 'Ruud Gullit look-alike' who plays his league soccer in France for Montpellier PSC, gathered a long crossfield ball and completed a great solo run by blasting the ball past the Emirates goalkeeper.

Colombia: Higuita; Herrera, Perea, Escobar, Gildardo Gómez, Alvarez, Gabriel Gómez, Valderrama, Redin, Iguarán(Estrada), Rincón.
Scorers: Redin, Valderrama
United Arab Emirates: Muhsin Mussabah Faraj; Eissa Meer Abdulrahman(Abdulla Ali Sultan), Ibrahim Meer Abdulrahman, Yousuf Hussain Mohamed, Khaleel Ghanim Mubarak, Abdulrahman Mohamed Abdullah, Nasser Khamis Mubarak, Hussain Ghuloum Abbas, Ali Thani Jumaa, Fahad Khamis Mubarak(Zuhair Bakheet Bilal), Adnan Khamis Al Talyani.
Referee: George Courtney (England)

WEST GERMANY 4   YUGOSLAVIA 1 (Half-time 2-0)
Stadio Giuseppe Meazza (San Siro), Milan, 10 June
Attendance: 74,765

NOTORIOUSLY slow starters in previous World Cup campaigns, the West Germans seemed to be repeating past performances in the opening 20 minutes when they allowed the young

Valderrama of Colombia.

and talented Yugoslav team to play the better football. But then Franz Beckenbauer's new team put their game together and took control. And from the moment their captain, Lothar Matthäus, opened the scoring in the 28th minute, there was never any doubt that the West Germans were on their way to victory — and in style.

Reuter set up the opening goal when he fed a good ball to his captain and Matthäus hit an accurate shot low to the outstretched 'keeper's right. Five minutes before the interval, Klinsmann made it 2-0 when he dived to deflect a cross from his Inter-Milan colleague, Brehme, into the net with Ivković stationary on the goal-line.

Germany went into the interval with that two-goal lead and were perhaps fortunate to still have 11 men on the field. Brehme, who had earlier been cautioned for a crunching tackle, went unpunished for a similar offence later in the half. Other players, notably from Cameroon and the United States, had been dismissed for offences far less severe than Brehme's first bookable offence, let alone for committing two of them.

Yugoslavia pulled a goal back ten minutes into the second half when Jozić outjumped Klinsmann to get his head to a floated free-kick from Stojković. But eight minutes later the Germans were two goals in front again, thanks to a superb solo effort from Matthäus.

He picked up the ball in his own half of the field and powered his way through the defence before unleashing a stunning shot from 25 yards. Völler made it 4-1 in the 70th minute, when he followed up a Brehme shot which the Yugoslav goalkeeper fumbled.

West Germany have an excellent World Cup record in recent tournaments and this impressive opening win suggested they would be one of the strongest contenders for the 14th tournament.

West Germany: Illgner; Reuter, Brehme, Augenthaler, Buchwald, Berthold, Hässler(Littbarski), Matthäus, Bein(Möller), Völler, Klinsmann.
Scorers: Matthäus 2, Klinsmann, Völler.
Yugoslavia: Ivković; Spasić, Vulić, Hadžibegić, Jozić, Susić(Prosinečki), Baljić, Stojković, Katanec, Vujović, Savićević(Brnović).
Scorer: Jozić
Referee: Peter Mikkelsen (Denmark)

YUGOSLAVIA 1   COLOMBIA 0 (Half-time 0-0)

Stadio Renato Dall'Ara, Bologna, 14 June
Attendance: 32,257

YUGOSLAVIA bounced back from their 4-1 drubbing by West Germany to play some attractive football and gain their first win of the series. Indeed, despite the close scoreline, they were far superior to their South American opponents.

The first 45 minutes proved yet another dull affair and Katanec's header was the only clear-cut chance of the half.

With the game seemingly heading for a goalless draw, Davor Jozić chested down a cross from Susić and volleyed the Europeans into the lead in the 73rd minute.

The goal was the spur Yugoslavia needed and they came close to adding a second when a Susić shot hit the foot of a post. Pančev also came close and then a Hadžibegić penalty, following a hand-ball by Perea, was easily saved by Colombia's long-haired extrovert goalkeeper, René Higuita.

Yugoslavia should have scored more than their solitary goal. However, they served up a warning to other teams that they could play good football and that the disappointment of the German defeat was well behind them.

Yugoslavia: Ivković; Stanojković, Spasić, Hadžibegić, Jozić, Brnović, Susić, Stojković, Vujović (Pančev), Katanec(Jarni), Šabanadžović.
Scorer: Jozić
Colombia: Higuita; Escobar, Gildardo Gómez, Herrera, Perea, Gabriel Gómez, Valderrama, Redin(Estrada), Alvarez, Rincón(Hernandez), Iguarán.
Referee: Luigi Agnolin (Italy)

WEST GERMANY 5   UNITED ARAB EMIRATES 1 (Half-time 2-0)

Stadio Giuseppe Meazza (San Siro), Milan, 15 June
Attendance: 71,167

FOR the first time in 61 games, Franz Beckenbauer was able to field an unchanged team and what a display of attacking football they gave, just as they had in their opening game against Yugoslavia.

In torrential rain the Germans attacked from the first whistle and had three clear-cut chances to open the scoring in the first five minutes. But they had to wait until the 35th minute before Völler eventually started the rout when he met a low cross from Klinsmann and beat the 'keeper to the ball.

Two minutes later, Klinsmann got his name on the score-sheet when he rose high to meet a cross from Reuter and brilliantly headed the ball down into the corner of the net.

The Emirates silenced the vast number of German supporters when, a minute after the start of the second half, Khalid Ismail Mubarak was on hand to hammer home a ball from a cross which bounced over the head of Hässler. But 30 seconds later the Germans' two-goal advantage was restored when Brehme and Matthäus, both playing on their home pitch, combined well for the German skipper to strike the ball past the 'keeper with the help of a deflection from Khaleel Mubarak.

Klinsmann of West Germany.

Alvarez of Colombia.

Thomas Hässler of West Germany.

Colombia's eccentric goalkeeper, Higuita.

Hans Pflügler of West Germany gets the better of a Colombian defender.

In the 58th minute, a powerful 20-yard shot from Bein saw Germany increase their lead to 4-1 and in the 74th minute, a Völler header from a Littbarski corner was helped into the net via two Emirates defenders.

This was a clinical display by the Germans, who now became many people's favourites to win the trophy. But all credit to the Emirates, who played open football when many expected them to produce a dour, defensive game.

West Germany: Illgner; Reuter, Brehme, Berthold(Littbarski), Augenthaler, Buchwald, Hässler, Bein, Völler, Matthäus, Klinsmann(Riedle).
Scorers: Völler 2, Klinsmann, Matthäus, Bein
United Arab Emirates: Muhsin Mussabah Faraj; Eissa Meer Abdulrahman, Khaleel Ghanim Mubarak, Yousuf Hussain Mohamed, Ibrahim Meer Abdulrahman(Abdulrhaman Al Haddad), Abdulrahman Mohamed Abdullah, Hussain Ghuloum Abbas, Nasser Khamis Mubarak, Khalid Ismail Mubarak(Hassan Mohamed Hussain), Adnan Khamis Al Talyani, Ali Thani Jumaa.
Scorer: Khalid Ismail Mubarak.
Referee: Alexei Spirin (Soviet Union)

COLOMBIA 1   WEST GERMANY   1 (Half-time 0-0)

Stadio Giuseppie Meazza (San Siro), Milan, 19 June
Attendance: 72,510

WITH their place in the second phase secure, West Germany did not display the form which had made them the top scorers of the opening group matches.

The Colombians, however, displayed the skills of which many suspected them capable, although those other aspects of South American football — the spoiling, time-wasting tactics — were far too evident and much of it came from their star player, Carlos Alberto Valderrama.

With the game heading for a goalless draw, which would have ensured Colombia a place in the second phase, the South Americans became victims of their own tactics when an 89th-minute goal was set up by Rudi Völler, and converted by Littbarski, who beat Higuita with a superb shot into the top corner of the goal.

The Colombians looked a beaten team but then, in the second minute of injury time, Valderrama, who had contributed little to the game, split the German defence with a superb ball to Rincón, who equalized with a shot that went straight through Illgner's legs.

Then Irish referee Alan Snoddy, who handled a potentially volatile South American-European clash well, blew for full-time with Colombia assured of the second-round place which, moments earlier, had looked beyond their grasp.

Colombia: Higuita; Escobar, Gildardo Gómez, Herrera, Perea, Gabriel Gómez, Valderrama, Fajardo, Alvarez, Estrada, Rincón.
Scorer: Rincón
West Germany: Illgner; Reuter, Berthold, Augenthaler, Buchwald, Pflügler, Hässler(Thon), Matthäus, Bein(Littbarski), Völler, Klinsmann.
Scorer: Littbarski
Referee: Alan Snoddy (Northern Ireland)

YUGOSLAVIA 4   UNITED ARAB EMIRATES 1 (Half-time 2-1)

Stadio Renato Dall'Ara, Bologna, 19 June
Attendance: 27,833

THERE were many who still thought Yugoslavia were a good outside bet to win the 1990 World Cup, even though they had lost to West Germany in their opening group match.

Since then the Yugoslavs had improved and, in beating the United Arab Emirates with ease, they showed themselves to be competent goalscorers.

Their place in the last 16 was secured with an efficient performance which saw them lead 2-0 after only eight minutes.

Sušić opened the scoring with the fastest goal of the tournament so far, in the fourth minute, when he had an easy header from a Sabanadžović cross from the by-line. Four minutes later, Pančev scored his first goal when, thanks to a bit of help from a defender, he was presented with an opportunity just inside the penalty area and side-footed the ball home.

Midway through the first half, however, the Europeans allowed the Emirates to pull a goal back when Thani Jumaa headed powerfully past Ivković. One minute into the second half, though, Yugoslavia restored their two-goal advantage when Vujović chested down the ball for Pančev to pounce and hammer home his side's third.

In injury-time, substitute Prosinečki's shot was deflected over the goalkeeper's head for a bizarre, but fully deserved, fourth goal for Yugoslavia.

The only unsavoury incident of the match saw Khaleel Ghanim Mubarak sent off for retaliation in the 75th minute. He thus earned the unwanted distinction of being the 50th player to have been dismissed in a World Cup finals.

Yugoslavia: Ivković; Stanojković, Spasić, Hadžibegić, Jozić, Brnović, Sušić, Stojković, Šabanadžović(Prosinečki), Pančev, Vujović(Vulić).
Scorers: Pančev 2, Sušić, Prosinečki
United Arab Emirates: Muhsin Mussabah Faraj; Eissa Meer Abdulrahman, Ibrahim Meer Abdulrahman, Abdulrhaman Al Haddad, Khaleel Ghanim Mubarak, Yousuf Hussain Mohamed, Nasser Khamis Mubarak(Abdullah Ali Sultan), Ali Thani Jumaa(Fahad Khamis Mubarak), Khalid Ismail Mubarak, Hussain Ghuloum Abbas, Adnan Khamis Al Talyani.
Scorer: Ali Thani Jumaa
Referee: Shizuo Takada (Japan)

Group E

BELGIUM 2   SOUTH KOREA 0 (Half-time 0-0)

Stadio Marc Antonio Bentegodi, Verona, 12 June
Attendance: 32,486

SOUTH Korea, still searching for their first victory in a World Cup finals, at the third attempt, were no match for Belgium, one of the surprise teams of the 1986 tournament.

The Belgians began impressively and came close to scoring in the opening minutes but then fell away a little and allowed the Koreans to get into the game although, even then, Preud'homme's goal was never threatened.

It was thanks largely to good defensive organization that the Koreans managed to go in

Group D – Final Table							
	P	W	D	L	F	A	Pts
W Germany	3	2	1	0	10	3	5
Yugoslavia	3	2	0	1	6	5	4
Colombia	3	1	1	1	3	2	3
UA Emirates	3	0	0	3	2	11	0

Jan Ceulemans of Belgium.

Marco Degryse (light shirt) fights his way past South Korea's Choi Soon-ho and Hwang Seon-hong.

Belgium's midfield dynamo Scifo in a battle with South Korea's Hwang Seon-hong.

Noh Soo-jin of South Korea.

Francisco Villarroya of Spain.

Alzamendi of Uruguay.

at the interval still level. And when Belgium introduced Ceulemans into the game in the second half the deadlock was broken, although it took a bizarre 52nd-minute goal to put the Belgians ahead.

Enzo Scifo sent a long pass to Degryse, who was 30 yards from goal when he collected the ball. As the Belgian moved forward, the Korean goalkeeper charged out of his area and Degryse lobbed the ball high into the air and into the net.

Twelve minutes later, Belgium went two goals ahead on the slippery pitch when their 32-year-old full-back, Michel De Wolf, won possession after an interception and finished off a great solo effort by blasting the ball into the net from 25 yards.

Belgium: Preud'homme; Gerets, Clijsters, Demol, De Wolf, Versavel, Van der Elst, Scifo, Degryse, Emmers, Van der Linden(Ceulemans).
Scorers: Degryse, De Wolf
South Korea: Choi In-young; Hong Myung-bo, Gu Sang-bum, Choi Kang-hee, Chung Young-hwan, Park Kyung-joon, Noh Soo-jin(Lee Tae-ho), Kim Joo-sung, Lee Young-jin(Cho Min-kook), Hwang Seon-hong, Choi Soon-ho.
Referee: Vincent Mauro (United States)

SPAIN 0 URUGUAY 0 (Half-time 0-0)

Stadio Friuli, Udine, 13 June
Attendance: 35,713

CONSIDERING that both Spain and Uruguay hate to lose, the second World Cup clash between the nations was expected to be a tight defensive affair — and it certainly 'lived down' to expectations.

Spain were exceptionally defensive and relied upon Butragueño to do all the front running, but he was given little support by his midfielders. And when he had a chance to open the scoring in the first half, he missed the target when well-placed.

However, the best chance in the opening 45 minutes of this dour tactical battle fell to Uruguay when, following a good run by Sosa, Alzamendi's shot was tipped on to the crossbar by Zubizarreta.

Uruguay, it must be said, played less defensively in the second half and a fine shot by Sosa was well saved as the South Americans went in search of the one goal that was always likely to decide this match. And when Herrera's 71st-minute header was handled on the line by Villarroya, it looked as though Uruguay would get their rightful reward. Instead, Ruben Sosa's spot-kick went sailing high over the bar.

So, the 14th World Cup saw its first goalless draw. Spain left the stadium to disapproving whistles from the Italian fans who did not like their negative attitude, which at times saw them resort to back-passes to their goalkeeper from the half-way line.

Spain: Zubizarreta; Chendo, Andrinúa, Sanchís, Jiménez, Míchel, Roberto, Villarroya(Rafael Paz), Martín Vázquez, Butragueño, Manolo(Górriz).
Uruguay: Alvez; Herrera, Gutiérrez, De Leon, Dominguez, Perdomo, Francescoli, Ruben Paz, Pereira(Correa), Alzamendi(Aguilera), Sosa.
Referee: Helmut Kohl (Austria)

SPAIN 3 SOUTH KOREA 1 (Half-time 1-1)

Stadio Friuli, Udine, 17 June
Attendance: 32,733

AT last Spain gave their manager, Luis Suarez, something to cheer as they found the net three times, all the goals coming from Míchel, the talented Real Madrid midfielder. It was the first hat-trick of the series.

After their drab opening game against Uruguay, it was good to see Spain playing attacking football which contained some deadly finishing from Míchel, who opened the scoring in the 24th minute when he met a cross from the left and volleyed it across the face of the goal and into the net at the end of a well-timed run.

However, it looked as though the 'minnows' were going to have their day once again when the Koreans equalized two minutes before the interval. Choi Soon-ho tapped a free-kick to Hwang Bo-kwan, who blasted a swerving shot from 25 yards, past Zubizarreta in the Spanish goal.

Despite losing their lead, Spain were still on top and it was from another free-kick, in the 62nd minute, that they went in front again. It was Míchel who struck the ball from 22 yards past the diving Korean 'keeper.

Julio Salinas and Martín Vázquez both had chances to increase the lead before Míchel completed his hat-trick in the 81st minute, when he collected a ball headed on from Salinas and dummied his way through the defence before blasting home from six yards.

Spain, so often one of the World Cup's fancied teams but never quite able to produce their best form when it mattered, showed yet again that they had the ability and talent to progress further.

Spain: Zubizarreta; Chendo, Andrinúa, Sanchís, Górriz, Míchel, Villarroya, Roberto(Bakero), Martín Vázquez, Butragueño(Gómez), Salinas.
Scorer: Míchel 3
South Korea: Choi In-young; Park Kyung-joon(Chung Jong-soo), Choi Kang-hee, Hong Myung-bo, Yoon Deuk-yeo, Chung Hae-won(Noh Soo-jin), Hwang Bo-kwan, Kim Joo-sung, Gu Sang-bum, Byun Byung-joo, Choi Soon-ho.
Scorer: Hwang Bo-kwan
Referee: Elias Guerrero (Ecuador)

BELGIUM 3   URUGUAY 1 (Half-time 2-0)
Stadio Marc Antonio Bentegodi, Verona, 17 June
Attendance: 33,759

DESPITE playing the entire second half with only ten men, Belgium moved into the second phase with a creditable performance against strongly-fancied Uruguay.

The Europeans were unfortunate to have full-back Eric Gerets sent off a couple of minutes before the interval, when he brought down Ruben Sosa, who followed the tackle with a typical Uruguayan 'Oscar-winning' dive. It was by no means a bad foul and Gerets went off having already received his first yellow card ten minutes earlier. Once again it brought into question the refereeing — or at least the referees' directives — at the 1990 World Cup.

By the time of Gerets' dismissal, Belgium were 2-0 ahead. The first goal was scored after 15 minutes, following a well-worked move with Ceulemans at the heart of it. It ended with Clijsters meeting a Demol cross and heading powerfully into the net.

Another clever passing movement yielded Belgium's second goal eight minutes later. This time it ended with Scifo blasting the ball into the net from 30 yards.

Despite being a man short, Belgium increased their lead less than two minutes into the second half when Ceulemans strode through a leaky Uruguayan defence to score a great solo goal.

Uruguay scored a consolation goal in the 72nd minute, when substitute Bengoechea side-footed a volley past Preud'homme, following a corner.

Belgium: Preud'homme; Gerets, Clijsters(Emmers), Demol, Grün, De Wolf, Versavel(Vervoort), Van der Elst, Scifo, Ceulemans, Degryse.
Scorers: Clijsters, Scifo, Ceulemans
Uruguay: Alvez; Gutiérrez, De Leon, Herrera, Dominguez, Perdomo, Ostolaza(Bengoechea), Francescoli, Ruben Paz, Alzamendi(Aguilera), Sosa.
Scorer: Bengoechea
Referee: Sigfried Kirschen (East Germany)

SPAIN 2   BELGIUM 1 (Half-time 2-1)
Stadio Marc Antonio Bentegodi, Verona, 21 June
Attendance: 35,950

WITH both teams through to the second phase there still remained the matter of resolving the top spot in the group. A point would have sufficed for Belgium, whereas Spain, playing in front of King Juan Carlos and Queen Sofia, needed a victory to ensure they headed the table.

The first half was one of the most entertaining of the series with the Spaniards producing some attractive football which confirmed them as one of the fancied outsiders.

Zubizarreta was outstanding in the Spanish goal and his point-blank save from Van der Elst in the 26th minute was the turning point of the match. From the resulting break, Julio Salinas was brought down in the penalty area by the Belgian 'keeper, Preud'homme, and Míchel made no mistake with the spot-kick. Spanish celebrations were short-lived, though, and three minutes later, a Vervoort free-kick was deflected past Zubizarreta for the Belgian equalizer.

Spain regained the lead six minutes before half-time when Górriz had a clear header from a Míchel corner, thanks to sloppy Belgian marking.

The pace slowed down in a second half dominated by the two goalkeepers, who brought off some fine saves. Belgium had their chance to draw level again in the 61st minute, when they were awarded a penalty after Andrinúa was judged to have tripped Staelens. Perhaps justice was done when Scifo's kick thundered against the bar and Spain held on for the win which took them to the top of the group.

Spain: Zubizarreta; Chendo, Sanchís, Andrinúa, Górriz, Villarroya, Míchel, Roberto, Butragueño(Alcorta), Martín Vázquez, Salinas(Pardeza).
Scorers: Míchel (pen), Górriz
Belgium: Preud'homme; Staelens(Van der Linden), De Wolf, Emmers(Plovie), Albert, Demol, Vervoort, Van der Elst, Ceulemans, Scifo, Degryse.
Scorer: Vervoort
Referee: Juan Carlos Loustau (Argentina)

Francescoli of Uruguay.

Emilio Butragueño of Spain.

Belgium's Scifo hits the crossbar with a 61st-minute penalty against Spain.

Group E - Final Table

	P	W	D	L	F	A	Pts
Spain	3	2	1	0	5	2	5
Belgium	3	2	0	1	6	3	4
Uruguay	3	1	1	1	2	3	3
South Korea	3	0	0	3	1	6	0

Ruben Sosa of Uruguay.

Right: Gary Lineker (falling, white shirt) has just chested forward a cross by Waddle and follows the ball into the net to give England the lead after only eight minutes against the Republic of Ireland. *Below:* Lineker is congratulated by teammate Peter Beardsley.

URUGUAY 1   SOUTH KOREA 0 (Half-time 0-0)

Stadio Friuli, Udine, 21 June
Attendance: 29,039

NEARLY 30,000 spectators were subjected to probably the worst match of the first phase. Considering that Uruguay had to win to stay in the tournament — and that the Koreans had to do so with a hatful of goals — it was surprising to see that neither side was prepared to show any adventure and go in search of goals.

Uruguay were even given the advantage of having an extra man when Yoon Deuk-yeo was sent off in the 72nd minute for time-wasting.

With the end of the boredom rapidly approaching, and with the game two minutes into injury time, Uruguay were awarded a free-kick. Dominguez's kick was floated across a packed penalty area and substitute Fonseca cleverly headed the ball wide of the diving 'keeper. The goal had a suspicion of offside about it, but it meant that Uruguay not only won their first World Cup match since beating the Soviet Union in 1970, but they also went through to the second phase and broke the hearts of many Scotsmen, who were relying on a draw to give their team a lifeline as one of the best third-placed clubs.

Uruguay: Alvez; Gutiérrez, De Leon, Herrera, Dominguez, Perdomo, Ostolaza(Aguilera), Francescoli, Ruben Paz, Sosa(Fonseca), Martinez.
Scorer: Fonseca
South Korea: Choi In-young; Park Kyung-joon, Choi Kang-hee, Yoon Deuk-yeo, Hong Myung-bo, Lee Heung-sil, Hwang Bo-kwan(Chung Hae-won), Chung Jong-soo, Kim Joo-sung, Choi Soon-ho, Byun Byung-joo(Hwang Seon-hong).
Referee: Tullio Lanese (Italy)

Group F

ENGLAND 1   REPUBLIC OF IRELAND 1 (Half-time 1-0)

Stadio Sant 'Elia, Cagliari, 11 June
Attendance: 35,238

ENGLAND had been humiliated by Jack Charlton's Irish side in the 1988 European Championships. Now they had a chance for revenge. And when Gary Lineker carried on where he had left off in Mexico four years previously, by scoring after eight minutes, it looked as though they were going to put the record straight. Instead, the game deteriorated as both teams gave under par performances.

Waddle started the move that led to Lineker's goal when his splendid pass caught McCarthy unawares with the Spurs man ready to pounce. Lineker took the ball on his chest, whilst under pressure from two defenders and the advancing Pat Bonner, before stabbing it over the line.

An electrical storm was followed by torrential rain and conditions became difficult. England

skipper Bryan Robson was under orders to play just in front of the back-four and not venture forward and the English midfield was ineffective. They were, however, perhaps unlucky not to have been awarded a penalty early in the second half when Moran brought down Waddle. But, as the second half wore on, there was a feeling that Ireland's equalizer was not far away.

In the 70th minute, Bobby Robson took off Peter Beardsley and replaced him with his Liverpool colleague, Steve McMahon. Two minutes later, with almost his first touch of the ball, McMahon lost control on the edge of the penalty area. Kevin Sheedy was on hand to fire in a lethal left-foot drive which beat Peter Shilton, who was playing in his 119th international match to equal Pat Jennings' record.

The match ground to a 1-1 draw, which was probably a fair result from a game which neither side deserved to win. But as one Irish supporter described it later: 'It was a great 1-1 win'. The shame was that both sides had served up the sort of football which suggested that there was a gulf between the British game and the rest of world.

England: Shilton; Stevens, Pearce, Walker, Butcher, Robson, Waddle, Gascoigne, Barnes, Lineker(Bull), Beardsley(McMahon).
Scorer: Lineker
Republic of Ireland: Bonner; Morris, Staunton, McCarthy, Moran, McGrath, Houghton, Townsend, Aldridge(McLoughlin), Cascarino, Sheedy.
Scorer: Sheedy
Referee: Aron Schmidhuber (West Germany)

The Republic of Ireland's Steve Staunton (left) and Andy Townsend.

EGYPT 1   HOLLAND 1 (Half-time 0-0)

Stadio Della Favorita, Palermo, 12 June
Attendance: 33,288

EGYPT arrived in Rome having beaten Scotland and Czechoslovakia as they prepared for the 1990 finals, but even then there were few who would have wagered money on them holding Holland, the European champions. But it was Egypt who were desperately unlucky not to win. The Dutch treated their opponents with little respect and the Egyptians showed just how much the African game has progressed in recent years.

It was Egypt's first appearance in the finals since 1934, when they played only one match, losing 4-2 to Hungary. But in those intervening years, the game in Egypt — and Africa generally — has developed beyond recognition. The Third World nations are rapidly becoming forces to be reckoned with in the world of soccer.

After a goalless first half it was apparent that Holland were playing below par. Most of their established stars were proving ineffective and there seemed to be a general lack of harmony in the Dutch camp. Gullit looked particularly out of touch. The Egyptians, however, played with flair and enterprise and El Kas, in particular, showed brilliant individual skills. However, the best chance of the half fell to Marco van Basten, who volleyed over the crossbar from six yards.

Completely against the run of play, Holland took the lead in the 58th minute when van Basten crossed from the left. Rijkaard missed his kick and the ball passed to second-half substitute Kieft, who drove it past Shobeir with the aid of a deflection.

Holland were expected to dominate after going in front and for a few minutes they did force their opponents back. But Egypt were soon on the attack again and had three good chances to level the scores. Only fine goalkeeping from van Breukelen saved the Dutch but in the 82nd minute, Egypt got their just rewards when they were awarded a penalty. Ronald Koeman pulled back Hossam Hassan and television replays suggested that the foul had been committed outside the area with Hassan falling into it. But overall justice was done when Abedelghani struck the perfect penalty to the goalkeeper's right.

Following Cameroon's win over Argentina, this match only confirmed that the African nations were no longer to be regarded as the underdogs of world football.

Egypt: Ahmed Shóbeir; Ibrahim Hassan, Rabie Yassein, Hany Ramzy, Ahmed Ramzy(Magdi Tolba), Hesham Yakan, Ismail Youssef, Magdi Abedelghani, Hossam Hassan, Gamal Abdelhamid(Adel Abdelrahman), Ahmed Abdou El Kas.
Scorer: Magdi Abedelghani (pen)
Holland: van Breukelen; van Aerle, Rijkaard, R.Koeman, van Tiggelen, Rutjes, Wouters, E.Koeman(Witschge), Vanenburg(Kieft), van Basten, Gullit.
Scorer: Kieft
Referee: Emilio Soriano Aladren (Spain)

ENGLAND 0   HOLLAND 0 (Half-time 0-0)

Stadio Sant 'Elia, Cagliari, 16 June
Attendance: 35,267

FOR the first time in his England managerial career, Bobby Robson played the sweeper system. He used Mark Wright in that role and the Derby County player gave an outstanding performance as the tactic proved successful. At the end of the game, Peter Shilton, having just won a record-breaking 120th full cap, said: "This is how we've got to play international football from now on."

Holland still appeared to have off-the-field problems that were carried on to the pitch, but the poor Dutch performance should not detract from England's great showing, notably

England's Chris Waddle (left) and Richard Witschge of Holland.

England's Gary Lineker (left) shoots the ball into the net but the attempt was ruled out for a handling offence.

Stuart Pearce of England.

from Paul Gascoigne, who never stopped running and had surely his best game for England to date.

England had two good chances to take the lead in the first ten minutes, when Barnes and Robson were fed by Lineker and Gascoigne respectively.

Five minutes into the second half, Lineker had the ball in the net but the 'goal' was disallowed because of hands by the England striker. Then both he and substitute Steve Bull had further good chances to put England in front. Only rarely did Gullit or Rijkaard look threatening and then they found Peter Shilton as safe as ever.

England lost skipper Bryan Robson, still troubled by a toe injury and now also suffering an Achilles tendon problem, but in the final minute it looked as though they had at last made the breakthrough. They were awarded a free-kick just outside the penalty area after an obstruction offence. Full-back Pearce struck the ball brilliantly and it beat the Dutch wall and the despairing dive of goalkeeper van Breukelen to thunder into the net. But the referee had clearly indicated that the kick was indirect and English celebrations were short-lived. The result was Group F's third consecutive draw.

England: Shilton; Pearce, Walker, Butcher, Parker, Wright, Robson(Platt), Waddle(Bull), Gascoigne, Lineker, Barnes.
Holland: van Breukelen; van Aerle, Rijkaard, R.Koeman, van Tiggelen, Wouters, Gullit, Witschge, van Basten, Van't Schip(Kieft), Gillhaus.
Referee: Zoran Petrović (Yugoslavia)

EGYPT 0   REPUBLIC OF IRELAND 0 (Half-time 0-0)

Stadio Della Favorita, Palermo, 17 June
Attendance: 33,288

AFTER frustrating England in their opening game, the Republic of Ireland were in turn frustrated by the tactics of the Egyptians who, after playing attractive football in drawing

Paul Gascoigne of England (white shirt) and Ronald Koeman of Holland.

Egypt gained draws against both Holland and the Republic of Ireland before narrowly losing to England. Here, Ireland's Kevin Sheedy is foiled by Hossam Hassan with Ismail Youssef ready to pounce.

1-1 with Holland, offered nothing in attack. Irish goalkeeper Pat Bonner did not have one save or cross to contend with in 90 minutes' football and at the end of the game, manager Jack Charlton was quick to condemn the Egyptians' tactics.

All the attacking came from Charlton's men but every foray was met by a penalty area packed with Egyptian players. Poor passing also let the Irish down at crucial moments.

Houghton, Aldridge, Cascarino, Staunton and Townsend all had chances to give the Republic the lead, but the best opportunity fell to Houghton in the 70th minute. He was put through by Sheedy but goalkeeper Shobeir was quickly off his line to block the shot.

Egypt: Ahmed Shobeir; Ibrahim Hassan, Rabie Yassein, Hany Ramzy, Hesham Yakan, Magdi Tolba(Taher Abouzeid), Ismail Youssef, Ahmed Abdou El Kas(Gamal Abdelhamid), Magdi Abdelghani, Hossam Hassan, Osama Oraby.
Republic of Ireland: Bonner; Morris, McCarthy, Moran, Staunton, Houghton, McGrath, Townsend, Sheedy, Aldridge(McLoughlin), Cascarino(Quinn).
Referee: Marcel van Langenhove (Belgium)

ENGLAND 1   EGYPT 0 (Half-time 0-0)
Stadio Sant 'Elia, Cagliari, 21 June
Attendance: 34,959

GOING into the last two matches, Group F was still wide open with all four teams having equal records and all still capable of qualifying for the next phase.

The Egyptians had shown what a difficult team they were to beat and, whilst not a great attacking force, they knew how to stop opponents and in Hany Ramzy boasted one of the outstanding defenders of Italia '90.

England manager Bobby Robson named Steve Bull in his starting line-up, but the man who loves to score goals received scant service from Barnes and Waddle and it was left to centre-half Mark Wright to score the only goal of the game.

The deadlock was broken in the 58th minute when Wright, the man who was passed fit to play in Italy only a few hours before the final squads had to be named, rose above the Egyptian defence to glance home a header from Paul Gascoigne's free-kick. It was Wright's first goal for England and what a crucial strike it turned out to be.

Egypt always seemed capable of breaking quickly but England, without injured skipper Bryan Robson, who was on the brink of returning home, held on to head a group which had promised so much, but in the end was probably the most disappointing one of all.

England: Shilton; Parker, Walker, Wright, Waddle(Platt), McMahon, Gascoigne, Barnes, Pearce, Bull(Beardsley), Lineker.
Scorer: Wright
Egypt: Ahmed Shobeir; Ibrahim Hassan, Rabie Yassein, Hany Ramzy, Hesham Yakan, Ahmed Ramzy, Ismail Youssef, Magdi Abdelghani, Hossam Hassan, Gamal Abdelhamid(Adel Abdelrahman), Ahmed Abdou El Kas(Tarek Soliman).
Referee: Kurt Roethlisberger (Switzerland)

HOLLAND 1   REPUBLIC OF IRELAND 1 (Half-time 1-0)
Stadio Della Favorita, Palermo, 21 June
Attendance: 33,288

THE Irish may not have won a lot of friends with their style of football, but for gritty determination there was no better outfit than Jackie Charlton's men, who, for the second time in the tournament, came from behind to snatch an equalizer.

When the Dutch took the lead in the tenth minute, after a brilliant piece of Gullit football, it looked as though the Irish were going to succumb to the experience of the 1988 European champions.

Holland's goal was masterminded and finished by Gullit, who indicated that his old pace had returned. From a Koeman free-kick, he played a one-two with Kieft before striding through the defence and hitting the ball superbly beyond the diving Bonner.

But, as this World Cup had shown, reputations counted for nothing and the Irish were far from overawed. They worked hard and defended well before Quinn's 71st-minute equalizer, which came from a long ball pumped upfield by Bonner, who was now emerging as the Irish 'play-maker' with his hefty kicks which were putting opposing defences under such pressure. This time Dutch defender van Aerle was hurried into a poor back-pass to van Breukelen which was not held by the 'keeper. The ball bounced loose and Quinn was on hand to stab it over the line.

Both teams thus ended with identical records and in order to decide final placings, lots were drawn. The Irish made second spot and looked forward to what looked the easier of the second-round matches, against Romania. Holland, meanwhile, were paired with the highly-rated West Germans.

Holland: van Breukelen; van Aerle, Rijkaard, R.Koeman, van Tiggelen, Witschge(Fräser), Wouters, Gullit, Kieft(van Loen), van Basten, Gillhaus.
Scorer: Gullit
Republic of Ireland: Bonner; Morris, McCarthy, Moran, Staunton, Houghton, McGrath, Townsend, Sheedy(Whelan), Quinn, Aldridge(Cascarino).
Scorer: Quinn
Referee: Michel Vautrot (France)

Group F - Final Table

	P	W	D	L	F	A	Pts
England	3	1	2	0	2	1	4
R of Ireland	3	0	3	0	2	2	3
Holland	3	0	3	0	2	2	3
Egypt	3	0	2	1	1	2	2

Second and third places decided by lots.

England's Paul Gascoigne, who began to blossom as a truly international star.

Hossam Hassan, one of Egypt's stars in the opening round of matches.

Louis-Paul M'Fede of Cameroon.

Round Two

CAMEROON 2   COLOMBIA 1 a.e.t. (Half-time 0-0; 90 mins 0-0)
Stadio San Paolo, Naples, 23 June
Attendance: 50,026

WHEN the 1990 tournament began, there could have been few people who imagined that Cameroon and Colombia would kick-off the knock-out stage of the 14th World Cup two weeks later. But both teams deserved their place on merit and after a lively first half it looked as though the South Americans were going to progress to their first-ever quarter-finals. Yet again, though, it was 38-year-old Roger Milla who made his presence felt and earned himself a place in World Cup folklore as he carried the Africans through.

Colombia created the better chances and deserved a first-half lead, particularly after a Rincón free-kick rattled the upright in the dying moments of the half. Valderrama was involved in many of the Colombian moves, but it was the arrival of Milla, as a 54th-minute substitute for M'Fede, which changed the course of the game.

After a goalless 90 minutes and then 15 barren minutes of extra-time, it looked as though the first penalty competition of the tournament was looming. But within 30 seconds of the start of the second period of extra-time, Milla became a national hero when he brilliantly finished a move, collecting a pass from Omam Biyik and striking home a superb left-foot drive. Three minutes later, Colombia's extrovert goalkeeper, Higuita, was caught in possession by Milla a clear ten yards out of his penalty area. The African star had little trouble in running in his fourth goal of the series.

Four minutes from time, Colombian substitute, Redin, scored a consolation goal but the day belonged to Cameroon, Africa's first-ever representatives in the World Cup quarter-finals. Most of all, it belonged to Roger Milla.

Alas, the game was marred, yet again, by some strange refereeing decisions which saw the Italian official excessively use the yellow card which resulted in four Cameroon players being banned from the quarter-final after receiving their second cautions.

Cameroon: N'Kono; Ebwelle, Onana, Akem N'Dip, Tataw, Kana Biyik, M'Bouh, M'Fede (Milla), Maboang, Makanaky(Djonkep), Omam Biyik.
Scorer: Milla 2
Colombia: Higuita; Herrera, Perea, Escobar, Gildardo Gómez, Gabriel Gómez(Redin), Alvarez, Valderrama, Rincón, Fajardo(Iguarán), Estrada.
Scorer: Redin
Referee: Tullio Lanese (Italy)

CZECHOSLOVAKIA 4   COSTA RICA 1 (Half-time 1-0)
Stadio Sant Nicola, Bari, 23 June
Attendance: 47,673

The scoreline may indicate a walk-over for Czechoslovakia in the World Cup's 450th game, but that was far from the case and this match was finely balanced until 15 minutes from time, when the Central Americans were trailing 2-1 and pushing for a second equalizer. In the end, though, Czech dominance showed and the highlight of the game was the tournament's second hat-trick — all headed goals — from Tomáš Skuhravý.

The Sparta Prague striker opened the scoring in the 11th minute, when he rose high

Above: Africa's most famous footballer, Roger Milla, the 38-year-old striker who was a two-goal hero against Colombia.
Opposite: Milla scored his second after robbing Colombia's eccentric goalkeeper, José Higuita.

above the defence to head powerfully past replacement goalkeeper, Barrantes. That was the only score at the interval, although the Czechs had another effort disallowed. But ten minutes into the second half, Costa Rica pulled themselves back into the game when Gonzalez, the youngest player in the tournament, powerfully headed home a Ramirez free-kick from the right.

Now the Costa Ricans began to play the better football but in the 63rd minute, Skuhravý scored his second goal when he glanced a header just inside the post after the ball had been accurately headed across the goal to him.

Both teams had plenty of chances to add to the score and 14 minutes from time, Czechoslovakia went 3-1 ahead. Justice was done after the referee refused to allow the advantage when Moravčik went on to put the ball in the net after Hašek had been hacked down by two Costa Rican defenders. From the ensuing free-kick, Kubíc bent the ball around the defensive wall and into the net with the goalkeeper almost motionless.

Skuhravý completed his hat-trick of headers with eight minutes remaining when he rose to meet a Chovanec corner. The Czechs went into the last eight having established themselves as one of the tournament's best teams behind Italy and West Germany.

The Costa Ricans went to the 1990 World Cup finals with no chance of winning the trophy. But they left soccer's finest stage with pride and their honour intact after giving a good account of themselves on their debut in the finals.

Czechoslovakia: Stéjskal; Kadlec, Kocian, Chovanec, Hašek, Bílek, Kubíc, Moravčik, Straka, Skuhravý, Knofliček.
Scorers: Skuhravý 3, Kubíc
Costa Rica: Barrantes; Flores, Montero, Obando(Medford), Chávez, Gonzalez, Chavarria (Guimaraes), Marchena, Cayasso, Ramirez, C.Jara.
Scorer: Gonzalez
Referee: Sigfried Kirschen (East Germany)

Ivo Knofliček, once a defector to England, now a star for his country.

ARGENTINA 1   BRAZIL 0 (Half-time 0-0)

Stadio Delle Alpi, Turin, 24 June
Attendance: 61,381

BRAZIL went to Italy with the reputation as one of the most entertaining and attacking soccer nations in the world. Sadly, they decided to play the European way and, despite creating countless chances, they had nobody of the Pelé, Jairzinho or Rivelino mould to put the ball into the back of the net. And they paid dearly for their inability to score goals.

In a game which they dominated for 80 minutes, the Brazilians should have had the defending champions packing their bags at half-time. Instead, Brazil could only count the cost of missed chances.

Maradona appeared a very ordinary player in a very ordinary team, but his one piece of brilliance turned the whole match. In the 80th minute, despite being under pressure, Maradona hit a pass which split the Brazilian defence and Caniggia, one of the revelations of the Argentine side, took the goal calmly as he rounded Taffarel, the Brazilian goalkeeper.

Minutes later the Brazilians' game collapsed completely when their captain, Ricardo Gomes, was sent off for a foul on Basualdo. In the dying minutes, Muller had an easy chance to level the scores but his shot was wide of the target. How they missed their goalscoring players of old.

After three previous World Cup meetings between the teams it was, indeed, sweet revenge

Above: Claudio Caniggia, one of the revelations of the Argentinian side. *Left:* Caniggia scores the only goal of the game against Brazil after taking a Maradona through-ball and rounding goalkeeper Taffarel.

Brazil's Dunga had a fine game against the Argentinians but his side still went out to Caniggia's goal.

Frank Rijkaard of Holland, who disgraced himself by spitting at West Germany's Rudi Völler and marred what was otherwise a splendid advertisement for soccer.

Jürgen Klinsmann beats off a challenge from Holland's Berry van Aerle to put West Germany ahead after five minutes of the second half.

for the Argentinians, who beat their arch-rivals for the first time in the tournament. On this form, though, they were going to find it tough to hold on to the trophy they won in Mexico four years earlier.

Argentina: Goycochea; Simón, Ruggeri, Monzon, Olarticoechea, Giusti, Troglio(Calderón), Caniggia, Basualdo, Burruchaga, Maradona.
Scorer: Caniggia
Brazil: Taffarel; Galvão(Renato), Ricardo Gomes, Rocha, Jorginho, Valdo, Dunga, Alemão (Silas), Branco, Careca, Muller.
Referee: Joël Quiniou (France)

WEST GERMANY 2   HOLLAND 1 (Half-time 0-0)

Stadio Giuseppe Meazza (San Siro), Milan, 24 June
Attendance: 74,559

TWO of Europe's finest teams gave one of the best and most pulsating displays of the 1990 World Cup to date. Sadly, the game, like many others, was marred by inconsistent and controversial refereeing, and also by a confrontation between Frank Rijkaard and Rudi Völler in the early stages.

After a whirlwind opening 15 minutes which saw Winter miss two chances for the Dutch, the game reached boiling point after 20 minutes when Rijkaard was booked for a bad foul on Völler who, in turn, was shown the yellow card for complaining that the Dutchman had spat at him.

Seconds later, the two were involved in a heated exchange after the German went for a ball which van Breukelen reached first. It looked a harmless enough challenge, but first Völler and then Rijkaard were ordered off in the ensuing row. As they left the field, Rijkaard again appeared to spit at Völler.

It was only a matter of time before the game's first goal and in the 38th minute, Littbarski had a chance to give the Germans the lead, but his volley from a Buchwald cross was remarkably saved by van Breukelen. However, the Germans eventually opened their account five minutes into the second half when Klinsmann was on the end of another Buchwald cross to cleverly beat a defender at the near post and slot the ball across the face of the goal and into the far corner of the net.

Klinsmann had a chance to increase the lead in the 75th minute, when his shot rattled the post during another pulsating 45 minutes football. And with the Dutch pressing forward for the equalizer, the Germans grabbed a second goal in the 84th minute. Van Breukelen had just brought off a great save from Littbarski, but the Dutch 'keeper was beaten when Brehme curled the ball around the defence and into the goal from just inside the area.

With German celebrations already underway, Holland broke clear and although Marco van Basten appeared to 'dive', they were awarded a penalty by the Argentine referee, who made some strange decisions, including a farcical booking of the German captain, Matthäus. Ronald Koeman converted the spot-kick with composure but it was all too late and the tournament's second favourites ran out winners.

It was a marvellous advertisement of football, spoiled only by that contretemps between Völler and Rijkaard.

West Germany: Illgner; Reuter, Brehme, Kohler, Augenthaler, Buchwald, Berthold, Littbarski, Völler, Matthäus, Klinsmann(Riedle).
Scorers: Klinsmann, Brehme
Holland: van Breukelen, van Aerle(Kieft), Rijkaard, R.Koeman, van Tiggelen, Wouters, Witschge(Gillhaus), Winter, Van't Schip, van Basten, Gullit.
Scorer: R.Koeman (pen)
Referee: Juan Carlos Loustau (Argentina)

REPUBLIC OF IRELAND 0   ROMANIA 0 a.e.t. (Half-time 0-0; 90 mins 0-0)
Republic of Ireland won 5-4 on penalties
Stadio Luigi Ferraris, Genoa, 25 June
Attendance: 31,818

FOR both sides there was the prospect of a place in the last eight of the World Cup for the first time in their history. And before the outcome was known, 26 sets of tired legs played through 120 minutes' football and endured a tense penalty competition. In the end, it was the World Cup newcomers from the Republic of Ireland who won through a monumental battle.

Both sides had limited opportunities during normal time and the Irish were saved on several occasions by goalkeeper Pat Bonner. In extra-time, however, it looked as though the tired legs of the Republic were going to succumb to the Romanians, who still showed some pace, notably from Hagi, who had an outstanding game. But the Irish held out and it came down to penalties.

Hagi converted the first kick and then Sheedy did likewise for the Irish. Lupu, Rotariu

Ruud Gullit, who was unable to revive the fortunes of a Dutch team that appeared to be suffering from off-the-field unrest.

Ray Houghton, one of the stars of a hard-working Irish team.

David O'Leary hits home the penalty that took the Irish into a quarter-final meeting with Italy in Rome.

Franco Baresi, the defender who helped Italy go through to their quarter-final as the only team still to concede a goal in the competition.

Spain's Míchel was his country's outstanding player but he could not prevent them from going out of the tournament.

and Lupsecu all made no mistakes with their kicks and Houghton, Townsend and Cascarino all scored for Ireland, although goalkeeper Lung came close to saving Cascarino's kick.

With the score balanced at 4-4, the agony of becoming the first to miss fell to the Romanian, Timofte, whose kick was well saved by Bonner. Now it was down to David O'Leary, one of the most experienced members of the Irish squad, to put his team into the quarter-finals. O'Leary, who had come on as a late substitute, coolly sent Lung the wrong way and the whole of Ireland, plus quite a few others, celebrated a fairy-tale victory.

A word of praise for the Brazilian referee, José Ramiz Wright, who did what many other referees in this tournament had failed to do — apply the law of commonsense instead of producing red and yellow cards at random.

Republic of Ireland: Bonner; Morris, Staunton(O'Leary), McCarthy, Moran, McGrath, Houghton, Townsend, Aldridge(Cascarino), Sheedy, Quinn.
Romania: Lung; Rednic, Klein, Andone, G.Popescu, Rotariu, Sabău(Timofte), Hagi, Lupescu, Răducioiu(Lupu), Balint.
Referee: José Ramiz Wright (Brazil)

ITALY 2   URUGUAY 0 (Half-time 0-0)
Stadio Olimpico, Rome, 25 June
Attendance: 73,303

THE reshuffled Uruguayan team which could find no place in the starting line-up for the two Rubens — Sosa and Paz — frustrated the hosts for an hour with their defensive tactics, coupled with some fine goalkeeping from Fernando Alvez.

The new strike force of Baggio and Schillaci nearly gave Italy the lead in the first minute, when Schillaci was on the end of a Baggio cross, but his volleyed shot went wide of the post. Schillaci and De Agostini both had further chances to put the hosts in front, but were denied by Alvez. Baggio had the ball in the net in the 15th minute from a free-kick but, like England's 'goal' against Holland, it was ruled out because it was indirect.

As time wore on, both sides engaged in some cynical tackling, notably by Perdomo and Berti, both of whom were booked by English referee, George Courtney.

The stadium erupted in the 67th minute when Schillaci scored for Italy. A clever pass by Serena went through the legs of Gutiérrez and Schillaci's left foot struck the ball superbly from 20 yards with Alvez powerless to do anything.

José Perdomo had two chances to snatch an equalizer for the Uruguayans before substitute Serena headed home a Giannini cross four minutes from time to make the match safe for Italy and ensure them a quarter-final match against the Republic of Ireland. In reaching that stage, Italy had done so without conceding a goal, the only team with such a record.

Italy: Zenga; Baresi, Bergomi, De Agostini, Ferri, Maldini, Berti(Serena), De Napoli, Giannini, Baggio(Vierchowod), Schillaci.
Scorers: Schillaci, Serena
Uruguay: Alvez; Gutiérrez, De Leon, Dominguez, Pintos, Perdomo, Ostolaza(Alzamendi), Francescoli, Pereira, Aguilera(Sosa), Fonseca.
Referee: George Courtney (England)

YUGOSLAVIA 2   SPAIN 1 a.e.t. (Half-time 0-0; 90 mins 1-1)
Stadio Marc Antonio Bentegodi, Verona, 26 June
Attendance: 35,500

FOR 77 minutes, Spain and Yugoslavia played a dour tactical battle in intense heat and at strolling pace, with goals never likely to be a prominent feature. Yet the game suddenly came alive to produce an exciting closing 13 minutes of normal time.

The best opportunities had fallen to Spain, notably to their skipper Butragueño, who missed a couple of second-half chances, including a header which hit a post. But it was Yugoslavia who took the lead in the 77th minute when Katanec headed on a Vujović cross to Stojković, who showed his £5 million class by beating Martín Vázquez before slotting the ball past Zubizarreta.

The goal was against the run of play and seven minutes from time, Spain had good cause to appeal for a penalty. Salinas was brought down by Vulić in the penalty area but the referee waved play on. However, two minutes later the Spaniards got their just reward when Martín Vázquez powered a shot across the area for Salinas to tap the ball into the net at the far post after the Yugoslav goalkeeper, Ivković, had stopped, believing Salinas to be offside.

The game went into extra-time and with only two minutes on the clock, the Yugoslavs regained the lead when a Stojković free-kick beat the poorly-organized defensive wall and gave the Spanish 'keeper no chance.

Yugoslavia spent the last 28 minutes holding on to their slender lead to set up a first-time World Cup meeting with Argentina in the quarter-finals.

Yugoslavia: Ivković; Spasić, Hadžibegić, Jozić, Brnović, Susić, Stojković, Katanec(Vulić), Šabanadžović, Pančev(Savićević), Vujović.
Scorer: Stojković 2
Spain: Zubizarreta; Chendo, Villarroya, Górriz, Andrinúa(Jiménez), Sanchís, Roberto, Martín Vázquez, Butragueño(Rafael Paz), Míchel, Salinas.
Scorer: Salinas
Referee: Aron Schmidhuber (West Germany)

ENGLAND 1   BELGIUM 0 a.e.t. (Half-time 0-0; 90 mins 0-0)

Stadio Dall'Ara, Bologna, 26 June
Attendance: 34,520

THE last quarter-final place was established after another tense, closely-fought match between two equally matched European sides. And what drama there was as England scored the winning goal 30 seconds from the end of extra-time, just at a point when everyone was bracing themselves for another nerve-racking penalty competition.

Almost from the first whistle, England, playing without injured skipper Bryan Robson, found themselves under pressure from the imaginative Belgians. Early on, Bobby Robson's team had to thank the woodwork which prevented them falling behind when a Ceulemans shot beat Peter Shilton. Belgium also felt unlucky not to have been awarded a penalty.

But, after allowing the Belgians to dominate the first half-hour, England found their way into the game and shortly before the interval, John Barnes put the ball in the net with a fierce volley, only for the effort to ruled out for offside. Television replays suggested that the linesman had been wrong, but Barnes could also look back to an earlier effort when he should have scored when ideally placed.

The woodwork saved England again in the second half when a marvellous curling shot by Scifo from 25 yards hit the post with Shilton again beaten. It was a superb strike, worthy of a goal.

The Belgians began extra-time where they had left off after 90 minutes, but still they could not penetrate Shilton's goal. As the seconds ticked away, England began to play the ball around at the back, seemingly resigned to penalties, but then they pushed forward and

Belgium's captain, Eric Gerets.

Mark Wright, who was asked to play sweeper for England and emerged as a world-class defender.

Left top: Wright clears the ball from Belgium's Stéphane Demol with John Barnes (left) and Gary Lineker looking on. The other Belgian player is Georges Grün. *Left bottom:* David Platt scores one of the best goals of Italia '90, volleying home Paul Gascoigne's free-kick to hit a last-gasp winner for England against Belgium.

David Platt, hero of England's passage to the quarter-final.

Gascoigne was fouled. He took the free-kick himself and substitute David Platt timed his run perfectly before swivelling to volley home one of the finest goals ever seen in the World Cup. It was certainly one of the most dramatic finishes to any match in the tournament, which was well handled by referee Mikkelsen, the youngest official in the series.

England: Shilton; Pearce, Walker, Butcher, Parker, Wright, Waddle, McMahon(Platt), Gascoigne, Lineker, Barnes(Bull).
Scorer: Platt
Belgium: Preud'homme; Gerets, Clijsters, Demol, Grün, De Wolf, Van der Elst, Scifo, Versavel (Vervoort), Degryse(Claesen), Ceulemans.
Referee: Peter Mikkelsen (Denmark)

Quarter-finals

ARGENTINA 0   YUGOSLAVIA 0 a.e.t. (Half-time 0-0; 90 mins 0-0)
Argentina won 3-2 on penalties
Stadio Comunale, Florence, 30 June
Attendance: 38,971

AFTER Argentina lost their opening game of the 1990 World Cup finals to Cameroon, many people felt that the South Americans' reign as world champions looked over. Yet they now found themselves in the semi-finals, despite another unimpressive performance.

Throughout the tournament Argentina had relied far too much on Maradona and now they were made to look a very moderate team indeed by a classy Yugoslavian side, who had to play for 90 minutes with only ten men when Šabanadžović was sent off after half an hour for committing his second yellow-card offence within a couple of minutes. But it was hard to tell which side was a man short because it was the Europeans who played the more attacking football. And the final outcome was a travesty because the Argentinians had posed the strong Yugoslav defence few problems.

Jozić had a great chance to put Yugoslavia in front in the first half and in extra-time Savićević had two further opportunities to open the scoring as they continued to play the more creative football. Argentina were too predictable and kept hoping for a piece of Maradona brilliance to win them the game. But the master was clearly off form and seemed to be struggling with knee problems.

At the end of 120 minutes' football, the tournament's second penalty competition was required and in an amazing turnaround, which saw both teams take the lead, it was Yugoslavia

Right: **Argentina's goalkeeper Sergio Goycochea (centre) celebrates his side's victory over Yugoslavia, flanked by Juan Simón (left) and reserve goalkeeper Fabian Cancelarich.**

Dragan Stojković of Yugoslavia.

who missed three of their penalties, whilst Argentina missed two, including Maradona's weak effort which was saved by Ivković, much to the delight of the Florentine crowd.

Argentina: Goycochea; Ruggeri, Simón, Olarticoechea(Troglio), Serrizuela, Giusti, Burruchaga, Basualdo, Calderón(Dezotti), Caniggia, Maradona.
Yugoslavia: Ivković; Spasić, Hadžibegić, Jozić, Vulić, Šabanadžović, Brnović, Susić(Savićević), Stojković, Prosinečki, Vujović.
Referee: Kurt Roethlisberger (Switzerland)

ITALY 1   REPUBLIC OF IRELAND 0 (Half-time 1-0)

Stadio Olimpico, Rome, 30 June
Attendance: 73,303

Unexpectedly called up after Nery Pumpido was injured, goalkeeper Sergio Goycochea was one of the few Argentinians to emerge from the 1990 World Cup with any credit.

THE Irish dream eventually faded in front of 73,000 fervent fans in the Olympic Stadium, Rome, but not before they had put up a great fight and inflicted the kind of pressure on the Italian defence which they had not previously been subjected to in Italia '90.

For the first 25 minutes, the Irish were on top and showed that they were capable of playing attractive and fluent football, so dissimilar to their style against England and Egypt. With the game played at a furious pace and in a stiffling Italian heat, the Irish put pressure on Walter Zenga, who still had to concede a goal in the tournament. But it was the new Italian superstar, Salvatori Schillaci, who scored the goal which carried Italy into the semi-finals.

In the 37th minute, Ireland's goalkeeper, Pat Bonner, could not hold a powerful, swerving shot from Donadoni. Bonner parried the ball to Schillaci, who placed a fine shot into the far corner of the net after the 'keeper had stumbled in making the first save and could not recover his ground.

Schillaci could have bagged a hat-trick and when his fierce shot from a second-half free-kick rattled the bar and bounced on to the line, many thought it was a goal, but referee

The Republic of Ireland's aerial onslaught was not enough to overcome Italy, although Tony Cascarino (*left, white shirt*) certainly made his presence felt against the tournament favourites.

Valente ruled in Ireland's favour. A bigger margin of defeat, though, would not have reflected the Republic's contribution to an entertaining game. Indeed, in the closing minutes they looked threatening and an equalizer even seemed a possibility. They were certainly a credit to the game and to the 1990 World Cup.

Italy: Zenga; Baresi, Bergomi, De Agostini, Ferri, Maldini, De Napoli, Giannini(Ancelotti), Baggio(Serena), Donadoni, Schillaci.
Scorer: Schillaci
Republic of Ireland: Bonner; Morris, Staunton, McCarthy, Moran, McGrath, Houghton, Townsend, Aldridge(Sheridan), Sheedy, Quinn(Cascarino).
Referee: Carlos Antonio Silva Valente (Portugal)

WEST GERMANY 1   CZECHOSLOVAKIA 0 (Half-time 1-0)

Stadio Giuseppe Meazza (San Siro), Milan, 1 July
Attendance: 73,347

WHILST the 1990 World Cup produced some awful games, there were occasional moments of magic and most of the outstanding performances were produced by Franz Beckenbauer's German team. In reaching their record ninth semi-final they gave another sizzling performance against a talented Czech team, who never gave up, despite playing with ten men for the last 25 minutes.

The game started at a blistering pace with the Germans dominating the opening play. After 20 minutes they should have taken the lead but a Buchwald effort was magnificently

Another goalkeeping hero, Pat Bonner of the Republic of Ireland. He was unlucky when his save from Donadoni rebounded for Schillaci to hit the winner for Italy.

Thomas Berthold of West Germany.

Jürgen Kohler of West Germany.

David Platt wheels away in delight after heading home Stuart Pearce's cross to give England a 26th-minute lead against Cameroon.

saved by goalkeeper Stéjskal, who had an outstanding game for the Czechs. From the resulting corner, Hašek cleared off the line.

Five minutes later, German pressure was rewarded with a goal when Klinsmann beat two defenders before being felled in the box and the referee had no hesitation in awarding a penalty. Skipper Lothar Matthäus blasted the ball past Stéjskal with the 'keeper going the wrong way.

Klinsmann came close to scoring a second goal for the Germans in first-half injury-time but Hašek cleared off the line again.

West Germany started the second half as they finished the first, with constant raids on the Czech goal, and two minutes after the restart they had another effort cleared off the line, this time by Bílek.

Czechoslovakia showed skill and always looked capable of producing an equalizer, despite the German superiority, but they were rocked in the 65th minute when Moravčik was harshly sent off for a foolish second bookable offence. Three minutes earlier, West Germany were unlucky not to have been awarded a penalty when Stéjskal appeared to bring down Bein in the area.

After so much pressure, it was therefore surprising that the game should be decided by that solitary goal from the penalty-spot.

West Germany: Illgner; Brehme, Kohler, Augenthaler, Buchwald, Berthold, Matthäus, Bein (Möller), Littbarski, Riedle, Klinsmann.
Scorer: Matthäus (pen)
Czechoslovakia: Stéjskal; Kadlec, Kocian, Straka, Hašek, Bílek(Němeček), Chovanec, Kubíc (Griga), Moravčik, Skuhravý, Knofliček.
Referee: Helmut Kohl (Austria)

ENGLAND 3   CAMEROON 2 a.e.t. (Half-time 1-0; 90 mins 2-2)

Stadio San Paolo, Naples, 1 July
Attendance: 55,205

ENGLAND came close to an embarrassing World Cup defeat that would have matched their 1-0 humiliation at the hands of the United States in 1950. But, at the end of 120 minutes' play, they edged out the talented Cameroons with a professional, if sometimes unconvincing, performance.

England got off to a great start when David Platt, their hero of the second round, headed home a Pearce cross in the 26th minute to open the scoring. Fifteen minutes before Platt's strike, however, Omam Biyik had found himself with plenty of room in front of England's goal and only a fine stop from Peter Shilton saved the day.

The English defence was having all sorts of problems, even after taking the lead, and Libiih had a great chance to equalize in the 38th minute, when he, too, was given plenty of room in the penalty area before sending his header over the bar.

The second half was soon to turn to disaster for England and in the 61st minute the Cameroons were rewarded for their enterprise when substitute Roger Milla was brought down in the penalty area by Paul Gascoigne and Kunde scored with the spot-kick, although Shilton came close to bringing off a memorable save.

Four minutes later the amazing Milla was involved in a quick and clever one-two with the other substitute, Ekeke, who strode through the defence to place the ball neatly past the advancing Shilton.

England were now in disarray and were being made to look second-rate at times, but they kept pushing forward and gradually crept back into the game. Nine minutes from time

Gary Lineker was upended in the box and picked himself up to tuck away the penalty. And it was Lineker who became England's saviour in the last minute of the first half of extra-time when, again, he was brought down in the area, this time by goalkeeper N'Kono, who was booked.

Lineker's second spot-kick went fairly straight but N'Kono had already committed himself and England, who finished the game with Mark Wright suffering from a bad cut under an eye, were through to the semi-finals of the World Cup. It was their first appearance in the last-four since 1966 and their first time on foreign soil. And it was only the second time in World Cup history that three penalties had been successfully converted in one game.

In a World Cup of shocks, the Cameroons treated us to some delicate skills, albeit that some of the tackling was over-robust at times, and England's struggle to beat them should not be taken lightly. Their presence in the last eight was far from a fluke.

England: Shilton; Pearce, Walker, Butcher(Steven), Parker, Wright, Waddle, Platt, Gascoigne, Lineker, Barnes(Beardsley).
Scorers: Lineker 2 (2 pens), Platt
Cameroon: N'Kono; Massing, Ebwelle, Kunde, Pagal, Tataw, M'Fede(Ekeke), Libiih, Makanaky, Maboang(Milla), Omam Biyik.
Scorers: Kunde (pen), Ekeke
Referee: Edgardo Codesal Mendez (Mexico)

Semi-finals

ARGENTINA 1   ITALY 1 a.e.t. (Half-time 0-1; 90 mins 1-1)
Argentina won 4-3 on penalties
Stadio San Paolo, Naples, 3 July
Attendance: 59,978

ITALY paid a heavy price for doing what they are normally most proficient at — sitting back on a slender lead. For whilst Diego Maradona was again only a shadow of his former self, Argentina gave their finest performance of the championship as the Italians buckled under the pressures of being both hosts and tournament favourites.

Yet the whole of Italy rejoiced in the 17th minute, when Schillaci scored his fifth goal of the series to put the hosts in front.

The new superstar of Italian football started the move which saw Giannini work hard before sending a back-header to Vialli, whose shot was only partially saved by Goycochea. Schillaci was on hand to snap up the rebound, although many felt that the referee should have ruled him offside as Vialli shot. Having allowed play to continue, the referee could hardly blow when the ball came back to Schillaci from an opponent.

Italy have always proved a difficult side to break down once they are in front, particularly in their own country. But this time, with a World Cup Final place beckoning, they showed signs of nerves.

Argentina began to look the better side and in the 67th minute they got a deserved equalizer when Caniggia glanced home a header from Olarticoechea's cross from the left. It was the first goal scored past Walter Zenga in 517 minutes of World Cup football, beating Peter Shilton's record by 18 minutes.

At the end of 90 minutes the scores were still level and, whilst the period of extra-time produced no further goals, it certainly provided plenty of incidents.

Terry Butcher, who took over the England captaincy after Bryan Robson went home injured.

England's Des Walker, who caught the eye as a world-class central defender, despite carrying an ankle injury for much of the tournament.

Sergio Goycochea dives to his left to save Donadoni's penalty.

Caniggia (right) glances a header past Walter Zenga and Argentina are level in the 67th minute. It was the first goal to be scored past Zenga in 517 minutes of World Cup football.

Rudi Völler limped off against England with a trapped nerve in his leg.

Joy and despair. England's Chris Waddle is consoled by West German skipper Lothar Matthäus after missing from the penalty-spot. Behind them the rest of the German team collapse in a heap on top of goalkeeper Bodo Illgner, who has just seen Waddle's effort fly over his bar.

The first half of the extra period was in its fourth minute of injury time when Ricardo Giusti was sent off for an off-the-ball incident involving Baggio. Linesman Peter Mikkelsen of Denmark gave referee Vautrot his account before the red card was produced and play was held up for a further three minutes whilst Maradona pleaded Giusti's case. Altogether the first period lasted almost 24 minutes and, overall, extra-time had been in stark contrast to the first 90 minutes, producing as it did, much that is bad about the game.

Argentina, engaging in their second successive penalty competition, again had luck on their side. After both teams successfully converted three kicks, Donadoni's shot was saved by Goycochea. Maradona then scored what turned out to be the winner, as Serena's shot was also saved by the Argentinian 'keeper. Called up following the injury to Pumpido, Goycochea was now his country's hero after starting the tournament in reserve.

Argentina reached their second successive World Cup Final having scored only five goals on the way, a record low for the competition. Their football had been negative and dull but now, for the first time, they had shown what they were capable of achieving. They were now one game away from becoming only the second South American nation, after Brazil in 1958, to win the trophy on European soil.

Argentina: Goycochea; Serrizuela, Ruggeri, Simón, Basualdo(Batista), Burruchaga, Maradona, Giusti, Olarticoechea, Caniggia, Calderón(Troglio).
Scorer: Caniggia
Italy: Zenga; Baresi, Bergomi, Ferri, Maldini, De Agostini, De Napoli, Giannini(Baggio), Vialli(Serena), Donadoni, Schillaci.
Scorer: Schillaci
Referee: Michel Vautrot (France)

WEST GERMANY 1   ENGLAND 1 a.e.t. (Half-time 0-0; 90 mins 1-1)
West Germany won 4-3 on penalties
Stadio Delle Alpi, Turin, 4 July
Attendance: 62,628

FOR the first time in World Cup history, both semi-finals were decided on the outcome of a penalty competition at the end of 120 minutes' play. However, unlike the first game, between Argentina and Italy, this second semi-final was a classic encounter between two old adversaries and contained none of the play-acting and cheating that had been evident 24 hours earlier.

It was also well refereed by an official who was prepared to let the game flow and allow players the benefit of the doubt on such a momentous occasion.

Undoubtedly, West Germany had been the team of the tournament so far, whereas England had been criticized for some indifferent performances. Indeed, many commentators put their appearance in the last four down to good fortune rather than good football. But Bobby Robson's men proved that English football was still amongst the best in the world as they matched the Germans in all departments.

England dominated from the start and held the advantage until the last ten minutes of the first half, when the Germans began to look dangerous on the break. They started the second half in the same fashion but it was only a cruel piece of luck which saw England fall behind in the 59th minute, when Brehme's free-kick was deflected off Parker and looped over Shilton's head into the net.

It seemed that England would bow out to that dreadful piece of ill fortune but ten minutes

from time, Parker's cross from the right found Lineker in the penalty area. Three German defenders made a hash of clearing the ball and the England striker fired a marvellous left-foot shot into the far corner of the net for the tenth World Cup goal of his career. Both sides came close to scoring the winner in extra-time. Waddle, who earlier might have had a penalty when he was brought down, struck the post with a shot, and then Buchwald's shot also hit an upright.

Once more the lottery of a penalty competition was required. Lineker, Beardsley and Platt scored England's first three, whilst Brehme, Matthäus and Riedle found the back of the net for the Germans. Then the English dream began to die. Pearce hit his shot against Illgner's leg, Thon put the Germans in front and then Waddle, who had the responsibility of keeping England in the tournament, fired his shot over the bar. West Germany were in a record sixth World Cup Final and were the first side to play in three consecutive Finals. They also set up a repeat of the 1986 Final against Argentina.

England gave by far their best international performance of recent times and came out of the game with great credit and pride. So did manager Bobby Robson, who, as the team left for Italy, had been pilloried by certain sections of the English Press after allegations about his private life.

But for a rare moment in Italia '90, it was nice to be able to say that the real winner was the game of football.

West Germany: Illgner; Brehme, Kohler, Augenthaler, Buchwald, Berthold, Matthäus, Hässler (Reuter), Thon, Völler(Riedle), Klinsmann.
Scorer: Brehme
England: Shilton; Pearce, Walker, Parker, Wright, Waddle, Butcher(Steven), Platt, Gascoigne, Beardsley, Lineker.
Scorer: Lineker
Referee: José Ramiz Wright (Brazil)

Third place play-off
ITALY 2   ENGLAND 1 (Half-time 0-0)
Stadio Sant Nicola, Bari, 7 July
Attendance: 51,426

OVER the years, what is often regarded as the World Cup's most irrelevant contest has produced some boring matches. But, considering the immense disappointment that these two teams had to overcome after losing their semi-finals in penalty competitions, Italy and England served up one of the better games of the 1990 tournament.

As in their semi-final, England served notice that their opening performances of the tournament were not a true indication of their capabilities. Playing with greater confidence and freedom, they showed once more that they could compete with the best in the world.

During a goalless first half in Bari, it was England who created the best chances, although they might have trailed at the interval, had Schillaci been able to get to a ball which rebounded off a post following Shilton's brilliant save.

Ironically, it was from an uncharacteristic Shilton error that Italy opened the scoring in the 70th minute. Playing in his 125th game for England before announcing his retirement from international soccer, Shilton was rolling the ball along the ground when Baggio sneaked in to steal it from him. The ball was passed to Shillaci, who returned it to Baggio. The Italian was now in an offside position but the referee allowed play to continue and Baggio's effort in beating off defenders to hammer the ball high into the net was a world-class strike for all that.

It would have been so sickening for England to have lost to a goal given away in such

STATISTICS

Goalscorers:
6 — Salvatore Schillaci (Italy).
5 — Tomáš Skuhravý (Czechoslovakia).
4 — Míchel (Spain); Roger Milla (Cameroon); Gary Lineker (England); Lothar Matthäus (West Germany).
3 — David Platt (England); Andreas Brehme, Rudi Völler, Jürgen Klinsmann (all West Germany).
2 — Davor Jozić, Dragan Stojković, Darko Pančev (all Yugoslavia); Bernardo Redin Valverde (Colombia); Careca, Muller (both Brazil); Marius Lăcătus, Gavril Balint (both Romania); Michal Bílek (Czechoslovakia); Roberto Baggio (Italy); Claudio Paul Caniggia (Argentina).
1 — Safet Susić, Robert Prosinečki (both Yugoslavia); Kevin Sheedy, Niall Quinn (both Republic of Ireland); Roger Flores, Ronald Gonzalez, Juan Arnoldo Cayasso, Hernán Medford (all Costa Rica); Leo Albert Jozef Clijsters, Michel Jean De Wolf, Vincenzo Scifo, Marc Gabriel Degryse, Jan Ceulemans, Patrick Felix Vervoort (all Belgium); Carlos Alberto Valderrama Palacio, Freddy Eusébio Rincón Valencia (both Colombia); Ronald Koeman, Willem Kieft, Ruud Gullit (all Holland); Pablo Bengoechea, Daniel Fonseca (both Uruguay); Alberto Górriz Echarte, Julio Salinas Fernandez (both Spain); Andreas Ogris, Gerhard Rodax (both Austria); Magdi Abedelghani (Egypt); Stuart McCall, Maurice Johnston (both Scotland); Hwang Bo-kwan (South Korea); Alexander Zavarov, Oleg Protasov, Igor Dobrovolsky, Andrei Zygmantovich (all Soviet Union); Glenn Strömberg, Tomas Brolin, Johnny Ekström (all Sweden); Ali Thani Jumaa, Khalid Ismail Mubarak (both United Arab Emirates); Paul Caligiuri, Bruce Murray (both United States); Ivan Hašek, Lubos Kubík, Milan Luhový (all Czechoslovakia); Emmanuel Kunde, François Omam Biyik, Eugene Ekete (all Cameroon); Mark Wright (England); Giuseppe Giannini, Aldo Serena (both Italy); Jorge Burruchaga, Pedro Damian Monzon, Pedro Antonio Troglio (all Argentina); Pierre Littbarski, Uwe Bein (both West Germany).

Own Goals:
None

Hat-tricks:
Míchel (Spain v South Korea), Tomáš Skuhravý (Czechoslovakia v Costa Rica).

Fastest goal
4 minutes — Safet Susić (Yugoslavia v United Arab Emirates).

Roberto Baggio is about to put the ball into the England net after Peter Shilton's uncharacteristic lapse of concentration. Baggio looked well offside when Schillaci returned the ball to him but the goal stood.

circumstances but nine minutes from time, David Platt scored a magnificent equalizer when he rose to head home Dorigo's cross from the left. It was a marvellous effort by England, who were now without Wright, who had gone off with a leg injury.

England's joy at pulling themselves back into the game was short-lived, however. Four minutes later, and with the prospect of extra-time looming once more — Paul Parker was adjudged to have brought down Schillaci in the penalty area. The new Italian scoring sensation picked himself up and took the spot kick, driving the ball past Shilton. It was Schillaci's sixth goal of the tournament and made him its leading scorer.

If England felt hard done to by that penalty decision, they could count themselves very fortunate when a Berti goal in injury time was ruled out for offside. The Italian was well onside when the ball was crossed to him and the decision by the linesman was hard to fathom.

At the end of the game, both team received their medals and then set up their own little 'Mexican wave' before taking off on a joint lap of honour. It was good to see the players mingling and perhaps served to remind people of the true values of the World Cup. England, especially, had played their part in this. They were rewarded with FIFA's Fair Play Award. And 24 hours later they were receiving a heroes' welcome on their home soil.

Italy: Zenga; Baresi, Bergomi, De Agostini(Berti), Ferrara, Maldini, Vierchowod, Ancelotti, Giannini(Ferri), Baggio, Schillaci.
Scorers: Baggio, Schillaci (pen)
England: Shilton; Stevens, Walker, Parker, Wright(Waddle), Dorigo, McMahon(Webb), Platt, Steven, Beardsley, Lineker.
Scorer: Platt
Referee: Joël Quiniou (France)

Final

WEST GERMANY 1   ARGENTINA 0 (Half-time 0-0)

Stadio Olimpico, Rome, 8 July
Attendance: 73,603

WHAT a sad ending this was to the 14th World Cup tournament. West Germany, for much of the time the outstanding team of the competition, failed to produce the form which had won them many admirers. Argentina, who boasted few admirers even before the game, had even less at the end of the 90 minutes and what should have been a celebration of the world's best in soccer turned out to be a dreadful advertisement for the game.

Argentina took full advantage of the rules of a tournament which made it possible for a team to lift the World Cup without winning a game in normal time, or even in extra-time. They made it clear from the kick-off that they were going to make no real effort to score. If they managed a goal, it would be from a breakaway or through a defensive lapse on the part of the Germans. It was appalling to watch.

West Germany, meanwhile, could not turn their chances into goals and on a good day, Völler might have scored a hat-trick. The Germans looked most dangerous from Brehme's magnificently placed free-kicks which he got around the defensive wall, but each time his forwards let him down.

As the half-time whistle blew, it seemed certain that the 73,000 fans, who had paid a world record £4 million in gate receipts, were going to witness the lowest-scoring World Cup Final of all time, for never before had a Final yielded less than three goals.

West Germany attacked from the start of a second half which would be played almost entirely in Argentina's half of the field. The Germans went close three times in the first five minutes, but then the game degenerated into its familiar first-half pattern with the Argentinians, although well organized in defence, contributing nothing.

Both sides had engaged in their fair share of play-acting and the unwanted distinction of being the first man to be sent off in a World Cup Final was not far away. After Klinsmann made a meal of a tackle by substitute Monzon in the 68th minute, the Argentinian was dismissed.

From that moment the Mexican referee, who had been having a good game, let the match slip from his grasp and in the 75th minute Argentina could count themselves unfortunate not to have been awarded a penalty when Calderón was tripped in the box.

Ten minutes later the referee did point to the spot when Völler was brought down by Sensini. It looked no greater an offence than the one for which Argentina had been denied a penalty, but after a long delay for the inevitable Argentinian protests, Brehme stepped up to slide home the spot-kick.

Two minutes later, Argentina's Dezotti also received his marching orders after aggressively trying to retrieve the ball from Köhler, who appeared to be time-wasting. The German went unpunished and as Dezotti left the field there was uproar. The referee was shoved by several Argentinian players, any one of whom might have joined his two colleagues in an early bath.

This was the first World Cup Final to be resolved by a single goal and it was also the worst Final in memory. The game did little for football but there was one consolation.

Argentina) *Referee: Kurt Roethlisberger (Switzerland)*. Lubomir Moravčik (Czechoslovakia v West Germany) *Referee: Helmut Kohl (Austria)*. Ricardo Giusti (Argentina v Italy) *Michel Vautrot (France)*. Pedro Damian Monzon (Argentina v West Germany) *Referee: Edgardo Codesal Mendez (Mexico)*. Gustavo Abel Dezotti (Argentina v West Germany) *Referee: Edgardo Codesal Mendez (Mexico)*.

Most players used
20 — Argentina

No of players used by Finalists
17 — West Germany
20 — Argentina

West German skipper Lothar Matthäus.

Had Argentina lifted the World Cup — with two wins and five goals from their seven matches — it would have been a catastrophe for the game. At least their awful approach to Italia '90 had gone unrewarded.

West Germany: Bodo Illgner; Andreas Brehme, Jürgen Kohler, Klaus Augenthaler, Guido Buchwald, Thomas Berthold(Stefan Reuter), Lothar Matthäus, Thomas Hässler, Pierre Littbarski, Rudi Völler, Jürgen Klinsmann.
Scorer: Brehme (pen)
Argentina: Sergio Javier Goycochea; Nestor Gabriel Lorenzo, Roberto Nestor Sensini, José Tiburcio Serrizuela, Oscar Ruggeri(Pedro Damian Monzon), Juan Ernesto Simón, José Horacio Basualdo, Jorge Burruchaga(Gabriel Humberto Calderón), Diego Armando Maradona, Pedro Antonio Troglio, Gustavo Abel Dezotti.
Referee: Edgardo Codesal Mendez (Mexico)

Andreas Brehme, stepped up to score from the penalty-spot to give West Germany the 1990 World Cup.

Top: Andreas Brehme scores the only goal of the 1990 World Cup Final with an 85th-minute penalty.

Below, left: West German celebrations: Lothar Matthäus and Rudi Völler acknowledge German fans in the 73,000 crowd. *Below, right:* Goalkeeper Bodo Illgner jumps for joy.

The victorious West German squad with their medals and the FIFA World Cup trophy.

A Look to the Future
USA 1994

*I*N 1994, the World Cup finals are scheduled to cross the Atlantic once again but, for the first time, the tournament will be staged in the United States of America. While geographically not a million miles from Uruguay's inaugural tournament of 1930, in every other respect, the event will be far removed from its humble South American origins *(writes Mark Shanahan).*

The greatest difference from all preceding tournaments is that the matches will be played in a country which, up until now, has been indifferent to the fortunes of world soccer. The 'World Game' has so far failed to penetrate the traditional sporting loves of the average American and, throughout its history, 'soccer' has been an extremely poor relation, dragging well behind gridiron football, baseball and ice hockey. For years the USA's isolation in terms of the distances to be travelled to compete in world sporting events meant that such hybrid games developed and, even though most immigrants would have come from soccer-playing countries, the United States has no tradition of 'street soccer', to coin a phrase used by Jim Lennox, one of the country's leading American-born soccer coaches.

True, USA qualification for the 1990 finals lifted the profile of the game in the eyes of the media, but the World Cup '94 authorities still face an uphill battle to put soccer at the forefront of the nation's thoughts by the time the World Cup circus rolls into town. The USA's showing in the 1990 finals did little to make that battle any easier, even after a creditable showing against Italy. Television, for instance, remains sceptical of the game's drawing power in North America and the ABC network chose not to bid for coverage rights.

As one American reporter said after his team had lost 5-1 to Czechoslovakia in their opening game: 'Now nobody back home will give a damn about soccer. What interest there was, other than at grass-roots level, will evaporate just as quickly as it flourished.'

FIFA has never before charged its most prestigious tournament to the care of a country where the game is regarded as a minority sport, fit only for schoolchildren and a rather chic game for college students. Thus, even if the game is flourishing at grass-roots level in some areas, it came as a surprise to many football watchers when the International Federation awarded the finals to America. Indeed, many people felt downright indignant that the showpiece should be given to probably the one nation on earth which does not regard soccer as a major sport.

However, in terms of facilities, TV and marketing opportunities and the immense off-field effort needed to accommodate players and supporters in comfort for more than a month, FIFA placed the United States ahead of Morocco, the only serious rival. The decision was announced in July 1988, appropriately enough, on US Independence Day. The Americans came top of the pile with ten votes to Morocco's seven and Brazil's two.

The one outstanding worry, though, is how the American public will react to soccer taking over their summer sporting schedules. Whilst outright hostility is not expected, utter indifference could be a major factor, and four years is not a long time to educate people into the delights of soccer as a spectator sport.

Planning for 1994

FOR 30 days in June and July 1994, 24 teams including the United States and West Germany, the current holders of the World Cup, will play out 52 matches in 12 cities to determine the champions of the 15th tournament.

City Bids

THE cities to host the 1994 World Cup matches were not due to be selected until mid-1991, although the World Cup '94 Organizing Committee, whose bid to stage the tournament was successful, was well on the way to selecting the successful candidates even before the 1990 competition got underway.

Sites were being selected from bids made by interested civic groups in each potential location and the final decisions were to be made after detailed checks by the committee, coupled with inspection visits to each site by FIFA's representatives.

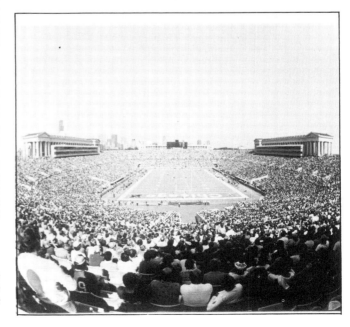

Soldier Field, Chicago, is the subject of another bid to stage World Cup soccer in 1994. *Above:* The stadium staged soccer as long ago as 1926 when the Czech side Sparta played there. *Below:* Soldier Field today, home of the Chicago Bears of the NFL.

Strict criteria were laid down for each bid to fulfil and these took into account far more than simply playing the game on grass.

The interested civic groups came from a range of backgrounds and included the Miami Tourist and Visitor Commission and the Los Angeles Sports Council. One stipulation from the authorities was that all significant soccer authorities in each city must form part of the bidding group.

Late in 1989, contracts were distributed to each of the interested groups, together with a package detailing the requirements each must meet for their bids to be considered.

As well as stadium and on-field requirements which demanded stadiums to cater for at least 30,000 seated spectators, cleanliness, spectator amenities, natural grass and a realistic construction or renovation timetable, each group had to supply details for their wider plans. The analysis required included a detailed business plan for local transportation, accommodation for World Cup staff, teams and supporters, office space before and during the event, local volunteer staff, promotional assistance and other logistical support.

Bidders also provided details of local and state government and civic support, evidence of the level of soccer participation in the area, population in the catchment area, geographical and community details as well as full climatic details. Las Vegas, for instance, bid for a slice of the action but the extremely hot, dry climate was seen as a major factor against the gambling city in the middle of the Nevada desert. Only by providing satisfactory responses to all those potential obstacles to success could any bid hope to succeed.

By May 1990, the venues being considered were:

Stadium	Venue	Capacity
Arrowhead	Kansas City, Missouri	78,067
Bobby Dodd	Atlanta, Georgia	45,000
Candlestick Park	San Francisco, California	61,000
Charlotte*	Charlotte, North Carolina	72,000
Citrus Bowl	Orlando, Florida	50,000
Cotton Bowl	Dallas, Texas	72,000
Cougar	Salt Lake City/Provo, Utah	65,000
Foxboro	Foxboro/Boston, Massachusetts	61,000
Franklin Field	Philadelphia, Pennsylvania	60,546
Husky	Seattle, Washington	72,000
Joe Robbie	Fort Lauderdale, Florida	73,000
Memorial	Baltimore, Maryland	60,000
Memorial Coliseum	Los Angeles, California	92,000
Michigan	Ann Arbor, Michigan	101,701
Minnesota Sports Complex*	Blaine, Minnesota	45,000
Navy-Marine Corps	Annapolis, Maryland	33,000
Neyland	Knoxville, Tennessee	91,910
Ohio	Columbus, Ohio	86,071
Orange Bowl	Miami, Florida	75,500
Palmer	Princeton, New Jersey	45,000
Parker	Corvallis, Oregon	40,593
RFK	Washington, DC	57,000
Rose Bowl	Pasadena, California	104,091
Sam Boyd Silver Bowl	Las Vegas, Nevada	32,000
Soldier Field	Chicago, Illinois	66,814
Stanford	Palo Alto, California	86,019
Sun Devil	Phoenix, Arizona	74,865
Tampa	Tampa, Florida	74,317
University at Buffalo*	Buffalo, New York	35,000
Wallace Wade	Raleigh-Durham, North Carolina	33,941
Yale Bowl	New Haven, Connecticut	70,896

*Planned or under construction

A number of completely new venues are planned throughout the USA, although in some cases these developments are not yet sufficiently advanced to feature in the strongest bids. What was noticeable was that cities such as New York and San Diego are not in the running, despite having cosmopolitan populations likely to support a major soccer event. The reason for this is that the organizers had stipulated that bids will not be accepted based on stadiums where other major sports will be competing in the summer of 1994.

This rule has meant that there are no major stadiums in either New York or San Diego which could support a city bid at the moment. Miami may also come under threat as the city is negotiating to launch a new baseball franchise, should the major leagues follow up their wish to expand in the next few years.

In February 1991, each of the bidding groups were due to make an oral presentation to the Organizing Committee. The Committee would make a confidential decision following this, and FIFA was due to make its final decision after visiting all the potential sites. This would leave at least two and a half years for each of the chosen cities to raise the profile of soccer both in their local communities and to the wider audience.

Winning the Media Battle

TV and, to a lesser extent, the Press, is all important to the success of any major event in America. They can make or break the fortunes of politicians and multi-million dollar businesses, so the success of hosting a major money-spinner like the World Cup finals tournament is bound to hinge largely on the mood of the media.

At present soccer features only on cable TV networks — and that applied even to the 1990 World Cup Final. Whilst these reach many homes in the States, the sport is still aimed at ethnic minorities such as the Hispanics, who have traditionally supported soccer, and the enthusiasts who have embraced the game since the rise of the North American Soccer League in the 1970s. However, the major networks chose not to cover the 1990 finals, despite the USA being represented for the first time since 1950.

The reasons for this stem from the American media's need to present the USA as the world's number one. This came across very strongly in TV's portrayal of the Los Angeles Olympics of 1984. For any non-Americans viewing, the games appeared to show a USA versus the Rest of the World match and sports where America was not strong were given short shrift indeed.

In America's home sporting mythology there is little place for foreign competition either. What other nation, for instance, would host a 'World Series' and not invite the rest of the world?

In 1990, the USA soccer team had no hope of lifting the World Cup and thus the fiercely patriotic media were largely not interested in their efforts. It is going to take some impressive powers of persuasion off the pitch and some equally impressive performances on it before 1994 if the TV networks are going to take a lead in introducing soccer to the non-playing masses of home-town USA.

It is fair to say that the game is once again on the rise in America. In 1989 more than 15 million Americans were actively involved in soccer with over nine million players under the age of 19. The growth is at grass-roots level and bodes well for the future. Taking kids to the ball game is a national pastime, and with more and more boys and girls playing soccer, the 'ball game' could soon become association football for an increasing number of parents.

Building National Heroes

AT national level, the USA is far from being a world power and will have to improve significantly to get beyond the first stages of the finals when 1994 comes around. However, where youth and inexperience were apparent in the USA's preparation for, and participation in, the 1990 finals, the same group of players will still be available for selection in 1994 and should have gained considerable experience by then.

For the Italian finals, the squad were strong in organization and team spirit but there was only a smattering of the necessary guile and experience gleaned from playing regularly at the top level. However, the matches against Czechoslovakia, Italy and Austria provided a shop window for the young Eagles to show their talent, and several such as Ramos, Meola and Harkes could well land contracts in Europe which will do them no harm in improving their games before they entertain the rest of the world as hosts.

Unlike almost every other nation where players are called up from professional clubs to play for their country, the Americans do not have a strong professional league and so contract their star players as a full-time national team. They prepare for major tournaments with a series of squad sessions and friendly internationals. As yet this has not taken off with the fans and a recent international against Finland, played at Tampa, drew a crowd of only 5,000. Tampa is a traditional soccer area where the Rowdies regularly drew crowds of over 30,000 to their NASL games back in the 1970s. The cynics would say that, as with the rest of the NASL, the faithful attended only to see the foreign stars, not the Americans in to make up the numbers.

It is against this background that the United States Soccer Federation (USSF) have to break down the barriers of apathy and interest ordinary Americans in a game that does not stop when the ads come on TV.

The USSF plan to introduce a nation-wide professional soccer league before the finals reach America's shores. At the moment, while High School and College soccer programmes are strong, there's very little soccer for young American stars to progress to when they leave University. The American Soccer League and Western Soccer League have risen out of the ashes of the NASL and are run along semi-professional lines, with member clubs participating often on a shoe-string budget. The two leagues have formally agreed to join together and it is hoped that major sponsorship and media support will enable them to grow to provide a coast-to-coast fully professional league.

Much has been learned since the collapse of the NASL in 1984 and the new league will be a platform for the top American players, rather than a final staging post for Europe and South America's ageing soccer statesmen.

If the league becomes a reality, it will undoubtedly strengthen the playing base for the USA. If this can be allied to a growth in the export of Stateside players to Europe, the traditional American virtues of fitness and strength, together with enviable expertise in planning could lead to the hosts springing a few surprises on the pitch in '94.

A coast-to-coast league of professionals should be more to the taste of the TV networks too, and if games are shown regularly on network television, it will help make the game as much a part of the normal sporting life as it is throughout the rest of the world. The fact that the game cannot be built around the demands of commercial breaks remains a problem still to be addressed both by the networks and the soccer authorities.

Off the pitch, much depends on the USSF's success in selling the game to the American public through a sympathetic media. It can be done, as two recent soccer events show. In 1984, the Olympic soccer tournament drew nine crowds of over 60,000 to matches and twice the crowd exceeded 100,000. More recently the USA played the USSR in front of more than 61,000 at Stanford Stadium in California.

If promotional flair is all-powerful, then there is no doubt that USA '94 will be a resounding success, for the Americans couple entrepreneurial skills with showmanship like no other nation. However, by the end of Italia '90 there were renewed mutterings that the USA did not deserve the World Cup. And even though they are backed by no less a figure than Henry Kissinger, a member of the organizing committee, there were thoughts that the American Dream might not come to pass after all.

Venue for the 1994 World Cup Final? The Joe Robbie Stadium in Florida, home of the NFL's Miami Dolphins, was built by a soccer-loving millionaire.

Uruguay, the 1930 winners. Back row (left to right): Figoli (masseur), Alvaro Gestido, José Nasazzi, Enrique Ballesteros, Ernesto Mascheroni, José Leandro Andrade, Lorenzo Fernández, Greco (masseur). Front row: Pablo Dorado, Héctor Scarone, Héctor Castro, Pedro Cea, Santos Iriarte.

Italy, the 1934 World Cup winners. Back row (left to right): Giampiero Combi, Luís Monti, Attilo Ferraris IV, Luigi Allemandi, Enrique Guaita, Giovanni Ferrari. Front row: Angelo Schiavio, Giuseppe Meazza, Eraldo Monzeglio, Luigi Bertolini, Raimundo Orsi.

The victorious Italian team of 1938. Back row (left to right, players only): Amedeo Biavati, Silvio Piola, Giovanni Ferrari, Gino Colaussi. Front row: Ugo Locatelli, Giuseppe Meazza, Alfredo Foni, Aldo Olivieri, Pietro Rava, Pietro Serantoni. Michele Andreolo is lying in front of Foni. Coach Vittorio Pozzo is holding the trophy.

Uruguay, winners in 1950. Back row (left to right, players only): Obdulio Jacinto Varela, Eusébio Tejera, Schubert Gambetta, Matías Gonzáles, Roque Gaston Máspoli, Victor Rodríguez Andrade. Front row: Alcides Edgardo Ghiggia, Julio Pérez, Omar Oscar Míguez, Juan Alberto Schiaffino, Rubén Morán.

West Germany, the 1954 World Cup winners. From left to right: Fritz Walter, Anton Turek, Horst Eckel, Helmut Rahn, Ottmar Walter, Werner Liebrich, Josef Posipal, Hans Schäfer, Werner Kohlmeyer, Karl Mai, Max Morlock.

Brazil, winners in 1958, wearing the unfamiliar blue strip in which they contested the Final. Back row (left to right): V.Feola (chief coach), D.Santos, Zito, Bellini, N.Santos, Orlando, Gilmar. Front row: Garrincha, Didí, Pelé, Vavá, Zagalo, Americo (trainer).

Brazil again, this time the 1962 World Cup-winning team. Back row (left to right): Djalmar Santos, Zito, Gilmar, Nilton Santos, Zózimo, Mauro. Front row: Americo (trainer), Garrincha, Didí, Vavá, Amarildo, Zagalo.

Victorious England in 1966. Skipper Bobby Moore holds aloft the trophy. Other players are (left to right) Jack Charlton, Nobby Stiles, Gordon Banks (hidden behind Alan Ball's arm), Alan Ball, Martin Peters, Geoff Hurst, Ray Wilson, George Cohen, Bobby Charlton.

Brazil, winners for the third time in 1970. Pictured is one their teams in the finals, back row (left to right): Carlos Alberto, Brito, Piazza, Felix, Clodoaldo, Everaldo, trainer. Front row: Jairzinho, Rivelino, Tostão, Pelé, Paulo Cesar.

West Germany's team which won the World Cup in 1974, their second success. Back row (left to right, players only): Maier, Müller, Grabowski, Breitner, Schwarzenbeck. Front row: Hoeness, Bonhof, Beckenbauer, Hölzenbein, Vogts, Overath.

Argentina, winners in 1978. Back row (left to right): Daniel Passarella, Daniel Bertoni, Jorge Olguín, Alberto Tarantini, Mario Kempes, Ubaldo Fillol. Front row: Américo Gallego, Osvaldo Ardíles, Leopoldo Luque, Oscar Ortíz, Luís Galván.

Italy, the 1982 winners. From left to right: Dino Zoff, Francesco Graziani, Bruno Conti, Fulvio Collovati, Gaetano Scirea, Claudio Gentile, Giuseppe Bergomi, Paolo Rossi, Gabriele Oriali, Antonio Cabrini, Marco Tardelli.

Argentina's 1986 winning team. Back row (left to right): Sergio Batista, José Cuciuffo, Julio Olarticoechea, Nery Pumpido, José Brown, Oscar Ruggeri, Diego Maradona. Front row: Jorge Burruchaga, Ricardo Giusti, Héctor Enrique, Jorge Valdano.

West Germany with the FIFA World Cup after beating Argentina in the 1990 Final. It was the Germans' sixth Final – a record – and their third in a row. It was also their third victory and Franz Beckenbauer became the first man to captain and then manage a winning side.

Garrincha – 'The Little Bird' – an immensely talented Brazilian star.

And perhaps the greatest of them all, Pelé. His name is synonymous with the famous Brazil triumphs of the past.

Bobby Moore, the West Ham United star who skippered England to their World Cup victory in 1966.

Franz Beckenbauer – 'The Kaiser' – who captained West Germany to World Cup success and then managed the side which won the trophy in 1990.

Portugal's Eusébio, one of the stars of the 1966 tournament in England.

Gerd Müller – 'Der Bomber' – West Germany's great goalscorer.

Roberto Rivelino of Brazil, his country's leading scorer in the 1974 World Cup.

Johann Cruyff of Holland, who took over from Pelé as the World Cup's leading star when he guided the Dutch to their first Final in 1974.

Italy's Paolo Rossi, another fine striker who wrote his name into World Cup history, scoring six goals in seven games in 1982 when the Italians won the trophy. Yet two years earlier, his career appeared to be in ruins after an alleged 'fixing' scandal rocked Italian soccer.

Mario Kempes of Argentina, star of the South Americans' success in 1978. Kempes was the tournament's leading scorer with six goals.

Socrates of Brazil, a doctor of medicine with an interest in politics as well as being one of the world's most creative midfielders. He score their first goal of the 1986 tournament.

Peter Shilton of England, the world record-holder for full international appearances. In the 1990 tournament, Shilton carried his total to 125 caps.

Karl-Heinz Rummenigge of West Germany, who scored five goals in the 1982 Finals and skippered his country to the Final. In the 1986 Final he made his 19th World Cup appearance.

Zico of Brazil, scored four goals in five games in the 1982 Finals, when Brazil returned to the attacking style which suited his wonderful skills.

Gary Lineker, England's leading scorer in World Cup matches. He first made his mark in the 1986 finals and was prominent again as England reached the semi-final in 1990.

Diego Maradona of Argentina. The winning skipper in 1986, he led his side to the 1990 Final but failed to become the first captain to lift the World Cup twice.

The Estadio Nacional in Santiago, pictured before the start of the 1962 World Cup Final.

Bobby Moore (6) and Gordon Banks parade the World Cup at Wembley in 1966. The other England players are Roger Hunt and Martin Peters.

Carlos Alberto's 76th-minute goal which gave Brazil a 4-1 lead in the 1970 World Cup Final.

Gerd Müller scores West Germany's winner against Holland in the 1974 Final.

Argentina's skipper, Daniel Passarella, with the World Cup in 1978, when the hosts won the trophy in Buenos Aires.

Italy's first goal of the 1982 Final, scored by Paolo Rossi.

Victorious skippers with the World Cup: *Left:* **Dino Zoff of Italy in 1982.** *Right:* **Diego Maradona in 1986.**

José Luis Brown scores for Argentina in the 1986 Final.

England and West Germany line-up before their exciting semi-final draw in the Stadio Delle Alpi, Turin. The game was eventually decided on penalties.

The goal that won the 1990 World Cup. Andreas Brehme scores from the penalty-spot with five minutes to go.

World Cup Records

*After extra-time.   †After replay.

ALGERIA

Finals Appearances: 2 (1982-86)
Biggest Win: 3-2 v Chile (1982)
Biggest Defeat: 0-3 v Spain (1986)
Record: P W D L F A
          6 2 1 3 6 10
Leading Scorer: 2 Salah Assad

1982	West Germany	won 2-1
	Austria	lost 0-2
	Chile	won 3-2
1986	Northern Ireland	drew 1-1
	Brazil	lost 0-1
	Spain	lost 0-3

In 1978, Argentina were the host nation and lifted the World Cup. Here, skipper Daniel Passarella proudly holds aloft the trophy. In 1986, when the competition was held in Mexico, Argentina won the World Cup for a second time.

ARGENTINA

Finals Appearances: 10 (1930-34, 1958-66, 1974-90)
Biggest Win: 6-0 v Peru (1978)
Biggest Defeat: 1-6 v Czechoslovakia (1958)
Record: P W D L F A
         48 24 9 15 82 59
Leading Scorer: 8 Guillermo Stàbile

1930	France	won 1-0
	Mexico	won 6-3
	Chile	won 3-1
	United States	won 6-1
	Uruguay	lost 2-4
1934	Sweden	lost 2-3
1958	West Germany	lost 1-3
	Northern Ireland	won 3-1
	Czechoslovakia	lost 1-6
1962	Bulgaria	won 1-0
	England	lost 1-3
	Hungary	drew 0-0
1966	Spain	won 2-1
	West Germany	drew 0-0
	Switzerland	won 2-0
	England	lost 0-1
1974	Poland	lost 2-3
	Italy	drew 1-1
	Haiti	won 4-1
	Holland	lost 0-4
	Brazil	lost 1-2
	East Germany	drew 1-1
1978	Hungary	won 2-1
	France	won 2-1
	Italy	lost 0-1
	Poland	won 2-0
	Brazil	drew 0-0
	Peru	won 6-0
	Holland	won *3-1
1982	Belgium	lost 0-1
	Hungary	won 4-1
	El Salvador	won 2-0
	Italy	lost 1-2
	Brazil	lost 1-3
1986	South Korea	won 3-1
	Italy	drew 1-1
	Bulgaria	won 2-0
	Uruguay	won 1-0
	England	won 2-1
	Belgium	won 2-0
	West Germany	won 3-2
1990	Cameroon	lost 0-1
	Soviet Union	won 2-0
	Romania	drew 1-1
	Brazil	won 1-0
	Yugoslavia	drew *0-0
		(won 3-2 on pens)
	Italy	drew *0-0
		(won 4-3 on pens)
	West Germany	lost 0-1

AUSTRALIA

Finals Appearances: 1 (1974)
Biggest Win: not won
Biggest Defeat: 0-3 v West Germany (1974)
Record: P W D L F A
         3 0 1 2 0 5
Leading Scorer: not scored

1974	East Germany	lost 0-2
	West Germany	lost 0-3
	Chile	drew 0-0

AUSTRIA

Finals Appearances: 6 (1934, 1954-58, 1978-82, 1990)
Biggest Win: 7-5 v Switzerland (1954)
Biggest Defeat: 1-6 v West Germany (1954)
Record: P W D L F A
         26 12 2 12 40 43
Leading Scorers: 5 Erich Probst, Hans Krankl

1934	France	won 3-2
	Hungary	won 2-1
	Italy	lost 0-1
	Germany	lost 2-3
1954	Scotland	won 1-0
	Czechoslovakia	won 5-0
	Switzerland	won 7-5
	West Germany	lost 1-6
	Uruguay	won 3-1
1958	Brazil	lost 0-3
	Soviet Union	lost 0-2
	England	drew 2-2
1978	Spain	won 2-1
	Sweden	won 1-0
	Brazil	lost 0-1
	Holland	lost 1-5
	Italy	lost 0-1
	West Germany	won 3-2
1982	Chile	won 1-0
	Algeria	won 2-0
	West Germany	lost 0-1
	France	lost 0-1
	Northern Ireland	drew 2-2
1990	Italy	lost 0-1
	Czechoslovakia	lost 0-1
	United States	won 2-1

BELGIUM

Finals Appearances: 8 (1930-38, 1954, 1970, 1982-90)
Biggest Win: 4-3 v Soviet Union (1986)
Biggest Defeat: 2-5 v Germany (1934)
Record: P W D L F A
         25 7 4 14 33 49
Leading Scorer: 4 Jan Ceulemans

1930	United States	lost 0-3
	Paraguay	lost 0-1
1934	Germany	lost 2-5
1938	France	lost 1-3
1954	England	drew 4-4
	Italy	lost 1-4
1970	El Salvador	won 3-0
	Soviet Union	lost 1-4
	Mexico	lost 0-1
1982	Argentina	won 1-0
	El Salvador	won 1-0
	Hungary	drew 1-1
	Poland	lost 0-3
	Soviet Union	lost 0-1
1986	Mexico	lost 1-2
	Iraq	won 2-1
	Paraguay	drew 2-2
	Soviet Union	won *4-3
	Spain	drew *1-1
		(won 5-4 on pens)
	Argentina	lost 0-2
	France	lost *2-4
1990	South Korea	won 2-0
	Uruguay	won 3-1
	Spain	lost 1-2
	England	lost *0-1

BOLIVIA

Finals Appearances: 2 (1930, 1950)
Biggest Win: not won
Biggest Defeat: 0-8 v Uruguay (1950)
Record: P W D L F A
         3 0 0 3 0 16
Leading Scorer: not scored

1930	Yugoslavia	lost 0-4
	Brazil	lost 0-4
1950	Uruguay	lost 0-8

BRAZIL

Finals Appearances: 14 (1930-90)
Biggest Win: 7-1 v Sweden (1950)
Biggest Defeat: 2-4 v Hungary (1954)
Record: P   W   D   L   F   A
            66   44   11   11   148 65
Leading Scorer: 12 Pelé

1930	Yugoslavia	lost 1-2
	Bolivia	won 4-0
1934	Spain	lost 1-3
1938	Poland	won *6-5
	Czechoslovakia	drew *1-1
	Czechoslovakia	won †2-1
	Italy	lost 1-2
	Sweden	won 4-2
1950	Mexico	won 4-0
	Switzerland	drew 2-2
	Yugoslavia	won 2-0
	Sweden	won 7-1
	Spain	won 6-1
	Uruguay	lost 1-2
1954	Mexico	won 5-0
	Yugoslavia	drew 1-1
	Hungary	lost 2-4
1958	Austria	won 3-0
	England	drew 0-0
	Soviet Union	won 2-0
	Wales	won 1-0
	France	won 5-2
	Sweden	won 5-2
1962	Mexico	won 2-0
	Czechoslovakia	drew 0-0
	Spain	won 2-1
	England	won 3-1
	Chile	won 4-2
	Czechoslovakia	won 3-1
1966	Bulgaria	won 2-0
	Hungary	lost 1-3
	Portugal	lost 1-3
1970	Czechoslovakia	won 4-1
	England	won 1-0
	Romania	won 3-2
	Peru	won 4-2
	Uruguay	won 3-1
	Italy	won 4-1
1974	Yugoslavia	drew 0-0
	Scotland	drew 0-0
	Zaïre	won 3-0
	East Germany	won 1-0
	Argentina	won 2-1
	Holland	lost 0-2
	Poland	lost 0-1
1978	Sweden	drew 1-1
	Spain	drew 0-0
	Austria	won 1-0
	Peru	won 3-0
	Argentina	drew 0-0
	Poland	won 3-1
	Italy	won 2-1
1982	Soviet Union	won 2-1
	Scotland	won 4-1
	New Zealand	won 4-0
	Argentina	won 3-1
	Italy	lost 2-3
1986	Spain	won 1-0
	Algeria	won 1-0
	Northern Ireland	won 3-0
	Poland	won 4-0
	France	drew *1-1
	(lost 4-3 on pens)	
1990	Sweden	won 2-1
	Costa Rica	won 1-0
	Scotland	won 1-0
	Argentina	lost 0-1

BULGARIA

Finals Appearances: 5 (1962-74, 1986)
Biggest Win: not won

Biggest Defeat: 1-6 v Hungary (1962)
Record: P   W   D   L   F   A
            16   0   6   10   11   35
Leading Scorer: 2 Christo Bonev

1962	Argentina	lost 0-1
	Hungary	lost 1-6
	England	drew 0-0
1966	Brazil	lost 0-2
	Portugal	lost 0-3
	Hungary	lost 1-3
1970	Peru	lost 2-3
	West Germany	lost 2-5
	Morocco	drew 1-1
1974	Sweden	drew 0-0
	Uruguay	drew 1-1
	Holland	lost 1-4
1986	Italy	drew 1-1
	South Korea	drew 1-1
	Argentina	lost 0-2
	Mexico	lost 0-2

CAMEROON

Finals Appearances: 2 (1938, 1990)
Biggest Win: 2-1 v Romania (1990), 2-1 v Colombia (1990)
Biggest Defeat: 0-4 v Soviet Union (1990)
Record: P   W   D   L   F   A
            8   3   3   2   8   10
Leading Scorer: 4 Roger Milla

1982	Peru	drew 0-0
	Poland	drew 0-0
	Italy	drew 1-1
1990	Argentina	won 1-0
	Romania	won 2-1
	Soviet Union	lost 0-4
	Colombia	won *2-1
	England	lost *2-3

CANADA

Finals Appearances: 1 (1986)
Biggest Win: not won
Biggest Defeat: 0-2 v Hungary (1986), 0-2 v Soviet Union (1986)
Record: P   W   D   L   F   A
            3   0   0   3   0   5
Leading Scorer: not scored

1986	France	lost 0-1
	Hungary	lost 0-2
	Soviet Union	lost 0-2

CHILE

Finals Appearances: 6 (1930, 1950, 1962-66, 1974, 1982)
Biggest Win: 5-2 v United States (1950)
Biggest Defeat: 1-4 v West Germany (1982)
Record: P   W   D   L   F   A
            21   7   3   11   26   32
Leading Scorers: 4 Guillermo Subiabre, Leonel Sánchez

1930	Mexico	won 3-0
	France	won 1-0
	Argentina	lost 1-3
1950	England	lost 0-2
	Spain	lost 0-2
	United States	won 5-2
1962	Switzerland	won 3-1
	Italy	won 2-0
	West Germany	lost 0-2
	Soviet Union	won 2-1
	Brazil	lost 2-4
	Yugoslavia	won 1-0
1966	Italy	lost 0-2
	North Korea	drew 1-1
	Soviet Union	lost 1-2
1974	West Germany	lost 0-1
	East Germany	drew 1-1
	Australia	drew 0-0
1982	Austria	lost 0-1
	West Germany	lost 1-4
	Algeria	lost 2-3

COLOMBIA

Finals Appearances: 2 (1962, 1990)
Biggest Win: 2-0 v United Arab Emirates (1990)
Biggest Defeat: 0-5 v Yugoslavia (1962)
Record: P   W   D   L   F   A
            7   1   2   4   9   15
Leading Scorer: 2 Bernardo Redin Valverde

1962	Uruguay	lost 1-2
	Soviet Union	drew 4-4
	Yugoslavia	lost 0-5
1990	United Arab Emirates	won 2-0
	Yugoslavia	lost 0-1
	West Germany	drew 1-1
	Cameroon	lost *1-2

When Chile hosted the finals in 1962, they reached the semi-final before losing to Brazil, who are seen here scoring one of their four goals. The Brazilians went on to retain the World Cup, beating Czechoslovakia 3-1 in the Final.

COSTA RICA

Finals Appearances: 1 (1990)
Biggest Win: 2-1 v Sweden (1990)
Biggest Defeat: 1-4 v Czechoslovakia (1990)
Record:

P	W	D	L	F	A
4	2	0	2	4	6

Leading Scorers: 1 Roger Flores, Ronald Gonzales, Juan Arnoldo Cayasso, Hernan Medford.

1990	Scotland	won 1-0
	Brazil	lost 0-1
	Sweden	won 2-1
	Czechoslovakia	lost 1-4

CUBA

Finals Appearances: 1 (1938)
Biggest Win: 2-1 v Romania (1938)
Biggest Defeat: 0-8 v Sweden (1938)
Record:

P	W	D	L	F	A
3	1	1	1	5	12

Leading Scorer: 2 Carlos Olivera Maquina

1938	Romania	drew *3-3
	Romania	won 2-1
	Sweden	lost 0-8

CZECHOSLOVAKIA

Finals Appearances: 8 (1934-38, 1954-62, 1970, 1982, 1990)
Biggest Win: 6-1 v Argentina (1958)
Biggest Defeat: 0-5 v Austria (1954)
Record:

P	W	D	L	F	A
30	11	5	14	44	45

Leading Scorer: 7 Oldrich Nejedly

1934	Romania	won 2-1
	Switzerland	won 3-2
	Germany	won 3-1
	Italy	lost *1-2
1938	Holland	won *3-0
	Brazil	drew *1-1
	Brazil	lost †1-2
1954	Uruguay	lost 0-2
	Austria	lost 0-5
1958	Northern Ireland	lost 0-1
	West Germany	drew 2-2
	Argentina	won 6-1
	Northern Ireland	lost *1-2
1962	Spain	won 1-0
	Brazil	drew 0-0
	Mexico	lost 1-3
	Hungary	won 1-0
	Yugoslavia	won 3-1
	Brazil	lost 1-3
1970	Brazil	lost 1-4
	Romania	lost 1-2
	England	lost 0-1
1982	Kuwait	drew 1-1
	England	lost 0-2
	France	drew 1-1
1990	United States	won 5-1
	Austria	won 1-0
	Italy	lost 0-2
	Costa Rica	won 4-1
	West Germany	lost 0-1

DENMARK

Finals Appearances: 1 (1986)
Biggest Win: 6-1 v Uruguay (1986)
Biggest Defeat: 1-5 v Spain (1986)
Record:

P	W	D	L	F	A
4	3	0	1	10	6

Leading Scorer: 4 Preben Elkjaer-Larsen

1986	Scotland	won 1-0
	Uruguay	won 6-1
	West Germany	won 2-0
	Spain	lost 1-5

DUTCH EAST INDIES

Finals Appearances: 1 (1938)
Biggest Win: not won
Biggest Defeat: 0-6 v Hungary (1938)
Record:

P	W	D	L	F	A
1	0	0	1	0	6

Leading Scorer: not scored

1938	Hungary	lost 0-6

EAST GERMANY

Finals Appearances: 1 (1974)
Biggest Win: 2-0 v Australia (1974)
Biggest Defeat: 0-2 v Holland (1974)
Record:

P	W	D	L	F	A
6	2	2	2	5	5

Leading Scorer: 2 Joachim Streich

1974	Australia	won 2-0
	Chile	drew 1-1
	West Germany	won 1-0
	Brazil	lost 0-1
	Holland	lost 0-2
	Argentina	drew 1-1

EGYPT

Finals Appearances: 2 (1934, 1990)
Biggest Win: not won
Biggest Defeat: 2-4 v Hungary (1934)
Record:

P	W	D	L	F	A
4	0	2	2	3	6

Leading Scorer: 2 Abdel Rahman Fawzi

1934	Hungary	lost 2-4
1990	Holland	drew 1-1
	Republic of Ireland	drew 0-0
	England	lost 0-1

EL SALVADOR

Finals Appearances: 2 (1970, 1982)
Biggest Win: not won
Biggest Defeat: 1-10 v Hungary (1982)
Record:

P	W	D	L	F	A
6	0	0	6	1	22

Leading Scorer: 1 Ramírez Zapata

1970	Belgium	lost 0-3
	Mexico	lost 0-4
	Soviet Union	lost 0-2
1982	Hungary	lost 1-10
	Belgium	lost 0-1
	Argentina	lost 0-2

ENGLAND

Finals Appearances: 9 (1950-70, 1982-90)
Biggest Win: 4-2 v West Germany (1966)
Biggest Defeat: 2-4 v Uruguay (1954)
Record:

P	W	D	L	F	A
41	18	12	11	55	38

Leading Scorer: 10 Gary Lineker

1950	Chile	won 2-0
	United States	lost 0-1
	Spain	lost 0-1
1954	Belgium	drew 4-4
	Switzerland	won 2-0
	Uruguay	lost 2-4
1958	Soviet Union	drew 2-2
	Brazil	drew 0-0
	Austria	drew 2-2
	Soviet Union	lost 0-1
1962	Hungary	lost 1-2
	Argentina	won 3-1
	Bulgaria	drew 0-0
	Brazil	lost 1-3
1966	Uruguay	drew 0-0
	Mexico	won 2-0
	France	won 2-0
	Argentina	won 1-0
	Portugal	won 2-1
	West Germany	won *4-2
1970	Romania	won 1-0
	Brazil	lost 0-1
	Czechoslovakia	won 1-0
	West Germany	lost *2-3
1982	France	won 3-1
	Czechoslovakia	won 2-0
	Kuwait	won 1-0
	West Germany	drew 0-0
	Spain	drew 0-0
1986	Portugal	lost 0-1
	Morocco	drew 0-0
	Poland	won 3-0
	Paraguay	won 3-0
	Argentina	lost 1-2
1990	Republic of Ireland	drew 1-1
	Holland	drew 0-0
	Egypt	won 1-0
	Belgium	won *1-0
	Cameroon	won *3-2
	West Germany	drew *1-1
		(lost 4-3 on pens)
	Italy	lost 1-2

England, winners in 1966, were thwarted in their attempt to retain the World Cup in Mexico four years later. They reached the quarter-final before West Germany fought back from 2-0 to win 3-2 after extra-time. *Right:* Alan Mullery (left, dark shirt) scores England's first goal watched by Francis Lee. Höttges is the fallen German defender.

Honduras relax for the camera of FIFA's official photographer, Peter Robinson, during a training session prior to their appearance in the 1982 finals. So determined were the Hondurans to do well that they spent the year before the finals together rather than play for their clubs. During that time they remained unbeaten and in Spain did well with two draws and only one defeat.

FRANCE

Finals Appearances: 9 (1930-38, 1954-58, 1966, 1978-86)
Biggest Win: 7-3 v Paraguay (1958)
Biggest Defeat: 2-5 v Brazil (1958)

Record:	P	W	D	L	F	A
	34	15	5	14	71	56

Leading Scorer: 13 Juste Fontaine

1930	Mexico	won 4-1
	Argentina	lost 0-1
	Chile	lost 0-1
1934	Austria	lost 2-3
1938	Belgium	won 3-1
	Italy	lost 1-3
1954	Yugoslavia	lost 0-1
	Mexico	won 3-2
1958	Paraguay	won 7-3
	Yugoslavia	lost 2-3
	Scotland	won 2-1
	Northern Ireland	won 4-0
	Brazil	lost 2-5
	West Germany	won 6-3
1966	Mexico	drew 1-1
	Uruguay	lost 1-2
	England	lost 0-2
1978	Italy	lost 1-2
	Argentina	lost 1-2
	Hungary	won 3-1
1982	England	lost 1-3
	Kuwait	won 4-1
	Czechoslovakia	drew 1-1
	Austria	won 1-0
	Northern Ireland	won 4-1
	West Germany	drew *3-3
		(lost 5-4 on pens)
	Poland	lost 2-3
1986	Canada	won 1-0
	Soviet Union	drew 1-1
	Hungary	won 3-0
	Italy	won 2-0
	Brazil	drew *1-1
		(won 4-3 on pens)
	West Germany	lost 0-2
	Belgium	won *4-2

HAITI

Finals Appearances: 1 (1974)
Biggest Win: not won
Biggest Defeat: 0-7 v Poland (1974)

Record:	P	W	D	L	F	A
	3	0	0	3	2	14

Leading Scorer: 2 Emmanuel Sanon

1974	Italy	lost 1-3
	Poland	lost 0-7
	Argentina	lost 1-4

HOLLAND

Finals Appearances: 5 (1934-38, 1974-78, 1990)
Biggest Win: 5-1 v Austria (1978)
Biggest Defeat: 0-3 v Czechoslovakia (1938)

Record:	P	W	D	L	F	A
	20	8	6	6	35	23

Leading Scorer: 7 Johannes Rep

1934	Switzerland	lost 2-3
1938	Czechoslovakia	lost *0-3
1974	Uruguay	won 2-0
	Sweden	drew 0-0

	Bulgaria	won 4-1
	Argentina	won 4-0
	East Germany	won 2-0
	Brazil	won 2-0
	West Germany	lost 1-2
1978	Iran	won 3-0
	Peru	drew 0-0
	Scotland	lost 2-3
	Austria	won 5-1
	West Germany	drew 2-2
	Italy	won 2-1
	Argentina	lost *1-3
1990	Egypt	drew 1-1
	England	drew 0-0
	Republic of Ireland	drew 1-1
	West Germany	lost 1-2

HONDURAS

Finals Appearances: 1 (1982)
Biggest Win: not won
Biggest Defeat: 0-1 v Yugoslavia (1982)

Record:	P	W	D	L	F	A
	3	0	2	1	2	3

Leading Scorers: 1 Tony Laing, Héctor Zelaya

1982	Spain	drew 1-1
	Northern Ireland	drew 1-1
	Yugoslavia	lost 0-1

HUNGARY

Finals Appearances: 9 (1934-38, 1954-66, 1978-86)
Biggest Win: 10-1 v El Salvador (1982)
Biggest Defeat: 0-6 v Soviet Union (1986)

Record:	P	W	D	L	F	A
	32	15	3	14	87	57

Leading Scorer: 11 Sandor Kocsis

1934	Egypt	won 4-2
	Austria	lost 1-2
1938	Dutch East Indies	won 6-0
	Switzerland	won 2-0
	Sweden	won 5-1
	Italy	lost 2-4
1954	South Korea	won 9-0
	West Germany	won 8-3
	Brazil	won 4-2
	Uruguay	won *4-2
	West Germany	lost 2-3

Ferenc Puskás (extreme right) is flattened during Hungary's 8-3 win over West Germany in 1954. The attentions of Kwiatkowski (22) and Liebrich (centre) combined to put Puskás out of the next two games. He recovered but was still not fully fit when the teams met again in the Final and West Germany gained revenge with a 3-2 victory.

1958	Wales	drew 1-1
	Sweden	lost 1-2
	Mexico	won 4-0
	Wales	lost 1-2
1962	England	won 2-1
	Bulgaria	won 6-1
	Argentina	drew 0-0
	Czechoslovakia	lost 0-1
1966	Portugal	lost 1-3
	Brazil	won 3-1
	Bulgaria	won 3-1
	Soviet Union	lost 1-2
1978	Argentina	lost 1-2
	Italy	lost 1-3
	France	lost 1-3
1982	El Salvador	won 10-1

	Argentina	lost 1-4
	Belgium	drew 1-1
1986	Soviet Union	lost 0-6
	Canada	won 2-0
	France	lost 0-3

Italy, rivalled only by West Germany as Europe's most successful World Cup nation, nevertheless suffered some disappointments along a road which has brought them three World Cup Final victories. *Below:* Jeppson of Sweden crosses after beating Parola during the Swedes' 3-2 win in the 1950 tournament, Italy's first-ever World Cup defeat. *Bottom:* Domenghini is shadowed by a Brazilian during Italy's 4-1 defeat by the eventual winners in 1970.

IRAN

Finals Appearances: 1 (1978)
Biggest Win: not won
Biggest Defeat: 1-4 v Peru (1978)

Record:	P	W	D	L	F	A
	3	0	1	2	2	8

Leading Scorers: 1 Iraj Danaifar, Hassan Rowshan

1978	Holland	lost 0-3
	Scotland	drew 1-1
	Peru	lost 1-4

IRAQ

Finals Appearances: 1 (1986)
Biggest Win: not won
Biggest Defeat: 1-2 v Belgium (1986)

Record:	P	W	D	L	F	A
	3	0	0	3	1	4

Leading Scorer: 1 Ahmed Amaiesh Rhadi

1986	Paraguay	lost 0-1
	Belgium	lost 1-2
	Mexico	lost 0-1

ISRAEL

Finals Appearances: 1 (1970)
Biggest Win: not won
Biggest Defeat: 0-2 v Uruguay (1970)

Record:	P	W	D	L	F	A
	3	0	2	1	1	3

Leading Scorer: 1 Mordechai Spiegler

1970	Uruguay	lost 0-2
	Sweden	drew 1-1
	Italy	drew 0-0

ITALY

Finals Appearances: 12 (1934-54, 1962-90)
Biggest Win: 7-1 v United States (1934)
Biggest Defeat: 1-4 v Switzerland (1954), 1-4 v Brazil (1970)

Record:	P	W	D	L	F	A
	54	31	12	11	89	54

Leading Scorer: 9 Paolo Rossi

1934	United States	won 7-1
	Spain	drew 1-1
	Spain	won †1-0
	Austria	won 1-0
	Czechoslovakia	won *2-1
1938	Norway	won *2-1
	France	won 3-1
	Brazil	won 2-1
	Hungary	won 4-2
1950	Sweden	lost 2-3
	Paraguay	won 2-0
1954	Switzerland	lost 1-2
	Belgium	won 4-1
	Switzerland	lost 1-4
1962	West Germany	drew 0-0
	Chile	lost 0-2
	Switzerland	won 3-0
1966	Chile	won 2-0
	Soviet Union	lost 0-1
	North Korea	lost 0-1
1970	Sweden	won 1-0
	Uruguay	drew 0-0
	Israel	drew 0-0
	Mexico	won 4-1
	West Germany	won *4-3
	Brazil	lost 1-4
1974	Haiti	won 3-1
	Argentina	drew 1-1
	Poland	lost 1-2
1978	France	won 2-1
	Hungary	won 3-1
	Argentina	won 1-0
	West Germany	drew 0-0

	Austria	won 1-0
	Holland	lost 1-2
	Brazil	lost 1-2
1982	Poland	drew 0-0
	Peru	drew 1-1
	Cameroon	drew 1-1
	Argentina	won 2-1
	Brazil	won 3-2
	Poland	won 2-0
	West Germany	won 3-1
1986	Bulgaria	drew 1-1
	Argentina	drew 1-1
	South Korea	won 3-2
	France	lost 0-2
1990	Austria	won 1-0
	United States	won 1-0
	Czechoslovakia	won 2-0
	Uruguay	won 2-0
	Republic of Ireland	won 1-0
	Argentina	drew *1-1
		(lost 4-3 on pens)
	England	won 2-1

KUWAIT

Finals Appearances: 1 (1982)
Biggest Win: not won
Biggest Defeat: 1-4 v France (1982)

Record:

P	W	D	L	F	A
3	0	1	2	2	6

Leading Scorers: 1 Abdullah Al Buloushi,
Faisad Al Dakhil.

1982	Czechoslovakia	drew 1-1
	France	lost 1-4
	England	lost 0-1

MEXICO

Finals Appearances: 9 (1930, 1950-70, 1978,
1986)
Biggest Win: 4-0 v El Salvador (1970)
Biggest Defeat: 0-6 v West Germany (1978)

Record:

P	W	D	L	F	A
29	6	6	17	27	64

Leading Scorers: 2 Horacio Casarin, Javier
Valdivia Huerta, Fernando Quirarte

1930	France	lost 1-4
	Chile	lost 0-3
	Argentina	lost 3-6

Italy's first World Cup Final win came in 1934, on home soil, and was achieved after an extra-time win over Czechoslovakia. Here the players are seen at the end of normal time with the scores locked at 1-1.

1950	Brazil	lost 0-4
	Yugoslavia	lost 1-4
	Switzerland	lost 1-2
1954	Brazil	lost 0-5
	France	lost 2-3
1958	Sweden	lost 0-3
	Wales	drew 1-1
	Hungary	lost 0-4
1962	Brazil	lost 0-2
	Spain	lost 0-1
	Czechoslovakia	won 3-1
1966	France	drew 1-1
	England	lost 0-2
	Uruguay	drew 0-0
1970	Soviet Union	drew 0-0
	El Salvador	won 4-0
	Belgium	won 1-0
	Italy	lost 1-4
1978	Tunisia	lost 1-3
	West Germany	lost 0-6
	Poland	lost 1-3
1986	Belgium	won 2-1
	Paraguay	drew 1-1
	Iraq	won 1-0
	Bulgaria	won 2-0
	West Germany	drew *0-0
		(lost 4-1 on pens)

MOROCCO

Finals Appearances: 2 (1970, 1986)
Biggest Win: 3-1 v Portugal (1986)
Biggest Defeat: 0-3 v Peru (1970)

Record:

P	W	D	L	F	A
7	1	3	3	5	8

Leading Scorer: 2 Abdelrazak Khairi

1970	West Germany	lost 1-2
	Peru	lost 0-3
	Bulgaria	drew 1-1
1986	Poland	drew 0-0
	England	drew 0-0
	Portugal	won 3-1
	West Germany	lost 0-1

Steve Wooddin of New Zealand netted a goal against Scotland. It made him the Kiwis' joint top scorer, along with Steve Sumner, in the World Cup finals.

NEW ZEALAND

Finals Appearances: 1 (1982)
Biggest Win: not won
Biggest Defeat: 2-5 v Scotland (1982)

Record:

P	W	D	L	F	A
3	0	0	3	2	12

Leading Scorers: 1 Steve Wooddin, Steve
Sumner.

1982	Scotland	lost 2-5
	Soviet Union	lost 0-3
	Brazil	lost 0-4

NORTHERN IRELAND

Finals Appearances: 3 (1958, 1982-86)
Biggest Win: 2-1 v Czechoslovakia (1958)
Biggest Defeat: 0-4 France (1958)
Record: P W D L F A
         13 3 5 5 13 23
Leading Scorer: 5 Peter McParland

1958	Czechoslovakia	won 1-0
	Argentina	lost 1-3
	West Germany	drew 2-2
	Czechoslovakia	won *2-1
	France	lost 0-4
1982	Yugoslavia	drew 0-0
	Honduras	drew 1-1
	Spain	won 1-0
	Austria	drew 2-2
	France	lost 1-4
1986	Algeria	drew 1-1
	Spain	lost 1-2
	Brazil	lost 0-3

NORTH KOREA

Finals Appearances: 1 (1966)
Biggest Win: 1-0 v Italy (1966)
Biggest Defeat: 3-5 v Portugal (1966)
Record: P W D L F A
          4 1 1 2 5 9
Leading Scorer: 2 Pak Seung-zin

1966	Soviet Union	lost 0-3
	Chile	drew 1-1
	Italy	won 1-0
	Portugal	lost 3-5

NORWAY

Finals Appearances: 1 (1938)
Biggest Win: not won
Biggest Defeat: 1-2 v Italy (1938)
Record: P W D L F A
          1 0 0 1 1 2
Leading Scorer: 1 Arne Brustad

| 1938 | Italy | lost *1-2 |

PARAGUAY

Finals Appearances: 4 (1930, 1950, 1958, 1986)
Biggest Win: 3-2 v Scotland (1958)
Biggest Defeat: 3-7 v France (1958)
Record: P W D L F A
         11 3 4 4 16 25
Leading Scorers: 2 Florencio Amarilla,
Jorgelino Romero, Juan Bautista Aguero,
José Parodi, Julio César Romero, Roberto
Cabañas

1930	United States	lost 0-3
	Belgium	won 1-0
1950	Sweden	drew 2-2
	Italy	lost 0-2
1958	France	lost 3-7
	Scotland	won 3-2
	Yugoslavia	drew 3-3
1986	Iraq	won 1-0
	Mexico	drew 1-1
	Belgium	drew 2-2
	England	lost 0-3

PERU

Finals Appearances: 4 (1930, 1970, 1978-82)
Biggest Win: 4-1 v Iran (1978)
Biggest Defeat: 0-6 v Argentina (1978)
Record: P W D L F A
         15 4 3 8 18 31
Leading Scorer: 10 Teófilo Cubillas

1930	Romania	lost 1-3
	Uruguay	lost 0-1
1970	Bulgaria	won 3-2
	Morocco	won 3-0
	West Germany	lost 1-3
	Brazil	lost 2-4
1978	Scotland	won 3-1
	Holland	drew 0-0
	Iran	won 4-1
	Brazil	lost 0-3
	Poland	lost 0-1
	Argentina	lost 0-6
1982	Cameroon	drew 0-0
	Italy	drew 1-1
	Poland	lost 1-5

Peru's world-class star, and their leading scorer in the final stages with ten goals, is Teófilo Cubillas, seen here in action during the 1970 game against West Germany. The German players are Wolfgang Overath (left) and Karl Schnellinger.

POLAND

Finals Appearances: 5 (1938, 1974-86)
Biggest Win: 7-0 v Haiti (1974)
Biggest Defeat: 5-6 v Brazil (1938)

Record:	P	W	D	L	F	A
	25	13	5	7	39	29

Leading Scorer: 10 Grzegorz Lato

1938	Brazil	lost *5-6
1974	Argentina	won 3-2
	Haiti	won 7-0
	Italy	won 2-1
	Sweden	won 1-0
	Yugoslavia	won 2-1
	West Germany	lost 0-1
	Brazil	won 1-0
1978	West Germany	drew 0-0
	Tunisia	won 1-0
	Mexico	won 3-1
	Argentina	lost 0-2
	Peru	won 1-0
	Brazil	lost 1-3
1982	Italy	drew 0-0
	Cameroon	drew 0-0
	Peru	won 5-1

Scotland's Kenny Dalglish, who made his name first with Celtic and then Liverpool. Dalglish steered Liverpool to more triumphs as manager and is many Scots' choice as national team manager.

	Belgium	won 3-0
	Soviet Union	drew 0-0
	Italy	lost 0-2
	France	won 3-2
1986	Morocco	drew 0-0
	Portugal	won 1-0
	England	lost 0-3
	Brazil	lost 0-4

PORTUGAL

Finals Appearances: 2 (1966, 1986)
Biggest Win: 5-3 v North Korea (1966)
Biggest Defeat: 1-3 v Morocco (1986)

Record:	P	W	D	L	F	A
	9	6	0	3	19	12

Leading Scorer: 9 Eusébio

1966	Hungary	won 3-1
	Bulgaria	won 3-0
	Brazil	won 3-1
	North Korea	won 5-3
	England	lost 1-2
	Soviet Union	won 2-1
1986	England	won 1-0
	Poland	lost 0-1
	Morocco	lost 1-3

REPUBLIC OF IRELAND

Finals Appearances: 1 (1990)

Biggest Win: not won
Biggest Defeat: 0-1 v Italy (1990)

Record:	P	W	D	L	F	A
	5	0	4	1	2	3

Leading Scorers: 1 Niall Quinn, Kevin Sheedy.

1990	England	drew 1-1
	Egypt	drew 0-0
	Holland	drew 1-1
	Romania	drew *0-0
		(won 5-4 on pens)
	Italy	lost 0-1

ROMANIA

Finals Appearances: 5 (1930-38, 1970, 1990)
Biggest Win: 3-1 v Peru (1930)
Biggest Defeat: 0-4 v Uruguay (1930)

Record:	P	W	D	L	F	A
	12	3	3	6	16	20

Leading Scorer: 3 Stefan Dobai

1930	Peru	won 3-1
	Uruguay	lost 0-4
1934	Czechoslovakia	lost 1-2
1938	Cuba	drew *3-3
	Cuba	lost 1-2
1970	England	lost 0-1
	Czechoslovakia	won 2-1
	Brazil	lost 2-3
1990	Soviet Union	won 2-0
	Cameroon	lost 1-2
	Argentina	drew 1-1
	Republic of Ireland	drew *0-0
		(lost 5-4 on pens)

SCOTLAND

Finals Appearances: 7 (1954-58, 1974-90)
Biggest Win: 5-2 v New Zealand (1982)
Biggest Defeat: 0-7 v Uruguay (1954)

Record:	P	W	D	L	F	A
	20	4	6	10	23	35

Leading Scorer: 4 Joe Jordan

1954	Austria	lost 0-1
	Uruguay	lost 0-7
1958	Yugoslavia	drew 1-1
	Paraguay	lost 2-3
	France	lost 1-2
1974	Zaïre	won 2-0
	Brazil	drew 0-0
	Yugoslavia	drew 1-1
1978	Peru	lost 1-3
	Iran	drew 1-1
	Holland	won 3-2
1982	New Zealand	won 5-2
	Brazil	lost 1-4
	Soviet Union	drew 2-2
1986	Denmark	lost 0-1
	West Germany	lost 1-2
	Uruguay	drew *0-0
1990	Costa Rica	lost *0-1
	Sweden	won 2-1
	Brazil	lost 0-1

SOUTH KOREA

Finals Appearances: 3 (1954, 1986-90)
Biggest Win: not won
Biggest Defeat: 0-9 v Hungary (1954)

Record:	P	W	D	L	F	A
	8	0	1	7	5	29

Leading Scorers: 1 Park Chang-sun, Kim Jong-boo, Choi Soon-ho, Huh Jung-moo, Hwang Bo-kwan.

1954	Hungary	lost 0-9
	Turkey	lost 0-7
1986	Argentina	lost 1-3
	Bulgaria	drew 1-1
	Italy	lost 2-3
1990	Belgium	lost 0-2
	Spain	lost 1-3
	Uruguay	lost 0-1

SOVIET UNION

Finals Appearances: 7 (1958-70, 1982-90)
Biggest Win: 6-0 v Hungary (1986)
Biggest Defeat: 3-4 v Belgium (1986)
Record:

P	W	D	L	F	A
31	15	6	10	53	34

Leading Scorer: 5 Valentin Ivanov

1958	England	drew 2-2
	Austria	won 2-0
	Brazil	lost 0-2
	England	won 1-0
	Sweden	lost 0-2
1962	Yugoslavia	won 2-0
	Colombia	drew 4-4
	Uruguay	won 2-1

	Chile	lost 1-2
1966	North Korea	won 3-0
	Italy	won 1-0
	Chile	won 2-1
	Hungary	won 2-1
	West Germany	lost 1-2
	Portugal	lost 1-2
1970	Mexico	drew 0-0
	Belgium	won 4-1
	El Salvador	won 2-0
	Uruguay	lost *0-1
1982	Brazil	lost 1-2
	New Zealand	won 3-0

Jesús María Satrustegui, Spanish forward in the 1982 finals.

	Scotland	drew 2-2
	Belgium	won 1-0
	Poland	drew 0-0
1986	Hungary	won 6-0
	France	drew 1-1
	Canada	won 2-0
	Belgium	lost *3-4
1990	Romania	lost 0-2
	Argentina	lost 0-2
	Cameroon	won 4-0

SPAIN

Finals Appearances: 8 (1934, 1950, 1962-66, 1978-90)
Biggest Win: 5-1 v Denmark (1986)
Biggest Defeat: 1-6 v Brazil (1950)
Record:

P	W	D	L	F	A
32	13	7	12	43	38

Leading Scorers: 5 Estanislao Basora, Emilio Butragueño.

1934	Brazil	won 3-1
	Italy	drew 1-1
	Italy	lost †0-1
1950	United States	won 3-1
	Chile	won 2-0
	England	won 1-0
	Uruguay	drew 2-2
	Brazil	lost 1-6
	Sweden	lost 1-3
1962	Czechoslovakia	lost 0-1
	Mexico	won 1-0
	Brazil	lost 1-2
1966	Argentina	lost 1-2
	Switzerland	won 2-1
	West Germany	lost 1-2
1978	Austria	lost 1-2
	Brazil	drew 0-0
	Sweden	won 1-0
1982	Honduras	drew 1-1
	Yugoslavia	won 2-1
	Northern Ireland	lost 0-1
	West Germany	lost 1-2
	England	drew 0-0
1986	Brazil	lost 0-1
	Northern Ireland	won 2-1
	Algeria	won 3-0
	Denmark	won 5-1
	Belgium	drew *1-1
		(lost 5-4 on pens)
1990	Uruguay	drew 0-0
	South Korea	won 3-1
	Belgium	won 2-1
	Yugoslavia	lost *1-2

SWEDEN

Finals Appearances: 8 (1934-50, 1958, 1970-78, 1990)
Biggest Win: 8-0 v Cuba (1938)
Biggest Defeat: 1-7 v Brazil (1950)
Record:

P	W	D	L	F	A
31	11	6	14	49	52

Leading Scorers: 4 Gustav Wetterström, Kurt Hamrin, Agne Simonsson, Sven Jonasson, Ralf Edström.

1934	Argentina	won 3-2
	Germany	lost 1-2
1938	Cuba	won 8-0
	Hungary	lost 1-5
	Brazil	lost 2-4
1950	Italy	won 3-2
	Paraguay	drew 2-2
	Brazil	lost 1-7

Tunisia's greatest moment was holding World Champions, West Germany to a goalless draw in 1978. Here, Kaabi tangles with West Germany's Fischer.

	Uruguay	lost 2-3
	Spain	won 3-1
1958	Mexico	won 3-0
	Hungary	won 2-1
	Wales	drew 0-0
	Soviet Union	won 2-0
	West Germany	won 3-1
	Brazil	lost 2-5
1970	Italy	lost 0-1
	Israel	drew 1-1
	Uruguay	won 1-0
1974	Bulgaria	drew 0-0
	Holland	drew 0-0
	Uruguay	won 3-0
	Poland	lost 0-1
	West Germany	lost 2-4
	Yugoslavia	won 2-1
1978	Brazil	drew 1-1
	Austria	lost 0-1
	Spain	lost 0-1
1990	Brazil	lost 1-2
	Scotland	lost 1-2
	Costa Rica	lost 1-2

SWITZERLAND

Finals Appearances: 6 (1934-54, 1962-66)
Biggest Win: 4-1 v Italy (1954)
Biggest Defeat: 5-7 v Austria (1954)
Record:
P	W	D	L	F	A
18	5	2	11	28	44
Leading Scorer: 6 Josef Hugi

1934	Holland	won 3-2
	Czechoslovakia	lost 2-3
1938	Germany	drew *1-1
	Germany	won †4-2
	Hungary	lost 0-2
1950	Yugoslavia	lost 0-3
	Brazil	drew 2-2
	Mexico	won 2-1
1954	Italy	won 2-1
	England	lost 0-2
	Italy	won 4-1
	Austria	lost 5-7

1962	Chile	lost 1-3
	West Germany	lost 1-2
	Italy	lost 0-3
1966	West Germany	lost 0-5
	Spain	lost 1-2
	Argentina	lost 0-2

TUNISIA

Finals Appearances: 1 (1978)
Biggest Win: 3-1 v Mexico (1978)
Biggest Defeat: 0-1 v Poland (1978)
Record:
P	W	D	L	F	A
3	1	1	1	3	2
Leading Scorers: 1 Mokhtar Dhouieb, Ali Kaabi, Nejib Ghommidh.

1978	Mexico	won 3-1
	Poland	lost 0-1
	West Germany	drew 0-0

TURKEY

Finals Appearances: 1 (1954)
Biggest Win: 7-0 v South Korea (1954)
Biggest Defeat: 2-7 v West Germany (1954)
Record:
P	W	D	L	F	A
3	1	0	2	10	11
Leading Scorers: 3 Mamat Suat, Sargun Burhan.

1954	West Germany	lost 1-4
	South Korea	won 7-0
	West Germany	lost 2-7

UNITED ARAB EMIRATES

Finals Appearances: 1 (1990)
Biggest Win: not won
Biggest Defeat: 1-5 v West Germany (1990)
Record:
P	W	D	L	F	A
3	0	0	3	2	11
Leading Scorers: Ali Thani Jumaa, Khalid Ismail Mubarak.

1990	Colombia	lost 0-2
	West Germany	lost 1-5
	Yugoslavia	lost 1-4

UNITED STATES

Finals Appearances: 4 (1930-34, 1950, 1990)
Biggest Win: 3-0 v Belgium (1930), 3-0 v Paraguay (1930)
Biggest Defeat: 1-7 v Italy (1934)
Record:
P	W	D	L	F	A
10	3	0	7	14	29
Leading Scorer: 3 Bert Patenaude

1930	Belgium	won 3-0
	Paraguay	won 3-0
	Argentina	lost 1-6
1934	Italy	lost 1-7
1950	Spain	lost 1-3
	England	won 1-0
	Chile	lost 2-5
1990	Czechoslovakia	lost 1-5
	Italy	lost 0-1
	Austria	lost 1-2

The USA's greatest day was undoubtedly their 1-0 win over England in 1950. Here, England goalkeeper Bert Williams clutches the ball to his chest in the Mineiro Stadium, Belo Horizonte.

Top: Uruguay's skipper José Nasazzi before the start of the 1930 Final in Montevideo. *Above:* Uruguay's 1966 line-up. Back row (left to right): Caetano, Troche, Alvarez, Ubiñas, Manicera, Sosa. Front row: Pérez, Rocha, Silva, Cortés, Urruzmendi.

URUGUAY

Finals Appearances: 9 (1930, 1950-54, 1962-74, 1986-90)
Biggest Win: 8-0 v Bolivia (1950)
Biggest Defeat: 1-6 v Denmark (1986)

Record:	P	W	D	L	F	A
	37	15	8	14	61	52

Leading Scorer: 7 Juan Alberto Schiaffino

1930	Peru	won 1-0
	Romania	won 4-0
	Yugoslavia	won 6-1
	Argentina	won 4-2
1950	Bolivia	won 8-0

	Spain	drew 2-2
	Sweden	won 3-2
	Brazil	won 2-1
1954	Czechoslovakia	won 2-0
	Scotland	won 7-0
	England	won 4-2
	Hungary	lost *2-4
	Austria	lost 1-3
1962	Colombia	won 2-1
	Yugoslavia	lost 1-3
	Soviet Union	lost 1-2
1966	England	drew 0-0
	France	won 2-1
	Mexico	drew 0-0
	West Germany	lost 0-4
1970	Israel	won 2-0
	Italy	drew 0-0
	Sweden	lost 0-1
	Soviet Union	won *1-0
	Brazil	lost 1-3
	West Germany	lost 0-1
1974	Holland	lost 0-2
	Bulgaria	drew 1-1
	Sweden	lost 0-3
1986	West Germany	drew 1-1
	Denmark	lost 1-6
	Scotland	drew 0-0
	Argentina	lost 0-1
1990	Spain	drew 0-0
	Belgium	lost 1-3
	South Korea	won 1-0
	Italy	lost 0-2

WALES

Finals Appearances: 1 (1958)
Biggest Win: 2-1 v Hungary (1958)
Biggest Defeat: 0-1 v Brazil (1958)

Record:	P	W	D	L	F	A
	5	1	3	1	4	4

Leading Scorer: 2 Ivor Allchurch

1958	Hungary	drew 1-1
	Mexico	drew 1-1
	Sweden	drew 0-0
	Hungary	won 2-1
	Brazil	lost 0-1

Davie Cooper's penalty beats Wales' Neville Southall at Ninian Park in September 1985 and Scotland's World Cup hopes are still alive. Alas, the night was marred by the sudden death of Scotland manager, Jock Stein.

WEST GERMANY

(Including GERMANY - 1934-38)
Finals Appearances: 12 (1934, 1938, 1954-90)
Biggest Win: 7-2 v Turkey (1954)
Biggest Defeat: 3-8 v Hungary (1954)

Record:	P	W	D	L	F	A
	68	39	15	14	145	90

Leading Scorer: 14 Gerd Müller

1934	Belgium	won 5-2
	Sweden	won 2-1
	Czechoslovakia	lost 1-3
	Austria	won 3-2
1938	Switzerland	drew *1-1
	Switzerland	lost †2-4
1954	Turkey	won 4-1
	Hungary	lost 3-8
	Turkey	won 7-2
	Yugoslavia	won 2-0
	Austria	won 6-1
	Hungary	won 3-2
1958	Argentina	won 3-1
	Czechoslovakia	drew 2-2
	Northern Ireland	drew 2-2
	Yugoslavia	won 1-0
	Sweden	lost 1-3
	France	lost 3-6
1962	Italy	drew 0-0
	Switzerland	won 2-1
	Chile	won 2-0
	Yugoslavia	lost 0-1
1966	Switzerland	won 5-0
	Argentina	drew 0-0
	Spain	won 2-1
	Uruguay	won 4-0
	Soviet Union	won 2-1
	England	lost *2-4
1970	Morocco	won 2-1
	Bulgaria	won 5-2
	Peru	won 3-1
	England	won *3-2
	Italy	lost *3-4
	Uruguay	won 1-0
1974	Chile	won 1-0
	Australia	won 3-0
	East Germany	lost 0-1
	Yugoslavia	won 2-0
	Sweden	won 4-2

	Poland	won 1-0
	Holland	won 2-1
1978	Poland	drew 0-0
	Mexico	won 6-0
	Tunisia	drew 0-0
	Italy	drew 0-0
	Holland	drew 2-2
	Austria	lost 2-3
1982	Algeria	lost 1-2
	Chile	won 4-1
	Austria	won 1-0
	England	drew 0-0
	Spain	won 2-1
	France	drew *3-3
		(won 5-4 on pens)
	Italy	lost 1-3
1986	Uruguay	drew 1-1
	Scotland	won 2-1
	Denmark	lost 0-2
	Morocco	won 1-0
	Mexico	drew *0-0
		(won 4-1 on pens)
	France	won 2-0
	Argentina	lost 2-3
1990	Yugoslavia	won 4-1
	United Arab Emirates	won 5-1
	Colombia	drew 1-1
	Holland	won 2-1
	Czechoslovakia	won 1-0
	England	drew *1-1
		(won 4-3 on pens)
	Argentina	won 1-0

YUGOSLAVIA

Finals Appearances: 8 (1930, 1950-62, 1974, 1982, 1990)
Biggest Win: 9-0 v Zaïre (1974)
Biggest Defeat: 1-6 v Uruguay (1930)

Record:	P	W	D	L	F	A
	33	14	7	12	55	44

Leading Scorer: 4 Drazan Jerković

1930	Brazil	won 2-1
	Bolivia	won 4-0
	Uruguay	lost 1-6
1950	Switzerland	won 3-0
	Mexico	won 4-1
	Brazil	lost 0-2

Jules Rimet presents West Germany skipper Fritz Walter with the World Cup trophy in 1954.

1954	France	won 1-0
	Brazil	drew 1-1
	West Germany	lost 0-2
1958	Scotland	drew 1-1
	France	won 3-2
	Paraguay	drew 3-3
	West Germany	lost 0-1
1962	Soviet Union	lost 0-2
	Uruguay	won 3-1
	Colombia	won 5-0
	West Germany	won 1-0
	Czechoslovakia	lost 1-3
	Chile	lost 0-1
1974	Brazil	drew 0-0
	Zaïre	won 9-0
	Scotland	drew 1-1
	West Germany	lost 0-2
	Poland	lost 1-2
	Sweden	lost 1-2
1982	Northern Ireland	drew 0-0
	Spain	lost 1-2
	Honduras	won 1-0
1990	West Germany	lost 1-4
	Colombia	won 1-0
	United Arab Emirates	won 4-1
	Spain	won *2-1
	Argentina	drew *0-0
		(lost 3-2 on pens)

ZAIRE

Finals Appearance: 1 (1974)
Biggest Win: not won
Biggest Defeat: 0-9 v Yugoslavia (1974)

Record:	P	W	D	L	F	A
	3	0	0	3	0	14

Leading Scorer: not scored

1974	Scotland	lost 0-2
	Yugoslavia	lost 0-9
	Brazil	lost 0-3

*After extra-time. Biggest win/defeats are based on most goals scored/conceded. For example, Switzerland's 7-5 defeat by Austria in 1954 is regarded as a bigger defeat than their 3-0 defeat by Italy in 1962.

APPEARANCES

MOST APPEARANCES IN THE FINALS:

21 Uwe Seeler (West Germany) 1958, 1962, 1966, 1970
21 Wladislaw Zmuda (Poland) 1974, 1978, 1982, 1986
20 Grzegorz Lato (Poland) 1974, 1978, 1982
19 Wolfgang Overath (West Germany) 1966, 1970, 1974
19 Hans-Hubert Vogts (West Germany) 1970, 1974, 1978
19 Karl-Heinz Rummenigge (West Germany) 1978, 1982, 1986
19 Diego Maradona (Argentina) 1982, 1986, 1990
18 Franz Beckenbauer (West Germany) 1966, 1970, 1974
18 Sepp Maier (West Germany) 1970, 1974, 1978
18 Mario Kempes (Argentina) 1974, 1978, 1982
18 Gaetano Scirea (Italy) 1978, 1982, 1986
18 Antonio Cabrini (Italy) 1978, 1982, 1986
18 Pierre Littbarski (West Germany) 1982, 1986, 1990

17 Karl-Heinz Schnellinger (West Germany) 1958, 1962, 1966, 1970
17 Dino Zoff (Italy) 1974, 1978, 1982
17 Peter Shilton (England) 1982, 1986, 1990
16 Jairzinho (Brazil) 1966, 1970, 1974
16 Zbigniew Boniek (Poland) 1978, 1982, 1986
16 Jan Ceulemans (Belgium) 1982, 1986, 1990
15 Didí (Brazil) 1954, 1958, 1962
15 Nilton Santos (Brazil) 1954, 1958, 1962
15 Hans Schäfer (West Germany) 1954, 1958, 1962
15 Roberto Rivelino (Brazil) 1970, 1974, 1978
15 Maxime Bossis (France) 1978, 1982, 1986
15 Lothar Matthäus (West Germany) 1982, 1986, 1990

Seeler's World Cup career is slightly longer than Zmuda's; 33 hours as opposed to 30 hours 7 minutes.

In addition to those mentioned above, the following have also appeared in four or more tournaments.
5 Antonio Carbajal (Mexico, 1950, 1954, 1958, 1962, 1966)
4 Djalma Santos (Brazil, 1954, 1958, 1962, 1966)
Pelé (Brazil, 1958, 1962, 1966, 1970)
Gianni Rivera (Italy, 1962, 1966, 1970, 1974)
Pedro Rocha (Uruguay, 1962, 1966, 1970, 1974)

Above: Victorious England skipper Bobby Moore in 1966. *Below (left to right):* West German stars Franz Beckenbauer, Hans-Hubert Vogts and Karl-Heinz Rummenigge.

The most tournaments by a British Isles player is: 3 by Tom Finney, Billy Wright, Bobby Moore, Bobby Charlton, Peter Shilton, Bryan Robson, Terry Butcher (all England) Kenny Dalglish, Joe Jordan, Graeme Souness, Alex McLeish (all Scotland).

WORLD CUP DEBUTANTS (Finals)

1930 Argentina; Belgium; Bolivia; Brazil; Chile, France; Mexico, Paraguay; Peru; Romania; United States; Uruguay; Yugoslavia.
1934 Austria; Czechoslovakia; Egypt; Germany; Holland; Hungary; Italy; Spain; Sweden; Switzerland.
1938 Cuba; Dutch East Indies; Norway; Poland.
1950 England.
1954 Scotland; South Korea; Turkey; West Germany.
1958 Northern Ireland; Soviet Union; Wales.
1962 Bulgaria; Colombia.
1966 North Korea; Portugal.
1970 El Salvador; Israel; Morocco.
1974 Australia; East Germany; Haiti; Zaïre.

1978 Iran; Tunisia.
1982 Algeria; Cameroon; Honduras; Kuwait; New Zealand.
1986 Canada; Denmark; Iraq.
1990 Republic of Ireland; United Arab Emirates; Costa Rica.

MOST TOURNAMENTS COMPETED IN (Nations)

14 Brazil	9 Uruguay	6 Austria
12 Italy	8 Belgium	6 Chile
12 West Germany	8 Czechoslovakia	6 Switzerland
10 Argentina	8 Spain	5 Bulgaria
9 England	8 Sweden	5 Holland
9 France	8 Yugoslavia	5 Poland
9 Hungary	7 Scotland	5 Romania
9 Mexico	7 Soviet Union	

PLAYED FOR TWO WINNING TEAMS

Giovanni Ferrari (Italy, 1934/1938)
Giuseppe Meazza (Italy, 1934/38)
Didí (Brazil, 1958/1962)
Garrincha (Brazil, 1958/1962)
Gilmar do Santos Neves (Brazil, 1958/1962)
Djalma Santos (Brazil, 1958/1962)
Nilton Santos (Brazil, 1958/1962)
Vavà (Brazil, 1958/1962)
Mario Zagalo (Brazil, 1958/1962)
Zito (Brazil, 1958/1962)
Pelé (Brazil, 1958/1962)

GOALSCORERS

MOST GOALS IN FINALS (Individual)

14 Gerd Müller (West Germany) 1970, 1974
13 Juste Fontaine (France) 1958
12 Pelé (Brazil) 1958, 1962, 1966, 1970
11 Sandor Kocsis (Hungary) 1954
10 Helmut Rahn (West Germany) 1954, 1958
10 Teófilo Cubillas (Peru) 1970, 1978

Grzegorz Lato of Poland.

10 Grzegorz Lato (Poland) 1974, 1978, 1982
10 Gary Lineker (England) 1986, 1990
9 Leónidas da Silva (Brazil) 1934, 1938
9 Ademir Marques de Menezes (Brazil) 1950
9 Vavà (Brazil) 1958, 1962
9 Eusébio (Portugal) 1966
9 Uwe Seeler (West Germany) 1958, 1962, 1966, 1970
9 Jairzinho (Brazil) 1970, 1974
9 Paolo Rossi (Italy) 1978, 1982
9 Karl-Heinz Rummenigge (West Germany) 1978, 1982, 1986

MOST GOALS IN ONE TOURNAMENT (Individual)

13 Juste Fontaine (France) 1958
11 Sandor Kocsis (Hungary) 1954
10 Gerd Müller (West Germany) 1970
9 Ademir Marques de Menezes (Brazil) 1950
9 Eusébio (Portugal) 1966
8 Guillermo Stàbile (Argentina) 1930
8 Leónidas da Silva (Brazil) 1938
7 Gyula Zsengeller (Hungary) 1938
7 Jairzinho (Brazil) 1970
7 Grzegorz Lato (Poland) 1974
6 Josef Hugi (Switzerland) 1954
6 Max Morlock (West Germany) 1954

Gerd Müller of West Germany.

6 Pelé (Brazil) 1958
6 Helmut Rahn (West Germany) 1958
6 Helmut Haller (West Germany) 1966
6 Mario Kempes (Argentina) 1978
6 Paolo Rossi (Italy) 1982
6 Gary Lineker (England) 1986
6 Salvatore Schillaci (Italy) 1990

Teófilo Cubillas (Peru) is the only player to score five goals or more in a tournament on two occasions, 1970 and 1978.

Paolo Rossi of Italy.

Jairzinho of Brazil.

Pelé (Brazil) and Uwe Seeler (West Germany) head the list of players who have scored in most tournaments.

PLAYERS WHO HAVE SCORED IN MOST TOURNAMENTS

4 Pelé (Brazil) 1958, 1962, 1966, 1970
4 Uwe Seeler (West Germany) 1958, 1962, 1966, 1970
3 Joe Jordan (Scotland) 1974, 1978, 1982
3 Grzegorz Lato (Poland) 1974, 1978, 1982
3 Andrzej Szarmach (Poland) 1974, 1978, 1982
3 Michel Platini (France) 1978, 1982, 1986
3 Dominique Rocheteau (France) 1978, 1982, 1986
3 Karl-Heinz Rummenigge (West Germany) 1978, 1982, 1986

MOST GOALS IN FINALS (Team)

148 Brazil
145 Germany/West Germany
89 Italy
87 Hungary
82 Argentina
71 France
61 Uruguay
55 England
55 Yugoslavia
53 Soviet Union
51 Sweden
44 Czechoslovakia
43 Spain
40 Austria
39 Poland
35 Holland

MOST GOALS IN ONE TOURNAMENT (Team)

27 Hungary (1954)
25 West Germany (1954)*
23 France (1958)
22 Brazil (1950)
19 Brazil (1970)*
18 Argentina (1930)
17 Austria (1954)
17 Portugal (1966)
17 West Germany (1970)
16 Uruguay (1954)
16 Brazil (1958)*
16 Poland (1974)
16 France (1982)
15 Uruguay (1930)*
15 Hungary (1938)
15 Uruguay (1950)*
15 West Germany (1966)
15 Holland (1974)
15 Argentina (1978) *
15 Holland (1978)
15 Brazil (1982)
15 West Germany (1990)*
*Denotes champions

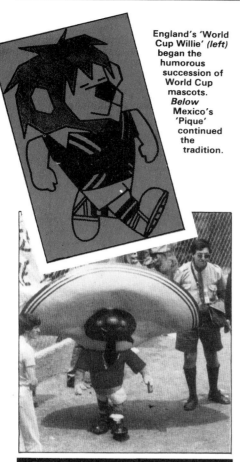

England's 'World Cup Willie' *(left)* began the humorous succession of World Cup mascots. *Below* Mexico's 'Pique' continued the tradition.

WORLD CUP MASCOTS

Introduced for the 8th World Cup in England in 1966 all Mascots have been:
1966 World Cup Willie
1970 Juanito
1974 Tip and Tap
1978 Pampita
1982 Naranjito
1986 Pique
1990 Ciao

MISCELLANY

OFFICIAL NAME OF THE COMPETITION

1930-70 FIFA World Championship
1974-90 FIFA World Cup

OFFICIAL NAME OF THE TROPHY

1930-38 FIFA World Cup
1950-70 Jules Rimet Cup
1974-90 FIFA World Cup

FIFA PRESIDENTS AT TIME OF EACH COMPETITION

1930-50 Jules Rimet (France)
1954   Rodolphe Seeldrayers (Belgium)
1958   Arthur Drewry (England)
1962-70 Sir Stanley Rous (England)
1974-90 João Havelange (Brazil)

REFEREES

MOST MATCHES OFFICIATED IN

7 Jean Langenus (Belgium) 1930, 1934, 1938
7 Mervyn Griffiths (Wales) 1950, 1954, 1958
7 Juan Gardeazabal Garay (Spain) 1958, 1962, 1966
6 Ivan Eklind (Sweden) 1934, 1938, 1950

England's Ray Wilkins was sent off against Morocco in 1986 and remains the only Englishman to receive his marching orders in the World Cup finals.

6 Arthur Ellis (England) 1950, 1954, 1958
6 Nikolai Latychev (Soviet Union) 1958, 1962
5 Ramon Barreto Ruiz (Uruguay) 1970, 1974, 1978
5 Gottfried Dienst (Switzerland) 1962, 1966
5 Abraham Klein (Israel) 1970, 1978, 1982
5 Nicolae Rainea (Romania) 1974, 1978, 1982
5 Michel Vautrot (France) 1986, 1990
5 Arturo Ladonado Yamasaki (Peru/Mexico) 1962, 1966, 1970
5 Istvan Zsolt (Hungary) 1954, 1958, 1966
Eklind is the only man to have refereed both before and after World War Two.

MOST TOURNAMENTS OFFICIATED IN

In addition to those above, the following have also officiated in three tournaments: Bob Davidson (Scotland, 1962, 1970, 1974); Kurt Tschenscher (West Germany, 1966, 1970, 1974); Karoly Palotai (Hungary, 1974, 1978, 1982); Erik Fredriksson (Sweden, 1982, 1986, 1990).

SENDINGS-OFF

A total of 60 players have received their marching orders in the World Cup finals. The South American nations certainly have the worst record with Brazil, Uruguay, Argentina, Peru, and Chile accounting for 38.33% of that total with 23 dismissals between them.

The worst nations have been:

Dismissals	Country
7	Brazil
7	Argentina
6	Uruguay
4	Czechoslovakia
4	Germany/West Germany
4	Hungary
3	Yugoslavia
2	Cameroon
2	Chile
2	Holland
2	Italy
2	Soviet Union

No player has been sent off twice.

Paul von Hertzka (Hungary) 1938, Arthur Ellis (England) 1950, and Michel Vautrot (France) 1990, are the only referees to have dismissed three players.

BIGGEST WINS

HIGHEST SCORES (all matches)

13-0 New Zealand v Fiji, 1982 (qualifying)
12-0 West Germany v Cyprus, 1970 (qualifying)
11-1 Hungary v Greece, 1938 (qualifying)
11-1 Trinidad v Antigua, 1974 (qualifying)

Steve Sumner, scorer of six goals when New Zealand hammered Fiji 13-0 in 1982.

10-0 Soviet Union v Finland (away), 1958 (qualifying)
10-0 Australia v Fiji, 1982 (qualifying)
10-1 Hungary v El Salvador, 1982
9-0 Spain v Portugal, 1934 (qualifying)
9-0 Hungary v South Korea, 1954
9-0 England v Luxembourg (away), 1962 (qualifying)
9-0 Holland v Norway, 1974 (qualifying)
9-0 Romania v Finland, 1974 (qualifying)
9-0 Yugoslavia v Zaïre, 1974
9-0 Austria v Malta, 1978 (qualifying)
9-0 East Germany v Malta, 1978 (qualifying)
9-0 South Korea v Nepal (away), 1990 (qualifying)
Fiji's 13-0 and 10-0 defeats were within two days of each other.

HIGHEST SCORES (Finals)

10-1 Hungary v El Salvador, 1982
9-0 Hungary v South Korea, 1954
9-0 Yugoslavia v Zaïre, 1974
8-0 Sweden v Cuba, 1938
8-0 Uruguay v Bolivia, 1950
8-3 Hungary v West Germany 1954
7-0 Turkey v South Korea, 1954
7-0 Uruguay v Scotland 1954
7-0 Poland v Haiti, 1974
7-1 Italy v United States, 1934
7-1 Brazil v Sweden, 1950
7-2 West Germany v Turkey, 1954
7-3 France v Paraguay, 1958
7-5 Austria v Switzerland, 1954

HIGHEST AGGREGATE SCORES (Finals)

12 goals — Austria 7 Switzerland 5, 1954
11 goals — Brazil 6 Poland 5, 1938
11 goals — Hungary 8 West Germany 3, 1954
11 goals — Hungary 10 El Salvador 1, 1982
10 goals — France 7 Paraguay 3, 1958
9 goals — Argentina 6 Mexico 3, 1930
9 goals — Hungary 9 South Korea 0, 1954
9 goals — France 6 West Germany 3, 1958
9 goals — Yugoslavia 9 Zaïre 0, 1974
9 goals — West Germany 7 Turkey 2, 1954
The highest scoring draws in the final stages are:
4-4 Belgium v England, 1954; Colombia v Soviet Union, 1962.

RECORDS IN FINAL STAGES

MOST TITLES

3 Brazil — 1958/1962/1970
3 Italy — 1934/1938/1982
3 West Germany — 1954/1974/1990
2 Argentina — 1978/1986
2 Uruguay — 1930/1950
1 England — 1966

FINAL APPEARANCES

6 West Germany
4 Argentina
4 Brazil
4 Italy
2 Czechoslovakia
2 Holland
2 Hungary
2 Uruguay*
1 England*
1 Sweden
* Undefeated

SEMI-FINAL APPEARANCES

9 West Germany‡
7 Brazil
6 Italy
4 Argentina*
4 Uruguay
3 France
3 Sweden
2 Austria
2 Czechoslovakia*
2 England
2 Holland*
2 Hungary*
2 Poland
2 Yugoslavia
1 Belgium
1 Chile
1 Portugal
1 Soviet Union
1 Spain
1 United States
* Undefeated
‡ Includes one as Germany
NB. The last four in the 1950 tournament are regarded as the semi-finalists and the final match between Uruguay and Brazil is regarded as the 'Final' for the purposes of the above.

MOST WINS IN FINAL STAGES

44 Brazil
39 Germany/West Germany
31 Italy
24 Argentina
18 England
15 France
15 Hungary
15 Soviet Union
15 Uruguay
14 Yugoslavia
13 Poland
13 Spain
12 Austria
11 Czechoslovakia
11 Sweden

MOST DEFEATS IN FINAL STAGES

17 Mexico
15 Argentina
14 Belgium
14 Czechoslovakia
14 France
14 Germany/West Germany
14 Hungary
14 Sweden
14 Uruguay

LEAST WINS

Nineteen teams have reached the final stages and not won a game. The following have played five or more matches and still not won:

16 Bulgaria
8 South Korea
6 El Salvador
5 Republic of Ireland

The following teams have all not won a point in the final stages. The figures in brackets indicate the number of matches played: Norway (1), Dutch East Indies (1), Bolivia (3), Canada (3), Haiti (3), Iraq (3), New Zealand (3), United Arab Emirates (3), Zaïre (3), El Salvador (6)

SEQUENCES

MOST SUCCESSIVE WINS

7 Italy, 1934-38
6 England, 1966-70
6 Brazil, 1970
6 Brazil, 1978-82
5 Uruguay, 1930 & 50
5 Uruguay, 1950-54
5 West Germany, 1954-58
5 Brazil, 1958-62

5 Brazil, 1962-66
5 Poland, 1974
5 Argentina, 1986
5 Italy, 1990

MOST SUCCESSIVE DEFEATS

9 Mexico, 1930 & 1950-58
7 Switzerland, 1954 & 1962-66
6 El Salvador, 1970 & 1982
5 Bulgaria, 1966-70
5 Sweden, 1978 & 1990

MOST SUCCESSIVE DRAWS

4 Republic of Ireland, 1990
3 England, 1958
3 Wales, 1958
3 Bulgaria, 1970-74
3 Morocco, 1970 & 1986
3 West Germany, 1978
3 Cameroon, 1982
3 Italy, 1982
3 Holland, 1990

MOST GAMES UNDEFEATED

13 Brazil, 1958-66 (won 11, drew 2)
11 Uruguay, 1930 & 1950-54 (won 10, drew 1)
11 Brazil 1970-74 (won 9 drew 2)
11 Brazil, 1978-82 (won 8 drew 3)
10 Italy, 1982-86 (won 5, drew 5)
9 Italy, 1934-38 (won 8, drew 1)
9 West Germany, 1974-78 (won 5, drew 4)
8 West Germany, 1954-58 (won 6, drew 2)
8 Brazil, 1986-90 (won 7, drew 1)

> Games decided on penalties are regarded as drawn matches.

MOST GAMES WITHOUT A WIN

*16 Bulgaria, 1962-74 & 1986 (lost 10 drew 6)
13 Mexico, 1930 & 1950-62 (lost 12, drew 1)
11 Uruguay, 1970-74 & 1986-90 (lost 7, drew 4)
9 Chile, 1966, 1974 & 1982 (lost 6, drew 3)
*8 South Korea, 1954 & 1986-90 (lost 7, drew 1)
7 Switzerland, 1954 & 1962-66 (lost 7)
7 Czechoslovakia, 1962, 1970 & 1982 (lost 5, drew 2)
6 England, 1954-62 (lost 3, drew 3)
*6 El Salvador, 1970 & 1982 (lost 6)
6 Yugoslavia, 1974 & 1982 (lost 4, drew 2)
6 Peru, 1978-82 (lost 4, drew 2)
6 Sweden, 1978 & 1990 (lost 5, drew 1)
*All their World Cup games

Despite letting in this Wisnieski header, Bulgarian goalkeeper Naidenov went to the 1962 World Cup finals in Chile, even though his side lost this qualifying match 3-0 to France in Paris. The Bulgarians have yet to win a game in the finals, though, in 16 attempts.